Handbook of Research on Institution Development for Sustainable and Inclusive Economic Growth in Africa

Evans S. Osabuohien
Covenant University, Nigeria

Emmanuel A. Oduntan
Covenant University, Nigeria

Obindah Gershon
Covenant University, Nigeria

Olaronke Onanuga
Covenant University, Nigeria

Oluyomi Ola-David
Covenant University, Nigeria

A volume in the Practice, Progress, and Proficiency in Sustainability (PPPS) Book Series

IGI Global
PUBLISHER of TIMELY KNOWLEDGE

Published in the United States of America by
IGI Global
Business Science Reference (an imprint of IGI Global)
701 E. Chocolate Avenue
Hershey PA, USA 17033
Tel: 717-533-8845
Fax: 717-533-8661
E-mail: cust@igi-global.com
Web site: http://www.igi-global.com

Library of Congress Cataloging-in-Publication Data

Names: Osabuohien, Evans, 1979- editor. | Oduntan, Emmanuel A., 1967- editor. | Gershon, Obindah, 1975- editor. | Onanuga, Olaronke Toyin, editor. | Ola-David, Oluyomi, 1983- editor.
Title: Handbook of research on institution development for sustainable and inclusive economic growth in Africa / Evans S. Osabuohien, Emmanuel A. Oduntan, Obindah Gershon, Olaronke Onanuga, and Oluyomi Ola-David, editors.
Description: Hershey : Information Science Reference, 2020. | Includes bibliographical references and index. | Summary: "This book focuses on institution development for sustainable and inclusive economic growth in Africa"-- Provided by publisher.
Identifiers: LCCN 2020012009 (print) | LCCN 2020012010 (ebook) | ISBN 9781799848172 (hardcover) | ISBN 9781799848189 (ebook)
Subjects: LCSH: Sustainable development--Africa, Sub-Saharan. | Women in development--Africa, Sub-Saharan. | Youth in development--Africa, Sub-Saharan. | Africa, Sub-Saharan--Economic conditions--21st century.
Classification: LCC HC800.Z9 E5468 2020 (print) | LCC HC800.Z9 (ebook) | DDC 338.967--dc23
LC record available at https://lccn.loc.gov/2020012009
LC ebook record available at https://lccn.loc.gov/2020012010

This book is published in the IGI Global book series Practice, Progress, and Proficiency in Sustainability (PPPS) (ISSN: 2330-3271; eISSN: 2330-328X)

British Cataloguing in Publication Data
A Cataloguing in Publication record for this book is available from the British Library.

Practice, Progress, and Proficiency in Sustainability (PPPS) Book Series

Ayman Batisha
International Sustainability Institute, Egypt

ISSN:2330-3271
EISSN:2330-328X

Mission

In a world where traditional business practices are reconsidered and economic activity is performed in a global context, new areas of economic developments are recognized as the key enablers of wealth and income production. This knowledge of information technologies provides infrastructures, systems, and services towards sustainable development.

The **Practices, Progress, and Proficiency in Sustainability (PPPS) Book Series** focuses on the local and global challenges, business opportunities, and societal needs surrounding international collaboration and sustainable development of technology. This series brings together academics, researchers, entrepreneurs, policy makers and government officers aiming to contribute to the progress and proficiency in sustainability.

Coverage

- Eco-Innovation
- Technological learning
- Strategic Management of IT
- Green Technology
- Socio-Economic
- Global Content and Knowledge Repositories
- Intellectual Capital
- Innovation Networks
- E-Development
- Knowledge clusters

IGI Global is currently accepting manuscripts for publication within this series. To submit a proposal for a volume in this series, please contact our Acquisition Editors at Acquisitions@igi-global.com or visit: http://www.igi-global.com/publish/.

The Practice, Progress, and Proficiency in Sustainability (PPPS) Book Series (ISSN 2330-3271) is published by IGI Global, 701 E. Chocolate Avenue, Hershey, PA 17033-1240, USA, www.igi-global.com. This series is composed of titles available for purchase individually; each title is edited to be contextually exclusive from any other title within the series. For pricing and ordering information please visit http://www.igi-global.com/book-series/practice-progress-proficiency-sustainability/73810. Postmaster: Send all address changes to above address.

Titles in this Series

For a list of additional titles in this series, please visit: www.igi-global.com/book-series

Examining Biophilia and Societal Indifference to Environmental Protection
Mary Ann Markey (Grand Canyon University, USA) and Lonny Douglas Meinecke (King University, USA)
Engineering Science Reference • © 2021 • 279pp • H/C (ISBN: 9781799844082) • US $195.00

Strategies for Business Sustainability in a Collaborative Economy
Ramona-Diana Leon (National School of Political and Administrative Studies, Romania)
Business Science Reference • © 2020 • 440pp • H/C (ISBN: 9781799845430) • US $225.00

Sustainability in the Entrepreneurial Ecosystem Operating Mechanisms and Enterprise Growth
Yang Gao (Dalian University of Technology, China) Sang-Bing Tsai (Regional Green Economy Development Research Center, Wuyi University, China & Research Center for Environment and Sustainable Development of the China Civil Aviation, Civil Aviation University of China, China) Xiaomin Du (Yingkou Institute of Technology, China) and Chunlin Xin (Beijing University of Chemical Technology, China)
Business Science Reference • © 2020 • 342pp • H/C (ISBN: 9781799834953) • US $215.00

Developing Sustainable Food Systems, Policies, and Securities
Abiodun Elijah Obayelu (Federal University of Agriculture, Abeokuta, Nigeria) and Oluwakemi Adeola Obayelu (University of Ibadan, Nigeria)
Engineering Science Reference • © 2020 • 292pp • H/C (ISBN: 9781799825999) • US $195.00

Building an Entrepreneurial and Sustainable Society
Brizeida R. Hernández-Sánchez (University of Salamanca, Spain) José C. Sánchez-García (University of Salamanca, Spain) and Antonio Carrizo Moreira (University of Aveiro, Portugal)
Business Science Reference • © 2020 • 369pp • H/C (ISBN: 9781799827047) • US $235.00

Toward Sustainability Through Digital Technologies and Practices in the Eurasian Region
Gainiya Tazhina (University of International Business, Kazakhstan) and Judith Parker (Teachers College, Columbia University, USA)
Information Science Reference • © 2020 • 294pp • H/C (ISBN: 9781799825517) • US $195.00

Examining the Environmental Impacts of Materials and Buildings
Blaine Erickson Brownell (University of Minnesota, USA)
Engineering Science Reference • © 2020 • 358pp • H/C (ISBN: 9781799824268) • US $245.00

IGI Global
PUBLISHER of TIMELY KNOWLEDGE

701 East Chocolate Avenue, Hershey, PA 17033, USA
Tel: 717-533-8845 x100 • Fax: 717-533-8661
E-Mail: cust@igi-global.com • www.igi-global.com

List of Contributors

Table of Contents

Section 2
Finance, Inclusive Growth, and Development

Section 3
Agricultural Development and Food Security

Section 4
Sustainable Resource Development, Energy, and Environment

Detailed Table of Contents

The hierarchical state-led model of governance that is used to address global policy issues has proved to be wanting on sustainable development. This chapter discusses the concept of transnational governance of sustainable development, focusing on the United Nations 2030 Agenda and Agenda 2063 in Africa. The premise is that implementation of the two agendas represents an enormous challenge to African governments in terms of resources, extent, and urgency. The chapter will make a reasonable case that transnational governance is required for active engagement of non-state actors and relevant institutions to mobilize resources to support the effective implementation and monitoring of the 2030 Agenda and Agenda 2063 in Africa.

There are few studies on the role of institutions in achieving sustainable development that infer that these institutions offer the mechanisms for resource and environmental management. Thus, twelve West African countries (Benin, Burkina Faso, Cote d'Ivoire, Gambia, Ghana, Liberia, Mali, Niger, Nigeria, Senegal, Sierra Leone, and Togo) are covered in the study using data from World Development Indicators and World Governance Indicators. Six main outcome variables are used. These are CO2 emissions per capita, CO2 emissions from electricity and heat production, CO2 emissions from liquid fuel consumption, CO2 emissions from manufacturing and construction, total greenhouse gas emissions (kt of CO2 equivalent), and CO2 intensity. A two-step generalised method of moment (GMM) found that governance effectiveness and regulatory quality as curtails the rate of CO2 emissions. Policy implications are discussed.

A cross-country comparison reveals the fact that high tertiary enrollment rates are associated with low corruption, and low tertiary enrollment rates are associated with high corruption. Such a comparison does not show whether an increase in higher education leads to lower or higher corruption. Hence, the aim of the study is to analyze the effect of higher education on corruption on best performing European Union countries and worst performing African Union countries. It is found that higher education has positive significant effect on corruption not only in African Union but also in European Union. Hence, it is concluded that the enticement of higher living standard prevails the moral principals and ethical values of individuals in the way of reaching it. The author advise a course on moral principals and ethical values to be included in the curriculum of higher education institutions to teach the meaning of virtue and the long-term gains of living with high moral standing rather than to be gravitated to the short-term gains of corruption as a policy implication.

This chapter explores the roles of institutional settings in renewable energy (RE) development in Sub-Saharan Africa, and the effects of RE development on forest cover changes in the region. The study finds that the slow but persistent growth in RE contribution to total energy bundles can be credited to the general improvements in institutional reforms and frameworks. It also finds that unlike biomass-based RE systems, the indirect deforestation effects associated with solar and wind energy systems, are largely offset by the environmental benefits that accrue from them. Based on these findings, the chapter recommends that coordinated institutional interventions should prioritize the deployment of more environmentally sustainable RE technologies such as solar and wind energies.

Economic transformation suggests sustainable and inclusive economic development. It includes the changes in the structures of the economy in favour of more productive sectors to ensure consistent economic progress. This has been the earnest desire of most African countries. However, achieving economic transformation will require strong institutions, among others. The channels through which institutions can influence the process of economic development using specific country analyses are still under-researched. Thus, this study examines the importance of institutions in the development and sustenance of some important sectors: finance, education, technology, industry, and trade, believed to

Poverty is no longer fashionable even in the less developed countries of the world. The world has deemed poverty-ridden regions of the world as 'anathema', forbidden, and ignoble. At the same time ways to get out of the menace are regularly strategised over a period of time. The developed countries of the world had been able to nip poverty to the bud significantly, but the developing countries still have a lot to do so as to overcome the menace. Poverty in the developing countries operates in a cycle of repetitions. This makes it difficult to curtail. How can poverty be reduced in the developing countries? This study reveals the reason while poverty has become a domestic phenomenon in developing countries and the way forward. The theory on poverty is evaluated alongside the present economic situation in Africa. The cycle of poverty, which includes the social cycle of poverty (SCP), political cycle of poverty (PCP), and the economic cycle of poverty (ECP), are examined. This study analyses the strategies to break the cycle of poverty in Africa and other developing countries.

Oluwabunmi Opeyemi Adejumo, Institute for Entrepreneurship and Development Studies, Obafemi Awolowo University, Ile-Ife, Nigeria & Centre for Economic Policy and Development Research (CEPDeR), Nigeria
Uchenna R. Efobi, College of Business and Social Sciences, Covenant University, Ota, Nigeria & Institute for Entrepreneurship and Development Studies, Obafemi Awolowo University, Ile-Ife, Nigeria & Centre for Economic Policy and Development Research (CEPDeR), Nigeria & Merian Institute for Advanced Study in Africa, University of Ghana, Ghana
Simplice A. Asongu, African Governance and Development Institute, Cameroon

Actualizing sustainable development in Africa will require enormous economic resources. This implies that there must be a clear balance of prioritization of financing options on what works best for development in this region without further escalating other societal problems. The authors argue in the chapter that though there has been some benefit from the traditional means of financing development in Africa, some drawbacks still exist considering the rising rate of inequality and poverty head-count in the region. On this note, this present study examines financing options that have previously been advocated for in financing development in the African region (i.e., taking stock), such as development assistance and foreign investment, by considering its implication on development outcomes like poverty, inequality, and aggregate human development indicator in the region.

Abba Yadou Barnabe, University of Dschang, Cameroon

The main objective of this chapter is to examine the effect of migrant remittances on financial inclusion in Africa from 2004 to 2017. Thus, the authors constructed a composite index of financial inclusion using principal component analysis (PCA). In addition, they examine the effect of remittances on financial inclusion using a system GMM and a pooled mean group (PMG). It is found that remittances have a negative effect on financial inclusion in the short run and a positive effect in the long run. Moreover, remittances have a negative long-term effect on the use of financial services and a positive long-term effect on access to financial services. This implies improved policies to both attract the flow of remittances through formal channels and improve financial inclusion.

Saharan Africa. Some countries like Kenya, Nigeria, South Africa, and Rwanda, and, to a lesser extent, Senegal are more advanced in this process of using ICT because they are relatively more economically stable. Finally, the constraints linked to the adoption of these ICTs as well as certain public policy recommendations were formulated.

The production of the food is majorly composite to the rural setting, and the consumption of this food is not only restricted to the rural area. This rural food production and urban area demand/consumption emphasises the need for rural-urban market linkages. This study employed mixed methods to investigate the role of road transport in the flow of food products from rural areas to the urban markets. Ten urban markets were sampled and 250 respondents from urban markets in Ibadan. The study revealed that household collaboration in the production and marketing of food produce exists in Ibadan. It was established that distance and transportation cost plays a vital role in supply volume, pricing, and delivery price. The variance in delivery cost is dependent on factors such as bargaining power, the season of the year, demand, destination, and road condition. In conclusion, improved roads condition and workable traffic policies that eliminate roadblocks are recommended.

Agriculture's importance to industrialization efforts in Tanzania goes far beyond its direct impact on the manufacturing sector, but on farmers' incomes, economic stability, and reduction of poverty. The challenges are on both sides; agricultural development initiatives are needed on one hand while manufacturing obstacles are supposed to be dealt with on the other hand. Using literature review approach, the study found that there should be a balance between infrastructure development and agricultural support so that the two may support well the industrialization process. Massive efforts have been myths to the smooth changes which call for serious attention to the planners to review strategies, policies and programme. On the other hand, the potentials of the agricultural sector are observed to support the industrialization process in Tanzania. The potentials include food security, private investments support, employment, and exports enhancement and supply strain stabilization through various crops and produce.

Preface

INTRODUCTION AND OBJECTIVE OF THE BOOK

Efficient institutional arrangements and the sustainable utilization of natural resources are essential for achieving sustainable development in Africa. Consequently, African countries have been pursuing some development agendas towards achieving economic growth - like Vision 2030 of Algeria, Kenya, and South Africa. These country-specific development agenda are in tandem with the African Union (AU) Agenda 2063 and the United Nations Sustainable Development Goals (SDGs). This book fundamentally assesses and evaluates the institutional arrangements within which African countries are pursuing their respective development agenda. Institutions generally entail formal, semi-formal and informal framework for sustainable and inclusive economic growth as it helps in the coordination of interrelationships among economic agents (Beecroft et al., 2020; Egbetokun et al., 2020; Karakara & Osabuohien, 2020; Olakojo & Onanuga, 2020; Osabohien et al., 2020; Osabuohien, 2020).

Even though the World Development Indicators and African Economic Outlook show that many African countries performed lower than other developing countries in the global south, research efforts have highlighted factors responsible for the low economic development in Africa. However, the vital process of building viable institutions - to serve as the fulcrum for managing Africa's resources and promoting sustainable economic growth that is inclusive - is yet to be unraveled. This is the objective of this book. The chapters proffer potential actionable solutions for Africa's developmental challenges with respect to sustainable and inclusive economic growth. It is a value-adding paradigm to the literature that will be useful to students, academics, policymakers, international organizations and development partners.

HIGHLIGHTS OF THE CHAPTERS IN THE BOOK

The chapters contained in the book are broadly divided into four thematic areas dubbed sections. They include: Institution, Governance and Africa's Development Agenda; Finance, Inclusive Growth and Development; Agricultural Development and Food Security; as well as Sustainable Resource Development, Energy and Environment.

The hierarchical state-led model of governance used to address global policy issues is apparently inadequate for sustainable development. So, Oluwaseun Oguntuase discusses the concept of transnational governance of sustainable development, focusing on the United Nations 2030 Agenda and African Union's Agenda 2063 in the first chapter. Subsequently, in the second chapter, Alhassan Karakara and Evans Osabuohien emphasize the relevance of institutional framework that offers mechanisms for resource and environmental management on environmental pollution and the unsustainable nature of institutions. In the chapter that follows, Adem Gök undertakes an analysis of tertiary school enrollment rates and how they are associated with corruption, comparing European Union countries and African Union countries. The sustenance of education in the face of competitive pressures requires that learning strategies equip students with relevant labour skills for the world of work.

The roles of institutional settings in renewable energy development and the effects of renewable energy development on forest cover changes in Sub-Saharan Africa is explored in Chapter Four by Evelyn Anyokwu and Chigozie Nweke-Eze. The slow but persistent growth in renewable energy contribution to total energy mix can be credited to general improvements in institutional reforms and frameworks. Ibukun Beecroft, Evans Osabuohien, Isaiah Olurinola, Uchenna Efobi, and Stephen Oluwatobi pen in Chapter Five the channels through which institutions can influence the process of economic development.

Economic diversification is a recipe for achieving inclusive growth, and the role of institutions in strengthening the process of diversification cannot be ruled out. Thus, Amaka Metu, Chekwube Madichie, Uchenna Anyanwu, Chris Kalu and Okezie Ihugba examine the role of institutions in facilitating economic diversification to achieve inclusive growth in Chapter Six. Furthermore, Naser Nuru and Hayelom Gereziher apply the Cholesky identification scheme to examine the effects of financial development in an open economy in Chapter Seven. Meanwhile, since poverty is no longer fashionable, in the eighth chapter, theories on poverty are evaluated by Opeyemi Aluko to identify how to break the cycle of poverty in Africa. Actualizing sustainable development in Africa will require enormous economic resources. This implies that there should be a clear prioritization of financing options on what works best for the continent's development. Uchenna Efobi, Oluwabunmi Adejumo and Simplice Asongu take stock of these financing options in Chapter Nine.

Taking the discourse further, Abba Barnabe examine the effect of migrant remittances on financial inclusion in Africa in the tenth chapter. While Msafiri Njoroge clarifies, in Chapter Eleven, how trade policies could be employed to promote the inclusiveness of the tourism sector. The chapter concludes that until local communities are allowed to participate fully in tourism activities - either through supplying goods and services or direct employment - inclusiveness of tourism business cannot be practically realized. It is notable that job-hopping between formal and informal sectors represents an essential driver of welfare and productivity changes. Consequently, Solomon Olakojo, Olaronke Onanuga and Abayomi Onanuga write the last chapter of Section Two on patterns, forms and drivers of informality, in addition to factors that determine hopping between formal and informal jobs.

The agriculture industry is dependent on weather and climate to produce food and fiber necessary to sustain human life in many African economies. So, the thirteenth chapter, by Zerihun Amare, dwells on climate adaptation for crop production, predictability of weather conditions, and the effect of climate change on land, water and temperature. To further highlight the importance of land to farmers in agricultural production, Abiodun Obayelu, Kamilu Bolarinwa, and Olalekan Oyekunle apply a combination of methods - expository, comparative and case analysis – in the fourteenth chapter. Their analysis and findings showed that land issues are delicate, demanding careful attention to avoid social or political conflicts. The study concludes that politicization of land is a significant cause of land dispute, but with good land governance; land policy reform becomes easier to implement.

Galinoma Lubawa analyzes the importance of business planning for family-owned food processing Small and Medium Enterprises (Fo-SMEs) in Chapter Fifteen. It demonstrates the establishment of an "integrated planning" strategy to link Fo-SMEs with a government support system for sustainable business development. The production of food is majorly a rural activity in Africa, but the demand and consumption of food cuts across both rural and urban areas. Hence, in Chapter Seventeen, Ayobami Popoola, Yamah Adeyemi, Femi Oni, Odunayo Omojola, Bamiji Adeleye, Samuel Medayese and Ojoma Popoola discuss the need for rural-urban market linkages. Amadou Tandjigora assesses technological innovations in general and more specifically, the use of information and communication technologies in agriculture while Nyanjige Mayala write on finding the balance between infrastructure development and agricultural support so that the two can support industrialization process in Chapters Sixteen and Eighteen, respectively.

Sustainable food systems contribute to addressing food security, poverty alleviation and economic growth. Therefore, Olubunmi Ajayi, Scott Baum and Cordia Ch, in Chapter Nineteen, discuss a food waste reduction program model, designed to deliver effective responses through relevant institutions. The chapter identifies significant policy opportunities for food waste management strategies and food waste guidelines. The twentieth chapter, by Alexis Beyuo, engages the ladder of participation as a framework to assess how knowledge co-creation between local farmers and agro-technocrats from non-governmental organizations (NGOs) is associated with farmers' environmental consciousness. Local powerholders are known to perpetuate non-participation in the management and use of forest resources. Samuel Medayese, Hangwelani Magidimisha-Chipungu, Ayobami Popoola, Lovemore Chipungu, and Bamiji Adeleye, in Chapter Twenty-One, make a chronological review of inclusiveness in urban development.

José Vargas-Hernández, in the twenty-second chapter, focuses on the implications of the transition of ecosystem services for urban agroecology. The author proposes that a transition from traditional and industrial agriculture towards urban agroecology is inevitable to improve ecological and environmental services, economic efficiency, social equity and justice, as well as environmental sustainability of cities. Chapter Twenty-Three, by Enoch Kosoe, Alexis Beyuo and Reginald Addy-Morton, extensively discuss the benefits of community participation and the impediments of lack of community cooperation in forest reserve management. In the last chapter, Chigozie Nweke-Eze assesses the implementation, experiences and impacts of neoliberal electricity-sector reforms in Sub-Saharan Africa. In sum, it identifies the reasons for the poor performance of the reforms, weak institutions, and non-existence of unhampered competition among players in the region's electricity markets.

CONCLUDING REMARKS

Considering the chapters contained in this book, researched areas and respective cases have contributed to enhancing existing literature by resolving the challenges specific to the attainment of sustainable and inclusive economic growth in Africa. The book points out some development challenges and proffers recommendations for sustainable, inclusive practices that would lead to prosperity in the continent. Institutional framework has varying effects in different sectors across African countries, but the book advocates that strong institutional framework is required for Africa's transition to sustainable and inclusive economic development.

There is the need for Africa to diversify its economies and create effective institutions to participate more actively in the international polity. Effective institutional frameworks should be such that encourage the citizenry (particularly female and youth) to: participate and co-manage projects in all sectors; ensure investment in climate-smart agriculture, energy and infrastructure for environmental quality; and allow the adoption of advanced information, communication and technology for economic stability purpose. This would ensure an investment-friendly environment, resulting in more jobs, better wages and improved standard of living in Africa.

Evans S. Osabuohien
Covenant University, Nigeria

Obindah Gershon
Covenant University, Nigeria

Olaronke Onanuga
Covenant University, Nigeria

Oluyomi Ola-David
Covenant University, Nigeria

Emmanuel A. Oduntan
Covenant University, Nigeria

REFERENCES

Beecroft, I., Osabuohien, E., Efobi, U., Olurinola, I., & Osabohien, R. (2020). Manufacturing Export and ICT Infrastructure in West Africa: Investigating the Roles of Economic and Political Institutions. *Institutions and Economies*, *12*(1), 1–36.

Egbetokun, S., Osabuohien, E., Onanuga, O., Akinbobola, T., Gershon, O., & Okafor, V. (2020). Environmental Pollution, Economic Growth and Institutional Quality: Exploring the Nexus in Nigeria. *Management of Environmental Quality*, *31*(1), 18–31.

Karakara, A. A., & Osabuohien, E. (2020). ICT Adoption, Competition and Innovation of Informal Firms in West Africa: Comparative Study of Ghana and Nigeria. *Journal of Enterprising Communities*, *14*(3), 397–414.

Olakojo, S. A., & Onanuga, O. T. (2020). Effects of Climate Change on the Long-run Crops' Yields in Nigeria. *International Journal on Food System Dynamics*, *11*(3), 270–296.

Osabohien, R., Onanuga, O., Aderounmu, B., Matthew, O., & Osabuohien, E. (2020). Social protection and employment in Africa's agricultural sector. *Business: Theory and Practice*, *21*(2), 494–502.

Osabuohien, E. (2020). *The Palgrave Handbook of Agricultural and Rural Development in Africa*. Palgrave Macmillan.

Acknowledgment

The editors acknowledge the help of numerous persons and organizations that made this edited volume a reality. First, we sincerely appreciate the concerted efforts of all the contributing authors and the reviewers for committing their valuable time to this project.

The conception of this book project stemmed from a conference on 'Sustainable Economic Development in Africa' organized by the Department of Economics and Development Studies in conjunction with the Centre for Economic Policy and Development Research (CEPDeR), both of Covenant University, Ota, Nigeria in June 2019. Our appreciation goes to the Management of Covenant University for creating an enabling environment necessary for the successful completion of the book project.

The call for chapters of this volume enjoyed a broad subscription from a diverse selection of authors across disciplines and geographical boundaries. Consequent to this, we appreciate the various online platforms, professional and social networks that helped feature and widely disseminate the call for chapters. Suffice to say that we navigated through over 90 chapter proposals and subsequent chapter submissions to arrive at the select papers included in this volume.

Even though COVID-19 *brouhaha* emerged in the process, the kind assistance and follow up provided by IGI Global and her publishing assistants was an essential boost to complete the project. Also, we acknowledge the Equipment Subsidy Grant from the Alexander von Humboldt Foundation [Ref: 3.4-8151/19047] to CEPDeR, Covenant University that facilitate CEPDeR's activities including this project.

We appreciate our families for their support and encouragement through it all.

Finally, we appreciate the Almighty God for the endowment of grace and strength to commence and conclude this book project.

Evans S. Osabuohien
Covenant University, Nigeria

Obindah Gershon
Covenant University, Nigeria

Olaronke Onanuga
Covenant University, Nigeria

Oluyomi Ola-David
Covenant University, Nigeria

Emmanuel A. Oduntan
Covenant University, Nigeria

Section 1
Institution, Governance, and Africa's Development Agenda

Chapter 1
Africa, 2030 Agenda and Agenda 2063:
The Imperative of Transnational Governance

Oluwaseun James Oguntuase
https://orcid.org/0000-0003-2225-7766
Lagos State University, Lagos, Nigeria

ABSTRACT

The hierarchical state-led model of governance that is used to address global policy issues has proved to be wanting on sustainable development. This chapter discusses the concept of transnational governance of sustainable development, focusing on the United Nations 2030 Agenda and Agenda 2063 in Africa. The premise is that implementation of the two agendas represents an enormous challenge to African governments in terms of resources, extent, and urgency. The chapter will make a reasonable case that transnational governance is required for active engagement of non-state actors and relevant institutions to mobilize resources to support the effective implementation and monitoring of the 2030 Agenda and Agenda 2063 in Africa.

INTRODUCTION

The link between governance and development is a two-way street in Africa The quality and characteristics of governance shape the level of development. The World Bank used the term "crisis in governance" for the first time in 1989 to sum up the litany of Africa's development problems (World Bank, 1989). The challenges besetting the continent of Africa are numerous, multifaceted and complex— ranging from poverty to climate change, food insecurity, energy insecurity, loss of biodiversity, lack of portable water, unemployment, rapid urbanization, gender inequality, violent conflict and over-exploitation (Osabohien et al, 2020; Osabuohien, 2020a). It therefore behooves on us to explore how to improve the governance of sustainable development on the continent.

DOI: 10.4018/978-1-7998-4817-2.ch001

This chapter focuses on a specific governance approach: the concept of transnational governance. In conceptualizing this chapter, transnational governance is defined as the transboundary institutional arrangements emerging from the interaction among private actors or between private and public actors that steer actors' behaviors in an issue-specific area (Falkner, 2003).

In 2013, the African Union endorsed the 2063 Agenda, the continent's shared strategic framework for inclusive growth and sustainable development. Two years later, the United Nations Sustainable Development Summit adopted the 2030 Agenda for Sustainable Development, popularly called the Sustainable Development Goals (SDGs). The United Nations' 2030 Agenda for Sustainable Development acknowledges the importance of the African Union Agenda 2063 and considers it an integral part of it. African countries have shown their commitments to both the Agenda 2030 and the Agenda 2063 (Osabuohien, 2020b).

Agendas 2030 and 2063 continue and reinforce the vision of the 1980s for sustainable development. They offer eminent platforms for African countries for setting a common course aimed at attaining sustainable development at national and continental levels. The relatability of sustainable development to human development goals has led to it becoming the ground norm of evaluating private and public, national and regional resource utilization. To achieve this, targets on socially and/or environmentally practices have been set at multi-national, national and regional levels (Pomare, 2018), making sustainable development a core concept within global development policy and agenda (Abubakar, 2017; Cerin, 2006).

There is need to reform governance in Africa to realize the aspirations stated in both 2030 Agenda and Agenda 2063. The large remit of the two Agendas demands that countries formulate good policy foundations; both in respect of individual goals and overall trajectories (for example, development plans). Most importantly, achieving the goals and targets in the Agendas will demand thorough implementation, monitoring, accountability and sustained long-term attention. In addition, they both recognize the importance of getting the governance dimensions right. From this perspective, this chapter presents transnational governance as innovation mechanisms to confront the challenges of governance in Africa towards the achievement of 2030 Agenda and Agenda 2063 in the continent.

GOVERNANCE OF SUSTAINABLE DEVELOPMENT

Governance is the various institutionalized modes of social coordination to produce and implement collectively binding rules, or to provide collective goods. It includes formal institutions and regimes empowered to enforce compliance, as well as informal arrangements that people and institutions either have agreed to or perceive to be in their interest (Commission on Global Governance, 1995). Governance consists of both structure and process. As a structure, it relates to institutions and actor constellations. Governance as process pinpoints the modes of social coordination by which actors engage in rulemaking and implementation and in the provision of collective goods (Börzel & Risse, 2010). In the words of Keping (2018), governance identifies the blurring of boundaries and responsibilities for tackling social and economic issues, which are key elements of sustainable development.

Although definitions abound with respect to sustainable development, the most often cited definition of the concept is the one proposed by the Brundtland Commission Report. It defines a development to be sustainable when "it meets the needs of the present without compromising the ability of future generations to meet their own needs" (World Commission on Environment and Development [WCED], 1987: p.8). Since the Brundtland Report brought the concept of sustainable development into public consciousness, the practices of sustainable development has continued to evolve, from tackling environmental issues, to dealing with the global strategic issue (Olawumi & Chan, 2018) and becoming a fundamental strategy to guide the world's social and economic transformation (Klarin, 2018).

Scholars have acknowledged the importance of global policy in the realization of sustainable development (Van den Brande, Happaerts, & Bruyninckx, 2008). Global policy is perceived as the strategy for realization of sustainable development strategies (Bochańczyk-Kupka & Pęciak, 2015). Governance at one level - local, national, supranational or global - is not sufficient for implementation of the idea of sustainable development. It requires synchronization and coordination of actions at multidimensional level (Bochańczyk-Kupka & Pęciak, 2015). In this context, governance has been referred to as the "fourth pillar of sustainable development" (Kanie, Zondervan, & Stevens, 2014: p.6).

CONCEPTUALISING TRANSNATIONAL GOVERNANCE

It has become increasingly difficult to separate what takes place within national boundaries and what takes place across and beyond nations. The neat opposition between "globalization" and "nations", often just beneath the surface in a number of debates, does not really make sense, whether empirically or analytically. Organizations, activities and individuals constantly span multiple levels, rendering obsolete older lines of demarcation (Djelic & Sahlin-Andersson, 2006). The label "transnational" suggests entanglement and blurred boundaries to a degree that the term "global" could not.

The concept of transnational governance focuses on the forms of regulation that emerge from the notion that states are no longer the exclusive sources of regulatory global authority (Cashore, 2002; Vogel, 2008) and that private authority is emerging alongside traditional governance (Green, 2013). Transnational governance does not imply that national autonomy is no longer predominant or that the nation state has lost its sovereignty, but seeks to highlight that governance processes are immersed in geopolitical relations and structures of interactions and institutions at multiple levels. (*e.g.*, local, national, global) (Gomes & Merchán, 2017).

In the transnational realm, governance is primarily organized through cross-border networks of different configurations of actors (Andonova, Betsill, & Bulkeley, 2009). They operate simultaneously across multiple scales, mobilizing resources to integrate new concepts into everyday worldviews and practices (Betsill & Bulkeley, 2004). To be considered a form of transnational governance, such networks must seek to address some form of public goal (though they may not accomplish it) (Andonova et al., 2009).

Transnational governance is characterized by two main aspects. First, the state is not the main actor involved in rule making; instead, it is especially private actors that develop rules. It involves regular interaction across national boundaries when at least one actor is a non-state agent or does not operate on behalf of a national government or intergovernmental organization (Risse-Kappen, 1995). Second, transnational governance is voluntary and relies on market forces and public scrutiny to exert pressure on the target group and generate public benefits (Kalfagianni, Partzsch, & Widerberg, 2020). Moreover, transnational governance can take two forms: (a) soft regulation (or soft law) in self-regulating (i.e., only pro-market actors) or co-regulated (i.e., when there are public and private authors); (b) legislation and its forms of command and control (hard law), which determine what is permitted or not permitted in a particular jurisdiction (Djelic & Sahlin-Andersson, 2006; Rasche & Gilbert, 2012).

Regardless of the form taken by transnational governance, three characteristics or dimensions can be highlighted: (a) it involves multiple actors, both the State and its agencies, as well as civil society organizations and businesses; (b) it is immersed in multilevel relations, that is, the local, national and global dimensions intertwine and it is often difficult to analytically separate what happens in each of them; and (c) decision making is not a result of imposition of a single actor (e.g. the state) but a result of negotiation and consensus building on the rules and norms that will guide the behavior of the actors (Gomes, & Merchán, 2017).

THE ROLE OF TRANSNATIONAL INSTITUTTIONS IN GOVERNANCE OF SUSTAINABLE DEVELOPMENT

The reconfiguration of the word "State" by globalization has led to emergence of new forms of authority through global and regional policy processes that co-exist alongside nation-state policy processes (Stone, 2008). These new forms of authority, transnational institutions, are seen as alternatives to state-based forms of governance because they provide many governance functions—such as rule-setting, dispute resolution, and public good provision—which are traditionally associated with national governments and intergovernmental organizations (Andonova, Hale, & Roger, 2017). Much of the literature on transnational governance assumes that non-state actors increase the effectiveness of governance because they bring in resources and knowledge that public actors lack (Dzebo, 2019).

This chapter aligns with Williamson (1975, 1985) in presenting transnational institutions as governance structures. The term transnational institutions (rather than networks, coalitions, or movements) is adopted to evoke the structured and structuring dimensions in the actions and to underscore the diversity of these institutions. These transnational institutions are labeled as social innovation, in which stakeholders come together to negotiate their own governance (Sauer & Hiete, 2020), establish new formal or informal rules that may lead to changes in practice (Shalley, Hitt, Zhou, Raffaelli, & Glynn, 2015), and drive change (Jacob et al., 2019).

Transgovernmental Networks

Transgovernmental networks are networks of state executives (government officials) from specialized ministerial departments or independent domestic regulatory agencies, who acting below the level of central government, established institutionalized links to exchange information, develop common regulatory standards, and assist one another in enforcing such standards in their respective jurisdictions (Freyburg, Krizic, Lavenex & O'flynn, 2017). The resulting networks range from more informal groupings which may lack a permanent secretariat or official by-laws, to more institutionalized organizations that share some of the characteristics of traditional intergovernmental organizations. In many cases a process of gradual institutionalization occurs (Hale & Held, 2011).

Slaughter (2004) noted that transgovernmental networks provide a fast and flexible alternative to the cumbersome formality of interstate cooperation. They tend to serve one of three functions: share information and best practices concerning challenges that all governments face; coordinate and harmonize policies across jurisdictions; and increase countries' enforcement capacities regarding transnational problems (Slaughter, 2004).

Multi-Stakeholders Initiatives

Multi-stakeholders initiatives bring together government, civil society, and the private sector to address complex development challenges that no one party alone has the capacity, resources, and know-how to do so more effectively (Thindwa, 2015). The composition – actors across the public and private sectors – ensure the governance and capabilities do not rely on one constituent actor (Biekart & Fowler, 2018). In so doing, MSIs come to complement, and not usurp the role of governments in achieving these ends (Thindwa, 2015).

Most MSIs are anchored on facilitating transparency, accountability and (stakeholder) participation – three critical ingredients for strengthening public sector governance in developing as well as developed countries (Thindwa, 2015). They represent a "transnational private regulation" that is "formally independent of government but not reducible to industry self-regulation, and regulatory in that it purports to set and enforce standards for performance" (Bartley, 2007; p. 302).

Voluntary Approaches

Voluntary approaches is a broad term that encompasses many different kinds of arrangements, such as self-regulation, voluntary initiatives, voluntary codes, environmental charters, voluntary accords, voluntary agreements, co-regulation, covenants, and negotiated environmental agreements, to name just a few (Higley, Convery, & Lévêque, 2001). In all, the parties voluntarily agree to participate, rather than being legally required or forced to do so (Segerson, 2013).

Voluntary approaches range from international agreements and programmes, to national policy, legislation and regulation, and financial sector lending and investment requirements, which can serve the purpose of improving the sustainable development practices and performance of industrial activities (Greene, Moffett, Meyer, & Middelkoop, 2002). These approaches ensure parties involved go beyond the law in producing positive externalities (Burke, 2016). Government reliance on voluntary approaches represents a significant shift in public policy: moving from command and control regulations to market-based mechanisms. They are developed from a need to address the market and governance failures that have occurred as a result of globalization and the increasingly penetrable nature of transnational borders (Burke, 2016).

THE AGENDA 2030 FOR SUSTAINBLE DEVELOPMENT

Many United Nations Millennium Development Goals (MDGs) have been absorbed into the SDGs. Where the aim of the MDGs was to reduce poverty, hunger, illiteracy, gender inequality and correct some developmental abnormalities, the SDGs shed light on the need for an inclusive, long-term, and sustainable development process. The 17 Goals and 169 targets address vital global issues and represent a big step forward on a long road toward an inclusive, equitable and resilient society. It can be argued from the SDGs that the goal of sustainable development is to achieve social progress, environmental equilibrium and economic growth (Mensah, 2019). Since its adoption in 2015, increasing numbers of stakeholders have adopted the SDGs as an eminent platform for setting a common course aimed at attaining sustainable development at national, regional and global levels (Josephsen, 2017).

While Africa made encouraging progress on the MDGs, the forerunner of the SDGs, the continent's starting point in the adoption of the SDGs was lower than those of other continents. Emerging evidence over the last four years (2015 – 2020) of tracking SDGs progress indicates that sustainability challenges still prevail in Africa, with several African countries not being on track to achieve the SDGs. The 2020 Africa SDG Index showed that the top-ranking countries in Africa are a combination of North African countries and small island states – Tunisia, Mauritius, Morocco, Algeria and Cabo Verde – but these top performers are still only about two-thirds on the way, on average, to achieving the SDGs. Low performers are South Sudan, Central African Republic, Chad, Somalia and Eritrea, mainly fragile states with high levels of poverty and conflicts in their territories (see Table 1). (The Sustainable Development Goals Center for Africa [SDGCA] and Sustainable Development Solutions Network [SDSN], 2020).

Table 1. SDGs performance of African countries (2020)

Rank	Country	Score	Rank	Country	Score	Rank	Country	Score	Rank	Country	Score
1	Tunisia	67.10	14	Gabon	58.07	27	Zambia	53.25	40	Guinea	50.20
2	Mauritius	66.79	15	Côte d'Ivoire	57.67	28	Mali	53.22	41	Liberia	49.33
3	Morocco	66.30	16	Rwanda	57.65	29	Eswatini	52.94	42	Nigeria	48.84
4	Algeria	65.90	17	Tanzania	57.00	30	Libya	52.70	43	Madagascar	47.94
5	Cabo Verde	65.59	18	Burkina Faso	55.90	31	Malawi	52.64	44	Sudan	47.85
6	Egypt	65.44	19	Uganda	55.71	32	Lesotho	52.43	45	Comoros	46.98
7	Botswana	63.93	20	The Gambia	55.53	33	Mozambique	52.17	46	Guinea-Bissau	46.37
8	Ghana	62.69	21	Togo	54.11	34	Sierra Leone	51.59	47	Democratic Rep. of Congo	44.83
9	South Africa	62.20	22	Ethiopia	54.15	35	Djibouti	51.30	48	Eritrea	44.17
10	São Tomé and Principe	61.61	23	Zimbabwe	53.79	36	Angola	51.18	49	Somalia	42.34
11	Senegal	58.69	24	Mauritania	53.78	37	Republic of Congo	50.81	50	Chad	40.34
12	Kenya	58.54	25	Benin	53.53	38	Niger	50.47	51	Central African Republic	38.05
13	Namibia	58.31	26	Cameroon	53.37	39	Burundi	50.37	52	South Sudan	32.36

There are 54 countries in Africa. The authors excluded Seychelles and Libya due to insufficient data availability

Source: SDGCA & SDSN (2020)

THE AFRICAN UNION AGENDA 2063

Agenda 2063 was adopted at the Golden Jubilee Summit (May 2013) of the Organization of African Unity (OAU)/African Union (AU) to guide Africa's development for the next half-century and to achieve the vision of *The Africa We Want.* The 50-year development framework, with 20 goals and 174 targets, aims to materialize Africa's vision of: an *integrated, prosperous and peaceful Africa, driven by its own citizens and representing a dynamic force in the world* (AU, UNECA, AfDP, & UNDP, 2016). The continental blueprint consolidates the earlier initiative, the New Partnership for Africa's Development (NEPAD) into a forward-looking transformational framework for Africa (AU, UNECA, AfDP, & UNDP, 2016). It provides a rallying point for African Union Member states, regional bodies and development stakeholders to garner investments and collective efforts towards a common development agenda. Furthermore, it is a concrete manifestation of the pan-African drive for unity, self-determination, freedom, progress and collective prosperity pursued under Pan-Africanism and African Renaissance (NEPAD, 2020).

The continent embarked on the implementation of her 50-year development blueprint through domesticating and implementing Agenda 2063 into national and regional development strategies. Fifty-four countries have signed and twenty-nine have ratified the agreement. The first six years of implementation witnessed remarkable progress towards the targets. The continent registered good progress in attaining several goals and targets defined in the First Ten-Year Implementation Plan of Agenda 2063 with an aggregate score of 32% against the 2019 targets. At the regional level, East Africa recorded the highest

Table 2. Aspirations of the African Union Agenda 2063

Aspiration 1	A prosperous Africa based on inclusive growth and sustainable development
Aspiration 2	An integrated continent; politically united and based on the ideals of Pan-Africanism and the vision of Africa's Renaissance
Aspiration 3	An Africa of good governance, democracy, respect for human rights, justice and the rule of law
Aspiration 4	A peaceful and secure Africa
Aspiration 5	An Africa with a strong cultural identity, common heritage, shared values and ethics
Aspiration 6	An Africa, whose development is people-driven, relying on the potential of African people, especially its women and youth, and caring for children
Aspiration 7	Africa as a strong, united, resilient and influential global player and partner

Source: African Union (2015)

performance in five out of the seven aspirations in Agenda 2063 First Ten Year Implementation Plan, with an aggregate score of 40% against the 2019 targets. The aggregate performance of West Africa stood at 34%, while the aggregate performance of North Africa stood at 27%. Southern and Central Africa both recorded an aggregate score of 25% against the 2019 targets (NEPAD, 2020).

Evidently, more efforts will be required to accelerate implementation for the continent to achieve the set of goals and targets defined in Agenda 2063. This will require concerted and coordinated efforts at sub-national, national, regional and continental levels to comprehensively address the identified challenges and harness the available opportunities (NEPAD, 2020).

AGENDAS 2030 AND 2063

Even though operating in very different time frames (just 15 years for the 2030 Agenda and 50 years for the Agenda 2063), the 17 SDGs fit neatly into the 20 goals of Agenda 2063. The degree of convergence between the two agendas depends on the level of disaggregation (goals, targets, indicators), and of course, the nature of their focus. A mapping exercise by the UN Economic Commission for Africa (2017) has shown that convergence is 100.0% at Goal level. Convergence reaches 69.8% at Target level and 67.2% at indicator level. The two agendas broadly converge on human development (poverty eradication, education, and health), sustainable economic opportunity (transforming economies, infrastructure, and rural sector), gender equality and youth empowerment, peaceful and inclusive societies, accountable institutions, justice and environmental sustainability. Hence by implementing Agenda 2063 African countries should ipso facto be meeting global obligations under the 2030 Agenda (Mo Ibrahim, 2019).

There are topics of divergence as well, with themes such as inequality (between and within nations), sustainable management of land ecosystems (desertification, biodiversity, and land degradation), responsible consumption and production and urgent climate action as central to the SDGs, but not as fully developed in Agenda 2063 (SDGCA & SDSN, 2019).

Recognizing the strong thematic overlaps in the Agendas 2030 and 2063 as shown in Table 2 above, in January 2018, the African Union Commission and the United Nations signed the *AU-UN Framework for the Implementation of Agenda 2063 and the 2030 Agenda for Sustainable Development.* This framework represents the development of a continent-wide, unified monitoring and evaluation reporting

Table 3. Comparison of the 2030 agenda and agenda 2063

Sustainable Development Goals	Strongly matched	Weakly matched	Total	No association
Number of Goals	11	6	17	0
Percentage of Goals	64.7	35.3	100.0	0.0
Number of targets	62	56	118	51
Percentage of targets	36.7	33.1	69.8	30.2
Number of indicators	96	66	162	79
Percentage of indicators	39.8	27.4	67.2	32.8

Source: UNECA (2017)

system which included a harmonized set of goals, indicators and targets, while avoiding duplication and policy incoherence.

IMPERATIVE OF TRANSNATIONAL GOVERNANCE TOWARDS 2030 AGENDA AND AGENDA 2063

The hierarchical state-led model of governance that is used to address global policy issues have been proving wanting on a range of pressing societal challenges (Hale & Held, 2011; Pattberg & Widerberg, 2016). Delivering collective public goods and achieving sustainable development in a highly interconnected globalized world need innovative approaches including new structures and systems in a global order. These factors make governance a crucial part of both 2030 Agenda and Agenda 2063, which are underpinned by an elaborate means of implementation including follow-up and review mechanism.

The social and environmental challenges which are targets of both 2030 Agenda and Agenda 2063 are global policy issues which many countries have contributed to, and no individual country can effectively address by acting alone. Transnational governance has gained popularity as mechanisms to address complex societal problems whose causes span diverse institutions and whose resolution requires the alignment and application of different competencies and locations of authority and power (Fowler & Biekart, 2017).

Transnational governance authoritatively steers constituents towards these public goals with the participation of non-state actors helping to overcome lack of accountability in global politics, and improving both the quality of public policies and the effectiveness of their implementation and monitoring. Both Agenda 2030 and Agenda 2063 are comprehensive, underpinned by an extensive consultation process, and share common aspirations of structural transformation and sustainable development. Implementing these agendas is set to rely on mechanisms bringing together diverse actors to actively align their efforts towards a shared objective. Transnational governance will help achieve this unity of purpose.

The implementation of 2030 Agenda and Agenda 2063 represents an enormous challenge in terms of resources, extent and urgency. There is a call for promoting adequate political decisions and launching effective, practical actions at all levels (Josephsen, 2017). Transnational governance is also important in promoting adequate political decisions and launching effective, practical actions at all levels. Governments face significant challenges, including fiscal constraints, political divisions, state fragility, corruption and institutional failures. These constraints point to the need for active engagement by civil society organizations and companies, not to replicate government responsibilities or let them "off the hook", but to advocate for policy reforms and public resources in support of the developmental agenda, and to unlock additional resources and enhance capabilities to achieve implementation.

Likewise, proponents of transnational governance argue that coalition and cooperation between government agencies, business actors, and civil society will increase the likelihood to stay within a 'safe operating space for humanity' (Rockström et al., 2009) as new collaborative arrangements are expected to forge more efficient, effective, and inclusive responses to solving global policy problems (Pattberg & Widerberg, 2016), as targeted by 2030 Agenda and Agenda 2063.

FURTHER RESEARCH DIRECTIONS

While the concept of transnational governance and institutions has the potential for addressing complex sustainable development problems, they have yet to reach their full potential. To achieve this, the question of credence, credibility and legitimacy must be answered considering the increasing number and diverse transnational institutions involved in sustainable development issues. There is need to explore the role of credence, credibility and legitimacy, and how transnational institutions could achieve them, towards the achievement of both 2030 Agenda and Agenda 2063, other developmental agenda, and overall quality of life in Africa.

CONCLUDING REMARKS

When it comes to development, Africa countries are still on unsustainable track. However, there are opportunities to bring together diverse actors to actively align their efforts towards a share objective. And, given the

All the significant international recent treaties, such as the United Nations 2030 Agenda for Sustainable Development and the Agenda 2063 in Africa, are structured over voluntary commitments. And, given the all-too-visible inadequacies of existing intergovernmental institutions in Africa and the enormous development problems facing the continent, then transnational governance has a major role to play in mobilizing the knowledge and resources required to solve the escalating societal challenges on the continent.

It is imperative for African leaders, scholars and all other relevant stakeholders to embrace, deepen and institutionalize transnational governance including its innovative mechanisms and institutions, to overcome crisis of governance on the continent. This will ensure the achievement of both 2030 Agenda and Agenda 2063 towards ensuring sustainable livelihoods of its over 1.33 billion people.

REFERENCES

Abubakar, I. R. (2017). Access to sanitation facilities among Nigerian households: Determinants and sustainability implications. *Sustainability*, *9*(4), 547. doi:10.3390/su9040547

African Union, Economic Commission for Africa, African Development Bank, & United Nations Development Programme. (2016). MDGs to Agenda 2063/SDGs Transition Report 2016. Towards an integrated and coherent approach to sustainable development in Africa. Addis Ababa: AU, ECA, AfDP, UNDP.

African Union Development Agency – NEPAD. (2020, February). First Continental Report on the Implementation of Agenda 2063. Midrand, South Africa: NEPAD.

Andonova, L. B., Betsill, M. M., & Bulkeley, H. (2009). Transnational climate governance. *Global Environmental Politics*, *9*(2), 52–73. doi:10.1162/glep.2009.9.2.52

Andonova, L. B., Hale, T. L., & Roger, C. B. (2017). National policy and transnational governance of climate change: Substitutes or complements? *International Studies Quarterly*, *61*(2), 253–268. Advance online publication. doi:10.1093/isq/sqx014

Bartley, T. (2007). Institutional emergence in an era of globalization: The rise of transnational private regulation of labour and environment conditions. *American Journal of Sociology*, *113*(2), 297–351. doi:10.1086/518871

Betsill, M. M., & Harriet Bulkeley, H. (2004). Transnational networks and global environmental governance: The cities for climate protection program. *International Studies Quarterly*, *48*(2), 471–493. doi:10.1111/j.0020-8833.2004.00310.x

Biekart, K., & Fowler, A. (2018). Ownership dynamics in local multi-stakeholder initiatives. *Third World Quarterly*, *39*(9), 1692–1910. doi:10.1080/01436597.2018.1450139

Bochańczyk-Kupka, D., & Pęciak, R. (2015). Institutions in the context of sustainable development. *The Macrotheme Review*, *4*(5), 29–41.

Börzel, T. A., & Risse, T. (2010). Governance without a state: Can it work? *Regulation & Governance*, *4*(2), 113–134. doi:10.1111/j.1748-5991.2010.01076.x

Burke, D. (2016). Voluntary initiatives in corporate global governance; a case study on the UN Global Compact. Erasmus University. https://thesis.eur.nl/pub/36662/DoreenBurkeThesis-26072016-1.pdf

Cashore, B. (2002). Legitimacy and the privatization of environmental governance: How non-state market-driven (NSMD) governance systems gain rule-making authority. *Governance: An International Journal of Policy, Administration and Institutions*, *15*(4), 503–529. doi:10.1111/1468-0491.00199

Cerin, P. (2006). Bringing economic opportunity into line with environmental influence: A discussion on the coase theorem and the Porter and van der Linde hypothesis. *Ecological Economics*, *56*(2), 209–225. doi:10.1016/j.ecolecon.2005.01.016

Commission on Global Governance (Ed.). (1995). *Our global neighborhood*. Oxford University Press.

Djelic, M.-L., & Sahlin-Andersson, K. (Eds.). (2006). *Transnational governance: institutional dynamics of regulation*. Cambridge University Press., doi:10.1017/CBO9780511488665.

Dzebo, A. (2019). Effective governance of transnational adaptation initiatives. *International Environmental Agreement: Politics, Law and Economics*, *19*(4-5), 447–466. doi:10.1007/s10784-019-09445-8

Falkner, R. (2003). Private environmental governance and international relations: Exploring the links. *Global Environmental Politics*, *3*(2), 72–87. doi:10.1162/152638003322068227

Fowler, A., & Biekart, K. (2017). Multi-stakeholder initiatives for Sustainable Development Goals: The importance of interlocutors. *Public Administration and Development*, *37*(2), 81–89. doi:10.1002/pad.1795

Freyburg, T., Krizic, I., Lavenex, S., & O'flynn, C. (2017, January). Democratic governance and trans-governmental networks. *SUPW and PEIO Conference*.

Gomes, M. V. P., & Merchán, C. R. (2017). Transnational governance: Definitions, approaches and research agenda. *Journal of Contemporary Management*, *12*(1). Advance online publication. doi:10.1590/1982-7849rac2017150332

Green, J. F. (2013). *Rethinking private authority: Agents and entrepreneurs in global environmental governance*. Princeton University Press.

Greene, G., Moffett, J., Meyer, S., & Middelkoop, M. J. (2002). Industry codes of practice and other voluntary initiatives: their application to the mining and metals sector. London: International Institute for Environment and Development (IIED).

Hales, T., & Held, D. (Eds.). (2011). *Handbook of transnational governance: Institutions and innovations*. Polity Press.

Higley, C. J., Convery, F., & Lévêque, F. (2001). Voluntary approaches: an introduction. In C. J. Higley & F. Lévêque (Eds.), Environmental Voluntary Approaches: Research Insights for Policy-Makers (pp. 4-13). Paris: Centre d'économie Industrielle.

Jacob, K., Guske, A. L., Antoni-Komar, I., Funcke, S., Gruchmann, T., Kny, J., Naber, E., Ruppert-Winkel, C., Sauer, P. C., Stumpf, K. H., & Volk, R. (2019). Governance for the sustainable economy. Institutional innovation from the bottom up? GAIA Ecological Perspectives on Science and Society, 28(1), 204–209. doi:10.14512/gaia.28.S1.6

Josephsen, L. (2017). Approaches to the implementation of the Sustainable Development Goals – some considerations on the theoretical underpinnings of the 2030 Agenda. Economics Discussion Papers, No 2017-60, Kiel Institute for the World Economy. http://www.economics-ejournal.org/economics/discussionpapers/2017-60

Kalfagianni, A., Partzsch, L., & Widerberg, O. (2020). Transnational institutions and networks. In F. Biermann & K. Rakhyun (Eds.), *Architectures of Earth System Governance: Institutional Complexity and Structural Transformation*. Cambridge University Press., doi:10.1017/9781108784641.004.

Kanie, N., Zondervan, R., & Stevens, C. (2014). Ideas on Governance 'of' and 'for' Sustainable Development Goals: UNU-IAS/POST2015 Conference Report. Tokyo: United Nations University Institute for the Advanced Study of Sustainability.

Keping, Y. (2018). Governance and good governance: A new framework for political analysis. Fudan Journal of the Humanities and Social Sciences, 11(1), 1–8. doi:10.1007/s40647-017-0197-4

Klarin, T. (2018). The concept of sustainable development: From its beginning to the contemporary issues. Zagreb International Review of Economics and Business, 21(1), 67–94. doi:10.2478/zireb-2018-0005

Mensah, J. (2019). Sustainable development: Meaning, history, principles, pillars, and implications for human action: Literature review. *Cogent Social Sciences, 5*. Advance online publication. doi:10.1080/23311886.2019.1653531

Mo Ibrahim Foundation. (2019, October). Agendas 2063 & 2030: Is Africa on track? The African Governance Report.

Olawumi, T. O., & Chan, D. W. M. (2018). A scientometric review of global research on sustainability and sustainable development. *Journal of Cleaner Production, 183*, 231–250. doi:10.1016/j.jclepro.2018.02.162

Osabohien, R., Matthew, O., Ohalete, P., & Osabuohien, E. (2020). Population-Poverty-Inequality Nexus and Social Protection in Africa. *Social Indicators Research, 151*(2), 575–598. Advance online publication. doi:10.1007/s11205-020-02381-0

Osabuohien, E. (2020a). *The Palgrave Handbook of Agricultural and Rural Development in Africa*. Palgrave Macmillan., doi:10.1007/978-3-030-41513-6.

Osabuohien, E. (2020b). Guest Editorial: Labour Issues in Africa's Agricultural and Rural Transformation. *African Journal of Economic and Management Studies, 11*(2), 185–191. doi:10.1108/AJEMS-06-2020-406

Pattberg, P., & Widerberg, O. (2016). Transnational multistakeholder partnerships for sustainable development: Conditions for success. *Ambio, 45*(1), 42–51. doi:10.1007/s13280-015-0684-2 PubMed

Pomare, C. (2018). A multiple framework approach to sustainable development goals (SDGs) and entrepreneurship. Entrepreneurship and the Sustainable Development Goals Contemporary Issues in Entrepreneurship Research, 8, 11–31. doi:10.1108/S2040-724620180000008006

Rasche, A., & Gilbert, D. U. (2012). Institutionalizing global governance: The role of the United Nations Global Compact. Business Ethics: The European Review, 21(1), 100–114. doi:10.1111/j.1467-8608.2011.01642.x

Risse-Kappen, T. (1995). Bringing transnational relations back. In *Bringing Transnational Relations Back In: Non-State Actors, Domestic Structures and International Institutions* (pp. 3–36). Cambridge University Press., doi:10.1017/CBO9780511598760.

Rockström, J., Steffen, W., Noone, K., Persson, A., Chapin, F. S. III, Lambin, E., Lenton, T. M., Scheffer, M., Folke, C., Schellnhuber, H. J., Nykvist, B., de Wit, C. A., Hughes, T., van der Leeuw, S., Rodhe, H., Sörlin, S., Snyder, P. K., Costanza, R., Svedin, U., ... Foley, J. (2009). Planetary boundaries: Exploring the safe operating space for humanity. *Ecology and Society, 14*(2), 32. doi:10.5751/ES-03180-140232

Sauer, P. C., & Hiete, M. (2020). Multi-stakeholder initiatives as social innovation for governance and practice: A review of responsible mining initiatives. *Sustainability, 12*(1), 236. doi:10.3390/su12010236

Segerson, K. (2013). Voluntary approaches to environmental protection and resource management. *Annual Review of Resource Economics, 5*(1), 161–180. doi:10.1146/annurev-resource-091912-151945

Shalley, C., Hitt, M. A., Zhou, J., Raffaelli, R., & Glynn, M. A. (2015). Institutional innovation. In C. Shalley, M. A. Hitt, & J. Zhou (Eds.), *The Oxford Handbook of Creativity, Innovation, and Entrepreneurship*. Oxford University Press., doi:10.1093/oxfordhb/9780199927678.013.0019.

Slaughter, A.-M. (2004). *A new world order*. Princeton University Press.

Stone, D. (2008). Global public policy, transnational policy communities, and their networks. *Policy Studies Journal: the Journal of the Policy Studies Organization*, *36*(1), 19–38. doi:10.1111/j.1541-0072.2007.00251.x

The African Union Commission (2015, September). Agenda 2063: The Africa We Want. First Ten-year Implementation Plan 2014-2023. Author.

The Sustainable Development Goals Center for Africa & Sustainable Development Solutions Network. (2020). *Africa SDG Index and Dashboards Report 2020*. SDGCA & SDSN.

Thindwa, J. (2015 July 7). Multi-stakeholders initiatives: Platforms of collective governance for development. World Bank Blogs. https://blogs.worldbank.org/governance/multi-stakeholder-initiatives-platforms-collective-governance-development

United Nations Economic Commission for Africa (UNECA). (2017). Integrating Agenda 2063 and 2030 Agenda for Sustainable Development into national development plans. http://mif.media/gr-2019-uneca.

Van den Brande, K., Happaerts, S., & Bruyninckx, H. (2008). The role of the subnational level of government in decision-making for sustainable development: a multi-level governance perspective. Katholieke Universiteit Leuven Working Paper No 4.

Vogel, D. (2008). Private global business regulation. *Annual Review of Political Science*, *11*(1), 261–282. doi:10.1146/annurev.polisci.11.053106.141706

Williamson, O. E. (1975). *Markets and hierarchies: Analysis and antitrust implications*. Free Press.

Williamson, O. E. (1985). *The economic institutions of capitalism*. Free Press.

World Bank. (1989). *From crisis to sustainable growth – sub Saharan Arica: a long-term perspective study*. The World Bank.

World Commission on Environment and Development. (1987). *Our common future*. Oxford University Press.

ADDITIONAL READING

Beisheim, M., & Simon, N. (2018). Multistakeholder partnership for the SDGs: Actors' views on UN metagovernance. *Global Governance*, *24*(4), 497–515. doi:10.1163/19426720-02404003

Brandi, C. A. (2017). Sustainability standards and sustainable development: Synergies and trade-offs of transnational governance. *Sustainable Development*, *25*(1), 25–34. doi:10.1002d.1639

Cleary, S. (2017). Reconceptualizing transnational governance: Making global institutions fit for purpose. *Economics: The Open-Access. Open-Assessment E-Journal*, *11*(21), 1–13. doi:10.5018/economics-ejournal.ja.2017-21

Dodds, F. (2015). Multi-stakeholders partnerships: Making them work for the Post-2015 Development Agenda. ECOSOC/United Nations.

Glass, L.-M., & Newig, J. (2019). Governance for achieving the Sustainable Development Goals: How important are participation, policy coherence, reflexivity, adaptation and democratic institutions? Earth System Governance, 2, 100031. doi:10.1016/j.esg.2019.100031

Monkelbaan, J. (2019). Overview of governance theories that are relevant for the SDGs. In *Governance for the Sustainable Development Goals: Exploring an integrative framework of theories, tools and contingencies* (pp. 21-48). Sustainable Development Goal Series. Singapore: Springer. doi:10.1007/978-981-13-0475-0_2

Osabohien, R., Onanuga, O., Aderounmu, B., Matthew, O., & Osabuohien, E. (2020). Social Protection and Employment in Africa's agricultural Sector. Business. *Theory into Practice*, *21*(2), 494–502. doi:10.3846/btp.2020.11945

van Zeijl-Rozema, A., Corvers, R., Kemp, R., & Martens, P. (2008). Governance for sustainable development: A framework. *Sustainable Development*, *16*(6), 410–421. doi:10.1002d.367

KEY TERMS AND DEFINITIONS

Agenda: An underlying often ideological plan or program.

Governance: The structures and processes of governing a state or organization.

Institution: A social structure in which people cooperate and which influences the behavior of people and the way they live.

Sustainable Development: Development that meets the needs of the present without compromising the ability of future generations to meet their own needs.

Transnational: Extending or operating across national boundaries.

Chapter 2
The Role of Institutions in the Discourse of Sustainable Development in West African Countries

Alhassan Abdulwakeel Karakara
https://orcid.org/0000-0001-7378-1678
University of Cape Coast, Ghana

Evans S. Osabuohien
https://orcid.org/0000-0002-3258-8326
Covenant University, Nigeria

ABSTRACT

There are few studies on the role of institutions in achieving sustainable development that infer that these institutions offer the mechanisms for resource and environmental management. Thus, twelve West African countries (Benin, Burkina Faso, Cote d'Ivoire, Gambia, Ghana, Liberia, Mali, Niger, Nigeria, Senegal, Sierra Leone, and Togo) are covered in the study using data from World Development Indicators and World Governance Indicators. Six main outcome variables are used. These are CO2 emissions per capita, CO2 emissions from electricity and heat production, CO2 emissions from liquid fuel consumption, CO2 emissions from manufacturing and construction, total greenhouse gas emissions (kt of CO2 equivalent), and CO2 intensity. A two-step generalised method of moment (GMM) found that governance effectiveness and regulatory quality as curtails the rate of CO2 emissions. Policy implications are discussed.

INTRODUCTION

This paper is motivated by issues bordering on economic development and the menace of environmental pollution in Sub-Saharan African (SSA) countries. Most literature on sustainable development has been established in two main ways. On the one hand, there are insights into the relationships between the pol-

DOI: 10.4018/978-1-7998-4817-2.ch002

lution of the environment and economic growth, with particular emphasis on the Environmental Kuznets Curve (EKC) assumption (Diao *et al.*, 2009; He & Richard, 2010; Osabuohien *et al.*, 2014; Egbetokun *et al.,* 2018; 2020). On the other hand, there has been concerned with the links between environmental pollution, energy consumption and economic growth (Apergis & Payne, 2009; Ozturk & Acaravci, 2010; Begum *et al.*, 2015; Akinyemi *et al.,* 2019a, 2019b) and the relationship between economic growth and the consumption of energy (Esso, 2010; Akinyemi *et al.*, 2017). Also, some other papers dwell on studying technology adoption and sustainable development in some cases (Binswanger, 2001; Karakara, 2017).

To the best of our knowledge, there is very scarce studies on the role of institutions in the discourse of achieving sustainable development. Even those few studies that highlight the importance of institutions in sustainable development have analogically inferred that these institutions offer the mechanisms for resource and environmental management (Anyanwu & Erhijakpor, 2014; Egbetokun *et al.,* 2018) and established that for institutions to be positively connected to economic development, one may need the consolidation of societal change (Efobi, 2015). Hence, Institutional frameworks, laws, regulations, conventions, customs and practices are essential for the efficient working of sustainable development strategies. One study (Asongu, 2017) explores comparative sustainable development in Sub-Saharan Africa, paying attention to regulatory quality and political stability as institutional variables. Our study differs as we measure, in addition to Asongu, (2017), rule of law, voice and accountability and government effectiveness. Again, we measured six different environmentally unsustainability as against four measures in Asongu (2017). Thus, our study has a wider coverage of variables of study than Asongu (2017).

The main causes of climate change in West Africa are known to be: greenhouse gases (GHG) emission from the use of energy from fossil fuels (coal, oil and gas) in industrial processes, transportation and in homes; and agricultural production and deforestation (UNFCCC, 2005). It is also important to note that low-income nations are less industrialized and therefore associated with lower CO_2 emissions, which require less mechanisms of CO_2 management (Asongu, 2017). Moreover, these nations are likely to attract corporations that exploit its weak environmental regulations/legislations to set up factories that employ dirty technologies. Therefore emissions may be higher than in higher-income countries.

There is a positive relationship between economic development and emissions since industrialization leads to a greater demand for energy, including fossil fuels (Huxster *et al.,* 2015; Holtz-Eakin & Selden, 1995; Wang *et al.,* 2017). Aye and Edoja (2017) studied 31 developing countries. They indicated that economic growth has a negative effect on CO2 emission in the low growth regime but a positive effect in the high growth regime with the marginal effect being higher in the high growth regime. They further asserted that energy consumption and population exert a positive and significant effect on CO2 emissions. Also, Antonakakis, Chatziantoniou, and Filis (2017) after studying 106 countries classified by different income groups over the period 1971–2011 concluded that the effects of the various types of energy consumption on economic growth and emissions are heterogeneous. They further asserted that total economic growth and energy consumption is bidirectional, thus making a case for the feedback hypothesis. Renewable energy consumption had no significant effect on economic growth, and there was no evidence in support of the EKC hypothesis. However, Kais and Ben Mbarek (2017) found interdependence between energy consumption and economic growth in the long run, a unidirectional causality running from economic growth to CO2 and a unidirectional causal relationship from energy consumption to CO2 emissions.

Many West African countries have low per capita GDPs and correspondingly low per capita emissions. Overall, the sub-region has not done very well in terms of environmental sustainability. This was confirmed by the 2010 Environmental Performance Index (EPI) of Yale University that ranked 163 countries on 25 performance indicators tracked across ten policy categories that covered both environmental public health and ecosystem vitality (United Nations Economic Commission for Africa-UNECA, 2012). Also, UNECA (2012) acknowledged that the economic, social and environmental pillars of the West African show that the sub-region has done quite well in resuscitating the growth of its economies. However, there are severe threats to the well-being of the population and environmental health. This study makes a contribution in this regard. The rest of the paper is captured as follows. The second section looks at an overview of sustainable development and institutions in West Africa. Data issues and methods are discussed in the third section, while the fourth section presents the empirical results with discussions on it. The last section concludes and highlights policy implications of the study.

THEORETICAL UNDERPINNINGS AND CONCEPTUAL FRAMEWORK

Theoretical Underpinnings

As pointed out earlier in the introduction, there are two categories of literature on the relationship between economic growth and environmental impact. Theoretically, an earlier work by Grossman and Krueger (1991) indicates that there is an inverted U-shaped curve between economic growth and environmental quality. They asserted that this inverted U-shaped is due to interaction between resource utilization, technology improvement and changes in economic structures (Stern, 2004; Xu & Song, 2011). This strand of the literature has been labelled the Environmental Kuznets Curve (EKC) theory and has been empirically replicated in many jurisdictions (Osabuohien *et al.*, 2014). However, some proponent scholars contested the shape of EKC (Moomaw & Unruh, 1997; Ajmi *et al.*, 2003) and others have the opinion that the EKC doesn't exist (Perman & Sterm 2003). The other strand of theoretical literature is based on analysis of the factors that influence resources and environment based on stochastic impacts by looking at population, affluence and technology. Thus, this model considers population, affluence and technology as the main factors affecting a region's environment (Wang *et al.*, 2017a, Fan *et al.*, 2006).

Empirical studies have also been conducted on the specific case of CO2 emissions and economic growth rather than general environmental impact (Wang *et al.*, 2017a). Among this strand of literature is the investigation of comparison of CO2 emissions across time, industries and regions (Long, Shao, & Chen, 2016; Ahmad *et al.*, 2016) with the general conclusion that CO2 is gradually increasing, however in changing patterns across industries and regions. Wang *et al.* (2018) indicated that the iñuence of economic growth on carbon productivity is highly nonlinear. They concluded that, from a longitudinal perspective, this nonlinear positive impact is further divided into three stages, transiting from a high regime to a low regime and then back to a high regime. The high regime is where economic growth has stronger positive iñuence on enhancing carbon productivity, is expected to last for a considerably longer time than the low regime stage. It is more probable for a low regime stage to transit to a high regime. Once the relation of carbon productivity and economic growth enters the high regime status, it becomes relatively stable there. Other empirical studies (Zhang & Da, 2015; Wang, Zhou, & Zhou, 2012) looked at the factors that determine CO2 emissions and assert that industry structure, energy consumption structure, technological level, macroeconomic policies and so on are the main determinants.

From the literature above, this study defines and conceptualizes carbon dioxide emissions, sustainable development and institutions in figure one. Carbon dioxide emissions refer to the environmental impact that human activities have. Human interactions with each other, as well as the environment, produce side effects like degradation, pollution, and erosion, which are harmful to the environment. Sustainable development, on the other hand, refers to economic development that is premised on achieving development and still be mindful of the environmental dangers that could arise from such development efforts. Institutions, as used in this paper, refer to the rules and political state that a country puts together to guide their social, economic, political and human interactions with others as well as human interactions with the environment. They include rule of law, government effectiveness, voice and accountability as well as corruption control. The interrelations between these concepts (CO2 emissions, sustainable development and institutions) are explained in figure 1.

Conceptual Framework

Figure 1 conceptualizes the interrelations between institutions and sustainable development. As a country harness its resources to achieve economic growth and development, the institutions that the country has played a crucial role in achieving this. If a country has strong institutions, it could manage its resources well as resource governance would play a vital role in the development agenda. Where rule of law works, there are regulations, government institutions are effective, and there is transparency (voice & accountability) in the management of resources, this will lead to sustainable development. Good resource governance will increase the likelihood of achieving sustainable development. On the other hand, 'bad' resource governance, brought about by weak institutions, could stifle sustainable development.

With fundamentally weak institutions, corruption could be rampant, resource tragedy of the commons could occur, environmental destruction without recourse and so on will lead to unsustainable development being witnessed. However, in the figure, the dotted line connecting strong institutions to the arrow indicates that with institutions becoming stronger, this could help achieve sustainable development in the long run. Thus, strong institutions bring about good resource governance and lessen corruptions and mismanagement as well as environmental destruction. This will help achieve sustainable development. But with fundamentally weak institutions, bad resource governance could be witnessed. This situation could create room for corruption, mismanagement and environmental destruction and hence unsustainable development. However, if institutions become stronger, this will in the long run yield sustainable development.

Sustainable Development and Institutions in West Africa

Our definition of sustainable development follows that of the Brundtland Commission as a 'development that meets the needs of the present generation without compromising the ability of future generations to meet their own needs' (Brundtland Commission, 1987). This definition is related to the context of this study because environmental unsustainability by means of CO_2 emissions can compromise the needs of future generations.

Table 1, shows the per capita CO_2 emissions for the 12 West African countries. Senegal accounts for the highest emissions per capita, followed by Nigeria and Ghana in the year 2010. There is a positive relationship between economic development and emission since industrialization leads to a greater demand for energy, including fossil fuels. However, many West African countries have low per capita GDPs and correspondingly low per capita emissions.

Figure 1. Conceptual Framework (Institutions in the discourse of sustainable development)
Source: *The Authors'*

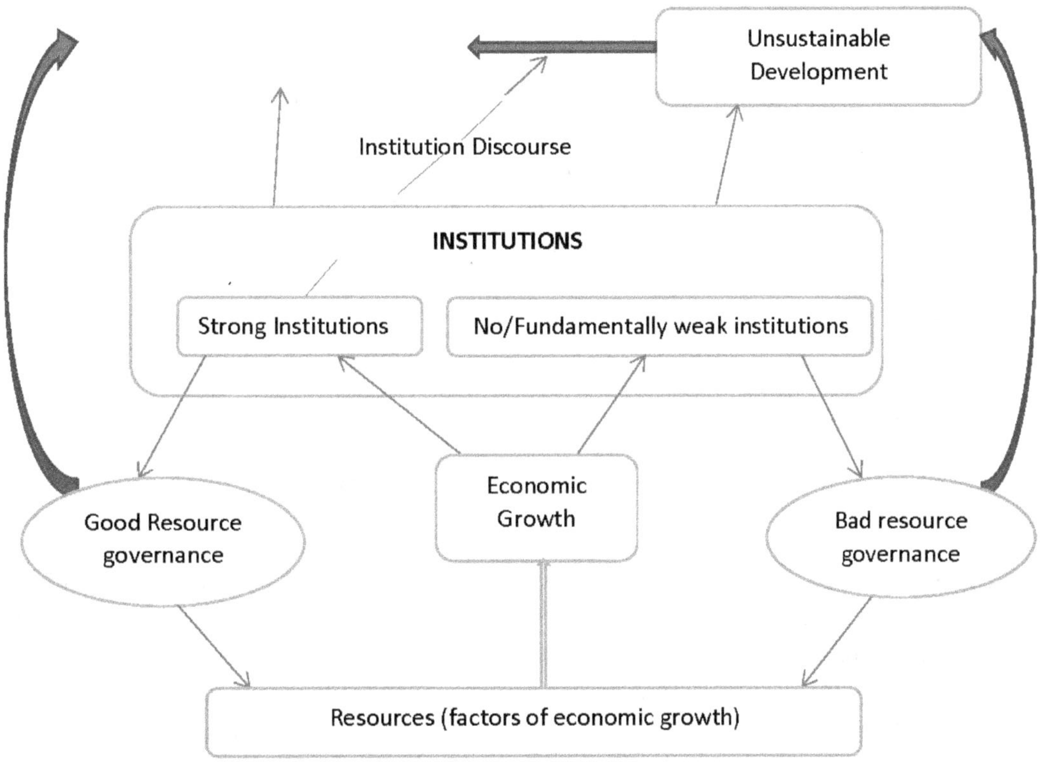

Table 1. CO_2 per capita emissions for 12 West African countries

Country	1996	1998	2000	2002	2004	2006	2008	2010
Benin	0.20	0.19	0.23	0.28	0.32	0.46	0.50	0.54
Burkina Faso	0.07	0.08	0.09	0.08	0.08	0.08	0.12	0.11
Cote d'Ivoire	0.56	0.44	0.41	0.42	0.43	0.38	0.36	0.29
Gambia	0.20	0.20	0.22	0.24	0.23	0.23	0.26	0.28
Ghana	0.34	0.36	0.33	0.38	0.35	0.43	0.40	0.42
Liberia	0.16	0.15	0.15	0.16	0.20	0.22	0.16	0.20
Mali	0.05	0.07	0.07	0.07	0.07	0.07	0.07	0.08
Niger	0.10	0.10	0.07	0.07	0.07	0.06	0.06	0.08
Nigeria	0.36	0.34	0.64	0.76	0.71	0.69	0.61	0.53
Senegal	0.42	0.37	0.40	0.44	0.48	0.41	0.44	0.64
Sierra Leone	0.10	0.100	0.10	0.14	0.13	0.14	0.12	0.13
Togo	0.24	0.25	0.28	0.24	0.26	0.21	0.29	0.27

Source: World Development Indicators, World Bank (2019)
Note: Figures are rounded to 2 decimals

It has been recognized that institutions are considered the spine for the efficient functioning of any system (Osabuohien & Efobi, 2013; Osabuohien *et al.,* 2013; 2014; 2015; Beecroft, 2020). The behavioural patterns of entities which pertain to both the formulation and implementation of frameworks, laws, regulations, conventions, customs and practices guide sustainable development (UNECA, 2012). Thus, it is imperative to study how institutions, particularly in SSA, foster environmentally benign to achieve sustainable development. This study regards income as one of the main determinants of a country's affluence and growth. Income level could show economic growth and to some extend development. Development comes with 'cost' to the environment. It is noted that the dynamics of CO_2 by country income categories indicates that high-income countries – in their aggregate figure – have slightly reduced their direct emissions in manufacturing sectors overall (Musolesi *et al.,* 2010), while both medium-low and medium high-income groups have witnessed increases.

DATA AND METHODOLOGY

Data

The study covers 12 West African countries based on data from World Development Indicators and World Governance Indicators of the World Bank for the period 2004-2014. The coverage of the data is due mainly to data availability for the outcome variables. The six main outcome variables used are: CO_2 emissions per capita; CO_2 emissions from electricity and heat production; CO_2 emissions from liquid fuel consumption, CO_2 emissions from manufacturing industries and construction (% of total fuel combustion), total greenhouse gas emissions (kt of CO_2 equivalent) and CO_2 intensity. Four main control variables are adopted in order to control for variable omission bias, namely: Gross Domestic Products (GDP) growth, population growth and educational and Income Levels. Institutional variables of interest included are; Government Effectiveness; Regulatory Quality; Rule of Law; and Voice and Accountability.

The country included are as follows: Benin, Burkina Faso, Cote d'Ivoire, Gambia, Ghana, Liberia, Mali, Niger, Nigeria, Senegal, Sierra Leone, and Togo. These countries are categorized into middle-income and lower-income countries. The middle-income countries include; Cote d'Ivoire, Ghana and Nigeria while the lower-income countries comprise Benin, Burkina Faso, Gambia, Liberia, Mali, Togo, Niger, Senegal, and Sierra Leone. The middle-income countries include those of lower middle and upper middle income.

Estimation Technique

A two-step Generalized Method of Moments (GMM) was used to investigate the problem mainly because; the GMM technique is in accordance with a panel data structure, cross-country differences are considered in the regressions; the estimation approach further takes account of endogeneity by controlling for simultaneity in the exploratory variables employing a process of instrumentation as well as controlling for the unobserved heterogeneity through time-invariant variables; inherent biases in the difference estimator are corrected with the system estimator.

The following equations in level (1) and first difference (2) summarise the standard system GMM estimation procedure as defined in equations (1) and (2):

$$CO_{i,t} = \sigma_0 + \sigma_1 CO_{i,t-\tau} + \sum_{h=1}^{5} \delta_h W_{h,i,t-\tau} + \sum_{h=1}^{7} \delta_h M_{h,i,t-\tau} + \mu_i + \theta_t + \varepsilon_{i,t} \quad (1)$$

$$\begin{aligned} CO_{i,t} - CO_{i,t-\tau} &= \sigma_1 \left(CO_{i,t-\tau} - CO_{i,t-2\tau} \right) + \sum_{h=1}^{5} \delta_h (W_{h,i,t-\tau} - W_{h,i,t-2\tau}) \\ &+ \sum_{h=1}^{7} \delta_h \left(M_{h,i,t-\tau} - M_{h,i,t-2\tau} \right) + \left(\theta_t - \theta_{t-\tau} \right) + \varepsilon_{i,t-\tau} \end{aligned} \quad (2)$$

Where; $CO_{i,t}$, is a CO_2 emissions indicator of country i at period t, σ_0 is a constant, W is the vector of control variables (GDP growth, population growth, education and regulation quality), M is the vector of control variables (GDP growth, population growth, education and regulation quality), τ represents the coefficient of auto-regression which is one of the specifications, θ_t shows the time-specific constant, μ_i indicates country-specific effect and $\varepsilon_{i,t}$ is the error term.

Empirical Result

Table 2 presents the econometric results. With the GMM estimation, it two criteria are used to validate the GMM method used. The second-order Arellano and Bond autocorrelation test (AR [2]) is more relevant as an information criterion than the first-order. And these two criteria are all valid showing that the GMM model is valid overall. Assessing the persistence of CO_2 emissions in the studied countries, it is established that the estimated lagged dependent variable has persistence. This is in line with what Asongu (2017) established. Thus, a higher magnitude of this estimated coefficient translates a higher degree of persistence because past values of the outcome variable have a more proportionate impact of future values. Again, for persistence to be established, the estimated lagged dependent variable should be within the convergence range. The convergence criterion is that the absolute value of the lagged estimated endogenous variable should be within the interval of zero and one (Asongu, 2013; 2017). Our estimated result has all the lagged dependent variables having coefficient falling between zero and one.

From the empirical estimation in Table 2, it can be established that middle-income countries have lower rates of CO2 emissions per capita, CO2 emissions from electricity and heat and CO2 emissions from liquid fuel consumption than lower-income countries. However, middle-income countries have moderately higher persistence of CO2 emissions intensity, CO2 emissions from manufacturing and construction and total GHG emissions than lower-income countries. This finding is so partly because middle-income countries, compared to lower-income countries, might have a higher capacity and engaged in manufacturing and commence where there are industries engaged in such. This finding is similar to what Asongu (2017) observed in their study.

Again, GDP growth is found to have a negative association with the environmental sustainability of a country. It thus means that the countries under study might have been achieving growth at the expense of the environment. However, this is not significant. A related finding was established by Aye and Edoja (2017). Increase in population is found to moderate the persistence level of environmental unsustainability. Large numbers of people could mean stress on the environment and thus higher levels of CO_2 emissions being witnessed. This is similar to what Wang *et al.,* (2017a) and Fan *et al.,* (2006) established in their studies.

Table 2. Econometric estimation of environmental sustainability with CO_2 emissions

	CO_2 per capita		CO_2 Elect_Heat		CO_2 Liq_Fuel_Con		CO_2 Man_Const		CO_2 intensity		Total GHG	
Variables	**LI**	**MI**	**LI**	**MI**	**LI**	**MI**	**LI**	**MI**	**LI**	**MI**	**LI**	**MI**
Constant	0.137* (0.03)	0.566* (0.67)	-0.23 (0.45)	0.97* (0.001)	0.398 (0.851)	-23.76 (0.042)	0.741 (0.032)	0.654 (0.041)	0.761** (0.004)	0.942 (0.078)	0.543 (0.034)	0.754 (0.042)
CO_2 per capita (-1)	0.890* (0.001)	0.902** (0.94)										
CO_2 Elect_ Heat (-1)			0.967** (0.002)	0.801*** (0.005)								
CO_2 Lig_ Fuel_Con (-1)					0.912** (0.0001)	0.076* (0.20)						
CO_2 Man_ Const (-1)							0.621** (0.034)	0.793*** (0.046)				
CO_2 Intensity (-1)									0.723** (0.052)	0.621** (0.061)		
Total GHG (-1)											0.741** (0.024)	0.810** (0.041)
GDP growth	-0.002 (0.46)	-0.034 (0.391)	0.002 (0.67)	-0.006* (0.05)	-0.213 (0.005)	-0.196 (0.223)	-0.084 (0.042)	-0.291 (0.054)	0.059 (0.002)	-0.302 (0.054)	-0.086 (0.052)	-0.871 (0.058)
Population growth	0.021 (0.89)	0.420 (0.42)	0.021 (0.62)	-0.321 (0.002)	2.91 (0.001)	8.10 (0.31)	0.851 (0.007)	0.652 (0.026)	0.734 (0.026)	2.084 (0.087)	0.382 (0.074)	3.142 (0.098)
Education (% of adult population)	-0.002 (0.25)	-0.012 (0.61)	0.283 (0.321)	-0.121** (0.791)	0.020 (0.52)	-0.741* (0.279)	-0.312 (0.061)	-0.0523* (0.004)	-0.0371 (0.063)	0.237 (0.071)	-0.0732 (0.062)	-0.421* (0.071)
Government effectiveness	0.092** (0.012)	0.32*** (0.543)	0.0862 (0.034)	0.0762 (0.041)	-1.130 (0.46)	13.87 (0.528)	0.934 (0.072)	4.210 (0.421)	1.024 (0.082)	7.213 (0.092)	0.871 (0.034)	6.128 (0.064)
Rule of law	0.002 (0.01)	0.054 (0.03)	0.060 (0.023)	0.0081 (0.021)	-2.042 (0.63)	4.623 (0.72)	0.0423 (0.027)	2.421 (0.92)	0.954 (0.071)	1.872 (0.046)	1.067 (0.054)	4.310 (0.025)
Regulatory Quality	-0.051 (0.034)	0.067** (0.041)	-0.082 (0.004)	0.045 (0.037)	0.842 (0.082)	0.765 (0.069)	0.0543 (0.021)	0.0641 (0.004)	0.087 (0.053)	0.094* (0.023)	0.0876 (0.061)	0.632* (0.028)
Voice and accountability	0.002 (0.0001)	0.0061 (0.003)	0.001 (0.005)	0.008 (0.009)	0.0107 (0.005)	0.091 (0.08)	0.0024 (0.006)	0.0521 (0.0071)	0.0641 (0.072)	0.0921 (0.057)	0.049 (0.081)	0.102 (0.068)
AR (1)	(0.212)	(0.301)	(0.082)	(0.498)	(0.342)	(0.620)	(0.221)	(0.512)	(0.641)	(0.721)	(0.564)	(0.743)
AR (2)	(0.313)	(0.891)	(0.150)	(0.390)	(0.410)	(0.781)	(0.421)	(0.721)	(0.452)	(0.324)	(0.571)	(0.347)
Sargan OIR	(0.014)	(0.004)	(0.986)	(0.324)	(0.042)	(0.0760)	(0.075)	(0.053)	(0.061)	(0.038)	(0.047)	(0.432)
Hansen OIR	(0.781)	(0.97)	(1.00)	(1.00)	(0.82)	(0.910)	(0.841)	(0.931)	(0.872)	(0.941)	(1.00)	(1.00)
Fisher	6289**	650**	176.40***	1676***	2341**	362**	7342***	4321***	5674**	452***	6342**	342***
Instruments	8	8	8	8	8	8	8	8	8	8	8	8
Countries	9	3	9	3	9	3	9	3	9	3	9	3
Observations	15	7	13	8	16	6	21	13	22	9	31	11

Note: LI=low income countries; MI=middle income countries; Elect_Heat= electricity and heat production; Liq_Fuel_Con= liquid fuel consumption; Man_Const=manufacturing industries and construction; OIR=over-identifying restriction test; *,**,***=significance at 10%, 5% and 1%.

Source: The Authors'

An educated populace is deemed to be aware of environmental unsustainability effects and may thus resort to behaviour that promotes sound environmental practice. It is established in table 2 that a higher percentage of adults being educated lead to low levels of CO_2 emissions being witnessed in both middle-income and low-income countries. On the institutional variables, it is established that they contribute positively to enhancing reduction in environmental unsustainability in the study countries. It is established that government being effective, rule of law working and there is quality in regulations as well as voice and accountability being prudent. Then there is a tendency to achieving low levels of CO_2 emissions in a country.

CONCLUSION AND POLICY IMPLICATION

Motivated by the unsustainable nature of economic development and the menace of environmental pollution in Sub-Saharan African (SSA) countries, this chapter used GMM estimation technique on data on 12 West African countries. Previous CO_2 emissions rate relates directly to current rates of CO_2 emissions. Thus, past unsustainability nature in West Africa is carried on to the coming years. The UNFCCC (2005) noted that greenhouse gases (GHG) emission from the use of energy from fossil fuels (coal, oil and gas) in industrial processes, transportation and in homes; and agricultural production and deforestation are the main cause of climate change in West Africa.

Higher growth in GDP of countries goes at the expense of environmental sustainability. Countries that have a high rate of educated adults are more likely to enjoy environmentally sustainable living. Also, higher population calls for more pollution and subsequently higher CO_2 emissions in a country. Institutional variables such as government effectiveness, rule of law, voice and accountability, and regulatory quality show that they affect environmental quality and subsequently sustainable development of the countries studied. Middle-income countries seem to have better institutions that manage the environment more sustainably than lower-income countries. Thus, middle-income countries are well developed and have the capacity to manage institutions well.

The governments of the countries should endeavour to strengthen their institutional capacity regarding the environment. A country with weak institutions calls for multinationals that go there in the name of FDI and tend to exploit the vulnerable environmental laws to their advantage. Thus, institutional capacities should be built. Also, the countries could harness the advantage of educating their populace. Such education may be much on environmental education and literacy.

ACKNOWLEDGMENT

This study is a beneficiary of the Mentorship Programme under the auspices of the African Finance and Economic Association (AFEA); thus, the authors appreciate the robust discussions on the platform. The second author acknowledges the Equipment Subsidy Grant from the Alexander von Humboldt Foundation [Ref: 3.4-8151/19047] to Centre for Economic Policy and Development Research (CEPDeR), Covenant University that facilitated the preparation of this chapter. The useful comments from the editors and anonymous reviewers that have improved the quality of the paper are much appreciated. The views expressed are the authors.

REFERENCES

Adeleye, N., Osabuohien, E., & Bowale, E. (2017). The Role of Institutions in the Finance-Inequality Nexus in Sub-Saharan Africa. *Journal of Contextual Economics, 137*(1-2), 173–192. doi:10.3790/jce.137.1-2.173

Ajmi, A. N., Hammoudeh, S., Nguyen, D. K., & Sato, J. R. (2015). On the relationships between CO2 emissions, energy consumption and income: The importance of time variation. *Energy Economics, 49*, 629–638. doi:10.1016/j.eneco.2015.02.007

Akinyemi, O., Efobi, U., Asongu, S., & Osabuohien, E. (2019b). Renewable energy, trade performance and the conditional role of finance and institutional capacity in sub-Sahara African Countries. *Energy Policy, 132*, 490–498. doi:10.1016/j.enpol.2019.06.012Akinyemi, O., Osabuohien, E., Alege, P., & Ogundipe, A. (2017). Energy Security, Trade and Transition to Green Economy in Africa. *International Journal of Energy Economics and Policy, 7*(3), 127–136.

Akinyemi, O., Efobi, U., Osabuohien, E., & Alege, P. (2019a). Regional Integration and Energy Sustainability in Africa: Exploring the Challenges and Prospects for ECOWAS. *African Development Review, 31*(4), 517–528. doi:10.1111/1467-8268.12406

Antonakakis, N., Chatziantoniou, I., & Filis, G. (2017). Energy consumption, CO2 emissions, and economic growth: An ethical dilemma. *Renewable and Sustainable Energy Reviews, 68,* 808–824. .rser.2016.09.105 doi:10.1016/j

Anyanwu, J., & Erhijakpor, A. (2014). Does Oil Wealth Affect Democracy in Africa? *African Development Review, 26*(1), 15–37. doi:10.1111/1467-8268.12061

Apergis, N., & Payne, J. (2009). CO_2 emissions, energy usage, and output in Central America. *Energy Policy, 37*(8), 3282–3286. doi:10.1016/j.enpol.2009.03.048

Asongu, S. A. (2013). African Stock Market Performance Dynamics: A Multidimensional Convergence Assessment. *Journal of African Business, 40*(3), 186–201. doi:10.1080/15228916.2013.844043

Asongu, S. A. (2017). *The Comparative Sustainable Development in Sub-Saharan Africa*. African Governance and Development Institute working paper no. WP/17/060

Aye, G. C. & Edoja, P. E. (2017). Effect of economic growth on CO2 emission in developing countries: Evidence from a dynamic panel threshold model. *Cogent Economics & Finance, 5*(1). DOI: doi:10.1080/23322039.2017.137923

Beecroft, I., Osabuohien, E., Efobi, U., Olurinola, I., & Osabohien, R. (2020). Manufacturing Export and ICT Infrastructure in West Africa: Investigating the Roles of Economic and Political Institutions. *Institutions, Etc., 12*(1), 1–36.

Begum, R. A., Sohag, K., Abdullah, S. M. S., & Jaafar, M. (2015). CO_2 emissions, energy consumption, economic and population growth in Malaysia. *Renewable & Sustainable Energy Reviews, 41*(January), 594–601. doi:10.1016/j.rser.2014.07.205

Binswanger, M. (2001). Technological progress and sustainable development: What about the rebound effect? *Ecological Economics*, *36*(1), 119–132. doi:10.1016/S0921-8009(00)00214-7

Brundtland Commission. (1987). *Our Common Future*. Oxford University Press.

Diao, X. D., Zeng, S. X., Tam, C. M., & Tam, V. W. Y. (2009). EKC Analysis for Studying Economic Growth and Environmental Quality: A Case Study in China. *Journal of Cleaner Production*, *17*(5), 541–548. doi:10.1016/j.jclepro.2008.09.007

Efobi, U. (2015). Politicians' Attributes and Institutional Quality in Africa: A Focus on Corruption. *Journal of Economic Issues*, *49*(3), 787–813. doi:10.1080/00213624.2015.1072393

Egbetokun, S., Osabuohien, E., & Akinboloa, T. (2018). Feasible Environmental Kuznets and Institutional Quality in North and Southern African Sub-regions. *International Journal of Energy Economics and Policy*, *8*(1), 104–115.

Egbetokun, S., Osabuohien, E., Onanuga, O., Akinbobola, T., Gershon, O., & Okafor, V. (2020). Environmental Pollution, Economic Growth and Institutional Quality: Exploring the Nexus in Nigeria. *Management of Environmental Quality*, *31*(1), 18–31. doi:10.1108/MEQ-02-2019-0050

Esso, L. J. (2010). Threshold cointegration and causality relationship between energy use and growth in seven African countries. *Energy Economics*, *32*(6), 1383–1391. doi:10.1016/j.eneco.2010.08.003

Fan, Y., Liu, L. C., Wu, G., & Wei, Y. M. (2006). Analyzing impact factors of CO_2 emissions using the STIRPAT model. *Environmental Impact Assessment Review*, *26*(4), 377–395. doi:10.1016/j.eiar.2005.11.007

Grossman, G. M., & Krueger, A. B. (1991). *Environmental Impacts of a North American Free Trade Agreement*. National Bureau of Economic Research. doi:10.3386/w3914

He, J., & Richard, P. (2010). Environmental Kuznets Curve for CO_2 in Canada. *Ecological Economics*, *69*(5), 1083–1093. doi:10.1016/j.ecolecon.2009.11.030

Holtz-Eakin, D., & Selden, T. M. (1995). Stoking the ðres? CO_2 emissions and economic growth. *Journal of Public Economics*, *57*(1), 85–101. doi:10.1016/0047-2727(94)01449-X

Huxster, J. K., Uribe-Zarain, X., & Kempton, W. (2015). Undergraduate Understanding of Climate Change: The Influences of College Major and Environmental Group Membership on Survey Knowledge Scores. *The Journal of Environmental Education*, *46*(3), 149–165. doi:10.1080/00958964.2015.1021661

Kais, S., & Ben Mbarek, M. (2017). Dynamic relationship between CO2 emissions, energy consumption and economic growth in three North African countries. *International Journal of Sustainable Energy*, *36*(9), 840–854. doi:10.1080/14786451.2015.1102910

Karakara, A. A. (2017). Technological Change and Sustainable Development: The Case of Plastic Products Producers in Ghana. *ADRRI Journal of Arts and Social Sciences, 5*(3), 17 – 33.

Moomaw, W. R., & Unruh, G. C. (1997). Are environmental Kuznets curves misleading us? The case of CO_2 emissions. *Environment and Development Economics*, *2*(4), 451–463. doi:10.1017/S1355770X97000247

Musolesi, A., Mazzanti, M., & Zoboli, R. (2010). A panel data heterogeneous Bayesian estimation of environmental Kuznets curves for CO_2 emissions. *Applied Economics*, *42*(18), 2275–2287. doi:10.1080/00036840701858034

Osabohien, R., Ufua, D., Moses, C. L., & Osabuohien, E. (2020). Accountability in agricultural governance and food security in Nigeria. *Brazilian Journal of Food Technology*, *23*, e2019054. doi:10.1590/1981-6723.08919

Osabuohien, E. S. (2014). Large-scale Agricultural Land Investments and Local Institutions in Africa: The Nigerian Case. *Land Use Policy*, *39*(July), 155–165. doi:10.1016/j.landusepol.2014.02.019

Osabuohien, E. S., & Efobi, U. R. (2013). Africa's Money in Africa. *The South African Journal of Economics*, *81*(2), 292–306. doi:10.1111aje.12012

Osabuohien, E. S., Efobi, U. R., & Gitau, C. M. W. (2013). External Intrusion, Internal Tragedy: Environmental Pollution and Multinational Corporations in Sub-Saharan Africa. In L. Leonard & M. A.Gonzalez-Perez (Eds.), Principles and Strategies to Balance Ethical, Social and Environmental Concerns with Corporate Requirements (pp. 93-118). Emerald Group Publishing doi:10.1108/S2051-5030(2013)0000012010

Osabuohien, E. S., Efobi, U. R., & Gitau, C. M. W. (2014). Beyond the Environmental Kuznets Curve in Africa: Evidence from Panel Cointegration. *Journal of Environmental Policy and Planning*, *16*(4), 517–538. doi:10.1080/1523908X.2013.867802

Osabuohien, E. S., Efobi, U. R., & Gitau, C. M. W. (2015). Environmental Challenges in Africa: Further Dimensions to the Trade, MNCs and Energy Debate. *Management of Environmental Quality*, *26*(1), 118–137. doi:10.1108/MEQ-04-2014-0058

Ozturk, I., & Acaravci, A. (2010). CO2 emissions, energy consumption and economic growth in Turkey. *Renewable & Sustainable Energy Reviews*, *14*(9), 3220–3225. doi:10.1016/j.rser.2010.07.005

Perman, R., & Stern, D. I. (2003). Evidence from panel unit root and cointegration tests that the Environmental Kuznets Curve does not exist. *The Australian Journal of Agricultural and Resource Economics*, *47*(3), 325–347. doi:10.1111/1467-8489.00216

Stern, D. I. (2004). The Rise and Fall of the Environmental Kuznets Curve. *World Development*, *32*(8), 1419–1439. doi:10.1016/j.worlddev.2004.03.004

United Nations Economic Commission for Africa. (2005). *Sustainable Development on Africa*. Author.

United Nations Economic Commission for Africa. (2012). *Progress towards Sustainable Development in West Africa*. United Nations Economic Commission for Africa.

Wang, C., Wang, F., Zhang, X., Yang, Y., Su, Y., Ye, Y., & Zhang, H. (2017b). Examining the driving factors of energy related carbon emissions using the extended STIRPAT model based on IPAT identity in Xinjiang. *Renewable & Sustainable Energy Reviews*, *67*, 51–61. doi:10.1016/j.rser.2016.09.006

Wang, C., Yang, S., Liu, C., & Li, S. (2018). How Would Economic Development Inñuence Carbon Productivity? A Case from Hubei in China. *International Journal of Environmental Research and Public Health*, *15*(8), 1730. doi:10.3390/ijerph15081730

Wang, Z. X., Hao, P., & Yao, P. Y. (2017a). Non-Linear Relationship between Economic Growth and CO2 Emissions in China: An Empirical Study Based on Panel Smooth Transition Regression Models. *International Journal of Environmental Research and Public Health*, *14*(12), 1568. doi:10.3390/ijerph14121568

Xu, G., & Song, D. (2011). An Empirical Study on the Environmental Kuznets Curve for China's Carbon Emissions: Based on Provincial Panel Data. *China Journal of Population and Resource Environment*, *9*(3), 66–76. doi:10.1080/10042857.2011.10685040

ADDITIONAL READING

Akbostanci, E., Turut-Asi, S., & Tunc, G. I. (2009). The Relationship between Income and Environment in Turkey: Is there an Environmental Kuznets Curve? *Energy Policy*, *37*(3), 861–867. doi:10.1016/j.enpol.2008.09.088

Akpan, G. E., & Akpan, U. F. (2012). Electricity Consumption, Carbon Emissions and Economic Growth in Nigeria. *International Journal of Energy Economics and Policy*, *2*(4), 292–306.

Ang, J. B. (2007). CO2 emissions, energy consumption, and output in France. *Energy Policy*, *35*(10), 4772–4778. doi:10.1016/j.enpol.2007.03.032

KEY TERMS AND DEFINITIONS

Carbon Dioxide Emission: This is the environmental impact that human activities have. Human interactions with each other as well as the environment produce side effects like degradation, pollution, erosion, etc. which are harmful to the environment.

Institutions: These are the rules and political state that a country puts together to guide their social, economic, political, and human interactions with others as well as human interactions with the environment. They include rule of law, government effectives, voice, and accountability as well as corruption control.

Sustainable Development: This is economic development that is premised on achieving development and still be mindful of the environmental dangers that could possibly arise from such development efforts.

Chapter 3 The Role of Higher Education on Corruption: Comparison of European Union and African Union

Adem Gök
https://orcid.org/0000-0002-3786-2507
Kırklareli University, Turkey

ABSTRACT

A cross-country comparison reveals the fact that high tertiary enrollment rates are associated with low corruption, and low tertiary enrollment rates are associated with high corruption. Such a comparison does not show whether an increase in higher education leads to lower or higher corruption. Hence, the aim of the study is to analyze the effect of higher education on corruption on best performing European Union countries and worst performing African Union countries. It is found that higher education has positive significant effect on corruption not only in African Union but also in European Union. Hence, it is concluded that the enticement of higher living standard prevails the moral principals and ethical values of individuals in the way of reaching it. The author advise a course on moral principals and ethical values to be included in the curriculum of higher education institutions to teach the meaning of virtue and the long-term gains of living with high moral standing rather than to be gravitated to the short-term gains of corruption as a policy implication.

INTRODUCTION

Corruption is more than simply misappropriation of money or abuse of power: corruption hinders people's right to affiliation, political participation, rule of law, nondiscrimination, and social, institutional and economic development (Cheung and Chan, 2008; Osabuohien, 2020). There are two opposing argument for the effect of higher education on corruption in the literature. The mainstream argument asserts that higher education is a moral enterprise that teaching the value of virtue by practicing knowledge and ex-

DOI: 10.4018/978-1-7998-4817-2.ch003

perience. The aim of higher education is to provide opportunities for students to learn about their social and ethical responsibilities to uphold their morality ideals (Cheung and Chan, 2008). Hence citizens with higher education most likely to hold higher moral values and they avoid conducting corrupt acts. Also, the increase in education and literacy, which development brings, will increase the likelihood of corrupt act to be discovered and punished (Elbahnasawy and Revier, 2012; Ejemeyovwi et al, 2018). The second argument asserts that graduation from a higher education institution grants better jobs with high potential corruption rents (Eicher et al., 2009). Hence increase in higher education increases the potential corruption rents, which increases the likelihood of corrupt acts.

A simple scatterplot of tertiary enrollment rates and corruption level as in Figure 1 (in the Appendix) reveal the fact that high tertiary enrollment rates are associated with low corruption and low tertiary enrollment rates are associated with high corruption. Hence there is a negative correlation between higher education and corruption. But it does not show whether an increase in higher education leads to lower or higher corruption.

In order to test the competing hypothesis for the effect of higher education on corruption, we took two samples from the population of all countries representing two extremes. First sample includes members of European Union (EU), where the level of higher education is highest and the level of corruption is lowest. Second sample includes members of African Union (AU), where the level of higher education is lowest and the level of corruption is highest. This sample selection also considers another fact; the members of EU are generally ex-colonizers and the members of AU are generally ex-colonies. The relationship between higher education and corruption is based on the relationship between higher education and governance institutions. The members of EU established good institutions and govern them effectively due to high level of human capital with high level of higher education. And the members of AU could not establish good institutions and govern them inefficiently due to low level of human capital with low level of higher education.

We expect that mainstream argument is valid for the members of European Union and second argument is valid for members of African Union.

Control of Corruption is a crucial dimension of governance. Good governance requires low corruption and vice versa. Only rich countries can afford better institutions (Acemoglu et al., 2001). Hence they argue that the level of income is the crucial factor in establishing better institutions. We argue that the level of education, especially higher education is the crucial factor in establishing and governing better institutions. Hence, only countries endowed with better educated citizens can establish and govern better institutions.

INSIGHTS FROM THE LITERATURE AND CONTRIBUTION OF THE STUDY

There are several studies in the literature analyzing the role of corruption on higher education. However, there is only one study in the literature analyzing the effect of higher education on corruption, which is as follows. For a cross sectional analysis of 56 countries, Cheung and Chan (2008) found that higher education has negative significant effect on corruption and concluded that as more people participated in tertiary education the lower its incidence of corruption across nations.

The rest of the studies in the literature analyzed the effect of education (not higher education) on corruption, which are as follows. For a cross sectional analysis of 41 developing countries, Shabbir and Anwar (2008) found that education has positive significant effect on perceived corruption and concluded that the level of corruption in developing countries is increased with the increase in the level of education. In a cross-country analysis, Ali and Isse (2003) concluded that education has negative significant effect on corruption and concluded that increase in education in the form of secondary school enrollment rates reduces the level of corruption.

In a panel fixed effect regression over 81 countries, Fréchette (2006) found that increase in education increases corruption and concluded that the finding of increasing income and education increases corruption suggests that some policy objectives might work against each other. In a cross section analysis of 46 countries, Evrensel (2010) concluded that countries with lower levels of education have higher levels of corruption. In a cross sectional analysis of 63 countries, Goel and Nelson (2005) found that educational attainment has no significant effect on corruption and concluded that holding development level constant, (lack of) educational attainment does not seem to contribute anything additional towards explaining corruption. By conducting a panel fixed effect regression for 104 countries, Rehman and Naveed (2007) found that secondary school enrolment and public spending has negative significant effect on corruption and concluded that a higher level of education fosters a sense of nationalism, self-importance and public duty in the community, which lead to decrease in the level of corruption.

The main issue of the study is to identify the role of higher education on the level of corruption. Since corruption is a structured institutional issue, we took two extreme case: one is the case of AU, which has lowest level of higher education and highest level of corruption, and second is the case of EU, which has highest level of higher education and lowest level of corruption. We expect that an increase in higher education should lead to lower corruption in EU countries in parallel to mainstream argument, and an increase in higher education should lead to higher corruption in AU countries as opposed to mainstream argument.

There is only one study in the literature analyzing the role of higher education on corruption and there are only few studies analyzing the role of education on corruption in a broader sense. These studies have following drawbacks as;

- The studies are mostly cross sectional analysis, which lacks of measuring the effect of education on corruption by time varying context. They are just improved versions of scatter plot analysis. They just show correlation not the effect of incremental change of independent variable on dependent variable through time.
- There are only one or two studies that considered the endogeneity problem stemming from reverse causality.
- None of the studies included lag of corruption as an independent variable.
- Most of the studies did not classify countries in estimation; rather they try to include as many countries as possible as long as they have data.

How the chapter tackles mentioned above drawbacks is as follows;

The chapter employs System GMM analysis that allows both overcoming endogeneity problem and including lag of corruption as a possible determinant of corruption. Hence it is not static but dynamic panel analysis.

The chapter takes two clusters of countries as AU and EU as mentioned above. The division of countries between bad performing AU and good performing EU on higher education – corruption nexus is not a mere coincidence. It goes back to the colonial origins of institutional setting. AU countries are generally ex-colonies that did not find a chance to establish their own governance infrastructure since they are ruled by the regimes of ex-colonizers, which are mostly EU countries (Gök, 2017). When they thought they won their independence, they were ruled by corrupt totalitarian regimes left behind and supported by several EU countries for sustaining political stability of the region or securing their economic interest (Beyer, 2008; Etzioni, 2008; Gök, 2017). The colonial state and extractive institutions persisted even after independence (Acemoglu et al., 2011; Beecroft et al, 2020).

EMPIRICAL ANALYSIS

Empirical Model

The general model to be estimated with System GMM is as below;

$$y_{it} = \alpha\, y_{i,t-1} + x'_{it}\beta + \varepsilon_{it} \tag{1}$$

$$\varepsilon_{it} = \mu_i + \nu_{it} \tag{2}$$

$$E(\mu_i) = E(\nu_{it}) = E(\mu_i \nu_{it}) = 0 \tag{3}$$

The disturbance term ε_{it} has two orthogonal components as the fixed effects, μ_i and idiosyncratic shocks, ν_{it}

$$\Delta y_{it} = (\alpha - 1)\, \Delta y_{i,t-1} + \Delta x'_{it}\beta + \Delta\nu_{it} \tag{4}$$

$$E[\Delta w_{it}\mu_i] = 0 \tag{5}$$

The System GMM estimator that is developed by Arellano and Bover (1995), Blundell and Bond (1998) augments the Difference GMM estimator that is developed by Arellano and Bond (1991) by making an additional assumption of the first differences of instrument variables are uncorrelated with the fixed effects (5), which allows the introduction of more instruments. Hence it can dramatically improve efficiency by building a system of two equations; one is the original equation (1), the other is the transformed one (4). While Arellano and Bond (1991) instruments differences with levels, Blundell and Bond (1998) instruments levels with differences (Rodman, 2009).

Validity depends on the assumption that the v_{it} is not serially correlated. If the v_{it} is serially correlated of order 1 then, for instance, $y_{i,t-2}$ is endogenous to the $v_{i,t-1}$ in the error term in differences, $\Delta\varepsilon_{it} = v_{it} - v_{i,t-1}$, making it a potentially invalid instrument. The researcher would need to restrict the instrument set starting with third lag or longer. If the researcher finds second order correlation, he or she would need to start with even longer lags (Rodman, 2009).

System GMM approach is preferred in the analysis since it tackles endogeneity issue due to lag of dependent variable and reverse causality running from dependent variable to independent variables. It also tackles multicollinearity issue and heteroscedasticity problem.

Reduced Form Equation for the effect of higher education on corruption with institutional control variables is as follows.

$$COR_{it} = \alpha\, COR_{i,t-1} + \beta\, TERT_{it} + \gamma\, INST_{it} + \varepsilon_{it} \tag{1.1}$$

$$\varepsilon_{it} = \mu_i + \nu_{it} \tag{2.1}$$

$$E(\mu_i) = E(\nu_{it}) = E(\mu_i \nu_{it}) = 0 \tag{3.1}$$

$$\Delta COR_{it} = \delta\, \Delta COR_{i,t-1} + \phi\, \Delta\, TERT_{it} + \varphi\, \Delta\, INST_{it} + \Delta\nu_{it} \tag{4.1}$$

$$E[\Delta w_{it} \mu_i] = 0 \tag{5.1}$$

Reduced Form Equation for the effect of higher education on corruption with economic control variables is as follows.

$$COR_{it} = \alpha\, COR_{i,t-1} + \beta\, TERT_{it} + \gamma\, ECON_{it} + \varepsilon_{it} \tag{1.2}$$

$$\varepsilon_{it} = \mu_i + \nu_{it} \tag{2.2}$$

$$E(\mu_i) = E(\nu_{it}) = E(\mu_i \nu_{it}) = 0 \tag{3.2}$$

$$\Delta COR_{it} = \delta\, \Delta COR_{i,t-1} + \phi\, \Delta\, TERT_{it} + \varphi\, \Delta\, ECON_{it} + \Delta\nu_{it} \tag{4.2}$$

$$E[\Delta w_{it} \mu_i] = 0 \tag{5.2}$$

COR_{it} and $COR_{i,t-1}$ represents level of corruption and its first lag for country i in year t. $TERT_{it}$ represents level of higher education for country i in year t. $INST_{it}$ represents institutional control variables including government effectiveness, political stability, regulatory quality, rule of law, and voice and accountability for country i in year t. $ECON_{it}$ represents economic control variables including per capita income, natural resource rents, trade openness, and foreign direct investment inflows for country i in year t.

Data and Variables

The empirical analysis covers 41 AU countries and 28 EU countries in two clusters over the period of 1996-2017. See Table 1 for the variables, their description and source.

Estimation Results

According to the estimation results in Table 2, the lag of corruption has positive significant impact on the current level of corruption both in AU and EU. The finding supports the theory of self-reinforcing corruption in the sense that past corruption levels become significant determinant of current corruption level due to strategic complementarity.

Higher education has positive significant effect on corruption both in AU and EU, contradicting our expectations for the case of EU. The reason might be that the enticement of higher living standard prevails the moral principals and ethical values of individuals in the way of reaching it. Since low moral standing in higher education for the case of corruption is valid for both ex-colonizers of EU and ex-colonies

Table 1. Source of the data

Variable	Description	Source
cor	Control of Corruption: Estimate	WGI (2019)
tert	School enrollment, tertiary (% gross)	WDI(2019)
govef	Government Effectiveness: Estimate	WGI (2019)
pols	Political Stability and Absence of Violence/Terrorism: Estimate	WGI (2019)
regq	Regulatory Quality: Estimate	WGI (2019)
rol	Rule of Law: Estimate	WGI (2019)
va	Voice and Accountability: Estimate	WGI (2019)
gdppc	GDP per capita (constant 2010 US$)	WDI(2019)
natur	Total natural resources rents (% of GDP)	WDI(2019)
trade	Trade (% of GDP)	WDI(2019)
fdi	Foreign direct investment, net inflows (% of GDP)	WDI(2019)

Notes: The data on corruption is obtained by multiplying the values of control of corruption with minus one.

of AU, it should be injected to ex-colonies by the ex-colonizers in a distant past. We may infer that this low moral standing against corruption is also valid for other countries as well since we analyzed it for both extreme cases.

Government effectiveness has negative significant effect on corruption for both AU and EU. Hence increase in the quality of public and civil services, and their dependence from political pressures, the quality of policy formulation and implementation, and the credibility of the government's commitment to such policies lead to decrease in corruption. Political stability has a positive significant effect on corruption for the case of EU. Hence it should be the case that the extended tenure of the public official due to political stability may give opportunity to build long lasting relationship with potential suppliers of bribe (Elbahnasawy and Revier, 2012).

Regulatory quality has positive significant effect on corruption in AU, while it has negative significant effect in EU. Since the variable captures the ability of government to formulate and implement sound policies, the policies should be designed for powerful elites not for the common citizen for the case of AU. That is why increase in regulatory quality leads to increase in corruption. Regulatory quality leads to decrease in corruption for the case of EU, because well functioning regulatory mechanism reduces the asymmetry of information and rent extraction related to provision of public goods, which reduces the incidence of corruption (Lederman et al., 2005).

Rule of law has negative significant effect on corruption for the case of EU. Because, better rule of law increases the likelihood of detection and punishment of illicit rent seeking behavior and a perception of strong rule of law decreases the incentives of corrupt acts (Elbahnasawy and Revier, 2012). Per capita income has negative significant effect on corruption for the case of EU. Because, public officials are well paid in rich countries of EU in contrast to poor countries, hence bureaucrats in rich countries do not accept bribes as a form of corruption due to the fact that the gain from the bribe is low compared to the outcome of being caught (Seldadyo and Haan, 2005).

Table 2. System GMM estimation results

	Dependent Variable: cor			
	African Union		European Union	
Variables	Institutional	Economic	Institutional	Economic
l.cor	0.4077**	0.8373***	0.4940***	0.8464***
	(0.1816)	(0.1452)	(0.0726)	(0.0751)
tert	0.0044**	0.0092*	0.0038***	0.0019**
	(0.0020)	(0.0050)	(0.0008)	(0.0009)
govef	-0.5059**		-0.3371***	
	(0.1952)		(0.0752)	
pols	0.0490		0.1606**	
	(0.0784)		(0.0720)	
regq	0.2409*		-0.2777*	
	(0.1263)		(0.1383)	
rol	-0.3217		-0.2230*	
	(0.2605)		(0.1103)	
va	0.0973		0.0733	
	(0.2443)		(0.0952)	
gdppc		2.1e-05		-8.7e-06**
		(4.2e-05)		(3.2e-06)
natur		0.01567**		-0.0146
		(0.00726)		(0.0426)
trade		-0.0060*		4.3e-06
		(0.0030)		(0.0002)
fdi		0.0260		-0.0010
		(0.0160)		(0.0007)
Prob>F	0.0000	0.0000	0.0000	0.0000
Countries	41	37	28	26
Instruments	21	16	27	26
Hansen	0.877	0.757	0.908	0.332
AR(#)	0.451	0.135	0.190	0.838

Source: Author's own calculations

Notes: The values in parenthesis are robust standard errors. ***, ** and * denote significance levels at % 1, % 5 and % 10 respectively. AR(#) is test for second or third order serial correlation in the second-differenced residuals, under the null of no serial correlation. Hansen test of over-identification is under the null that all instruments are valid. All independent variables are treated endogenously. Second and deeper lags are instrumented according to AR(2) or AR(3) test of serial correlation.

Natural resources rent has positive significant effect on corruption for the case of AU. Because, the higher extent of natural resources increases the level of corruption for AU countries by creating opportunities for rent-seeking corrupt behavior (Elbahnasawy and Revier, 2012). Trade openness has negative significant effect on corruption for the case of AU. Because, greater foreign competition reduces potential economic rents and decreases potential gains from bribes (Elbahnasawy and Revier, 2012).

CONCLUSION

Actually the results are surprising especially for the case of EU. Even in the case of highest levels of higher education and lowest levels of corruption, increase in higher education still leads to higher corruption. We may conclude that the enticement of higher living standard prevails the moral principals and ethical values of individuals in the way of reaching it. Since low moral standing in higher education for the case of corruption is valid for both ex-colonizers of EU and ex-colonies of AU, it should be injected to ex-colonies by the ex-colonizers in a distant past. We may conclude that this low moral standing against corruption is also valid for other countries as well since we analyzed it for both extreme cases. Hence, as a policy implication, we advise a course on moral principals and ethical values to be included in the curriculum of higher education institutions to teach the meaning of virtue and the long term gains of living with high moral standing rather than to be gravitated to the short-term gains of corruption.

We have found that an increase in political stability leads to increase in the level of corruption for EU countries. A further study based on this shocking result might be taken as an opportunity.

ACKNOWLEDGMENT

This research received no specific grant from any funding agency in the public, commercial, or not-for-profit sectors.

REFERENCES

Acemoglu, D., Johnson, S., & Robinson, J. A. (2001). The colonial origins of comparative development: An empirical investigation. *The American Economic Review*, *91*(5), 1369–1401. doi:10.1257/aer.91.5.1369

Ali, A. M., & Isse, H. S. (2003). Determinants of Economic Corruption: A Cross-Country Comparison. *The Cato Journal*, *22*(3), 449–466.

Arellano, M., & Bond, S. (1991). Some tests of specification for panel data: Monte Carlo evidence and an application to employment equations. *The Review of Economic Studies*, *58*(2), 277–297. doi:10.2307/2297968

Arellano, M., & Bover, O. (1995). Another look at the instrumental variable estimation of error-components models. *Journal of Econometrics*, *68*(1), 29–51. doi:10.1016/0304-4076(94)01642-D

Beecroft, I., Osabuohien, E., Efobi, U., Olurinola, I., & Osabohien, R. (2020). Manufacturing Export and ICT Infrastructure in West Africa: Investigating the Roles of Economic and Political Institutions. *Institutions, Etc.*, *12*(1), 1–36.

Beyer, C. (2016). *Violent globalisms: conflict in response to empire*. Routledge. doi:10.4324/9781315548111

Blundell, R., & Bond, S. (1998). Initial conditions and moment restrictions in dynamic panel data models. *Journal of Econometrics*, *87*(1), 115–143. doi:10.1016/S0304-4076(98)00009-8

Cheung, H. Y., & Chan, A. W. (2008). Corruption across countries: Impacts from education and cultural dimensions. *The Social Science Journal*, *45*(2), 223–239. doi:10.1016/j.soscij.2008.03.002

Ejemeyovwi, J. O., Osabuohien, E. S., & Osabohien, R. (2018). ICT Investments, Human Capital Development and Institutions in ECOWAS. *International Journal of E-Business Research*, *15*(4), 463–474.

Elbahnasawy, N. G., & Revier, C. F. (2012). The determinants of corruption: Cross-country-panel-data analysis. *The Developing Economies*, *50*(4), 311–333. doi:10.1111/j.1746-1049.2012.00177.x

Etzioni, A. (2008). *Security first: for a muscular, moral foreign policy*. Yale University Press.

Eicher, T., García-Peñalosa, C., & Van Ypersele, T. (2009). Education, corruption, and the distribution of income. *Journal of Economic Growth*, *14*(3), 205–231. doi:10.100710887-009-9043-0

Evrensel, A. Y. (2010). Institutional and economic determinants of corruption: A cross-section analysis. *Applied Economics Letters*, *17*(6), 551–554. doi:10.1080/13504850802297814

Frechette, G. R. (2006). *Panel data analysis of the time-varying determinants of corruption (No. 2006s-28)*. Cirano.

Goel, R. K., & Nelson, M. A. (2005). Economic freedom versus political freedom: Cross-country influences on corruption. *Australian Economic Papers*, *44*(2), 121–133. doi:10.1111/j.1467-8454.2005.00253.x

Gök, A. (2017). The Role of Governance on Outward Foreign Direct Investment in Emerging Market Economies. In Outward Foreign Direct Investment (FDI) in Emerging Market Economies (pp. 77-101). IGI Global.

Lederman, D., Loayza, N. V., & Soares, R. R. (2005). Accountability and corruption: Political institutions matter. *Economics and Politics*, *17*(1), 1–35. doi:10.1111/j.1468-0343.2005.00145.x

Osabuohien, E. (2020). *The Palgrave Handbook of Agricultural and Rural Development in Africa*. Palgrave Macmillan., doi:10.1007/978-3-030-41513-6

Rehman, H. U., & Naveed, A. (2007). Determinants of corruption and its relation to GDP (A panel study). *Journal of Political Studies*, *12*(2), 27–59.

Roodman, D. (2009). How to do xtabond2: An introduction to difference and system GMM in Stata. *The Stata Journal*, *9*(1), 86–136. doi:10.1177/1536867X0900900106

Seldadyo, H., & De Haan, J. (2005). The determinants of corruption. *The Economist, 66*, 1-60.

Shabbir, G., & Anwar, M. (2007). Determinants of corruption in developing countries. *Pakistan Development Review*, *46*(4II), 751–764. doi:10.30541/v46i4IIpp.751-764

WDI. (2019). *Worldwide Development Indicators, World Bank.* Retrieved from https://databank.worldbank.org/reports.aspx?source=2&series=SI.POV.DDAY&country=WLD

WGI. (2019). *Worldwide Governance Indicators, World Bank.* Retrieved from https://databank.worldbank.org/source/worldwide-governance-indicators/Type/TABLE/preview/on

KEY TERMS AND DEFINITIONS

AU: African Union.

Colonial Origin: The roots of countries in the age of colonization.

EU: European Union.

Ex-Colonies: Mostly, African countries that were colonized in 19th century and afterwards mainly for exploitation of natural resources or slave labor.

Ex-Colonizers: European countries that colonized African countries (mostly) in 19th century and afterwards mainly for economic and political hegemony.

Extractive Institutions: Type of institutional setup, in which a powerful elite exploits the rest of the population.

Higher Education: Enrollment in an educational institution above the level of high school.

Tertiary Enrollment: Enrollment in higher education.

APPENDIX

Figure 1. Scatterplot of higher education and corruption in the world
Source: Author's own calculations based on WDI (2019) and WGI (2019)
Notes: The values of corruption are obtained by multiplying the values of control of corruption with minus one. Higher education represents school enrollment, tertiary (% gross).

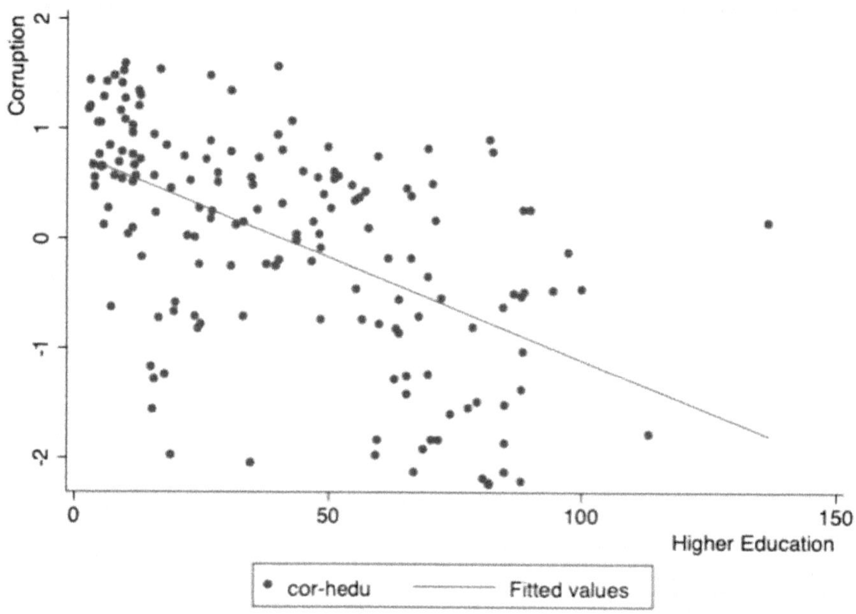

Chapter 4
Institutional Settings, Renewable Energy Development, and Forest Cover Changes in Sub-Saharan Africa

Ewere Evelyn Anyokwu
Center for Development Research (ZEF), University of Bonn, Germany

Chigozie Nweke-Eze
Institute of Geography, University of Bonn, Germany

ABSTRACT

This chapter explores the roles of institutional settings in renewable energy (RE) development in Sub-Saharan Africa, and the effects of RE development on forest cover changes in the region. The study finds that the slow but persistent growth in RE contribution to total energy bundles can be credited to the general improvements in institutional reforms and frameworks. It also finds that unlike biomass-based RE systems, the indirect deforestation effects associated with solar and wind energy systems, are largely offset by the environmental benefits that accrue from them. Based on these findings, the chapter recommends that coordinated institutional interventions should prioritize the deployment of more environmentally sustainable RE technologies such as solar and wind energies.

INTRODUCTION

Forests are indispensable natural resources; covering only about 30% of the earth' land area but hosting almost 80% global biodiversity (The European Union Action Plan, 2019. Despite the importance of the forest ecosystem, the world forest area continues to decline due to anthropogenic and natural factors including logging for wood products, mineral resources extraction, urbanization, volcanic eruption, and cropland expansion, leading to a condition sometimes referred to as forest cover change (Kayiranga et al., 2018). This is particularly more challenging in Sub-Sahara Africa (SSA) where there is slow prog-

DOI: 10.4018/978-1-7998-4817-2.ch004

ress in executing sustainable forest management and an increasing rate of forest loss. While forest areas may stabilize and increase in many transition countries of Asia and the Pacific, most of the low and middle-income forest-rich countries will probably witness a persistent decline in their forest area due to agricultural expansion. Forest resources in Europe are expected to continue to increase given their rising concern for environmental protection and well-structured institutional and policy frameworks (Food and Agriculture Organisation – FAO, 2009). Many other studies have suggested that global forest cover is probably changing more rapidly than the last decade and scientists believe that this trend could even peak in the next twenty years. For instance, Kayiranga et al. (2018), found that while the net deforestation rate was about 1.9%, the net annual rate of forest regeneration was about 1.8% from 1986-2000 in central and East Africa. This accounted for about 0.2% loss in the forest area between 2000 and 2015.

This growing trend of deforestation could pose bigger problems to the climate, the environment, humanity, global economy, social wellbeing and others (Negasi et al., 2018). Searchinger et al. (2018) and Waheed et al. (2017) think that harvesting wood from the forest for burning would probably increase carbon in the atmosphere for decades. This is further emphasized by FAO (2007) who opines that the possible effect of increasing the recovery of biomass from forests include biodiversity loss, scarcity of nutrient, changes to ecosystem function and difficulties in forest regeneration. Sharma et al. (1994) also identify the possibility of strong interlinkages between deforestation, environmental degradation, and long-run economic decline. In the face of these likely problems, the field of energy seems to demand more research because of the possible need for more solutions that would address the seemingly increasing forest cover changes, as highlighted by Moon & Solomon (2018). It is also argued that some of these solutions could emanate from the effective deployment of renewable energy options. For instance, Maiwada et al. (2014) believe that exploiting other renewable energy sources like biofuels, solar and wind technologies could lead to a reduction in the overreliance on forests for fuelwood and still slow down deforestation and climate change.

Renewable energy is being promoted as a possible significant way of addressing environmental and forest security concerns (OECD Policy Brief, 2015). Scholars of energy sciences often state that renewable energy deployment has been quite massive in the 21st Century and is likely to be an excellent approach towards meeting the energy demand of future generations (Owusu & Asumadu-Sarkodie, 2016). Gasparatos et al. (2017) have argued that there seems to be a rapid increase in the level of renewable energy penetration in the global energy landscape. Renewable energy deployment could provide better energy services for a sustainable social and economic development path (Moomaw et al., 2011). According to the United Nations Economic Commission for Europe - UNECE Report (2014), some European countries seem to have had their shares of renewable energy in total final energy consumption exceeding 50% as of 2012. However, compared to developed contries, renewable energy deployment and utilization remains low in Sub-Sahara Africa.

Some studies have attempted to explore the causes of the growth pattern in the renewable energy sector in Africa focusing on the production and consumption aggregates (Ackah & Kizys, 2015; da Silva, Cerqueira, & Ogbe, 2018; Rahut, Behera, & Ali, 2017). For example, Ackah & Kizys (2015) found that real income per capita, energy resource depletion per capita, carbon dioxide (CO_2) emissions per capita, and energy prices were the major drivers of renewable energy consumption in oil-producing African countries. Similar evidence was reported in a household level analysis by Rahut et al., (2017). While income and other factors may be important in determining the growth of renewable energy use, the role of institutions in promoting these technologies have been less accessed. Development of renewable energy and fostering environmental integrity requires not just more money but policy attention and massive political effort from both domestic and international actors - all of which are embodied and embedded in institutions (AfDB 2017, Davidson & Sokona, 2002; Brew-Hammond 2010; Brew-Hammond & Kemausuor, 2009). Strong institutions and packages of policies are needed to promote clean energy access, including electricity for productive uses and a full range of technical solutions – notably off-grid and mini-grid renewables (Eberhard et al. 2008; Elias & Victor, 2005). Evidence suggests that institutional frameworks are necessary for the achievement of the goals of renewable energy development (Akinyemi et al. 2019). Yet, the role of institutions is unclear when associated with renewable energy deployment and development in the SSA context.

Furthermore, earlier studies on the determinants of RE deployment focused on the total bundle of renewable energies(Adewuyi & Adeniyi, 2015; Adewuyi & Awodumi, 2017; Opeyemi, Uchenna, Simplice, & Evans, 2019; Salim & Rafiq, 2012). However, renewable energies are a collection of technology types, each with specific and peculiar drivers and impacts. Depending on the aggregate RE bundles again provides little information for environmental sustainability of renewable energy transitions. For example, while all types of renewable energies may have CO_2 saving capability, ecosystem effects may defer between solar, wind and biomass-based RE systems. Yet these disaggregated effects have received little attention in the RE literature. Likewise, studies that discuss these effects have mostly focused on economic effects (Opeyemi et al., 2019; Adewuyi and Adeniyi, 2015) with narrowly focused evidence on environmental effects (Inglesi-Lotz & Dogan, 2018; Yazdi & Beygi, 2017). For instance, the estimation of the effects of renewable energy on CO_2 emissions, (Inglesi-Lotz & Dogan, 2018; Yazdi & Beygi, 2017) found the environmental improving effect of renewable energy relative to non-renewable consumption.

Given this background and recollections on literature gaps, this chapter explores the roles of institutional settings and development in renewable energy development, on the one hand; and the effects of renewable energy development on forest cover changes, on the other hand. In doing so, we differentiate and disaggregate the roles and contributions of the different types of renewable energy and their technologies to capture their individual effects on forest cover changes. The analyses of the paper are based on the review of literature and documents as well as case study analyses, and descriptive data presentations.

CONCEPTUAL AND ANALYTICAL FRAMEWORK

Renewable Energy Development/Deployment

Renewable Energy (RE) could be referred to as energy that is derived from resources which are naturally replenished on a human timescale, with examples as sunlight, wind, rain, tides, geothermal heat etc., known as renewable resources. In other words, renewable energy development could be seen as the activities of a country or region to increase the uptake of renewable energy and hence, improve its share in the country's total energy mix. Most times, the increased deployment of renewable energy may imply a decrease in the adoption of non-renewable energy and a higher possibility of a safer environment.

Institutions/Institutional Framework

In the context of renewable energy deployment, institutions could be seen as those organizations founded by both the government and the private sector that mobilize and encourage renewable energy investments and a smooth transition to renewable energy consumption. On a larger scale, it could also be referred to as an institutional framework, which includes the system of formal laws, regulations and procedures, and convention, norms and customs that shape the production and consumption, demand and supply of renewable energy in a particular country.

Forest Cover Changes (Afforestation, Deforestation and Reforestation)

Forests are said to expand naturally if they follow a natural succession onto previously non-forested lands, usually unused land for agriculture. This growth of forest in the previously non-forested area could be termed afforestation. On the other hand, forest cover could also be reduced when they are cut down or through natural disasters; known as deforestation. All of these factors lead to the forest cover changes, a distortion of the previous composition of forests.

Climate Change

This has been described in different ways by different organizations. Notable among them is that given to it by NASA, as the wide range of global occurrences created mainly by the use of fossil fuels for energy generation, which lead to the accumulation of greenhouse gases in the earth's atmosphere. They listed some of those phenomena to include the steady trend of rising temperature emphasized by global warming, sea-level rise and other extreme weather events.

Environmental Degradation

This describes the deterioration of the environment caused by the overuse of resources such as air, water and soil; the destruction of ecosystems and habitats, the extinction of wildlife species and the outright pollution of both land and water bodies.

The conceptual framework below shows the linkages between these core concepts of our study.

The Energy industry is one of the most thriving industries globally, and this is not surprising because energy is needed in almost all facets of human endeavours. Primarily, the energy industry focuses on increasing global energy access, either by intensifying its efforts towards the expansion of the already mature and dominant non-renewable energy sector or the promotion and development of the renewable energy sector. The latter option tends to encourage a gradual but smooth transition from burning fossil fuels to the use of renewables. Expansion of the energy sector through the development of either renewable energy or non-renewable energy like in other economic sectors requires a great deal of procedures, mostly in the forms of policy formulation and implementation, legal assessments and regulations, as well as the public and private sector institutions and investments. These are referred to as the policy framework, the legal framework and the institutional framework, respectively (Karekezi & Kithyoma, 2003).

In the course of developing renewable energy, the different types of renewable energy are explored, and they include the bioenergy, wind energy, solar energy and hydro energy. Others are the tidal and geothermal energy, which are still very nascent in Africa. The generation of these different renewable energy types have a strong relationship with forest cover changes in Africa and may lead to deforestations, as evidenced by the studies reviewed above. Deforestation itself may contribute to climate and other forms of environmental degradation, just as the development of non-renewable energy mostly in the form of fossil fuels would cause.

Figure 1. The conceptual framework for connection among institutional settings, renewable energy deployment and forest cover change (Authors own)

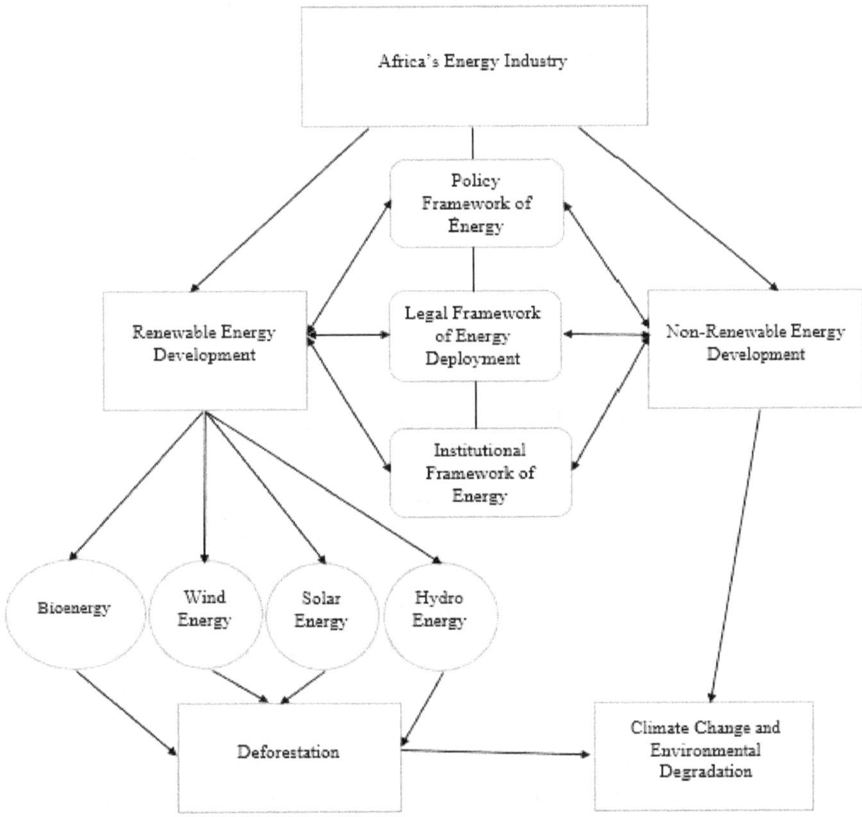

INSTITUTIONS AND RENEWABLE ENERGY DEVELOPMENT IN SUB-SAHARAN AFRICA

Roles of Institutional Settings and Activities on Renewable Energy Development in SSA

In this section, we discuss the role of institutional contexts, policies, strategies, rules and regulations, in the governing of the operation and development of renewable energy systems. There already exists a diversity of renewable energy-related institutional building efforts in many SSA countries, supported by governments, various global and international development finance institutions, the private sector and civil society organizations. However, these efforts are unevenly spread across the SSA countries and taken together, still fall far short of reaching the required context required for renewable energy deployment to happen in its full scale. Therefore, there is need for significant scaling up of efforts and accelerated proposition and implementation of required institutional frameworks among SSA countries, in a manner that all countries are carried along and support each other in solidarity in achieving their RE leveraging goals.

In the process of discussing the roles, this section will also discuss clusters of activities that will need to be further designed, funded, and implemented. In practice, countries will need to select and combine specific elements into comprehensive, nationally determined policy packages. Considering the dynamic and multifaceted challenges of implementing an energy transition, a variety of complementary and interrelated approaches are required. Activities should take place at both the national and sub-regional levels, to provide technical and financial resources for policy development and incentive creation and execution, building on replicable and effective best practices in Africa and other regions.

Both public and private investors will need to benefit from enabling and strengthening institutional activities, which come in the form of favorable and promoting policies, regulatory frameworks, incentives and supports. These institutional activities create stability and certainty in their investment environment, thereby making the countries attractive for renewable energy investment. A fundamental element is a strong regulatory environment that respects contracts and the rule of law. Investors need confidence that contracts will be honored. We discuss both enabling and strengthening institutional settings and activities in the following clusters of activities.

Provision of Investment Security and Incentives

Although there is often already a clear business case for renewable energy based on lifetime costs, efforts to accelerate renewable energy deployment must address the difference in cost structure between fossil fuels and renewable energy sources (Raza et al., 2015; El-katiri, 2011; Arnold, 2015). That the cost of renewable energy projects is dominated by the upfront capital costs of the equipment rather than fuel and other operating costs presents a risk to investors (Dulal et al. 2013; Raza et al. 2015). Investors and developers (constituting households, communities, cooperatives, small and medium scale enterprises (SMEs) or larger companies) need both certainties of off-take of produced energy and certainty on the tariff (price) on which the produced energy can be sold (Suzuki, 2013).

For ambitious roll-out of renewable energy in Africa, these risks need to be addressed in a comprehensive, predictable, and long-term manner through targeted support and incentives. De-risking, time-bound payment guarantees such as those offered through power purchase agreements (PPAs) can provide secure investment conditions for both small and large investors and developers (Ohunakin et al., 2014). Many African countries already have or are planning for such results-based incentives using feed-in tariff (FIT) or auction-based systems. For example, as at year 2013, Kenya, Tanzania and Uganda already had existing FIT systems with more countries including Ghana and Botswana completing processes for its introduction (Meyer-Renschhausen, 2017). If these measures are scaled-up, they will provide a leeway for the flowing-in of significant investments from international and national, public and private actors. Other incentives that countries may consider include indirect support measures such as tax rebates, insurance, various forms of risk guarantees, low-cost loans and concessional financing, and, seldomly used cost-efficient, direct support measures such as cash subsidies (Sun & Nie, 2015; Ansari et al., 2016; Raza et al., 2015).

Besides, countries can consider a range of policy measures that further enhance long-term investment conditions by ensuring that national RE goals are formulated for both short-term and long-term, and enforcing uniform standards for important processes such as PPAs, off-take and tariffs requirements (Stokes, 2013; Sun & Nie, 2015). Design and application of these instruments will need to be financed through a mix of national and international climate/ development funding, which will in turn, leverage much larger public and private investment. It is crucial in designing policy frameworks and incentives to involve stakeholders through participatory processes and address issues of affordability, socio-economic benefits, environmental soundness, regional cooperation, and technology transfer elements (Goldsmith, 2015; Nesamalar et al., 2017; Jianjun & Chen 2014).

Provision of Financing and Access to Credits

In the short run, financial resources in the form of new and additional concessional credits and grants would be needed for the required analytical, preparatory and planning work and to provide incentives and financial investment support (Sun & Nie, 2015; Painuly, 2001). Based on experiences in Africa and other developing countries, these efforts could be expected to attract private and public sector financing and lead to the installation of new and additional RE generation capacity in African countries (Zhang et al., 2014).

To fully leverage on renewable energy opportunities, the access-to-credit bottleneck faced by RE investors across the continent needs to be resolved. Many African credit institutions are reluctant and inexperienced in lending for RE investments, resulting in many RE potential projects never occurring due to either the non-availability of credit or excessively high-interest rates (Ohunakin et al., 2014; Suzuki, 2013). This is particularly true for small-scale investments in distributed RE systems, which is a modern, unproven field for many financial institutions, and where borrowers/creditors are often relatively weak and inexperienced economic entities like SMEs, cooperatives, societies and households (Suzuki, 2013). Further credit-related problems include lack of access to foreign exchange, strict lending conditions which often involve collaterals, as well as questions and risks of off-taker creditworthiness (Ohunakin et al., 2014).

Capacity Building

Achieving a transition to sustainable, renewable energy systems in Africa is a challenge that will take unparalleled commitment and capacity building across sectors and at all levels of people and institutions. Doing so would increase overall costs, but the benefits from robust institutional and human capacity are significant (Ansari et al., 2016). The sustained expansion of renewable energy projects in Africa would more than cover the costs; therefore, they are better seen as investments. A significant capacity-building effort would require considerable support from the international public to complement domestic resources (Karakaya & Sriwanawit, 2015). Although international expertise, including South-South cooperation and the sharing of information, is important, it is equally crucial that Africa develop its own skills base and expertise (Nasirov et al. 2015). National ownership means African institutions are taking control of the technical effort required to expand the renewable energy sector (Paravantis et al., 2014).

There is a need to develop comprehensive strategic plans and programmes for enhancing skills, education and training, with the involvement of top national and international experts (Nasirov et al. 2015). It is also essential to support mobilizing and, as appropriate channeling, public financial support for scaled-up renewable energy education and training at universities and other relevant institutions, and foster international and interdisciplinary collaboration, such as the creation of interchangeable job and training specifications, harmonization of curricula, and development of common quality standards for training programmes and trainers (Paravantis et al., 2014, Ansari et al. 2016; Karakaya & Sriwanawit, 2015). Another critical point is to build the capacity of researchers to produce, access, and communicate evidence that informs policy-making, and strengthen capacity to monitor and evaluate progress and achievements at all levels of the RE development plans (Ahlborg & Hammar, 2014; Nesamalar et al., 2017).

Improving Technical Capacities for Uptake

Achieving the ambitious vision of a future with a high penetration of renewable energy in Africa requires long-term planning and entails major investments in upgrading existing grids and developing new smart grids, both regional mini-grids and national ones (Zhao et al. 2016; Izadbakhsh et al., 2015). Although this will mean higher short-term costs, it will create a robust African energy network (Bhandari et al., 2015). For smart grids, the energy infrastructure can support both large-scale RE installations and modern, small-scale generators that are both consumers and electricity producers (Nasirov et al., 2015).

Localized networks may, therefore, tackle non-technical disadvantages including non-metered and unbilled usage more efficiently. The energy system can accommodate significantly higher amounts of renewable energy by developing new and smarter grids and upgrading old grids. Based on a greater range of renewable energy sources and intelligent design, the device would be able to provide reliability and baseload capability. Stand-alone installations will interconnect, even at the household level, and mini-grids and can ultimately connect to the national grid (Izadbakhsh et al., 2015).

As is the case in many other developing countries, accelerated roll-out and funding for mini-grids for many African countries would be a major part of the renewable energy transition (Izadbakhsh et al., 2015). Mini-grid regulations and support schemes must ensure safe investments for developers (whether by the community, small and medium-sized enterprise or a larger enterprise) and promote economically and technically feasible future grid connections, (Sen & Bhattacharyya, 2014; Cho et al., 2013; Halabi et al., 2015).

Coordination and Review of Institutional Activities

This cluster stresses the importance of enhancing coordination with and build on the outcome of the various institutional programmes and initiatives on the development of renewable energy that already exists in SSA, including bilateral and multilateral cooperation. Regionally coordinated development and review of existing institutional framework will prevent costly duplication of efforts in renewable energy promotion across the region. These efforts will ensure the assessment of current and emerging technologies, RE policies, regulations, and experiences in the African region drawing on existing information as well as commissioning new assessments of approaches to determine success factors and lessons learned (Ahlborg & Hammar, 2014; Goldsmith, 2015; Nesamalar et al., 2017). Reviewing past institutional activities will help to determine the most promising and replicable approaches among existing initiatives, assess the level of effort, gaps, and priorities of the different RE programmes and identifying areas that can be further strengthened through partnerships and collaborations (Emodi et al., 2014; Huang et al. 2013). Effective coordination among stakeholders will also facilitate the exchange of best-practice policies by supporting the participation of policymakers in peer-exchange networks. Organized consultative events on policy design and implementation that bring together national, regional and international decision-makers, managers, regulators, investors, private sector and the civil society is also necessary to enhance coordination (Ahlborg & Hammar, 2014; Goldsmith, 2015; Nesamalar et al., 2017).

Institutions and Mechanisms for Renewable Energy Development in Africa

Many institutions have emerged in Africa over the years to contribute to the global agenda on renewable energy adoption to combat climate change effectively. According to the CEIF Report (2008), three of

the core objectives of the African Development Fund (AfDF), a subsidiary of the African Development Bank (AfDB) Group, are rural electrification in Africa, multi-national grid interconnections and renewable energy development. This is behind 12% of the fund's budget between 1967 and 2007 allocated to the energy sector, out of which more than 25% was channelled towards renewable energy development. In addition to their independent activities, the Bank has also collaborated with governments to initiate programs aimed at renewable energy development. One of such programs is the FINESSE Africa Program, financed by the Dutch Government with the main aim of promoting the mainstreaming of renewable energy and energy efficiency into the Bank Group's energy sector operations. This program was vital in developing a portfolio of renewable energy projects for the Bank. In no order of importance, the program developed the US$5.9 million renewable energy component under the Madagascar rural water supply and sanitation project approved in 2005 (with 250 solar water pumps and four wind generation). Also, a US$500,000 solar component of Uganda's Education Project Fund approved in 2005 was also supported. The Ugandan project's was aimed at providing rural basic education institutions with lighting, laboratory equipment and solar powered computers. It also covered the initiation of "renewable energy packages" for a rural market place for agro-processing, approved in 2007. The Bank also launched other renewable energy projects in other African countries such as Lesotho (rural electrification with micro-hydro, wind and solar), Tanzania (through a renewable energy component of rural water supply and sanitation project), Mozambique (through support to sugar-cane for the production of bio-ethanol) and others.

The African Renewable Energy Initiative (AREI) is another strong institutional mechanism for promoting renewable energy deployment in Africa. It is under the mandate of the African Union and endorsed by the African Heads of State and Government on Climate Change (CAHOSCC) and is set to increase Africa's renewable energy generation capacity by 300GW at least, by 2030. The initiative aimed to achieve two main objectives. First, it was designed to assist African countries rapidly move towards low-carbon development strategies including bundles of renewable energy systems that enhance energy and economic security. Secondly, the goal was (to ensure universal access to sufficient amounts of clean, appropriate and affordable energy in Africa and thus, help in achieving sustainable development in the continent (AREI Framework, 2015).

From the international arena, various institutions have also played a role in Africa's renewable energy development. One of such is the International Renewable Energy Agency (IRENA). Her engagement with Africa on renewables started almost when the organization was founded in 2009. In July 2011, the organization convened a forum in which African nations and development partners formulated renewable energy priorities, which smoothened IRENA's renewable energy development activities in Africa (IRENA Impact Report, 2019)

Apart from the above-mentioned institutional arrangements and initiatives, it is also important to reveal that many African countries have introduced national support instruments for renewable energy – covering renewable energy targets, fiscal incentives, regulatory policies and public investment into renewable energy. This renewable energy targets exist in about 40 countries, most of which focus on electricity from renewable sources. For this, the dominant instruments include tendering (in 12 countries), premiums/feed-in-tariffs (in nine countries) and net metering (seven countries). Additionally, about 30 African countries have adopted tax reductions as an instrument for renewable energy promotion. More than twenty African countries also adopt grants or loans, while about 13 countries use rebates and capital subsidies. Unfortunately, for the transport and heat sectors, renewable energy remains grossly unpopular. Nine countries have adopted biofuels obligations or mandates, while three countries have renewable heat obligations and mandates (Quitzow et al., 2016).

Specific Institutional Setup for the Different Renewable Energy Development in Sub-Saharan Africa

Renewable energy sources are essential for global climate stabilization and a greener environment. However, while renewable energy deployment is speeding up in the global north, the global south, especially the region commonly referred to as sub-Saharan Africa, seems to lag (both in absolute renewable energy development indices and technology differentials), evidenced by the fact that the region could only record about 30.5% electrification rate in 2016, far below the rate in other regions (Chirambo, 2016). One of the factors that could have attributed to this is the region's inability to attract enough energy sector investments. SSA is mostly perceived to have minimal opportunities to reduce GHG emissions since the region currently contributes just a little to global greenhouse gas emissions. Consequently, the region constantly misses out on attracting climate and renewable energy finance projects (Chirambo, 2016). Karekezi & Kithyoma (2003) further identified other factors as inadequate planning policies for renewable energy adoption, poor infrastructure and institutional framework, lack of skilled workforce and insufficient baseline information. Also, according to Khellaf (2018), higher capital costs are, most times, required for renewable energy deployment than non-renewable energy deployment and Africa may not have the financial capability to do so much towards a rapid uptake of renewable energy. This is summarised in Table 1.

Table 1. Capital cost for renewable and non-renewable power generation systems

Source	Technology	Installation cost ($/W)
Conventional source	Nuclear plant	4.27-7.93
	Natural gas combustion turbine	0.49-0.81
	Natural gas combined cycle	0.91-1.54
	Coal-fired power plant	1.88-3.90
Renewable source	Stand-alone biomass power plant	2.87-5.75
	Geothermal power plant	5.94
	Hydropower	2.28-4.73
	Solar PV power plant	2.12-3.54
	Solar PV home system	3.6-17.0
	Grid-connected solar PV rooftop system	2.0-3.0
	Mini-grid system	2.5-2.9
	CSP trough with storage power plant	4.59-8.12
	CSP tower with storage power plant	4.58-8.10
	Wind onshore power plant	1.49-2.48
	Wind fixed bottom off shore power plant	2.15-4.47
	Wind floating platform offshore power plant	2.73-5.67

Source: Khellaf, (2018).

Figure 2. Global renewable energy investment (Source: IRENA Africa Impact Report 2020)

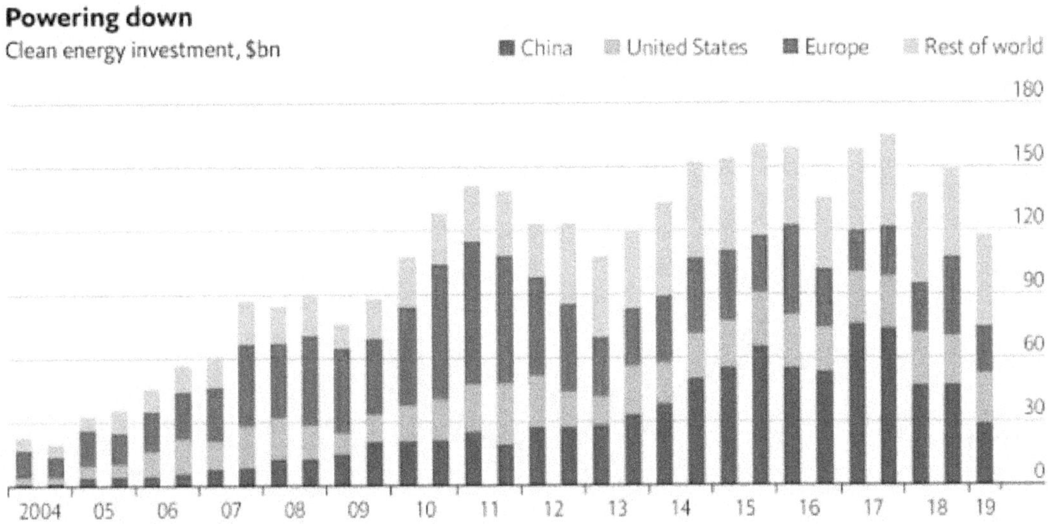

Figure 3. Africa's energy mix 2016 (Source: IRENA Impact Report, 2019)

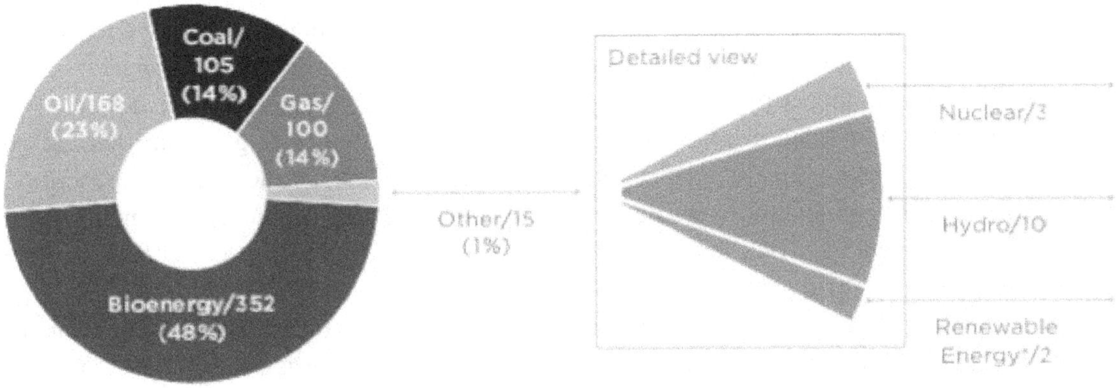

The excessive use of bioenergy as reflected in the figure 3 is mainly within the traditional biomass consumption, not in the form of clean energy coming from bioenergy sources. This excessive biomass consumption in Africa poses a danger to human health while causing environmental damages through deforestation (World Bank Energy Report 2018).

More notably, renewable energy deployment in Africa is mostly dependent on national and international support. Hence, institutions are essential for this development, but these are less understood in the African context. More importantly, renewable energy deployment may have some critical impact which has been poorly explored. It is, therefore, essential to examine the specific institutions that champion the development of the individual renewable energy sources.

Figure 4. EU energy mix 2017 (Source: IRENA Impact Report 2019)

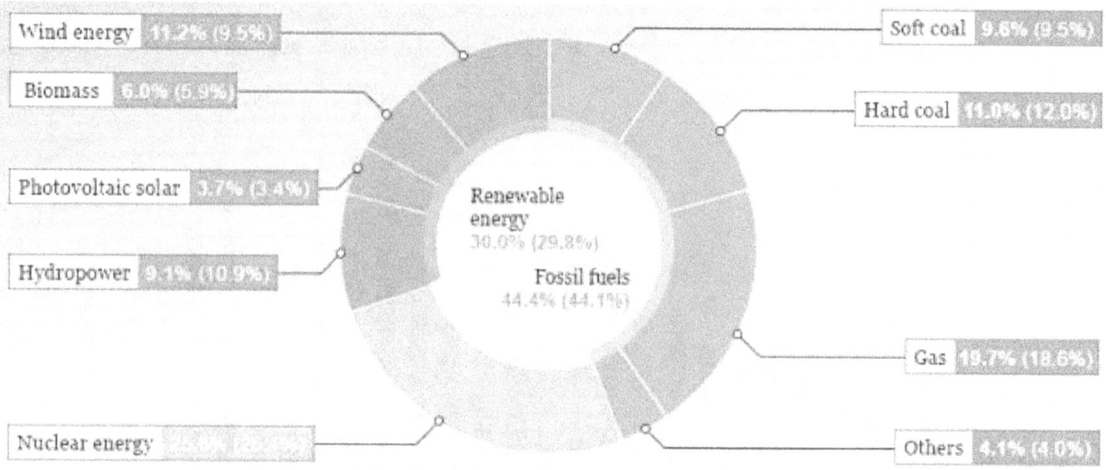

Specific Institutions for Solar Energy Development in Sub-Saharan Africa

As already mentioned, the African Development Bank (AfDB) is a major stakeholder in Africa's renewable energy development and as such, has made giant strides in the different renewable energy sectors, ranging from solar and wind energy to geothermal. In the quest for solar energy development in Africa, the Bank's Private Sector Department (OPSM), with the assistance from the Danish Renewable Energy Technical Assistance, compiled a project pipeline for 2008-2012 comprising a solar thermal power plant in Morocco as well as rural electrification in Tanzania with mainly the solar component (CEIF Report, 2018). The International Renewable Energy Agency (IRENA) is equally very instrumental in solar energy development in Africa, as the document in the IRENA Africa Impact Report (2020), especially in the aspect of off-grid solar energy solutions for African rural communities (IRENA Off-Grid RE Solutions, 2018). There is also the presence of the private sector in the development of solar energy in Africa, and indeed other renewable energy sources. They mainly participate either as sponsors or partners of Public-Private-Partnerships – PPPs (Mukasa et al., 2012). IEA is also a vital institution for solar energy development in Africa.

Specific Institutions for Wind Energy Development in Sub-Saharan Africa

Some of the AfDB renewable energy development projects in Africa also include small-to-large-scale wind power projects expected to generate about 921MW of electricity, launched within the 2007-2008 project pipeline. Others include a wind energy project in Madagascar involved in the Bank's pipeline of clean energy operations appraised from 2008-2012, and a renewable energy project in the Gambia comprising of wind, solar and hydro energy (CEIF Report, 2018). Other institutions involved in wind energy development in Africa also include the European Investment Bank (EIB), East African Development Bank (the co-founders of the largest wind farm in Africa), regional Development Finance Institutions (DFIs), DEG (German), and FMO (Dutch) (Kazimierczuk, (2019). Generally, there has been a gradual shift from the use of concessional to non-concessional funding from DFIs and greater use of specialized and Clean Development Mechanism (CDM) funds on wind energy projects in Africa (Mukasa et al., 2013).

Figure 5. Population served by and capacity of off-grid renewable energy solutions in Africa (Source: IRENA Impact Report, 2019)

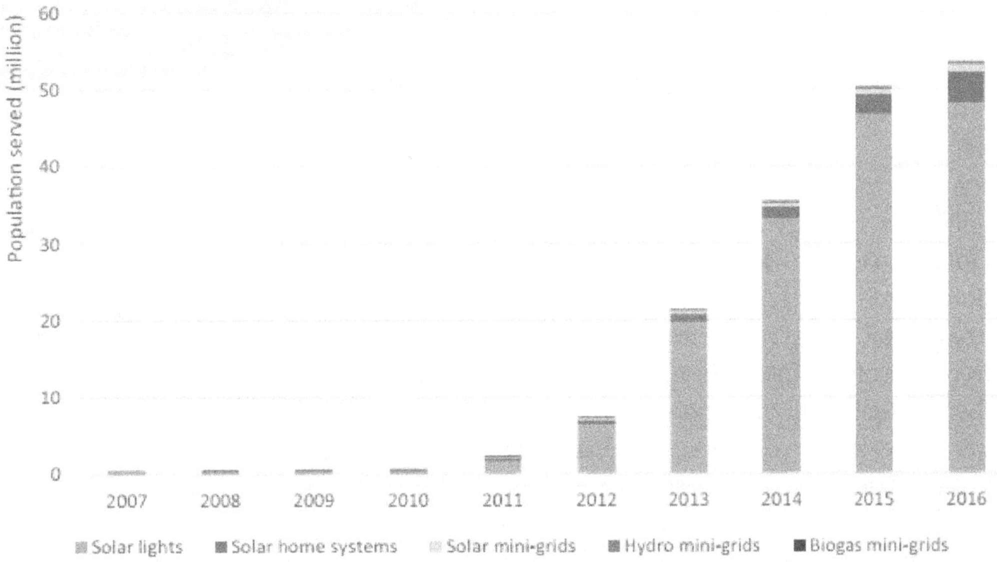

Specific Institutions for Bioenergy Development in Sub-Saharan Africa

The AfDB's partnership with the Danish Renewable Energy Technical Assistance was also beneficial to the bioenergy sector in Africa. Through their interventions, bioenergy projects were launched in some parts of Africa. For example, the development of energy cogeneration utilizing bagasse from sugar factories as a fuel in Gabon and many community forestry management projects in Benin, Burkina Faso and Ghana were supported by the duo (CEIF Report, 2018). The European Union (EU), through her EU Energy Initiative - EUEI (2012) has been playing a vital role in the development of renewable energy projects in Africa. Some of the African countries that have benefited from their bioenergy projects include Burundi, Ethiopia, Mozambique and Tanzania. They also initiated combined renewable energy projects in Madagascar, Ghana, Guinea, DR Congo, The Gambia, Kenya, Nigeria, Rwanda, Senegal, Sierra Leone and Uganda. National institutions are also involved in the bioenergy development in Africa, as is the case with South Africa where the Department of Energy, the Department of Agriculture, Forestry and Fisheries and the National Energy Regulator play critical roles in attracting investment into bioenergy (OECD/IEA, FAO, 2017).

The African Union Commission (AU) in partnership with the UN Economic Commission for Africa (ECA) and NEPAD Planning and Coordinating Agency (NPCA) launched a program aimed at reviving Africa's bioenergy sector in 2011. This further led to the development of the African Bioenergy Framework and Policy Guidelines in 2013. Some of the tangible outputs of this program in Africa include the adaptation of bioenergy resolution by AU Assembly on January 13, 2014, enhancement of biofuels for household and transport sectors in Africa (with case studies in Arusha, Accra, Cairo, Dakar, Gaborone, Kampala and Antananarivo) (AU Energy Report, 2015).

Specific Institutions for Hydro Energy Development in Sub-Saharan Africa

One of the notable institutions positively influencing hydro energy development in Africa is still the African Development Bank (AfDB). This is evidenced by the plethora of hydro projects implemented in the different regions of Africa within the period 2007-2012. Some of them include hydro-power projects in Sierra Leone and Uganda, Micro-hydro project in Madagascar, and some mini and micro hydro-power plants in Gabon (CEIF Report). The New Partnership for Africa's Development (NEPAD) is an economic development program of the African Union. It was adopted at the 37th session of the Assembly of Heads of State and Government in July 2001 in Lusaka, Zambia. Her vision for Africa's energy sector has targeted the exploitation of the continent's vast hydropower potential to address the socio-economic problems therein while promoting clean energy effectively. This programme, therefore, remains very crucial in increasing trend of hydro energy development in Africa (AfDB Report, 2008). The UK Department for International Development (DFID) also supports hydropower development in Africa, as highlighted in the report (DFID Report, 2007). Also, the World Bank Group, comprising of the World Bank, IFC and MIGA, recognizes this as a timely and important period for hydro-power development in Africa, and are initiating projects in that direction (World Bank, 2009).

Generally, there is the scarcity of institutions focused on the deployment of specific renewable energies, which puts renewable energy in a disadvantaged position. More worrisome is the fact that the energy sectors are still fully engrossed in fossil fuel generation, despite the global call for a reduction in the burning of fossil fuels and the recent but drastic drop in global oil price due to the novel coronavirus (COVID-19) pandemic. In these countries, even the power utilities most times do not accept power produced by solar, biomass and wind technologies because of their small size, and the resistance to change that is common in any well-established institution or society. They argue that it is challenging to match power from those sources with the usual peak load due to problems of intermittency in renewable supply (UNIDO, 2009).

Trends in the Development of Renewable Energy in Sub-Saharan Africa

This subsection presents an overview of renewable energy development in Africa (including (1) the charts that show the trend of Renewable Energy in Ghana, Nigeria and South Africa from 2000 to 2018, and (2) the share of renewable energy in the energy consumption sectors of Nigeria, Ghana and South Africa.

Energy and electricity are arguably among the topical issues on the African continent in recent times given that about two-thirds of its population lack access to electricity, according to the World Bank. The situation in Sub-Saharan Africa seems even worse, especially in the rural areas, as almost half of all energy use therein includes the consumption of traditional biomass, which could be dangerous for human health while causing damages to the environment through deforestation (GIZ, 2018). Many scholars in the field of energy have argued that solutions to the energy access issues in Africa lie in the smooth transition to renewable energy since the potential is available, as highlighted in the Sustainable Energy Regulation and Policymaking-SERP training manual (2005). Some of these renewable energy resources include hydro energy, bioenergy, wind energy and solar energy. The IRENA Africa 2030 Renewable Energy Roadmap (2015) suggests that given the changing economy, changing lifestyles and the growing need for reliable modern energy access, Africa is expected to at least double her current energy supply and triple her electricity production by 2030, with renewable energy as the only hope of making it happen.

Figure 6. The trend of renewable energy in ghana, Nigeria and South Africa from 2000 to 2018 (Source: IRENA Data and Statistics)

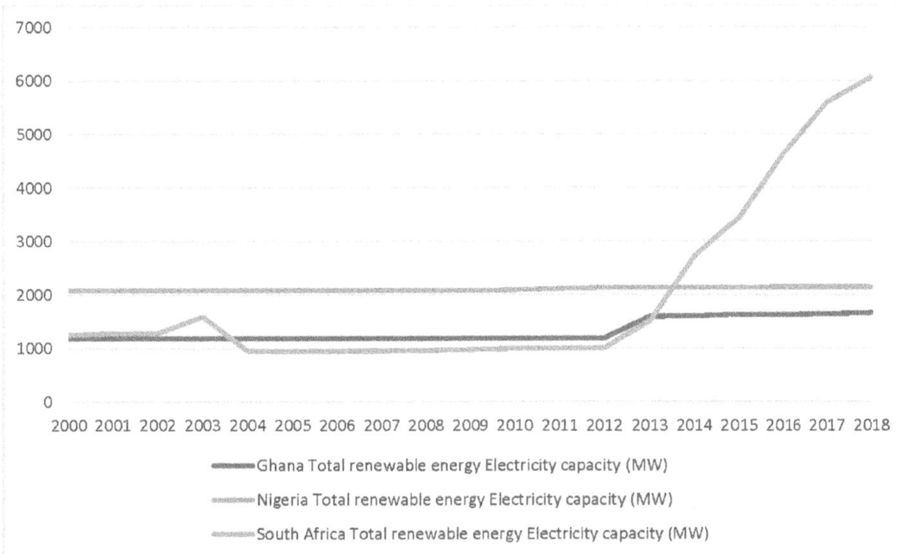

Figure 7. Renewable energy targets of African countries (Source: GIZ, 2018).

	Share of total energy	Share of electricity	Planned capacity	Target year	Notes
Algeria	40			2030	5% by 2017
Benin				2025	50% of rural electricity
Burundi	2.1			2020	4 MW biomass, 212 MW hydropower, 40 MW PV and 10 MW wind
Cabo Verde		50		2020	
Côte d' Ivoire	5, 15, 20			2015, 2020, 2030	
Djibouti	30			2017	(solar PV off-grid)
Egypt	14			2020	(hydropower: 2.8 GW by 2020; PV: 220 MW by 2020, 700 MW by 2027; CSP: 1.1 GW by 2020, 2.8 GW by 2027; wind: 7.2 GW by 2020)
Eritrea		50		n.d.	From wind power
Ethiopia			6810 MW	2013	760 MW of wind, 5600 MW of hydropower, and 450 MW of geothermal capacity addition
Gabon	80			2020	
Ghana		10		2020	
Guinea		8		2025	6% of PV and 2% of wind
Guinea-Bissau	2			2015	From solar PV
Kenya			5000 MW geothermal	2030	Double installed renewable energy capacity by 2012 and 5000 MW of geothermal capacity by 2030
Lesotho		35		2020	Share of rural electricity
Libya	10			2020	
Madagascar	54			2020	
Malawi	7			2020	
Mali	15			2020	
Mauritania	20			2020	15% by 2015 (excl. biomass)
Mauritius		35		2025	
Morocco		42		2020	20% by 2012
Mozambique			6000 MW and others	na	6000 MW of wind, solar and hydro capacity (2000 MW each) and installation of 82000 solar PV systems, 1000 biodigesters, 3000 wind pumping systems, 5000 renewable-based productive systems and 100000 solar heaters in rural areas
Namibia			40 MW	2011	Excluding hydro power
Niger	10			2020	
Nigeria		20		2030	18% by 2025
Rwanda		90		2012	
Senegal	15			2025	
Seychelles		15		2030	
South Africa		13		2020	
Swaziland				2014	20% of all public buildings installed with solar water heaters
Tunisia		25		2030	11% by 2016
Uganda		61		2017	
Zimbabwe		10		2015	10% share of biofuels in liquid fuels

According to the SERP training manual (2005), the industrial subsector seems one of the three major energy-consuming subsectors in the sub-Saharan region, the other two being the transport and residential sectors. This present pattern of energy consumption seems far from efficient. More worrisome is the fact that the share of renewable energy in this sectorial energy consumption in Africa, as studies have shown, remains at a very minimal level. The figures below reveal the small quantity of the share of renewable energy in energy production and consumption of three African countries: Ghana, Nigeria and South Africa. It is worthy of mention though, that South Africa seems to be making much more tremendous progress than most other sub-Saharan African countries, as evidenced by the existing literature.

Figure 8. Electricity Generation and Consumption in Ghana from 2010 to 2015 (Source: Ahmed & Gong, 2017)

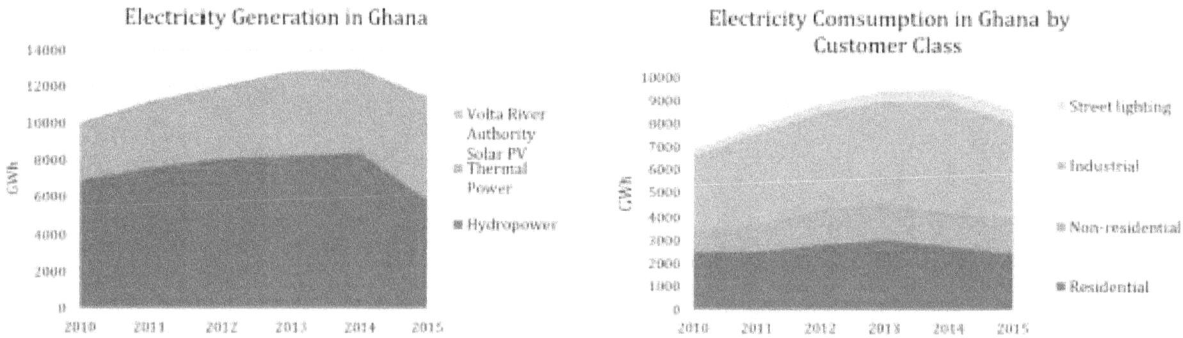

Figure 9. Trends of electricity generation in Ghana (Source: Asumadu-Sarkodie & Owusu, 2016)

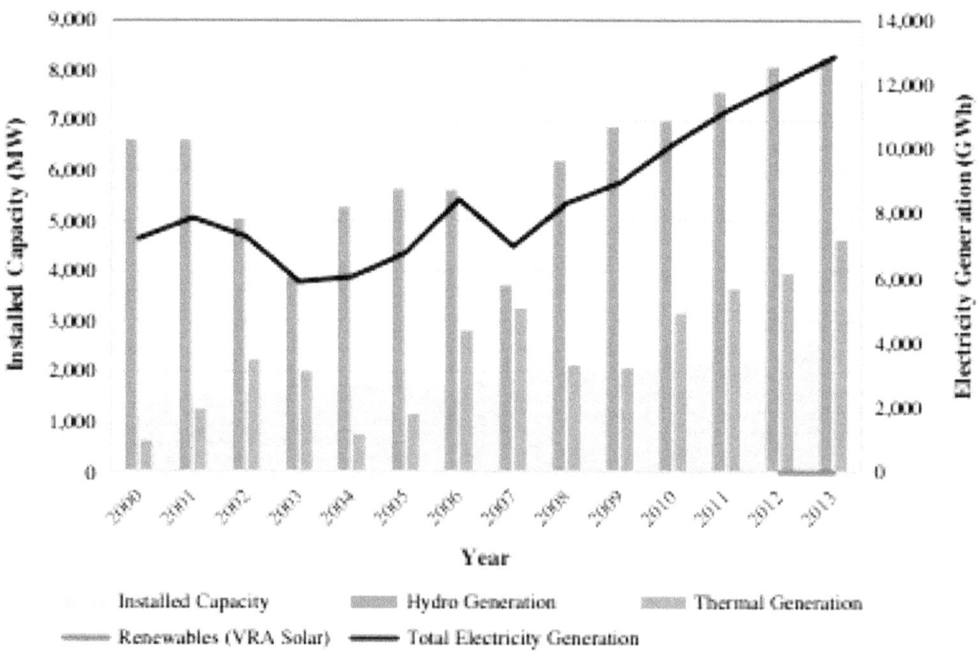

Figure 10. Projected total generation in the least cost scenario including renewable energy (Source: Castalia-GIZ and Government of Ghana, 2015)

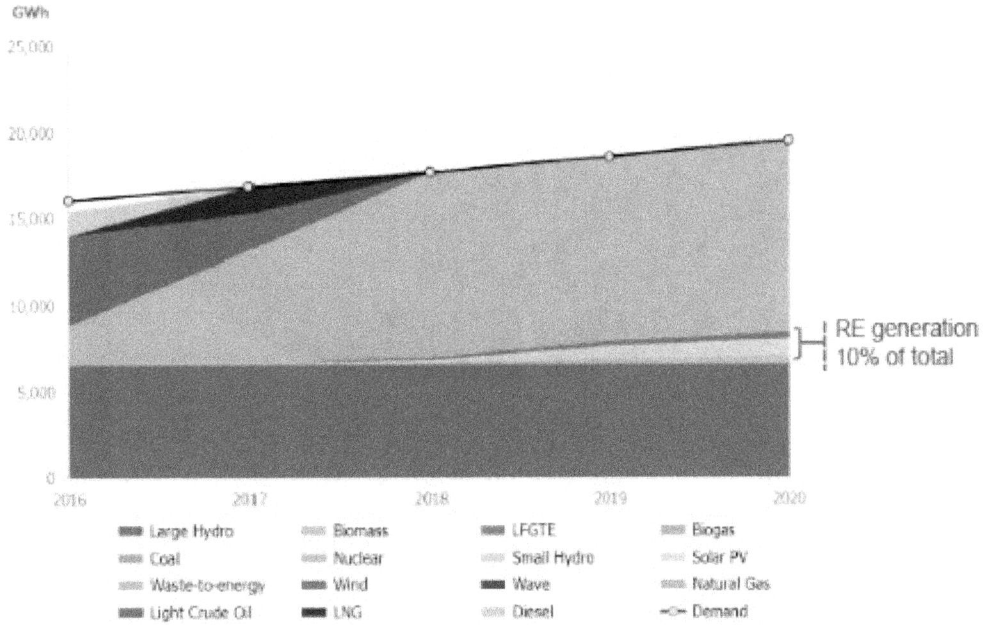

Figure 11. Electricity installed capacity (MW) and consumption by sector in Nigeria in 2010

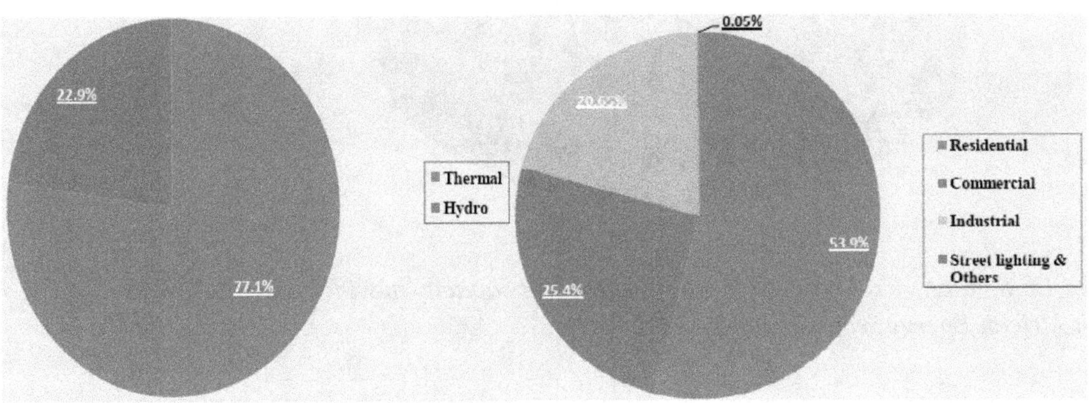

The African Renewable Energy Initiative, led by institutions including the African Union and the United Nations Environment Programme, has set a goal of 300 GW of renewable energy capacity by 2030 (The Economist Intelligent Unit, 2016). In order to achieve this goal, efforts could be directed at understanding the current players in Africa's renewable energy sector, the market evolution, the potential challenges, and the right strategies for success (Akinyemi, Efobi, Osabuohien & Alege, 2019; Akinyemi, Efobi, Asongu & Osabuohien, 2019).

Figure 12. Energy demand by sectors in South Africa (Source: South African Energy Report, 2018)

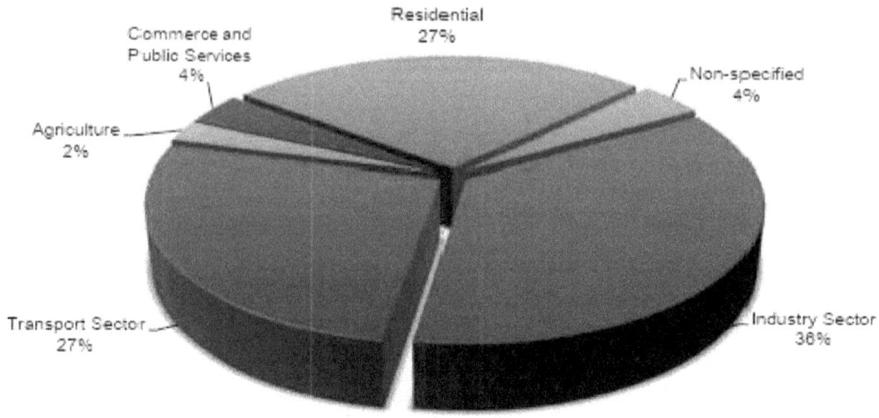

Figure 13. Energy demand in the residential sector in South Africa (South African Energy Report, 2018)

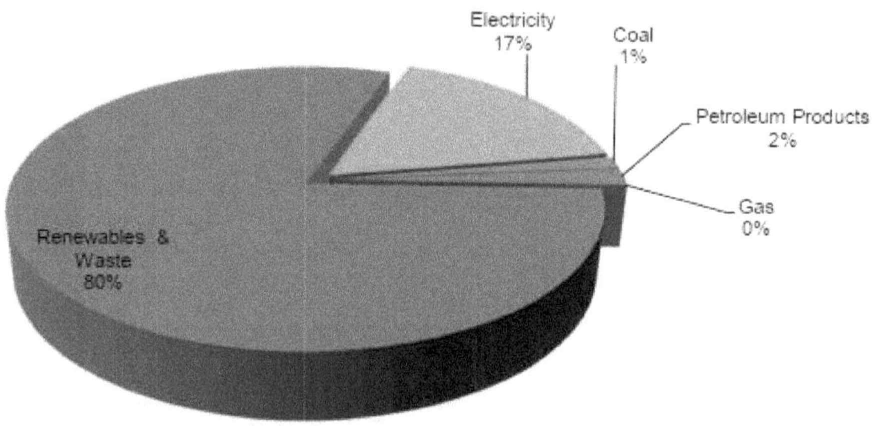

Figure 14. South Africa's renewable energy allocated capacity in windows 1, 2, 3 and 4, 2017 (Source: South African Energy Sector Report, 2018)

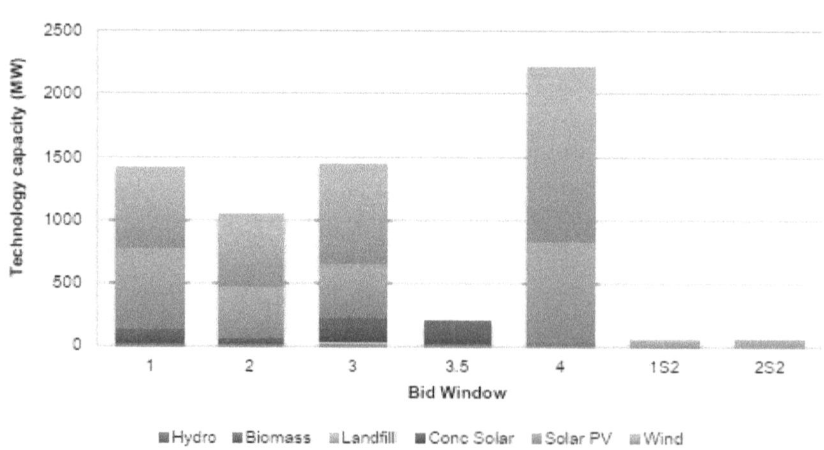

Figure 15. South Africa's renewable energy generation in comparable emerging markets (Source: WWF Technical Report, 2014)

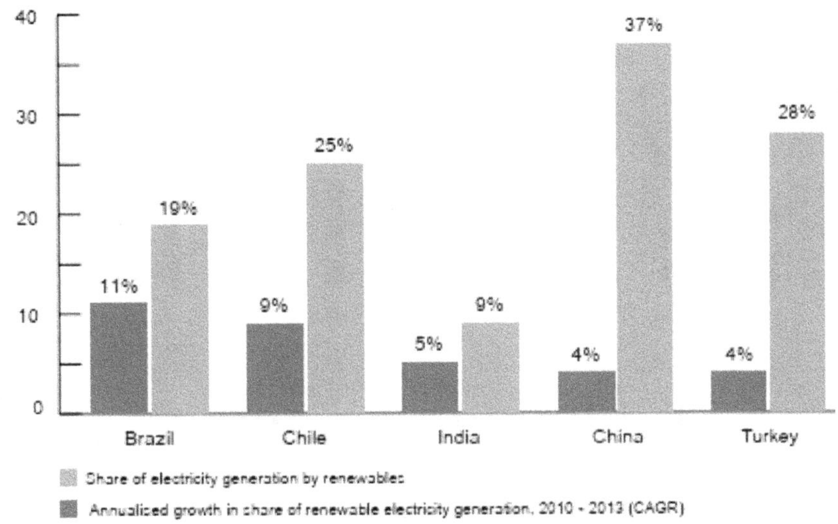

EFFECTS OF RENEWABLE ENERGY DEVELOPMENTS ON FOREST COVER CHANGES

Effects of Bioenergy on Forest Cover Changes

It is often argued that extensive bioenergy production may have serious impacts on food supply and the environment. One of such possible environmental impacts identified by Popp et al. (2014) is increased deforestation. Other studies have also suggested that deforestation of the high latitudes could lead to a global cooling due to the increased albedo of deforested land which has some form of dominance over other biogeochemical and geophysical mechanisms in the energy balance (Dass et al., 2013). Ii may be difficult to examine the effects of bioenergy without identifying policies that promote its production. Okoro et al. (2018) have argued that bioenergy policies have intensified the competition for land while increasing the risk of adverse environmental effects resulting from greenhouse gas emissions (GHGs) and deforestation. High deforestation rates in Brazil have also been strongly linked to the country's high consumption of bioenergy, being one of the largest consumers of biomass energy in the world (Ceccon & Miramontes, 2008). In the European Union (EU), the use of wood for heat and electricity generation in modern technologies has increased remarkably in the last five years (Brack, 2017). It has the prospects of continuing that way (Brack, 2017). In addition, the EU has been, and remains the major global source of wood demand, given its targets for renewable energy (Brack 2017). This demand is met mainly by its forest resources to the point of much pressure, supplemented by imports from Canada, Russia and the US (Brack, 2017). Stewart et al. (2011) have claimed the likely environmental impacts of the use of biomass for renewable energy generation could be both positive and negative. One notable potential environmental benefit is a decline in the loss of forest carbon storage to wildfires, insect disease infestations, and severe weather events; while the major concern could be that, it erodes essential wildlife habitat and biodiversity elements across the larger landscape (Stewart et al. 2011; Herrmann, Jumbe, Bruentrup & Osabuohien, 2018).

Figure 16. Trend of biomass supply in Ghana (Source: Asumadu-Sarkodie & Owusu, 2016)

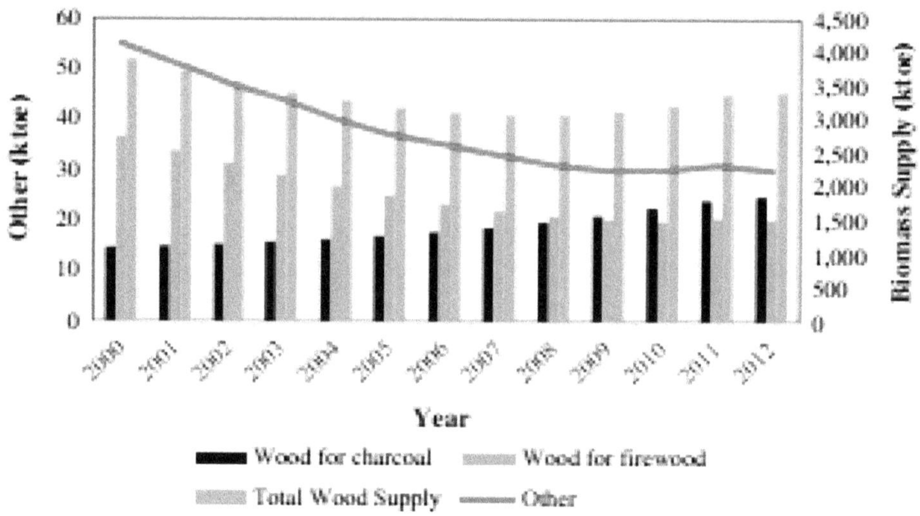

Most of the studies reviewed above indicate that bioenergy production and utilization most likely affects forest cover changes tremendously. However, they may not have quantitatively investigated the extent of the effects, which calls for further research.

Effects of Hydropower Energy on Forest Cover Changes

Mercado-Bettin et al. (2017), in their study aimed at synthesizing the forest cover effects on long-term water balance partitioning in large basis, found that forest cover may be an effective descriptor of basin attributes essential for characterizing long-term balance partitioning in large basins of the world. They, however, described the effects of hydro energy on forest cover as a possible uncertainty worthy of investigation. Hydropower is often seen as a clear choice for the generation of clean energy, yet may pose serious negative environmental impacts (Collier, 2004; World Bank Report, 2016). Vietnam converted a large area of natural forest into the development of hydropower and initiated a reforestation programme to cover for the loss of natural forest. Unfortunately, by 2013, only about 3.7% of the converted forest areas had been reforested, thus implying a net forest loss in the bid to generate hydro energy (Ty & Nghi, 2017). Stickler et al. (2013) has further opined that the seeming reliability of hydropower plants as energy sources must take into account their strong relationship with forests, as either a cause or an effect. Analysis carried out by researchers at Climate Policy Initiative (CPI), covering a period of nine years (2003-2011), in Amazon Brazil, reveals that the arrival of hydropower plants may have multiple effects on forests, depending on the specific details of individual plants and how behaviours and circumstances lead to such different consequences. Going further, they believe that while some hydropower projects encourage deforestation, others help to avoid it, thus, making it necessary for public policies to ally environmental protection and economic development.

Figure 17. Hydropower plant development and forest recompensing plantation in Vietnam (Source: Ty & Nghi, 2017)

Effects of Solar Energy on Forest Cover Changes

The environmental issues associated with the generation of solar energy may not have been extensively discussed in the literature (Turney & Fthenakis, 2011). A study conducted by Suuronen (2017) has suggested that there could be a strong relationship between the generation of solar energy, especially from solar PV plants and the ecological environment. They specifically found that fixed-mount solar power plants' shade conditions can act as a refuge to some arthropod species, but for vegetations, shade conditions may also disturb their fluorescence. The removal of forests to make spaces for solar power have been reported to cause CO_2 emissions as high as 36g CO_2 KWh^{-1}, which is a crucial contribution to the life cycle CO_2 emissions of solar power (Turney & Fthenakis, 2011). Hernandez et al. (2013) further suggest that there could be both adverse and beneficial effects of utility-scale solar energy (USSE) development on land use and land cover change. They further note that improving the environmental compatibility of USSE systems will maximize the efficacy of this main renewable energy source in reducing global environmental change (Hernandez et al. 2013). Close attention during the planning, construction and operation phase of most large-scale solar energy projects. Can minimize their effects on vegetation and forest covers (Tsoutsos et al., 2009).

Effects of Wind Energy on Forest Cover Changes

Wind energy, like many other renewable energy sources, can have positive impacts on the environment. However, there may still be some uncertainty about the negative ecological of the construction and operation of land-based and offshore wind energy on forests and wildlife (Allison et al., 2009). Wind projects have been developed in forests in some countries because of the perceived difficulties of developing an onshore wind farm without forest interference and in a bid to keep them far away from residential areas (Enevoldsen, 2017). This study further opines that even though there are many risks and challenges involved in siting wind turbines in forests, these have not been thoroughly addressed empirically by the academia. This is possibly because of the difficulty in estimating wind flows above forest canopies, especially if the forest formation is heterogenous with clearing and different tree heights and types. Going forward, the study suggests that it could be possible to estimate the changes in wind conditions above forest canopies using specific methods with high-quality data input regarding tree heights and leaf area densities.

Figure 18. Summary of the aggregate impact of solar power in forested environments compared to traditional US power generation (Source: Turney & Fthenakis, 2011)

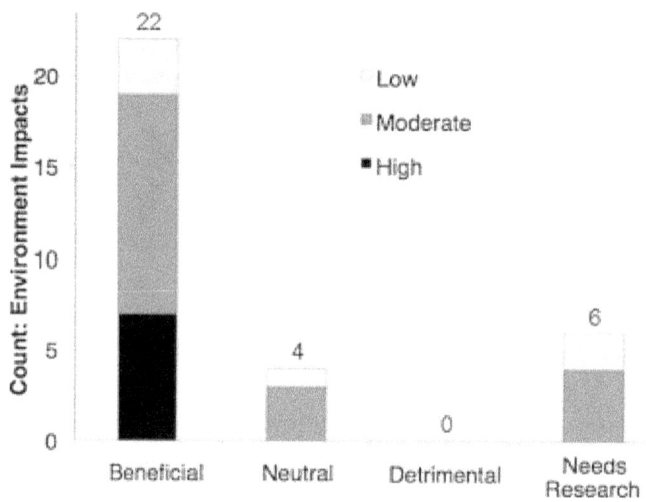

Figure 19. Wind power in forests (Source: Energiforsk Report, 2018)

SUMMARY AND CONCLUSION

In this chapter, we first reviewed and assessed the roles and implications of institutional settings on renewable energy development in Sub-Saharan Africa. As a step forward, we further looked at the effects of disaggregated renewable energy technologies on the environmental factors focusing on forest cover changes (deforestation). To achieve this, the paper reviewed literatures and documents and used case studies and descriptive presentations to come to its findings. In general, we find that although renewable energy development in Africa is still slow in Africa compared to global averages, the rate of transitions to renewable energies is increasing due to improvements in institutional settings. There are, however, still room for improvement in institutional settings and mechanisms for the deployment of renewable energy, especially in Africa. By disaggregating the different renewable energy technologies, we find that different renewable energy technologies have different effects and implications for deforestation. Specifically, we find that renewable energies that are based on biomass, such as biofuel, have more negative effects and implications on forest cover changes – increasing deforestation rates across the continent. All other types of renewable (especially solar and wind systems) also have direct or indirect influences on deforestation; however, the benefits that come from there use offsets the loss of the environment. With the right sets of institutions, Sub-Saharan Africa can be able to leapfrog to the adoption of the cleanest form of renewable energies, which will have the least impacts on the environmental outcomes, including on forest and ecosystems. This will imply the adoption of renewable energy technologies other than biomass and biofuels, which are currently being favoured in sub-Saharan Africa.

REFERENCES

Action Plan, E. U. (2019). Stepping up EU Action to Protect and Restore the World's Forests. Communication from the Commission to the European Parliament, the Council, the European Economic and Social Committee and the Committee of the Regions.

IRENA Africa Impact Report. (2020). *Scaling Up Renewable Energy Deployment in Africa: Detailed Overview of IRENA's Engagement and Impact*. Author.

African Development Bank -AfDB Report. (2008). *Hydropower Resource Assessment in Africa*. Report of the Ministerial Conference, Libyan Arab Jamahiriya.

Ahlborg, H., & Hammar, L. (2014). Drivers and barriers to rural electrification in Tanzania and Mozambique: Grid extension, off-grid and renewable energy technologies. *Renewable Energy*, *61*, 117–124. doi:10.1016/j.renene.2012.09.057

Ahmed, A., & Gong, J. (2017). Assessment of Electricity Generation Mix in Ghana. Degree Project in Technology, First Cycle, 15 Credits, Stockholm, Sweden.

Akinyemi, O., Efobi, U., Asongu, S., & Osabuohien, E. (2019). Renewable energy, trade performance and the conditional role of finance and institutional capacity in sub-Sahara African Countries. *Energy Policy*, *132*, 490–498. doi:10.1016/j.enpol.2019.06.012

Akinyemi, O., Efobi, U., Osabuohien, E., & Alege, P. (2019). Regional Integration and Energy Sustainability in Africa: Exploring the Challenges and Prospects for ECOWAS. *African Development Review*, *31*(4), 517–528. doi:10.1111/1467-8268.12406

Allison, T. D., Diffendorfer, J. E., Baerwald, E. F., Beston, J. A., Drake, D., Hale, A. M., Hein, C. D., Huso, M. M., Loss, S. R., Lovich, J. E., Strickland, M. D., Williams, K. A., & Winder, V. L. (2009). *Impacts to Wildlife of Wind Energy Siting and Operation in the United States.* Issues in Ecology, Report No 21, Fall 2009.

Ansari, M. F., Kharb, R. K., Luthra, S., Shimmi, S. L., & Chatterji, S. (2016). Analysis of barriers to implement solar power installations in India using interpretive structural modeling technique. *Renewable & Sustainable Energy Reviews*, *27*, 163–174. doi:10.1016/j.rser.2013.07.002

Arnold, U., & Yildiz, Ö. (2015). Economic risk analysis of decentralized renewable energy infrastructures: A Monte Carlo simulation approach. *Renewable Energy*, *77*, 227–239. doi:10.1016/j.renene.2014.11.059

Asumadu-Sarkodie, S., & Owusu, A. (2016). A Review of Ghana's Energy Sector National Energy Statistics and Policy Framework. *Cogent Engineering*, *3*(1), 1155274. doi:10.1080/23311916.2016.1155274

Bhandari, B., Lee, K., Lee, G., Cho, Y., & Ahn, S. (2015). Optimization of hybrid renewable energy power systems: A review. *Int. J. Precis. Eng. Manuf. Green Technol.*, *2*(1), 99–112. doi:10.100740684-015-0013-z

Bodart, C., Brink, A. B., Donnay, F., Lupi, A., Mayaux, P., & Achard, F. (2013). Continental Estimates of Forest Cover Changes in the Dry Ecosystems of Africa Between 1990 and 2000. *Journal of Biogeography*, *40*(6), 1036–1047. doi:10.1111/jbi.12084 PMID:23935237

Brack, D. (2017). *The Impacts of the Demand for Woody Biomass for Power and Heat on Climate and \forests.* Environment, Energy and Resources Department.

Castalia-GIZ & Government of Ghana, (2015). *Renewable Energy Policy Review, Identification of Gaps and Solutions in Ghana*. Author.

Ceccon, E., & Miramontes, O. (2008). Revenue Déforestation? Bioenergy and Society in Two Brazilian Models. *Ecological Economics*, *67*(2), 311–317. doi:10.1016/j.ecolecon.2007.12.008

CEIF Report, . (2008). *Proposals for Clean Energy Investment Framework for Africa: Role of African Development Bank Group*. Final Version.

Chauhan, A., & Saini, R. P. (2015). Renewable energy based off-grid rural electrification in Uttarakhand state of India: Technology options, modelling method, barriers and recommendations. *Renewable & Sustainable Energy Reviews*, *51*(December), 662–681. doi:10.1016/j.rser.2015.06.043

Chirambo, D. (2016). Addressing the Renewable Energy Financing Gap in Africa to Promote Universal Energy Access: Integrated Renewable Energy Financing in Malawi. *Renewable & Sustainable Energy Reviews*, *62*, 793–803. doi:10.1016/j.rser.2016.05.046

Cho, C., Yang, L., Chu, Y., & Yang, H. (2013). Renewable energy and renewable R&D in EU countries. *Cointegrat. Anal.*, *2*(1), 10–16.

Collier, U. (2004). *Hydropower and the Environment: Towards Better Decision-making*. Paper submitted to the United Nations Symposium on Hydropower and Sustainable Development, Beijing, China.

Dass, P., Muller, C., Brovkin, V., & Cramer, W. (2013). Can Bioenergy Cropping Compensate High Carbon Emissions from Large Scale Deforestation of High Latitudes? *Earth System Dynamics*, *4*(2), 409–424. doi:10.5194/esd-4-409-2013

Dulal, H. B., Shah, K. U., Sapkota, C., Uma, G., & Kandel, B. R. (2013). Renewable energy diffusion in Asia: Can it happen without government support? *Energy Policy*, *59*(April), 301–311. doi:10.1016/j.enpol.2013.03.040

El-katiri, L. (2014). *A roadmap for renewable energy in the Middle East and North Africa*. Academic Press.

Emodi, V. N., Yusuf, S. D., & Boo, K. (2014). The necessity of the development of standards for renewable energy technologies in Nigeria. *Smart Grid and Renewable Energy*, *5*(November), 259–274. doi:10.4236gre.2014.511024

AU Energy Report. (2015). *The African Union Bioenergy Development in Africa Programme*. Author.

Enevoldsen, P. (2017). *Managing Risks of Wind Farms in Forested Areas: Design Principles for Northern Europe*. Industrial PhD Dissertation at the School of Business and Social Sciences, Aarhus University.

EUEI. (2017). *Partnership Dialogue Facility (EUEI PDF), Phase II bis report*. EUEI.

FAO. (2007). *Forests and Energy in OECD Countries*. Forests and Energy Working Paper 1.

FAO. (2009). State of the World's Forests. Viale delle Terme di Caracalla.

AREI Framework. (2015). *A Framework for Transforming Africa Towards a Renewable Energy Powered Future with Access to All*. Author.

Gasparatos, A., Doll, C. N. H., Esteban, M., Ahmed, A., & Olang, T. A. (2017). Renewable Energy and Biodiversity: Implications for Transitioning to a Green Economy. *Renewable & Sustainable Energy Reviews*, *70*, 161–184. doi:10.1016/j.rser.2016.08.030

GIZ. (2018). *Best Practises on Renewable Energy in Africa*. GIZ.

Goldsmiths, K.R. (2015). *Barriers and solutions to the development of renewable energy technologies in the Caribbean*. Academic Press.

Halabi, M. A., Al-qattan, A., & Al-otaibi, A. (2015). Application of solar energy in the oil industry: Current status and future prospects. *Renewable & Sustainable Energy Reviews*, *43*, 296–314. doi:10.1016/j.rser.2014.11.030

Hernandez, R. R., Easter, S. B., & Murphy-Mariscal, M. L. (2013). Environmental Impacts of Utility-Scale Solar Energy. *Renewable & Sustainable Energy Reviews*, *29*. Advance online publication. doi:10.1016/j.rser.2013.08.041

Herrmann, R., Jumbe, C., Bruentrup, M., & Osabuohien, E. (2018). Competition between Biofuel Feedstock and Food Production: Empirical Evidence from Sugarcane Outgrower Settings in Malawi. *Biomass and Bioenergy*, *114*(July), 100–111. doi:10.1016/j.biombioe.2017.09.002

Huang, S., Lo, S., & Lin, Y. (2013). To re-explore the causality between barriers to renewable energy eevelopment: A case study of wind energy. *Energies*, *6*(9), 4465–4488. doi:10.3390/en6094465

IRENA Impact Report. (2019). *Scaling Up Renewable Energy Deployment in Africa: Impact of IRENA's Engagement*. Author.

Izadbakhsh, M., Gandomkar, M., Rezvani, A., & Ahmadi, A. (2015). Short-term resource scheduling of a renewable energy based micro grid. *Renewable Energy*, *75*(March), 598–606. doi:10.1016/j.renene.2014.10.043

Jianjun, J., & Chen, D. S. (2014). Willingness to pay for renewable electricity: A contingent valuation study in Beijing, China. *Energy Policy*, *68*(May), 340–347.

Karakaya, E., & Sriwannawit, P. (2015). Barriers to the adoption of photovoltaic systems: The state of the art. *Renewable & Sustainable Energy Reviews*, *49*, 60–66. doi:10.1016/j.rser.2015.04.058

Karekezi, S., & Kithyoma, W. (2003). Renewable Energy in Africa: Prospects and Limits. The Workshop for African Energy Experts on Operationalising the NEPAD Energy Initiative, 2-4 June 2003, Novetel, Dakar, Senegal.

Kayiranga, A., Kurban, A., Nahayo, L., & Ndayisaba, F. (2018). Assessing Forest Cover Changes in Volcanoes Parks Region of East-central Africa Using Landsat Imagery. *Journal of Environmental Protection and Sustainable Development*, *4*(2), 16–25.

Kazimierczuk, A. H. (2019). Wind Energy in Kenya: A Status and Policy Framework Review. *Renewable & Sustainable Energy Reviews*, *107*, 434–445. doi:10.1016/j.rser.2018.12.061

Khellaf, A. (2018). Overview of Economic Viability and Social Impact of Renewable Energy Deployment in Africa. *Africa-EU Renewable Energy Research and Innovation Symposium*.

Maiwada, N. A., El-Ladan, A. H., & Abdullahi, U. S. (2014). The Role of Renewable Energy in Mitigating Deforestation and Climate Change in Nigeria. *Journal of Natural Sciences Research*, *4*(24).

Mercado-Bettin, D., Salazar, J. F., & Villegas, J. C. (2017). Global Synthesis of Forest Cover Effects on Long-term Water Balance Partitioning in Large Basins. *Hydrology and Earth System Sciences Discussions*, *550*. Advance online publication. doi:10.5194/hess-2017-550

Moomaw, W., Yamba, F., Kamimoto, M., Maurice, L., Nyboer, J., Urama, K., & Weir, T. (2011). Introduction. In *IPCC Special Report on Renewable Energy Sources and Climate Change Mitigation*. Cambridge University Press.

Moon, H., & Solomon, T. (2018). Forest Decline in Africa: Trends and Impacts of Foreign Direct Investment: A Review. *International Journal of Current Advanced Research*, *7*(11), 16356–16361. doi:10.24327/ijcar.2018

Mukasa, A. D., Mutambatsere, E., Arvanitis, Y., & Triki, T. (2012). *Development of Wind Energy in Africa.* African Development Bank Group Working Paper Series No 152- June, 2012.

Mukasa, A. D., Mutambatsere, E., Arvanitis, Y., & Triki, T. (2013). *Development of Wind Energy in Africa.* African Development Bank Group Working Paper Series No 170- March 2013.

Nasirov, S., Silva, C., & Agostini, C. A. (2015). Investors' perspectives on barriers to the deployment of renewable energy sources in Chile. *Energies*, *8*(5), 3794–3814. doi:10.3390/en8053794

Negasi, S., Hishe, H., Annang, T., Pabi, O., Asante, I. K., & Birhane, E. (2018). Forest Cover Change, Key Drivers and Community Perception of Wujig Mahgo Waren Forest of Northern Ethiopia. *Land (Basel)*, *7*(1), 32. doi:10.3390/land7010032

Nesamalar, J. J. D., Venkatesh, P., & Raja, S. C. (2017). The drive of renewable energy in Tamilnadu: Status, barriers and future prospect. *Renewable & Sustainable Energy Reviews*, *73*(June), 115–124. doi:10.1016/j.rser.2017.01.123

OECD Policy Brief. (2015). *Linking Renewable Energy to Rural Development*. Author.

OECD/IEA. (2017). *FAO*. Bioenergy Roadmap Development and Implementation.

Ohunakin, O. S., Adaramola, M. S., Oyewola, O. M., & Fagbenle, R. O. (2014). Solar energy applications and development in Nigeria: Drivers and barriers. *Renewable & Sustainable Energy Reviews*, *32*, 294–301. doi:10.1016/j.rser.2014.01.014

Okoro, S. U., Schickhoff, U., & Schneider, A. (2018). Impacts of Bioenergy Policies on Land- Use Change in Nigeria. *Energies*, *11*(152). Advance online publication. doi:10.3390/en11010152

Owusu, P. A., & Asumadu-Sarkodie, S. (2016). A Review of Renewable Energy Sources, Sustainability Issues and Climate Change Mitigation. *Cogent Engineering*, *3*(1), 1167990. doi:10.1080/23311916.2016.1167990

Painuly, J. P. (2001). Barriers to renewable energy penetration; a framework for analysis. *Renewable Energy*, *24*(1), 73–89. doi:10.1016/S0960-1481(00)00186-5

Paravantis, J., Stigka, E., Mihalakakou, G. (2014). An analysis of public attitudes towards renewable energy in Western Greece. *Renew. Sustain. Energy Rev.*, *32*(March), 100-106.

Popp, J., Lakner, Z., Harangi-Rakos, M., & Fari, M. (2014). The Effect of Bioenergy Expansion: Food, Energy and Environment. *Renewable & Sustainable Energy Reviews*, *32*, 559–578. doi:10.1016/j.rser.2014.01.056

Quitzow, R., Roehrkasten, S., Jacobs, D, Bayer, B., Jamea, E., Waweru, Y. & Matschoss, P. (2016). *The Future of Africa's Energy Supply*. Institute for Advanced Sustainability Studies (IASS).

Rapid Assessment and Gap Analysis – RAGA. (2013). *Sustainable Energy for All in Nigeria*. Author.

Raza, W., Saula, H., Islam, S. U., Ayub, M., Saleem, M., & Raza, N. (2015). Renewable energy resources: Current status and barriers in their adaptation for Pakistan. *J. Bioprocess. Chem. Eng*, *3*(3), 1–9.

DFID Report. (2007). *Water Storage and: Supporting Growth, Resilience and Low Carbon Development*. A DFID Evidence-into-Action Paper.

Energiforsk Report. (2018). *Wind Power in Forests II*. Author.

UNECE Report. (2014). *Development of Renewable Energy: The Water-Energy-Food- Ecosystem Nexus Approach to Support the Sustainable Development Goals*. Author.

Searchinger, T. D., Beringer, T., Holtsmark, B., Kammen, D. M., Lambiri, E. F., Lucht, W., Raven, P., & van Ypersele, J. (2018). Europe's Renewable Energy Directive Poised to Harm Global Forests. *Nature Communications*, *9*(3741). Advance online publication. doi:10.103841467-018- 06175-4 PMID:30209361

Sen, R., & Bhattacharyya, S. C. (2014). Off-grid electricity generation with renewable energy technologies in India: An application of HOMER. *Renewable Energy*, *62*, 388–398. doi:10.1016/j.renene.2013.07.028

Sharma, N. P., Rietbergen, S., Heimo, C. R., & Patel, J. (1994). *A Strategy for the Forest Sector in Sub-Saharan Africa*. World Bank Technical Paper Number 251, Africa Technical Department Series.

South African Energy Sector Report. (2018). *Energy Data Collection, Management and Analysis*. Author.

Stewart, W., Powers, R.F., McGown, K., Chiono, L. & Chuang, T. (2011). *Potential Positive and Negative Environmental Impacts of Increased Woody Biomass Use for California*. Public Interest Energy Research – PIER Program Final project report.

Stickler, C.M., Coe, M.T., Costa, M.H., Nepstad, D.C., McGrath, D.G., Dias, L.C.P., Rodrigues, H.O. & Soares-Filho, B.S. (2013). Dependence of Hydropower Energy Generation on Forests in the Amazon Basin at Local and Regional Scales. *PNAS Early Edition,* 1-6.

Stokes, L. C. (2013). The politics of renewable energy policies: The case of feed-in tariffs in Ontario, Canada. *Energy Policy*, *56*, 490–500. doi:10.1016/j.enpol.2013.01.009

Sun, P., & Nie, P. (2015). A comparative study of feed-in tariff and renewable portfolio standard policy in renewable energy industry. *Renewable Energy*, *74*(February), 255–262. doi:10.1016/j.renene.2014.08.027

Sustainable Energy Regulation Policymaking -SERP. (2005). *Overview of Renewable Energy and Energy Efficiency*. Academic Press.

Suuronen, A. (2017). Ecological and Social Impacts of Photovoltaic Solar Power Plants and Optimization of their Locations in Northern Chile. *Jyvaskyla Studies in Biological and Environmental Science, 338.*

Suzuki, M. (2013). *What are the roles of national and international institutions to overcome barriers in diffusing clean energy technologies in Asia? Matching barriers in technology diffusion with the roles of institutions*. Retrieved from: http://cdn.intechopen.com/pdfs/43765/InTech-What_are_the_roles_of_national_and_international_institution s_to_overcome_barriers_in_diffusing_clean_energy_technologies_in_asia_matching_barriers_in_technology_diffusion_with_the_roles_of_institutions.pdf

The Economist Intelligent Unit. (2016). *Power Up: Delivering Renewable Energy in Africa*. Author.

Tsoutsos, T., Frantzeskaki, N., & Gekas, V. (2009). Environmental Impacts from the Solar Energy Technologies. *Energy Policy*, *33*(3), 289–296. doi:10.1016/S0301-4215(03)00241-6

Turney, D., & Fthenakis, V. (2011). Environmental Impacts from the Installation and Operation of Large-scale Solar Power Plants. *Renewable & Sustainable Energy Reviews*, *15*(6), 3261–3270. doi:10.1016/j.rser.2011.04.023

Ty, P.H. & Nghi, T.H. (2017). Hydropower Plant Development and Forest Recompensing Plantation in Vietnam. *Tropics of Vietnam.*

UNIDO. (2009). *Scaling Up Renewable Energy in Africa.* 12th Ordinary Session of Heads of State and Governments of the African Union, Addis Ababa, Ethiopia.

Waheed, R., Chang, D., Sarwar, S., & Chen, W. (2017). Forest, Agriculture, Renewable Energy and CO_2 Emission. *Journal of Cleaner Production*, 1–8.

World Bank. (2009). *Directions in Scaling Up for Development.* Water Working Notes 49017, No. 21, June 2009.

World Bank Energy Report. (2018). Best Practises on Renewable Energy in Africa. *The Status.*

World Bank Report. (2016). *Managing Environmental and Social Impacts of Hydro-power in Bhutan.* A Final Report Prepared in Collaboration with the Royal Government of Bhutan.

WWF Technical Report. (2014). *Renewable Energy Vision 2030 – South Africa.* Author.

Zhang, H., Li, L., Zhou, D., & Zhou, P. (2014). Political connections, government subsidies and firm financial performance: Evidence from renewable energy manufacturing in. *Renewable Energy*, *63*, 330–336. doi:10.1016/j.renene.2013.09.029

Zhao, Z., Chang, R., & Chen, Y. (2016). What hinders the further development of wind power in China? A socio-technical barrier study. *Energy Policy*, *88*(January), 465–476. doi:10.1016/j.enpol.2015.11.004

Chapter 5
Institutions and Economic Transformation in Africa:
Sectoral Analysis From Nigeria

Ibukun Beecroft
Centre for Economic Policy and Development Research (CEPDeR), Covenant University, Nigeria

Evans S. Osabuohien
https://orcid.org/0000-0002-3258-8326
Covenant University, Nigeria

Isaiah O. Olurinola
Covenant University, Nigeria

Uchenna R. Efobi
Covenant University, Nigeria

Stephen Oluwatobi
Covenant University, Nigeria

ABSTRACT

Economic transformation suggests sustainable and inclusive economic development. It includes the changes in the structures of the economy in favour of more productive sectors to ensure consistent economic progress. This has been the earnest desire of most African countries. However, achieving economic transformation will require strong institutions, among others. The channels through which institutions can influence the process of economic development using specific country analyses are still under-researched. Thus, this study examines the importance of institutions in the development and sustenance of some important sectors: finance, education, technology, industry, and trade, believed to drive economic transformation. Drawing evidence from Nigeria, the study submits that institutions have varying influence on all the selected sectors. Thus, the role of specific sectoral planning based on a strong institutional framework cannot be overemphasised in a country's quest for economic transformation.

DOI: 10.4018/978-1-7998-4817-2.ch005

INTRODUCTION

Economic transformation simply suggests the sustainable process of moving resources to higher productive sectors, which includes the changes in the structures of the economy in favour of more productive sectors to ensure consistent economic progress (Beecroft et al., 2020; Tan and Phang, 2005). The effects of economic transformation are numerous: it includes trade competitiveness, industrialization, human capital development to foster innovation and creativity, improved financial sector development and technology.

To say that 'strong' institutions are relevant for the achievement of transformation is almost stating the obvious, especially comparing the institutional performances *vis-à-vis* economic outcomes in South Korea versus North Korea as well as Botswana versus Zimbabwe (Beecroft et al., 2020; Osabuohien, 2020a). Institutions, formal and informal rules and codes of conduct that affect the behaviours of economic actors, matter as market dynamics are made up of socially constructed institutions and conventions that are established to ensure the protection of individuals against moral hazards (Beecroft et al., 2020; Beecroft, Osabuohien and Olurinola, 2018; Ejemeyovwi, Osabuohien and Osabohien, 2018; North, 1991; Osabuohien and Efobi, 2013). Moral hazards imply that the consequences of a transaction or the actions of a party to a transaction can be detrimental to other parties (Osabuohien, Okorie and Osabohien, 2018). This has been eloquently discussed in Asongu (2016) regarding how the rule of law can affect investment in Africa as well as by Efobi and Osabuohien (2016) as well as Beecroft et al. (2020) who related it to manufacturing exports and infrastructures in Economic Community of West African States (ECOWAS).

Consequently, the study of institutions in relation to economic progress has almost reached consensus. Some of these studies have engaged cross-country analyses in reaching the conclusions on the role of institutions in economic growth and development (Cavalcanti, Magalhaes and Tavares, 2008; North, 1990). Amid these are the part institutions play in attracting foreign finance and improving (for instance) remittance utilization (Asiedu, 2005; Catrinescu *et al.*, 2009; Osabuohien and Efobi, 2013); enhancing trade competitiveness and outcome (Akinyemi *et al.*, 2017; Osabuohien and Efobi, 2011), and so on. Prodded by the above, this study contributes to existing knowledge by making a case for the role of institutional development in Nigeria's economic transformation agenda and comparing some specific indicators with Ghana and South Africa. Also, it underscores the relevance of this approach, considering the economic and political influence that these countries have in common on the African continent. This is to bring a broader perspective to the discussion on the sustainable growth of Nigeria and to further the consensus on how institutional development matters in this process. The study focuses on five drivers of economic transformation: trade, industry, finance, education and technology.

This study is motivated by the need for African countries to consider transformation by industrial development, improved trade competitiveness, and attract finance, among others. However, there is a need to understand that economic transformation does not occur in a vacuum as institutions matter a great deal. Also, institutional development can account for the disparities in the outcomes of the respective sectors of an economy, thereby making its assessment critical *as per* specific policy actions. The study is essential for the following reasons: the five economic drivers that form the focus of the analysis are crucial for economic transformation. For instance, the industrial development has been noted for absorbing resources from the agricultural sector and converting same into finished products that are suitable for export and local consumption (Aigbokhan, 2004; Ogunrinola and Osabuohien, 2010; Beecroft et al., 2020; Osabuohien, 2020b). Also, the development of the industrial sector will improve Nigeria's competitiveness in global trade through multi-product lines and innovation for enhanced production capacity.

The financial sector is also crucial as this sector is involved in financial mediation, which will affect the quality of investment in the country; reduce poverty and inequality (Beck, Demirguc-Kunt and Levine, 2007); and foster higher economic growth (Levine, 2005), to mention a few. The significance of trade for economic transformation cannot be overemphasized as trade has been noted to improve economic growth (Frankel and Romer, 1999, Williamson, 2011); improve employment opportunities, and create platforms for female empowerment (Randriamaro, 2006; Tran-Nguyen and Zampetti, 2004).

Education and technology are also essential for economic transformation. Education promotes innovation and creativity, which can result in knowledge-driven development (Ejemeyovwi et al., 2019; Ejemejovwi and Osabuohien, 2020; 2020; Karakara and Osabuohien, 2019). The experience of the 'Asian Tigers' is enlightening in this regard as they have experienced sustainable economic growth by investing in human capital and research and development, among others. Technology is also fundamental as it boosts the productivity of the other sectors. It has been noted that technology is one of the factors that account for disparities across countries (Baliamoune-Lutz, 2003; Ejemeyovwi and Osabuohien, 2020; Guerrieri *et al.*, 2011; Osabuohien and Efobi, 2012).

The main interest of the scope of this study stems from Nigeria's pivotal role to the African narratives, due to her population size and vastness of her economy, particularly in terms of market potential. Moreover, Nigeria's institutional development has witnessed significant setbacks. This is specifically with respect to the rising rate of corruption and the prevalence of other forms of non-adherence to constitutional dictates, such as excessive extra-budgetary spending in the public sector (Beecroft, Olurinola and Osabuohien, 2018; Osabuohien and Ike, 2011; Sala-i-Martin and Subramanian, 2013). The above will affect economic transformation and can halt the desired economic progress needed for sustainable development. The next section presents the link between institutions and the selected sectors (the drivers) based on an analytical model. The third section gives an overview of the trends of the designated five drivers of economic transformation. The fourth section draws further evidences from Nigeria's policy and economic outcomes while relating it to the institutional structures. The last section concludes with policy recommendations.

INSTITUTIONS AND ECONOMIC TRANSFORMATION

To attain sustainable economic growth and transformation, the development of Nigeria's institutional framework is paramount. This is following the stance of institutional theorists such as: Acemoglu and Robinson (2012), North (1990), and Williamson (2000) that have mentioned the role of institutions in a country's sustainable growth. By institutions, we refer to those humanly formulated structures that are crafted to create peaceful economic interactions and reduce uncertainty in the exchange of values (Acemoglu and Johnson, 2005; Osabuohien and Efobi, 2011; 2013; Williamson, 2000). These consist of informal measures such as sanctions, customs, and traditions as well as formal rules such as constitutions, laws, and property rights (Karakara and Osabuohien, 2020; North, 1991).

Institutions do not occur in a vacuum but are driven by individuals-public agents, who have the constitutional right to ensure the 'well-being' of the country (Acemoglu and Robinson, 2012; Efobi and Osabuohien, 2016). Occurrences in most African countries are such that public officers pursue self-interest at the expense of the State (Akinyemi et al., 2019; Asongu, 2016; Van, 2007). Nigeria's situation is no different as her level of institutional development may need to be improved to enforce the required economic transformation, which has resulted in poor economic conditions from rent-seeking and even the curse of natural resources, among others (Osabuohien and Ike, 2011; Sala-i-Martin and Subramanian, 2013).

Using measures of government commitment, regulatory quality, rule of law and corruption rating, Table 1 presents Nigeria's situation[1]. The outlook from Table 1 reveals that the Nigerian government has consistently performed poorly with regards to policy formulation and its commitment to pursue such policies. Likewise, the government's commitment to formulating policies for the promotion of private sector development (regulatory quality) and the measure for rule of law was poor. During the same period, Ghana and South Africa witnessed a better institutional development as the values for South Africa were positive for most of the years, and Ghana's values were close to 0 especially for the period 2006-2010; signifying fair performance. The same trend was exhibited for the measure of corruption. The values for Nigeria were negatively higher than in other countries (South Africa and Ghana) for the entire period. In recent years, Nigeria ranks 13 (of 100) in government effectiveness, 18 (of 100) in regulatory quality, 14 (of 100) in rule of law, and 13 (of 100) in control of corruption: South Africa and Ghana outperform Nigeria in these measures.

Table 1. Indicators of institutional quality

	Government Effectiveness			Regulatory Quality			Rule of Law			Control of Corruption		
	2000-05	2006-09	2010-15	2000-05	2006-09	2010-15	2000-05	2006-09	2010-15	2000-05	2006-09	2010-15
World	0.00	-0.01	n.a	-0.02	-0.01	n.a	-0.03	-0.03	n.a	n.a	n.a	n.a
East Asia-Pacific	-0.5	-0.53	n.a	-0.65	-0.69	n.a	-0.33	-0.25	n.a	n.a	n.a	n.a
Europe and Central Asia	-0.44	-0.31	n.a	-0.40	-0.10	n.a	-0.64	-0.45	n.a	n.a	n.a	n.a
Latin America and Caribbean	-0.20	-0.10	n.a	-0.05	-0.12	n.a	-0.31	-0.36	n.a	n.a	n.a	n.a
Middle East and North Africa	-0.57	-0.61	n.a	-0.72	-0.63	n.a	-0.47	-0.54	n.a	n.a	n.a	n.a
Sub-Saharan Africa	-0.72	-0.78	n.a	-0.68	-0.70	n.a	-0.73	-0.74	n.a	n.a	n.a	n.a
South Africa*	0.70	0.49	0.36	0.64	0.47	0.36	0.10	0.12	0.14	0.12	0.2	0.00
Ghana*	-0.19	0.00	-0.13	-0.26	0.01	0.07	-0.06	-0.04	0.05	-0.01	0.03	-0.1
Nigeria*	-1.01	-0.98	-1.07	-1.11	-0.62	-0.74	-1.43	-1.12	-1.10	-0.22	-0.96	-1.16

Note: the values range from -2.5 (worst) to +2.5 (best), i.e. the higher the better.
The values for each region/country were the averages for the respective periods.
* were averages for the period. n.a: not available.
Sources: Authors' compilation from Worldwide Governance Indicators of the World Bank (2017a)

To better understand how institutional structures, affect some sectors in the economy, we present in Figure 1 such linkage between Nigeria's institutional development and some of the critical drivers of her economic transformation as shown in Figure 1. This is developed as a framework for the economic transformation of Nigeria (Central Bank of Nigeria-CBN, 2012). From the Figure, we noted that the general framework of Nigeria's institution is embedded in her colonial history, culture, traditions and norms and the State in general. By the State, we imply the general acceptable framework of the governance structure, which is expected to align with the generally proper system of governance and best

Figure 1.

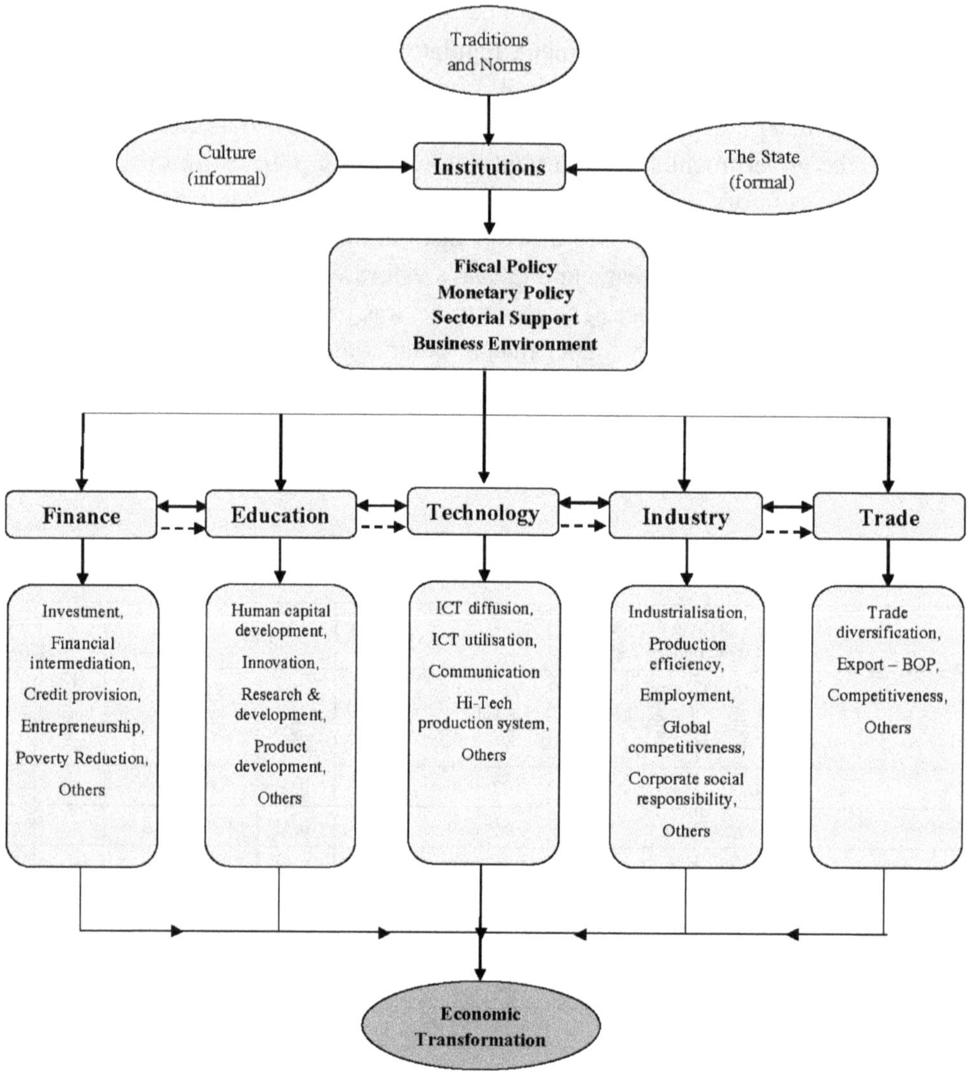

practice around the world. The combination of these factors is what brings about the rules, policies and regulations expected to translate into economic progress.

The situation (with reported cases of corrupt practices especially within the political class) in Nigeria questions the extent to which her economic progress can be achieved (Adewole and Osabuohien, 2007; Iyoha *et al.*, 2015; Osabuohien and Ike, 2011), especially knowing that there is a strong correlation between institutional development and the growth of the different sectors (as depicted in Figure 2 in the Appendix)[2]. This is because some actions that are bizarre to Nigeria's culture and traditions are being accepted as the norm, and they informally influence policies and guidelines. For instance, the issue of bribery, favouritism and other forms of corruption have informally structured the operation of the public administration in Nigeria. Oyinola (2011) examined the causes of corruption and noted that trade policies, wage policies, government subsidies and price controls are all instigated by corrupt intentions.

Figure 2.

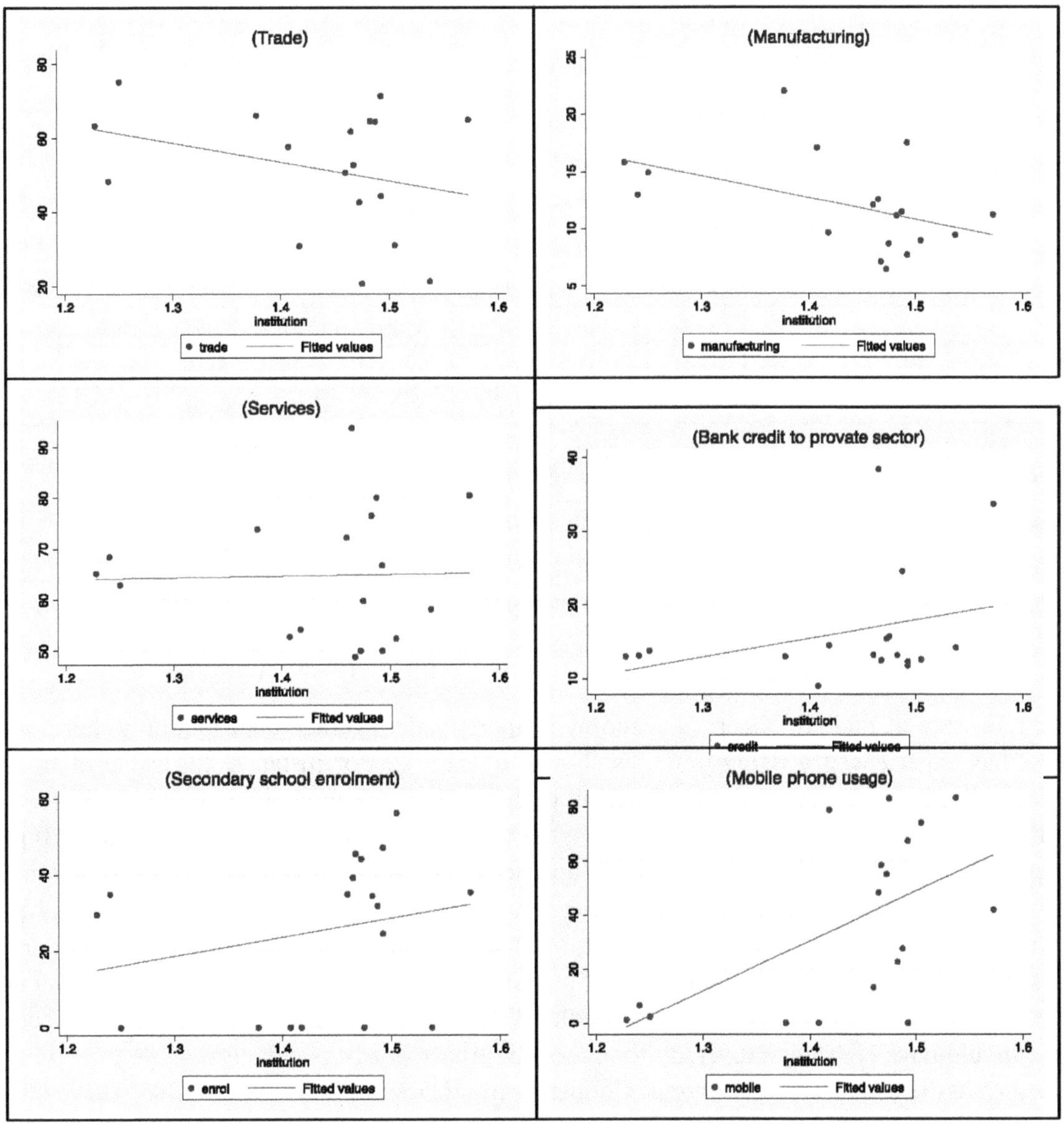

To improve on the current institutional framework in Nigeria, there is the need for a broad mix of both the formal and informal institutions, such that indigenous value systems are embedded in the formal institutions (Karakara and Osabuohien, 2020; Osabuohien, Okorie and Osabohien, 2018). As a result, other macroeconomic policies and structural transformation can arise from such process, such that will bring about improved fiscal policy, monetary policy, sectoral support and a business environment conducive enough to encourage investment: they have varying impacts on the drivers of transformation as presented by straight-line arrows in the Figure. The broken arrows in the Figure demonstrate the connectedness of the different drivers. They indicate that an impulse on one sector will have a corresponding impact on the other sectors.

TRENDS OF THE 'DRIVERS' OF ECONOMIC TRANSFORMATION

Based on the areas of focus, the study presents an overview of the trends of the drivers of economic transformation. Starting with trade, the percentage contribution of trade to the gross domestic products (GDP) is used to compare Nigeria's trend with the averages of countries in other regions of the world.

Table 2. Indicator of trade performance (Trade as a % of GDP)

	1970-75	1976-80	1981-85	1986-90	1991-95	1996-00	2001-05	2006-10	2011 - 15
World	30.37	35.93	38.66	37.29	39.89	45.51	49.95	56.05	61.32
East Asia & Pacific	32.43	38.31	41.81	38.84	40.42	45.18	53.10	62.53	62.28
Europe & Central Asia	44.58	50.82	56.73	53.37	55.28	64.13	69.91	76.98	79.96
Latin America & Caribbean	24.84	28.40	30.14	32.23	35.86	42.43	46.95	48.59	44.23
Middle East & North Africa	70.56	81.25	73.96	62.41	67.01	60.47	73.02	87.05	83.57
Sub-Saharan Africa	50.41	58.33	53.70	52.61	54.28	59.87	64.42	68.63	61.32
Nigeria	**29.84**	**45.06**	**35.05**	**53.22**	**83.52**	**78.78**	**75.09**	**68.31**	36.09

Notes: Averages were computed by the authors based on the years available for each variable per country/region.
Source: Authors' compilations from World Bank (2017b)

The relevance of trade to Nigeria's economy is appreciable, as trade contribution to her economic progress has experienced a rising trend, as shown in Table 2. For instance, the value of trade as a percentage of GDP improved from 29.8 percent in the early 1970s to about 83.0 percent in the period 1991-1995. However, due to the financial crisis, the value experienced a decline to about 68.0 percent in the period 2006-2010, and a further reduction to 36.09 in 2011-2015. Other countries experienced a similar decline. In comparing Nigeria's dependence on trade with countries from other regions, she has performed fairly. However, Nigeria's trade sector has mostly been dominated by the export of crude oil and gas, and the importation of a wide range of manufactured goods; this has somewhat heightened the neglect of her non-oil exports (Efobi and Osabuohien, 2011; Osabuohien *et al.*, 2018). It is expected that Nigeria should have high trade diversity for economic transformation and sustainable growth. Policy-makers such as the Organisation Economic Cooperation and Development-OECD (2011) have reiterated this by noting that for African countries to ensure sustainable growth, they would require the boosting of non-traditional sectors and the expansion of the range of their exportable products. It could, thus, be inferred that Nigeria's performance has not been impressive in this regard.

Using the Herfindahl-Hirschman Index-HHI, which measures the level of market concentration, with values ranging from 0 (perfect competition) to 1 (perfect monopoly); statistics from World Integrated Trade Solutions (WITS) reveal that the index for Nigeria was above 0.50 in the period 2000-2010. Specifically, in 2000, Nigeria had an HHI index of 0.987, but it later declined to 0.672 in 2010. From the trend, we can insinuate a shortfall in her level of trade competitiveness, as competition will bring about diversity that will enhance production for export.

Investigating another critical driver of industrial transformation, it is observed that Nigeria has experienced marginal performance in the development of her industry. Worthy of mention is the recent firm migration from Nigeria to other neighbouring African countries based on her poor infrastructural development, will affect the rate of her industrialization and economic transformation.

Table 3. Indicators of Industrial Development

	Manufacturing Value Added (% GDP)			Industry Value Added (% Growth)			Services Value Added (% Growth)		
	2001-05	**2006-10**	**2011-15**	**2001-05**	**2006-10**	**2011-15**	**2001-05**	**2006-10**	**2011-15**
World	17.79	16.84	15.577	2.480	1.940	26.759	2.940	2.490	63.785
East Asia & Pacific	22.71	22.18	23.541	5.460	2.030	34.588	3.300	3.180	58.365
Europe & Central Asia	18.05	16.63	13.868	1.660	0.090	23.308	2.390	1.850	64.290
Latin America & Caribbean	19	17.69	13.184	2.210	2.980	27.475	2.730	4.390	57.368
Middle East & North Africa	11.32	10.94	10.672	2.730	NA	46.673	4.840	5.630	46.064
Sub-Saharan Africa	13.85	13.08	9.829	5.020	4.470	24.716	4.870	4.420	52.018
South Africa	19.16	16.15	11.873	3.000	1.750	26.576	5.200	2.510	61.143
Ghana	9.81	8.22	5.295	**NA**	7.810	25.369	**NA**	7.760	48.483
Nigeria	**3.18**	**2.58**	8.559	**NA**	**-1.970**	25.110	**14.520**	**12.650**	52.690

Notes: Averages were computed by the authors based on the years available for each variable per country/region.
NA: Not available
Source: Authors' compilations from World Bank (2017b)

The statistics presented in Table 3 reveal Nigeria's poor industrial performance when compared with countries from other regions of the world. This is predominantly with regard to her manufacturing sector, which had a percentage contribution to GDP of less than 5 percent for the period 2001-2010, but later increased marginally to about 9 percent in the period 2011-2015. The value implies that the output from Nigeria's manufacturing sector, after accounting for intermediate inputs, increased by a marginal 4 percent of her GDP. The study also considered the trend of industry value-added, which is more encompassing as it includes the output less input from manufacturing, mining, construction and other sectors of the economy. The growth rate of industry value added was examined, as data for the percentage of GDP was unavailable. Also, from Table 3, it is evident that in the latter period presented, Nigeria did not perform very well. She experienced a negative growth rate on the average but witnessed a sudden increase in 2011-2015. Such an increase is likely attributable to the flow of foreign direct investment, especially in the real sector, which must have spurred industrial value addition.

It can be said that the service sector is very crucial for Nigeria because it performed impressively comparing it with the averages of other countries. Nigeria's average service value added for the period 2001-05 was 14.52 percent. In the latter period (2006-10), it decreased to 12.65 percent but later witnessed a sporadic increase to about 53 percent in the period 2011-2015. However, her value was still the highest compared to Ghana. The success of this sector can be traceable, to the development experienced in the financial sector, especially for the banks and capital market, and the telecommunication industry, which has boosted the output of other service firms. Some of the banks have branches across other countries in Africa, and the capital market is rated amongst the most developed in Africa.

In the context of global competitiveness and sustainable development, this study questions the relevance of the Nigerian services sector, particularly the financial sector, in performing their role of financial intermediation. It is observed that though the financial sector has experienced a growth rate in its value-added, its impact on Nigeria's economy has not been too substantial. This statement is based on the evidence from Table 4, using indices for financial development as a percentage of GDP. From the Table, Nigeria had an average domestic credit from bank to the private sector of less than 25 percent of GDP during the entire period 1996-2010, which later reduced to 13 percent in the period 2011-15. Within this period, Ghana had above 25 percent while the volume for South Africa was significantly higher than the GDP for the entire period, except for the period 2011-15, when there was a decrease to 68 percent. The averages of countries from other regions (except for the Middle East and North African countries) revealed that their banks issued out volumes of credit that were above 50 percent of the GDP, especially for the period 2001 to 2010.

Table 4. Domestic credit provided by banking sector as a % of GDP

	1981-85	1986-90	1991-95	1996-2000	2001-05	2006-10	2011-15
World	105.33	130.28	141.6	153.27	161.99	162.68	83.13
East Asia & Pacific	149.04	196.9	213.75	219.97	217.59	193.44	119.54
Europe & Central Asia	87.70	93.58	101.78	107.59	116.25	135.74	97.53
Latin America & Caribbean	49.94	91.84	59.73	47.43	48.69	61.46	44.06
Middle East & North Africa	29.25	62.51	53.91	55.47	53.08	43.86	46.86
Sub-Saharan Africa	53.93	57.51	73.74	71.98	75.73	74.05	28.72
South Africa	88.24	94.85	104.78	144.49	171.08	185.56	67.75
Ghana	20.84	22.31	19.11	28.05	31.78	25.76	16.73
Nigeria	**42.61**	**33.20**	**27.52**	**14.70**	**15.76**	**24.68**	**13.10**

Note and Source: Same as Table 2

The discussion is taken further by considering the human capital development of Nigeria in relation to countries of other regions. It examines the statistics of the average school enrolment rate and level of adult literacy to conclude the situation of Nigeria. Further, we present in Table 5 the statistics for the measures of human capital development for the period when data were available. The enrolment rate in Nigerian schools declined as individuals progressed in their level of educational attainment. For instance, the primary school enrolment rate was about 65 percent of the total individuals expected to enrol for this level of education; however, the enrolment rate decreased to 34 percent for secondary school and further reduced to about 9 percent for tertiary institutions. Although other countries from other regions of the world experienced a general decrease in enrolment rate across the different stages of education, their rates were many folds higher than that of Nigeria.

Focusing on another aspect of human capital-the adult literacy rate, Nigeria has performed fairly well as about 61 percent of her adult population is literate. Ghana had an adult literacy rate of about 67 percent, while that of South Africa was 89 percent. The rate for entire sub-Saharan Africa (SSA) was about 70 percent and countries from other regions, maintained rates above 70 percent. The performance of Nigeria in this regard, questions the country's capacity to be involved in innovation and creativity that can bring about product development for global competitiveness.

Assessing the extent of scientific investigations, which is a significant component of human capital that results in the creation of new knowledge, products and processes for economic transformation; Nigeria was at the lower echelon. Out of a million population, only about 39 researchers were involved in scientific research. Comparing this value with South Africa and the averages of countries from other regions, we can observe a wide margin of disparity. On average, South Africa recorded about 356 re-

Table 5. Indicators of human capital

	Primary Enrolment	Secondary Enrolment	Tertiary Enrolment	Adult Literacy	Researchers (Per Million People
	2000-15	2000-15	2000-15	2000-15	2000-15
World	103.01	67.81	27.12	83.76	1187.49
East Asia & Pacific	106.52	75.66	26.35	93.92	1336.13
Europe & Central Asia	102.18	98.15	57.72	98.47	2635.58
Latin America & Caribbean	114.67	88.53	35.53	91.06	418.90
Middle East & North Africa	102.07	73.95	28.08	75.03	NA
Sub-Saharan Africa	93.26	35.28	6.84	59.49	NA
South Africa	101.16	91.44	19.80	92.83	372.99
Ghana	95.38	46.46	10.62	64.70	28.05
Nigeria	**94.35**	**37.31**	**9.97**	**52.93**	**38.58**

Note and Source: Same as Table 2

searchers, while Latin American countries had about 450 researchers, as evidenced in Table 5. Countries in other parts of the world recorded above 1000 researchers from a million population.

The results of low human capital are numerous; among which include a low level of innovation and creativity, which is evidenced in the level of technology penetration and utilization in the country. This is because technology will diffuse faster in countries where the level of human capital is high since the utilization of technology is sometimes complicated and will require technical know-how of the potential user. Some authors, such as Baliamoune-Lutz (2003) and Guerrieri *et al.* (2011) have echoed this fact in their studies. Osabuohien and Efobi (2012) also noted that innovation is an essential component of technology diffusion as it can enhance the speedy implementation of the technology to a particular process.

Measuring the extent of technology utilization in Nigeria-based on telephone and internet usage, on the average, only about 1 person from 100 persons has access to the use of telephone (see Table 6). The average rate of diffusion of mobile phone was higher, as about 39 users from 100 persons were accounted for in the period 2006-2010, which later rose to about 72 users per 100 persons in the period 2011-15. Comparing this value with the global average, Nigeria has recorded some level of progress. However, countries like South Africa had about 138 users, while Ghana recorded close to 106 users. Focusing on Internet usage, the rate of diffusion was generally low in SSA countries; on average, less than 10 persons from a gathering of 100 persons have access to the Internet. Nigeria recorded an average usage rate of 17 users per 100 persons in the period 2006-2010, which later decreased to less than 1 user per 100 persons in the period 2011-15.

The level of technology output as a result of innovation and high human capital development using high technology export is also examined. Nigeria's total manufactured export comprises about 1 percent of high technology products. In the period 2006-2010, the value increased to about 3 percent. Considering that all measures of technology experienced an increase during the periods, Nigeria has the potential to perform better with regards to technology utilization and innovation for production: the onus rests on her level of institutional development.

Table 6. Indicators of technology utilisation and production

	Telephone Usage			Mobile Cellular Subscriptions			Internet Usage			High-technology Exports		
	2001-05	2006-10	2011-15	2001-05	2006-10	2011-15	2001-05	2006-10	2011-15	2001-05	2006-10	2011-15
World	18.01	18.34	15.73	21.57	18.15	91.48	12.13	23.65	12.47	21.57	18.15	21.48
East Asia & Pacific	19.75	23.14	19.50	25.03	57.59	96.10	10.85	25.56	13.17	30.59	27.34	24.63
Europe & Central Asia	38.24	37.4	35.01	58.48	112.38	123.70	27.01	47.81	22.66	18.14	14.79	15.64
Latin America & Caribbean	16.95	18.12	17.66	26.71	77.84	110.50	11.37	27.21	9.236	13.69	11.21	10.68
Middle East & North Africa	13.15	16.7	15.76	15.73	69.26	104.99	5.46	18.43	5.177	4.69	2.90	2.88
Sub-Saharan Africa	1.46	1.48	1.18	6.10	31.19	64.04	1.33	6.97	0.314	3.52	4.65	4.20
South Africa	10.49	9.08	7.96	41.46	91.58	139.80	7.28	9.36	2.501	5.73	5.36	5.52
Ghana	1.40	1.22	1.05	5.67	48.32	105.94	1.15	5.17	0.262	2.17	1.67	4.64
Nigeria	0.66	0.94	0.22	4.76	39.04	72.38	1.16	17.01	0.01	0.75	2.56	1.98

Note: Telephone, Mobile Cellular Subscriptions and Internet Usage were measured based on users per 100 persons. High technology export was measured as a percentage of total manufacturing export.

Source: Same as Table 2

ECONOMIC TRANSFORMATION THROUGH STRONG INSTITUTIONS

Fiscal Policy

The outcomes from a sound fiscal policy cannot be overemphasized. They include infrastructural development, enhanced government expenditure on specific sectors, improved government revenue, counter-cyclical and public debt reduction (Arpaia and Turrini, 2008). These factors affect the drivers of economic transformation (Okorie, Osabuohien and Oaikhenan, 2020). A close look at the component of the Nigerian government revenue and expenditure, as presented in Table 7, reveals that the Nigerian government practices a fiscal policy structure, with the average total revenue as a percentage of GDP increasing from 21.31 (1971-1975) to 35.01 (2001-2005) and latter to 27.34 (2006-2010). In the same period, total government expenditure as a percentage of GDP was 19.06, 15.14 and 12.79, respectively.

Sustainable revenue, such as domestically mobilized revenue in the form of tax, is required for Nigeria to ensure economic transformation (Areo, Gershon and Osabuohien, 2020). The advantage of this kind of revenue is that it is less volatile and makes public officers more accountable (Culpeper and Bhushan, 2010; Henri-Bernard, 2010). However, the Nigerian government has mostly depended on oil revenue and debt financing, as depicted in Table 7. The pitfall of this source of revenue is that it is susceptible to market shocks, and sometimes, the influence of the lending organization supersedes national interest.

Paying attention to government expenditure, it is essential to note that an economy will require substantial government expenditure to ensure sustainable industrialization and growth (Serena and Andrea, 2011). Public spending in the form of grants, subsidies, tax exemptions, creation of social goods and other forms of infrastructures pave the way for sustainable growth of the drivers of economic transformation. For instance, government spending on education will enhance research and development, innovation

Table 7. Classifications of central government accounts (% GDP)

	1971-75	1976-80	1981-85	1986-90	1991-95	1996-00	2001-05	2006-10	2011-15
Total Federally Collected Revenue	21.31	25.79	22.41	24.74	28.51	25.72	35.01	27.34	15.31
Total Expenditure	19.06	25.69	20.45	21.16	19.49	18.14	15.14	12.79	7.60
Components of Public Revenue									
Oil Revenue	13.95	19.73	15.50	17.80	23.12	19.88	28.09	21.66	10.84
Non-Oil Revenue	1.98	1.78	1.57	0.86	1.16	1.05	1.24	1.63	4.47
Components of Expenditure									
Recurrent Expenditure	11.69	10.36	10.26	13.10	11.76	6.45	8.41	7.16	5.55
Capital Expenditure	7.38	9.89	11.81	13.51	14.22	9.89	3.95	3.42	1.42
Components of Recurrent Expenditure									
Administration	3.65	1.74	1.94	3.05	2.42	2.90	3.40	3.26	1.82
Social and Community Service	0.38	0.81	0.62	1.14	1.02	1.25	1.46	1.30	1.26
Economic Services	0.39	0.27	0.37	0.64	0.57	0.83	0.80	1.07	0.43
Transfers	7.26	7.56	7.32	8.27	7.75	3.21	4.62	2.63	3.16
Components of Capital Expenditure									
Administration	1.78	2.86	1.10	1.15	0.98	1.22	1.11	1.13	0.37
Social and Community Service	1.49	2.98	1.75	0.88	0.49	0.52	0.60	0.51	0.17
Economic Services	2.84	9.15	3.91	1.66	1.87	6.08	2.61	1.76	0.62
Transfers	1.25	0.33	3.45	4.37	4.40	2.13	0.37	0.26	0.27

Source: Authors' Computation from Central Bank of Nigeria Statistical Bulletin (2017)

and inventions, which will boost the technology diffusion and utilization, industrial capacity and then the overall export. This is denoted by the straight-line flowing through the drivers of economic transformation in Figure 1, earlier presented. However, the outlook of the component of Nigeria's government expenditure reveals a disturbing trend.

The Nigerian government has hitherto focused its attention on recurrent expenditure with significant emphasis on transfers and administrative expenses. Table 8 reveals that administrative and recurrent expenditure was over two-fold more than other components. When considering economic transformation, this component of expenditure does not matter much as it includes the cost of government, national security and cost of public debt (e.g. interest on debt). This trend can explain the low level of development of education, infrastructure and industrialization in Nigeria.

Economic transformation will require not only sufficiency but also accountability in government expenditure on social goods and economic services such as agriculture, infrastructure and construction. A close examination of the capital expenditure reveals a higher trend than other components but at a decreasing rate. For instance, in the period 1976-1980, expenditure on economic services was 9.15 percent of GDP, but as at 2000-2010, the value was 1.76. In this period, the cost of administration was 1.13 percent of GDP. The rising rate of administrative cost for both recurrent and capital expenditure cannot be disassociated with corruption, which has drastically heightened the cost of running the government.

Table 8. Recurrent government expenditure on structures (% of GDP)

	1971-75	1976-80	1981-85	1986-90	1991-95	1996-00	2001-05	2006-10	2011-15
Education	0.20	0.59	0.35	0.79	0.62	0.97	1.03	0.73	0.55
Health	0.16	0.13	0.18	0.20	0.24	0.30	0.55	0.43	0.34
Agriculture	0.10	0.04	0.03	0.06	0.13	0.52	0.15	0.17	0.06
Transport and Communication	0.07	0.05	0.07	0.13	0.12	0.14	0.37	0.33	0.03

Source: Authors' Computation from Central Bank of Nigeria Statistical Bulletin (2017)

Monetary Policy

Consensus has it that the weak transmission of monetary policy in African countries is as a result of the thin financial sector and structural factors (Iyoboyi and Pedro, 2013). The authors noted that the Central Banks of most African countries are unable to mobilize domestic credit. Monetary policies in Nigeria are also prodded by this situation and are challenged by poor institutions. The recent corporate governance failure by chief executives of some banks in Nigeria and former directors of the Nigerian Stock Exchange exemplifies the fact that sometimes, corrupt executives impede monetary policies.

Some other evidences from the score in the World Bank financial sector rating[3]; reveals the fact that information asymmetry between the financial firms and their customers is an inhibitor to the performance of their financial intermediation responsibility. It may be inferred that Nigerian banks' poor credit to the private sector is attributed to information asymmetry and fear of moral hazard in the provision of credit, which are components of poor institutional development. This position was supported by the World Bank Doing Business Statistics, which reveals that between 2004 and 2010, the depth of credit information index was 0[4] (World Bank, 2016). Connoting that high credit information for both firms and individuals, to facilitate lending decisions are unavailable or inaccessible. In this case, banks will grant these credits to individuals and business organization based on personal recommendation and interest, without resort to equity and fairness.

Focusing on financial inclusion and some policy stance, Nigeria is currently experiencing an adult exclusion rate of 46.3 percent (CBN, 2012). This rate has instigated some policy response as the Central Bank of Nigeria (CBN) has started up a financial inclusion strategy, which involves driving on the reduction of information asymmetry, re-digitization of customers account, encourage the use of debit cards, removal of charges for inter-bank teller machine transactions and inter-connectedness of the banks (CBN, 2012). The effect of this policy response includes growth in domestic investment and bank sustainability.

Considering the inflation rate in Nigeria, which remained a double-digit in the period 2000-2010 (World Bank 2017); the influence of institutional failure can be traced to this scenario. Based on economic theory, competition brings about price reduction, as market forces can determine the prices of goods (Olayiwola, Osabuohien and Efobi, 2012). However, in some sectors of the Nigerian economy-household consumables, there is an almost perfect monopoly. Anecdote evidence suggests that corruption, in the form of cabals, who control these sectors and do not grant access to new market entrants. This act is perpetrated with the support of the government (by implication) based on the fact that some of these cabals fund the government and as a reward, the government protects their stake in these sectors.

Sectoral Supports

To access the extent to which institutional development in Nigeria has affected structural transformation, we focus attention on education, health, agriculture and transport and communication. The focus on these sectors is because they have a direct effect on the drivers of economic transformation, as have been identified in Figure 1. For instance, the structural transformation of the health sector is noted to affect the level of industry productivity because healthy workers are more productive than sick workers (Asiedu, Jin and Kanyama, 2015). Likewise, the transformation of the agricultural sector will result in improved trade performance, employment generation and reduction in gender poverty and production of quality input material for industrial consumption (Aigbokhan, 2004). Structural improvement in the transport and communication sector will have an immediate impact on the five drivers of transformation. The experience of South Korea is informative, as the government's investment in high-tech infrastructure has paid off in her economic transformation process (Osabuohien and Ike, 2011).

The analysis is based on whether public policies have been conducive to promote structural changes in the four sectors. We present the trend of the total government expenditure in these four sectors in Table 9. From the Table, it can be observed that the volume of government expenditure in these structures is very low. This is based on the values in the Table, which were all less than 1 percent of GDP (except for education in the period 2001-2005). Considering the education sector, the government tried to improve fiscal policy performance in this regard, resulting in an improvement from 0.20 in 1971-1975 to 0.73 in 2006-2010. Generally, the Nigerian government has paid little attention to these structures. This trend may explain the reason for the poor performance of the drivers of economic transformation when compared with other countries.

Table 9. Government expenditure on sectors (% of total recurrent government expenditure)

	1971-75	**1976-80**	**1981-85**	**1986-90**	**1991-95**	**1996-00**	**2001-05**	**2006-10**	**2011-15**	**Priority**
Education	1.76	5.43	3.41	6.12	5.23	9.70	7.84	7.44	NA	First
Health	1.37	1.19	1.74	1.56	1.93	2.91	4.26	4.33	NA	Second
Agriculture	0.84	0.41	0.27	0.46	1.04	3.75	1.17	1.68	NA	Fourth
Transport and Communication	0.55	0.52	0.67	0.98	0.90	1.37	2.76	3.06	NA	Third

Source: Authors' Computation from Central Bank of Nigeria Statistical Bulletin (2017)

The study goes further to examine the priority list of the government by considering the percentages of government expenditure on the sectors in relation to the total government expenditure. The trend provides evidence that the government placed more priority on education, followed by health, transport and communication, and then agriculture. Even though the government's emphasis is on education, the magnitude of the total recurrent expenditure is intangible compared to the total expenditure. The percentage of this structure varied between 1.76 of total expenditure in 1971-1975 to 7.44 in 2006-2010. For the entire period, they maintained a less than 10 percent composition of the total recurrent expenditure. The same experience was observed in other sectors. The output from this trend, questions Nigeria's ability to effectively compete globally and ensure sustainable development.

Business Environment

The business environment includes the regulations, protection of rights of economic agents and other forms of economic institutions that are available in a particular country to encourage investment and economic relations. This kind of environment thrives with developed institutions. This is based on the submission of extant studies that institutions are critical for shaping the relationship between economic agents to reduce potential moral hazards and adverse selection (North, 1991; Osabuohien and Efobi, 2013; Rodrik, 1998).

Considering some aspects of the business environment in Nigeria, a trend of these aspects using data from World Bank Business Enterprise Survey is presented. It starts with the rating of the main business obstacles to establishing the most prevalent inhibitor for business growth. Table 10 reveals that among the main inhibitors of business growth is infrastructural development, especially electricity. This calls for a redirection of fiscal policy towards infrastructural development. The second major constraint is access to finance and transportation. Focusing on infrastructure, Table 10 records 25.2 percent of businesses that have experienced at least one electrical outage in a typical month. 85.6 percent of the businesses in Nigeria own a generator set. Considering the level of technology utilization by the businesses, it is observed that less than 30 percent are Information Technology (IT) oriented. Only 26 percent use email, and less than 10 percent have their website.

Table 10. Business environment in Nigeria

	Access to Finance	Access to Land	Electricity	Tax rates	Transportation
Biggest Obstacle to Business	15.6	2.9	63.6	2.2	7.5
	Monthly Electrical Outages	Own Generator	% Electricity from Generator	Electricity as a Major Constraint	Transport as a Major constraint
Infrastructure	25.2	85.6	52.1	75.9	28.1
	Internationally Recognized Quality Certification	Using technology licensed from foreign companies	Firms having their own website	Firms using email to interact	Firms with Audited financial statement
Technology and Innovation	8.5	10.7	9.7	26.0	17.0

Source: Authors' Computation from World Bank Enterprise Survey (2012)

A policy stance on infrastructural development will have a mammoth influence on industrial development in Nigeria. Likewise, technology development will thrive on infrastructure and hence, position Nigeria towards sustainable development and global competitiveness. The situation of Nigeria's institutional condition on industrial development is presented in Table 11. From the Table, we observe that there is a prevalence of requisition for a bribe and giving of gifts to public officials, before business operation is carried out. The statistics from the Table reveal that more than 40 percent of the businesses in Nigeria are either expected to give gifts or pay bribes to public officials to get things done, to secure government contracts, to get an operating licence, to secure a construction permit, or for some form of services.

Table 11. Institutional framework and business environment

Sectors	A	B	C	D	E	F	G	H	I	J
	40.9	**22.9**	**44.3**	**4.7**	**40.3**	**53.0**	**39.3**	**30.1**	**40.0**	**24.7**
Food	37.3	20.2	41.8	3.3	33.5	49.3	35.8	27.4	37.5	24.6
Garments	32.3	19.6	44.0	4.6	34.2	48.9	33.0	26.6	36.4	24.2
Other Manufacturing	38.4	20.1	45.1	4.8	37.1	52.9	35.8	27.4	37.0	24.1
Retail	39.1	23.2	38.5	3.8	42.0	42.1	40.6	30.5	40.3	25.7
Other Services	47.2	26.7	48.8	5.6	45.6	59.1	43.3	33.5	43.7	24.5
Small (5-19)	42.0	23.9	46.8	4.9	47.3	51.6	42.3	31.5	41.4	27.2
Medium (20-99)	39.9	21.3	38.3	4.2	28.8	55.5	32.4	27.5	38.1	17.4
Large (100+)	15.2	7.2	17.2	1.9	10.2	n.a.	9.7	10.8	13.3	9.2

Note: A-% of firms expected to give gifts to public officials to get things done; **B**-% of firms expected to give gifts in meetings with tax officials; **C**- Percent of firms expected to give gifts to secure government contract; **D**- Value of gifts given to secure contract as % of total contract value; **E**- % of firms expected to give gifts to get an operating license; **F**- % of firms expected to give gifts to secure a construction permit; **G**- % of firms expected to give gifts to secure electricity; **H**- % of public transactions that require gifts or bribe to be paid; I- % of firms experiencing at-least one bribe payment; J- % of firms identifying corruption as a major obstacle.

It is important to note that a developed business environment will promote the drivers of economic transformation, especially industry, trade, technology and finance. Likewise, burdensome institutions are a vital constraint to private sector development. There is, therefore, the need to enhance government commitment towards ensuring a business environment that encourages fair competition, the security of rights and properties, and private investment. This calls for policy action by the government. One of the required steps in this regard will be to expedite the cooperation among government agencies, the private sector and the people (in terms of value re-orientation and adherence to law and order). All of these are essential catalysts for a country's desired economic transformation.

CONCLUSION

This paper made efforts in drawing a possible linkage between institutional development in Nigeria and economic transformation focusing on five main drivers: namely: finance, education, technology, industry and trade. A framework was developed, which showed a linkage between institutions and the development of the drivers.

From the analysis, we cannot disassociate economic transformation from institutional development. This is following the findings that institutional development transmits to economic transformation, through its drivers. The government responsiveness, especially in the form of fiscal and monetary policies, structural transformation, and conducive business environment that will enhance private investment, export, exchange rate stability, poverty reduction, among others, is underlined. Thus, the roles of the government in creating the structures that can lead to transformation involving the highlighted sectors are essential. Notably, education and infrastructural development should be upheld as this can lead to the speedy realization of the transformation process. On the other hand, this process of economic transformation can be expedited with the cooperation of the government, the private sector and the people, in terms of value re-orientation and adherence to law and order, which are *sine qua non* for a country's economic transformation agenda.

ACKNOWLEDGMENT

The authors acknowledge the supports from Covenant University Centre for Research, Innovation and Discovery (CUCRID) during the preparation of the manuscript. The second author appreciates the Alexander von Humboldt Foundation for supporting his visiting research fellowship at Witten/Herdecke University, Witten, Germany [Ref 3.4-1147508-NGA-GF-P] as well as Equipment Subsidy Grant to the Centre for Economic Policy and Development Research (CEPDeR), Covenant University [[REF: 3.4-8151/19047]. The views expressed are those of the authors.

REFERENCES

Acemoglu, D., & Johnson, S. (2005). Unbundling Institutions. *Journal of Political Economy*, *113*(5), 949–995. doi:10.1086/432166

Acemoglu, D., & Robinson, J. (2012). *Why Nations Fail: The Origins of Power, Prosperity, and Poverty*. Crown Business Publisher.

Adewole, M. A., & Osabuohien, E. S. (2007). Analysis of the Cost of Governance and Options for Its Reduction in Nigeria. *The Nigerian Journal of Economic and Social Studies*, *49*(1), 137–159.

Aigbokhan, B. E. (2004). Wage Determination in Nigerian Manufacturing Sector: A Test of Competing Theories. *The Nigerian Journal of Economic and Social Studies*, *46*(2), 105–124.

Akinyemi, O., Efobi, U., Asongu, S., & Osabuohien, E. (2019). Renewable energy, trade performance and the conditional role of finance and institutional capacity in sub-Sahara African Countries. *Energy Policy*, *132*, 490–498. doi:10.1016/j.enpol.2019.06.012

Akinyemi, O., Osabuohien, E., Alege, P., & Ogundipe, A. (2017). Energy Security, Trade and Transition to Green Economy in Africa. *International Journal of Energy Economics and Policy*, *7*(3), 127–136.

Areo, F., Gershon, O., & Osabuohien, E. (2020). Improved Public Services and Tax Compliance of Small and Medium Scale Enterprises in Nigeria: A Generalised Ordered Logistic Regression. *Asian Economic and Financial Review*, *10*(7), 833–860. doi:10.18488/journal.aefr.2020.107.833.860

Arpaia, A., & Turrini, A. (2008). *Government Expenditure and Economic Growth in the EU: Long-Run Tendencies and Short-Term Adjustment. Economic Papers 300*. European Commission.

Asiedu, E. (2005). Foreign Direct Investment in Africa: The Role of Natural Resources, Market Size, Government Policy, Institutions and Political Instability. *World Economy*, *29*(1), 63–77. doi:10.1111/j.1467-9701.2006.00758.x

Asiedu, E., Jin, Y., & Kanyama, I. (2015). The Impact of HIV/AIDS on Foreign Direct Investment in Developing Countries. *Journal of African Trade*, *2*(1), 1–17. doi:10.1016/j.joat.2015.01.001

Asongu, S. A. (2016). Law and investment in Africa. *Institutions, Etc.*, *8*(2), 91–120.

Baliamoune-Lutz, M. (2003). An Analysis of the Determinants and Effects of ICT Diffusion in Developing Countries. *Information Technology for Development*, *10*(3), 151–169. doi:10.1002/itdj.1590100303

Beck, T., Demirguc-Kunt, A., & Levine, R. (2007). Finance, Inequality and the Poor. *Journal of Economic Growth, 12*(1), 27–49. doi:10.100710887-007-9010-6

Beecroft, I., Osabuohien, E., Efobi, U., Olurinola, I., & Osabohien, R. (2020). Manufacturing Export and ICT Infrastructure in West Africa: Investigating the Roles of Economic and Political Institutions. *Institutions, Etc., 12*(1), 1–36.

Beecroft, I., Osabuohien, E. S., & Olurinola, I. O. (2018). Institutions, Fiscal Performance and Development Trajectories in ECOWAS: Implications for Sustainability. In U. R. Efobi & S. Asongu (Eds.), *Financing Sustainable Development in Africa* (pp. 121–141). Palgrave-Macmillan. doi:10.1007/978-3-319-78843-2_6

Catrinescu, N., Leon-Ledesma, M., Piracha, M., & Quillin, B. (2009). Remittances, Institutions and Economic Growth. *World Development, 37*(1), 81–92. doi:10.1016/j.worlddev.2008.02.004

Cavalcanti, T., Magalhaes, A. M., & Tavares, J. (2008). Institutions and Economic Development in Brazil. *The Quarterly Review of Economics and Finance, 48*(2), 412–432. doi:10.1016/j.qref.2006.12.019

Central Bank of Nigeria. (2017). *Statistical Bulletin*. Central Bank of Nigeria.

Culpeper, R., & Bhushan, A. (2010). Why Enhance Domestic Resource Mobilisation in Africa? *Trade Negotiations Insights, 9*(6), 5–7.

Efobi, U., & Osabuohien, E. (2011). Promotion of Non-Oil Export in Nigeria: Empirical Assessment of Agricultural Credit Guarantee Scheme Fund. *Current Research Journal of Economic Theory, 3*(1), 20–28.

Efobi, U., & Osabuohien, E. (2016). Manufacturing exports, Infrastructure and Institutions in Africa: Reflections from ECOWAS. In D. Seck (Ed.), *In Accelerated Economic Growth in West Africa* (pp. 157–179). Springer International Publishing. doi:10.1007/978-3-319-16826-5_8

Ejemeyovwi, J. O., & Osabuohien, E. S. (2020). Investigating the Relevance of Mobile Technology Adoption on Inclusive Growth in West Africa. *Contemporary Social Science, 15*(1), 48–61. doi:10.1080/21582041.2018.1503320

Ejemeyovwi, J. O., Osabuohien, E. S., Johnson, O. D., & Bowale, E. I. K. (2019). Internet Usage, Innovation and Human Development Nexus in Africa: The Case of ECOWAS. *Journal of Economic Structures, 8*(5). Advance online publication. doi:10.118640008-019-0146-2

Ejemeyovwi, J. O., Osabuohien, E. S., & Osabohien, R. (2018). ICT Investments, Human Capital Development and Institutions in ECOWAS. *International Journal of E-Business Research, 15*(4), 463–474.

Frankel, J., & Romer, D. (1999). Does Trade Cause Growth. *The American Economic Review, 39*(3), 379–399. doi:10.1257/aer.89.3.379

Guerrieri, P., Luciani, M., & Meliciani, V. (2011). *The Determinants of Investment in Information and Communication Technologies. Bruges European Economic* Research Papers. Nos. 16.

Henri-Bernard, S. L. (2010). Taxation for Development in Africa: A Shared Responsibility. *Trade Negotiations Insights, 9*(6), 3–4.

Iyoboyi, M., & Pedro, L. M. (2013). The Demand for Money in the Nigeria: Evidence from Bounds Testing Approach. *Business and Economic Journal*, *76*, 1–13.

Iyoha, F. O., Gberevbie, D. E., Iruonagbe, C. T., & Egharevba, M. E. (2015). Cost of Governance in Nigeria: In Whose Interest? International Journal of Social, Education, Economics and Management Engineering, 9(1), 252-259.

Karakara, A. A., & Osabuohien, E. (2019). Households' ICT Access and Bank Patronage in West Africa: Empirical Insights from Burkina Faso and Ghana. *Technology in Society*, *56*, 116–125. doi:10.1016/j.techsoc.2018.09.010

Karakara, A. A., & Osabuohien, E. (2020). ICT Adoption, Competition and Innovation of Informal Firms in West Africa: Comparative Study of Ghana and Nigeria. *Journal of Enterprising Communities*, *14*(3), 397–414. doi:10.1108/JEC-03-2020-0022

Levine, R. (2005). Finance and Growth: Theory and Evidence. In P. Aghion & S. Durlauf (Eds.), *Handbook of Economic Growth*. Elsevier Science.

North, D. C. (1990). *Institutions, Institutional Change and Economic Performance*. University Press. doi:10.1017/CBO9780511808678

North, D. C. (1991). Institutions. *The Journal of Economic Perspectives*, *5*(1), 97–112. doi:10.1257/jep.5.1.97

Ogunrinola, I. O., & Osabuohien, E. S. (2010). Globalization and Employment Generation in Nigeria's Manufacturing Sector (1990-2006). *European Journal of Soil Science*, *12*(4), 581–593.

Okorie, U., Osabuohien, E., & Oaikhenan, H. (2020). Electricity Consumption, Public Agricultural Expenditure and Output in Nigeria: A Time Series Dynamic Approach. *International Journal Energy Economics and Policy*, *10*(2), 113–123. doi:10.32479/ijeep.8436

Olayiwola, W., Osabuohien, E., & Efobi, U. (2012). Inflation and Financial Development in Nigeria. In O. Olaniyan, A. O. Lawson, & B. Alayande (Eds.), *Financial Sector Issues and Economic Development in Nigeria II* (pp. 49–67). University Press.

Organization for Economic Cooperation & Development-OECD. (2011). *Economic Diversification in Africa: A Review of Selected Countries*. OECD Publishing.

Osabuohien, E. (2020a). *The Palgrave Handbook of Agricultural and Rural Development in Africa*. Palgrave Macmillan. doi:10.1007/978-3-030-41513-6

Osabuohien, E. (2020b). Guest Editorial: Labour Issues in Africa's Agricultural and Rural Transformation. *African Journal of Economic and Management Studies*, *11*(2), 185–191. doi:10.1108/AJEMS-06-2020-406

Osabuohien, E., & Efobi, U. (2011). Trade Outcomes in Africa's Regional Economic Communities and Institutional Quality: Some Policy Prescriptions. *Economic Insights - Trends and Challenges*, *LXIII*(4), 19–32.

Osabuohien, E., & Efobi, U. (2012). Technology Diffusion and Economic Progress in Africa: Challenges and Opportunities. In N. Ekekwe & N. Islam (Eds.), *Disruptive Technologies, Innovation and Global Redesign: Emerging Implications* (pp. 425–440). Information Science Reference. doi:10.4018/978-1-4666-0134-5.ch024

Osabuohien, E., & Efobi, U. (2013). Africa's Money in Africa. *The South African Journal of Economics, 81*(2), 292–306. doi:10.1111aje.12012

Osabuohien, E., & Ike, D. N. (2011). Economic Transformation and Institutional Framework in Nigeria – Lessons from Botswana and South Korea. *Selected Papers at the 2011 Annual Conference of Nigerian Economic Society,* 382-414.

Osabuohien, E., Obiekwe, E., Urhie, E., & Osabohien, R. (2018, Spring). Inflation Rate, Exchange Rate Volatility and Exchange Rate Pass-Through Interactions: The Nigerian experience. *Journal of Applied Economic Sciences, 13*(2), 574–585.

Osabuohien, E., Okorie, U., & Osabohien, R. (2018). Rice Production and Processing in Ogun State, Nigeria: Qualitative Insights from Farmers' Association. In E. Obayelu (Ed.), *Food Systems Sustainability and Environmental Policies in Modern Economics* (pp. 188–216). IGI Global. doi:10.4018/978-1-5225-3631-4.ch009

Oyinola, O. A. (2011). Corruption Eradication in Nigeria: An Appraisal. *Library Philosophy and Practice.* Available at http://www.webpages.uidaho.edu/~mbolin/ayobami.htm

Randriamaro, Z. (2006). *Gender and Trade: Overview Report. Bridge.* University of Sussex.

Rodrik, D. (1998). Why is Trade Reform so difficult in Africa? *Journal of African Economies, 7*(Supplement 1), 10–36. doi:10.1093/jafeco/7.suppl_1.10

Sala-i-Martin, X., & Subramanian, A. (2013). Addressing the Natural Resource Curse: An Illustration from Nigeria. *Journal of African Economies, 22*(4, Supplement 1), 15–48. doi:10.1093/jae/ejs033

Serena, L., & Andrea, Z. (2011). Increasing Public Expenditures: Wagner's Law in OECD Countries. *German Economic Review, 12*(2), 149–164. doi:10.1111/j.1468-0475.2010.00517.x

Tan, K., & Phang, S. (2005). *From Efficiency-Driven to Innovation-Driven Economic Growth: Perspectives from Singapore.* Policy, Research Working Paper No. WPS 3569. Washington, DC: World Bank.

Tran-Nguyen, A. N., & Zampetti, A. B. (2004). *Trade and Gender: Opportunities and Challenges for Developing Countries.* UNCTAD.

Van, W. J-A. (2007). Political Leaders in Africa: Presidents, Patrons and Profiteers? Durban: ACCORD.

Williamson, J. (2011). *Trade and Poverty: When the Third World Fell Behind.* MIT Press. doi:10.7551/mitpress/9780262015158.001.0001

Williamson, O. E. (2000). The New Institutional Economics: Taking Stock, Looking Ahead. *Journal of Economic Literature, 38*(3), 595–613. doi:10.1257/jel.38.3.595

World Bank. (2016). *Doing Business: Measuring Business Regulations.* The World Bank.

World Bank. (2017a). *Worldwide Governance Indicators*. The World Bank.

World Bank. (2017b). *World Development Indicators*. The World Bank.

ENDNOTES

1 **Government effectiveness** measures the quality of policy formulation and the credibility of the government's commitment to such policies; **regulatory quality** reflects the government's commitment to formulate sound policies and regulations that will promote private sector development; **rule of law** measures the quality of contract enforcement, property rights protection, among others; **Control of Corruption** reflects the extent to which public power is exercised for private gain as well as 'capture' of the state by the elites and private interests. It is possible to use other indicators of institutions from other sources (e.g. Political Rights and Civil Liberty from Freedom House). However, those from the Worldwide Governance Indicators (WGI) of the World Bank (2017a) were also used in this study to complement the rest of the data sources.

2 The negative correlation seen for institutions and trade to GDP can be tied to the dominance of the primary sector in the trade regime of Nigeria, which is mostly linked to the corruption seen in the country. Hence, once the institutional structure is improved, it has a negative effect on the output for export in this sector, which will have a strong effect on trade outcomes.

3 This statistic assesses the structure of the financial sector and the policies and regulations that affect it. The values range from 1 (low) to 6 (high).

4 The index ranges from 0 to 6, with higher values indicating the availability of more credit information, from either a public credit registry or a private credit bureau, to facilitate lending decisions.

Section 2

Finance, Inclusive Growth, and Development

Chapter 6
Economic Diversification and Inclusive Growth in Nigeria:
Does Institutional Quality Matter?

Amaka G. Metu
Nnamdi Azikiwe University, Nigeria

Chekwube V. Madichie
https://orcid.org/0000-0001-9405-6264
Nnamdi Azikiwe University, Nigeria

Uchenna N. Anyanwu
Nnamdi Azikiwe University, Nigeria

Chris U. Kalu
Nnamdi Azikiwe University, Nigeria

Okezie A. Ihugba
Alvan Ikoku Federal College of Education, Owerri, Nigeria

ABSTRACT

Economic diversification is identified as a recipe for achieving inclusive growth and the role of institutions in strengthening the process of diversification cannot be ruled out. This study examined the role of institutions in helping economic diversification to achieve inclusive growth in Nigeria. Inclusive growth was measured using the growth rate of the inequality-adjusted human development index. Based on the Solow growth model and adopting the Johansen cointegration test, the results show that economic diversification in Nigeria does not significantly contribute to inclusive growth. The interaction of diversification with the institutions gave a positive significant result meaning that effective institutions will help economic diversification contribute to inclusive growth. Hence, the government using appropriate institutions can ensure an investment-friendly environment to support economic diversification and encourage inclusive growth in Nigeria.

DOI: 10.4018/978-1-7998-4817-2.ch006

BACKGROUND AND JUSTIFICATION

In any country's development matrix, economic diversification, institutional quality and inclusive growth are significant variables. Developed countries of North America, Europe and the Asian Tigers have shown that economic diversification is necessary for inclusive growth. But, developing countries, especially for countries dominated by primary products, economic diversification remains one of their biggest economic challenges (World Bank, 2019). Nigeria is blessed with abundant human and natural resources such as crude oil, natural gas, lead, coal, and so many others. The country's superior climatic conditions are viable for agricultural proceeds including cocoa, groundnut, tobacco, oil palm and different live stocks.

The availability of the different resources and introduction of technology gave rise to industries such as oil and gas, furniture, construction and building, food and beverages. Slowly, growth became pronounced in the production of consumer goods. Hence an economy which depended on agriculture delved into industrialisation which boomed despite many infrastructural challenges. Industrialisation is identified as the key object to the economic development of any nation and by the 1970s, oil became the biggest foreign exchange earner and completely replaced palm products, groundnut, cocoa and hides and skin (Oyebola et al, 2020; Adeleye et al, 2020). The oil boom of 1974 led to an increase in revenue and flood of wealth, resulting in a structural transformation of the Nigeria economy from a third world country to an appreciable position in terms of development and international politics (Oparah, 2018). Much of the revenue which was intended for investment and to diversify the economy also spurred increased government expenditure, inflation and inequalities in the country.

Nigeria continued to rely on a single source of revenue which exposed the economy to macroeconomic instability (Metu, Maduka, Eze & Ajudua, 2019). The oil boom was short-lived as the 2008 global economic crisis crashed commodity prices, including oil. Brainard and Cooper (1968) argued that countries rich in natural resources, such as oil, are more vulnerable to economic fluctuations especially high level of primary product export concentration. Similarly, the collapse in crude oil price coupled with low productivity contracted the average annual growth rate of GDP and the country witnessed another recession after 25 years (World Bank, 2019). Economic diversification in developing countries is linked with the structural transformation of their economies and the achievement of higher levels of productivity as a result of the movement of economic resources within and across different sectors.

Before the recession, despite the growth trajectories for almost 15 years, there was little economic development even with the rebasing of the GDP at 2010 constant prices, the structure of the economy remained undiversified; peasant agriculture dominates the economy, manufacturing contributes less than 10% to GDP while the 50% contribution of the services sector to GDP needs to be interpreted with caution (Ekpo, 2016). Data also shows poor economic performance indicator was less than 80% while both unemployment and underemployment averaged 27% in 2015 (National Bureau of Statistics, 2016).

The oil price volatility has frequently led the country's resource expectation into avoidable difficulties resulting in the resurgence of calls for the diversification of the Nigeria revenue base. This is not the first discussion or call on the Nigerian government to embrace economic diversification as a tool to stabilize the Nigerian economy, but the recent economic crises resulting from the decline in global oil prices have heightened the call. Some of the difficulties developing countries experience in attempts at economic diversification include poor infrastructure, poor macroeconomic policies and weak institutions. Economic and political institutions raise business confidence and encourage the improvement of new business activities by generating a friendly investment atmosphere and environment (Cramer, 1999).

Examining the role of institutions is fundamental since a successful diversification process aimed at achieving inclusive and sustainable growth requires a robust efficient and effective institution (Beecroft et al, 2020; Okorie et al, 2020). The 2016 report of United Nations Economic Commission for Africa focused on the importance of implementing and putting in practice the principles of good governance, highlight how effective economic governance institutions are essential for structural transformation and inclusive development in Africa (Food and Agricultural Organisation 2018).

Despite the growing level of concern in understanding the role of institutions in the process of diversification, empirical evidence on the role of institutions in the link between diversification and inclusive growth appears to be limited, as available studies mostly focused on either the link between diversification and the economy or the link between institutions and the economy (see Abubakar, 2020; Isukul, Chizea & Agbugba, 2019; Osabohien, Osabuohien & Ohalete, 2019; Madichie, Osagu & Eze, 2018; Moghaddasi et al, 2017; Eregha & Mesagan (2017; Clark et al, 2016; Uzonwanne, 2015; Esanow, 2012). This paper without claiming to be exhaustive, examines the role institutions play in economic diversification towards achieving inclusive growth in Nigeria using data from 1990 to 2019. In examining the role of institutions in the nexus between economic diversification and inclusive growth, this study particularly relates with a strand of literature (Beecroft, Osabuohien, Efobi, Olurinola & Osabohien, 2020; Osabohien, Osabuohien & Ohalete, 2019; Adeleye, Osabuohien & Bowale, 2017) where the role of institutions is measured as its interactions with some key explanatory variables in relation to the targeted explained variable.

REVIEW OF RELATED LITERATURE

Theoretical Literature

Economic Diversification

Many poor countries which depend so much on primary agriculture or minerals tend to concentrate on economic structure. This exposes them to shocks such as sudden price shocks for minerals or weather-related challenges for those that depend on agriculture. According to Imbs and Wacziarg (2003), for a country with abundant natural resources to experience long term sustainable development, it must first embark on what is called broad-based economic development or more technically, economic diversification. Economic diversification is identified as a key measure of economic development in which a country evolves to a less concentrated production and trade structure. In this regard, a less concentrated production structure would mean a diversified source of earning revenues from different sectors of the economy (Isukul, Chizea & Agbugba, 2019). Economic diversification is the shift to a more varied production, structure, involving the introduction of new or expansion of pre-existing products including higher quality products (International Monetary Fund, 2014). Diversification is a development instrument for providing a stable path for sustainable growth and development as well as mitigate economic challenges such as worsening poverty and unemployment problems.

African Development Bank (2018) suggests that economic diversification is a medium to long term process that requires a transformation from natural resource assets towards a more balanced portfolio of physical and human capital, especially among commodity-exporting nations. In this context, economic diversification is considered an important factor towards improving infrastructure, health, education,

and regulatory framework, thereby leading to inclusive growth. Economic diversification could be a key element of economic development during which a country moves to a more diverse trade and production structure. Successful diversification is imperative to increase the quality and number of job opportunities given the recent slowing of global growth. Expansion in trade can create higher productivity jobs that will facilitate growth through structural changes in the country. For instance, countries in East Asia made such growth transition within the 1990s by moving labour from low productivity employment, mainly in agriculture, to higher labour-intensive manufactures.

Therefore, the authors conceptualise economic diversification as a situation in which an economy has different sources through which they earn revenue without depending on a single source. For instance, Nigeria's heavy dependence on the exportation of crude oil is nowhere near diversification. To be diversified, a country with natural resources like Nigeria should have a modern agricultural sector, a strong manufacturing base and a vibrant dynamic services sector. This is what Ekpo (2016) referred to as economic complexity. To drive the process of economic diversification, the government through the institution has a critical role to play. Ekpo suggested that while diversification is fundamental for sustained and inclusive development, the process must be compelled by the government. Hence, the call for state actions through effective institutions, as well as policy reforms that support a more diversified economy, remains centrally important towards achieving inclusive growth in Nigeria.

Institutions

The concept of institutions has been discussed in different fields but the most common and widely used can be credited to the pioneering work of Douglas North (1990) who defined institutions as the rules of the game in a society, the humanly devised constraints that shape human interaction. They regulate the implementation of contracts, government bureaucracies, property right and rules of law and may have heterogeneous impacts on labour reallocation in the different sectors of an economy. North identifies a set of formal and informal rules that governs individual and organizational behaviours. The formal rules include constitutions, political systems and laws; while the informal institutions refer to as social norms, values and beliefs (Kolawole, 2016). Ostrom (1990) explains institution as a set of working rules used to make decisions in some arena, the usable rules, the actions that should be allowed or constrained, the procedures that must be followed, the information to be provided, as well as the pay-offs to be assigned to individuals depending on their actions. Most times, the conceptualization of institutions allows for the view that institutions are all laws or modes of behaviour, designed to minimize ambiguity arising from incomplete knowledge, regulate the environment and social contact, as well as lower transaction costs (Menard & Shirly, 2005). Institutions structure the incentives which affect behaviour and provide the foundation for economic exchanges. Hence, good institutions, as well as sound policies create an environment that fosters economic sustainable and inclusive growth through efficient and productive use of resources (Egbetokun et al, 2018; 2020). The institutional environment defines how the superstructure operates, how infrastructure is assigned, and the rules of the game would, in turn, determine the nature and structure of economic transformation (Metu, Igbanugo & Okonji, 2018). In other words, institutional differences play an important role in shaping innovation intensity and technological patterns which are top requirements for industrialization and economic growth.

Diversification and Inclusive Growth in the Nigerian Economy

The main aim of engaging in economic diversification is to reduce the negative external shocks that may arise from the losses in export revenues and growth volatility (Briguglio, 2016). But, the magnitude of exposure to this vulnerability depends on the level of export concentration of that economy. Most developing countries are mono-resource economies, depend so much on a single or very few commodities for export earnings and become vulnerable to external commodity price shocks. The rate of economic growth and the volatility of a country's export earnings tend to be directly related to the country's export concentration. We discuss the trend of Nigeria's economic diversification using export concentration index and compared it with some selected sub-Sahara African countries with peculiar developmental challenges as Nigeria. To measure the export concentration levels, we use the Herfindahl-Hirschmann Index (HHI) to capture the degree of product concentration in developing countries by benchmarking the level of economic diversification and growth resilience (change in GDP overtime) (Isukul et al., 2019).

Table 1. Export concentration index for some selected sub-saharan African countries (1995-2017)

Country	1995	2000	2005	2010	2016	2017*	2018*	2019*
Angola	0.85	0.92	0.80	0.88	0.73	0.75	0.72	0.70
Botswana	0.71	0.67	0.78	0.61	0.88	0.81	0.84	0.87
Burkina Faso	0.56	0.54	0.75	0.57	0.75	0.76	0.80	0.84
Equatorial Guinea	0.45	0.80	0.92	0.74	0.68	0.84	0.88	0.92
Ethiopia	0.56	0.48	0.38	0.36	0.30	0.22	0.16	0.10
Gabon	0.81	0.76	0.78	0.82	0.76	0.77	0.77	0.77
Guinea Bissau	0.50	0.59	0.88	0.87	0.88	1.06	1.16	1.26
Liberia	0.80	0.56	0.84	0.41	0.33	0.26	0.15	0.04
Malawi	0.66	0.60	0.56	0.53	0.41	0.38	0.32	0.27
Mali	0.72	0.61	0.58	0.65	0.74	0.68	0.69	0.70
Nigeria	0.85	0.92	0.88	0.80	0.73	0.73	0.69	0.66
Sierra Leone	0.28	0.46	0.47	0.24	0.66	0.58	0.64	0.69
South Africa	0.11	0.14	0.14	0.14	0.12	0.14	0.14	0.14
Sudan	0.30	0.46	0.60	0.81	0.65	0.88	0.98	1.09
Zambia	0.75	0.45	0.52	0.67	0.66	0.62	0.63	0.63

*forecasted figures
Source: UNCTAD (2018), http://unctadstat.unctad.org. (2018)

Table 1 shows that some SSA countries have made some measurable degrees of progress in reducing their export concentration indices in recent years. For instance, countries like Ethiopia, Liberia and Malawi have made some measurable progress in reducing the index of their export concentration. Ethiopia's index reduced from 0.56 in 1995 to 0.30 in 2016 while Malawi reduced its export concentration from 0.66 in 1995 to 0.41 in 2016. Contrary to this, some resource-based countries like Nigeria, Angola and Botswana still have a high export concentration up till 2016. This shows that economic diversification remains a very big challenge for SSA including Nigeria. The continual concentration of exports in a few sectors

has serious implications for inclusive growth, particularly as it limits trade potentials, undermines the ability to create jobs and most of all, it increases the economy's exposure to external economic shocks.

Evidence shows that the Nigerian economy is not diversified making it highly vulnerable to external shocks. Without an improvement in extreme poverty reduction and many of the population still struggling to meet basic needs; sustained, productivity-enhancing economic growth for an improved standard of living becomes critical. Sustained economic growth is a major driver of human development and remains the surest route out of poverty (Metu et al., 2019). Economic growth in Nigeria is subdued and remains potential thereby hampering the achievement of the Sustainable Development Goals (SDGs). Looking at the incidence of inclusive growth, Nigeria is not on the right track towards meeting the SDGs by 2030. There has been a deceleration of extreme poverty reduction in Nigeria even before the economy slipped into a recession in 2016 and missed the 7.4% average GDP growth achieved in 2014. For instance, according to the 2018 World Bank report, almost half the population of Nigeria is living below US$2 per day and unemployment peaked at 23.1% (World Bank, 2018).

Given these unfavourable data, the target of achieving inclusive and sustained growth and development will almost certainly be missed if drastic measures are not taken. Economic growth does not happen in a vacuum, some basic building blocks are needed to jumpstart the process as well as to sustain economic development, particularly for low-income countries (World Economic Forum [WEF], 2019). There is a need to build economic resilience through improved competitiveness given the current volatile geopolitical context we find ourselves as a nation. To assess the drivers of productivity and long-term prosperity, the Global Competitiveness Index (GCI) measures a nation's competitiveness and is defined as the set of institutions, policies, and factors that determine the level of productivity in an economy (WEF, 2019). Building on four decades of benchmarking competitiveness, the new GCI 4.0 sheds light on emerging factors so dire for productivity in the Fourth Industrial Revolution (4IR) and offers a tool for evaluating them. The 2019 GCI 4.0 assess 141 economies using 103 indicators classified into 12 pillars with 3 sub-indexes namely: (i) Enabling environment consisting of institutions, infrastructure, ICT adoption, macroeconomic stability; (ii) Human capital consisting of health and skill; (iii) Markets consisting of product market, labour, financial system, market size; (iv) Innovation and ecosystem consisting of business dynamism and innovation capacity. The GCI 4.0 introduces a new progress score ranging from 0 to 100 representing policy targets. Table 2 shows five pillars of the Global Competitiveness Index for Nigeria compared with some selected oil-producing countries in SSA for 2019.

Table 2. Global competitiveness index 4.0 for some selected SSA countries, 2019

		Enabling Environment			Human Capital	
Country	**GCI Rank**	**INS.**	**ICT**	**MES**	**HEA**	**Sk**
Algeria	89	111	76	102	56	85
Angola	136	135	123	137	127	140
Gabon	119	129	85	77	113	105
Cameroon	123	117	132	79	130	114
Nigeria	116	128	118	130	127	129
Congo DR	139	138	138	140	134	121
Chad	141	137	141	64	138	141

NOTE: INS=Institutions; ICT= ICT Adoption; MES=Macroeconomic Stability; HEA= Health; SK=Skills
Source: World Economic Forum, (2019)

Data on Table 2 shows that on the overall 2019 ranking, Nigeria has not performed any better because it ranks 116 out of 141 economies that participated in the survey. But when we compare it with the previous year's ranking, it is an improvement in global competitiveness. For instance, Nigeria ranked 120 out of 148 countries in the 2013-2014 survey, despite having a favourable GDP growth rate but slipped to 125th position out of 137 countries in the 2016-2017 survey. Nigeria was among the African countries that participated in the 2018-2019 survey. Then in comparison to oil-exporting countries in SSA, Nigeria ranks only behind Algeria (89th) beating Gabon (119), Cameroon (123), and Congo Dr (139) that were above in ranking in previous years. An in-depth analysis of the individual pillars shows that Nigeria performed poorly both in providing the enabling environment and the development of human capital which are very critical for productivity and long-term growth. The country continues to register a profound institutional and infrastructural deficit. The institution remained weak at 128th out of 141 countries with a high level of corruption, insecurity, insufficiently protected property rights, and undue government influences. It also underperformed significantly in providing health and basic education needed for skills development. The country benefited from its large market size (32nd) which is an important factor for economies of scale and bound to attract investment if properly utilized. Nigeria also benefited from the financial market with the financial system recovering after the 2009 crisis. The country requires efforts across many areas to place the country on a sustainable growth path, going forward. More efforts are required to increase long term competitiveness because countries that rank poorly on GCI are less likely to have a productive, competitive, and diversified economy (Isukul et al., 2019).

Empirical Studies

There are a plethora of studies either on the link between diversification and the economy or on the link between institutions and the economy. In either case, there seems to be a consensus that diversification and institutions have a significant positive influence on the overall economy (Abubakar, 2020; Isukul, Chizea & Agbugba, 2019; Osabohien, Osabuohien & Ohalete, 2019; Madichie, et al. 2018; Moghaddasi et al, 2017; Eregha & Mesagan (2017; Clark et al, 2016; Uzonwanne, 2015; Esanow, 2012). With the aim of unbundling institutional framework in the infrastructure-export nexus, Beecrof, et al. (2020) empirically examined the relationship between manufacturing export and ICT infrastructure, and how economic and political institutions influence such interaction, using data from 14 West African countries. The study used the Systems Generalized Method of Moments (SGMM) technique to address possible issues of endogeneity due to reverse causality. The study revealed that, in the face of improved economic and political institutions, particularly those related to enforcement of contracts, the influence of ICT infrastructure in strengthening the exporting capacity from the manufacturing sector is greater.

Abubakar (2020) examined the directional effect of institutional quality through contract intensive money and effective governance index to economic growth in Nigeria using annual time series data covering the period 1979 to 2018. The study hinges on both the Solow-Swan neoclassical growth model and Washington Consensus to provide insight on the policy necessity for institutional quality. The study employed both the Johansen Cointegration and Ordinary Least Square (OLS) approach and the results show that economic growth responds positively significantly to institutional quality (contract intensive money), while effective governance index exerts positive and insignificant influence on the economy. The study further revealed that economic growth responds positively and negative to the effect of the variables of domestic investment and foreign direct investment, although the negative effect was significant.

Isukul, et al. (2019) employed a case study methodology to examine diversification in developing countries, to draw lessons from countries who have failed to make the diversification and from those who have made the diversification to Nigeria. The study revealed that diversification is not only a Nigerian problem as several African countries have diversification issues. While noting that diversification is a complex process which needs an enabling environment, the study identified a right institutional mix (financial, legal, regulatory and market institutions), good infrastructure, human capital development, entrepreneurship combined with the right policy mix sustained over a considerable period as the necessary factors for a successful diversification.

Osabohien, et al. (2019) examined how the performance of the agricultural sector can be enhanced in the long-run through institutional framework thereby ensuring food security in Nigeria. They employed the ARDL (Autoregressive Distributed Lag) to estimate food security as a function of agricultural sector performance, institutional framework and population. The findings show that in the long-run, agriculture production and agriculture credit (agriculture variables) will increase food security by reducing the number of people undernourished by 2% and 18%, respectively. In terms of the institutional framework; political stability and absence of violence and rule of law increased food security by reducing undernourishment by approximately 69% and 29%, respectively; control of corruption and voice and accountability tends to reduce food security by increasing the number of the people undernourished by 74%, 51% and 63% respectively.

Madichie, et al. (2018) examined the imperative of economic diversification in trade and industrial policies in Nigeria. Based on annualized secondary time series, spanning from 1970 to 2015, the study employed the Autoregressive Distributed Lag (ARDL) model in achieving its objective. The results show that manufacturing output, crude petroleum and natural gas production, as well as mining production, have significant positive longrun impact on economic growth in Nigeria.

Ejemeyovwi, Osabuohien, and Osabohien (2018) explored the linkage between the investment in information and telecommunication technology (ICT) and human capital development on economic transformation in Economic Communities of West African States (ECOWAS). This study engaged the generalized method of moments (GMM) in achieving its objective. The study found, among other things, that investment in ICT did not have a statistically significant relationship with human development. The study pointed out that factors responsible for the non-significant impact of investment in telecommunications on human development could be attributed to the relatively low investment in telecommunications accompanied with a high cost of acquisition of the technology in ECOWAS and harsh policy environment.

Adeleye, et al. (2017) employed the system-generalized method of moments (sys-GMM) technique to examine the role of institutions in the finance-inequality nexus based on a sample of 42 Sub-Saharan African (SSA) countries from 1996 to 2015. The study found that inequality is persistent in the region; financial development does not significantly reduce income inequality; and the control of corruption and its interaction with domestic credit exhibit an Inverted-U relation with income inequality.

Moghaddasi et al, (2017) examined the export diversification and agricultural growth in developed countries using a panel data set of 20 developed countries from 2000 to 2014. The study used the Herfindahl index for export diversity and GLS method to examine dynamic interactions among the variables. Main results showed that openness, export diversification, rainfall, capital stock, total factor productivity and EU membership had a positive effect on agricultural growth while labour force was negatively related to it. The study recommended that governments should support entrepreneurship and provide all prerequisites to motivate investments in new kind of activities and products in agriculture.

Eregha and Mesagan (2017) analysed the issues involved in inclusive growth as well as the challenges faced by Nigeria. The study identified and discussed issues like economic growth, green growth, inclusive green growth and inclusive growth using the descriptive method. The study concluded that human capital investment, job creation, structural transformation, social protection and quality institutions were the key determinants of inclusive growth in Nigeria. The study further posited that Nigeria is still far away from realistically being able to achieve inclusive growth given that dependency ratio, poverty and depletion of natural capital is very high in the country.

Clark et al, (2016) examined the relationship between three manufacturing diversification stages and level of economic development for 29 African countries. Considerable differences in diversification were found over the first stage at the low end of the per capita income scale. The study recommends that diversification alone will not encourage development in poorer countries until obstacles such as weak institutions, poor governance and lack of infrastructure are addressed. The results further showed that countries further along the African economic development path successfully diversified in manufacturing. However, greater openness and resource intensity were found to encourage diversification. On the contrary, Ansu (2013) argued that Structural Adjustment Programme (SAP) imposed by the International Monetary Fund (IMF) and World Bank may have limited manufacturing diversification by discouraging the use of targeted industrial policies to support specific activities.

Uzonwanne (2015) examined out how diversification of the economy will enhance stable and viable economic growth in Nigeria. The descriptive statistical method was employed for the study and like other similar studies found that there exists a positive relationship between economic growth in Nigeria and diversification. According to the study, the Nigerian economy was healthy and vibrant due to proper management of human resources, huge investment and concentration on agriculture. Esanow (2012) in examining the determinants and dynamics of economic diversification discovered that the quality of institutions and infrastructure are important determinants of economic diversification.

DATA TYPE AND METHODOLOGY

Theoretical Framework and the Model

To explore the link between diversification and inclusive growth, the study adopts the simple Solow growth model. Hence efficient institutional quality with diversification can boost economic growth. The Solow growth model can be represented in a mathematical form using the Cobb-Douglas production function as follows:

$$Y = A\,F\,(K, L) \tag{1}$$

Where, Y, K, L are aggregate real output, capital and labour respectively while A is the technical progress or total factor productivity.

Modern economic growth depends on the accumulation of physical capital and an increase in the labour force with improved technology without which labour cannot be effective. Economic growth and distribution, in turn, depends on policy and non-policy factors (UNECA, 2019). Hence, it will not be out of place to say that inclusiveness of growth is influenced by policy and non-policy factors that affect economic growth. The framework for this study is adopted from Haung and Quibria (2013) which suggest that inclusive growth measurement must enhance benefit sharing and participation. The authors included three indicators – income, poverty and inequality - in their analysis. The measurement of inclusive growth is inspired by the work of Haung and Quibria (2013) which is modified to reflect the Nigerian economy. Inclusive growth is measured in terms of the percentage change in the inequality-adjusted human development index (*IHDI*). To determine the impact of economic diversification on inclusive growth with particular reference to the role of institutions, we develop two models as specified in Equations 2 and 3. Equation 2 is an inclusive growth model for determining the individual impact of economic diversification, institutions and other control variables. Equation 3 is an interactive model where the interaction between economic diversification and institution is incorporated to determine the role of institutions in facilitating the process of diversification. Thus, the models of this study are specified as follows:

Model 1:

$$INCGR = f\,(EDI,\ INS,\ IND,\ TRA,\ INF) \qquad (2)$$

Model 2:

$$INCGR = f\,(EDI{*}INS,\ IND,\ TRA,\ INF) \qquad (3)$$

In the equations, *INCGR* denotes the inclusive growth variable which is obtained as the percentage change in the inequality-adjusted human development index. Following the United Nations Development Programme (2011), the authors calculated the annual data for the Inequality-Adjusted Human Development Index (*IHDI*) following the work of Haung and Quibria (2013). The IHDI means that the human development index is adjusted for inequality element to ensure that the measure of inclusive growth implies that inclusiveness requires that the benefits of growth are equitably shared by everyone (Metu et al., 2019).

The *EDI* stands for the economic diversification index measured in terms of export diversification index. The *EDI* signals whether the structure of exports by the products of a given country or group of countries differ from the structure of the products of the world. The *EDI* is computed by measuring the absolute deviation of a country's share from the world's structure. The score of the diversification index, which ranges from 0 to 1, reveals the extent of the differences between the structure of trade of a country or country group and the world average. The index value closer to 1 indicates a higher difference from the world average. It is constructed as the inverse of a Herfindahl index, using disaggregated exports (World Bank, 2018). A diversified export base is expected to spur domestic output as well as create jobs and raise the income for most vulnerable groups, especially in labour-intensive sectors. Imbs and Wacziarg (2003) show that no country has been able to achieve significant growth and poverty reduction without economic diversification and structural transformation.

The *INS* denotes institutions which are measured in scores to show the quality of public administration, business environment and transparency in the conduct of public policy. The *INS* score ranges from 1 to 6, with 1 indicating poor quality of institutions and 6 indicating excellent quality of institutions. The inclusive growth agenda entails establishing standards and conditions to foster resource mobilisation, build strong institutions and enhance greater participation to promote broad-based growth (AfDB, 2012). Excellent public administration, conducive business environment and transparency in the conduct of public policy will encourage job creation, create a more stable and secure society and promote public participation.

The *TRA* stands for trade openness, which is defined as the ratio of total trade (export plus import) to gross domestic product (GDP). The *TRA* shows the extent to which a country is open to cross-board trade. The trade openness which has been argued to be a key recipe for an increase in economies of scale, technology transfer and other positive externalities that positively affect growth (UNECA, 2019). Trade openness is expected to increase diversity for intermediate inputs that will yield greater productivity, increased growth which will have a trickle-down effect on the people.

The *IND* stands for industry value-added and was added because as industrialisation takes place, the structure of the economy changes, leading to diversification, income growth, and overall improvements in standards of living. The *IND* measures the contribution of the private industry or government sector to overall GDP. The components of value-added consist of compensation of employees, taxes on production and imports less subsidies, as well as gross operating surplus. Value-added equals the difference between the industry's gross output (consisting of sales or receipts and other operating income, commodity taxes, and inventory change) and the cost of its intermediate inputs (including energy, raw materials, semi-finished goods, and services that are purchased from all sources) (AfDB, 2012).

The *INF* stands for infrastructure and is defined as a set of fundamental facilities and systems that are made up of public and private physical structures serving a country, including the services and facilities such as roads, railways, bridges, tunnels, water supply, sewers, electrical grids, and telecommunication (including internet connectivity and broadband speeds), which are necessary for the economy to function. The *INF* is measured in the form of an index of infrastructure on a range of values from 0 to 1, with 0 indicating the poorest level of infrastructure and 1 indicating the highest level of infrastructure. Improved infrastructure will increase the rate of productivity and competitiveness in an economy, lower the cost of doing business, facilitate trade activities and encourage investments that will create employment opportunities and spread to the members of the society (AfDB, 2012). While poor quality and unevenly distributed infrastructure is a constraint to the growth of commercial and informal activities.

The *EDI*INS*, as shown in Equation 2, is the interaction effect of economic diversification *EDI* and institutions *INS* to account for the role of institutions in the diversification process. It is measured as the product of *EDI* and *INS*. In specifying Equation 2, we removed *EDI* and *INS* from Equation 1 and replace them with a single variable *EDI*INS*, which is the product of *EDI* and *INS* to account for the role of institutions in the diversification process. The omission of *EDI* and *INS* from Equation 2 was to avoid the potential problem of multicollinearity that may arise due to the near-perfect association that is likely to exist between *EDI* and *EDI*INS*, and/or *INS* and *EDI*INS*.

Specifying our models in their full econometric forms and applying the natural log-linear transformation of all variables, our empirical models become:

$$LINCGR = \beta_0 + \beta_1 LEDI + \beta_2 LINS + \beta_3 LIND + \beta_4 LTRA + \beta_5 LINF + \mu \quad (4)$$

$$LINCGR = \alpha_0 + \alpha_1 L(EDI * INS) + \alpha_2 LIND + \alpha_3 LTRA + \alpha_4 LINF + \nu \quad (5)$$

Where, *L* denotes natural log notation; βi and αi (where $i = 0, 1, 2...5$) stand for the parameter estimates, and μ and ν are the uncorrelated random error disturbances (with usual properties: $N[0, \sigma^2]$). It should be noted that the log-linear transformation of the models is necessary to overcome any possible problem of the wide variation in data, as well as for the easy interpretation of coefficients as elasticities. The data relating to the relevant variables were obtained from the African Development Bank Socio-Economic Database (2020), and the United Nations Conference on Trade and Development, (2018).

Estimation Technique

Before the estimation of the models, we investigate the time-series properties of the relevant data to ensure consistency in subsequent econometric modelling. The Augmented Dickey-Fuller (ADF) unit root procedure was employed to determine the stationarity properties of the relevant time series as well as identify the order of integration of those time series. It is widely known meaningful economic policy can barely be generated from an OLS regression involving non-stationary time series.

Given that statistic underpinning of modern time-series analyses requires data to be covariance stationary, and that most economic time series display significant trends has led to the use of first difference stationary time series before estimating economic models. As pointed out by Engle and Granger (1987), even though economic series may wander over time, economic theory often provides a rationale as to why certain variables should obey equilibrium constraints. In other words, there may exist some linear combinations of variables that, over time, converge to equilibrium. If the individual non-stationary economic series becomes stationary after differencing, but the linear combination of their levels is stationary, then the series is said to be cointegrated. However, this test for cointegration proposed by Engle and Granger (EG) does not reveal the existence of more than one cointegrating vectors, and more importantly, their test relies on a super-convergence result and usually applies the OLS to obtain the estimates of the cointegrating vector. These OLS estimates, in practice, will differ with the arbitrary normalization implicit in the selection of the left-hand-side variables for the regression equation; and besides, different arbitrary normalization may, in practice, alter the EG test results (Nwaobi, 2001).

In contrast, Johansen and Juselius (1990) provide an alternative procedure for examining the question of cointegration in a multivariate setting. The Johansen approach yields the maximum likelihood estimators of the unconstrained cointegrating vector, as well as allows one to explicitly test for the number of cointegrating vectors. This approach does not rely on an arbitrary normalization, and test of certain restrictions suggested by economic theory such as the signs and magnitude of the estimated parameters may also be conducted (Nwaobi, 2001). In the light of the foregoing, this study employed the Johansen cointegration test for determining the existence of a long-run relationship between the dependent and independent variables, as well as generates the normalized cointegrating coefficients of the Johansen procedure. The Johansen cointegration test is based on estimating the following vector autoregressive (VAR) model:

$$Zt = A1Zt\text{-}1 + \text{- - - -} + ApZt\text{-}p + \beta Yt + \mu t \qquad (6)$$

Where: Zt is a k-vector of non-stationary variables; Yt is a d-vector of deterministic variables, and μt is a vector of innovations.

RESULT AND DISCUSSION

Table 3 presents evidence on the presence of unit roots in our variables based on the commonly used test, the Augmented Dickey-Fuller test. Looking at the levels of the variables, there is (not surprising though) strong evidence in favour of the null hypothesis of non-stationarity. This is because all the test statistics (absolute values) were less than the critical values at the 5% levels. However, the tests generally provide support for the rejection of the null hypothesis of non-stationarity of the series at their first differences, meaning that all the original series are all *I(1)*.

Table 3. ADF unit root test results

Variable	ADF Statistic		Order of Integration I(d)
	Level	1st diff.	
LINCGR	-1.805423	-4.761155**	I(1)
LEDI	1.509228	-4.982250*	I(1)
L_EDI_INS	-1.305539	-6.143075**	I(1)
LIND	-0.551111	-4.890016**	I(1)
LTRA	-2.641468	-5.895076**	I(1)
LINF	-1.029964	-5.070169**	I(1)
LINS	-1.881009	-6.425659**	I(1)

NB: **(*) implies significant at 1%(5%) level.
Source: Authors' Computation using EVIEWS 10

Following the test of the unit root above, we present the results of the Johansen cointegration tests for the two models of this study in Table 4. In the first model which deals with the individual impact of economic diversification and institution on inclusive growth, the variables are ordered as follows: *LINCGR, LEDI, LINS, LIND, LTRA, LINF*, with the assumption of linear deterministic trend and lag interval between 1 and 2. The second model which interacts diversification with institutions (the role institution in diversification process) has its variables ordered as follows: *LINCGR, L_EDI_INS, LIND, LTRA, LINF*, with the assumption of linear deterministic trend and lag interval between 1 and 2. These results are based on trace statistic and are reported in Table 4 as follows:

Table 4. Results of cointegration tests

Hypothesized No. of CE(s): Model 1	Trace Statistic	0.05 Critical Value	Hypothesized No. of CE(s): Model 2	Trace Statistic	0.05 Critical Value
None*	190.6634	95.75366	None*	95.96114	69.81889
At most 1*	127.1327	69.81889	At most 1*	53.94467	47.85613
At most 2*	79.46498	47.85613	At most 2	23.74276	29.79707
At most 3*	40.26392	29.79707	At most 3	6.865180	15.49471
At most 4	14.87008	15.49471	At most 4	1.401979	3.841466
At most 5	0.392952	3.841466			

Trace test indicates 4 cointegrating eqn(s) in Model 1 and 2 cointegrating eqn(s) in Model 2 at the 0.05 level.
* denotes rejection of the hypothesis at the 0.05 level.
Source: Authors' Computation using EVIEWS 10

As shown in Table 4, the null hypothesis of no cointegration among the relevant variables is rejected as the trace statistic indicates 4 cointegrating equations in Model 1 and 2 cointegrating equations in Model 2. This implies that consistent and meaningful estimates of both long-run and short-run coefficients can be generated from both models, even in the face of non-stationary variables, as a deviation from equilibrium is expected to be a temporal phenomenon given that equilibrium must be re-established in the long-run. Therefore, it becomes safe to report the normalized cointegrating coefficients of the Johansen procedure as follows:

Table 5. Normalized cointegrating coefficients of the Johansen procedure

Variable	Model 1 (Individual Impact of EDI & INS)	Model 2 (The Role of Institution: EDI*INS)
LEDI	0.115306 (1.748351)	
LINS	0.217016** (4.535855)	
LIND	0.937325* (2.184940)	0.229790* (2.013096)
LTRA	0.188608** (2.910872)	0.260286** (3.015061)
LINF	0.328136* (2.051083)	0.164086* (2.518553)
L_EDI_INS		0.932561** (4.411914)
Log-likelihood	237.5146	126.6097
Dependent Variable: LINCGR		

NB: **(*) implies significant at 1%(5%) level.
Figures in parenthesis () are the t-statistics.
Source: Authors' Computation using EVIEWS 10

Table 5 presents the normalized cointegrating coefficients of the Johansen procedure for Models 1 and 2. The normalized cointegrating coefficients are usually reported as the long-run model of cointegrated variables respect to the variable of interests (core dependent variables). These coefficients are generated by multiplying both sides of the equation of the normalized segment of the Johansen output by -1. The robustness of these estimates is usually determined by observing the value of the log-likelihood that measures the goodness of fit of a statistical model to a sample of data for the given values of the unknown parameters. In the case of this study, the log-likelihood for both Models 1 and 2 are positive and reasonably high, meaning that the long-run coefficients are based on a good fit. Also, it should be observed that the signs of the coefficients of the control variables remained the same for Models 1 and 2.

From Model 1 which shows the individual impact of diversification and institution on inclusive growth in Nigeria, all the estimated coefficients are individually statistically significant at either 1% or 5% level of significance except the coefficient of economic diversification (*LEDI*), which is not statistically significant. In line with the a priori expectation, all the estimated coefficients are rightly signed. More elaborately, this result shows that economic diversification has a significant positive impact on inclusive growth in the long run. In terms of magnitude, a percentage increase in diversification index is, by this result, expected to bring about a 0.12% increase in inclusive growth rate in Nigeria over the long-run. Also, the result shows that institution has a significant positive impact on inclusive growth rate in Nigeria in the long-run. Thus, a percentage increase in the performance score of institutions is expected to significantly translate to about 0.22% increase in inclusive growth in the long-run. Other significant determinants of inclusive growth incorporated in Model 1 include the industry value-added (*LIND*), trade openness (*LTRA*), and the level of infrastructure (*LINF*). For instance, a percentage rise in industry value-added could improve inclusive growth by 0.94% percentage. This may be attributed to the relatively more employment opportunities created in the industrial sector. Trade openness also has a significant positive effect on inclusive growth. This is not surprising given that Nigeria has enjoyed tremendous benefits from trading with other nations.

Model 2 shows the role of institutions in the diversification process, by way of interaction between diversification and institution, as well as how this interaction affects the inclusive growth rate in Nigeria. The essence of Model 2, as stated in the previous section, is to unveil how the interplay between economic diversification and institution affects the inclusive growth rate. In Model 2, the control variables (*LIND, LTRA & LINF*) of Model 1 were retained, and the signs of their estimated coefficients remained the same as in Model 1. The variables, *LEDI* and *LINS*, were removed and replaced with their interaction variable (*L_EDI_INS*) in Model 2 to avoid the likely problem of multicollinearity. The result shows that the interactive coefficient of economic diversification and institution (*L_EDI_INS*) has a significant positive impact on inclusive growth rate in Nigeria over the long-run. In terms of magnitude, a percentage increase in the interaction between economic diversification and institution is expected to significantly translate to about 0.93% increase in inclusive growth rate. Interestingly, economic diversification in Nigeria does not generate a significant impact on inclusive growth in Nigeria. This is not an entirely peculiar phenomenon as efforts towards economic diversification in Nigeria has never been met despite the attendant revenue generated from the sale of crude oil over the years. According to Ekpo (2016), Nigeria dependence on the export of crude petroleum is not diversification. Interestingly, when diversification interacted with institutions, the result shows a positive and significant effect on achieving inclusive growth. The study by ECA, (2019) found a similar result, although they did not interact institution with diversification which is different from the present study. The present result shows that the institutions have critical role to play in aiding diversification, especially to achieve inclusive growth in Nigeria.

Following the Johansen cointegration test and the report of the normalized cointegrating coefficients, we proceeded to the estimation of the short-run dynamics for Models 1 and 2, which are based on the parsimonious error correction specifications. The parsimonious error correction models (PECMs) were derived from the over-parameterized models through the general-to-specific framework of specifications. The major concern of the PECMs was to establish whether a strong feedback effect of deviation of the dependent variable *(LINCGR)* from its long-run growth path could be consistently generated, as well as to ascertain the speed of adjustment from short-run shocks to long-run equilibrium. For the estimated PECMs, the values of the error correction terms, *ECM(-1)*, from Models 1 and 2 were about -0.1358 and -0.1417 respectively, and were statistically significant at the 5% level, meaning that about 13.58% and 14.17% of the disequilibrium arising from short-run shocks in Models 1 and 2 were corrected in each period (annually).

CONCLUSION AND RECOMMENDATIONS

The study investigated the role of institutions in the target of inclusive growth through the process of economic diversification in Nigeria. This study was motivated by the fact that poor inclusive growth rates remain a source of concern in Nigeria given that a greater percentage of economic agents are being excluded in the growth process of the economy. In identifying economic diversification as a key recipe towards achieving the objective of inclusive growth in Nigeria, the role of institutions in strengthening the process of diversification was not ruled out. In this study, we developed an interactive model of inclusive growth where the interaction between economic diversification and institution is observed, such that the impact the interaction has on inclusive growth could be empirically investigated. The study is based on time-series data obtained from the AfDB Socio-Economic Database (2020) and UNCTAD (2018) over the period 1990 – 2019. The ADF test of unit root, and the Johansen cointegration test were carried out to determine the stationarity characteristics of the relevant variables, as well as establish the existence of a long-run relationship between the dependent and independent variables. The results show that economic diversification in Nigeria does not significantly contribute to inclusive growth, but a successful interaction with the institution yielded a positive significant result. This means that the role of institutions in strengthening the positive impact of economic diversification on inclusive growth is never in doubt.

The authors, therefore, conclude that economic diversification cannot sufficiently translate to inclusive growth without the institutions. Infrastructure and trade openness was also found to enhance inclusive growth in Nigeria. Based on the findings, it is recommended that government should formulate and implement institution strengthening policies in the area of public administration to support economic diversification and encourage inclusive growth. The government should provide infrastructures and business-friendly environment to encourage investment. Both domestic and foreign investment will help develop Nigeria into a vibrant economy, create more employment and in turn translate to economic growth and social well-being. Essentially, diversification should be export-driven, but the government should be cautious in exporting natural resources and agricultural products without value addition. Amongst all, there must be a serious commitment from stakeholders and the government for the diversification to help in achieving sustainable and inclusive growth.

REFERENCES

Abubakar, S. (2020). Institutional Quality and Economic Growth: Evidence from Nigeria. *African Journal of Economic Review*, *8*(I).

Adeleye, N., Osabuohien, E., & Asongu, S. (2020). Agro-Industrialisation and Financial Intermediation in Nigeria. *African Journal of Economic and Management Studies*, *11*(3), 443–456. Advance online publication. doi:10.1108/AJEMS-02-2019-0078

Adeleye, N., Osabuohien, E., & Bowale, E. (2017). The role of institutions in the finance-inequality nexus in sub-Saharan Africa. *Journal of Contextual Economics*, *137*(1-2), 173–192. doi:10.3790/jce.137.1-2.173

African Development Bank (AfDB). (2018). *African economic outlook, 2018*. African Development Bank. Retrieved from www.afdb.org

African Development Bank (AfDB). (2020). *Socio-economic database*. Retrieved from: https://dataportal.opendataforafrica.org/nbyenxf/afdb-socio-economic-database-1960-2020

Ansu, Y. (2013). Industrial policy and economic transformation in Africa: Strategies for development and a research agenda. In J. E. Stiglitz, J. L. Yifu, & E. Patel (Eds.), *The industrial policy revolution II. International Economic Association Series*. Palgrave Macmillan. doi:10.1057/9781137335234_19

Beecroft, I., Osabuohien, E. S., Efobi, U. R., Olurinola, I., & Osabohien, R. A. (2020). Manufacturing export and ICT infrastructure in West Africa: Investigating the roles of economic and political institutions. *Institutions, Etc.*, *12*(1), 1–36.

Brainard, W. & Cooper, R. (1968). Uncertainty and diversification of international trade. *Food Research Institute Studies in Agricultural Economics, Trade, and Development, 8,* 257-85.

Briguglio, L. P. (2016). Exposure to external shocks and economic resilience of countries: Evidence from global indicators. *Journal of Economic Studies (Glasgow, Scotland)*, *43*(6), 1057–1078. doi:10.1108/JES-12-2014-0203

Clark, D., Renato, L., & Charles, S. (2016). Stages of diversification in Africa. *Economics Letters*, *144*, 68–70. doi:10.1016/j.econlet.2016.05.001

Cramer, C. (1999). *The economics of political economy of conflict in sub-Saharan Africa.* CDPR Discussion Paper 1099. Retrieved from www.soas.ac.uk

Egbetokun, S., Osabuohien, E., & Akinbobola, T. (2018). Feasible Environmental Kuznets and Institutional Quality in North and Southern African Sub-regions. *International Journal of Energy Economics and Policy*, *8*(1), 104–115.

Egbetokun, S., Osabuohien, E., Onanuga, O., Akinbobola, T., Gershon, O., & Okafor, V. (2020). Environmental Pollution, Economic Growth and Institutional Quality: Exploring the Nexus in Nigeria. *Management of Environmental Quality*, *31*(1), 18–31. doi:10.1108/MEQ-02-2019-0050

Ejemeyovwi, J. O., Osabuohien, E. S., & Osabohien, R. (2018). ICT investments, human capital development and institutions in ECOWAS. *International Journal of E-Business Research*, *15*(4), 463.

Ekpo, A. H. (2013). *Rethinking institutions and economic development: is there a new framework?* Paper presented at the 54th Annual Conference of the Nigerian Economic Society, Abuja.

Ekpo, A. H. (2016). Education and economic diversification for self-reliance in Nigeria. *West African Financial and Economic Review*, *11*(2), 1–22.

Engel, R. F., & Granger, C. W. J. (1987). Cointegration and error correction representation, estimation and testing. *Econometrica*, *55*(2), 251–276. doi:10.2307/1913236

Eregha, P. B., & Mesagan, E. P. (2017). *The emergence of inclusive growth: Issues, challenges and policy options for Nigeria.* Munich Personal RePEc Archive (MPRA), Paper No. 95671. Available at: https://www.researchgate.net/deref/https%3A%2F%2Fmpra.ub.uni muenchen.de%2F95671%2F

Esanow, A. (2012). *Economic diversification: Dynamics, determinants and policy implications*. Review Watch Institute.

Food and Agricultural Organisation. (2018). *Institutions, economic freedom and structural transformation in 11 SSA countries.* FAO Agricultural Development Economics Working Paper 18-01. Rome: Food and Agricultural Organisation of United Nations.

Huang, Y., & Quibria, M. G. (2013). *The global partnership for inclusive growth.* WIDER Working Paper No. 2013/059.

Imbs, J., & Wacziarg, R. (2003). Stages of diversification. *The American Economic Review*, *93*(1), 63–86. doi:10.1257/000282803321455160

International Monetary Fund (IMF). (2014). *Long-run growth and macroeconomic stability in low-income countries: The role of structural transformation and diversification. IMF Policy Paper*. International Monetary Fund.

Isukul, A. C., Chizea, J. J., & Agbugba, I. K. (2019). Economic diversification in Nigeria: Lessons from other countries of Africa. *DBN Journal of Economics and Sustainable Development.* Retrieved from www.devbankng.com

Johansen, S., & Juselius, K. (1990). Maximum likelihood estimation and inference on cointegration with application to the demand for money. *Oxford Bulletin of Economics and Statistics*, *52*(2), 169–210. doi:10.1111/j.1468-0084.1990.mp52002003.x

Kolawole, B. O. (2016). Public spending, institutional quality and inclusive growth in Nigeria: An econometric assessment. *Proceedings of the 2015 Nigerian Economic Society Conference*, 235-264.

Madichie, C. V., Osagu, F., & Eze, A. E. (2018). Economic diversification: Imperative for trade and industrial policies in Nigeria. *Timisoara Journal of Economics and Business*, *11*(1), 67–86. doi:10.2478/tjeb-2018-0005

Menard, C., & Shirley, M. M. (2005). *Handbook of new institutional economics.* Springer. doi:10.1007/b106770

Metu, A. G., Igbanugo, I. C., & Okonji, S. O. (2018). Economic diversification, institutional environment and industrialization in Nigeria. *International Journal of Economics, Commerce and Management*, *6*(12), 10-25. Retrieved from http://ijecm.co.uk/

Metu, A. G., Maduka, O. D., Eze, A. E., & Ajudua, E. (2019). Impact of fiscal policy on inclusive growth in Nigeria. *African Journal of Sustainable Development*, *9*(2).

Moghaddasi, R., Sadeghi, E., Hosseini, S., & Mohammadi, A. (2017). Export diversification and agricultural growth: Evidence from developed countries. *Journal of Economics*, *1*, 1–13. doi:10.1016/j.econ.2017.07.001

North, D. (1990). *Institutions, institutional change and economic performance.* Cambridge University Press. doi:10.1017/CBO9780511808678

Nwaobi, G. C. (2001). Modern econometric modelling for developing economies I. Lagos: Quantitative Economic Research Bureau (QUANTERB).

Okorie, U., Osabuohien, E., & Oaikhenan, H. (2020). Electricity Consumption, Public Agricultural Expenditure and Output in Nigeria: A Time Series Dynamic Approach. *International Journal Energy Economics and Policy*, *10*(2), 113–123. doi:10.32479/ijeep.8436

Oparah, E. N. (2018). Diversification of the Nigerian economy: The role of Nigerian institute of Leather and Science Technology (NILEST), Zaria Kaduna Nigeria. In B. Anan & A. S. Antai (Eds.), The Nigerian economy: Recession, recovery and growth plan (pp. 2-8). KEJA Publications.

Osabohien, R., Osabuohien, E., & Ohalete, P. (2019). Agricultural Sector Performance, Institutional Framework and Food Security in Nigeria. *Bio-Based and Applied Economics*, *8*(2), 161–178.

Ostrom, E. (1990). *Governing the commons: The evolution of institutions for collective action*. Cambridge University Press. doi:10.1017/CBO9780511807763

Oyebola, P. O., Osabuohien, E., & Obasaju, B. (2020). Employment and Income Effects of Nigeria's Agricultural Transformation Agenda: Evidence from Cattle Value Chain. *African Journal of Economic and Management Studies*, *11*(2), 317–329. doi:10.1108/AJEMS-12-2018-0402

United Nations Conference on Trade and Development. (2018). *Trade and development report 2018*. UNCTAD. Retrieved from www.unctad.org

United Nations Development Programme. (2011). *Sustainability and equity: A better future for all*. Palgrave Macmillan.

United Nations Economic Commission for Africa. (2019). *Drivers of inclusive growth in Africa*. Economic Commission for Africa.

Uzonwanne, M. C. (2015). Economic diversification in Nigeria in the face of dwindling oil revenue. *Journal of Economics and Sustainable Development*, *6*(4), 61–67.

World Bank. (2018). *Strengthening economic diversification in Nigeria through connectivity*. Retrieved from https://www.worldbank.org/en/country/nigeria/publication/strengthening-economic-diversification-in-nigeria-through-connectivity

World Bank. (2019). *The World Bank in Nigeria*. Retrieved from https://www.worldbank.org/en/country/nigeria/overview

World Economic Forum. (2019). *The global competitiveness report 2019*. World Economic Forum. Retried from www.weforum.org/gcr

Chapter 7
The Growth Effects of Financial Development Over Economic Cycle in South Africa

Naser Yenus Nuru
Adigrat University, Ethiopia

Hayelom Yrgaw Gereziher
Adigrat University, Ethiopia

ABSTRACT

This study examines the effects of financial development, proxied by domestic credit, on growth for South Africa across the states of the economy over the sample period 1970Q1-2019Q3. To address this point, the authors use Jorda's local projection method to generate impulse response functions for this small developing open economy. The shocks, however, are identified by applying short-run contemporaneous restrictions in a vector autoregressive model based on Cholesky identification scheme. The states of the economy are determined by a threshold variable, namely output growth. The results indicate that one standard deviation shock in domestic credit leads to a significant increment in output in this economy. This effect, though, is a bit pronounced in recession than the expansion state. One standard deviation shock in domestic credit leads to around 0.8 and 0.5% increment in output in recession and expansion states at the fourth quarter and on impact, respectively. The results are also robust to an alternative proxy variable of financial development.

INTRODUCTION

The unanswered intuition behind the long-run sustainable economic growth and reasons for cross country growth differences between countries has always attracted considerable attention in the literature. Since the economic performance of a country determines the welfare of a country substantially researchers and economists are striving to determine the source of economic growth to implement accurate economic policies (Betül, 2014).

DOI: 10.4018/978-1-7998-4817-2.ch007

In the literature of economic growth, so many explanations and empirical investigations are stated about the sources of economic growth and development. The financial crisis that has happened in the 1970s marked the fall of the Keynesian view and rise of the neoclassical (Brian and Odhiambo, 2018). As a result, according to the neoclassical theory, countries transformed their policies towards trade liberalization after the 1980s. Hence, an interaction between the financial sector and the real sector is observed recently and considerable attention is given in the finance-growth literature. The financial crisis of 2008 made economists interested in reexamining the effect of financial development on the real economy. Prior to the financial crisis, there was a strong belief that financial development leads every economy to growth and development since information asymmetry and transaction costs are minimal in financially advanced systems (Ebru, 2016).

According to Demirgüç-Kunt and Levine (2008), the overall functions of the financial system is to reduce information and transaction costs impeding economic activity. It has five core functions played by the financial system (i) financial systems produce information and allocate capita, (ii) financial systems monitor firm behavior and exert corporate governance, (iii) financial instruments, intermediaries, and markets can facilitate the trading, (iv) financial systems pool or mobilize savings from different savers for investment, and (v) at a more fundamental level, financial instruments, intermediaries, and markets can stimulate specialization, innovation, and growth by reducing transactions costs. On the other hand, Beck, *et al.* (2014) argued that an oversized financial system leads to instability, imperfect competition, wastage of resources, rent extraction, negative externalities from auxiliary financial services and implicit insurances due to bailouts. Such externalities from auxiliary financial services, for example, can be useful for some clients but not for the whole society as it may lead the financial sector to grow too large relative to its social optimum. Hence, there could be limits to the financial benefits.

Therefore, the growth effects of financial development cannot be generalized for all countries. The differences across countries lead to the unique transmission mechanism of financial development on economic growth (José, *et al.* 2019; Al-Yousif, 2002). Another explanation for the puzzling results of previous studies is that the empirical results of the growth impact of financial development are sensitive to the choice of financial development indicator (Adu *et al.*, 2013). Furthermore, previous studies, at least for South Africa, ignore the effects of economic cycles on the finance-growth nexus. According to the finance constraint theory, the economic cycle has inconsistent impacts on agents depending on their exposure to agency problem and asymmetric information. Hence, agents may respond to shocks in a financial sector differently across different cycles of the economy. This gap is going to be addressed in this paper by using the case of South Africa.

Similar to other developing countries, South Africa faced the effects of the 2008 global financial crisis, which disrupted – and in some cases reverse – the achievement of Millennium Development Goals, including decent work for all. This is of particular concern given that, even in the pre-crisis period, growth patterns in certain regions, notably in Africa, led to only negligible reductions in poverty. Decent living and working conditions still remain out of reach for large numbers of people. Importantly, the crisis spread throughout the real economy by important mutually-reinforcing transmission channels including limited availability of credit for working capital and many countries attempted financial–rescue measures to restore credit liquidity (Khatiwada, 2009). Hence, it is quite essential to see how growth can be affected by financial development during such slump times in economies like South Africa.

By studying the growth effect of financial development over the economic cycle, this paper has several significant contributions to the literature and the policy practice of central bankers in South Africa. First of all, it distinguishes the impact of financial development on economic growth over expansions and recessions. The findings answer a crucial question of whether policymakers should be flexible in designing the financial policy. Moreover, the paper provides evidence about the sensitivity of estimations to the choice of the proxy for financial development in the setting of time-series analysis.

This chapter is organized as follows. The literature review is presented in section 2. The data and methodology are presented in section 3. Results are presented and discussed in section 4. In section 5, conclusions and policy relevance are presented.

REVIEW OF RELATED LITERATURE

Theoretical Literature

Financial development is defined as any improvements in the functions performed by the financial system, such as savings pooling, funds mobilization, liquidity, and information generation. Its relationship with economic growth dates back since Adam Smith (1776) wrote his masterpiece entitled "An Inquiry into the Nature and Causes of Wealth of Nations" and the works of Schumpeter (1912). Substantial theoretical, as well as empirical investigations, are discussed to purify the interaction between financial development and economic growth. In the 1950s, the leading neoclassical theory, states that long-run sustainable economic growth depends on continuous technological improvements and other factors that determine economic growth. However, in an economic model, the endogenous growth theory which emerged in the 1980s allowed endogeneity of other possible variables determining economic growth. The effect of financial development can be better explained in this way.

There are two dominant theories that postulate the causal relationship between financial development and economic growth. The first view is the supply-leading view, which elaborates the existence of positive effect running from financial development towards economic growth (Schumpeter, 1911; King and Levine, 1993; Calderon and Liu, 2003). This effect is generated by improvements in the efficiency of capital accumulation, an increase in the rate of investment and savings. To the other extreme, the demand-side viewpoint demonstrates that financial improvement are resulted from a change in the real sector, indicating a reverse causal relationship running from economic growth towards financial development (Jung, 1986; Ireland, 1994). Accordingly, an improvement in the real sector brought a significant positive effect on financial services which makes the financial sector to expand.

Apart from the causal relationship, there are also two other extreme viewpoints about the effect of financial development on economic growth in the literature. Some argue financial development certainly assures the promotion of economic growth. There exist channels at which financial integration positively affects economic growth through its effect on factors of production (Henry, 2006; Prasad *et al.*, 2006). The various channels can be grouped into two broad views. The first channel, by the standard neoclassical framework, is regarded as the direct channel. In accordance to this channel, financial integration stimulates economic growth by boosting domestic investment which augments domestic saving which in return reduces cost of capital. The second channel argument is based on the intuition that financial integration serves as a catalyst for certain collateral benefits like macroeconomic discipline, better governance and domestic institutional development, which affects economic growth. In line with the second channel, the impact of financial integration can be felt in a given country after some critical point of macroeconomic policies and institutional development are in place (Prasad *et al.*, 2006).

Schumpeter (1912), besides, believes that the services provided by the intermediaries of the financial system are highly crucial for innovation and development. According to Bagehot (1873) and Hicks (1969), advancement in the financial system played a critical role in industrializing England through high capital mobilization. On the other hand, Van Wijnberg (1983) and Buffie (1984) believe that financial system development brought economic growth deterioration in a given country's economy. Accordingly, advancement in the financial system promotes risk amelioration and efficient allocation of resources, which can actually reduce the rate of savings and risk, consequently leading to a low level of economic growth.

EMPIRICAL LITERATURE

Although most empirical evidence demonstrates that financial development has a positive long-run impact on economic growth, there is no consensus in both theoretical and empirical evidence on the effect of financial structure on economic growth. In support of the above two extreme theories, much of researches were undertaken in different countries over a different time horizon both at a country and panel of countries level. Hence, below there is a review of related empirical researches done on the areas of nexus between financial development and economic growth.

Guru and Yadav (2019) examined the relationship between financial development and economic growth for five major emerging economies (BRICS) for the period 1993 to 2014 using banking sector and stock market development indicators and by employing system GMM model. For the banking sector indicators, the size of the financial intermediaries, credit to deposit ratio and domestic credit to the private sector were used, whereas for the stock market development, values of shares traded and turn over ratios were employed. Beside some macroeconomic control variables like inflation, exports and enrolment in secondary education were used. Results from the estimates of the dynamic one-step system GMM confirm that all the financial intermediaries positively and significantly affect economic growth. Overall, the results signify that banking sector development and stock market development indicators are complementary to each other in stimulating economic growth.

Romualdas *et al.* (2019) investigated the relationship between financial and economic development in the European Union countries using annual data over the period 1998-2016. The results reveal that the highest financial development was achieved by middle-income countries and different directional causality relationships among economic growth and financial development in various European Union countries.

Ibrahim and Alagidede (2018) examined the overall economic growth effect of the disproportionate financial and real sector growth relying on a panel of 29 Sub-Saharan African countries over the period 1980-2014. The results from the estimation of system GMM reveal that, even though it depends on the simultaneous growth of real and financial sectors, the financial sector was found to support economic growth in almost all countries strongly. Besides, the elasticity of growth to changes in either size of the real sector or financial sector is found to be higher under balanced sectoral growth.

Jagadish and Robert (2018) investigated the relationship between financial development and economic growth for a panel of 16 selected low income African and non-African countries by employing OLS, panel unit root and cointegration analysis over the period 1995 to 2014. According to the results of the study, the existence of cross-sectional dependence across countries was assured and long-run cointegration was found. The long-run panel estimates indicate that, even if a low level of credit in the region, financial development has a positive and significant effect on economic growth.

Rodgers *et al.* (2014) investigated the relationship between financial development and economic growth from a cross-section of 50 African countries over the period 1980-2008. By employing two proxies of financial development, namely ratio of private sector credit to total GDP and ratio of broad money (M2) to total GDP, they show a positive relationship between financial development and economic growth. However, a strong relationship between private sector credit and the economic sector has been identified. Generally, the results exhibit that, for Africa, both the real sector and the financial sector is crucial in influencing Africa's current as well as future growth. Nabila and Zakir (2014) assessed the causal relationship between financial development and economic growth in developing countries by applying panel cointegration test over the period 1978-2012. The results indicate the existence of a long-run relationship between financial development and economic growth in developing countries.

Mandiefe (2015), using a vector error correction model, assessed short-run and long-run impact of financial sector development on economic growth for Cameron and South Africa. Only a long-run relationship between financial development and economic growth was noticed in Cameron, while both short-run and long-run in South Africa over the study period. Besides, the results reveal that the South African economy converges to its long-run equilibrium faster after economic shocks due to its good financial developed economy. Ghatey (2015) examined the contribution of financial development on economic growth in South Africa over the period 1965 to 2007, after accounting for unknown exogenous structural changes. The results reveal that, in the short-run "demand following" hypothesis is confirmed, whereas in the long-run, the results are in favor of the "supply-leading" phenomenon.

Tafirenyika (2012) assessed the nexus between financial sector development and economic growth in South Africa over the period 1975 to 2010 by employing error correction and cointegration together with granger causality test. The findings show that economic growth is positively determined by the proxies of financial development (broad money supply as percentage of GDP and total credit to the private sector as percentage of GDP). Besides, the granger causality test indicates the existence of bidirectional relationship between financial sector development and economic growth.

Contrary to the above positive research findings obtained on the relationship between financial development and economic growth, there are many other kinds of research which witness a negative correlation between financial development and economic growth. Adu (2013) examined the effect of financial development on economic growth for Ghana over the period 1961-2010 using an autoregressive model. According to the estimates of the model, money supply, which is the proxy for financial development was found to have a negative effect on economic growth for Ghana over the study period. De Gregorio and Guidotti (1995), using a panel of large countries, investigated the relationship between financial development and economic growth using random effect model. Accordingly, for Latin America, a negative and significant effect running from financial development towards economic growth was found. Besides, Adusei (2013) found a negative impact of financial development on economic growth for Ghana.

From the preceding empirical review, we can deduce the following two main points. First, the results are inconclusive as to the effect of financial development on economic growth. Second, there are no researches undertaken to examine the effect of financial development on economic growth considering the economy at different states (expansion vs. recession states). Hence, this research paper potentially addresses the problem of non-linear effect of financial development on economic growth. Additionally, it employs a newly introduced methodology, local linear projection method, which has many advantages over the standard vector autoregressive approach. Beside to its accommodation of non-linearity, consistent impulse responses are obtained and the estimation is basically on robust standard errors under the local projection method. Last but not least, to come up with robust results, robustness checks for variable misspecification, taking money supply (M3) as an alternative proxy for financial development is conducted in this study.

DATA AND METHODOLOGY

Data Type and Source

The sample period that is used in the estimation is from 1970Q1 to 2019Q3. To keep the analysis as parsimonious as possible, the researchers employ four variables in our baseline model, namely real output, inflation, domestic credit and real effective exchange rate. The inflation rate is the quarterly first difference of the logarithm of the consumer price index. Domestic credit is used as a proxy for financial development. In a robustness check section, the authors also include broad money (M3) as a proxy for financial development. The reason behind the use of quarterly data is that, a given shock less likely affects variables with a quarter data than variables with annual data (Blanchard and Perotti, 2002). In addition, quarterly data can avoid the vanishing degrees of freedom in estimation that mostly resulted from small sample size. The variables are seasonally adjusted from the source. The data is obtained from the South African reserve bank and the International Monetary Fund.

The researchers apply the logarithm to all series and employ the standard unit-root methodology, i.e., the augmented Dickey-Fuller and Phillips-Perron tests. Hence, the researchers specify the number of augmentation lags to account for serial correlation in the Dickey-Fuller regressions, for which the authors employ the schwarz information criterion (SIC). Table 1 shows the results for the unit root tests. The values indicate that the series are non-stationary by accepting the null hypothesis of the existence of a unit root except for inflation. The non-stationary variables, however, are found to be stationary after first difference.

Table 1. Unit-root tests

	ADF			Phillips-Perron	
	Lags (SIC)	**t-statistic**	**p-value**	**t-statistic**	**p-value**
Real GDP	1	-1. 205296	0.9061	-1.159318	0.9151
Inflation	2	-3.358069	0.0137	-7.479049	0.0000
Domestic credit	2	2.246972	1.0000	2.831604	1.0000
Real effective exchange rate	0	-2.398877	0.1434	-2.613787	0.0919
Broad mjoney supply	3	1.259256	1.0000	2.048709	1.0000

H_0: Series has a unit root

ECONOMETRIC STRATEGY

Specification of the Baseline Local Projection Model

Jordà's (2005) local projection method is used to examine the effect of financial development on economic growth for South Africa. The local projection method requires running a sequence of predictive regressions of a variable of interest on a structural shock for different prediction horizons. The impulse response is then obtained from the sequence of regression coefficients of the structural shock (Aye and Harris, 2019; Aye, 2019). Therefore, the method can produce the response of output to domestic credit shock at different horizons.

As clearly explained in (Auerbach and Gorodnichenko, 2013; Ramey and Zubairy, 2018), this method has some advantages compared to conventional VAR model. First, the estimation relies on robust standard errors and is simple to implement. Second, it is robust to misspecification of the data generating process. Third, the joint or point-wise analytic inference is simple. Fourth, it can more easily accommodate non-linearities. Last but not least, impulse responses from the local projection are consistent and asymptotically normal.

The baseline local projection model can be written as follows:

$$x_{t+h} = \alpha_h + \varphi_h(L)y_{t-1} + \beta_h shock_t + \varepsilon_{t+h} \quad (1)$$

where x denotes the variable of interest, y represents a vector of control variables, $\varphi(L)$ is a polynomial in the lag operator, and shock is the VAR-based domestic credit shock. In our study, x contains domestic credit and output, y consists of lags of the values of domestic credit, output, and inflation. The coefficient βh $_r$epresents the response of x *a*t time t + *h t*o the shock at time t. Hence, one can construct impulse responses by estimating a set of regressions for each horizon h. *T*he researchers include a constant αh i$_n$ the model. The order of the polynomial φ(L) *is* determined by corrected Akaike information criterion (AICc) and set to be one. Following Ramey and Zubairy (2018), the authors use the Newey-West correction for standard errors to eliminate the possibility of serial correlation in the error terms.

STRUCTURAL IDENTIFICATION

To construct domestic credit shock, the authors use VAR-based domestic credit shock and establish a four-variable VAR framework.

Consider SVAR of the following form:

$$\mathbf{Ay}_t = \beta + \varphi t + B1\mathbf{y}_{t-1} + B2\mathbf{y}_{t-2} + \ldots\ldots\ldots\ldots + Bp\mathbf{y}_{t-p} + \mathbf{Bet},$$

where **yt** is an n x 1 vector of macroeconomic variables at time t; β is an n x 1 vector of constants; φt *i*s an n x 1 vector of time trends; A **and** Bl $_a$re each an n x n matrix of parameters for l = 1,...., p; et $_i$s an n x 1 vector of structural shocks with et~$_N$(0,BE($\mathbf{e}_t\mathbf{e}_t'$) $\mathbf{B}'$). The reduced-form equation is given by

$$\mathbf{y}_t = \mathbf{A}^{-1}\beta + \mathbf{A}^{-1}\varphi t + \mathbf{A}^{-1}\mathbf{B}_1\mathbf{y}_{t-1} + \mathbf{A}^{-1}\mathbf{B}_2\mathbf{y}_{t-2} + \ldots\ldots + \mathbf{A}^{-1}\mathbf{B}_p\mathbf{y}_{t-p} + \mathbf{A}^{-1}\mathbf{Be}_t$$

or, equivalently,

$$\mathbf{y_t} = \alpha + \gamma t + \mathbf{A}_1\mathbf{y}_{t-1} + \mathbf{A}_2\mathbf{y}_{t-2} + ... + \mathbf{A}_p\mathbf{y}_{t-p} + \mathrm{u_t}$$

with $\mathbf{A}_l = \mathbf{A}^{-1}\mathbf{B}_l$, $\mathrm{u_t} = \mathbf{A}^{-1}\mathbf{B}\mathbf{e}_t$ and $E(\mathbf{u_t}\mathbf{u_t'}) = \mathbf{A}^{-1}\mathbf{B}E(\mathbf{e_t}\mathbf{e_t'})\ \mathbf{B}'\mathbf{A}'^{-1}$.

The reduced-form residuals have little economic significance in that they are linear combinations of structural shocks. In order to identify the structural shocks, recursive (Cholesky decomposition) approach is employed which restricts B to a k-dimensional identity matrix and A to a lower triangular matrix. The recursive approach implies a causal ordering of the model variables. Hence, the output is ordered first followed by inflation, domestic credit and lastly real effective exchange rate. In a similar fashion, to identify broad money supply shocks for our robustness check exercise, the authors order output first followed by inflation, broad money supply and lastly real effective exchange rate. Accordingly, the authors impose the following contemporaneous zero-value restrictions for $\mathbf{A}\mathrm{u}_t = \mathbf{B}\mathbf{e}_t$:

$$\begin{bmatrix} -\alpha_{GDP,GDP} & 0 & 0 & 0 \\ -\alpha_{\inf,GDP} & -\alpha_{\inf,\inf} & 0 & 0 \\ -\alpha_{dcr,GDP} & -\alpha_{dcr,\inf} & -\alpha_{dcr,dcr} & 0 \\ -\alpha_{reer,GDP} & -\alpha_{reer,\inf} & -\alpha_{reer,dcr} & -\alpha_{reer,reer} \end{bmatrix} = \begin{bmatrix} u_t^{GDP} \\ u_t^{\inf} \\ u_t^{dcr} \\ u_t^{reer} \end{bmatrix}$$

$$\begin{bmatrix} 1 & 0 & 0 & 0 \\ 0 & 1 & 0 & 0 \\ 0 & 0 & 1 & 0 \\ 0 & 0 & 0 & 1 \end{bmatrix} = \begin{bmatrix} e_t^{GDP} \\ e_t^{inf} \\ e_t^{dcr} \\ e_t^{reer} \end{bmatrix}$$

This particular ordering of the variables has the following implications: (i) output does not react instantaneously to shocks to other variables in the system, (ii) inflation does not react instantaneously to domestic credit and real exchange rate shocks, but is affected instantaneously by output shock, (iii) domestic credit does not react instantaneously to exchange rate shock, but is affected instantaneously by output and inflation shocks, and (iv) the exchange rate is affected instantaneously by all shocks in the system. Note that after the initial period the variables in the system are allowed to interact freely, i.e., for example, inflation shocks can affect output in all periods after the one in which the shock occurred.

ASYMMETRIC EFFECTS OF FINANCIAL DEVELOPMENT ON GROWTH

The asymmetric effects of financial development on economic growth depending on the state of the economy (expansion vs recession regimes) are also investigated in this study. To examine the effects depending on the state of the economy, the researchers modify our baseline LP model (1) as follows:

$$x_{t+h} = \alpha_h + \varphi_h(L)y_{t-1} + \beta_h D_{it} shock_t + \beta_h (1 - D_{it}) shock_t + \varepsilon_{t+h} \quad (2)$$

where D is a dummy variable that takes value one for expansion regime and zero otherwise. The states of the economy are determined by a threshold variable (in our case output growth). One lag of the threshold variable is taken to account for economic rigidities. Positive output changes are considered as expansion regime while negative output changes are assumed as recession regime. Hence, 45 observations fall under the recession state and the remaining ones fall under the expansionary state.

RESULTS AND DISCUSSION

The researchers identify structural shocks in a vector autoregressive model and impulse response functions are generated from our local projection model. Impulse response functions over 12 horizons for the symmetric and asymmetric effects of financial development on economic growth are provided in figures 1-4. Each shock is the size of one standard deviation and the confidence bands in the graphs are 95% wide. The dark thick lines represent the point estimates of the mean of the impulse response while the light black lines are the 5th and 95th percentiles from standard errors calculated from local linear projections and their Newey-West corrected standard errors. The vertical axis indicates changes in the response variable to shocks and the horizontal axis represents the impulse response horizon. It is essential to consider that for brevity, only the responses of the endogenous variables to the variable of interest shock (domestic credit shock) are reported and as robustness check for broad money supply shock. The authors explain the graphs going row by row, moving from the top to the bottom of each row in each figure.

Figure 1 shows the linear response of economic growth as well as different macroeconomic control variables to a shock in domestic credit. Accordingly, real GDP responds significantly and positively on impact to a shock in domestic credit. As can be seen from the result, one standard deviation shock in domestic credit leads to around 0.25 per cent increment in real GDP on impact. This result confirms the findings of different researches done recently on the area of finance and growth as well as the Schumpeterian finance-led growth hypothesis (Schumpeter, 1912; Shaw, 1973; McKinnon, 1973; Gerschenkron, 1962; Patrick, 1966). In line with the findings of (Guo and Stepanyan, 2011; Iossifov and Khamis, 2009), domestic credit also has a positive and significant effect on inflation. Since domestic credit provision creates a huge demand as well as purchasing power, the general price level will inevitably go up. The domestic credit shock is not persistent. Finally, real effective exchange rate responds positively but insignificantly to a one standard deviation shock in domestic credit.

The effects of financial development on economic growth across the state of the economy (expansion vs recession regimes) are also examined in this study. Hence, as it can be seen from figure 2 below, one standard deviation shock in domestic credit is found to have positive and significant (about 0.5 per cent on impact) effect in the time of expansions. To the contrary, in the time of recession, one standard deviation shock in domestic credit leads to around 0.8 per cent incremental change in economic growth at the fourth quarter. These findings indicate that financial development is more powerful to affect economic growth in the time of recession than in the time of expansion, by waking the aggregate demand up.

Figure 1. Impulse responses to one standard deviation domestic credit shock with 95 per cent confidence bands

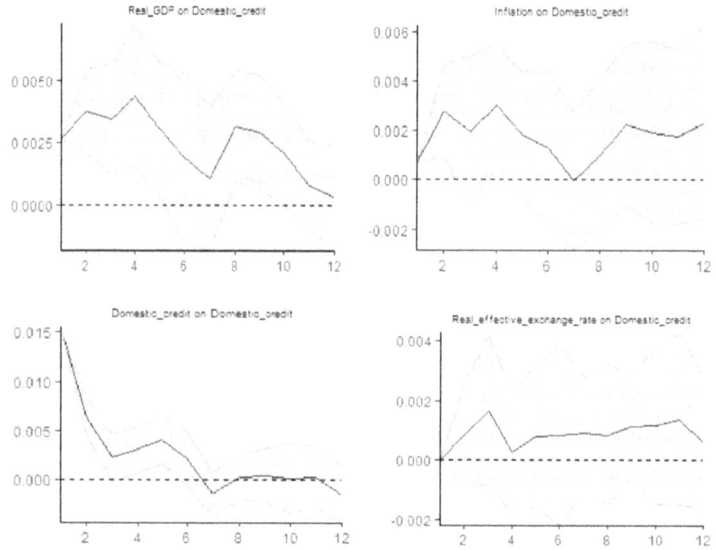

Figure 2. Impulse responses to one standard deviation domestic credit shock with 95 per cent confidence bands over economic cycle

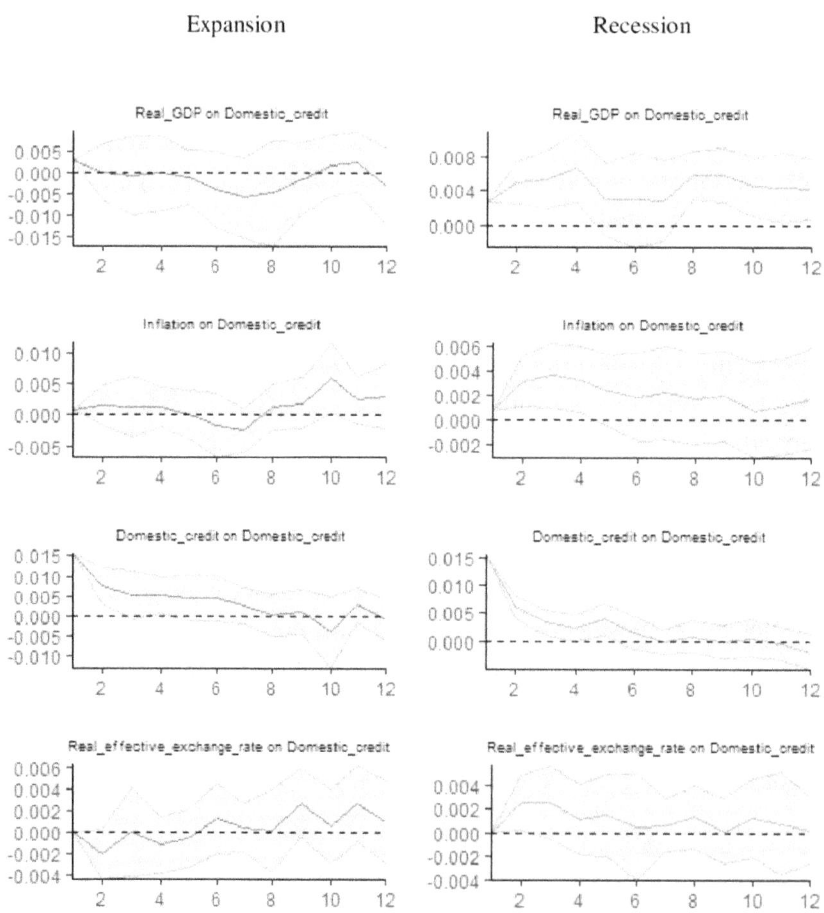

Finally, to explore the robustness of our results, the authors also use broad money supply (M3) as an alternative measure of financial development. The authors find the results are broadly similar to that of our baseline model. One standard deviation shock in broad money supply brings a positive effect on impact on output. The magnitude of the effect, however, is bigger under the downturn than the upturn. One standard deviation shock in broad money supply leads to around 0.6 per cent increment in the downturn in the seventh quarter while it is only approximately 0.5 per cent in the upturn in the third quarter.

Figure 3. Impulse responses to one standard deviation broad money supply shock with 95 per cent confidence bands

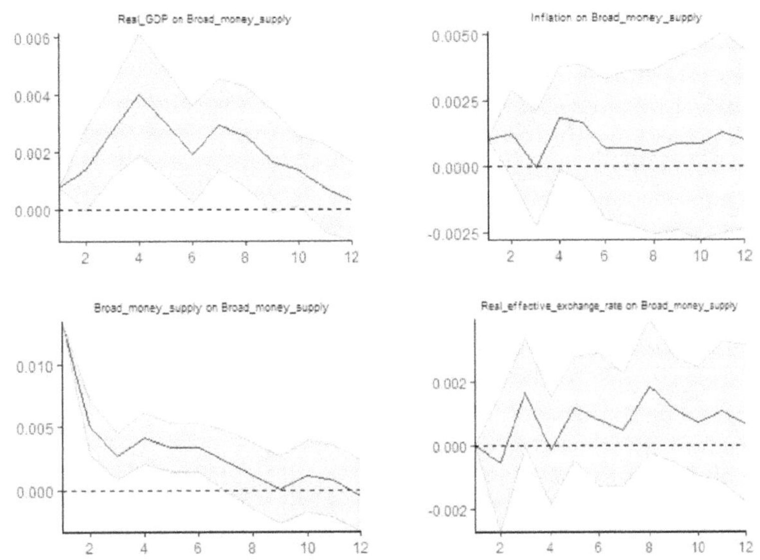

CONCLUSION

This paper investigates the effect of financial development, proxied by domestic credit, on economic growth in South Africa over the economic cycle for the period 1970Q1-2019Q3. To address this objective, Jordà's (2005) local projection method is employed to generate impulse response functions from our vector autoregressive (VAR) model. The domestic credit shock in our VAR model is identified recursively. Hence, the output is ordered first followed by inflation, domestic credit and finally real effective exchange rate in our baseline model. The states of the economy are determined using a threshold variable (in our case output growth). Positive output growth periods are considered as periods of expansion while periods of low output expansions are regarded as periods of recession.

The results indicate that one standard deviation shock in domestic credit leads to a positive and significant increment of output for the South African economy. The results, however, differ a bit across the state of the economy. While, during the expansion period, one standard deviation shock in domestic credit brings around 0.5 per cent increment in output on impact, it leads to about 0.8 per cent increase in output at the fourth quarter during the recession state. This implies that policymakers should be flexible

Figure 4. Impulse responses to one standard deviation broad money supply shock with 95 per cent confidence bands over economic cycle

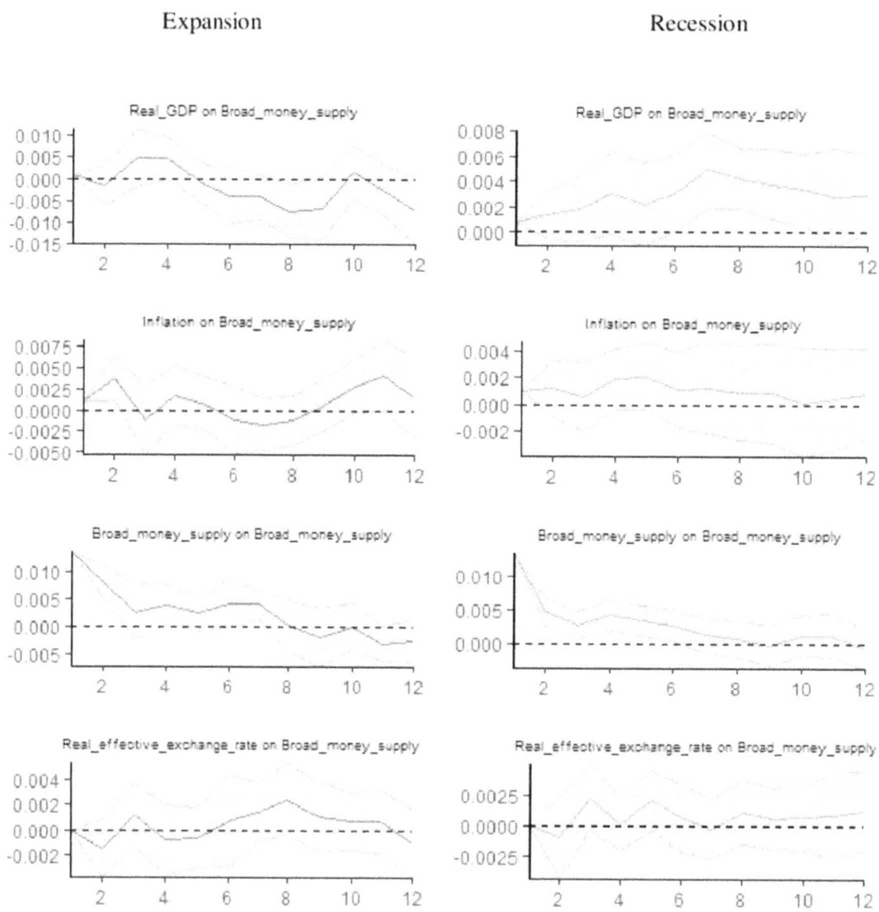

in designing financial policy in this economy. It has also practical implications for practitioners in the sense that financial institutions better to extend credit to economic agents in times of downturn times as this will have significant positive effect on the economy. These results are also broadly similar to the other specification of our baseline model based on an alternative proxy variable of financial development.

REFERENCES

Adu, G., Marbuah, G., & Mensah, J. T. (2013). Financial development and economic growth in Ghana: Does the measure of financial development matter? *Review of Development Finance*, *3*(4), 192–203. doi:10.1016/j.rdf.2013.11.001

Adusei, M. (2013). Financial development and economic growth: Evidence from Ghana. *International Journal of Business and Finance Research*, *7*(5), 61–76.

Al-Yousif, Y. K. (2002). Financial development and economic growth: Another look at the evidence from developing countries. *Review of Financial Economics*, *11*(2), 131–150. doi:10.1016/S1058-3300(02)00039-3

Auerbach, A. J., & Gorodnichenko, Y. (2013). Fiscal multipliers in recession and expansion. In A. Alesina & F. Giavazzi (Eds.), *Fiscal Policy after the Financial Crisis* (pp. 63–98). University of Chicago Press. doi:10.7208/chicago/9780226018584.003.0003

Aye, C. (2019). *Fiscal policy uncertainty and economic activity in South Africa: An asymmetric analysis* (UP Working Paper No.2019/22). Retrieved from https://www.up.ac.za/media/shared/61/WP/wp_2019_22.zp170505.pdf

Aye, C., & Harris, L. (2019). *The effect of real exchange rate uncertainty on income distribution in South Africa* (WIDER Working Paper No. 2019/29). Retrieved from https://www.wider.unu.edu/publication/effect-real-exchange-rate-volatility-income-distribution-south-africa

Bagehot, W. (1873). *Lombard street: a description of the money market*. John Murray.

Beck, T., Hans, D., & Christiane, K. (2014). Is more finance better? Disentangling intermediation and size effects of financial systems. *Journal of Financial Stability*, *10*, 50–64. doi:10.1016/j.jfs.2013.03.005

Betül, M. (2014). The relationship between financial development and economic growth for Turkey. *Journal of Economic Policy Researches*, *1*(2), 85–115.

Blanchard, O., & Perotti, R. (2002). An empirical characterization of the dynamic effects of changes in government spending and taxes on output. *The Quarterly Journal of Economics*, *117*(4), 1329–1368. doi:10.1162/003355302320935043

Brian, M., & Odhiambo, N. M. (2018). South Africa's financial development and its role in investment. *Journal of Central Banking Theory and Practice*, *7*(1), 101–120. doi:10.2478/jcbtp-2018-0005

Buffie, E. F. (1984). Financial repression, the new structuralist, and stabilization policy in semi- industrialized economies. *Journal of Development Economics*, *14*(3), 305–322. doi:10.1016/0304-3878(84)90061-0

Calderon, C., & Liu, L. (2003). The direction of causality between financial development and economic growth. *Journal of Development Economics*, *72*(1), 321–334. doi:10.1016/S0304-3878(03)00079-8

De Gregorio, J., & Guidotti, P. E. (1995). Financial development and economic growth. *World Development*, *23*(3), 433–448. doi:10.1016/0305-750X(94)00132-I

Demirgüç-Kunt, A., & Levine, R. (2008). *Finance, financial sector policies, and long-run growth* (WB Policy Research Working Paper No. 4469). doi:10.1596/1813-9450-4469

Ebru, T. (2016). Reexamining finance-growth nexus: A new literature survey. *EcoForum*, *5*, 1–7.

Gerschenkron, A. (1962). *Economic backwardness in historical perspective. A Book of Essays*. The Belknap Press of Harvard University Press.

Ghartey, E. E. (2015). Causal relationship between financial development and economic growth in South Africa. *Applied Econometrics and International Development*, *15*(1), 1255–142.

Guo, K., & Stepanyan, V. (2011). *Determinants of bank credit in emerging market economies* (IMF Working Paper No. 11/51). Retrieved from https://www.imf.org/en/Publications/WP/Issues/2016/12/31/Determinants-of-Bank-Credit-in-Emerging-Market-Economies-24698

Guru, B., & Yadav, I. (2019). Financial development and economic growth: Panel evidence from BRICS. *Journal of Economics, Finance and Administrative Science*, *24*(47), 113–126. doi:10.1108/JEFAS-12-2017-0125

Henry, B. P. (2006). *Capital account liberalization: Theory, evidence, and speculation* (NBER Working Paper No. 12698). Retrieved from https://www.nber.org/papers/w12698.pdf

Hicks, J. (1969). *A theory of economic history*. Claredon Press.

Ibrahim, M., & Alagidede, P. (2018). *Effect of financial development on economic growth in sub-Saharan Africa: Does sectoral growth Matter?* (ERSA working paper No.754). Retrieved from https://www.econrsa.org/system/files/publications/working_papers/working_paper_754.pdf

Iossifov, P. K., & Khamis, M. Y. (2009). *Credit growth in sub-Saharan Africa - sources, risks, and policy responses* (IMF Working Paper No. 09/180). Retrieved from https://www.imf.org/en/Publications/WP/Issues/2016/12/31/Credit-Growth-in-Sub-Saharan-Africa-Sources-Risks-and-Policy-Responses-23229

Ireland, P. N. (1994). Money and growth: An alternative approach. *The American Economic Review*, *84*(1), 47–65.

Jagadish, P. B. (2018). Financial development and economic growth: Evidence from a panel of 16 African and non-African low-income countries. *Cogent Economics and Finance*, *6*(1), 1449780–144. doi:10.1080/23322039.2018.1449780

Jordà, Ò. (2005). Estimation and inference of impulse responses by local projections. *The American Economic Review*, *95*(1), 161–182. doi:10.1257/0002828053828518

José, A.F., Miguel, D.F., Matheus, B., & António, C.M. (2019). The nexus between financial development and economic growth: Evidence from European countries. *Journal of Economics Studies and Research*.

Jung, W. S. (1986). Financial development and economic growth: International evidence. *Economic Development and Cultural Change*, *34*(2), 334–346. doi:10.1086/451531

Khatiwada, S. (2009). *Stimulus packages to counter global economic crisis: A review* (Discussion Paper 196). Retrieved from https://www.ilo.org/ inst/publication/discussion-papers/WCMS_193154/lang--en/index.htm

King, R. G., & Levine, R. (1993). Finance, entrepreneurship and growth. *Journal of Monetary Economics*, *32*(3), 30–71. doi:10.1016/0304-3932(93)90028-E

Mandiefe, P. S. (2015). *The impact of financial sector development on economic growth: analysis of the financial development gap between Cameroon and South Africa* (MPRA Paper No. 64694). Retrieved from https://mpra.ub.uni-muenchen.de/64694/

McKinnon, R. I. (1973). *Money and capital in economic development*. Brookings Institution Press.

Nabila, A., & Zakir, H. (2014). Financial development, trade openness and economic growth in developing countries: Recent evidence from panel data. *Pakistan Economic and Social Review*, *52*(2), 99–126.

Patrick, H. T. (1966). Financial development and economic growth in underdeveloped countries. *Economic Development and Cultural Change*, *14*(2), 174–189. doi:10.1086/450153

Prasad, A., Rogoff, K., Wei, S., & Kose, M. A. (2004). *Financial globalization, growth and volatility in developing countries* (Working Paper Series No. 10942). doi:10.3386/w10942

Ramey, V. A., & Zubairy, S. (2018). Government spending multipliers in good times and in bad: Evidence from U.S. historical data. *Journal of Political Economy*, *126*(2), 850–901. doi:10.1086/696277

Rodgers, A.M., Esman, M.N., & Eliud, D.M. (2014). The relationship between financial development and economic growth in Africa. *Research in Applied Economics, 6*(2).

Romualdas, G., Gitana, D., Martin, S., & Kęstutis, P. (2019). The inter-linkages between financial and economic development in the European Union countries. *Economic Research-EkonomskaIstraživanja*, *32*(1), 3309–3326.

Ross, L. (2005). Finance and growth: Theory and evidence. In Handbook of Economic Growth, (pp. 865-934). Elsevier.

Schumpeter, J. (1911). *The theory of economic development: An inquiry into profits, capital, credit, interest and the business cycle*. Oxford University Press.

Schumpeter, J. (1912). Theorie der Wirtschaftlichen, Entwicklung [The theory of economic development]. Leipzig: Dunker and Humblot.

Shaw, E. S. (1973). *Financial deepening in economic development*. Oxford University Press.

Smith, A. (1776). *An inquiry into the nature and the causes of the wealth of nations*. University of Chicago Press. doi:10.1093/oseo/instance.00043218

Tafirenyika, S. (2012). *Financial sector development and economic growth nexus in South Africa* (MPRA Paper No. 86633). Retrieved from https://mpra.ub.uni-muenchen.de/86633/

Van, W. S. (1983). Credit policy, inflation and growth in a financially repressed economy. *Journal of Development Economics*, *13*(1-2), 45–65. doi:10.1016/0304-3878(83)90049-4

ADDITIONAL READING

Adeleye, N., Osabuohien, E., & Asongu, S. (2020). Agro-industrialization and financial intermediation in Nigeria. *African Journal of Economic and Management Studies*, *11*(3), 443–456. Advance online publication. doi:10.1108/AJEMS-02-2019-0078

Adeleye, N., Osabuohien, E., & Bowale, E. (2017). The role of institutions in the finance-inequality nexus in Sub-Saharan Africa. *Journal of Contextual Economics*, *137*(1-2), 173–192. doi:10.3790/jce.137.1-2.173

Akinyemi, O., Efobi, U., Asongu, S., & Osabuohien, E. (2019). Renewable energy, trade performance and the conditional role of finance and institutional capacity in sub-Sahara African Countries. *Energy Policy*, *132*, 490–498. doi:10.1016/j.enpol.2019.06.012

Bonin, J., Hasan, I., & Wachtel, P. (2005). Privatization matters: Bank performance in transition countries. *Journal of Banking & Finance*, *29*(8-9), 2153–2178. doi:10.1016/j.jbankfin.2005.03.012

Caporale, G. M., Rault, C., Sova, R., & Sova, A. (2015). Financial development and economic growth: Evidence from ten new EU members. *International Journal of Finance & Economics*, *20*(1), 48–60. doi:10.1002/ijfe.1498

Dutta, N., & Roy, S. (2009). The impact of financial development on domestic investment: A quantile regression approach. *Indian Macroeconomics Annual*, *6*, 107–130.

Ejemeyovwi, J. O., & Osabuohien, E. S. (2020). Investigating the relevance of mobile technology adoption on inclusive growth in West Africa. *Contemporary Social Science*, *15*(1), 48–61. doi:10.1080/21582041.2018.1503320

Karakara, A. A., & Osabuohien, E. (2019). Households' ICT access and bank patronage in West Africa: Empirical insights from Burkina Faso and Ghana. *Technology in Society*, *56*, 116–125. doi:10.1016/j.techsoc.2018.09.010

King, R. G., & Levine, R. (1993). Finance and growth: Schumpeter might be right. *The Quarterly Journal of Economics*, *108*(3), 717–737. doi:10.2307/2118406

Masih, A. M. (1979). An econometric model of the role of financial institutions in financing private investment in Pakistan. *Pakistan Development Review*, *18*(3), 191–214. doi:10.30541/v18i3pp.191-214

Muyambiri, B., & Odhiambo, N. M. (2014). A chronological analysis of monetary policy and the financial system in South Africa. *Public and Municipal Finance*, *3*(2), 19–29.

KEY TERMS AND DEFINITIONS

Cholesky Decomposition: In linear algebra, the Cholesky decomposition or Cholesky factorization is a decomposition of a Hermitian, positive-definite matrix into the product of a lower triangular matrix and its conjugate transpose, which is useful for efficient numerical solutions, e.g., Monte Carlo simulations.

Economic Cycle: Is the fluctuation of the economy between periods of expansion (growth) and contraction (recession).

Economic Growth: Is an increase in the production of economic goods and services, compared from one period of time to another.

Financial Development: Is about overcoming "costs" incurred in the financial system. This process of reducing the costs of acquiring information, enforcing contracts, and making transactions resulted in the emergence of financial contracts, markets, and intermediaries.

Impulse Response Functions: Are used to describe how the economy reacts over time to exogenous impulses, which economists usually call shocks, and are often modeled in the context of a vector autoregression.

Small Open Economy: Is an economy that participates in international trade, but is small enough compared to its trading partners that its policies do not alter world prices, interest rates, or incomes, e.g., South Africa.

Vector Autoregression: Is a stochastic process model used to capture the linear interdependencies among multiple time series.

Chapter 8
Cycle of Poverty in Developing Countries

Opeyemi Idowu Aluko
Ajayi Crowther University, Nigeria

ABSTRACT

Poverty is no longer fashionable even in the less developed countries of the world. The world has deemed poverty-ridden regions of the world as 'anathema', forbidden, and ignoble. At the same time ways to get out of the menace are regularly strategised over a period of time. The developed countries of the world had been able to nip poverty to the bud significantly, but the developing countries still have a lot to do so as to overcome the menace. Poverty in the developing countries operates in a cycle of repetitions. This makes it difficult to curtail. How can poverty be reduced in the developing countries? This study reveals the reason while poverty has become a domestic phenomenon in developing countries and the way forward. The theory on poverty is evaluated alongside the present economic situation in Africa. The cycle of poverty, which includes the social cycle of poverty (SCP), political cycle of poverty (PCP), and the economic cycle of poverty (ECP), are examined. This study analyses the strategies to break the cycle of poverty in Africa and other developing countries.

INTRODUCTION

Poverty inhibits development in all its forms, be it; mentally, socially, economically or politically. Every poor country or individual will not have access to some basic amenities essential to his development. In fact, people living in poverty lines are making real efforts to come out of the menace. There are some zones of the world that had been tracked over a period of time to be in poverty base on the measurement of livelihood, which is below one dollar per day. Such zones are regarded as undeveloped, less developed, underdeveloped or developing countries of the world (Fields, 2019; Kim, 2019).

However, poverty is no longer fashionable even in the less developed countries of the world because of the stigma accompanying such classification. Even though the developed countries and some concerned world organization such as World Bank International Monetary Fund among others do vote some consensus fund for the poverty-ridden countries of the world to relieve their pain and alleviate their poverty

DOI: 10.4018/978-1-7998-4817-2.ch008

but all of such are with prices to be paid. Such largesse might be grievous in the long run but palliative in the short-run (Aluko, 2015; Gnangnon, 2019; Desai and Rudra, 2019). The prices to be paid include high-interest rate, devaluation of the currency, and increase in tax system mostly in favour of the rich against the poor, privatisation and commercialisation of public services which are not convenient to the citizens of such country as such. Others are restriction in international visibility, the brain drain from the less developed countries to the developed countries, external control of the political policy processes, and external control of the economic resources, among others.

In such regards, developing countries spread across the Global South of the world are pressing forward to mitigate the effects of poverty and the largesse of the Global West. Both political and economic measures are employed to curtail the effects. A prominent means is the international economic cooperation among the developing countries such as the Economic Community of West Africa States (ECOWAS), Africa Union (AU) in Africa, among others. The major quest of such organizations is to alleviate poverty and promote peaceful coexistence among its member.

Aluko, (2018); Attwoodet al. (2019); Masron and Subramaniam, (2019) and Mazumdar, (2020) opined that the world as well as clone poverty-ridden regions of the world as 'anathema', forbidden and ignoble. Some of such places are placed on the travel ban, stringent travel policy to the developed countries and economic partnership restrictions. Citizens of such countries are seen as living in the third world. This implies that they are so much poor to be able to afford a convenient livelihood. The developed countries opined that for the developing countries to be able to overcome the third world poverty and mentality, they will require some drastic measures which include a strong attachment to the first world countries political economy and a century of intensive investment which is nearly impossible. Therefore, the cycle of poverty in developing countries seems to be an unending paradigm (Aluko and Mawere, 2017).

The United Nation, which is a global body that comprises of both the developed and the developing countries but under the security control of few countries majorly in the developed countries such as the United States of America (USA), Britain, Russia and Germany, among others is an oligarchy structure. At the same time, over a period of time, it strategizes ways to get out of the menace of poverty. This is done by the principles of bridging the gap of development by sponsoring and supporting developmental programmes such as Millennium Development Goals (MDGs) and Sustainable Development Goals (SDGs). These goals in practice have put the developed countries than the developing countries more on their toes not to decline in their rate of development (Datt, Ravallion and Murgai, 2020; Osabohien, et al, 2020; Osabuohien, 2020).

No doubt, the developed countries of the world had been able to nip poverty to the bud significantly. The reason is that they have the economic capability and the political grips of world politics. The developing countries are seen as the market place and merchant for the developed countries. This is because the currency of the global market is controlled by developed countries. The leadership structure in the developing countries is also a melting point to their developmental crises (Aguilar and Sumner, 2020). Therefore, the developing countries still have a lot to do so as to overcome the menace.

To this end, poverty in the developing countries operates in a cycle of repetitions. This implies that a type of poverty has its cycle and operates in a cycle. This makes it difficult to curtail. Their spheres of occurrence are usually difficult to overcome because of the hydra-headed nature (Aluko and Mawere, 2017). If a cycle of poverty is curtailed, poverty has the potential of erupting from another cycle and gets integrated into the economic and political system. If the cycles of poverty are not curtailed effectively, it breeds another variant or dimension of poverty but of the same root cause in relations to the initial one. However, if the cycles of poverty are not curtailed at all, such a country will remain submerged in the murky waters of undeveloped, underdeveloped or developing status.

The cycle of poverty discussed in this study include the Social Cycle of Poverty (SCP), Political Cycle of Poverty (PCP) and the Economic Cycle of Poverty (ECP). How can poverty be reduced in developing countries? This study reveals the reason while poverty has become a domestic phenomenon in developing countries and the way forward. This study interrogates the concept of poverty and its theories, analyses the strategies to break the cycle of poverty in Africa and other developing countries. It as well uses the data from Afrobarometer 2018 data series to analyse Africa's present economic condition. Conclusions and recommendations are premised on developing the local economy through good leadership, consistent investment in the local content, education of the citizens and less dependence on the developed country's largesse.

INTERROGATING POVERTY'S CONCEPTS AND THEORY

Poverty, like many concepts in social sciences has a multivariate perspective and conceptualization. Several scholars have their perspectives to what the variable entails, what poverty is and or what it should be. Scholars are highly influenced by the different schools of thought they belong to, and this reflects in the definition of poverty that each of them utilizes. Adam Smith opined that poverty is 'the inability to purchase necessities required by nature or custom' (Smith, 1776). This view is over blotted, too large and generalized to have encapsulated the entire world to be poor because nobody is self-sufficient by nature and might not be able to get a basic necessity at a particular time though he has the wherewithal.

Poverty, as opined by Sen, (1983), is the absolute deprivation in terms of a person's capabilities to get a basic necessity of life which emanates from relative deprivation in terms of commodities, incomes and resources. This view implies that relative deprivation is a stage of poverty that proceeds to an absolute deprivation. This assertion corroborates what Peter Townsend defines poverty to be. He said it is what starts as a purely relative measure of deprivation or lack of the resources necessary to facilitate the participation of an individual in the activities, customs and food commonly approved by the community (Townsend, 1979).

Other contemporary scholars such as Bluemenstock, (2016) view poverty as a relative phenomenon where someone's resources are so negligible and seriously below those required for survival of the average individual or family and are excluded from the regular mode of living and association, customs and activities. This view strongly emphasized on social exclusion as a fundamental yardstick for relative poverty. Resources availability is stressed, especially when they are seriously below average as a symptom of relative poverty. But there may be situations of below-average livelihood, which is better than some other categories but of the two poverty situation, the below-average category implies a level of poverty.

The World Bank states that a common method used to measure poverty is based on incomes or the consumption levels of individuals or household. A person is considered poor if his or her consumption or income level falls below certain minimum level and which incapacitate in meeting basic needs. When estimating poverty worldwide, the same benchmark poverty line has to be used and expressed in a common unit across countries. Therefore, for the purpose of global aggregation and comparison, the World Bank uses yardstick set between $1.25 and $2 per day. Didia (2015) explained that any person living below the minimum level, which is usually called the poverty line is poor. However, this measurement might not be pronounced in the developed countries like United Kingdom (UK) and United States of America (USA) among other as compared to the developing countries of Africa and other parts of the world.

The European Commission view of poverty claims that;

People are poor if their income and resources are so inadequate or insufficient so as to preclude them from having a standard of living considered acceptable in the society in which they live. Due to the poverty level, they are susceptible to experience multiple disadvantaged through unemployment, low income, poor housing, inadequate health care and barriers to lifelong learning, culture, sport and recreation. – Joint report by the Commission and the Council on social inclusion, (2004)

This perception of poverty might essentially be a Eurocentric view of poverty, but a more comprehensive and balanced view of poverty is the United Nations, (1995) perception, published in the Copenhagen Declaration of the United Nations in 1995. It attempts to encompass both the developing and developed country contexts. At the summit, it was agreed that poverty includes:

Lack of income and productive resources to ensure sustainable livelihoods; hunger and malnutrition; ill health; limited or lack of access to education and other basic services; increased morbidity and mortality from illness; homelessness and inadequate housing; unsafe environments and social discrimination and exclusion, it is also characterized by lack of participation in decision making and in civil, social and cultural life. – (United Nations, 1995)

This declaration also highlights how poverty occurs in all countries. In many developing countries it occurs as mass poverty, in developed countries, it occurs as pockets of poverty amid wealth, it occurs when there is loss of livelihood as a result of pandemic or economic recession, sudden poverty as a result of disaster or conflict, the poverty due to low income workers, and the utter destitution of people who fall outside family support systems, social institutions and public or private safety nets.

THE THEORY OF POVERTY

There are different platforms and notion through which the theory of poverty has been discussed. These include the Marxian point of view, the moral point of view, and the liberal point of view among others. The view that there should be a communal support to help or assist anyone deprived when others have the means to prevent it, or that a community should rally round such individual is a moral view. This notion only assumes that poverty is inevitable and requires ongoing remediation, compassion, and charity. It also recognizes the claim that those in needs-the poor, the sick, the very old, and the very young-have a moral claim against the larger community. The moral duty to assist the poor in the society is a personal obligation of one individual to another, rather than the obligation of state to an individual. The obligation is, therefore, voluntary (Osabohien, et al, 2020; Aluko, 2020a). If the donor declines to give, there is no legal claim or entitlement. Moral argument to help the poor or the needy is not a coercive approach to assist the would-be benefactor. They are based on compassion and empathy.

Townsend (1979) from an economic point of view, opined that poverty is about much more than simply a lack of economic resources. For Townsend, poverty was, 'the experience of lacking resources to obtain the types of diet, participate in the activities and have the living conditions and amenities which are customary, or are at least widely encouraged and approved in societies to which they belong'. Townsend from the nineteenth-century behavioural school perspectives remarked that poverty was necessary because otherwise the labourers would not be motivated to work. Poverty Policy was, therefore interwoven with notions of laissez-faire.

From the sociological point of view, Welshman (2013) identified six variations in the terminology used to describe disadvantaged groups: the social residuum of the 1880s; the social problem group of the 1930s; the problem family of the 1950s; the culture of poverty thesis of the 1960s; the cycle of deprivation thesis of 1970s; and the underclass debates of the 1980s. During the later 1990s, the less stigmatising and pejorative term 'social exclusion' took centre stage as a way of talking about those experiencing multiple disadvantages. Furthermore, the notion gets better with the views of factors beyond individual behaviour analysis vied as important in understanding poverty, to the point that by the early 2000s the idea had become a common part of political debates in Europe and especially in Britain (Burchardt, Le Grand and Piachaud 2002).

Lewis (1961) also opined in his theory of the culture of poverty that being in a state of Poverty tends to create a way of living which becomes a culture of its own. This culture is mostly learned, shared and socially or generationally transmitted as a form of behaviour of the social group. People living in this culture perceived themselves as a separate part of society. This is evident in their utilization of the basic amenities for the elites. He stated that the urban poor makes little use of institutions such as banks, hospitals, museums and art galleries. In this way, Lewis opined that the poor segregate themselves from mainstream society. This gives rise to two distinct schools of taught on poverty. The first school perceived poverty as an individual phenomenon while the second school perceived poverty as a structural phenomenon.

The first school of taught purported that poverty is an individual causative phenomenon (Ryan 2014; Bruenig 2014). It opined that people are in poverty because they are lazy, uneducated, ignorant, or otherwise inferior in some manner. Therefore poverty is a self-inflicted hardship by an individual on himself. If this theory were true, it will mean that the impoverished people are constant and basically the same people or group of people every year. Their poverty will become perpetual and forever in their generation. By implications, the government and other international communities have no apportioned blame as to who caused the state of poverty. The whole duty of escaping poverty resides on the individual even though the government and the international community had provided some palliative measures against individual poverty. The individual, therefore, needs to break off from being lazy, uneducated, ignorant, or otherwise inferior to the rich in the community.

The second school of taught purported that poverty is a structural phenomenon (Ryan 2014; Bruenig 2014; Aluko, 2019). On this view, people are in poverty because they find themselves in holes in the economic system that delivers them inadequate income (Ryan 2014). However, because individual lives are dynamic, people do not remain in those holes forever. One year they are in a low-income hole, but the next year they've found a job or gotten a promotion and become rich or not poor anymore. The poverty holes that they were in the previous year do not go away. Others inevitably find themselves in that hole because it is a persistent defect in the economic structure of the society. Therefore the structural school of poverty believed that impoverished people are not the same people every year. The school further opined that the only way to reduce poverty is to alter the economic structure so as to reduce the number of low-income holes in society.

Cycle of Poverty

Poverty moves, Trans-generate and regenerate in a cycle. The cycles have their catalyst that activates poverty reaction and lifespan in a country or an individual. In Africa, there are many reasons that make some countries on the continent to be poor while others are somewhat rich. Many of such factors are more of domestic policies which the foreign policies externalities capitalise upon so as to override the domestic economies and causes cyclically inflict poverty. There may be many such possible cycles, but there are three most prominent cycles which inflict and regenerates poverty if the catalysts are activated in any country's economy. The three cycles of poverty have their components, manifestations and regeneration strategies in Africa. The cycle of poverty includes the Social Cycle of Poverty (SCP), Political Cycle of Poverty (PCP) and the Economic Cycle of Poverty (ECP). The strategies to break the cycle of poverty in Africa and other developing countries are as well analysed.

The Social Cycle of Poverty (SCP)

The Social Cycle of Poverty (SCP) operates in a cultural milieu of life patterned around neglect of basic work ethics and regular duties that can boost personal and national income generated (Barbier and Hochard, 2019). The major component of the social cycle of poverty is the Culture of Excessive Public Holidays (CEPH). The Culture of Excessive Public Holidays in the Social Cycle of Poverty is the catalyst that promotes absconding and neglect of duties by public and private workers. The CEPH that leads to poverty prominent in Africa and other developing countries manifests in six cyclical ways. The CEPH leads to Reduce Work Input (RWI). The time taken off the duty post is lost in the productive sector, if the time off is excessive, then the work input will be far lesser than expected. The Reduce Work Input (RWI) therefore leads to Reduce Work Output (RWO). As every working system always have inputs and outputs, if the input is reduced, the output will be reduced, and if the input multiplies, the output also multiplies. Once there is a reduction in work outputs, there will be a definite decline in net growth; this implies a Reduce Net Growth (RNG).

Reduce Net Growth (RNG) in the economy is a factor of poor input and non-commiserating outputs over a period of time. Net growth covers round all the sector of the economy;therefore development will be retarded and ascetic. At this point of development, there will be a glaring increase in the poverty rate and high rate of dependency on externalities for aids and bailouts. In essence, Reduce Net Growth (RNG) in the economy results in Increase Poverty and Dependency (IPD). At this manifestation of the social poverty cycle, there is a need for drastic government policy and interventions so as to correct the anomalies (Sutter, Bruton and Chen, 2019). If the intervention(s) results in poor policy or no policy to reduce the CEPH, then the cycle regenerates. The Poor/No policy to Reduce CEPH (PNP-CEPH) are the regenerating stage in the SCP. This simply continues the old status quo of the culture of an excessive public holiday. Figure I shows the flow system of the Social Cycle of Poverty (SCP).

The Political Cycle of Poverty (PCP)

The Political Cycle of Poverty (PCP) is a political-institutional cycle that determines policies, growth and development. The PCP indicates how poverty is permitted and accommodated in a political institution. PCP has seven components, and it starts with Government Policy (GP). These include regulatory, directional, corrective and other types of policies. The policy statement will indicate the commitment of

Figure 1. The social cycle of poverty (SCP)

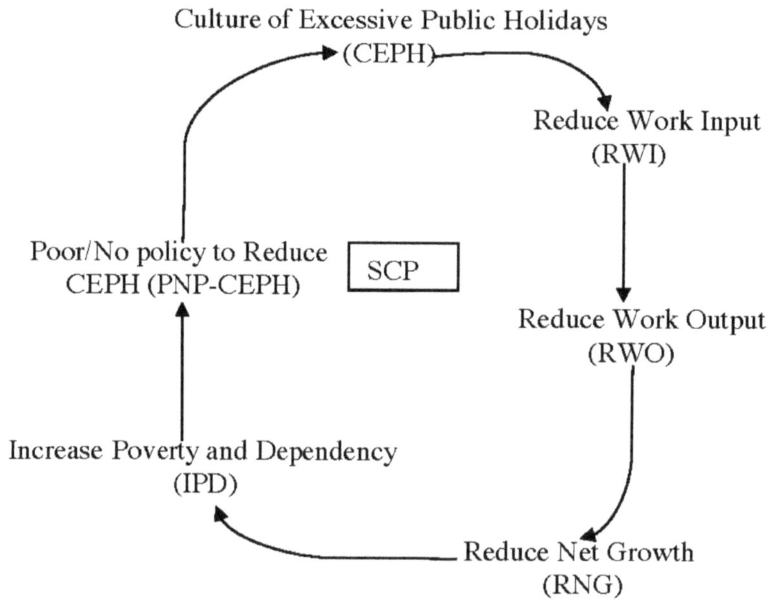

the government to solve a societal problem. The level of commitment of the policy actors, the capability of the political class and the political will to implement such policies are also vital in curbing poverty. The next component is the strength of the policy. The commitment of the policy actors, the capability of the political class and the political will are the yardstick to measure the strength of the policy. A Weak Government Policy (WGP) will encourage laxity and lackadaisical attitude by the policymakers to policy statement. Thereafter, the other determining component of PCP will become weak. It will result in a Weak Government Institution (WGI). WGI will further endanger the level of implementation of the policy (Onakoya, Johnson, Ogundajo, 2019; Aluko, (2020b). Porosity in the government policy will be capitalised on, this leads to the next component, which is the Unethical/Corrupt Political Environment (U-CPE). This type of environment endangers the entire society on whether the government policy will succeed or not.

A U-CPE will, therefore, encourage the environment of secrecy in public transactions, embezzlements and diversion of public funds and non-transparency. This leads to and makes up the next component of PCP which is Increase in Back Door Politics (IBDP). Back Door politics is a kind of patron-client relations, patrimonial politics and prebendal activities. The rich will be getting richer due to the circumventing of the entire national wealth into the covers of a group of people. The duties of the executives, legislatures, and judiciary will be circumvented from the normal procedure and best practices to become a venture for the privileged few to benefit at the expense of the entire country. The resultant effect is the poor attitude to work, and this leads to Low Commitment and Productivity (LCP). LCP is a great challenge to national development because it will endanger the per capita income, the gross domestic product (GDP) and the net income (NI) of the country. When all of the economic growth indicators are low, Increase in Poverty (IP) as the final component is inevitable. The IP can be curb as fast and effective as possible if Government Policy (GP) is strong. Figure II shows the Political Cycle of Poverty (PCP).

Figure 2. The political cycle of poverty (PCP)

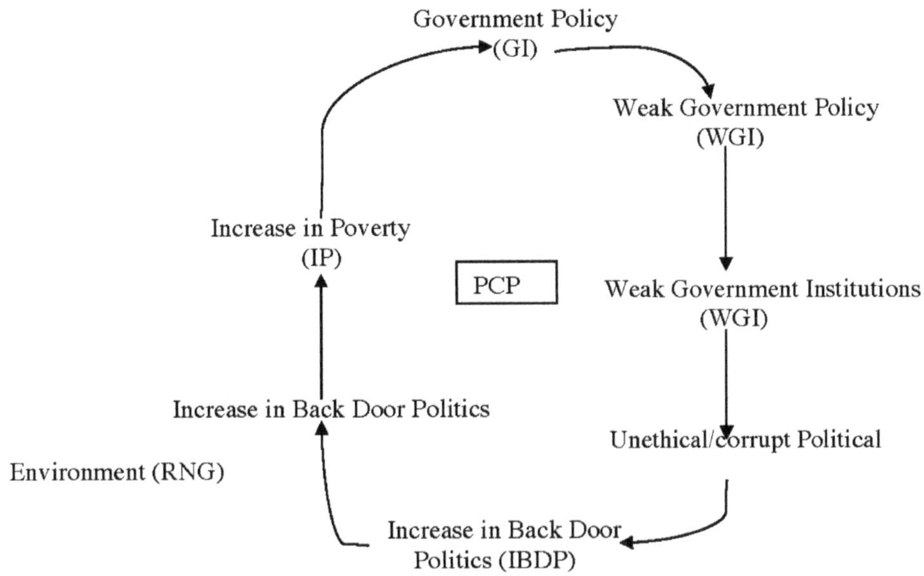

The Economic Cycle of Poverty (ECP)

The Economic Cycle of Poverty (ECP) on the other hand, is a major cycle which encapsulates essential economic activities of a country and thereby dictates the pathway to growth, development, dependency and or poverty. ECP has eight major components that deter a country from adequate growth and development. The first and major catalyst is the government economic plan/policy. A Weak Economic Plan/Policy (WEP-P) will endanger the nation into a weak strategy and implementations. This will lead to the dependence on the externalities and foreign governments for help, aid or assistance. This leads to Excessive External Dependency (EED), which dictates what posture the local economy of the country should take. Over time, this will result in an External Control of the Economy (ECE). The major sectors of the economy will be dominated by the external governments and the price and products of the local industries will not be able to compete favourably with those of the foreign goods (Pender, Hazell and Garrett, 2020). Eventually, this will as well lead to Reduced Indigenous Industries/Experts (RII-E).

Many of the indigenous industries will fold up and become moribund. The local expertise will be out of business because foreign expatriates have dominated the country's economic sector. Therefore there will be drastic repatriation of the profit out of the local economy to foreign homeland. This component of ECP is called External Profit Repatriation (EPR). No doubt EPR will eventually lead to a Shortage of Economic Capital (SEC) in the local economy of the country. The shortage of capital will prevent major and important capital intensive developmental activities fromtaking place. Eventually, this will lead to the next component of Stagnant Economic Growth (SEG).

At Stagnant Economic Growth (SEG) level in the economic cycle of poverty, a drastic measure is required to be taken so as to curb serious crises in the country especially if the stagnation lingers for a long time to the extent of dilapidation of government infrastructure, wind up of private investments, famine and or war in the country. At this critical stage, the last effect in the ECP is Increase in Poverty

(IP). A drastic measure from the government is needed to curb this menace (Sekkat, 2017; Aluko and Aderinola, 2019). If the response from the government is a weak economic plan or policy, the cycle of poverty will be *ad infinitum*. Figure III shows the Economic Cycle of Poverty (PCP).

Figure 3. The economic cycle of poverty (PCP)

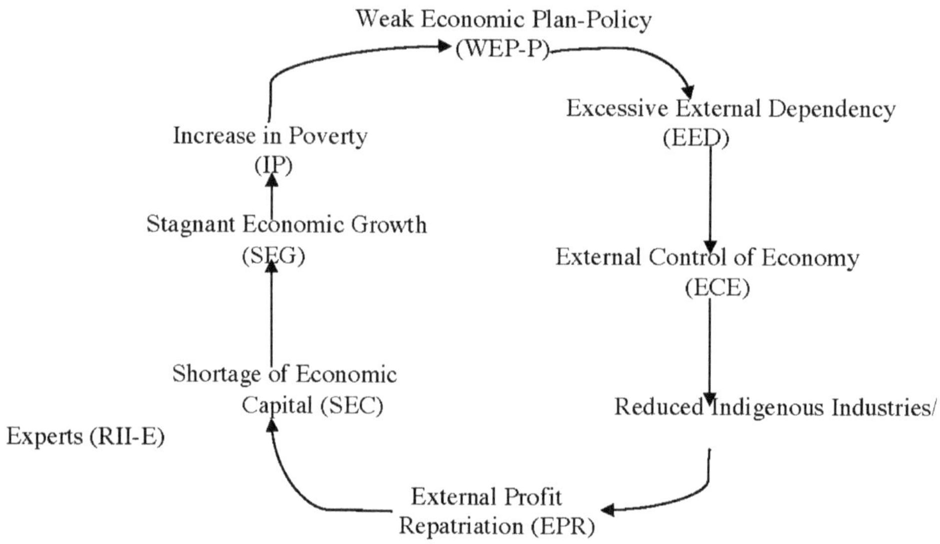

AFRICA'S PRESENT ECONOMIC CONDITION

The research methodology adopted utilises data from Afrobarometer socio-political and economic database 2018-2019 data. The Afrobarometer research network surveyed 37 countries in Africa. This covers about 76% of the entire Africa population. A total of socio-political and economic data centres about 54,000 survey responses on the present economic condition of Africa were obtained. A descriptive overview analysis is adopted to present and express the poverty and development status in Africa, and its implication on the continent.

Table 1. Africa's present economic condition Source: Afrobarometer data (2018/2019)

"In general, how would you describe: The present economic condition of Africa?"	**Total- Africa**
Very bad	23.9%
Fairly bad	27.9%
Neither good nor bad	14.9%
Fairly good	26.7%
Very good	5.0%
Don´t know	1.5%

Figure 4. Africa's present economic condition

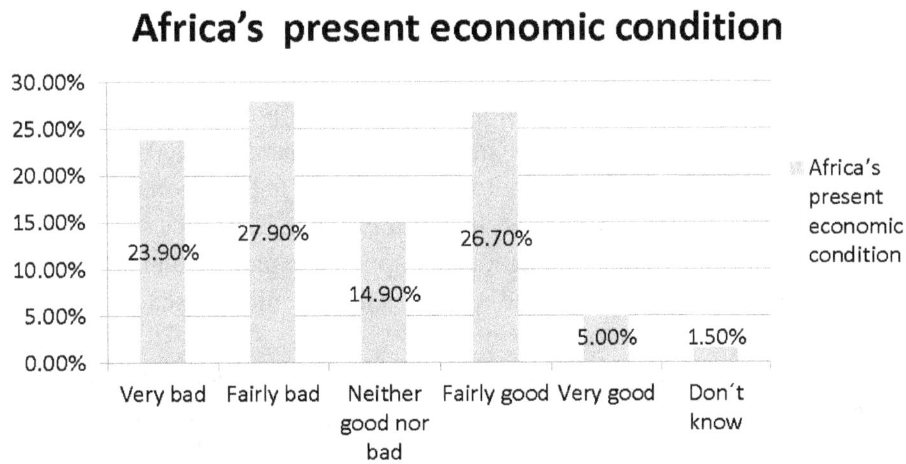

The Afrobarometer data presents the present economic condition in Africa, as shown above. It is observed that about twenty-four percent (23.9%) of Africans opined that the present economic situation in Africa is very bad. About twenty-eight percent (27.9%) of Africans perceived the economy to be fairly bad. This implies that a total of about fifty-two percent (51.8%) of African opined that the present economic condition of the continent is bad. Also, about twenty-seven percent (26.7%) of Africans opined that the present economic condition of the continent is fairly good while a less significant five percent (5%) perceived that the present economic situation is good. This implies that about thirty-two percent (31.7%) of Africans opined that the economic condition of Africa is good. About fifteen percent (14.9%) purported that it is neither good nor bad while about two percent (1.5%) do not know what the present economic situation of Africa is.

The present African economic condition is a reflection of the poverty level in the continent. From the analysis above, more than fifty percent (50%) of the respondents across the continent remarked that the present economic condition of their country is bad. Therefore, there must be some reasons for making such claims to be valid. This include; bad leadership, selfish political class, over-dependence on foreign loans, reliance on foreign direct investments, mono-economy, bureaucratic corruption, patrimonial politics, ethnic chauvinism, religious bigotry, embezzlement of public funds, poor maintenance culture and frequent or protracted urban violence or civil unrest.

The problem of bad leadership as a cause of poverty in the developing country cumulates into bad decision-making process which jeopardises the welfare of the people (Cabrera et al., 2017; Mahembe, and Odhiambo, 2018). The selfish political class is another problem which will ensure in most cases the blockage of new ideas which are against their class agenda and will block new membership by ensuring that political and juicy public offices are reserved for a member of such class through the circulation of elites. Also, the problem of over-dependence on foreign loans as a cause of poverty in the developing country makes the recipient countries slaves of the donor countries. Stringent rules of engagements and interests make the economic value of such loans to be deficient in merit.

The problem of reliance on foreign direct investments as a cause of poverty in the developing country makes the local contents in the country to become valueless, and the indigenous ideas become extinctions (Dhrifi, et al. 2020). This will as well lead to brain drain and dominance of foreign personnel in the economy and the reliance on the foreign donor country for expertise services. This in the short run drains the economy off to the foreign land because the profits are not reinvested to the local economy but the homeland economy of the foreign expertise.

Furthermore, the problem of the mono-economy as a cause of poverty in the developing country is centred on having a single source of income as a major means of financing daily governmental expenses by the developing countries (Fosu, 2017; Arndt and Tarp, 2017). This mono-economy is usually on Crude Oil or other mineral resources. However, this will promote indolence and lack of innovation to improve the economy. The problem of bureaucratic corruption and patrimonial politics are ready means of impoverishing and extorting the masses. The resources that should be used for general development will be assessable to only a few privileged few in society.

Also, the problem of ethnic chauvinism and religious bigotry are the twin pillar of stagnation that fuels enmity within the country. It affects the selection for employments, distribution of economic and political resources and the level of suspiciousness in the country. The embezzlement of public funds is another problem resulting in poverty. A course is the lack of public morality by the public, and private office holders lead to embezzlements, extortions and delay in wages and salary payment which in turn affects the forces of demand and supply in the country.

Moreover, poor maintenance culture of public structures and utilities such as road, hospitals, schools, among others makes the government and the citizens look irresponsible to the social welfare of themselves and their environmental safety. Dilapidated structures and houses are the reflections of poor economy or poor maintenance culture (Singh and Chudasama, 2020). Finally, another major source of poverty in Africa is the frequent or protracted urban violence or civil unrest and terrorism attacks. Violence cripples the economy and the government. Protracted violence will cost the government a fortune before it can recuperate. This implies that the citizens will lose their lives, properties and other means of livelihood; many will be internally displaced while others will become a refugee in another country. All of this rapidly increases poverty in a country, and by contraction, it affects the neighbouring countries.

CONCLUSION AND RECOMMENDATIONS

Poverty is a state of powerlessness, helplessness, 'moneylessness' and hopelessness of an individual or a State. This can as well be a widespread of poverty in a continent where almost all of the countries are submerged in the menace of powerlessness and hopelessness for a period of time. The African continent is in this category of the poverty-ridden continent and it is trying all efforts to curtail this menace. The efforts are in various categories such as each country measures, the regional measures such as the ECOWAS, SADC, among others. The continent's joint effort through the African Union (AU) and the international collaborations through programmes such as Millennium development goals and the Sustainable development goals are measured to suppress poverty across continents and countries.

The evil of poverty is evident in the political system, the economic sphere and the social milieu in Africa. This include; inflation, poor health care and facilities, poor road facilities, large scale of unemployment, high death rate, uncontrolled birth rate, poor educational facility, large scale of brain drain, high crime rate, high sexual violence, high rate of communal clashes, kidnapping and suicide to mention a few. The level or proportion of any or all of the evils of poverty occurrence in countries in Africa and other developing countries of the world may vary; however, it has brought down the countries into peasantries and punditries.

This study identified that the factors contributing to the poverty state in Africa include the following among others; bad leadership, selfish political class, over-dependence on foreign loans, reliance on foreign direct investments, mono-economy, bureaucratic corruption, patrimonial politics, ethnic chauvinism, religious bigotry, embezzlement of public funds, poor maintenance culture and frequent or protracted urban violence or civil unrest. Many African countries and indeed other developing countries of the world are decorated with such factorials. Apparently, for the solution from poverty to being achieved, all of the factors must be reduced gradually until they are finally eradicated.

Finally, in other to gradually reduce and eventually eradicate the menace of poverty in any country, the three cycles of poverty must be identified and broken. The cycle of poverty includes the Social Cycle of Poverty (SCP), Political Cycle of Poverty (PCP) and the Economic Cycle of Poverty (ECP). To break the cycle of poverty, decisive strategies in terms of strong policies, indigenised or localise ideals and political will must be employed so as to break the cycle of poverty in Africa and other developing countries. In fact, if policies will be imported from other climes, it must be domesticated, and test runs on a small scale before a large amount of money and other resources are committed into such policy implementation.

REFERENCES

Aguilar, G. R., & Sumner, A. (2020). Who are the world's poor? A new profile of global multidimensional poverty. *World Development, 126*, 104716. doi:10.1016/j.worlddev.2019.104716

Aluko, O. I. (2015). Political Economy of Crony Capitalism: The Prospect and the Bane. *Journal of Economics Library*, *2*(3), 192–197.

Aluko, O.I. (2018). Entangled in the "New World Order": Africa's (In-) Security Quandaries and Prospects. *Rethinking Securities in an Emergent Technoscientific New World Order: Retracing the Contours for Africa's Hi-jacked Futures, 171.*

Aluko O.I (2019) Caging the Leviathan. *Dynamics of Public Administration*, *39*(1).

Aluko, O. I. (2020a). Backdoor Politics: Permitting Informalities for Formal Development in African Democracy *TEME. Journal for Social Sciences*, *44*(1), 209–229.

Aluko, O. I. (2020b). Breaking the Cycle of Corruption in Nigeria. *The Myth and Reality Journal of Co-operative and Business Studies*, *5*(1), 115–125.

Aluko, O. I., & Aderinola, G. T. (2019). E-Governance and Corruption Impasse in Nigeria: A Developmental Expedition Synopsis. In Security Frameworks in Contemporary Electronic Government (pp. 129-149). IGI Global. doi:10.4018/978-1-5225-5984-9.ch006

Aluko O., I., & Mawere, M. (2017). Breaking the Cycle of Poverty: Rethinking Africa's Socio-political Economy. *The Political Economy of Poverty, Vulnerability and Disaster Risk Management: Building Bridges of Resilience, Entrepreneurship, 63.*

Arndt, C., & Tarp, F. (2017). Measuring Poverty and Wellbeing in Developing Countries: Motivation and Overview. In *Measuring Poverty and Wellbeing in Developing Countries*. Oxford University Press.

Attwood, D. W., Bruneau, T. C., Galaty, J. G., & Attwood, D. W. (2019). *Power and poverty: development and development projects in the Third World*. Routledge. doi:10.4324/9780429302817

Barbier, E. B., & Hochard, J. P. (2019). Poverty-Environment Traps. *Environmental and Resource Economics*, *74*(3), 1239–1271. doi:10.100710640-019-00366-3

Bluemenstock, J. E. (2016). Fighting Poverty with Data. *Science*, *353*(6301), 753–754. doi:10.1126cience.aah5217 PMID:27540154

Bruenig, M. (2014). *Two Theories of Poverty*. https://www.demos.org/policy-shop/Matt%20Bruenig

Burchardt, T., Le Grand, J., & Piachaud, C. (2002). Degrees of exclusion: developing a dynamic multidimensional measure. In J. Hills, J. Le Grand, & D. Piachaud (Eds.), *Understanding Social Exclusion*. Oxford University Press.

Cabrera, J. J. V., Herrero, S. P., Gómez, I. P., & Camacho, X. G. O. (2017). Causal attributions of poverty in less developed countries: Comparing among undergraduates from nations with different development levels. *The Journal of Psychology*, *51*(1), 4.

Datt, G., Ravallion, M., & Murgai, R. (2020). Poverty and Growth in India over Six Decades. *American Journal of Agricultural Economics*, *102*(1), 4–27. doi:10.1093/ajae/aaz043

Desai, R. M., & Rudra, N. (2019). Trade, poverty, and social protection in developing countries. *European Journal of Political Economy*, *60*, 101744. doi:10.1016/j.ejpoleco.2018.08.008

Dhrifi, A., Jaziri, R., & Alnahdi, S. (2020). Does foreign direct investment and environmental degradation matter for poverty? Evidence from developing countries. *Structural Change and Economic Dynamics*, *52*, 13–21. doi:10.1016/j.strueco.2019.09.008

Didia, O. D. (2015). *Ten reasons why sub-Saharan Africa has failed to develop economically: Can Africans succeed by themselves?* Edwin Mellen Press.

Fields, G. S. (2019). *Self-employment and poverty in developing countries*. IZA World of Labor. doi:10.15185/izawol.60.v2

Fosu, A. K. (2017). Growth, inequality, and poverty reduction in developing countries: Recent global evidence. *Research in Economics*, *71*(2), 306–336. doi:10.1016/j.rie.2016.05.005

Gnangnon, S. K. (2019). Does multilateral trade liberalization help reduce poverty in developing countries? *Oxford Development Studies*, *47*(4), 435–451. doi:10.1080/13600818.2019.1612866

Kim, H. (2019). Beyond monetary poverty analysis: The dynamics of multidimensional child poverty in developing countries. *Social Indicators Research*, *141*(3), 1107–1136. doi:10.100711205-018-1878-3

Lewis, O. (1961). *Five families: Mexican case studies in the culture of poverty*. Basic Books.

Mahembe, E., & Odhiambo, N. M. (2018). The dynamics of extreme poverty in developing countries. Studia Universitatis „Vasile Goldis. *Arad–Economics Series*, *28*(2), 18–35.

Masron, T. A., & Subramaniam, Y. (2019). Does poverty cause environmental degradation? Evidence from developing countries. *Journal of Poverty*, *23*(1), 44–64. doi:10.1080/10875549.2018.1500969

Mazumdar, D. (2020). The Problems of Development Gap between Developed and Developing Nations: Is There Any Sign of Convergence? In Wealth Creation and Poverty Reduction: Breakthroughs in Research and Practice (pp. 515-536). IGI Global.

Onakoya, A., Johnson, B., & Ogundajo, G. (2019). Poverty and trade liberalization: Empirical evidence from 21 African countries. *Economic research-. Ekonomska Istrazivanja*, *32*(1), 635–656. doi:10.1080/1331677X.2018.1561320

Osabohien, R., Matthew, O., Ohalete, P., & Osabuohien, E. (2020). Population-Poverty-Inequality Nexus and Social Protection in Africa. *Social Indicators Research*, *151*(2), 575–598. Advance online publication. doi:10.100711205-020-02381-0

Osabohien, R., Onanuga, O., Aderounmu, B., Matthew, O., & Osabuohien, E. (2020). Social Protection and Employment in Africa's agricultural Sector. *Business: Theory and Practice*, *21*(2), 494–502. doi:10.3846/btp.2020.11945

Osabuohien, E. (2020). *The Palgrave Handbook of Agricultural and Rural Development in Africa*. Palgrave Macmillan., doi:10.1007/978-3-030-41513-6

Pender, J., Hazell, P., & Garrett, J. L. (2020). *Reducing Poverty and Protecting the Environment. The overlooked potential of less-favoured lands*. Unfinished Agenda IFPRI Publication.

Ryan, P. (2014). *Do Not Block Grant and Expanding Opportunity in America*. http://budget.house.gov/uploadedfiles/expanding_opportunity_in_america.pdfhttp://www.demos.org/blog/7/24/14/response-paul-ryan-expand-eitc-do-not-block-grant-anything Assessed on 12/6/2017

Sekkat, K. (2017). Urban concentration and poverty in developing countries. *Growth and Change*, *48*(3), 435–458. doi:10.1111/grow.12166

Sen, A. (1981). *Poverty and Famines: An Essay on Entitlement and Deprivation*. Oxford University Press.

Singh, P. K., & Chudasama, H. (2020). Evaluating poverty alleviation strategies in a developing country. *PLoS One*, *15*(1), e0227176. doi:10.1371/journal.pone.0227176 PMID:31929549

Sutter, C., Bruton, G. D., & Chen, J. (2019). Entrepreneurship as a solution to extreme poverty: A review and future research directions. *Journal of Business Venturing*, *34*(1), 197–214. doi:10.1016/j.jbusvent.2018.06.003

Townsend, P. (1979). *Poverty in the United Kingdom: a survey of household resources and standards of living*. Penguin.

Welshman, J. (2013). From the Cycle of Deprivation to Troubled Families: Ethnicity and the underclass concept. In Migration, Health and Ethnicity in the ModernWorld (pp. 174-194). Palgrave Macmillan.

Chapter 9
Financing Sustainable Development in Africa:
Taking Stock and Looking Forward

Oluwabunmi Opeyemi Adejumo
Institute for Entrepreneurship and Development Studies, Obafemi Awolowo University, Ile-Ife, Nigeria & Centre for Economic Policy and Development Research (CEPDeR), Nigeria

Uchenna R. Efobi
College of Business and Social Sciences, Covenant University, Ota, Nigeria & Institute for Entrepreneurship and Development Studies, Obafemi Awolowo University, Ile-Ife, Nigeria & Centre for Economic Policy and Development Research (CEPDeR), Nigeria & Merian Institute for Advanced Study in Africa, University of Ghana, Ghana

Simplice A. Asongu
African Governance and Development Institute, Cameroon

ABSTRACT

Actualizing sustainable development in Africa will require enormous economic resources. This implies that there must be a clear balance of prioritization of financing options on what works best for development in this region without further escalating other societal problems. The authors argue in the chapter that though there has been some benefit from the traditional means of financing development in Africa, some drawbacks still exist considering the rising rate of inequality and poverty head-count in the region. On this note, this present study examines financing options that have previously been advocated for in financing development in the African region (i.e., taking stock), such as development assistance and foreign investment, by considering its implication on development outcomes like poverty, inequality, and aggregate human development indicator in the region.

DOI: 10.4018/978-1-7998-4817-2.ch009

INTRODUCTION

Sustainable development in Africa, which includes the ability to meet present economic, social and environmental needs without compromising the capacity of future generations to meet their own prevailing needs, will require enormous economic resources to fund it. This implies that there must be a clear balance of prioritization of financing options on what works best for development in this region without further escalating other societal problems. The vast majority of the literature has focused on traditional financing means such as development aids (Alesina and Dollar, 2000), Foreign Direct Investment (Velde, 2006), even remittances from migrants (Maphosa, 2007; Osabuohien and Efobi, 2013; 2014; Efobi et al, 2015), and to a large extent, foreign debt from bilateral and multilateral institutions (Chipumbu, 1993; Omotola and Saliu, 2009).

The puzzle in this chapter is not that the current means have not favored African development – because it has, but that a significant fraction of these funds has not been channeled for development structures that will facilitate sustainability. For instance, Kharas (2007) notes that despite the magnanimous flow of foreign aid to developing countries, a significant number of them channel these funds to debt forgiveness and other unprecedented natural occurrences, leaving out issues like infrastructural development and even education and health care development. Also, Safiq, Mansoon & Rafique (2013) observed that apart from national debts and inflation that continuously threatens the gross domestic product (GDP) of developing economies, foreign direct investment negatively affects economic performance. The limiting prospects of foreign funds for financing sustainable development is largely hampered by government instability, internal and external conflict, corruption and ethnic tensions, bureaucracies, unresponsiveness and unaccountability of government (Busse & Hefeker, 2007)

This chapter, therefore, sets out findings from an examination of the traditional funding options that African countries have relied on overtime, and then discuss new funding options by taking cases on how they have worked in specific African countries. For instance, issues like empowering cooperative societies and mutual support networks, agricultural cooperatives, crowdfunding, fiscal responsibility, other forms of informal banking alternatives, were considered for sustainability in Africa. These issues are essential considering that the set-up of African countries is unique and the specific structures are different from countries in other regions (Asiedu, 2002; Nkume, 2018; Akinyemi, et al, 2019), and policies that work in other regions may not be adaptable for this region because the circumstances and informal institutions (i.e. the foundations on which policies thrive) differ so much.

The remainder of the chapter is distributed as follows: the next section discusses the trends in traditional means of financing development in Africa, which is followed by the linkage between these means of financing development and key indicators of human development. The fourth section discusses some relevant case studies of other financing option that can fit the development trajectories of African countries, while the fifth section concludes the paper with policy recommendations.

Trends in Traditional Financing Option for African Countries

The level and composition of this alternative financing means has changed markedly over time, which implies development, which will be discussed subsequently. Despite the increasing flow of finances to the African region, there is still the need for alternative financing means considering the issues surrounding these traditional means of financing, which will be discussed later. This section, therefore, presents the traditional finance means based on a historical perspective, and compares the trend with other regions of the world. Considering the inflow of official development assistance[1] at constant 2015 US$ to countries in the African region (and compared to other regions) as seen in Figure 1, there has been a reasonably stable increase in the volume of this financial flow compared to other regions. In absolute terms, there has been about a four-fold increase in the value of this development assistance since 1975, from 11.9 billion to 45.8 billion in 2015.

Countries in other regions do not experience such a stable increase in foreign aid flow as compared to countries in the SSA region, as seen in Figure 1. Seeing the trend of foreign aid flow for MENA for instance, there is a sharp decline from about 30.1 billion in 2005 to approximately 12.7 billion in 2012, after which there was an improvement in the volume. The countries in the other regions like South Asia, Latin America and the Caribbean, and the East Asia and the Pacific all had a steady, but marginal, rise in their volume of aid flow. When compared to the value that flows to the SSA, there is about 5-fold difference in the value of aid flow to SSA countries compared to the value in East Asia and the Pacific countries.

Figure 1. Aid Flow to SSA and some other regions of the world

Notes: *ODA is defined as Net official development assistance and official aid received (constant 2015 US$).* **SSA**- *Sub Sahara Africa;* **MENA** – *Middle East and North Africa;* **SA** – *South Asia;* **LAC** – *Latin America and Caribbean;* **EAP** – *East Asia and Pacific*

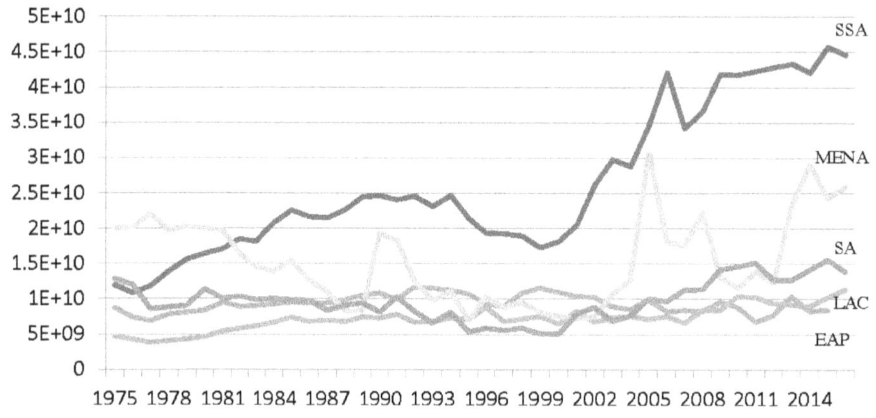

Meanwhile, the ODA flow to African countries in 2014 was highest in Ethiopia and Egypt, comprising about 7 percent of the total ODA flow to the region from Table 1. The remaining countries like Kenya, Tanzania, and Nigeria all receive about 5 percent of the total foreign aid flow to the region, and Congo, Morocco, Mozambique, and South Sudan receive 4 percent inflow. In comparison, the rest countries in the region receive less than 3 percent of the total aid flow. Countries like the United States of America was the highest aid donor to the region, with the European Union countries giving about 12 percent of the total aid flow. The aid direction to the SSA region is unevenly dispersed with the top 10 recipients receiving about 47 percent of the entire aid flow to the region. The implication of this skewed aid flows could indicate that some countries are not only more privileged or positioned for such opportunities, but could also have an edge in funding requirements compared to other countries that have not received. Therefore, in addition to considering alternative funding path for sustainable development, it is worthwhile for donors to consider the direction, spread and even nature of their donations.

Table 1. Aid flow and aid donors to African countries

Top 10 ODA receipts by recipient			Top 10 ODA donors		
USD million, net disbursements in 2014			USD million, net disbursements in 2014		
Ethiopia	3585	7%	United States	9338	17%
Egypt	3532	7%	EU Institutions	6737	12%
Kenya	2665	5%	IDA	6386	12%
Tanzania	2648	5%	United Kingdom	4346	8%
Nigeria	2476	5%	United Arab Emirates	3787	7%
Democratic Republic of Congo	2398	4%	Germany	3018	6%
Morocco	2247	4%	France	2929	5%
Mozambique	2103	4%	African Dev. Bank	2042	4%
South Sudan	1964	4%	Global Fund	1957	4%
Uganda	1633	3%	Japan	1558	3%
Other recipients	28941	53%	Other Donors	12098	22%

Unlike foreign aids, the inflow of foreign direct investment (FDI) to the African region has been a low trend in the volume of inflow in the past two decades compared to other regions; and more recently, the region has witnessed even more decreases. Generally, compared to other regions of the World, countries in SSA (for instance) see less foreign investment flow, which is about 13 times lower than those flow to EAP in 2015 alone.

Figure 2. Trend in foreign direct investment (Net inflows) across regions
Notes: SSA- *Sub Sahara Africa;* **MENA** – *Middle East and North Africa;* **LAC** – *Latin America and Caribbean;* **EAP** – *East Asia and Pacific*

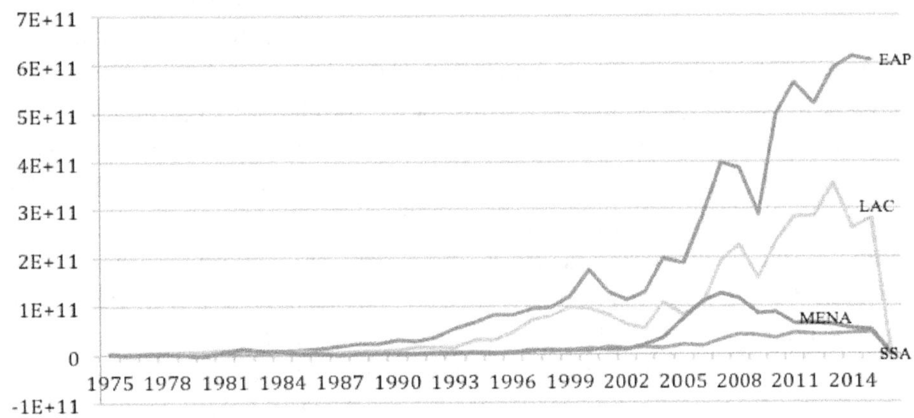

Countries in Africa is still expected to receive less foreign investment compared to those in other regions when considering the projection of foreign investment flow across regions in Table 2. From Table 2, the foreign investment flows to Africa are estimated to increase by about 19 per cent in 2018 to $50 billion from 42 billion in 2017. Despite this increase, African countries are seriously lagging when compared to countries in other regions. The projection for Africa is bolstered by the expectation of a continued fair recovery in the prices of commodity in the international market (despite that commodity dependence will cause FDI to remain cyclical), and by favorable macroeconomic fundamentals (UNCTAD, 2018). Importantly, the recent signing of the African Continental Free Trade Area (AfCFTA) by 44 African countries could encourage a more improved FDI flows.

Table 2. FDI inflows, projections (2015–2018) in billions of dollars and percent

	2015	2016	2017	2018*
World	1921	1868	1430	1450 to 1570
Developed Economies	1141	1133	712	740 to 800
Europe	595	565	334	380
North America	511	494	300	320
Developing Countries	744	670	671	640 to 690
Africa	57	53	42	50
Asia	516	475	476	470
Latin America and the Caribbean	169	140	151	140

Note: * is the 2018 projected value.
Source: UNCTAD (2018)

Despite the benefits embedded in FDI inflows for developing economies, the observed pattern of FDI inflow into the African continent courts urgent concerns as a dependable and sustainable source of financing. Apart from FDI being an outward and unpredictable form of finance for developing economies, governments within host economies have no control whatsoever on the capitalist choices of when and where to invest. Thus, owing to the volatility of this form of financing, the onus lies on developing economies to stir real endogenous economic growth. Studies have further proven other funds such as remittances as more predictable then FDI (Vaknin, 2008; Büthe & Milne, 2008). Therefore, rather than depending on external funding sources, it is imperative that developing economies are more inward looking via indigenous and frugal approaches to financing, production and economic outputs. Vaknin (2008) also noted that FDI does not necessarily metamorphose to net foreign exchange inflows given that some Multinational Corporations (MNCs) borrow from local funds at appreciable interest rates to finance their investment; thereby, constituting further threats to local firms and crowds out domestic firms from credit opportunities. Meanwhile, Büthe & Milner (2008) adds that variations in FDI inflows are largely attributed it to international trade agreements than local/host agreements or policies such as General Agreement on Tariff and Trade, World Trade Organisation (WTO) and African Continental Free Trade Area (AfCTA). This is because international commitments are passed as more worthwhile than local policies; thus, leaving host economies largely at the dictates of foreign investors especially where their activities are not so consistent with local objectives.

Another source of foreign revenue inflow to Africa is remittance inflow, which is one of the most stable forms of foreign capital to African countries. For instance, unlike foreign aid and foreign investment that depends on the economic condition of the originating countries, remittance inflow remains stable, in terms of its volume, considering that it includes those monetary funds sent to the home countries by its nationals for different purposes, including altruistic motive, investments, and other human capital development funding. Despite, remittance inflow to African countries is still considerably lower than those of other regions of the world (see Figure 3). Over the years, there has been a consistent increase in the trend of global remittance inflow, which makes this form of foreign capital flow to be an important source of countries development funding option.

Figure 3. Remittance inflow across regions
Notes: SSA- *Sub Sahara Africa;* **MENA** – *Middle East and North Africa;* **SA** – *South Asia;* **LAC** – *Latin America and Caribbean;* **EAP** – *East Asia and Pacific*

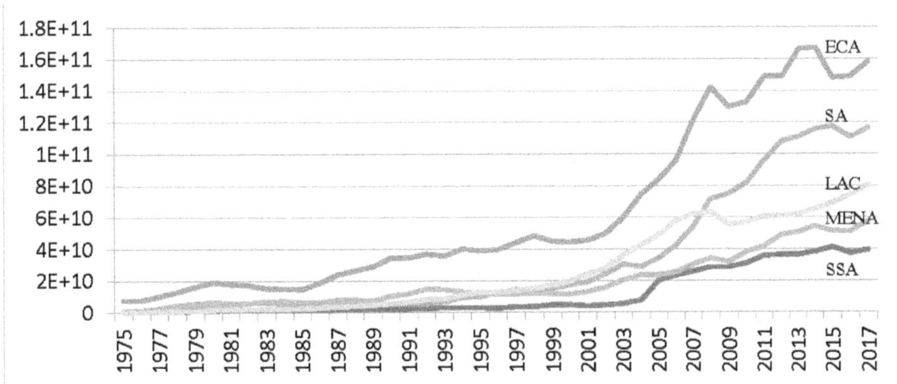

Considering the combined distribution of the three most important sources of foreign financial inflow to African countries as presented in Figure 4, we see from the trend that, as earlier noted, official development assistance is still the most important foreign capital flow to the region. As at 2016 alone, the volume of official development flow to African countries was about 19 percent more than remittance inflow, and about 16 percent more than the total foreign direct investment. In terms of stability of the flows, Figure 4 shows that the trend of remittance inflow is smoother than the other funds, which confirms the earlier assertion that remittance inflow is more stable than the other funds.

As laudable as remittances appears, the flow to SSA have been adjudged as low when compared to the flows in other regions of the world like LAC and EAP. In addition, the sustainability of this capital source is a puzzling phenomenon given that remittances are largely dependent on a number of factors such as family reunification, immigration policies, (Docquier, Rapoport & Salomone, 2012) continual viability of the remitter or remitting organization and the host economy. Meanwhile, the *remittance decay hypothesis* which captures the remitting behaviour of migrants argues that the amount of remittances sent by migrants to their countries of origin declines through time. While some studies have validated the remittance decay hypothesis (Chami, Fullenkamp & Jahjah, 2005; Arun & Ulku, 2011; Makina &Masenge, 2015); others have argued otherwise in favour of the *remittance theory* (Docquier, Rapoport & Salomone, 2012, Hunte, 2004). Irrespective the direction of argument, the budding issue of interest within this chapter is the reliability and sustainability of this source of finance; hence, the subsequent section delves more into funds that emanate locally and are somewhat reliable and sustainable in developing economies.

Figure 4. Remittance inflow across regions

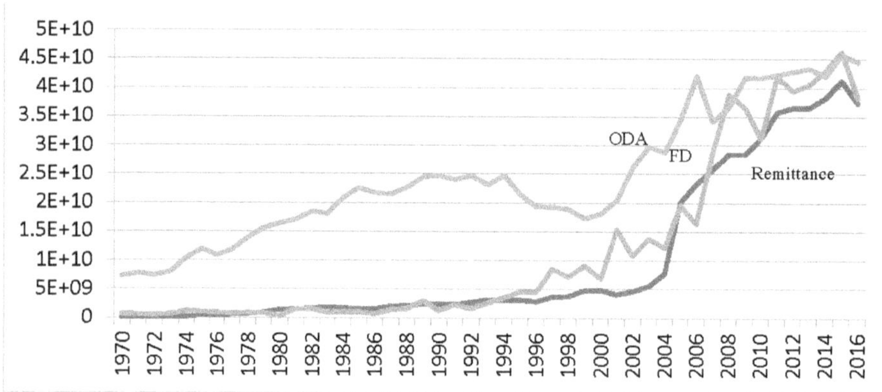

LINKAGE: TRADITIONAL FINANCE MEANS AND KEY INDICATORS OF HUMAN DEVELOPMENT

When observing the relationship between the different indicators of financial flow and development, it is important to consider the type and volume of these financial flows because the impact they have on the recipient countries depend on these characteristics. However, this study is not a rigorous examination of the importance of these financial flows, hence our inquiry is to observe the pairwise association between the different financial flows (especially the most popular ones in Africa) and the indicators of human development as suggested UNCTAD (2016) while taking into consideration health care and per capita income in the respective countries.

In Panel A of Figure 5:

- Upward association between ODA and infant mortality in the sampled countries- suggesting impaired financial sustainability for development.
- Swanson (2015) argued that aid directed at helping poor countries might be hurting and slowing their growth
- FDI to African countries, in terms of reduces under-five mortality rate; Suggesting that FDIcan assist and not necessarily hurt the recipient countries.
- African countries receive less of this form of foreign capital flow compared to other regions of the world

The findings from this plot support the consensus in the literature that advocates for foreign investment as a complementaryfinancial flow to assist African development (OECD, 2002; Torabi, 2015).

Another important development outcome that we consider in this section is the per capita income of African countries, which is a measure of the average income level of the population. Using a similar sample as presented in Figure 4, the scatter plots for the per capita GDP and the different financial flow indicators are in Figure 5. Foreign aid flow still maintains a significant negative relationship with per capita GDP of the respective countries in the African region, implying that this form of financial flow does not have a positive effect on the income level of the recipient countries in the region. In sharp contrast, we find a positive relationship between the volume of foreign direct investment and the income

Figure 5. Scatter Plot – ODA, FDI, and Infant Mortality (2015)

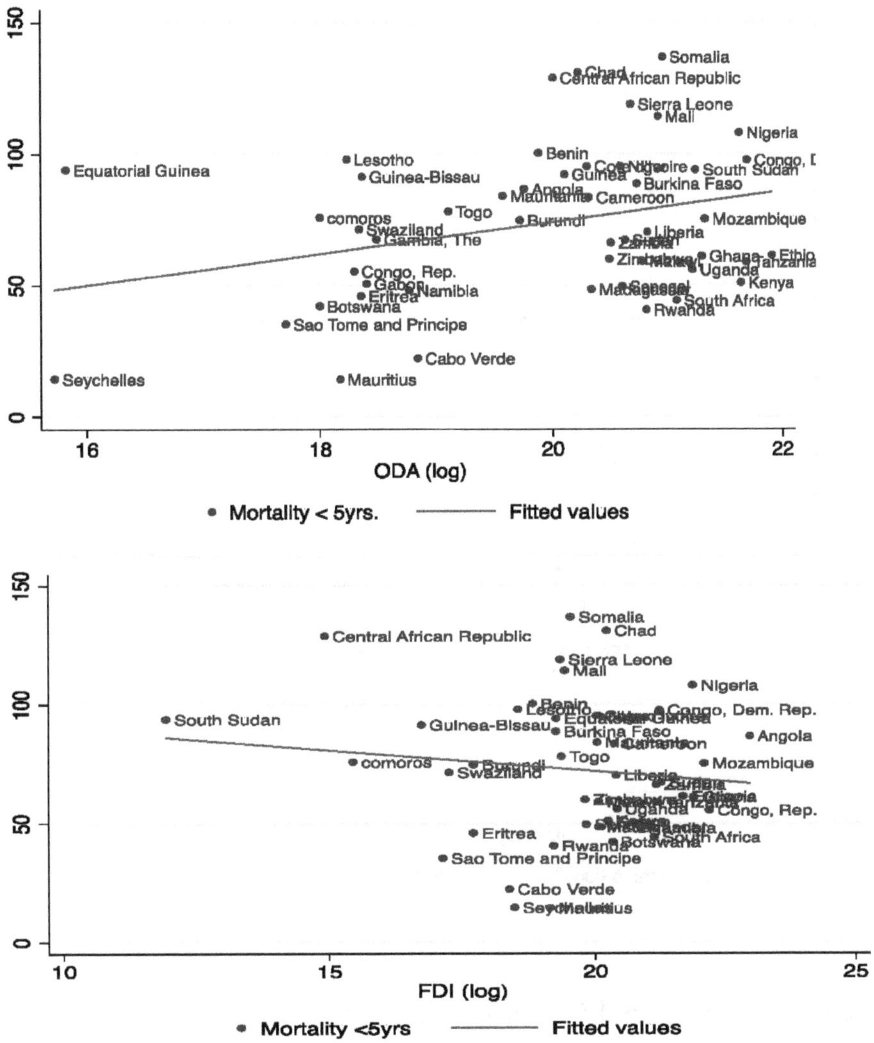

level of the respective African countries. This suggests that the average income of the population of the sampled countries increases at a consistent rate with the level of foreign direct investment inflow.

The negative relationship seen between foreign aid and the measures of development, and in contrast, seeing a positive relationship between foreign investment and the measures of development further reiterates the need to consider financing sustainable development in Africa effectively. The traditional means of finance do not consistently show an improvement in the measures of development, which reinforces the need to consider alternative means of financing sustainable development in Africa – which will be broadly discussed in the subsequent session. Finally, it is fair to say that there are immense literature that criticize the ability of foreign aid to deliver its development outcomes in the recipient countries. For instance, these studies point to the fact that international politics, governance and heightened public sector corruption is a major factor to be considered in ensuring the effectiveness of foreign aid in recipient African countries (see Kaufmann, 2009; Bauhr, 2016; Kenny, 2017).

Figure 6. Scatter Plot – ODA, FDI, and Per Capita GDP (2015)

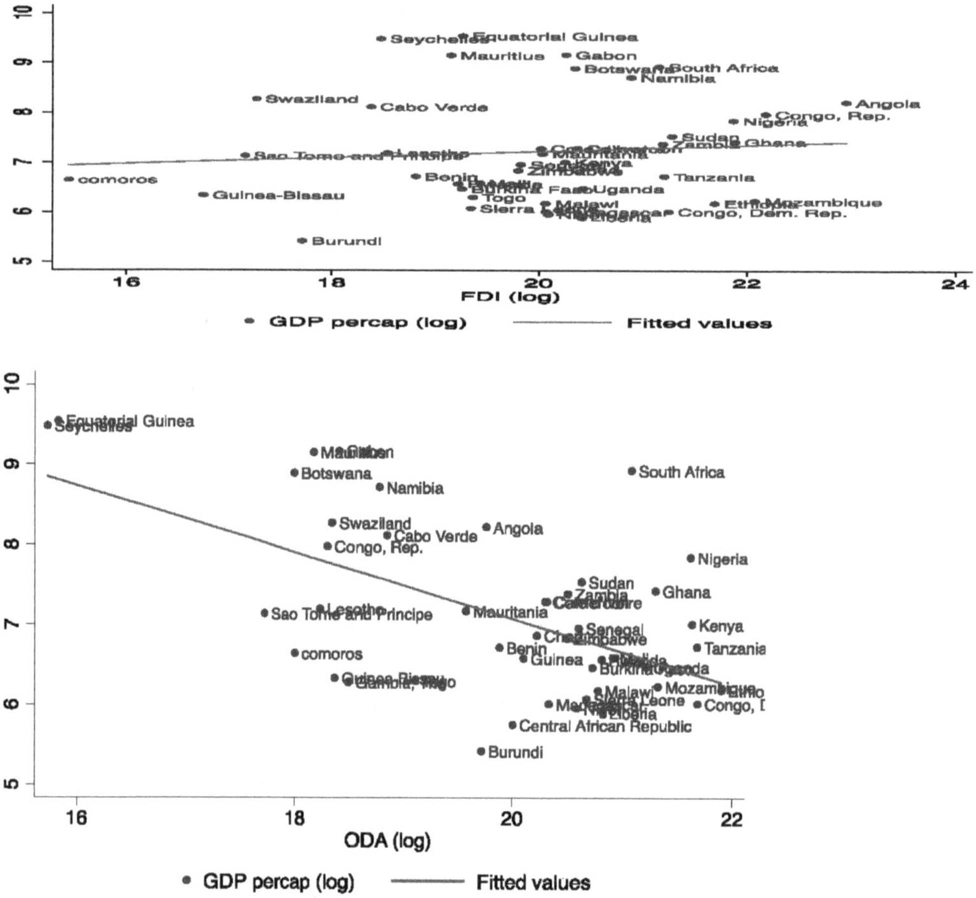

ALTERNATIVE PATH FOR SUSTAINABLE DEVELOPMENT IN AFRICA

There are different alternative, and more stable funding means that can help the sustainability of African countries. These alternative funding means have been used by some non-African countries and has worked in so many instances with accrued benefit and cost. However, when considering the cost, in relation to the cyclicality of the traditional means of finance, which was earlier elaborated in the document. The first funding option for African countries to consider is the sovereign wealth fund (SWF) as finely elaborated in Nkume (2018). SWF, which are those investment fund in real and financial assets like stocks, bonds, real estate, precious metals, or in alternative investments like private equity fund or hedge funds that are managed by the state. These SWF are expected to be funded by excess revenue from commodity exports or foreign reserves that are held by the central bank to be used for future development projects.

African countries are beginning to think in this direction, especially with the increasing number that subscribes to this important funding option. According to Nkume (2018) countries like Algeria, Botswana, Libya, Ghana, Angola, Senegal, Tanzania, Kenya, and Mozambique, with countries like South Africa still in the process of structuring how the SWF would be structured in their economy. Taking

Nigeria, for instance, there is a Nigeria Sovereign Investment Authority (NSIA) set up to manage this fund through the excess earnings from crude oil. The mechanism of operating this account is such that the NSIA receive monthly funding of a significant portion of the excess oil and gas revenue above the budgeted revenue (NSIA, 2018), with the three sovereign funds under the NSIA being future generation funds, Nigerian infrastructure fund, and stabilization fund. Apart from Nigeria, the SWFs contributes about 40 percent of Botswana's and 100 percent of Libyan gross national income and even makes up a quarter of Algerian national income (Fourie, 2016). To ensure these funds are effectively managed and to reduce the incidence of rent-seeking and corruption practices that plague other traditional means of funding development, there is the need for such funds to be administered by an independent financial body.

Another important concept to consider in funding sustainable development is the awakening of responsible state capacity in driving the development process in African countries. Unfortunately, most political leaders in African countries are short-term thinking, and many lack strategic ideas in propelling the development process of their respective countries (Jo-Ansie, 2007; Efobi, 2015). This has to change for there to be sustainable development in the continent. Reinventing responsible state capacity is all about the state being involved in deciding strategic competencies, and then enabling the private sector to get involved in such competency. A vivid example of countries where this has worked in Brazil: in the 1970s the government pursued an aggressive export-oriented industrialisation strategy by identifying sectors that they want to build competencies in (i.e. non-ferrous metals, chemicals and petrochemicals, paper, and machinery and equipment) and then mobilised Brazil's national bank to offer medium- and long- term financing to projects initiated by the private sector in these competencies. This initiative was successful in establishing a thriving steel industry in Brazil, which has boosted their export performance, and there has been an efficient development of other industries as a result of this initiative such as the automobile industry and even the aero industry. Brazil greatly contributes to the global supply chain of aircraft, which is a significant industrial revolution that places them as among the fast-emerging economies of the world (UNCTAD, 2016).

India also have a similar success story like Brazil, where the state got involved in the development of specialised financial institutions who were tasked with the responsibility of providing long-term finance to specific industries that were identified as strategic for national development (Chandrasekhar, 2015). In some other instances, the Indian government engaged in state-owned enterprises to develop such competencies, which then spill over to an industrial revolution. For instance, Amsden (2001) records that there were technological and human capital investments undertaken by the state had a great impact on local firms through the supply of trained workforce in the specific industry that the government got involved – in this case, the pharmaceutical industry. Similar spillover was also recorded for Ethiopia, where certain technologies that were first initiated in the state-owned enterprises were later adopted and advanced by the private sector (UNCTAD, 2016).

The miracle of cooperative societies and informal mutual support network is another important alternative source of funding development in African countries. Unlike the formal financial institutions, the informal support networks are a form of pool funds by members to provide a type of insurance for its members in cases of cyclicality, and in cases where huge funds are needed for investment needs (see Mangasini, 2018).

CONCLUSION

Sustainable development in Africa includes the ability to meet present economic, social and environmental needs without compromising the capacity of future generations to meet their own prevailing needs. However, achieving these development goals will require enormous economic resources. Hence, the need to balance the prioritization of financing options based on what works best for development in this region. Indeed, there have been beneficial outcome from some of the finance means: for instance, while we find negative relationship between foreign aid and some development outcomes, foreign direct investment was found to have positive association with similar development outcomes. We therefore argue for the consideration of other finance means like improving the effectiveness of mutual support networks, sovereign wealth funds, improving state capacity to chart development course. We conclude that despite the importance of traditional means of financing development in the African region, their wide spread impact on non-mainstream groups (like those involved in the informal sector, rural populace, and even the disadvantaged group) is not effectively felt; hence, the rising rate of inequality and exclusive development. However, these alternative means of financing development could be a viable policy option to bridge these gaps; thereby mainstreaming the process for financial inclusion and sustainability.

REFERENCES

Akinyemi, O., Efobi, U., Asongu, S., & Osabuohien, E. (2019). Renewable energy, trade performance and the conditional role of finance and institutional capacity in sub-Sahara African Countries. *Energy Policy*, *132*, 490–498. doi:10.1016/j.enpol.2019.06.012

Alesina, A., & Dollar, D. (2000). Who gives Foreign Aid to Whom and Why? *Journal of Economic Growth*, *5*(1), 33–63. doi:10.1023/A:1009874203400

Amsden, A. (2001). *The Rise of "The Rest:" Challenges to the West from Late-Industrializing Economies*. Oxford University Press. doi:10.1093/0195139690.001.0001

Arun, T., & Ulku, H. (2011). Determinants of Remittances: The Case of the South Asian Community in Manchester. *The Journal of Development Studies*, *47*(6), 894–912. doi:10.1080/00220388.2010.527951

Asiedu, E. (2002). On the Determinants of Foreign Direct Investment to Developing Countries: Is Africa Different? *World Development*, *30*(1), 107–199. doi:10.1016/S0305-750X(01)00100-0

Bauhr, M. (2016). *Does Corruption reduce Public Support for Foreign Aid? Aid Effectiveness, Accountability and Foreign Aid Cuts*. Paper Presented at "Public Opinion and Foreign Aid: Policy and Methodology Perspectives" Conference. Retrieved from https://ncgg-new.princeton.edu/sites/ncgg/files/media/bauhr_public_opinion_and_foreign_aid.pdf

Busse, M., & Hefeker, C. (2007). Political Risk, Institutions and Foreign Direct Investment. *European Journal of Political Economy*, *23*(2), 397–415. doi:10.1016/j.ejpoleco.2006.02.003

Büthe, T., & Milner, H. V. (2008). The politics of foreign direct investment into developing countries: Increasing FDI through international trade agreements? *American Journal of Political Science*, *52*(4), 741–762. doi:10.1111/j.1540-5907.2008.00340.x

Chami, R., Fullenkamp, C., & Jahjah, S. (2005). Are Immigrant Remittance Flows a Source of Capital for Development? *IMF Economic Review*, *52*, 55–81. doi:10.2307/30035948

Chandrasekhar, C. P. (2015). National Development Banks in a Comparative Perspective. In Rethinking Development Strategies after the Financial Crisis. United Nations Conference on Trade and Development and Fachhochschule für Technik und Wirtschaft Berlin.

Chipumbu, G. M. (1993). The Impact of External Debt on African Economies. *International Journal on World Peace*, *10*(1), 43–56.

Docquier, F., Rapoport, H., & Salomone, S. (2012). Remittances, Migrants' Education and Immigration Policy: Theory and Evidence from Bilateral Data. *Regional Science and Urban Economics*, *42*(5), 817–828. doi:10.1016/j.regsciurbeco.2011.10.005

Efobi, U. R. (2015). Politicians' Attributes and Institutional Quality in Africa: A Focus on Corruption. *Journal of Economic Issues*, *49*(3), 787–813. doi:10.1080/00213624.2015.1072393

Efobi, U. R., Osabuohien, E. S., & Oluwatobi, S. (2015). One Dollar, One Bank Account: Remittance and Bank Breadth in Nigeria. *Journal of International Migration and Integration*, *16*(3), 761–781. doi:10.100712134-014-0358-0

Fourie, J. (2016). *Finweek*. Retrieved from https://www.pressreader.com/south-africa/finweek-english-edition/20160908/281492160750259

Hunte, C. K. (2004). Workers' Remittances, Remittance Decay and Financial Deepening in Developing Countries. *The American Economist*, *48*(2), 82–94. doi:10.1177/056943450404800208

Jo-Ansie. (2007). *Political Leaders in Africa: Presidents, Patrons and Profiteers?* Occasional Paper Series 2, 1. African Centre for the Constructive Resolution of Disputes (ACCORD).

Kaufmann, D. (2009). Aid Effectiveness and Governance: The Good, the Bad and the Ugly. *Development Outreach*, *11*(1), 26–29. doi:10.1596/1020-797X-11_1_26

Kenny, C. (2017). How Much Aid is Really Lost to Corruption? *Centre for Global Development*. Retrieved from https://www.cgdev.org/blog/how-much-aid-really-lost-corruption

Makina, D., & Masenge, A. (2015). The Time Pattern of Remittances and the Decay Hypothesis: Evidence from Migrants in South Africa. *Migration Letters: An International Journal of Migration Studies*, *12*(1), 79–90. doi:10.33182/ml.v12i1.258

Maphosa, F. (2007). Remittances and development: The impact of migration to South Africa on rural livelihoods in southern Zimbabwe. *Development Southern Africa*, *24*(1), 123–136. doi:10.1080/03768350601165942

Nigeria Sovereign Investment Authority – NSIA. (2018). *Background on Nigeria Sovereign Investment Authority*. Retrieved from https://www.swfinstitute.org/swfs/excess-crude-account/

Nkume, N. (2018). Financing Mechanisms African Governments Should Pursue in Financing Sustainable Development in the Next 20 Years. In Financing Sustainable Development in Africa. Palgrave Macmillan.

OECD. (2002). *Foreign Direct Investment for Development: Maximising Benefits, Minimising Costs*. OECD.

Omotola, J. S., & Saliu, H. (2009). Foreign aid, debt relief and Africa's development: Problems and prospects. *South African Journal of International Affairs*, *16*(1), 87–102. doi:10.1080/10220460902986180

Osabuohien, E. S., & Efobi, U. R. (2013). Africa's Money in Africa. *The South African Journal of Economics*, *81*(2), 292–306. doi:10.1111aje.12012

Osabuohien, E. S., & Efobi, U. R. (2014). Africa's Money in Africa: Human and Physical Capital Dimensions. In S. Sahoo & B. K. Pattanaik (Eds.), *Global Diaspora and Development: Socioeconomic, Cultural and Policy Perspectives* (pp. 87–104). Springer. doi:10.1007/978-81-322-1047-4_5

Saqib, N., Masnoon, M., & Rafique, N. (2013). Impact of foreign direct investment on economic growth of Pakistan. *Advances in Management & Applied Economics*, *3*(1), 35–45.

Swanson, A. (2015). Why trying to help poor countries might actually hurt them. *Washington Post*. Retrieved from https://www.washingtonpost.com/news/wonk/wp/2015/10/13/why-trying-to-help-poor-countries-might-actually-hurt-them/?noredirect=on&utm_term=.cdc7a88cc142

Torabi, G. (2015). Foreign Direct Investment and Human Development: The Law and Economics of International Investment Agreements. *Journal of Human Development and Capabilities: A Multi-Disciplinary Journal for People-Centered Development, 16*(2) doi:10.1080/19452829.2015.1028813

UNCTAD. (2016). *Structural Transformation and Industrial Policy*. UNCTAD.

UNCTAD. (2018). World Investment Report – Investment and New Industrial Policies, Geneva: UNCTAD Mangasini, K., (2018), The Role of Cooperative Organizations in Tanzania's Industrialization. In U. Efobi & S. Asongu (Eds.), *Financing Sustainable Development in Africa*. Palgrave Macmillan.

Vaknin, S. (2007, May). *Foreign direct investments (FDI)-Pros and Cons*. In Based on a lecture given at the Euro College Student Union Business Forum, Kumanovo, Macedonia.

Velde, D. W. (2006). *Foreign Direct Investment and Development: An Historical Perspective*. Overseas Development Institute, Working Paper. Retrieved from https://www.odi.org/sites/odi.org.uk/files/odi-assets/publications-opinion-files/850.pdf

ENDNOTE

1 Which are those monetary transfers from wealthy nations and rich countries to poorer countries that are broadly corresponding to low and middle income countries for development related issues like education, infrastructural development, and health care growth in the recipient countries. However, it is important to also note that foreign aid covers a multitude of different types of transfers - not all of which go directly to poor countries (Kharas, 2007). For instance, other administrative overhead costs of development agencies, and their domestic efforts to advocate in favor of more assistance, are also regarded as "aid."

Chapter 10
Migrant Remittances and Financial Inclusion in Africa:
A Dynamic and Long-Run Approach

Abba Yadou Barnabe
University of Dschang, Cameroon

ABSTRACT

The main objective of this chapter is to examine the effect of migrant remittances on financial inclusion in Africa from 2004 to 2017. Thus, the authors constructed a composite index of financial inclusion using principal component analysis (PCA). In addition, they examine the effect of remittances on financial inclusion using a system GMM and a pooled mean group (PMG). It is found that remittances have a negative effect on financial inclusion in the short run and a positive effect in the long run. Moreover, remittances have a negative long-term effect on the use of financial services and a positive long-term effect on access to financial services. This implies improved policies to both attract the flow of remittances through formal channels and improve financial inclusion.

INTRODUCTION

The growth and low volatility of migrant remittances in recent decades pose a real challenge for developing economies, which receive 74% of remittances and account for 27% of GDP (World Bank, 2014). Indeed, migrant remittances are one of the sources of external financing of economies and are broader than foreign direct investment and official development assistance. For example, in 2019, migrant remittances to low- and middle-income countries reached $550 billion, surpassing foreign direct investment and official development assistance in those countries (World Bank and Knomad, 2019). All six regions have seen an increase in migrant remittances due in particular to the growing economic situation in the United States and the rebound in remittances from some Gulf Cooperation Council countries. Official statistics on the amount of migrant remittances is underestimated due to the preponderance of informal remittance flows. Indeed, the flow of migrant remittances through non-financial institutions and informal

DOI: 10.4018/978-1-7998-4817-2.ch010

channels accounts for 50% of this flow in Sub-Saharan Africa (Ratha et al., 2010). Moreover, this flow of migrant remittances is about 50 to 250% of official statistics, according to Freund and Spatafora (2008).

Besides, financial inclusion at the G20 summit in Seoul was placed high on the global development agenda. Financial inclusion is defined as access for individuals and enterprises previously excluded from the formal financial system to a range of useful and responsive financial products and services (transactions, payments, savings, credit and insurance) offered by formal financial intermediaries. For Sarma and Pais (2011), financial inclusion is a process that ensures the ease of access, availability and use of the formal financial system by all individuals in an economy. An inclusive financial system facilitates the efficient allocation of productive resources and thus has the potential to reduce the cost of capital (Sarma, 2008). In addition, it has been recognized that remittances from migrants play an essential development role and financial inclusion is vital (Global Migration Group, 2017; Efobi et al, 2015).

Previous studies have examined the link between migrant remittances and financial inclusion in a superficial way by not considering all aspects of financial inclusion. A study that takes into account the different dimensions of financial inclusion should produce a more explicit understanding of this relationship. Moreover, apart from the work of Chuc et al. (2019), taking into account the different aspects of financial inclusion in Middle-Income Countries (MICs), this study takes Africa into account.

Previous studies have considered the relationship between migrant remittances and financial inclusion by taking into account a financial inclusion indicator (Gemechu et al., 2014; Ambrosius et al., 2014; Inoue et al. 2016; Inoue and Hamori, 2016; Kwesi et al., 2020); and therefore provides incomplete information on financial inclusion (Sarma, 2008), based on a country (Anzoategui et al., 2014; Ajefu and Ogebe 2019) and taking into account a composite index. In addition to the work of Chuc et al. (2019) based on the case of middle-income countries (MICs), this study takes into account Africa composed of low-income countries (LICs) and low- and middle-income countries (LMICs). Moreover, in this study, we take into account the dynamic and long-term impact of the relationship between migrant remittances and financial inclusion.

LITERATURE REVIEW

Reasons for the positive impact of migrant remittances on financial inclusion include the increasing amount that leads to a demand for a bank account (Efobi et al. 2015; Ambrosius and Cuecuecha, 2016), reducing the risk of information asymmetry (Roa, 2015) which increases the creditworthiness of remittance recipients with lenders (Orozco and Fedewa, 2006; Chuc et al. 2019). Finally, it leads to the promotion of financial literacy that eventually leads to financial inclusion (Yoshino et al., 2017).

Theoretical Review

Theoretically, this study is based on the theories of asymmetry of information and pure altruism.

The theory of information asymmetry has its roots in the work of George Akerlof on Lemons markets in 1970. This theory refers to the effect of moral hazard between market participants, where one of the market participants holds information not known by the parties and which leads to market inefficiency. Many arguments argue that a regular flow of migrant remittances makes it easier for financial institutions to hold information on the income of the recipients of these flows, thereby establishing their creditworthiness (Anzoategui et al. 2014; Ambrosius and Cuecuecha, 2016). Also, remittances can be considered as collateral for obtaining credit, which aims to reduce problems of information asymmetry (Misati and Kamau, 2018; Toxopeus and Lensink, 2008). Such information could make financial institutions willing and able to provide credit and other financial products to remittance recipients (Brown et al., 2013). Besides, increased remittances may increase demand for bank deposit accounts as households need services to safeguard their temporary surplus income (Aggarwal et al. 2011; Anzoategui et al., 2014; Ambrosius and Cuecuecha, 2016).

The theory of pure altruism comes from the work of Lucas and Stark on the motivations for sending remittances to Botswana. In their study, they divided the theories of remittances into three groups, namely pure altruism, pure self-interest and temperate altruism. According to the pure altruism theory, the migrant's satisfaction depends on the satisfaction of his or her family in the country of origin (Lucas and Stark, 1985). Thus, migrant remittances act as insurance for recipient households to cope with shocks by diversifying sources of income (Stark, 1991).

In pure self-interest, migrant remittances play a role in acquiring assets for the migrant such as land, houses, and investment in a project. According to Lucas and Stack (1985), pure altruism or pure self-interest cannot explain the growth of this flow and its variability. They propose a theory of tempered altruism whereby remittances are seen as part of an agreement between the migrant and the recipients in his or her country of origin. Thus, unlike remittances through the informal channel, remittances through bank accounts can encourage savings and investment (World Bank, 2005). Estimates show that 10% of remittance recipients save, invest and use them for entrepreneurial activity (Orozco and Fedewa, 2006).

Empirical Review

The impact of remittances on financial inclusion has been little developed. Still, studies have focused more on access to financial services, often taking into account a dimension of financial inclusion, such as the possession of an account or the availability of financial institutions by increasing the branches of commercial banks and their impact on credit ((Inou and Hamori, 2016; Brown et al., 2013; Ambrosius and Cuecuecha, 2016). Empirical studies on the impact of remittances on financial inclusion can be divided into two main parts. One part focuses on a simple approach based on a financial inclusion indicator, and the other part focuses on a multidimensional approach. The development of financial sector and institutional development are also essential (Akinyemi et al, 2019; Karakara and Osabuohien, 2019).

Migrant remittances increase access to financial services (bank account ownership, increase in banking branches). The work of Anzoategui et al. (2014) examining the impact of remittances on access to financial services in El Salvador shows that receiving migrant remittances increases the probability of having an account by 11%. Also, Ambrosius (2016) using data from Mexico, finds that the impact of remittances increases the holding of savings accounts. However, remittances play a catalytic role for access to formal financial services if recipients are aware of the importance of formal finance (Inoue and Hamori, 2016).

Nevertheless, some work shows that remittances do not increase borrowing (Ambrosius, 2016; Anzoategui et al., 2014; Durga, 2019). Using household survey data in Mexico, Ambrosius and Cuecuecha (2016) study the effect of remittances on the use of formal and informal financial services. Their results show that remittances have a positive and significant impact on informal borrowing. However, studies by Aggarwal et al. (2011), show that remittances from migrants increase the aggregate level of deposit and credit with financial institutions. Moreover, Gupta et al. (2009), Demirguc-kunt et al. (2011) confirm this.

Previous studies do not consider financial inclusion on a multidimensional level, and some work is limited to a single period, such as the work of Durga (2019). These indicators of financial inclusion used individually provide partial information on financial inclusion and can lead to misinterpretation of the scope of financial inclusion (Sarma, 2008). Recent studies by Chuc et al. (2019) attempt to close this gap, although they ignore the geographical dimension of financial inclusion. Indeed, studies by Chuc et al. (2019) show that remittance flows and financial inclusion are positively related to economic development. Moreover, using a generalized moment model and a Structural Equation Model (SEM), they show that remittance flows can boost financial inclusion. They construct a financial inclusion index following the approach of Wang and Guan (2017), which takes into account two dimensions of financial inclusion. Financial inclusion in their work takes into account the access and use aspect of formal financial institutions. They disregard the geographical dimension of financial inclusion, which is captured by the proximity of financial services, which itself according to Global Findex (2017) is a reason for financial exclusion.

METHODOLOGY

Our sample covers 29 African countries from 2004 to 2017 due to data availability. Variables are drawn from several data sources such as the World Development Indicator (WDI), Financial Access Survey (FAS), Global Financial Development Database (GFDD) and International Country Risk Guide (ICRG).

Measuring Financial Inclusion

Several works have been undertaken to construct the financial inclusion index, such as the work of Sarma (2008). Sarma (2008) considers three dimensions of financial inclusion: banking penetration, availability of banking services, and the use of banking services. The first and second dimensions are similar. Thus, in this study, we consider two dimensions, namely access to and use of financial services. The use of banking services is motivated by two reasons, one of which refers to the notion of under-banked developed by Kempson et al. (2004) and the second to the fact that the possession of a bank account is not sufficient for financial inclusion. In the dimension of access to financial services, we take into account demographic (Sarma, 2008) and geographical (Mialou et al., 2017) indicators. The indicators of the availability of banking services in terms of demographics come from the FAS database. They include the number of bank branches per 100,000 adults and the number of ATMs per 100,000 adults. Indicators of financial services availability in terms of geography are the number of bank machines and the number of ATMs per 1,000 km2.

Like Sarma (2015), the financial services utilization dimension considers the volume of credit and deposits as a function of GDP. In this study, we take into account for the use dimension financial sector deposits as a percentage of GDP from the Global Financial Development Database (GFDD), domestic credit as a percentage of GDP from the World Development Indicator (WDI) and mobile banking. The increase in the use of mobile banking in Sub-Saharan Africa. For mobile banking, we use the mobile service subscription per 100 people from WDI. This indicator has been used by several studies on financial inclusion (Andrianaivo and Kpodar, 2012; Lenk and Barik, 2018). For the construction of the financial inclusion variable (FII), we use the Principal Component Analysis (PCA) approach.

Control Variables

Population growth (POPGROWTH) and population density (POPDENSITY) measures the demographic effect and population concentration on banking penetration. Some authors such as Beck et al. (2005) find a correlation between banking availability and the size of the economy and especially population density. We take into account government investment (goveexp) measured by government spending as a proportion of GDP and inflation (inflation) measured as an annual percentage of the consumer price index to account for economic uncertainty. We consider the Human Development Index (HDI) because there is a positive correlation between human development and financial inclusion (Arindam, 2015). We measure the quality of institutions by taking the average of seven variables from the ICRG database, which include: corruption, law and order, government stability, democratic accountability, quality of bureaucracy, socio-economic conditions, and internal conflict. Internet access and subscription to mobile services have a positive impact on financial inclusion (Olaniyi, 2018). Thus, we measure internet access (internet) by individual internet use as a percentage of the population. Our variable of interest migrant remittances (remit) is measured as a percentage of GDP. FII, FIIusage and FIIaccess represent the financial inclusion index, the financial services usage index and the financial services access index, respectively.

Methodological Approach using GMM and PMG

This section specifies the methodology adapted to examine the link between migrant remittances and financial inclusion. In this study, we adopt a system GMM to examine the dynamic effect of remittances on financial inclusion. Then for robustness, we consider the short- and long-term effect by adopting a Pooled Mean Group (PMG). The PMG allows us to see whether the results obtained with the GMM are short- or long-term results.

System GMM

We use a GMM in system as well as the work of Chuc et al. (2019) to take into account the potential endogeneity problem. Our equation takes this form:

$$FII_{it} = \beta_0 + \beta_1 FII_{i,t-1} + \beta_2 remit_{it} + X_{it} + \varepsilon_{it} \tag{1}$$

With FII_{it} who represents the financial inclusion index of country i in year t, $remit_{it}$ represents migrants' remittances, X_{it} represents the control variables and εi_t represents the error term.

Pooled Mean Group (PMG)

The GMM method just captures the short-term dynamics and ignores the long-term dynamics. To take into account the long-term dynamics, it is, therefore, appropriate to use a Pooled Mean Group (PMG) model developed by Pesaran et al. (1999). Indeed, Pesaran et al. (1999) suggest that for a large cross-section and a dynamic panel, panel regression, and an error-correction model can be combined by applying an Auto Regressive Distributive Lag ($ARDL_{p,q}$). The model can be written as follows:

$$FII_{i,t} = \varphi^i \left[FII_{i,t-1} \left\{ \beta_0^i + \beta_1^i X_{i,t-1} \right\} \right] + \sum_{j=1}^{p-1} \gamma_j^i FII_{i,t-j} + \sum_{j=0}^{q-1} \delta_j^i \Delta X_{i,t-j} + \mu_i + \varepsilon_{it} \quad (2)$$

FII, the financial inclusion index δ and γ represents respectively the short-term coefficient of the lagged independent and dependent variable, β represents the long-term coefficient, p and q represent respectively the lagged dependent and independent variable, φ is the coefficient of the speed of adjustment towards long-term equilibrium and εit th$_e$ error term.

Specifically, our equation (2) becomes equation (3) below:

$$\begin{aligned} \Delta FII_{i,t} &= \alpha_i + \sum_{j=1}^{m-1} \beta_{ij} \Delta FII_{i,t-j} + \sum_{l=0}^{n-1} \varphi_{il} \Delta remit_{i,t-l} + \sum_{r=0}^{p-1} \gamma_{ir} \Delta POPGROWTH_{i,t-r} + \sum_{u=0}^{s-1} \theta_{iu} \Delta HDI_{i,t-u} \\ &+ \sum_{w=0}^{v-1} \delta_{iw} \Delta \inf lation_{i,t-w} + \sum_{z=0}^{x-1} \varphi_{iz} \Delta \operatorname{int} ernet_{i,t-z} + \sigma_1 remit_{i,t-1} + \sigma_2 HDI_{i,t-1} \\ &+ \sigma_3 POPDENSITY_{i,t-1} + \sigma_4 POGROWTH_{i,t-1} + \sigma_5 gove \exp_{i,t-1} + \sigma_6 \inf lation_{i,t-1} \\ &+ \sigma_7 \operatorname{int} ernet_{i,t-1} + \sigma_8 ICRGmean_{i,t-1} \varepsilon_{i,t} \end{aligned} \quad (3)$$

To examine the effect of remittances on the use of financial services, we adopt the following model:

$$\begin{aligned} \Delta FIIusage_{i,t} &= \alpha_i + \sum_{j=1}^{m-1} \beta_{ij} \Delta FIIusage_{i,t-j} + \sum_{l=0}^{n-1} \varphi_{il} \Delta remit_{i,t-l} + \sum_{r=0}^{p-1} \gamma_{ir} \Delta POPGROWTH_{i,t-r} \\ &+ \sigma_1 remit_{i,t-1} + \sigma_2 HDI_{i,t-1} + \sigma_3 POPDENSITY_{i,t-1} + \sigma_4 POGROWTH_{i,t-1} \\ &+ \sigma_5 gove \exp_{i,t-1} + \sigma_6 \inf lation_{i,t-1} + \sigma_7 \operatorname{int} ernet_{i,t-1} + \sigma_8 ICRGmean_{i,t-1} \varepsilon_{i,t} \end{aligned} \quad (4)$$

To examine the impact of remittances on access to financial services, we adopt equation (5) below:

$$\begin{aligned} \Delta FIIaccess_{i,t} &= \alpha_i + \sum_{j=1}^{m-1} \beta_{ij} \Delta FIIaccess_{i,t-j} + \sum_{l=0}^{n-1} \varphi_{il} \Delta remit_{i,t-l} + \sum_{r=0}^{p-1} \gamma_{ir} \Delta POPGROWTH_{i,t-r} \\ &+ \sigma_1 remit_{i,t-1} + \sigma_2 HDI_{i,t-1} + \sigma_3 POPDENSITY_{i,t-1} + \sigma_4 POGROWTH_{i,t-1} \\ &+ \sigma_5 gove \exp_{i,t-1} + \sigma_6 \inf lation_{i,t-1} + \sigma_7 \operatorname{int} ernet_{i,t-1} + \sigma_8 ICRGmean_{i,t-1} \varepsilon_{i,t} \end{aligned} \quad (5)$$

RESULTS FROM EMPIRICAL ANALYSES

Preliminary Tests

The list of countries in the sample include: Angola, Botswana, Burkina Faso, Cote d'Ivoire, Malawi, Mali, Niger, Democratic Republic of Congo, Senegal, Sierra Leone, South Africa, Algeria, Cameroon, Congo, Egypt, Gabon, Ghana, Kenya, Madagascar, Morocco, Namibia, Nigeria, Sudan, Tanzania, Togo,

Tunisia, Uganda, Zambia and Zimbabwe. Table 1 show the description of the variables, while Table 2 provide their descriptive statistics.

Table 1b shows that remittances from migrants contribute on average 2.853919 of the percentage of GDP in the sampled countries. Moreover, the correlation matrix in Table 2 indicates that there is a low correlation between the variables used.

Table 1. Description of the variables

Variable Name	Description/Measurement	Sources
FII	Financial inclusion	Author
FIIaccess	Financial access	Author
FIIusage	Financial usage	Author
remit	Remittances comprise personal transfers and compensation of employees (as % GDP)	WDI
POPDENSITY	Density of population per 100 km2	WDI
POPGROWTH	Growth of population	WDI
internet	Internet subscriptions (per 100 people)	WDI
ICRGmean	Institution measured by mean of six variables of ICRG	ICRG
goveexp	Government expenditures are government final consumption expenditure (as % GDP)	WDI
inflation	Inflation is measured by the annual growth of consumer price	WDI
HDI	Human development index	UNHDI

Table 2. Descriptive statistics

Variables	Observations	Mean	Std error	Min	Max
remit	406	2.853919	3.109463	.0001832	13.61145
POPDENSITY	406	58.62275	50.42111	2.440486	213.759
POPGROWTH	406	2.534945	.7258959	.780902	4.51511
FII	406	.2069662	.1575069	1.00e-09	1
internet	406	12.66746	14.03159	.1899337	61.76221
ICRGmean	406	4.228727	.722095	2.5	5.857143
FIIusage	406	.275301	.178766	1.11e-08	1
FIIaccess	406	.2508143	.1887087	2.47e-09	1
goveexp	406	14.03169	4.627847	2.047121	26.24226
inflation	406	6.797134	6.77604	-23.08492	43.54211
HDI	406	.522532	.1087294	.274	.754

Source: The Authors'

Table 3. Pearson correlation matrix

	FII	remit	goveexp	inflation	HDI	popdensity	popgrowth
FII	1.0000						
remit	0.0733	1.0000					
goveexp	-0.0164	-0.0727	1.0000				
inflation	-0.0127	-0.2066	-0.2900	1.0000			
HDI	0.0191	-0.0907	0.2946	-0.0337	1.0000		
POPDENSITY	0.1876	0.3361	-0.3660	0.1968	-0.1439	1.0000	
POPGROWTH	0.0496	-0.1681	-0.3141	0.1476	-0.6274	0.0649	1.0000
ICRGmean	0.0602	-0.1751	0.4244	-0.0554	0.4445	-0.1806	-0.4049
FIIusage	0.3696	-0.0506	-0.0044	-0.0257	-0.0292	-0.0135	0.0038
FIIaccess	0.4974	0.0956	0.0487	-0.0510	0.0391	0.0034	-0.0577
internet	0.0316	0.1346	0.2663	-0.0970	0.6612	0.0615	-0.4809
	ICRGmean	FIIusage	FIIaccess	internet	mobile		
ICRGmean	1.0000						
FIIusage	0.0616	1.0000					
FIIaccess	0.0591	0.2569	1.0000				
internet	0.1371	0.0037	0.0647	1.0000			

Source: The Authors'

Test of Cross-Section Dependence and Unit Root Test

Table 4 shows the cross-section dependence test, according to Pesaran (2004) and Pesaran (2015). Indeed, the Pesaran (2004) test the strong existence of a cross-sectional dependence or the Pesaran (2015) test residuals or a variable for weak cross-sectional dependence in a panel data.

Table 4. Cross-section dependence test of Pesaran (2004) and Pesaran (2015)

Variables	Pesaran (2004)	Pesaran (2015)
remit	1.68*	61.782***
FII	19.21***	54.996***
HDI	73.55***	75.360***
goveexp	4.20***	73.015***
inflation	10.92***	54.840***
POPDENSITY	75.29***	75.336***
POPGROWTH	9.65***	74.626***
internet	69.05***	71.347***
ICRGmean	27.38***	75.162***
FIIusage	26.44***	59.910***
FIIaccess	20.94***	52.470***
Note: *** p<0.01, ** p<0.05 and ** p<0.1		

Source: The Authors'

This analysis shows that all the variables in our study have strong and weak cross-sectional dependence.

In the presence of cross-sectional dependence, the first-generation unit root test is biased, so it is essential to perform a second-generation unit root test. For this fact, we use the unit root tests of Pesaran (2003) and Pesaran (2007). It appears that our variables are stationary in level and difference. Table 5 shows the results of the different variables.

Table 5. Unit root test of Pesaran (2003, 2007)

Variables	Pesaran (2003)		Pesaran (2007)		Decision
	At Level	1st Difference	At Level	1st Difference	
remit	1.089	-0.597	-2.401***	-3.664***	I (0)
FII	-3.394***	-4.351***	-2.659***	-3.118***	I (0)
HDI	0.440	-0.680	-1.765	-2.817***	I (1)
goveexp	-3.614***	-5.428***	-2.055	-3.335***	I (0)
inflation	-2.731***	-2.881***	-2.667***	-3.988***	I (0)
POPDENSITY	-8.789***	-5.745***	-1.248	-0.937	I (0)
POPGROWTH	-4.802***	-4.156***	-1.208	-0.532	I (0)
internet	2.810	-0.749	-1.116	-2.685***	I (1)
ICRGmean	-4.389***	-3.952***	-2.347***	-3.343***	I (0)
FIIusage	-2.558***	-6.615***	-2.178*	-3.837***	I (0)
FIIaccess	-3.323***	-2.918***	-2.512***	-2.972***	I (0)

*** $p<0.01$
Source: The Authors'

Remittances and Financial Inclusion Nexus: System GMM Estimation Result

There is no evidence of a second serial correlation, but strong evidence of a first correlation. Then, regression analysis successfully passes the Sargan specification test as well as error term serial correlation tests (AR1 and AR2) and confirm the validity of instruments.

The results of the GMM system show us that remittances from migrants have a negative impact on financial inclusion in Africa. Indeed, remittances to Africa according to Ratha et al. (2010) in sub-Saharan African countries is more than 50%, and remittances via the informal channel occupy 50 to 250% of the official statistics of migrant remittances according to Freund and Spatafora (2008). Thus, the more remittances pass through the informal sector, the more recipient households do not find it necessary to use financial intermediaries to deposit their surplus income. However, it should also be taken into account that the cost of sending international remittances is high and thus discourages migrants from using formal channels. Also, according to the World Bank and Knomad (2019), the average overall cost of remittances is about 7% in the first quarter of 2019. Moreover, remittances to Sub-Saharan Africa are 9.3%, representing three times the target of the Sustainable Development Goals (SDGs).

According to the work of Lukman and Adeyemi (2019), remittances do not have a significant impact on financial inclusion in SSA. Furthermore, Kwesi et al. (2020) show that remittances from formal migrants in Kenya have a positive impact on financial inclusion due to the policies implemented by the

Table 6. GMM estimate of the relationship between remittances and financial inclusion

	GMM		
	FII	**FIIusage**	**FIIaccess**
L.FII	0.669***		
	(0.172)		
L.FIIusage		0.755***	
		(0.140)	
L.FIIaccess			0.762***
			(0.144)
remit	-0.0795**	0.0882*	0.0158
	(0.0310)	(0.0475)	(0.0378)
HDI	0.0434	0.285	0.320
	(0.176)	(0.200)	(0.225)
inflation	-0.00830***	-0.00631**	-0.00335
	(0.00274)	(0.00284)	(0.00270)
POPDENSITY	0.00216***	-0.00164*	-0.000151
	(0.000733)	(0.000999)	(0.000796)
POPGROWTH	-0.0425	0.112**	0.0337
	(0.0423)	(0.0517)	(0.0430)
ICRGmean	0.0139	0.0174	-0.0248
	(0.0347)	(0.0473)	(0.0425)
Constant	0.247	-0.567	-0.110
	(0.347)	(0.397)	(0.354)
AR1 (p-value)	5.05e-05	1.75e-05	1.44e-05
AR2 (p-value) value)	0.461	0.217	0.766
Sargan (p-value)	0.563	0.496	0.131
Number of countries	29	29	29
Observations	375	375	375

Standards errors in parentheses ***p<0.01, **p<0.05, ***p<0.1
Source: The Authors'

government. Removing barriers and reducing the cost of remittances can improve access to and use of financial services (Ajefu and Ogebe, 2019). Therefore, with the high cost of remittances and a large share of this flow passing through the informal channel, this reduces its impact on financial inclusion.

Furthermore, our results show that remittances from migrants have a positive impact on the use of financial services but have no impact on access to services, although the latter is positive. Our results are contrary to the findings of Chuc et al. (2019) which shows that remittances are a substitute for credit. In this work, it appears that remittances can play a complementary role in the use of financial services by reducing the liquidity constraint. But this effect on the use of financial services is positively small.

ROBUSTNESS OF RESULTS

Pooled Mean Group Estimation Result

However, it should be noted that these results refer to short-term effects using a GMM in the system. To see the long term and short-term impact, we use a Pooled Mean Group (PMG), model. Also, we add in the control variables the effect of internet access on financial inclusion (Olaniyi, 2018) and government investment as is the case in the work of Chuc et al. (2019).

Table 7. Remittances and financial inclusion: Pooled Mean Group estimation

	Variables	FII	FII	FIIaccess	FIIusage
Long run	remit	.0656782*** (.0021599)	.0522351*** (.0027108)	.0262164*** (.0080475)	-.0262044*** (.0030172)
	inflation	-.002897*** (.000318)	-.0026334*** (.0002919)		
	HDI	.1132031*** (.013756)			
	internet		.0020735*** (.000211)		
	POPGROWTH			-1.082425*** (.0276823)	-.177262*** (.0290421)
Short-run	ECT	-.6637885*** (.1511034)	-.6716655*** (.1515667)	-.5323233*** (.1704227)	-.8372684*** (.1423727)
	remit	-.2204385* (.1265524)	-.1265116* (.0689137)	-.1025458 (.0805059)	.0877918 (.2004535)
	HDI	-1.267322 (4.776106)	-.9909363 (4.64577)	12.3204 (8.3409)	-6.391084 (6.635059)
	POPDENSITY	-.2413485 (.3089223)	-.2182577 (.3080472)	1.308874 (1.594743)	1.000009 (1.310518)
	POPGROWTH	-.0767951 (1.273814)	-.0122939 (1.281167)	-2.75797 (3.297486)	.9049065 (1.705061)
	goveexp	-.012881 (.0131241)	-.0128341 (.013365)	-.0241944 (.0207876)	.0213577 (.0191577)
	inflation	.0055576 (.0036285)	.0053944 (.0037587)	.0079969 (.0073231)	.0079969 (.0051013)
	internet	-.0043198 (.0105461)	-.0051738 (.0105585)	-.0432451 (.0338187)	.0066893 (.0155689)
	ICRGmean	.119903 (.0927137)	.1165681 (.0919859)	-.2138048 (.1378558)	.1505801 (.1324114)
	cons	.2190276 (.2806209)	.2673282 (.285533)	1.387273 (1.052887)	.6663214 (.4367653)

Standards errors in parentheses ***p<0.01, **p<0.05, ***p<0.1
Source: The Authors'

The results of the PMG model show us that the results found using the GMM in-system model are short-term effects except for the access to financial services dimension. The PMG results show us that migrant remittances have a negative short-term impact on financial inclusion but a positive long-term impact. Moreover, by adding the variable internet access, we find that internet access increases financial inclusion (Olaniyi, 2018). Furthermore, remittances may have a negative effect on financial service use in the long run because this flow would act as a substitute for the demand for credit. Indeed, even as the receipt of remittances leads to the demand for a deposit account (Demirguc-Kunt et al., 2011), it is also a substitute for credit in countries with greater credit constraints (Giuliano and Ruiz-Arranz 2009) and hence a lower demand for credit. Moreover, according to Ambrosius and Cuecuecha (2016), the effect of remittances on credit is driven by informal finance to the detriment of traditional lending through formal financial intermediaries. Thus, the increase in migrant remittances is unlikely to encourage the use of formal financial services (Chuc et al., 2019).

Dumitrescu and Hurlin Causality Test (2012)

This study also uses the panel causality test of Dumitrescu and Hurlin (2012) to examine the potential link between migrant remittances and financial inclusion in Africa. Indeed, the study of causality allows for more appropriate economic policy recommendations. Dumitrescu and Hurlin's (2012) test is based on the null hypothesis of no causality for the panel versus the alternative hypothesis of causality for at least one unit in the panel. It is based on a linear dynamic panel test in which the following equation is used:

$$y_{it} = \alpha_i + \sum_{k=1}^{k} \beta_{ik} y_{i(t-k)} + \sum_{k=1}^{k} \gamma_{ik} x_{i(t-k)} + \varepsilon_{it}$$

Where k is the number of delays and εi_t the error term, the above equation allows us to examine the causal effect of variable X on variable Y. Dumitrescu and Hurlin (2012) proposed a mean statistic of Wald's test to test the null hypothesis. Wald's statistic is given as follows:

$$\overline{W}_{NT} = \frac{1}{N} \sum_{i=1}^{N} W_{iT}$$

Where's W_{iT} the Wald individual statistic for Granger's causality test. The Wald test statistic is independently and identically distributed, and the panel causality test is:

$$\overline{Z} = \sqrt{\frac{N}{2K}} (\overline{W}_{NT} - K)$$

Furthermore, the causality test of Dumitrescu and Hurlin (2012) has the advantage of taking into account the potential problem of cross-section dependency by implementing a bootstrap procedure to calculate the critical values of the test. Before implementing this causality test, the cross-section dependency test is conducted for each variable (see Table 3) using the CD test of Pesaran (2004 and 2015).

Table 8. Dumitrescu et Hurlin (2012) Granger non-causality test results

Null Hypothesis	z-bar	lag
FII does not Granger-cause remit.	1.5463	1
remit does not Granger-cause FII	4.3616***	1
FIIusage does not Granger-cause remit.	3.6639***	1
remit does not Granger-cause FIIusage.	-0.0431	1
FIIaccess does not Granger-cause remit	1.5939	1
remit does not Granger-cause FIIaccess.	8.3551***	1
H0: internet does not Granger-cause FII	17.0063***	1
H0: FII does not Granger-cause internet	3.0010***	1

Source: Authors

Dumitrescu and Hurlin's (2012) causality test shows us that there is a unidirectional causality between remittances and financial inclusion. Moreover, the use of financial services impacts the receipt of remittances. There is a unidirectional causality between remittances and access to financial services. Also, there is a two-way relationship between financial inclusion and internet access.

CONCLUSION

In this study, we examine the dynamic effect and the short- and long-term effect of migrant remittances on financial inclusion in a sample of 29 African countries from 2004 to 2017. Based on a GMM system model that solves the potential endogeneity problem and the PMG model that allows us to observe the short- and long-term dynamics, we find that remittances have a negative short-term impact on financial inclusion but a positive long-term impact.

Furthermore, by considering our two dimensions of financial inclusion (access and use of financial services) separately, we find that in the long run, remittances have a negative impact on the use of financial services but a positive impact on access to financial services. Thus, remittances play a role as a substitute for the use of financial services. To benefit from remittances, governments will need to implement a policy of attracting remittances to formal channels by removing barriers and reducing the costs of sending remittances.

REFERENCES

Aga & Peria. (2014). *International remittances and financial inclusion in Africa*. World Bank.

Aggarwal, R., Demirguc-Kunt, A., Soledad, M., & Peria, M. (2011). Do Emittances Promote Financial Development? *Journal of Development Economics*, *96*(2), 255–264. doi:10.1016/j.jdeveco.2010.10.005

Ajefu, J. B., & Ogebe, J. (2019). Migrant Remittances and Financial Inclusion among Households in Nigeria. *Oxford Development Studies*, *47*(3), 319–335. doi:10.1080/13600818.2019.1575349

Akinyemi, O., Efobi, U., Asongu, S., & Osabuohien, E. (2019). Renewable energy, trade performance and the conditional role of finance and institutional capacity in sub-Sahara African Countries. *Energy Policy*, *132*, 490–498. doi:10.1016/j.enpol.2019.06.012

Ambrosius, C. (2016). Remittances and financial access: Is there really a link and for whom? Evidence from Mexican household data. *World Economy*, *39*(7), 964–982. doi:10.1111/twec.12287

Ambrosius, C., & Cuecuecha, A. (2016). Remittances and the Use of Formal and Informal Financial Services. *World Development*, *77*, 80–98. doi:10.1016/j.worlddev.2015.08.010

Ambrosius, C., Fritz, B., & Stiegler, U. (2014). Remittances for Financial Access: Lessons from Latin American Microfinance. *Development Policy Review*, *32*(6), 733–753. doi:10.1111/dpr.12087

André, M., Amidzic, G., & Massara, A. (2017). Assessing Countries' Financial Inclusion Standing – A New Composite Index. *Journal of Banking and Financial Economics*, *2*(8), 105–126. doi:10.7172/23536845.jbfe.2017.2.5

Andrianaivo, M., & Kpodar, K. (2012). Mobile phone use spurs economic growth through financial inclusion. *Revista de Economia Institucional*, *3*(2).

Anzoategui, D., Demirguc-Kunt, A., & Peria, M. S. M. (2014). Remittances and Financial Inclusion: Evidence from El Salvador. *World Development*, *54*, 338–349. doi:10.1016/j.worlddev.2013.10.006

Arthur, K. E., Musau, S. M., & Wanjohi, F. M. (2020). Diaspora Remittances and Financial Inclusion in Kenya. *European Journal of Business and Management Research*, *5*(2). Advance online publication. doi:10.24018/ejbmr.2020.5.2.289

Beck, T., Demirguc-Kunt, A., & Peria, M. S. M. (2007). Reaching out: Access to and use of banking services across countries. *Journal of Financial Economics*, *85*(1), 234–266. doi:10.1016/j.jfineco.2006.07.002

Brown, R. P. C., Carmignani, F., & Fayad, G. (2013). Migrants' Remittances and Financial Development: Macro- and Micro-level Evidence of a Perverse Relationship. *World Economy*, *36*(5), 636–660. doi:10.1111/twec.12016

Demirguc-Kunt, A., Lopez Cordova, E., Martınez Perıa, M. S., & Woodruff, C. (2011). Remittances and Banking Sector Breadth and Depth: Evidence from Mexico. *Journal of Development Economics*, *95*(2), 229–241. doi:10.1016/j.jdeveco.2010.04.002

Dumitrescu, E.-I., & Hurlin, C. (2012). Testing for Granger non-causality in heterogeneous panels. *Economic Modelling*, *29*(4), 1450–1460. doi:10.1016/j.econmod.2012.02.014

Efobi, U. R., Osabuohien, E. S., & Oluwatobi, S. (2015). One Dollar, One Bank Account: Remittance and Bank Breadth in Nigeria. *Journal of International Migration and Integration*, *16*(3), 761–781. doi:10.100712134-014-0358-0

Evans, O. (2018). *connecting the poor: the internet, mobile phones and financial inclusion in Africa*. Digital Policy Regulation and Governance.

Findex, G. (2017). Measuring financial inclusion and Fintex revolution. Academic Press.

Freund, C., & Spatafora, N. (2008). Remittances, transaction costs, and informality. *Journal of Development Economics*, *86*(2), 356–366. doi:10.1016/j.jdeveco.2007.09.002

Gautam, D. P. (2019). *Do remittances promote financial inclusion?* (J. C. Hall & S. Harper, Eds.). Economic and Political Institutions and Development., doi:10.1007/978-3-030-06049-7_6

Giuliano, P., & Ruiz-Arranz, M. (2009). Remittances, Financial Development, and Growth. *Journal of Development Economics*, *90*(1), 144–152. doi:10.1016/j.jdeveco.2008.10.005

Global Migration Group. (2017). *Migration, remittances and financial inclusion: challenges and opportunities for women's Economic Empowerment.* GMG Report.

Gupta, S., Pattillo, C., & Wagh, S. (2009). Effect of Remittances on Poverty and Financial Development in Sub-Saharan Africa. *World Development*, *37*(1), 104–115. doi:10.1016/j.worlddev.2008.05.007

Inoue, T., & Hamori, S. (2016). Do Workers' Remittances Promote Access to Finance? Evidence from Asia-Pacific Developing Countries. *Emerging Markets Finance & Trade*, *52*(3), 765–774. doi:10.1080/1540496X.2016.1116287

Karakara, A. A., & Osabuohien, E. (2019). Households' ICT Access and Bank Patronage in West Africa: Empirical Insights from Burkina Faso and Ghana. *Technology in Society*, *56*, 116–125. doi:10.1016/j.techsoc.2018.09.010

Kempson, E., Atkinson, A., & Pilley, O. (2004). Policy level response to financial exclusion in developed economies: lessons for developing countries. Report of Personal Finance Research Centre, University of Bristol.

Kpodar, K., & Andrianaivo, M. (2011). *ICT, Financial Inclusion, and Growth Evidence from African Countries.* IMF Working Paper/11/73.

Laha. (2015). Association between financial inclusion and human development in south asia: A cross-country analysis with special reference to India. *Journal of Economic Policy and Research*, *10*(2).

Lenk, S. K., & Barik, R. (2018). Has expansion of mobile phone and internet use spurred financial inclusion in the SAARC countries? *Financial Innovation*, *4*(5), 5. Advance online publication. doi:10.118640854-018-0089-x

Lucas, R. E. B., & Stark, O. (1985). Motivations to Remit: Evidence from Botswana. *Journal of Political Economy*, *93*(5), 901–918. doi:10.1086/261341

Mandira, S. (2015). Measuring financial inclusion. *Economic Bulletin*, *35*(1), 604–611.

Misati, R., & Kamau, A. (2018). *Do Migrant Remittances Matter for Financial Development in Kenya?* The Kenya Bankers Association (KBA) Working Papers, no. 30, WPS/08/18.

Orozco & Fedewa. (2006). *Leveraging Efforts on Remittances and Financial Intermediation.* INTAL-ITD: Inter-American Development Bank.

Oyelami & Ogundipe. (2020). An empirical investigation of remittances and financial inclusion nexus in Sub-Saharan Africa. *Cogent Business & Management.* doi:10.1080/23311975.2020.1712126

Pesaran, M. H. (2003). *Estimation and inference in large heterogenous panels with cross section dependence.* CESifo Working Paper Series.

Pesaran, M. H. (2004). *General diagnostic tests for cross section dependence in panels*. CESifo working paper series No 1219.

Pesaran, M. H. (2007). A simple panel unit root test in the presence of cross-sectional dependence. *Journal of Applied Econometrics*, *22*(2), 265–312. doi:10.1002/jae.951

Pesaran, M. H. (2015). Testing weak cross-sectional dependence in large panels. *Econometric Reviews*, *34*(6-10), 1089–1117. doi:10.1080/07474938.2014.956623

Pesaran, M. H., Shin, Y., & Smith, R. P. (1999). Pooled mean group estimation of dynamic heterogeneous panels. *Journal of the American Statistical Association*, *94*(446), 621–634. doi:10.1080/01621459.1999.10474156

Pesaran, M. H., Shin, Y., & Smith, R. P. (1999). Pooled mean group estimation of dynamic heterogeneous panels. *Journal of the American Statistical Association*, *94*(446), 621–634. doi:10.1080/01621459.1999.10474156

Ratha, D., Mohapatra, S., & Silwal, A. (2010). *Migration and remittances factbook 2011*. World Bank Group.

Roa, M. J. (2015). *Financial Inclusion in Latin America and the Caribbean: Access, Usage and Quality. Research Papers 19*. CEMLA.

Sarma, M. (2008). *Index of Financial Inclusion*. ICRIER Working Paper 215.

Sarma, M., & Pais, J. (2011). Financial Inclusion and Development. *Journal of International Development*, *23*(5), 613–628. doi:10.1002/jid.1698

Stark, O. (1991). The Economics of International Labour Migration. *Population Studies*, *44*(1), 181–182. doi:10.1080/0032472031000144516

Tu, C. A., Nguyet, T. M. P., Tuan, L. Q., Yoshino, N., Sarker, T., & Taghizadeh-Hesary, F. (2019). *Remittance inflows, financial inclusion, and economic development: an empirical analysis of the world sample*. ADBI Working Paper Series, No. 1000.

Wang, X., & Guan, J. (2017). Financial Inclusion: Measurement, spatial effects, and influencing factors. *Applied Economics*, *49*(18), 1751–1762. doi:10.1080/00036846.2016.1226488

World Bank. (2005). *Global Economic Prospects Report 2006: Economic Implications of Remittances and Migration*. World Bank.

World Bank. (2014). *Global Economic Prospectus*. Author.

World Bank & Knomad. (2019). *Migration and remittances: recent developments and outlook. Migration and Development Brief 31*. Author.

Yoshino, N., Morgan, P. J., & Trinh, L. Q. (2017). *Financial Literacy in Japan: Determinants and Impacts*. ADBI Working Paper 796.

Yoshino, T.-H. & Otsuka. (2017). *International Remittances and Poverty Reduction: Evidence from Asian Developing Countries*. ADBI Working Paper 759. Tokyo: Asian Development Bank Institute.

Chapter 11
The Role of Trade Policy in Sustainable Tourism Inclusivity in Africa

Msafiri Njoroge
The Open University of Tanzania, Tanzania

ABSTRACT

When local communities are allowed to participate fully in tourism trade activities either through supplying goods and services or direct employment in the tourism sector-inclusiveness of tourism, trade can be realized in a practical sense. Research indicates that, in most tourist destinations in Africa, the tourism trade continues to be characterized by environmental and social-cultural degradation and inadequate local community participation associated with revenue leakages and weak economic linkages. The mechanism on how tourism trade contributes inclusively on local communities' benefits such as inclusive growth and poverty alleviation remains unclear. Despite destination economies engaging in services liberalization, little evidence exists on how such trade policies have been beneficial at enhancing inclusive benefits of the tourism trade. Therefore, this chapter aims to clarify how trade policies can be employed to promote the inclusiveness of the tourism trade.

INTRODUCTION

For decades, the tourism sector has recorded a remarkable contribution to the national and global economy on employment, foreign exchange earnings, gross domestic product, and investments (WTTC, 2019). Tourism trade however faces several impediments that limit its inclusiveness to local communities within the destination economies. Generally, inclusiveness entails widening the access to the economic system by relatively marginalized society such as the poor, the unemployed, women, people with disabilities, minority ethnic groups, indigenous populations, and youth in a more beneficial way (Draper *et al.*, 2019). Accordingly, this chapter conceptualizes trade inclusiveness as trade in tourism services that contributes to sustainable growth and poverty alleviation in an inclusive manner (OECD/WTO, 2017). In other words, inclusive trade must have a positive impact on the achievement of several UN sustainable

DOI: 10.4018/978-1-7998-4817-2.ch011

development goals (SDGs) including no hunger (SDG1), decent work and economic growth (SDG8), reduced inequalities (SDG10), and sustainable communities (SDG11).

In developing countries, the realization of SDGs depends on the performance of trade in services as manipulation of service trade policies (Fiorini and Hoekman, 2018; Martin, 2019). OECD/WTO (2017) indicate that services trade policies play a fundamental role in facilitating or restricting international trade and the achievement of UN SDGs. However, the growth in service trade portrays significant differential contributions across 2030 SDGs. For instance, in 2027 only 25 percent of respondents of the OECD/WTO aid-for trade monitoring exercise considered that trade in services has a significant contribution to ensuring sustainable cities and communities (SDG-11). In a similar vein, only 33.3 percent agree that service trade promotes responsible consumption and production (SDG-12). Until very recent inequalities continue to deepen among vulnerable populations especially for countries with weaker health systems and those facing existing humanitarian crises (UN, 2020).

The first impediment is relatively low governments' prioritization of the travel and tourism sector. This is inherently the case for African destinations like Tanzania, Kenya, Botswana, South Africa, Rwanda, Mauritius, and Seychelles (WEF, 2019). Evidence suggests that the inability to recognize tourism as a priority industry not only erodes its potential economic contribution but also can easily and negatively affect the health of tourism unintentionally (WTO, 2009). On the other hand, the tourism trade is highly fragmented, embracing several different industries such as transportation, accommodation, food services, travel trade (tour operators and travel agencies), recreation, and entertainment. This makes it difficult, if not impossible, for the industry to have one common voice to the government in an effort to articulate the needs of the tourism sector in an inclusive way. Furthermore, tourism trade is highly vulnerable to external forces, including acts of terrorism, economic trends, natural disasters, weather and climate, and competitive pressure from regional destinations (WTO, 2009).

Studies in Africa also reveal that the tourism trade is often associated with insufficient local benefits; revenue leakages; and weak inter-sectoral linkages (Luvanga and Shitundu, 2003; Anderson and Juma, 2011; Kazuzuru, 2014; Anderson, 2018). Likewise, community-based tourism initiatives tend to yield minimal inclusive outcomes (Imbaya *et al.*, 2019) due to a mismatch between local supply and industry demands (Anderson, 2018). Linking tourism trade with other sectors of the economy through a value chain approach is considered an essential means in making the industry more economically inclusive (Anderson, 2018). While such linkage is theoretically appealing, in practice there is no straight forward framework on how it can be achieved. So, the question is, how can trade in tourism be made more inclusive in order to enhance its local economic benefits. In other words, how can trade policies promote inclusive tourism trade in developing countries like African destinations?

It is doubtless that, when marginalized local communities are given an opportunity to engage in tourism trade activities either through supplying goods and services or direct employment in the tourism sector-inclusiveness of tourism trade can be practical and real (Anderson, 2018). In essence, this is the role of trade policy as articulated in this chapter. The chapter is based on the assertion that the linkage between the tourism sector and the rest of the local economy is largely a non-automatic process. That is unless it is complemented with appropriately targeted and purposeful policies such as trade and tourism policies. This chapter thus aims to clarify how national trade policies can enhance the contribution of the tourism trade in benefiting the local host communities inclusively. Such an approach can be crucial in poverty alleviation initiatives.

LITERATURE

This section provides broad definitions of key concepts in the chapter- service trade policy and tourism trade, and trade inclusiveness in tourism. Then trade policy and GATS commitments in tourism for selected African destinations are reviewed. Next, the chapter reviews the empirical literature on the relationship between trade liberalization and inclusiveness in tourism.

Tourism Services and National Trade Policies

This chapter follows the World Trade Organization (WTO) classification of tourism services trade as part of trade in services. The General Agreements on Trade in Services (GATS) defines trade in services as the supply of a service through any of the four modes of supply: cross border, consumption abroad, commercial presence, and the presence of natural persons. Tourism trade is therefore broadly construed to consist of various activities as detailed in the WTO product classification list (S/CSS/W/19) issued on 5 December 2000. According to the WTO and the United Nations Statistical Commission, tourism and travel-related services include tourism characteristic products supplied by hotels and restaurants (including catering), travel agencies and tour operator services, tourist guide services, and other related services. This embraces tourism industries defined by UN Tourism Satellite Account (TSA) through WTO document S/C/W/298 which includes transportation, accommodation, food and beverage services, travel trade (tour operators and travel agencies), as well as recreation and entertainment (WTO, 2009).

Trade policy refers to commercial policy (regulations and agreements) that control both domestic and international trade (imports and exports to foreign countries). General trade policy objectives involve reduced trade protection, achieving a more outward-oriented trade regime, increased market access for exports, and greater global integration, aimed at boosting economic efficiency, competitiveness, and export-led growth (URT, 2003; MITC, 2017). The impacts of trade policy on the pattern and direction of trade depend on trade policy instruments employed by a particular nation. Trade policy instruments are measures taken by governments to influence the direction and pattern of trade development often aimed at stimulating domestic production, promote exports, safeguard domestic industry against dumping practices, protect consumers as well as for government revenue. By their nature, trade policy instruments offer protection on the domestic economy against trade from the rest of the world.

In this chapter selected trade policies for competing tourism destinations in Africa (Tanzania, Kenya, Mauritius, South Africa, and Seychelles) are analyzed. For the countries analyzed, trade policies embrace both domestic and international trade policies. Trade policy instruments are broadly categorized into tariff measures and non-tariff measures (NTBs); bilateral, regional, and multilateral trade agreements; trade facilitation and development measures. All trade policies are based on national developmental visions. Based on the respective objectives of various trade policies, it is evident to a large extent they are all focused at ensuring trade inclusiveness as an essential dimension in a diversified competitive export-led economy, increased competitiveness, sustainable economic growth, and poverty eradication. Whether these policy aspirations have been translated into reality, is a question dealt with in this chapter.

Destinations' National Trade Policies

Table 1.

Trade Policy [Time frame]	Objective	Indicators for Inclusiveness Focus
Tanzania Trade Policy, 2003 [5 years]	• Based on National Development Vision 2025 -poverty eradication • Objectives of trade policy - increase efficiency; -widen linkages in domestic production; - diversified competitive export sector; -stimulate higher growth and development • Priority Sectors - increase agricultural exports -promote value addition in mining -stimulate investments in tourism - modernisation of the services industry	-inclusion in production and trade -poverty eradication -improve living standards - inclusion of poor communities in a commercialised domestic economy and international markets
Kenya Trade Policy, 2017	• Based on the Kenya Vision 2030 • Objectives of trade policy - poverty eradication and sustainable economic development - increased employment and competitiveness - recognizes the important role that trade in services including tourism - make Kenya an efficient domestic market and export-led competitive economy • Priority Sectors - tourism; transport and communications; trade and related services; and financial and business services	-full participation and gender inclusivity of women in the formal trade sector -youth inclusivity in trade - promotion of gender equality in trade development - promote the competitiveness of supply chains
Mauritius National Exports Strategy, 2017 [5 years]	• Based on Mauritius Vision 2030: the transition towards a knowledge-based and high-income economy • Objectives of trade policy - translate export-led success into sustainable and inclusive growth -move Mauritius to a knowledge-based economy thriving on innovation and value addition -transform Mauritius into a strategic hub for international trade. • Priority Sectors -product sectors e.g. fisheries, agro-processing, sugar, textiles -service sectors e.g. cultural tourism, financial services	-selection of priority sectors based on social-economic impact criteria -maintaining inclusiveness to tackle the rising inequality gap -emphasis on linkages to global value chains via long-term trade and industrial policies, coupled with pro-poor export-led growth -invest in higher-value services, country's competitiveness, and public revenues generation -invest more in research and development (R&D) and innovation -improve the quality of investment in the education system
South Africa Trade Policy, 2010	• Based on the National Development Plan: to eliminate poverty and reduce inequality by 2030 • Objectives of trade policy -ensure the long term sustainability and mutual benefits -economic upgrading and diversification -enhance market access for products of export interests -negotiate WTO rules that perpetuate imbalances -promote sustainable development -nurturing downstream and labour-intensive industries • Priority Sectors -wholesale and retail trade, financial services, tourism -infrastructural development, agriculture, mining, manufacturing, promotion of a green economy	trade policy contribution on: -inclusive economic growth and development -industrial upgrading and diversification -poverty reduction and extreme inequalities -sustainable employment and creation of decent jobs -inclusiveness of people and marginalised regions in the mainstream economy - linkages between trade and environment
Seychelles Trade Policy	• Objectives of trade policy -establish an interdependent trade regime conducive for businesses productivity and growth -stimulate economic growth prospects via the reallocation of investment resources from non-tradable to tradable sectors -regional integration and diversification of trading partners - facilitate private sector trade, boost the local trade environment, and - promote innovation and stimulate benefits for local consumers and producers • Priority Sectors - tourism and fisheries industries	-readiness to reduce the cost of living and income poverty - empowering women and single parents

Destinations' GATS Commitments in Tourism Services

For developing countries, GATS Article V requires Members, inter alia, to negotiate specific commitments relating to the strengthening of developing countries' domestic services capacity; the improvement of developing countries' access to distribution channels and information networks; and the liberalization of market access in areas of export interest to these countries. Moreover, Article XIX provides that liberalization takes place with due respect for national policy objectives and Members' development levels, both overall and in individual sectors.

Tanzania and Kenya: Based on the WTO trade policy review (TPR) of 2019, East African Community (EAC) countries under the GATS, have undertaken individual commitments in liberalizing trade in the tourism and travel sector. Based on the EAC Common Market Protocol, partner States are committed to liberalizing service sectors including communication, financial services, transport, and tourism services across all modes of supply. Tanzania and Kenya are willing to open up and committed to liberalizing the tourism and travel sector across all modes of supply by end-2015. By 2019 Tanzania has liberalized all the four sub-sectors of tourism while Kenya has liberalized 3 sub-sectors. Moreover, EAC members are committed to refrain from introducing any new restrictions on services provision.

Moreover, under the EAC Treaty, countries coordinate their tourism policies including the use of a common code of conduct for tour and travel operators, standardizing hotel classifications, and harmonizing the professional standards of agents in the industry. Common criteria for the classification of tourist accommodation establishments and restaurants have been developed by Kenya, Rwanda, Uganda, and Tanzania. During the review period, the EAC States took a number of initiatives to strengthen their tourism subsector. A single tourist visa was introduced in 2014 on a pilot basis between Kenya, Uganda, and Rwanda. Under the initiative, tourists can choose between a single country visa or an EAC tourist visa. On the other hand, under the EAC Customs Management Act, hotel equipment imported by licensed establishments is exempted from import duties.

Mauritius: WTO TPR in 2019 indicates that following the Uruguay Round, Mauritius bound measures that restrict consumption abroad of all types of tourism services. This was done without limitations on market access and national treatment Measures on the presence of natural persons are unbound. Certain restrictions have been maintained on market access and/or national treatment for cross-border provision of tourism services and commercial presence. Another requirement is that foreign travel agencies, arranging for services in Mauritius, must work with local agents. Domestic regulations require foreign hotels and restaurants to predominantly employ Mauritians. Likewise, tour-operating services, tourist guide services, provision of car rental services, and yacht and cruise services are reserved for Mauritian nationals. However, commercial presence is allowed for foreign operators subject to a permit from responsible ministries.

South Africa: The World Economic Forum's Travel and Tourism Competitiveness Report of 2019 indicated that the strengths of South Africa's tourism industry lie in its natural and cultural tourism resources, price competitiveness, ICT readiness, good air transport infrastructure, and favourable policy rules and regulations. WTO TPR of 2016 indicates that South Africa's tourism legislative framework is conducive for the sector's development as the country has improved its laws and regulations, with well-protected property rights and few visa requirements. Moreover, tourism is one of the five priority sectors driving economic growth. WTO TPR of 2009 and 2016, foreigners can only register as tour guides if they possess a valid work permit, and completed the accredited guiding training. Foreign travel agents must register (like most other businesses) under the South African Companies Act, and comply with any relevant regulations including those of IATA.

Empirical Studies on Trade Liberalization and Inclusiveness in Tourism

Trade policies that are pro-growth and development and predictable can enable the attainment of SDGs. Despite the challenges to developing economies in implementing international agreements and the adoption of efficient production processes that minimize environmental risks (Akinyemi et al., 2019), some tourist destinations have made tremendous progress in liberalizing trade in tourism services (WTO, 2019). What is unclear is how much such liberalization in the tourism trade has been inclusive in nature. In other words, how appropriate are destinations' trade policies in promoting trade inclusiveness that benefits the majority of local but marginalized communities in Africa?

A range of factors influences the inclusiveness of trade for the benefit of wider society. Evidence suggests that drivers of inclusiveness include economic growth, technology, structural change, political economy complemented with quality of infrastructure, human capital, and skilled workforce as well as macroeconomic stability (Draper, 2019). Similarly, trade policies coupled with responsible production and consumption patterns are expected to stimulate economic growth in an inclusive and sustainable manner (Akinyemi *et al.,* 2019). Moreover, Fiorini and Hoekman (2018) noted that lower trade restrictiveness is an important tool that can promote the performance of domestic services sectors and consequently the attainment of UN SDGs including inclusive economic growth, reduced inequalities, and sustainable communities. For trade to be essential for economic development and promote inclusiveness, particularly in the area of employment generation, poverty reduction, income redistribution, and economic growth (Osabuohien *et al.,* 2018), domestics trade policies must be tailored to specific national circumstances (Draper, 2019). Inequality associated with an unjust distribution of income and wealth is a problem and can lead to a lack of inclusiveness through marginalization. Improving connectivity (digital and physical) can enhance more trade inclusiveness and lead to larger trade gains to developing countries, in particular for the most isolated groups like women and people living in rural areas (OECD/WTO, 2017).

Countries' decision to implement trade liberalization policies depends on several pre-conditions. Common factors cited in the literature include the level of economic growth, institutional maturity in the country, trade performance, adjustment costs, and anticipated benefits (Osabuohien *et al.,* 2018). Legal bindings typically found in services trade agreements tend to have a positive impact on trade (exports and imports) even if no actual liberalisation has taken place (WTO, 2019). Theoretically, this may imply that commitment to GATS requirements is associated with trade inclusiveness. On the contrary, some empirical evidence indicates that trade liberalization can also lead to undesirable outcomes on the country's economy. For instance, in their study on impacts of the general agreement on trade in services on sustainable development of tourism, George and Henthorne (2007) reveal that such agreements are in tune with the business goals of the small and medium tourism firms in developing economies.

Brundtland report recognizes the role of institutions in ensuring that the development of tourism facilities and services are achieved in co-operation with the local community; inter-sectoral linkages; economic and ecological concerns are integrated during decision-making; exploitation of public and private resources is lined-up with socio-cultural contexts; locals are empowered to participate in large-scale projects. In particular, WCED emphasizes that nations' environmental objectives must be built into taxation, prior approval on investment and technology choice, foreign trade incentives, and all components of development policy. Broadly, factors that can enhance sustainable tourism benefits are summarized in Figure 1. Sustainable tourism can thus be enhanced if:

- Tourism activities benefit the local host communities both economically and socially,
- Policies are focused on protecting national and local cultural and natural resources,
- Policies and strategies should focus on environmental conservation and responsible consumption of scarce resources.
- Stakeholder participation embraces a coordinated and integrated approach between the various concerned Government departments, as well as public-private partnerships.
- Tourism development and investments take into account the needs and concerns of local communities to support employment opportunities.
- National policies are geared to conserve tourism resources and encourage resource management, biodiversity, and environmental protection
- National policies and strategies promote environmentally sustainable tourism emphasizing on recreational activities with low environmental impacts
- Governments emphasize on infrastructural investments (airports, harbours, electricity and water and sewage) and related services (communication, technology) to meet the needs of increasing tourist arrivals and enhance the quality of hospitality services.
- National strategies promote entrepreneurial training and skills development through education and vocational training, on-the-job training and transfer of knowledge from research institutions to local practitioners and entrepreneurs

Figure 1. Enhancers of inclusive tourism benefits

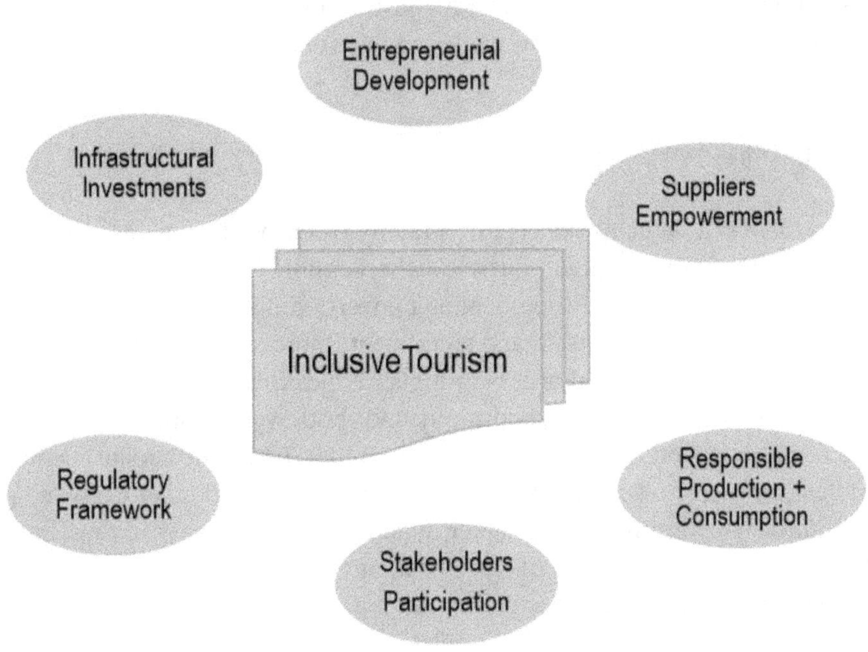

A question that remains unattended is how trade policy can be employed to promote the inclusiveness of tourism trade to the local community in a manner that is sustainable. Trade has long been considered as a central and essential pillar in the attainment of higher efficiency, productivity, and international competitiveness (OECD/WTO, 2017; WEF, 2019). In clarifying the role of trade policy on inclusive tourism, trade policies for competing tourism destinations (Tanzania, Kenya, Mauritius, Seychelles, and South Africa) are analyzed and compared to establish their complementary role in promoting the tourism inclusiveness. That is, trade policies are examined to determine the extent to which trade policies are focused on ensuring the local people, local entrepreneurs and businesses benefit from tourism trade activities and how tourism can be integrated with other commercial activities in the economy in an inclusive way.

METHODOLOGY

Measures

Trade Policy

In this chapter, trade policy is measured by two components, namely price competitiveness and business environment pillars-based on Travel and Tourism Competitiveness Report (WEF, 2019) which are respectively herein referred to as trade policy competitiveness and trade policy enabling environment. Trade policy competitiveness consists of a) ticket taxes and airport charges, b) hotel price index, c) relative purchasing power parity, and d) price levels for most widely sold diesel fuels. On the other, business environment entails a) the impact of rules on foreign direct investments; b) efficiency of the legal framework; c) time and cost associated with construction permits and starting a business; d) the extent and effect of taxation on incentives to work and investments; e) total commercial profits taxable (tax burden).

Inclusiveness in Tourism Trade

Inclusiveness in tourism is a valuable concept in a family of terms such as responsible tourism, social tourism, peace through tourism, pro-poor tourism, and accessible tourism that aim to foster the tourism industry's potential to contribute to development and poverty reduction. Inclusive trade should lead to a lower incidence of poverty, broad-based, and significant improvement in health outcomes, universal access for children to school, increased access to higher education, and improved standards of education. It should also be reflected in better opportunities for both wage employment and livelihoods and in improvement in the provision of basic amenities like water, electricity, roads, sanitation, and housing. Particular attention needs to be paid to the needs of minorities and other excluded population such as women and children. Accordingly, this chapter quantifies inclusiveness in tourism based on Travel and Tourism Competitiveness Report (WEF, 2019). It entails various issues including a) primary and secondary education enrolment rates; b) extent in training and employee development; c) treatment of customers; d) hiring and firing practices; e) pay related to employee productivity and f) female labour force participation.

ANALYSES OF NATIONAL TRADE POLICIES

The analysis of the role of trade policy on trade inclusiveness is based on secondary data collected by the World Economic Forum as reported in the Travel and Tourism Competitiveness Report of 2019. In analysing the role of trade policies of the selected economies, data from the Travel and Tourism Competitiveness Report (WEF, 2019) are utilized. Trade policy is thus captured by two dimensions: policy competitiveness, and policy environment.

Trade Policy Competitiveness and Inclusiveness

Figure 2 illustrates the analysis between trade policy competitiveness and tourism trade inclusiveness. Results indicate that the convergence between trade policy competitiveness and inclusiveness in the tourism trade differs substantially across regional competitors. The contribution of trade policy in countries like Tanzania and South Africa is relatively marginal compared to destinations such as Mauritius. Consistent with the WTO trade policy review of 2019, Mauritius put a strong emphasis on local communities' benefits. Trade policy competitiveness is also enhanced by lower costs related to travel. This in turn increases destinations' attractiveness for many travellers and investors in the tourism sectors. Among the dimensions of trade policy competitiveness are airfare ticket taxes and airport charges, which make flight tickets much more expensive; the relative cost of hotel accommodation; the cost of living measured by purchasing power parity; and fuel price costs influence the cost of travel. Ceteris paribus, the lack of destinations' attractiveness to tourists can be linked to the inability of the tourism industry to contribute inclusively within the destination economies.

Figure 2. Trade policy competitiveness versus trade inclusiveness

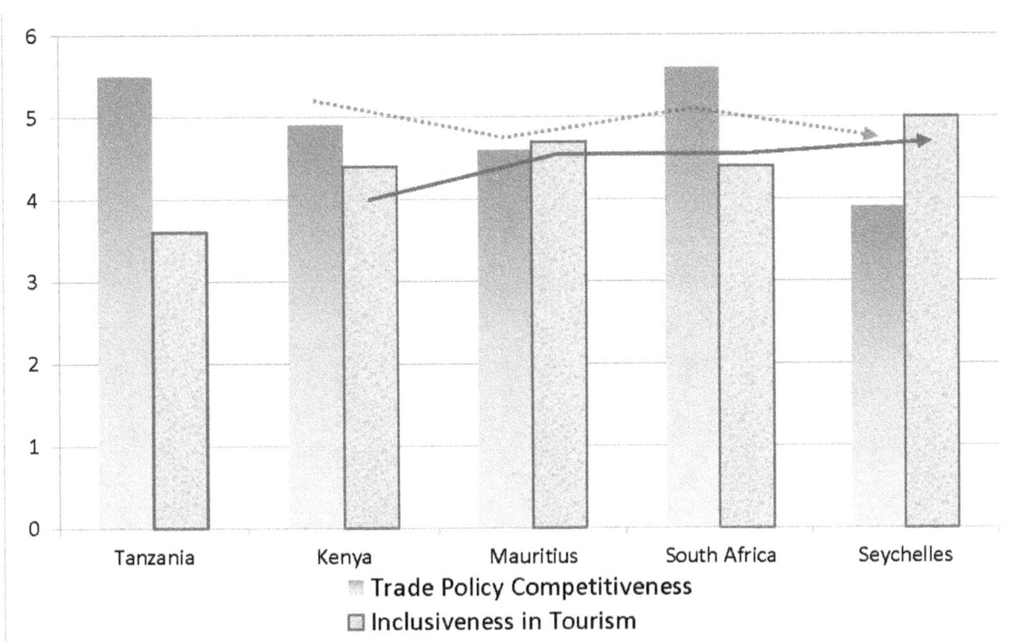

Moreover, some destinations (e.g. Tanzania and South Africa) fail to combine effectively their natural and cultural resources base with strong trade policy competitiveness in order to guarantee the inclusiveness of the tourism industry to a wider population. A probable reason is that natural resources assets cannot be created, but if not managed well can be depleted rapidly. The ability to create demand and generate value from these assets depends heavily on the enforcement of environmental policies as well as the capability to effectively ensure sustainable production and consumption. Thus, the adequate emphasis is required to conserve natural resources if they are to contribute meaningfully to the inclusiveness and overall competitiveness performance of a destination.

Trade Policy Environment and Inclusiveness

The analysis is illustrated in Figure 3 is evident that inclusiveness in the tourism industry is driven and increases depending on the conduciveness of trade policy environment. Among the selected destinations, Seychelles ranks 1st on tourism inclusiveness due to relatively qualified labour and a good labour market mainly defined by a high female participation rate. Seychelles' performance can be linked with its relatively good trade policy environment (ranking 2nd among regional competitors). Mauritius is the highest-ranked destination among Sub-Saharan Africa countries of tourism competitiveness but 2nd on tourism inclusiveness relative to regional competitors. As revealed in Figure 5, Mauritius is one of the most developed destination in the region in terms of the policy enabling environment aspect with an optimal balance between trade policy and tourism inclusiveness. It boasts a good business environment-defined by a low impact of taxes on business and profit and an effective legal and administrative system. All of which encourage investment in its tourism industry as well as inclusiveness of the industry within the local economy.

Figure 3. Trade policy environment vs. trade inclusiveness

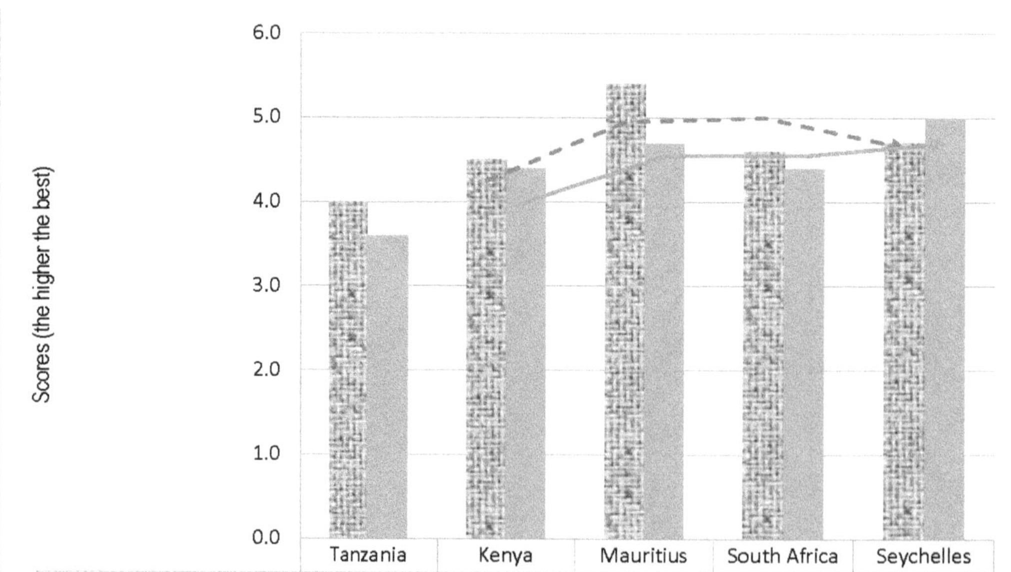

	Tanzania	Kenya	Mauritius	South Africa	Seychelles
Trade Policy Environment	4.0	4.5	5.4	4.6	4.7
Inclusiveness in Tourism	3.6	4.4	4.7	4.4	5.0

This analysis thus implies that the conduciveness of trade policy is important to support companies to conduct business within a particular destination. The linkage between business performance and good policy environment as manifested via protection of property rights; the efficiency of the legal framework; the cost of doing business; and un-distortive taxation and competition policies. A conducive trade policy environment not only is important on investment attraction but also an enabler for business efficiency and productivity in all sectors, including tourism.

RECOMMENDATIONS

Based on the analysis conducted in this chapter, a framework linking trade policy and inclusive tourism is developed and illustrated (Figure 4). It captures key mechanisms that can be utilized in fostering the inclusiveness of the tourism industry by capitalizing on destinations' trade policy. Most trade policies embrace instruments that are meant to affect the direction and trade patterns of merchandise products as opposed to service trade including tourism activities. On the contrary, the developed framework focus on trade in services (herein tourism) and how this can be an important pathway to the inclusive tourism trade.

Figure 4. Conceptual framework

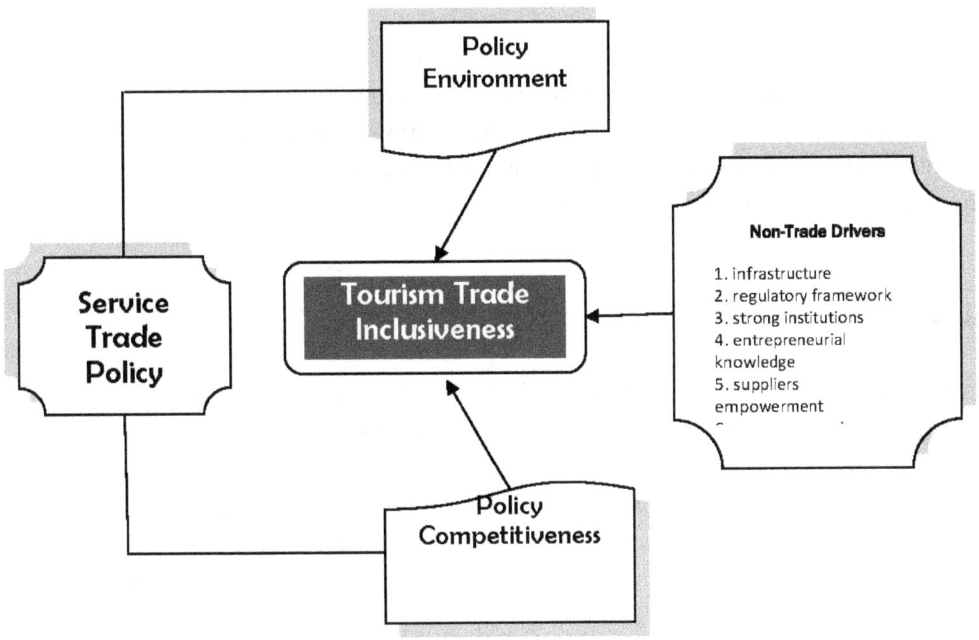

Specifically, to improve the role of trade policy in promoting inclusivity in tourism trade it is recommended that:

- Trade policies must be formulated in a way that enables local entrepreneurs to benefit by selling goods or services directly to tourists and hotel chains. This is crucial to promote high levels of leakage of tourist spending in the local economy.
- Trade policies should be geared at promoting local entrepreneurial activities within the tourism industry characterized by innovative products and services; encouraging new ideas; anticipating market trends, capitalizing on first-mover advantages; emphasizing customer satisfaction based on quality and standardized services.
- Trade policies must promote pro-poor and responsible tourism. Strategies should be put in place to ensure the empowerment of local suppliers to meet supply demands and standards.
- Trade policies can be linked with tourism activities to promote local commercial opportunities for sustainable tourism and ecotourism development, enhance new businesses, employment, and income generation opportunities.
- Effective management and marketing of tourist destinations should focus on supporting the local small and medium tourism enterprises.
- Tourist destinations in Africa can create a much more conducive environment that inclusively fosters entrepreneurial businesses.
- Trade policy should be linked to national efforts on resource efficiency and environmental protection. National and local programmes should aim at improving energy efficiency, greater use of renewable energy sources, enhanced water conservation, appropriate local waste treatment, and waste minimization.
- Sustainable tourism and local entrepreneurship must be linked through several channels (a) markets for other major economic sectors such as agriculture where the majority of poor are largely employed (b) increasing the direct and indirect employment in the tourism sector (c) promoting entrepreneurial local businesses to access and serve high-value markets in the sector and (d) ensuring stable linkages along the tourism value chains.

CONCLUSION

Tourism is often experienced as an exclusive activity. To make it more inclusive, trade policies must be formulated and implemented in a way that promotes tourism trade inclusiveness. This chapter developed a framework that clarifies key dimensions (policy environment and competitiveness) of service trade policies. For trade in tourism services, besides GATS commitments, there are several other drivers of trade inclusiveness including a conducive policy environment and enhanced competitiveness, physical and digital connectivity as well as human and institutional capabilities. This framework can be utilized by academia and practitioners in tourism destinations in Africa in making informed decisions in the formulation and implementation of service trade policies.

This chapter however recommends future research to test the concept of inclusiveness by conducting a detailed country-wise analysis. Future research can greatly benefit by employing longitudinal data covering a prolonged period. This crucial to understand the dynamism of trade policy relative to inclusiveness in the tourism industries.

REFERENCES

Akinyemi, O., Efobi, U., Asongu, S., & Osabuohien, E. (2019). Renewable energy, trade performance, and the conditional role of finance and institutional capacity in sub-Sahara African countries. *Energy Policy*, *132*, 490–498. doi:10.1016/j.enpol.2019.06.012

Anderson, W. (2018). Linkages between tourism and agriculture for inclusive development in Tanzania: A value chain perspective. *Journal of Hospitality and Tourism Insights*, *1*(2), 168–184. doi:10.1108/JHTI-11-2017-0021

Anderson, W., & Juma, S. (2011). Factors Constraining the Linkages between the Tourism Industry and Local Suppliers of Meats in Zanzibar. *New Alliances for Tourism, Conservation, and Development in Eastern and Southern Africa*, 49-62.

Bakker, M. (2019). A conceptual framework for identifying the binding constraints to tourism-driven inclusive growth. *Tourism Planning & Development*, *16*(5), 575–590. doi:10.1080/21568316.2018.1541817

Biddulph, R., & Scheyvens, R. (2018). Introducing inclusive tourism. *Tourism Geographies*, *20*(4), 583–588. doi:10.1080/14616688.2018.1486880

Draper, P., Freytag, A., Dörffel, C., & Schuhmann, S. (2019). Trade, Inclusive Development, and the Global Order. *Global Summitry*, *4*(1), 30–49. doi:10.1093/global/guz001

Fiorini, M., & Hoekman, B. (2018). *Restrictiveness of Services Trade Policy and the Sustainable Development Goals. ADBI Working Paper 903*. Asian Development Bank Institute. Available https://www.adb.org/publications/restrictiveness-services-trade-policy-sustainable-development-goals

George, B. P., & Henthorne, T. L. (2007). Tourism and the general agreement on trade in services: Sustainability and other developmental concerns. *International Journal of Social Economics*, *34*(3), 136–146. doi:10.1108/03068290710726702

Imbaya, B. O., Nthiga, R. W., Sitati, N. W., & Lenaiyasa, P. (2019). Capacity building for inclusive growth in community-based tourism initiatives in Kenya. *Tourism Management Perspectives*, *30*, 11–18. doi:10.1016/j.tmp.2019.01.003

International Trade Centre. (2017). Trade and sustainable tourism. International Trade Centre.

Kazuzuru, B. (2014). History, Performance, and Challenges of Tourism Industry in Tanzania. *International Journal of Business and Social Science*, *5*(11), 120–131.

Kim, K. B., Zhai, F., & Huynh, P. (2016). Regional Trade Agreements, Employment, and Inclusiveness. In ASEAN Economic Community (pp. 175-195). Palgrave Macmillan.

Luvanga, N. E., & Shitundu, J. L. (2003). *The role of tourism in poverty alleviation in Tanzania* (Vol. 3). Mkuki Na Nyoka Publications.

Njoroge, M. (2019). *Linking entrepreneurial orientation and corporate sustainability: A study of tourist hotels in Tanzania* [Unpublished doctoral thesis]. University of Dar es Salaam, Dar es Salaam, Tanzania.

Njoroge, M. (in press). Tourism Sustainability: Reconceptualization and Measurements In Tourism, and Sustainable Development in Tanzania. Academic Press.

OECD/WTO. (2017). *Aid for Trade at a Glance 2017: Promoting Trade, Inclusiveness and Connectivity for Sustainable Development*. WTO/OECD Publishing.

Osabuohien, E. S., Beecroft, I., & Efobi, U. R. (2018). Global trade and trade protection in a globalised world. *Transnational Corporations Review*, *10*(1), 43–52. doi:10.1080/19186444.2018.1436650

Scheyvens, R., & Biddulph, R. (2018). Inclusive tourism development. *Tourism Geographies*, *20*(4), 589–609. doi:10.1080/14616688.2017.1381985

UNEP and WTO. (2005). *Making Tourism More Sustainable: A Guide to Policy Makers*. International Policy Publishing.

WCED. (1987). *Our Common Future*. Oxford University Press.

World Economic Forum. (2019). *Travel and Tourism Competitiveness Report*. World Economic Forum.

WTO. (2019). *Trade Policy Review Report for the East African Community* (WT/TPR/S/384/Rev.1). WTO.

WTTC. (2019). *Economic Impact of Travel & Tourism World Report 2018*. WTTC.

Zapata Campos, M. J., Hall, C. M., & Backlund, S. (2018). Can MNCs promote more inclusive tourism? Apollo tour operator's sustainability work. *Tourism Geographies*, *20*(4), 630–652. doi:10.1080/14616688.2018.1457074

Chapter 12
Determinants and Implications of Hopping Between Formal and Informal Jobs in Nigeria

Solomon Abayomi Olakojo
https://orcid.org/0000-0002-4170-750X
University of Ibadan, Nigeria

Olaronke Onanuga
https://orcid.org/0000-0002-1687-3952
Center for Economic Policy and Development Research, Nigeria

Abayomi Toyin Onanuga
https://orcid.org/0000-0002-4023-9054
Olabisi Onabanjo University, Nigeria

ABSTRACT

Job hopping between formal and informal sectors represents an important driver of welfare and productivity changes. The study investigates the patterns, forms, and drivers of informality and factors determining hopping between formal and informal jobs in Nigeria. The data obtained from the general household surveys (GHS) was estimated with binary logistic regression technique within and between waves of each GHS across 13 primary economic activities in the formal and informal employment. The authors found high hopping from informal to formal in six sectors including manufacturing, buying and selling, construction, financial services, professional services, and education. Focus was also on dividing the households into three stages of life course. There is a greater hopping among early adulthood than any other age categories. Hence, bottlenecks to performance and productivity of the identified sectors should be adequately tacked to engender an improved formal sector characterised with better remuneration and living standards of its workers.

DOI: 10.4018/978-1-7998-4817-2.ch012

INTRODUCTION

Job hopping between formal and informal sectors is a necessary dynamic characterising labour market and could represent an important driver of welfare and productivity changes. For instance, the informal sector largely does not operate under existing legal or regulatory framework making certain labour laws such as minimum wage not to be strictly adhered to. Even where informal sector employers can afford to pay the minimum wage they shy away from it as they prefer to pay lower wages. This is perhaps one of the reasons for job hopping among others. There is convincing evidence of earning gaps between formal and informal sector (see Nordman, Rakotomanana and Roubaud, 2016). Therefore, any opportunity for an informal worker to hop to formal sector will imply enhanced welfare through provision of decent and remunerative jobs.

Besides, job-switching between formal and informal sector is not a one sided issue but an incredibly important channel by which better skills and practices can be deployed. For example, an individual may decide to be self-employed by establishing an informal enterprise having worked in the formal sector. The skills and knowledge previously gained in the formal sector can be deployed in the informal sector leading to productivity increase (Osabuohien et al., 2019). The evidence from Latin America indicates that a substantial share of workers voluntarily exits paid employment in the formal sector and form their own small informal businesses, this is however rare in West Africa (African Development Forum, 2012). From a policy perspective, facilitating employee mobility might be an important way to stimulate growth of the informal sector.

There is a gender dimension to the issue. Non-remunerative work undertaken in an income-producing enterprise is one of the characteristics of informal sector. In certain instances, informal family businesses headed by male (husbands) often engage female (wives) who are not remunerated. However, there is no consensus on whether male or female are more in (in)formal employment or not. For instance, while Nordman, Rakotomanana and Roubaud (2016) found that female workers have more opportunity to get informal sector jobs in the case of Madagascar, ILO (2018) indicated that informal employment is a greater source of employment for men (63.0%) than for women (58.1%)[1]. This implies that the relationship between gender and (in)formal employment may be context specific.

The size of informal economy varies from one region to another and from one country to another. In Africa, 85.8% of employment is informal, while the proportion is 68.2%, 68.6%, 40.0% and 25.1% in Asia and Pacific, the Arab States, the Americas, and Europe and Central Asia, respectively (ILO, 2018). In selected African countries, informality range from a low of 20% to 25% in Mauritius, South Africa, Namibia, and to a high of 50 to 65% in Benin, Tanzania and Nigeria (Medina, Jonelis, and Cangul, 2016). Specifically, Schneider (2002) estimated the size of Nigeria's informal sector at 57.9% of its gross national product (GNP), which was equivalent of US$212.6 billion. The arguments in the literature show possibility of bi-directional causality between poverty and informality in developing countries. While high incidence of informality is a challenge for the realization of decent work and inclusive development that reduces poverty, pervasive informality in developing African countries is traceable to poverty where people see informal enterprises and poorly paid casual jobs as a way of surviving.

The above shows that labour mobility from informal to formal sectors which guarantee decent and remunerative work remains an unmet need and a policy challenge in many African countries including Nigeria.

THE PROBLEM STATEMENT AND OBJECTIVES

The high level of employment in the informal sector (with no job security, retirement plans, and other benefits) in Nigeria is traceable to declining labour recruitment in the formal sector. For instance, between quarter three of 2012 and quarter one of 2016, the informal sector which, by definition, consists of low technical skills and low paying wages with little or limited structures recorded an average of 214,707 new jobs, while new jobs in the formal sector were only 97,313 within the same period (NBS, 2016)[2]. That is, formal employment only accounts for 31.2% of all new jobs created. This implies that there is a shortage in the demand for labour by firms in the Nigerian formal labour markets relative to the informal (Karakara and Osabuohien, 2020). The imbalance between formal and informal sectors' job creation is a motivation for occupational mobility between them given high and increasing number of tertiary education graduates unable to secure formal jobs employment.

In this study, we propose to focus on the labour force (worker) rather than on the employer. This is because the study's objective is to analyse the determinants of job switch between the Nigerian formal and informal economy sectors during the 2010/11-2015/16 period. The key research questions this study proposes to address are: what are the different forms of informality in Nigeria? What are the factors explaining employment in the (in)formal sector in the country? What factors explain the movement of labour between formal and informal employment in Nigeria? Does gender matter in explaining job hopping between formal and informal sector? Nigeria will be used as a case study being the largest populated country in Africa and it equally has a high degree of informality. Also, it has a huge youth population that has a high propensity of hopping between jobs.

Related studies such as Partida and Pacheco (2017), Nordman, Rakotomanana and Roubaud (2016) and Liang, Appleton and Song (2016) investigated hopping between formal and informal economic sectors in Mexico, earnings gaps between formal and informal sector in Madagascar, and trends, patterns and determinants of entry into informal sector in China, respectively. However, none of these studies deeply investigated the issue focusing on Nigeria. Hence, this study, besides contributing to the empirical literature, will be an important input in polity of ensuring inclusive growth that enhances welfare through the provision of decent jobs for Nigerian households.

LITERATURE REVIEW AND FRAMEWORK OF ANALYSIS

Empirical Review

The rapid growth in Nigeria's population led to an increase in its working age population. The increasing working age population is greater than the job offers available. Tokman (1979, 2004) posited that an economy without the ability to absorb the public's demand for jobs would have a labour market segmented into formal and informal sectors. The traditional view argued that those who cannot secure jobs in the formal sector turn to the informal sector. Aside from having surplus labour, the traditional view also believes that the informal sector yields subsistence income to those in the sector because it is not as productive as the formal sector (Chandra and Khan, 1993). The Marxist supports the traditional view and argued that the formal sector subcontract and or employ full time from the informal sector's abundant cheaper labour (Fields, 1975; Harris and Todaro, 1970). Considering the argument of the

Marxist, scholars came up with an alternative view that labour can choose to transit between the formal and informal sectors (Fajnzylber et al., 2006; Maloney, 1999).

The alternative view believes that the formal sector offers compensation packages like annual bonus, paid holiday, and severance pay which the informal sector does not offer (Tansel and Ozdemir, 2014). Meanwhile, the informal sector is compensated with the opportunity to evade tax, work flexible hours, and access to social funds (Maloney, 1997). According to Tansel and Ozdemir (2014), for this to be true, workers in the informal sector should be highly satisfied with their jobs and not want to hop to the formal sector. Pnad (1990) argued that Maloney (1997) would be the case for self-employed workers and not wage workers in the informal sector, hence the reason for a switch to a formal job.

Considering Mexico, Partida and Pacheco (2017) disentangled formal employment into non-manual highly-skilled, non-manual semi-skilled, manual skilled and manual low-skilled and informal employment into non-manual and manual, and the population is divided into three stages of life. There is a high mobility among the categories. Early adulthood exhibit a lower mobility than youth, mature adulthood and old age. An average Mexican wants to remain in formal jobs because it gives stability, social security, and bonus. For the same country, Coubès (2005) considered time line by observing the histories of three generations. Chances of moving from an informal sector to the formal sector were higher during 1936-1938 than 1951-1953 and 1966-1968. Chances of moving from the formal sector to the informal sector were higher during 1951-1953 and 1966-1968 than 1936-1938. Levy and Székely (2016) claim that there is labour mobility between the formal and informal sectors in Mexico but this may not be so in other countries.

Tansel and Ozdemir (2014) observed a highly static nature for the Egyptian labour market. A different segmentation from the traditional view was given. Most individuals remain in their initial labour market state except for those in the informal private wage work and the unemployed who transit to other labour market states. There is a higher probability of transiting from formal to informal private regular wage work than transiting from informal to formal private regular wage work. This implies that the switch indicated by the alternative view can be both ways. Due to limited employment opportunities in the formal sector, the probability of moving from the state of being unemployed to informal private regular wage work is higher than moving from being unemployed to formal private regular wage work. There is a reduced probability of moving from a formal wage work into self-employment for females.

Tansel and Ozdemir (2014) claims that tertiary education reduces the probability of moving from a formal wage work to an informal wage work, a formal wage work to unemployment, and self-employment to informal wage work and increases the probability of moving from informal to formal wage work and self-employment to formal wage work. That is, education plays an important role in reducing transition into informal sector and unemployment in Egypt. Experience decreases the probability of moving from an informal wage work to unemployment, from self-employment to informal wage work, from government employment to formal or informal wage work or self-employment and increases the probability of moving from unemployment. Considering sectors like services, they increase the probability of a transition from a formal to an informal wage work. Agriculture and construction sectors have a reduced probability of a transition from an informal to a formal wage work as these sectors are mostly informal (Osabohien et al., 2020). Agriculture and services have an increased probability of a transition from an informal wage work to a self-employment while services reduce the probability of moving from self-employment to an informal wage work.

Assuming that workers are better off with a formal job, Soares (2015) assessed queue estimates and the desire of informal workers to switch to a formal job in Brazil. The estimates of the job queue "length" for selected groups show that non-white, female, illiterate, new entrants and former informal workers have a lower probability of being chosen from the queue and may be on the queue for a longer period. This is truer for workers whose last job was in the informal sector. This shows that workers who are likely to benefit more from the formal sector are not chosen; hence formal employers should be encouraged to give these groups special attention.

Gutierrez, Kumar, Mahmud, Munshi and Nataraj (2019) provided evidence that Bangladesh is consistent with both the traditional and alternative views as the labour market is segmented and has a lower prospect for productivity but it is an entrepreneurial alternative to wage employment. Workers that change jobs are likely to remain in the same type of employment. Transiting from private wage employment (which could be formal or informal) to casual work is popular among those with lower levels of education, whereas transiting to self-employment is popular among those who have been in their jobs for a longer period.

Gutierrez et al. (2019) found that about half of the workers that transit out of private sector employment retain the same employment benefit as it is in their previous jobs or exhibit gains in earnings. This is consistent with voluntary resignation being associated with higher employment benefits. This is tagged upward mobility. Downward mobility indicates those that leave for lower employment benefits, especially those that transit to casual work as it is more hazardous and less remunerative. Those with higher levels of education, in Bangladesh, were found to move out of casual work to private wage employment and self-employment. Gutierrez et al. (2019) claim that self-employment is not a last resort job but mostly voluntary in Bangladesh. This is supported by the finding that most leave their wage jobs because they got a preferred job or they have the desire to start a business. In contrast, those that leave their self-employed jobs claim that the business did not make a profit.

Aside from studying the switch between the formal and informal sectors, scholars like Stumbitz, Lewis, Kyei, and Lyon (2018) explored the alternative view of Maloney (1997) by studying the patterns of maternity support between the formal and informal sectors in Ghana. Employers in the formal sector are likely to offer maternity support in line of legal requirements while that of the informal sector requires family support. Nordman, Rakotomanana and Roubaud (2016) tried to identify the income structure of the informal sector vis-à-vis the formal sector in Latin American, Asian or some African countries. The sign and magnitude of the formal–informal sector earnings gaps are highly dependent on the workers' employment status and on their relative position in the earnings distribution.

The Framework of Analysis

There are four theoretical models of job mobility—the reward-resource model, the limited opportunity model, and the vacancy competition model discussed by Hachen (1990) and the standard dualistic (also called segmented) labour market theory. The reward-resource model is an individual-based analysis that considers factors from the job holder's perspective which may limit or foster the job holder's ability to move from a job to another. These factors are the job holder's level of education (resource) relative to the rewards expected (e.g. higher income, higher position, etc.). The limited opportunity model considers macro societal determinants like gender issues, racial differences, religion matters, etc. that can constrain an individual's opportunity to explore job mobility. The vacancy competition model considers organisational and industrial factors like the type of labour market one is currently employed (Hachen, 1990).

The dualistic labour market theory proposes that the labour market can be divided into two groups (Blaauw, 2006). The theory's traditional division is into Primary and secondary markets whereby primary jobs have stable working conditions, relatively higher wages, and opportunities for promotion while secondary jobs are otherwise (Reich, Gordon and Edwards, 1973). In this study, the focus is to divide the labour market into the formal sector and informal sector. The study also depicts that further segmentation is also applicable within each of the markets.

Hence, the reward-resource model and vacancy competition model significantly apply the assumptions of a perfectly competitive market. The limited opportunity model and dualistic labour market theory are labour mobility models rooted in labour market failure. This better captures the problem within the policy space relating to the Nigerian labour market. The market failure is due to restrictions traceable to macrosocial factors such as dead-end nature of jobs held by a particular section of the labour market and internalized stereotypes with implications on lower rates of labour leaving their (informal) jobs because the opportunities to obtain better (formal) jobs are limited and makes moving to better jobs less likely. This further generates gaps in wages leading to significant inequality between the formal and informal sectors of the labour market.

However, in the mid-1990s, there were arguments that informality should be rethought in the context of a new emerging reality, especially in the developing countries, as an implementation of productive restructuring programs. For instance, Pérez (1996) formulated five fields of work ranging from emerging sector of tradable, to subordinated neo informality, to agglomerations, to the traditional formal sector, and to the subsistence informality. Importantly, informality is a necessary intermediate productive economic activity in the course of global value chain.

To conceptualize the formal/informal dichotomy and labour hopping between the formal and informal sectors, this study assumes that there are two work sectors: formal and informal sector. Also, there are two sets of labour: labour working in formal and those working in informal sector. Both formal and informal goods and services are produced using capital and labour. The amount of each good produced, given how much capital and labour are employed in each sector, is determined by a production function for each good as:

$$Q_F = Q_F\,(K_F, L_F) \tag{1}$$

$$Q_{NF} = Q_{NF}\,(K_{NF}, L_{NF}) \tag{2}$$

Where Q_F and Q_{NF} are the output levels of the formal and informal sector, respectively, K_F and L_F are the amounts of capital and labour employed in the formal sector, and K_{NF} and L_{NF} are the amounts of capital and labour employed in the informal sector. Overall, the economy has a fixed supply of capital K and labour L that is divided between employments in the two sectors.

The value of the economy's production is

$$Q = P_F * Q_F + P_{NF} * Q_{NF} \tag{3}$$

Where P_F and P_{NF} are the prices of the formal and informal sector, respectively. An isoline—a line along which the value of output is constant—has a slope of $-P_F / P_{NF.}$ The economy produces at a point, say Q, on the concave[3] production possibility frontier that touches the highest possible isoline where the slope of the production possibility frontier is equal to $-P_F / P_{NF}$. The slope of the production possibility frontier is negative indicating that producing goods and services belonging to the formal sector implies producing less of goods and services belonging to the informal sector. So the opportunity cost of producing additional unit of formal sector goods or services is equal to the relative price of formal sector in terms of informal sector prices. Hence, the relative price determines what the economy can produce. If prices of the formal sector increase relative to the informal sector, economy produces more of formal goods and services relative to the informal sector's goods and services because the labour will want to work in the sector that pays higher wages. This is assuming no hindrance to labour mobility and full employment in the labour market where factor prices strictly determine the input choices.

However, if there is an increase in labour supply and the economy is characterised with a situation in which limited employment opportunities exist in the formal sector and unemployment is generally high, labour movement to formal is hindered. Thus, the informal sector is overcrowded. The effect of this on the production possibility is ambiguous. On one hand, the increase in labour available in the informal sector may not necessarily make the production possibility to be significantly biased toward goods and services produced by the informal sector since such sectors are often characterised with production inefficiencies. In this case, increase in labour in the informal sector may not translate to welfare gain of the labour in the sector. In order words, the informal sector is crowded with labour, the average product of each worker will be very low and the marginal product tends to zero. As such, the formal sector could acquire cheap labour from the informal sector at a subsistence wage, at a rate approximately commensurate to what he earns in the informal sector. This is one way by which informal labour can hop to formal sector.

However, as the formal sector was able to match formerly informal labour with capital, productivity and output would rise, consumer prices would fall, and demand will rise leading to welfare increase and higher profit in the formal sector. A profit maximising producer in the formal sector would re-invest profits in capital to take advantage of cheap informal labour (assuming that other labour characteristics such as age, sex, education level, and place of residence are fixed) thus further increasing its output and revenues. This process would continue until excess supply of labour in the informal sector is depleted leading to increase in wages in the informal sector above subsistence levels. The outcome would be an increase in formality, biased expansion of production possibility frontier in favour of the formal sector, rise in the level of employment and labour welfare.

On the other hand, however, improved efficiency in the informal market may drive the production possibility in favour of informal sector. In this case, production possibility frontier will be biased toward informality making the labour in the sector to be better off. This may serve as incentive for the formal sector labour to hop into the informal sector.

METHODOLOGY AND DATA

This study investigates the patterns, forms and drivers of informality and factors determining hopping between formal and informal jobs. To implement the objectives, this study will use descriptive analysis focusing on the cross-tabulations. In terms of forms, the cross-tabulation analysis will focus on the main activity sector (agriculture, miming, manufacturing, etc.) a household engages in and applies measures of informality (of whether there is a contract, pension, and insurance coverage for the representative household's job, etc.). We will equally check whether informality is more of rural or urban. This is relevant in understanding informal morphologies and adaptations. Pattern of informality also has to do with age group, gender, education level as well as other socio-economic statuses of the households engaging in informality. We assume that these factors also determine hopping between formal and informal jobs. Hence, cross tabulations of age and gender with informality as well as hopping will be performed. Hopping will be a binary number taking the value of 1 if a household has changed status of its informality within and between any of the two waves (or seasons) of GHS and zero otherwise. This is necessary for adequate mapping of households engaging in informality for policy purpose.

Further, the study employs data consistent framework rooted in the limited opportunity model and dualistic labour market theory of labour mobility. This model is analysed utilizing binary logistic regression which is adequate in situations in which the observed outcome for a dependent variable can have only two possible types, "0" and "1" (which represent, working in informal versus working in formal jobs or no hop versus hop between jobs within the period under consideration). Since logistics regression command is generally preferred to the logit command because the former presents the estimates in terms of odds ratios rather than coefficients, the study obtains the corresponding coefficients by adding logit without additional arguments after logistic commands. The model can be specified as:

$$P_i = \Pr\left(Y = \frac{1}{X} = x_i\right) \tag{4}$$

Equation (4) can be written as:

$$\log(\frac{P_i}{1-P_i}) = logit\left(P_i\right) = \beta_0 + \beta_1 x_i + \mu_i \tag{5}$$

Where Pi is the probability of hopping between formal and informal job, and xi is other characteristics of representative households such as sex, and place of residence. Therefore, the parameter β_0 gives the log odds of a male representative household (for instance) hopping between jobs (when xi =0) and β1 shows how these odds differ for female (when xi =1). μi is not normally distributed as assumed to be for linear regression.

The logit model can be written in logistic form in terms of odds as:

$$\frac{P_i}{1-P_i} = Exp\left(\beta_0 + \beta_1 x_i\right) \tag{6}$$

Further, this technique is adequate when one or more predictor variables are either continuous (e.g. households' age) or categorical (e.g. household level of education, population life course—youth (15–24 years of age), early adulthood (25–44 years), and mature adulthood or old age (45 and above years). Dummies of main sector where a representative household work and hopping between different sectors will equally be generated. For instance, this will take the value of ''1'' if a household work in the manufacturing sector and ''0'' otherwise.

The Data

The data for the study was obtained from the General Household Survey (GHS) surveys of 2015/2016, 2010/2011 and 2012/2013. The GHS-Panel is a nationally representative survey of 5,000 Nigerian households, across the six geopolitical zones (at both the urban and rural level). The panel GHS is a sub-sample of the overall GHS sample households. It is a long-term project that collects panel data on households, their characteristics, welfare and their agricultural activities. Data for each wave is collected at two rounds– post planting (from October to November 2015) and post-harvest (from mid-April to May 2016). The proposed study will be utilizing households' questionnaire with specific attention on labour sub-section. There are specific questions characterising informality such as whether the representative household enrolled in a pension scheme on his job, has a written contract/agreement or letter of appointment, number of hours worked, and whether the employer provide health insurance coverage.

RESULTS AND DISCUSSION

In order to identify the households that have hop between jobs between visits and waves, the attention was on the households that have worked for someone in an enterprise, company, the government or any other individual. While those that have contract/agreement or letter of appointment were categorised as formal employment, those that do not have were categorised as informal. There are other forms of identifying formal or informal employment such as whether employers provide full or partial health insurance coverage or not, whether employees are enrolled in a pension scheme or not, number of people working in an enterprise ranging from 1-5, 6-10, 11-20 and above 20 employees. While none of the measures totally captures formal-informal dichotomy, we were convinced that a formal employment should have at least a written contract or employment letter.

Hopping between formal and informal jobs were analysed between visits (post-planting and post-harvest) and waves (wave 1 and 2, 1 and 3, and 2 and 3). The outcome, across gender, is presented in Table 1. Between wave 1 visits 1,435 (29.8%) households hop from informal to formal sector, 2,810 (58.4%) maintained their statuses while only 567 (11.8%) households hop from formal to informal sector. This could be due to job loss in the formal sector. Meanwhile, hopping from informal to formal sector is assumed to be characterised with better living standards. Between wave 2 visits, 1,135 (23.9%) households hop from informal to formal sector, the 2,783 (58.7) maintained their statuses while 826 (17.4%) households hop from formal to informal sector. Between wave 3 visits, 1,042 (21.1%) households hop from informal to formal sector, 2,985 (60.5%) maintained their statuses while 903 (18.3%) households hop from formal to informal job sector. Comparing waves, between wave 1 and wave 2, a total of 2026 (45.05) hop from informal to formal jobs, 1783 (41.9%) hops between wave 1 and 3, while 1725 (35.4%) hopped between wave 2 and 3. The decline in hopping from informal labour sector to formal sector could be due to rising limited opportunities in the formal sector. Also, hopping is more across waves than between waves.

There is significant gender, age, education and place of residence differences in jobs hopping. That is, male, young people, educated and urban residents hop more than female, older people, less educated, and rural residents, respectively. For instance, more of male hop from informal to formal sector and from formal to informal sector, except in the case of wave 2 between planting and harvest period. However, more females are retained, except for wave 1. This shows that job turn-over of male representative households are higher than females'.

Further, it is discovered that hopping from informal to formal sector is highest among households of age category of early adulthood (Table 2). This is followed by those in the age below 25 years, while it is least among the age category of old age. Among the households retaining their job statuses, the category of old age is the highest. However, this category is also highest among the households hop-

Table 1. Households hopping between formal and informal jobs across gender

	Wave 1 (Between Post-planting and harvest)	Wave 2 (Between Post-planting and harvest)	Wave 3 (Between Post-planting and harvest)	Wave 1 & 2	Wave 1 & 3	Wave 2 & 3
Hopping from informal to formal						
Male	984	873	756	1132	1082	992
Female	451	262	286	894	701	733
Sub-Total	1435	1135	1042	2026	1783	1725
Retention						
Male	1519	1034	1314	862	732	982
Female	1291	1749	1671	925	892	1044
Sub-Total	2810	2783	2985	1787	1624	2026
Hopping from formal to informal						
Male	268	341	658	365	427	652
Female	281	485	245	326	422	473
Sub-Total	567	826	903	691	849	1125
Total Households	**4812**	**4744**	**4930**	**4504**	**4256**	**4876**

Source: Computed by the Authors

ping from formal to informal jobs. This could be associated with retirement from formal jobs to join the informal sector. Related to the outcome in Table 1, hopping is equally higher, on the average, between waves than within waves.

Table 3 shows that the educated household representatives hop more from informal to formal jobs than the less educated households. The ratio is about 3 to 1. This is also indicated in the retention level of the less educated being higher than the educated households. This is because the educated have what it takes to hop between jobs than the less educated households. Although (most) less educated households are in the informal sector, their hopping from formal to informal sector are lesser compared to educated households. This supports that the less educated households may not be willing to give up the job security and entitlement benefits they enjoy in the formal sector to move into the informal sector.

The outcome in Table 4 reveals that hopping between formal and informal jobs is higher among urban residents than rural residents. However, while retention between waves is higher between waves among both urban and rural residents, retention is far higher within waves among rural residents than between waves. This can be explained by rural urban migration between waves bearing in mind that wave 3 (2015/2016) was the second round of panel surveys of previously conducted wave 1 surveys in 2010/11 and wave 2 surveys in 2012/13. Also, hopping from formal to informal is higher among urban residents than the rural residents.

The above shows that hopping from formal to informal sector is terse in Nigeria compared to hopping from informal to formal sector, this corroborates African Development Forum (2012) that the number of households exiting paid employment in the formal sector to form their own small informal businesses is rare in West Africa. Also, while the above shows that variations in the jobs hopping between formal and informal jobs vary across households' socio-economic characteristics; it doesn't give an idea of the causes of job hopping. This is considered subsequently.

Table 2. Hopping within and between waves across age range

	Wave 1 (Between Post-planting and harvest)	Wave 2 (Between Post-planting and harvest)	Wave 3 (Between Post-planting and harvest)	Wave 1 & 2	Wave 1 & 3	Wave 2 & 3
Hopping from informal to formal						
Youth (less than 25)	784	773	756	862	632	582
Early adulthood (25 to 44)	1,419	1004	1114	1226	1386	1325
Old age (above 45)	251	162	246	230	163	128
Sub-Total	2454	1939	2116	2318	2181	2035
Retention						
Youth (less than 25)	342	252	252	321	346	323
Early adulthood (25 to 44)	603	457	574	685	584	754
Old age (above 45)	991	1249	1271	925	892	1044
Sub-Total	1936	1958	2097	1931	1822	2121
Hopping from formal to informal						
Youth (less than 25)	57	78	74	69	85	79
Early adulthood (25 to 44)	93	89	97	96	105	98
Old age (above 45)	281	485	245	326	422	473
Sub-Total	431	652	416	491	612	650
Total Households	**4403**	**4549**	**4629**	**4353**	**4256**	**4892**

Table 3. Hopping within and between waves across education level

	Wave 1 (Between Post-planting and harvest)	Wave 2 (Between Post-planting and harvest)	Wave 3 (Between Post-planting and harvest)	Wave 1 & 2	Wave 1 & 3	Wave 2 & 3
Hopping from informal to formal						
Educated (first degree/HND and above)	1124	1013	1082	1184	1092	1192
Less Educated (less than first degree/HND)	442	378	399	594	601	533
Sub-Total	1566	1391	1481	1778	1693	1725
Retention						
Educated (first degree/HND and above)	892	783	981	1517	1134	1214
Less Educated (less than first degree/HND)	925	892	1044	1091	1049	1371
Sub-Total	1817	1675	2025	1517	2183	2585
Hopping from formal to informal						
Educated (first degree/HND and above)	368	391	558	365	423	554
Less Educated (less than first degree/HND)	281	485	237	357	412	473
Sub-Total	649	875	795	722	835	1027
Total Households	**4032**	**3941**	**4301**	**4017**	**4717**	**4577**

Source: Computed by the Authors

Table 4. Hopping within and between waves across place of residence

	Wave 1 (Between Post-planting and harvest)	Wave 2 (Between Post-planting and harvest)	Wave 3 (Between Post-planting and harvest)	Wave 1 & 2	Wave 1 & 3	Wave 2 & 3
Hopping from informal to formal						
Rural	351	362	388	794	831	937
Urban	1083	973	876	1102	1072	1082
Sub-Total	1434	1335	1264	1996	1903	2019
Retention						
Rural	1,619	1234	1114	872	737	782
Urban	1391	1049	1271	926	892	944
Sub-Total	1619	2283	2385	1798	1629	1726
Hopping from formal to informal						
Rural	458	473	453	365	427	452
Urban	683	786	673	564	462	663
Sub-Total	1141	1259	1126	929	889	1115
Total Households	**4194**	**4877**	**4775**	**4723**	**4421**	**4860**

Source: Computed by the Authors

Informal-Formal Job Hopping Determinants

Table 5 shows the estimations of informal-formal job hopping within waves visits. As indicated, age is significantly influencing hopping between informal and formal jobs. That is, as household's age increases we expect 0.342, 0.141 and 0.494 increases in the log-odds of job hopping from informal to formal sector between two visits of wave 1, 2 and 3 surveys, respectively. In other words, the odds of older households hopping from informal to formal jobs are: exp(0.34, 0.14, 0.49) = 1.40, 1.15, 1.63. This implies that the odds for an older households hopping are 1.40, 1.15, 1.63 times as high as they are for younger households. Also, the results show that male representative household hopping between informal and formal job differ from female representative households by log odds 0.28, 0.17 and 0.26 between two visits of wave 1, 2 and 3 surveys, respectively. Hence, the odds of a male having hopped from informal to formal jobs are: exp(0.28, 0.17, 0.26) = 1.32, 1.19, 1.30. Alternatively, it implies that the odds for male households hopping are 1.32, 1.19, 1.30 times higher than female households. Similar results were obtained for the urban residence. However, education level doesn't have significant impact on jobs hopping between any two visits of the waves surveys.

Unbundling the age into three categories of life cycles of youth (15–24 years of age), early adulthood (25–44 years), and mature adulthood and old age (45 years and above) revealed a different outcome. It was found that the early adulthood hop more than any other category from informal to formal jobs, while other age categories were not significant to job hopping. Across the main economic activities in which households are engaged, being in the agricultural sector was not found to be significantly influencing hopping. This may be due to the dominance of informality in the agricultural sector jobs. However, households working in the manufacturing, professional services (such as advertising professionals, architects, accountants, financial advisers, engineers, and consultants), buying and selling and

Table 5. Logit regression of hopping between waves visits

	Wave 1		Wave 2		Wave 3	
Variables (Hop=1)	**Coef.**	**z-value**	**Coef.**	**z-value**	**Coef.**	**z-value**
Log(Age)	0.342	3.31**	0.141	2.33**	0.494	5.44***
Sex (male= 1)	0.281	2.78**	0.172	2.08**	0.261	2.78**
Education Level (high=1)	0.012	1.07	0.112	1.67*	0.048	1.07
Urban (Urban=1)	0.232	3.01**	0.103	2.01**	0.232	3.01**
Age structure						
Youth (less than 25=1)	0.002	0.01	0.220	0.67*	0.000	0.09
Early adulthood (25 to 44=1)	0.062	5.98***	0.153	4.5***	0.092	5.63***
Old age (above 45=1)	-0.124	-0.78*	-0.140	-0.56	-0.109	1.72*
Main activities sector						
Agriculture (agric=1)	-0.110	-1.42	0.041	-1.34	-0.065	-1.42
Personal services (PS=1)	0.251	2.01**	0.104	2.42**	0.081	2.01**
Education (Edu=1)	0.011	1.04	0.051	1.54	0.065	1.21
Health (Health=1)	0.134	1.76*	-0.001	1.86*	0.028	1.52
Public Admin (PA=1)	-0.001	-0.12	0.047	-0.12	-0.241	-0.32
Mining (Mining=1)	0.100	1.08	0.013	1.18	0.688	2.03**
Manufacturing (man=1)	0.291	2.08**	0.231	2.72**	0.721	2.12**
Professional (Prof.=1)	0.182	1.98**	0.021	1.99**	0.232	1.99**
Electricity (Elec=1)	0.193	1.89*	0.063	1.86*	0.061	1.82*
Construction (Con.=1)	0.122	1.64*	0.105	1.99**	0.111	2.00**
Transportation (Trans=1)	0.021	0.13	0.084	0.18	0.168	0.13
Buying and Selling (B&S=1)	0.102	1.99**	0.205	1.99**	0.225	1.99**
Financial services (FS=1)	0.048	2.11**	0.074	2.76**	0.013	1.97**
Regions						
South-West (SW=1)	0.125	2.14**	0.439	3.45**	0.221	2.05**
South-East (SE=1)	0.002	0.13	0.115	0.47	0.013	0.96
South-South (SS=1)	0.050	0.93	0.000	0.04	0.021	0.90
North-Central (NC=1)	0.101	1.69*	0.045	1.69*	0.084	1.69*
North-East (NE=1)	0.211	1.10	-0.013	-1.93*	-0.002	-2.50**
North-West (NW=1)	0.021	1.20	0.088	1.43	0.063	1.20
Constant	1.204	1.32	0.056	1.66*	1.534	1.77*
Log-likelihood	-986.07		-783.08		-976.98	
Pseudo R^2	0.45		0.57		0.62	
$chi^2(26)$	79.465***		82.98***		98.66***	
Observations	3293		3519		3715	

Source: Computed by the author

Note: *,**,*** implies significance at 10%, 5%, and 1% level, respectively

financial services sectors have significant positive hopping log odds between visits of the three waves. Also, construction has significant positive log odds (coefficients) in the last two waves while mining has in wave 3 only. This shows that these sectors have the potential of making those working within the sector to earn better living in their formal sectors.

Across the geopolitical zones of Nigeria, log odds of hopping between informal to formal jobs are significant and positive in South West than in any other parts of Nigeria. This may be connected to high level of urbanization and industrialization in the zone. In the North Eastern part of the country, however, especially between visits in the wave 3, hopping log odds is significant and negative. The implication of negative sign is that many households slide from formal to informal job sector instead of the opposite and the odd ratio for the region compared to any other region is exp(-0.000)= 1.0. This could be traced to the rising insecurity in the region which could have made many of the formal sectors to relocate to other safer regions. Hence, the households in this region could have taken solace in informal jobs for survival.

Overall, the Pseudo R2 shows that about 45%, 57% and 62%, variations in informal-formal jobs hopping can be explained by the explanatory variables as estimated in the models, for wave 1, 2 and 3, respectively.

Informal-formal jobs hopping between waves are presented in Table 6. Unlike within waves' jobs hopping, between waves' jobs hopping log odd ratios (coefficients) are higher. This can be attributed to the difference in the length of time in between waves which gives households room to hop between jobs unlike the time within waves which is less than a year. It is revealed that the odds ratio of older households hopping from informal to formal jobs is 2.9, 6.42, and 3.7 between wave 1 and 2, 1 and 3, and 2 and 3, respectively after taking exponentials of the respective coefficients. That is, the odds for an older households hopping between informal to formal jobs are 6.42, 2.9, 3.7 times as high as they are for younger households across the indicated wave pairs. Similar to results obtained in the within the waves estimation, the male households hop significantly more than female household representatives. There are chances that male households will hop between informal to formal jobs about 3.22, 3.74, and 3.53 more than female household representatives across the wave pairs. Education is also important to hopping between formal and informal employment. The educated hop more than the less educated.

The age category shows that household representatives in early adulthood hop more than any other age categories, while those of old age hop less than any other age categories. Hopping is highest in the manufacturing jobs followed by buying and selling, construction, financial services, professional services and education, while it is least in agricultural sector. Across the geopolitical zones, hopping is highest in South-West, followed by South East, North Central, and North-West and it is least in North East.

In sum, the estimated models fit well given the values of Pseudo R^2 and Chi-square.

CONCLUSION AND POLICY RECOMMENDATIONS

This study contributed to the policy debate on the dynamics of informality in Nigeria, especially in terms of effectively mapping informality, moving labour force from informal to formal sector, as well as policies that can stimulate growth of the informal sector. The study found that hopping from informal to formal sector is highest among male, early adulthood and educated households. This outcome is related to the findings of Partida and Pacheco (2016). Hence, policies to help the households with potential hopping should be well targeted to further enhance their abilities to hop. The policies should address factors (such as family ties and culture) hindering the female and other categories of households to hop

Table 6. Logit regression of hopping between waves

	Wave 1&2		Wave 1&3		Wave 2&3	
Variables (Hop=1)	**Coef**	**z-value**	**Coef.**	**z-value**	**Coef.**	**z-value**
Log(Age)	1.061	1.99**	1.862	2.97**	1.321	3.04***
Sex (male= 1)	1.168	3.05***	1.328	2.08**	1.261	2.78**
Education Level (high=1)	1.248	5.07***	1.158	5.14***	1.371	4.07***
Urban (Urban=1)	1.508	3.01**	1.691	3.76***	1.340	2.91**
Age structure						
Youth (less than 25=1)	0.867	1.78*	0.220	2.21**	0.025	1.69*
Early adulthood (25 to 44=1)	1.530	5.98***	1.653	4.5***	1.192	5.63***
Old age (above 45=1)	-2.242	-3.78***	-0.956	-2.23**	-0.109	-2.72*
Main activities sector						
Agriculture (agric=1)	-0.310	-2.65**	-0.834	-2.97**	-0.265	-1.42
Personal services (PS=1)	0.245	3.06**	0.954	3.42**	0.081	2.01**
Education (Edu=1)	0.608	4.44***	0.544	5.85***	0.352	2.45**
Health (Health=1)	-0.106	-1.76*	-0.453	1.77*	0.128	1.52
Public Admin (PA=1)	-0.083	-0.18	0.147	0.19	-0.031	-0.22
Mining (Mining=1)	0.370	1.67*	0.793	1.88*	0.980	1.66*
Manufacturing (man=1)	1.213	5.08***	1.672	2.72**	1.600	3.12**
Professional (Prof.=1)	1.182	2.45**	1.333	1.99**	0.432	2.04**
Electricity (Elec=1)	0.193	1.89*	0.318	1.66*	0.160	1.92*
Construction (Con.=1)	1.522	2.19**	0.141	2.22**	0.111	2.00**
Transportation (Trans=1)	0.021	0.13	0.011	0.56	0.100	1.72*
Buying and Selling (B&S=1)	1.202	2.23**	1.323	2.06**	0.103	2.32**
Financial services (FS=1)	1.054	2.98**	1.074	2.76**	0.013	1.97**
Regions						
South-West (SW=1)	1.125	2.87**	2.439	3.45**	0.300	2.85**
South-East (SE=1)	0.076	2.00**	0.291	2.47**	0.314	1.96**
South-South (SS=1)	0.036	0.34	0.102	1.99**	0.231	1.83*
North-Central (NC=1)	0.049	1.69*	0.145	2.69**	0.114	1.09
North-East (NE=1)	-0.007	1.84*	-0.013	-1.93*	-0.192	-2.10**
North-West (NW=1)	0.341	1.40	0.360	2.12**	-0.063	-1.68*
Constant	2.076	1.88*	0.329	1.66	1.984	1.79*
Log-likelihood	-956		-803.05		-635.24	
Pseudo R^2	0.66		0.71		0.68	
$chi^2(26)$	85.867***		94.03***		87.63***	
Observations	3764		3325		3885	

Source: Computed by the author

Note: *,**,*** implies significance at 10%, 5%, and 1% level, respectively

for formal jobs characterised with better pay. Moreover, some sectors such as manufacturing, buying and selling, construction, financial services, professional services and education are potential sectors to make Nigerian growth inclusive in terms of providing remunerative jobs that minimizes poverty and inequality in the formal sector. Therefore, bottlenecks to performance and productivity of these sectors should be adequately tacked by formulating some pertinent policies:

- That will focus on attracting more investments in the wholesale and retail businesses from within and outside the economy;
- that will allow firms and prospective entrepreneurs to overcome infrastructural bottlenecks that is hindering the development of real sector especially agricultural, manufacturing and export sector;
- That will engender experienced staff to hop from formal to informal by using the operational experienced obtained in the formal sector for entrepreneurial development in order to reduce unemployment challenges in Nigeria;
- On national employment that will align employment markets in order to standardize improved working conditions and equitable employment opportunities with a view to discourage hopping between formal and informal.

REFERENCES

Blaauw, P.F. (2006). The dual labour market theory and the informal sector in South Africa. *Acta Commercii*, 248-257.

Chandra, V., & Khan, M. A. (1993). Foreign investment in the presence of an informal sector. *Economica*, *60*(237), 79–103. doi:10.2307/2554732

Coubès, M. L. (2005). Movilidad en la trayectoria laboral: Transición entre sector formal-informal del empleo. In M. L. Coubès, M. E. Zavala, & R. Zenteno (Eds.), *Cambio demográfico y social en México en el siglo XX. Una perspectiva de historias de vida* (pp. 259–282). Cámara de Diputados EGAP, Tecnológico de Monterrey, El Colegio de la Frontera Norte, Miguel Ángel Porrúa. Available from http://bibliotecasibe.ecosur.mx/sibe/book/000038678

Fajnzylber, P., Maloney, W., & Rojas, G. M. (2006). Microenterprise dynamics in developing countries: How similar are they to those in the industrialized world? Evidence from Mexico. *fir. Economic Review (Federal Reserve Bank of Atlanta)*, *20*(3), 389–419. doi:10.1093/wber/lhl005

Fields, G. S. (1975). Rural-urban migration, urban unemployment and underemployment, and job-search activity in LDCs. *Journal of Development Economics*, *2*(2), 165–187. doi:10.1016/0304-3878(75)90014-0 PMID:12265914

Gutierrez, I. A., Kumar, K. B., Mahmud, M., Munshi, F., & Nataraj, S. (2019). Transitions between informal and formal employment: Result from a worker survey in Bangladesh. *IZA Journal of Development and Migration*, *9*(3), 2–27. doi:10.118640176-019-0141-2

Hachen, D. S. Jr. (1990). Three Models of Job Mobility in Labour Markets. *Work and Occupations*, *17*(3), 320–354. doi:10.1177/0730888490017003004

Harris, J. R., & Todaro, M. P. (1970). Migration, unemployment and development: A two-sector analysis. *The American Economic Review*, *60*(1), 126–142.

Industrial Labour Organisation (ILO). (2014). Global Employment Trends 2014: Risk of a jobless recovery? International Labour Office.

Karakara, A. A., & Osabuohien, E. (2020). ICT Adoption, Competition and Innovation of Informal Firms in West Africa: Comparative Study of Ghana and Nigeria. *Journal of Enterprising Communities*, *14*(3), 397–414. doi:10.1108/JEC-03-2020-0022

Levy, S., & Székely, M. (2016, October 19). Más escolaridad, menos informalidad Un análisis de cohortes para México y América Latina. *El Trimestre Economico*, *332*(332), 499–548. doi:10.20430/ete.v83i332.232

Liang, Z., Appleton, S., & Song, L. (2016). *Informal Employment in China: Trends, Patterns and Determinants of Entry*. IZA DP No. 10139.

Maloney, W. F. (1997). *The Structure of Labor Market in Developing Countries: Time Series Evidence on Competing Views. Mimeo*. World Bank.

Maloney, W. F. (1999). Does informality imply segmentation in urban labor markets? Evidence from sectoral transitions in Mexico. *The World Bank Economic Review*, *13*(2), 275–302. doi:10.1093/wber/13.2.275

Medina, L., Jonelis, A., & Cangul, M. (2016). *The Informal Economy in Sub-Saharan Africa: Size and Determinants*. IMF working paper 156. (WP/17/156).

Nordman, C. J., Rakotomanana, F., & Roubaud, F. (2016). *Informal versus Formal: A Panel Data Analysis of Earnings Gaps in Madagascar. IZA Discussion Papers, No. 9970. Institute for the Study of Labour*. IZA.

Nordman, C. J., Rakotomanana, F., & Roubaud, F. (2016). Informal versus formal: A panel data analysis of earnings gaps in Madagascar. *World Development*, *86*, 1–17. doi:10.1016/j.worlddev.2016.05.006

Osabohien, R., Onanuga, O., Aderounmu, B., Matthew, O., & Osabuohien, E. (2020). Social Protection and Employment in Africa's agricultural Sector. *Business: Theory and Practice*, *21*(2), 494–502. doi:10.3846/btp.2020.11945

Osabuohien, E., Efobi, U. R., Herrmann, R., & Gitau, C. M. (2019). Female Labour Outcomes and Large-scale Agricultural Land Investments: Macro-Micro Evidence from Tanzania. *Land Use Policy*, *82*, 716–728. doi:10.1016/j.landusepol.2019.01.005

Partida, V., & Pacheco, M. E. (2016). *Changing Jobs in Mexico: Hopping between Formal and Informal Economic Sectors, Unemployment - Perspectives and Solutions*. Intech Open. Available from: https://www.intechopen.com/books/unemployment-perspectives-and-solutions/changing-jobs-in-mexico-hopping-between-formal-and-informal-economic-sectors

Reich, M., Gordon, D. M., & Edwards, R. C. (1973). *Dual labour markets: A theory of labour market segmentation. Economics Department Faculty Publications, Economics Commons*. University of Nebraska.

Soares, F. V. (2015). *Do informal workers queue for formal jobs in Brazil?* Discussion Paper No. 130, Institute for Applied Economic Research, Brazil.

Stumbitz, B., Lewis, S., Kyei, A. A., & Lyon, F. (2018). Maternity protection in formal and informal economy workplaces: The case of Ghana. *World Development, 110*, 373–378. doi:10.1016/j.worlddev.2018.06.007

Tansel, A., & Ozdemir, Z. A. (2014). *Determinant of transitions across formal / informal sectors in Egypt*. Working Paper 899, Economic Research Forum.

Tokman, V. (1979). Dinámica del mercado de trabajo urbano: El sector informal urbano en América Latina. In K. Rubén & J. L. Reyna (Eds.), *Fuerza de trabajo y movimientos laborales en América Latina* (pp. 68–102). El Colegio de México. doi:10.2307/j.ctv233mg4.6

Tokman, V. (2004). Una voz en el camino. Empleo y equidad en América Latina: 40 años de búsqueda. México: Fondo de Cultura Económica, 389.

World Economic Forum. (2012). *The Informal Sector in Francophone Africa, Firm Size, Productivity, and Institutions*. International Bank for Reconstruction and Development / The World Bank. Retrieved from. https://documents.worldbank.org/curated/en/737371468202815116/pdf/699350PUB0Publ067869B09780821395370.pdf

ENDNOTES

1 https://www.ilo.org/global/about-the-ilo/newsroom/news/WCMS_627189/lang--en/index.htm

2 National Bureau of Statistics Job Creation Survey, June 2016.

3 The production possibility frontier is concave and negatively slopped reflecting the law of diminishing returns to variable factor (labour) assuming capital is fixed in the short run. Recall that production in each sector requires labour and capital inputs as indicated in equation (1) and (2).

APPENDIX

Table A1.

	Wave 1 (Between Post-planting and harvest)	Wave 2 (Between Post-planting and harvest)	Wave 3 (Between Post-planting and harvest)	Wave 1 & 2	Wave 1 & 3	Wave 2 & 3
Hopping from informal to formal						
% of Male Hopping from informal to formal	20.4	18.4	15.3	25.1	25.4	20.3
% of Female Hopping from informal to formal	9.4	5.5	5.8	19.8	16.5	15.0
% of People Hopping from informal to formal	29.8	23.9	21.1	45.0	41.9	35.4
Retention						
% of Male Retained	31.6	21.8	26.7	19.1	17.2	20.1
% of Female Retained	26.8	36.9	33.9	20.5	21.0	21.4
% of People Retained	58.4	58.7	60.5	39.7	38.2	41.6
Hopping from formal to informal						
% of Male Hopping from formal to informal	5.6	7.2	13.3	8.1	10.0	13.4
% of Female Hopping from formal to informal	5.8	10.2	5.0	7.2	9.9	9.7
% of People Hopping from formal to informal	11.8	17.4	18.3	15.3	19.9	23.1

Table A2.

	Wave 1 (Between Post-planting and harvest)	Wave 2 (Between Post-planting and harvest)	Wave 3 (Between Post-planting and harvest)	Wave 1 & 2	Wave 1 & 3	Wave 2 & 3
Hopping from informal to formal						
% of Youth Hopping from informal to formal	17.8	17.0	16.3	19.8	14.8	11.9
% of Early Adulthood Hopping from informal to formal	32.2	22.1	24.1	28.2	32.6	27.1
% of Old Age Hopping from informal to formal	5.7	3.6	5.3	5.3	3.8	2.6
% of Households Hopping from informal to formal	55.7	42.6	45.7	53.3	51.2	41.6
Retention						
% of Youth Retained	7.8	5.5	5.4	7.4	8.1	6.6
% of Early Adulthood Retained	13.7	10.0	12.4	15.7	13.7	15.4
% of Old Age Retained	22.5	27.5	27.5	21.2	21.0	21.3
% of Households Retained	44.0	43.0	45.3	44.4	42.8	43.4
Hopping from formal to informal						
% of Youth Hopping from formal to informal	1.3	1.7	1.6	1.6	2.0	1.6
% of Early Adulthood Hopping from formal to informal	2.1	2.0	2.1	2.2	2.5	2.0
% of Old Age Hopping from formal to informal	6.4	10.7	5.3	7.5	9.9	9.7
% of Households Hopping from formal to informal	9.8	14.3	9.0	11.3	14.4	13.3

Table A3.

	Wave 1 (Between Post-planting and harvest)	Wave 2 (Between Post-planting and harvest)	Wave 3 (Between Post-planting and harvest)	Wave 1 & 2	Wave 1 & 3	Wave 2 & 3
Hopping from informal to formal						
% of Educated Hopping from informal to formal	27.9	25.7	25.2	29.5	23.2	26.0
% of Less Educated Hopping from informal to formal	11.0	9.6	9.3	14.8	12.7	11.6
% of Households Hopping from informal to formal	38.8	35.3	34.4	44.3	35.9	37.7
Retention						
% of Educated with a Retained job	22.1	19.9	22.8	37.8	24.0	26.5
% of Less Educated with a Retained job	22.9	22.6	24.3	27.2	22.2	30.0
% of Households with a Retained job	45.1	42.5	47.1	37.8	46.3	56.5
Hopping from formal to informal						
% of Educated Hopping from formal to informal	9.1	9.9	13.0	9.1	9.0	12.1
% of Less Educated Hopping from formal to informal	7.0	12.3	5.5	8.9	8.7	10.3
% of Households Hopping from formal to informal	16.1	22.2	18.5	18.0	17.7	22.4

Table A4.

	Wave 1 (Between Post-planting and harvest)	Wave 2 (Between Post-planting and harvest)	Wave 3 (Between Post-planting and harvest)	Wave 1 & 2	Wave 1 & 3	Wave 2 & 3
Hopping from informal to formal						
% of Rural Households Hopping from informal to formal	8.4	7.4	8.1	16.8	18.8	19.3
% of Urban Households Hopping from informal to formal	25.8	20.0	18.3	23.3	24.2	22.3
% of Households Hopping from informal to formal	34.2	27.4	26.5	42.3	43.0	41.5
Retention						
% of Rural Households with Retained jobs	38.6	25.3	23.3	18.5	16.7	16.1
% of Urban Households with Retained jobs	33.2	21.5	26.6	19.6	20.2	19.4
% of Households with Retained jobs	38.6	46.8	49.9	38.1	36.8	35.5
Hopping from formal to informal						
% of Rural Households Hopping from formal to informal	10.9	9.7	9.5	7.7	9.7	9.3
% of Urban Households Hopping from formal to informal	16.3	16.1	14.1	11.9	10.5	13.6
% of Households Hopping from formal to informal	27.2	25.8	23.6	19.7	20.1	22.9

Section 3
Agricultural Development and Food Security

Chapter 13
Climate Change and Crop Production in Africa

Zerihun Yohannes Amare
Institute of Disaster Risk Management and Food Security Studies, Bahir Dar University, Ethiopia

ABSTRACT

Agriculture, particularly crop production, is an economic activity that is highly dependent upon weather and climate in order to produce the food and fiber necessary to sustain human life. The vulnerability of agriculture to climate change and variability is an issue of major importance to the international scientific community. Greenhouse gas (GHG)-induced climate change would very likely result in significant damage in the agricultural sector in sub-Saharan Africa because the region already endures high heat and low precipitation. General circulation models (GCMs) are the primary source of climate change scenarios which make projections about the degree and timing of climate change. Agriculture has always been dependent on the variability of the climate for the growing season and the state of the land at the start of the growing season. The key for adaptation for crop production to climate change is the predictability of the conditions. What is required is an understanding of the effect on the changing climate on land, water, and temperature.

INTRODUCTION

Climate change impacts and adaptation strategies are increasingly becoming major areas of scientific concern. Climate variability is one of the most significant factors influencing year to year crop production, even in high yield and high-technology agricultural areas (Kang *et al.* 2009; Herrmann *et al*, 2018).The two fundamental response options to the risks posed by anthropogenic climate change are mitigation of climate change and adaptation to climate change. Mitigation refers to limiting global climate change by reducing the emissions of greenhouse gases (GHGs) and enhancing their sinks. Adaptation primarily aims at moderating the adverse effects of climate change through a wide range of actions that are targeted at the vulnerable system (Füssel 2007; Egbetokun et al, 2018; 2020). This implies mitigation addresses causes while adaptation addresses effects.

DOI: 10.4018/978-1-7998-4817-2.ch013

Adaptation has now emerged as an urgent policy priority, prompting action both within and outside the climate change negotiations (Parry et al., 2004). Owing to the significant differences in temporal and spatial scales at which mitigation and adaptation take place, and in their respective information needs, policies are formulated independently of each other (Cairns *et al.* 2012). This separation is also reflected in the structure of the Intergovernmental Panel on Climate Change (IPCC), where Working Group III addresses mitigation. In contrast, the assessment of adaptation lies within the responsibility of Working Group II.

However, adaptation has recently been covered more extensively and has an essential place in the fourth assessment report of the IPCC (2007). As a result, the Parties to the United Nations Framework Convention on Climate Change have identified adaptation as one of the fundamental key building block required to strengthen the future response to climate change (Israel climate change information Centre (ICCIC 2014; Akinyemi et al, 2019). In the face of these challenges, the paradigm is envisaged to advance beyond 2012 successfully with the incorporation of some initiatives and rearrangement (Rahman 2013). In the aspects of the literature, adaptation to climate change is given increasing international attention as the confidence in climate change projections is getting higher.

High temperatures under condition of global warming will encourage high rates evapotranspiration. Consequently, there may be decrease in the length of the growing season. In contrast, high temperatures would increase the length of the growing seasons in the middle and high latitudes as well as areas of high elevations as the number of frost-free days would increase. The sub-humid climatic zone of Africa permits the cultivation of a variety of crops in a pattern that emerged earlier centuries in response to local conditions (Karienye *et al.* 2018). This vulnerability is particularly high in Africa where agriculture production is the primary source of livelihoods for 66 percent of the total active population (Osabuohien, 2020).

This study provided an understanding of the relationship between rainfall variability and farmers' adaptation strategies to rainfall variability for crop production that would lead to high yields hence improving the family livelihoods. Furthermore, the study will serve as a useful reference material and guide to future prospective researchers who would want to research into similar thematic areas related to climate variability influence and adaptation in various regions in the world. Specifically, the study will benefit the ministry of Agriculture, farmers, and policy implementers in improving crop production in areas that are characterized by varying rainfall patterns.

CLIMATE CHANGE IMPACTS AND ADAPTATION STRATEGIES

In spite of recent technological and scientific advances, weather is still the most important variable in crop production. The climatic factor affects crop and determines the adequacy of food supplies into major ways. One is through weather hazards to crops and the other is the control exercised by climate on the type of agriculture feasible or viable in a given area. Climatic parameters have an influence on all stages of the crop production chain including land preparation, sowing, crop growth and management, harvesting, storage, transport and marketing. To improve communities' resilience, decision-makers must anticipate the impacts and encourage decisions that improve the region will enhance to cope and adapt, such as the development of early warning systems. Adaptation can either be proactive or reactive, and the form, of response, can take place within natural systems or within humans. Reactions within the human system can be motivated by either public or private interests, and they can be planned or autonomous.

The Impacts of Climate Change on Crop Production

Climate change increase uncertainty with respect to food production. Water availability will be one of the limiting constraints for crop production and food security (Reddy and Pachepsky 2000). Knowing current moisture trends is critical in forecasting future crop production in fluctuating climatic conditions (Iizumi and Ramankutty 2015, Nhamo et al. 2019).

The scarcity of water depends on the demand and supply (Fujihara et al. 2008). This implies, when the irrigated area is expanded, the efficiency of irrigation should consider the expansion of irrigated land. Therefore, it is urgent to determine the impacts of climate change on crop production and water resources to develop possible adaptation strategies. The reduction in crop production due to climate change and variability can influence global and regional food access and production. This is supported by related literatures like Abraha and Savage (2006) and Hassan and Nhemachena (2008). Increased diversification of crops, using drought and diseases resistant crops were suggested by Amare et al. (2018) and Hassan and Nhemachena (2008) to reduce the reduction of crop production due to harsh climatic conditions.

Climate change affects different varieties of crops differently. For example, Ortiz *et al.* (2008) stated that wheat production affected by climate change are mainly concerned with future CO2 concentrations. The authors recommend how wheat can adapt to climate change in Indo-Gangetic Plains for the 2050s and suggested that global warming is beneficial for wheat crop production in some regions but may reduce productivity in critical temperature areas. Therefore, it is urgent to develop some extreme heat-tolerant wheat germplasm to mitigate climate change impacts on crop production. The climate change will increase crop production in one region and decrease in others which are concerned with the latitude of the area and irrigation application (Kang *et al.* 2009). This implies, there is a regional variation on the impacts of climate change on crop yield. This is because of the geographical location and adaptive capacity of the region.

The main component of adaptation is building communities' resilience, the capacity of a system to absorb disturbance and shocks without collapsing (Folke et al. 2010). Adapting to impacts brought by the change in climate are possibly by adopting strategies like Shifting planting dates and cultivar substitution and climate-smart agriculture and livelihood diversification and encouraging change in shifts in the diet (Nhamo *et al.* 2019). Climate change adaptation strategies like irrigation help framers protect against crop losses due to extreme temperature and decreasing rainfall (Amare *et al.* 2018, Benhin 2006, Hassan and Nhemachena 2008). This implies the availability of irrigation application can explain the adaptive capacity. The crop yield can be increased with irrigation application and precipitation increase during the crop growth; meanwhile, crop yield is more sensitive to the precipitation than temperature. Therefore, if water availability is reduced in the future, the soil of high-water holding capacity will be better to reduce the frequency and severity of drought and improve the crop yield.

The Rational of Climate Change Adaptation

There are many convincing arguments for a more comprehensive consideration of adaptation as a response measure to climate change. Firstly, given the amount of past greenhouse gas emissions and the inertia of the climate system, we are already bound to some level of climate change, which can no longer be prevented even by the most ambitious emission reductions (Füssel 2007). Second, the effect of emission reductions takes several decades to fully manifest, whereas most adaptation measures have more immediate and sustainable benefits (Rahman 2013).

Third, Climate change adaptations are effectively implemented at local scale compared to mitigation measures. This implies adaptation can be practiced without the prior approval of the national and international community. Whereas, mitigation requires international cooperation and national government commitment to reduce emission sources. Therefore, adaptation is more efficient than mitigation. Fourth, risks associated with the current climate change and variability can be reduced through adaptations. These ideas were supported by IPCC (2007), (IPCC 2014). The role of mitigation in reducing risks of climate change and vulnerability to nature and society is inevitable if practiced efficiently. However, the benefits of climate change adaptation are largely local to regional in scale, but they can be immediate (IPCC 2007, IPCC 2014). The increasing interest in adaptation to climate change is reflected in the evolution of the theory and practice of climate change vulnerability assessments (IPCC 2007, IPCC 2014, Rahman 2013). Recently, the two response options to climate change in the policy highlights are mitigation and adaptation with priority for adaptation.

Climate Change Adaptation to Increase Crop Productivity

The changes in climate alone will not determine the adverse effects of climate variability and change on human welfare and natural systems. The sensitivity and adaptability of the human system to climate change can also determine the impact (Füssel 2007, IPCC 2001, Klein 2003). Therefore, adaptation is one of the fundamental response options to reduce the risks posed by anthropogenic climate change.

The scarcity of water depends on the demand and supply (Fujihara et al. 2008). This implies, when the irrigated area is expanded, the efficiency of irrigation should consider the expansion of irrigated land. Therefore, it is urgent to determine the impacts of climate change on crop production and water resources in order to develop possible adaptation strategies. The reduction in crop production due to climate change and variability has the possibility to influence on global and regional food access and production. This is supported by related literatures like Abraha and Savage (2006) and Hassan and Nhemachena (2008). Increased diversification of crops, using drought and diseases resistant crops were suggested by Amare et al. (2018) and Hassan and Nhemachena (2008) to reduce reduction of crop production due to harsh climatic conditions.

Inter-governmental Panel on Climate Change (IPCC 2001) highlighted potential adaptation options to reduce the negative impact of climate change or exploit the positive opportunities to places or sectors. For example, about 228 different adaptation measures, whether they are passive, reactive, anticipatory, planned or autonomous, were identified. There are various ways to classify climate change adaptation options. Depending on their timing, goal, and motive of implementation. Smit *et al.* (1999) and Klein (2003) classified adaptation strategies as reactive and proactive.

Reactive (ex-post) adaptation takes place after impacts of climate change have been observed. Provision of emergency assistance (relief) to flood victims and drought-affected people (share losses) and measures to rehabilitate and reconstruct the damaged property and communities are part of this adaptation process (United Nation Environment Programme (UNEP 1998).

Reactive adaptation is informed by direct experience; hence, resources can be allocated to known risks. In this sense, adaptation historically has been largely, but not entirely reactive (Burton *et al.* 2006). On the contrary, proactive (anticipatory) adaptation takes place before the impact of climate change is observed. Proactive adaptation, unlike reactive adaptation, is forward-looking and takes into account the inherent uncertainties associated with anticipated change(Burton *et al.* 2006). This means, it aims to reduce exposure to forthcoming risks; for instance, by avoiding development on flood-prone lands.

Table 1. Adaptation strategies based on timing

Reactive adaptation (Ex-post)	Anticipatory/proactive adaptation
Erosion control	Development of tolerant/resistant crops (to drought, salt, insect/ pests)
Dam construction for irrigation	Research and development
Changes in fertilizer use and application	Soil-water management
Introduction of new crops	Diversification and intensification of food and plantation crops
Soil fertility maintenance	Policy measures, tax incentives/subsidies, free market
Changes in planting and harvesting times	Development of early warning systems
Switch to different cultivars	
Educational and outreach programmes on conservation and management of soil and water	

Source: United Nations Framework Convention on Climate Change (UNFCC 2007)

Experience suggests that proactive adaptations require a greater initial investment, but is more effective at reducing potential risks(Burton *et al.* 2006). Therefore, adaptation strategies should give priority to proactive actions aimed at reducing future threat, but as risks will remain, reactive approaches also help vulnerable populations recover from the unavoidable impact. However, it is difficult to demarcate a clear boundary between reactive and proactive adaptation strategies. The reason is that actions after one event may also serve as preparation for the next occurrence. For example, bringing relief and rehabilitation to affected people is essential to take advantage of the opportunity to make them less vulnerable and to take care not to increase future vulnerability(UNEP 1998).

Depending on their degree of spontaneity, adaptation can be autonomous and planned(Smit *et al.* 1999, Smit and Wandel 2006). Autonomous (spontaneous) adaptation involves the changes that natural and most human systems will undergo in response to changing conditions irrespective of any policy, plan, or decision. Instead, autonomous adaptation will be triggered by ecological changes in natural systems and by the market or welfare changes in the human system induced by climate change.

Planned adaptation on the other hand, is the result of a deliberate policy decision, based on an awareness that conditions have changed or are about to change and that action is required to return to, maintain, or achieve the desired state(Burton *et al.* 2006, Smit *et al.* 1999). This distinction between planned and autonomous may be applied at different levels of decision-making. For example, from the perspective of Ministry of Agriculture in any developing countries that depends on agriculture as a livelihood, autonomous adaptation may refer to those actions that farmers undertake without state intervention. In this case, Relatively inexpensive adaptation measures such as change in planting dates to avoid higher temperature stress during the flowering and grain filling stages can reduce the adverse impact on crop yields due to climate change (UNEP 1998).

The third distinction can be based on the system in which the adaptation takes place: the natural system in which adaptation is by definition reactive or the human system in which both reactive and anticipatory adaptations are practical(Klein 2003). The fourth classification can be based on scales and actors involved in adaptation. There are private and public adaptation types(Klein 2003). Private adaptation is initiated and implemented by individual households and private companies usually in the actor's rational self-interest in response to threats to the climate, often triggered by extreme events (Adger 2003, Burton *et al.* 2006).

Others are public adaptations, which are initiated and implemented by the governments on behalf of society at all levels usually directed at collective needs, sometimes in anticipation of climate change and often in response to human and non-human populations(Adger 2003, Burton *et al.* 2006). Thus, autonomous and planned adaptations largely correspond to private and public adaptation respectively. Autonomous adaptation is the base for evaluating the need for planned anticipatory adaptation(Klein 2003).

Studies in Africa like (Madison 2006), in the Sahel region (Mertz *et al.* 2009), and Ethiopia (Yesuf *et al.* 2008) identified different climate change adaptation strategies (reactive or proactive and planned or autonomous). The most common adaptation methods used by almost all countries were crop planting, soil conservation, manure application, irrigation, rainwater harvesting, change planting dates (proactive) and replanting (reactive). To modify the threat/prevent the effect; planting different crop varieties, changing crop variety, engaging in non-farm activities (prevent the effect – proactive or reactive), migration (Change location), change farming type (from crop to livestock and vice-versa) - change use, and adaptation of new technologies.

Different planting dates are important adaptation practices in Egypt, Kenya, and Senegal. Adopting a shorter growing crop variety is practiced in Senegal. In Egypt, the majority of respondents have practiced non-farm activities while in Kenya and South Africa, large numbers of farmers have used irrigation. There is increasing use of water conservation in Burkina Faso, Kenya, and Niger. In Burkina Faso, Kenya, Senegal, and Niger, soil conservations are largely practiced. Increased use of weather insurance is almost exclusive to Egypt(Madison 2006). Prayer and ritual offerings are also made in Senegal and Niger. Every Egyptian and every Ethiopian respondent claimed to have made at least one adaptation strategy, which contradicts to other studies(Yesuf *et al.* 2008).

On the other hand, based on Daron (2014), an improved understanding of traditional mechanisms for coping with climate hazards, coupled with effectively designed strategies for dissemination of indigenous knowledge, could support vulnerability reduction for the country's population. However, the term "adaptation" and "coping "are sometimes used interchangeably, leading to confusion about the similarities and differences between these two important concepts. The list of characteristics (Table 2) was a compilation of brainstorming sessions by groups of development practitioners in Ghana, Niger, and Nepal.

Table 2. Characteristics of 'coping' and 'adaptation'

Coping	Adaptation
Short term and immediate	Oriented towards long-term livelihood security
Orientated towards survival	A continues process
Not continued	Results are sustained
Motivated by crises	Uses resources efficiently and sustainably
Often degrades resource base	Involves planning
Prompted by a lot of alternatives	Combined old and new strategies
	Focused on a study finding alternatives

Source: CAREInternational (2009)

The selling of productive assets (like livestock) and boosting incomes through artisanal charcoaling are two examples of "traditional coping mechanisms" common across much of semi-arid Africa. But while these strategies may work well enough when drought occurs only once every five or so years, they are a dead-end when it comes to dealing with the "adaptation" forces us to think outside the box and identify sustainable solutions to long-term climate change(Taylor *et al.* 2009).

CONCLUSION

Climate change will induce several of changes that will affect the evaporative environment in which plant leaves will evolve. Understanding climate change and the process by which plants control their water loss is needed, in particular to achieve tighter control. Climate change will also affect the pattern of cropping cycle. Breeding for short maturing crops will likely be increasingly important and this should largely mitigate the negative effects of climate change on crop yield. With increasing likelihood of drought, a key will be to understand the dynamics of water uptake and how water taken up at key developmental stages affects the yield under stress.

REFERENCES

Abraha, M., & Savage, M. (2006). Potential impacts of climate change on the grain yield of maize for the midlands of KwaZulu-Natal, South Africa. *Agriculture, Ecosystems & Environment*, *115*(1-4), 150–160. doi:10.1016/j.agee.2005.12.020

Adger, W. N. (2003). Social Capital, Collective Action, and Adaptation to Climate Change. *Economic Geography*, *79*(4), 387–404. doi:10.1111/j.1944-8287.2003.tb00220.x

Akinyemi, O., Efobi, U., Asongu, S., & Osabuohien, E. (2019). Renewable energy, trade performance and the conditional role of finance and institutional capacity in sub-Sahara African Countries. *Energy Policy*, *132*, 490–498. doi:10.1016/j.enpol.2019.06.012

Amare, Z. Y., Ayoade, J. O., Adelekan, I. O., & Zeleke, M. T. (2018). Barriers to and determinants of the choice of crop management strategies to combat climate change in Dejen District, Nile Basin of Ethiopia. *Agriculture & Food Security*, *7*(1), 37. doi:10.118640066-018-0188-y

Benhin, J. K. (2006). *Climate change and South African agriculture: Impacts and adaptation options*. CEEPA discussion paper.

Burton, I. (2006). *Adaptation to climate change: international policy options*. Citeseer.

Cairns, J. E. (2012). Maize production in a changing climate: impacts, adaptation, and mitigation strategies. Advances in Agronomy, 114, 1-58. doi:10.1016/B978-0-12-394275-3.00006-7

CAREInternational. (2009). *CARE International. Climate vulnerability and Adaptive capacity Analysis*. Handbook.

Daron, D. (2014). *Regional Climate Messages: East Africa. Scientific report from the CARIAA Adaptation at Scale in Semi-Arid Regions (ASSAR) Project, December 2014, Cape Town, South Africa.* Retrieved from http://www. uct. ac.za

Egbetokun, S., Osabuohien, E., & Akinbobola, T. (2018). Feasible Environmental Kuznets and Institutional Quality in North and Southern African Sub-regions. *International Journal of Energy Economics and Policy*, *8*(1), 104–115.

Egbetokun, S., Osabuohien, E., Onanuga, O., Akinbobola, T., Gershon, O., & Okafor, V. (2020). Environmental Pollution, Economic Growth and Institutional Quality: Exploring the Nexus in Nigeria. *Management of Environmental Quality*, *31*(1), 18–31. doi:10.1108/MEQ-02-2019-0050

Folke, C., Carpenter, S. R., Walker, B., Scheffer, M., Chapin, T., & Rockström, J. (2010). Resilience thinking: Integrating resilience, adaptability and transformability. *Ecology and Society*, *15*(4), art20. doi:10.5751/ES-03610-150420

Fujihara, Y., Tanaka, K., Watanabe, T., Nagano, T., & Kojiri, T. (2008). Assessing the impacts of climate change on the water resources of the Seyhan River Basin in Turkey: Use of dynamically downscaled data for hydrologic simulations. *Journal of Hydrology (Amsterdam)*, *353*(1-2), 33–48. doi:10.1016/j.jhydrol.2008.01.024

Füssel, H.-M. (2007). Vulnerability: A generally applicable conceptual framework for climate change research. *Global Environmental Change*, *17*(2), 155–167. doi:10.1016/j.gloenvcha.2006.05.002

Hassan & Nhemachena. (2008). Determinants of African farmers' strategies for adapting to climate change: Multinomial choice analysis. *African Journal of Agricultural and Resource Economics, 2*, 83.

Herrmann, R., Jumbe, C., Bruentrup, M., & Osabuohien, E. (2018). Competition between Biofuel Feedstock and Food Production: Empirical Evidence from Sugarcane Outgrower Settings in Malawi. *Biomass and Bioenergy*, *114*(July), 100–111. doi:10.1016/j.biombioe.2017.09.002

ICCIC. (2014). *Israeli Climate Change Information Center (ICCIC). 2014. Adaptation to climate change in Israel recommendations and knowledge gaps, Jerusalem, Israel.* ICCIC.

Iizumi, T., & Ramankutty, N. (2015). How do weather and climate influence cropping area and intensity? *Global Food Security*, *4*, 46–50. doi:10.1016/j.gfs.2014.11.003

IPCC. (2001). Intergovernmental Panel On Climate. *Climatic Change*, 2007.

IPCC. (2007). Intergovernmental Panel on Climate Change, Mitigation of Climate Change.

IPCC. (2007). *Solomon, Susan,climate change the physical science basis*. AGU Fall Meeting Abstracts.

Kang, Y., Khan, S., & Ma, X. (2009). Climate change impacts on crop yield, crop water productivity and food security–A review. *Progress in Natural Science*, *19*(12), 1665–1674. doi:10.1016/j.pnsc.2009.08.001

Karienye, J. M. (2018). Influence of Rainfall Variability on Tomato Production among Small Scale Farmers in Kieni East Sub County. Academic Press.

Klein, R. J. (2003). Adaptation to climate variability and change: what is optimal and appropriate. *Climate Change in the Mediterranean: Socio-Economic Perspectives of Impacts, Vulnerability and Adaptation, 32*.

Madison, D. (2006). *The Perception and Adaptation to Climate Change in Africa*. Policy Research Working Paper 4308. University of Pretoria: Centre for Environmental Economics and Policy in Africa.

Mertz, O., Mbow, C., Reenberg, A., & Diouf, A. (2009). Farmers' perceptions of climate change and agricultural adaptation strategies in rural Sahel. *Environmental Management*, *43*(5), 804–816. doi:10.100700267-008-9197-0 PMID:18810526

Nhamo, L. (2019). Preparedness or repeated short-term relief aid? Building drought resilience through early warning in southern Africa. *Water S.A.*, *45*(1), 75–85.

Nhamo, L., Mathcaya, G., Mabhaudhi, T., Nhlengethwa, S., Nhemachena, C., & Mpandeli, S. (2019). Cereal production trends under climate change: Impacts and adaptation strategies in southern Africa. *Agriculture*, *9*(2), 30. doi:10.3390/agriculture9020030

Niang, Ruppel, Abdrabo, Essel, Lennard, Padgham, & Urquhart. (2014). Africa. In Climate Change: Impacts, Adaptation, and Vulnerability (pp. 1199–1265). Cambridge University Press.

Ortiz, R., Sayre, K. D., Govaerts, B., Gupta, R., Subbarao, G. V., Ban, T., Hodson, D., Dixon, J. M., Iván Ortiz-Monasterio, J., & Reynolds, M. (2008). Climate change: Can wheat beat the heat? *Agriculture, Ecosystems & Environment*, *126*(1-2), 46–58. doi:10.1016/j.agee.2008.01.019

Osabuohien, E. (2020). *The Palgrave Handbook of Agricultural and Rural Development in Africa*. Palgrave Macmillan., doi:10.1007/978-3-030-41513-6

Rahman, M. I. (2013). Climate change: A theoretical review. *Interdisciplinary Description of Complex Systems: INDECS*, *11*(1), 1–13. doi:10.7906/indecs.11.1.1

Reddy, V., & Pachepsky, Y. A. (2000). Predicting crop yields under climate change conditions from monthly GCM weather projections. *Environmental Modelling & Software*, *15*(1), 79–86. doi:10.1016/S1364-8152(99)00011-0

Smit, B., Burton, I., Klein, R. J. T., & Street, R. (1999). The science of adaptation: A framework for assessment. *Mitigation and Adaptation Strategies for Global Change*, *4*(3-4), 199–213. doi:10.1023/A:1009652531101

Smit, B., & Wandel, J. (2006). Adaptation, adaptive capacity and vulnerability. *Global Environmental Change*, *16*(3), 282–292. doi:10.1016/j.gloenvcha.2006.03.008

Taylor. (2009). *Adaptation key terms*. Retrieved 29 May2019 from https://www.weadapt.org/knowledge-base/adaptation-decision-making/adaptation-versus-coping

UNEP. (1998). *United Nations Environmental Program (UNDP). Hand Book on Methods for Climate Change Impact Assessment and Adaptation Strategies*. UNEP and IES.

UNFCC. (2007). *United Nations Framework Convention on Climate Change (UNFCC). Climate Change: Impacts, Vulnerabilities, and Adaptation in Developing Countries*. United Nations Framework Convention on Climate Change Secretariat.

Yesuf, M. (2008). *The impact of climate change and adaptation on food production in low-income countries: evidence from the Nile Basin*. Intl Food Policy Res Inst.

Chapter 14
Political Economy of Land Policy Reform and Governance in Nigeria

Abiodun Elijah Obayelu
https://orcid.org/0000-0003-3328-7717
Federal University of Agriculture, Abeokuta, Nigeria

Kamilu Kolade Bolarinwa
Federal University of Agriculture, Abeokuta, Nigeria

Olalekan Oyekunle
Federal University of Agriculture, Abeokuta, Nigeria

ABSTRACT

Land is the most important asset of farmers that plays an indispensable role in agricultural production. Nigerian land system has strong social and cultural attraction making it difficult to separate from political, social, cultural, and economic effects. Politics and the process of politicking influence the course and outcome of government decision on land policy. This study examines the political economy of agricultural land policy reforms and governance in Nigeria. The study used a combination of methods, such as expository, comparative, and case analysis. Findings showed that land issues are delicate, demanding careful attention to avoid social or political conflicts. Politicization of land is a major cause of land dispute but with good land governance, land policy reform become easier to implement. Political will of government is crucial for land policy to succeed. Transparent, fair, and equitable land policy is necessary to continue on the path of peace, stability, and increase agricultural productivity.

INTRODUCTION

Land is one of the most valuable and disputed single natural resource that affects every facet of live (Ostrom, and Schlager, 1992) and cannot be isolated from agricultural production. Major development is creating pressure over land and this has resulted to an increase in competition for land between different

DOI: 10.4018/978-1-7998-4817-2.ch014

groups, such as multiple land users (farmers, herders), urban elites and foreign investors (Wells-Dang, 2016, Cotula *et al.,* 2004). Agricultural land (the share of land area that is arable, under permanent crops, and under permanent pastures) in Nigeria is reported to be 77.74% of the total land area as at 2016 (World Bank, 2016) and the main natural asset of farmers (Nzeh *et al.,* 2017). This resource, is a vehicle for human and rural development (Obayelu *et al.,* 2017) and source of political power that need to be reformed whenever there is a conflict on it as in the case of Nigeria. Ownership of land and the way it is managed affect agricultural development of a nation (Subedi, 2016, Nzeh *et al.,* 2017). Land ownership affects land use, farming systems, level of production and the volume of agricultural credit especially where the existing credit systems place undue emphasis on land as a form of collateral (Michie and Loboa, 2012).

Land policy is 'a set of agreed principles to govern ownership, use and management of land resources, and usually contains a statement of vision and objectives for the country' (AUC-ECA-AfDB Consortium, 2011). It is a significant tool in the transmission of wealth in addition to ensuring food security (Adeleye *et al.,* 2020). Land policy determines who has legal rights of access or ownership to land resources, how these rights are managed and the ways land is distributed among diverse stakeholders (French Development Cooperation, 2009). Land policy articulates political choices of power distribution between the state, the local systems of authority and its citizens (Lund, 2011a, 2011b). The multidimensional nature of land requires a careful and well implemented approach that looks at land within the broader historical, political economic and social context (EU Taskforce, 2004).

Land governance on the other hand is about power and the political economy of land. While the power structure of the society is revealed in the rules of land tenure, the quality of governance upsets the distribution of power in society (Palmer, Fricska and Wehrmann, 2009). Land governance has to do with decisions that are made about access to land and its use, the manner in which the decisions are implemented and the way competing interests are managed (Ukaejiofo, 2010).

Political economy of land policy reform and governance as used in this study entails how complex political nature in terms of power and authority influences decision making on access to land and its use, formulation of new land policy and amendments of the existing land reform in Nigeria going by the existing level of development.

Research Problem Statement

Many of the present challenges facing Nigeria have a clear land dimension: unequal access to land; insecurity of tenure; unsustainable land use; weak institutions for land administration, dispute and conflict resolution, et cetera and responses to these challenges are difficult when the governance of land is weak and have political undertone. Management of land is perceived as one of the most corrupt government activities (Wren-Lewis, 2013), and corrupt land systems/administration have a negative impact on both rural and urban agricultural production (Nzeh *et al.,* 2017). Successful land policy and good land governance is usually of a technical, procedural and political nature (Massay 2020; Kironde, 2009; Moyo and Yeros 2005). To this end, land management reforms are necessary to change the institutional structure governing man's relationship with the land, involving intervention in the prevailing pattern of land ownership, control and usage in order to change the structure of holdings, improve land productivity and broaden the distribution of benefits (World Bank, 1996). Land reform requires getting policies right or removal of policies that create market distortions and imperfections (de Janvry *et al.,* 2001; World Bank 2003). Modification or replacement of existing institutional arrangement governing possession, use and title are some of the common features of land reform but the Nigerian land reform program has faced many problems which hinder its success.

The study addressed the following questions:

1. What is the history and nature of land reforms in Nigeria?
2. What are the challenges and implications of the Nigerian Land Use Act?
3. What is the politics behinds land policy and governance in Nigeria?
4. How do key actors on land perceived the Nigeria land policy and governance?
5. Are there case studies on land policies in African countries where lessons can be learnt?

Objectives of the Paper

The goal of this study is to examine land policy reforms and governance in Nigeria through the application of the concept of political economy.

Specifically, the study has the following objectives:

1. Examine the nature, challenges and implications of the Land Use Act in Nigeria,
2. Generate insights into the political economy of land policy and governance in Nigeria,
3. Analyse the perceptions among key actors on the land policy and governance in Nigeria.
4. Assess case studies of land policies in some African countries and draw some lessons for Nigeria.

Justification of the Study

Unlike other studies (such as Obayelu *et al.*, 2017, Ghebru, and Akumo, 2016, Mabogunje, 2010, Uchendu, 1979) on land policy reform and other related issues in Nigeria, work on how political institutions affect land reform and governance in Nigeria have not yet received much attention as far as we know. This study was therefore undertaken to know how politics shapes and influences land management reforms in Nigeria. The study is important because it reveals the underlying interests and institutions that enable or frustrate changes in land policy reforms and governance in Nigeria. Such insights are important if Nigeria is going to overcome the challenging issues around land governance, and agricultural production which do not lend themselves to technical solutions alone. The outcomes from the study will support more effective and politically feasible strategies, as well as inform more realistic expectations of what can be achieved between politics, land reform and land governance.

For a better understanding, the study followed three frameworks which are: (i) analysis of the broad country context, the types of tenure and land reforms that exist and the operation of land markets; (ii) how a governance and political economy perspective can be applied to a land reform considering stakeholders' perceptions; and (iii) how to manage land reform process.

MATERIALS AND METHODS

The study was carried out in Nigeria. The country has a total land area of 910,800 square kilometres (Central Intelligence Agency [CIA], 2018, USAID, 2014), and more than 80% of the land is appropriate for production of both crops and livestock (USAID, 2010). Information on the past and current land-related legislation was primarily obtained from secondary sources. Sources include published articles and books, unpublished discussion papers, research reports, policy documents, position papers, complemented with primary data from personal discussions with some stakeholders. The information gathered covers a range of conceptual and empirical issues on land policy and governance. The study used a combination of techniques, such as expository analysis, comparative analysis and case analysis to analyse the information collected.

RESULTS AND DISCUSSION

The History and Nature of Land Policy in Nigeria

Land tenure strategy everywhere in the world is one of the basis of agricultural production and natural resource management (Norton, 2014). Going through memory lane, during the pre-colonial period in Nigeria, land was primarily regulated with the use of customary laws, making land governance the sole obligation of the indigenous people (Ghebru and Okumo, 2016, Ghebru *et al.,* 2014). However, during the colonial period, a blend of customary and legal laws was utilized to regulate land. While the customary laws were utilized in the communities, the legal laws were passed to permit land exchange between the indigenes and non-indigenes (Maduekwe, 2014, Abugu, 2012).

Between 1960 when Nigeria secured her independence and 1978 when the Land Use Act was enacted, land was governed through three major sources. These were: Customary Law (which varied from one custom to another), English received law (which is made up of common law private ownership in the south, and Crown ownership in the north) and local legislation. The Islamic law and custom (Crown ownership) in the north oversees all interest influencing land and the customary law in the south emphasized collective ownership among family and social groups (Abugu, 2012). Under these land management systems, lands were acquired either by inheritance, first settler, gift, outright purchase or long possession leading to conflicts and violence in terms of ownership (Nwocha, 2016). The systems impeded investment and prevented an equitable allocation of land among citizens which led to the enactment of the Nigerian Land Use Act (LUA) in1978 (Land Use Act, 1978) which is still the principal legislation that regulates contemporary land tenure in Nigeria till date. The Act is a modified version of the Land Tenure Law of 1962 in the southern and the State Law of 1915 in the northern parts of Nigeria. The Land Use Act provides the opportunities to own lands without recourse to families and communal land holdings.

The Act nationalized all land in Nigeria, and attempted to do away with customary land tenure, established a ceiling on individual landholdings, and gave state officials the authority to issue and revoke customary certificates of occupancy (Okonkwo, 2013). 'The Act vested all land in each state (except land vested in the federal government or its agencies) solely in the governor of the state, to hold land in trust for the people and be responsible for allocation of land in all urban areas to individual's resident in the state and to organisations for residential, agriculture, commercial and other purposes (Federal Government of Nigeria' [FGN], 1990). Similar powers with respect to non-urban areas were conferred on local governments.

The Act has several significant outcomes for land market development.

It terminated private ownership of land and established statutory and customary rights of occupancy that may be withdrawn in market only with the official written consent of the state governor or local government (Butler, 2013). Finding has shown that more than 70 percent of land transactions in Nigeria are in the informal market (Butler, 2013). This is in line with the evolutionary theory of property rights summarized by Platteau (1996) and Durand-Lasserve, (2003) who observed that customary or informal land markets account for 30–90 percent of all land transactions in sub-Saharan Africa due to land reforms. The Act has also increased credit opportunities (Myers, 1991). The Act helps to address the problem of inconsistency in the laws administering ownership and land-use; issue of uncontrolled theory in urban land; the subject of admittance to land rights by Nigerians on equivalent legitimate premise; the issue of discontinuity of fragmentation of rural lands emerging from either the utilization of conventional standards of inheritance or population growth and the outcomes of pressure on land (Uchendu 1979, Francis 1978, FAO, 2010, Nwocha, 2016).

The Act delegates authority over land allocation to all the states and their local governments in an effort to ensure that rural and urban populations had access and secure tenure to land. Land-allocation advisory committees under the Act are constituted to assist in the issuance of customary certificates of occupancy to applicants, reduction of speculation and streamlining access to land.

Implications and Associated Challenges of the Nigerian Land Use Act

The Land Use Act in Nigeria was promulgated with the aims of reducing land conflicts among citizens; unifying and simplifying land tenure concepts and land administration procedures throughout the country; achieving a more equitable distribution of and access to land rights for all citizens regardless of wealth or position; and facilitating greater government control over land use and development (Land Use Act, 1978). However, the limitations of the Act have negatively affected agricultural production. For instance, the Act imposed a ceiling on urban and rural landholdings. By the Act, no individual can hold more than 0.5 hectares of undeveloped urban land, 500 hectares of non-urban land, or 5000 hectares of grazing land (USAID, 2014, Afemikhe Consulting, 2016). This has limited the expansion of agricultural land and overuse of land in order to meet the growing population's food need. The Act does not care for small scale peasant farmers who frequently lose their farm lands through acquisition for urban expansion and large-scale acquisition of land for commercial agriculture with no adequate compensation (Atilola, 2010).

The Act changed the existing land laws in both Northern and Southern part of the country by removing corporate groups, families, chiefs and emirs from the trusteeship of land and replaced them with the state governors (Land Use Act, 1978). This may not be unconnected with the frequent land disputes and often violent in many parts of Nigeria. For instance, there have been land dispute in Benue and Taraba States between pastoralists and sedentary farmers, dispute among family members over inheritance and partition of land based on the nature of the Act. Some land tenants have also been reported to default at paying rent to landlords on the theory that the Act had nationalized land (Amnesty International, 2006).

Land acquired without a Certificate of Occupancy by implication in the Act shows that the buyer has no ownership rights as such merely translate to a lease. The Act has indirectly exposed marginal farmers to losing their only means for economic survival and made land to be very expensive. The LUA does not specify if a certificate of occupancy granted can be renewed after the expiration of the 99-year leasehold, leaving the Governor with the option to renew or not (Land Use Act, 1978). Many governors do not give the urgent attention needed to their responsibility of granting consent for land assignments thereby impeding the development of an effective land market (Nzeh *et al.,* 2017). The deferral by certain Governors in allowing assent within a short period of time and the granting of consent by the Governor is not automatic. The delay in the issuance of ownership right under the Land Use Act may not be unconnected to high-level corruption. Some state governors may use the provision in the Act as a way of rewarding their party loyalist and to deal with the opposition. Some may use the process as a device for imposing heavy charges on political enemies before granting such consent to develop acquired land. This is reducing the use of land for agrarian activities and thereby leading to reduction in the agricultural production.

To obtain statutory or customary rights of occupancy of land under the existing Land Use Act in Nigeria requires long procedures starting with the production of a survey plan of the land, payment of different fees ranging from the opening of file, the application fee and the survey fee to various additional charges (World Bank, 2017). The cumulative fees in some cases are closer to the land value. The number of days required to complete land title registration is equally observed to be longer in Nigeria than most countries in the world (Figure 1). While it takes less than 16 days to process registration of land title in some countries, that of Nigeria is an average of 69 days. This illustrates probably the low level of innovation and inefficiency in the land registration process in Nigeria.

Figure 1. Ease of registering land in selected countries
Source: World Bank (2017)

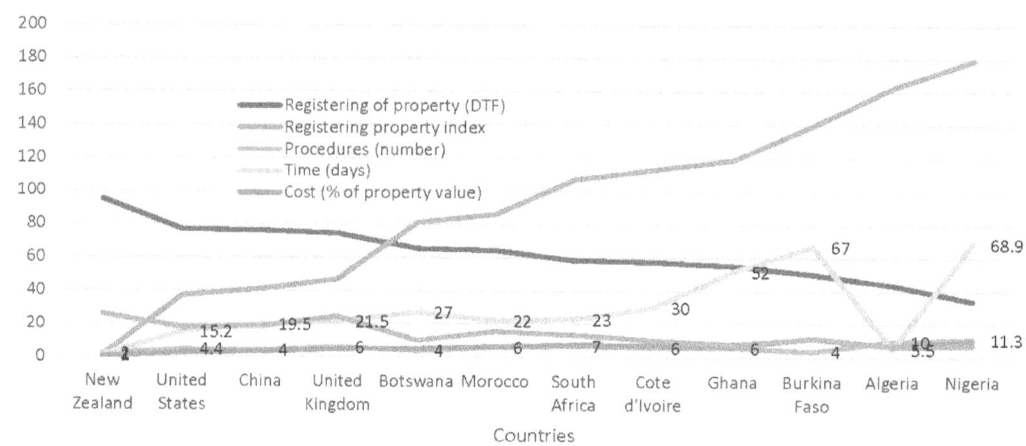

The Act is seen as one of the biggest impediments to converting land resources into individual wealth in the country as it hinders transferability of ownership rights in landed property because of government interference.

Government at all levels embarked on massive acquisition of land for the purpose of development under the Act but most of the acquired land remained undeveloped while original owners look for land for farming, building houses and other businesses (Udo, 1990).

To Oyebola *et al.,* (2019), the disadvantages of the Nigerian Land Use Act to the local community in terms of investment involving large-scale land acquisitions have also been identified to outweigh the few benefits. Adeleye *et al.,* (2020) opined that disputes between the members of the community and the investor often arise where only the governments are involved in Large-scale Land Investments (LLIs) dealings but land contract system is good if there is good collaboration between investors and community members. Under such scenario, the LLI investors stand the chance of making good profits;

enjoy hardworking labor with virtually no labor unrest as community members who are employed tend to see the project as one of their own.

Findings (such as Chikaire *et al.*, 2014, Nzeh *et al.*, 2017) have also shown that the Nigeria Land Use Act does not take the farm structure and landholding patterns and their implications for productivity and economic security into serious consideration. The Act also failed to address the problem of 'fragmented holdings' which is most prevalent in Nigerian farming system (Chikaire *et al.*, 2014).

Politics of Repealing/Amending the Land Use Policy in Nigeria

The Land Tenure Law of 1962 and Land Use Act of 1978 were the two land laws passed after independence in 1960 with the sole aim of making land freely accessible for all Nigerians through redistribution of land. This fundamental objective has however not yet been achieved (Myers, 1991). Nigerian government have made several efforts to remove or amend the contentious areas in the Land Use Act following the challenges created by the Act but with little or no success. The Nigerian Constitution of 1999 which gave the entire citizen the right to acquire and own immovable property is making reform or repeal of Land Use Act very difficult or impossible.

In 2007, the Nigeria government 7-Point Agenda included land reforms that will allow access of land to private sector for commercial farming or any other large-scale but the amendment has not been passed into law by the federal law makers till date (THISDAY Newspaper, 2017).

In response to the challenges posed by the existence of the LUA, a land reform program was also initiated in 2009 with two forms of reform: 1) expunging the LUA from the Constitution and amending all clauses that empower the state Governors to consent to mortgage transactions and assignments of land, and 2) making provision for all Nigerians to continue to enjoy their possessory and use rights to their land (Mabogunje, 2010). Little or no success was also achieved probably due to change in government and politics.

A Presidential Technical Committee on Land Reform in 2010 was constituted to advise the government on registration of landholdings, and the development of mechanisms for land valuation and conflict resolution but the effort was also futile (Ghebru *et al.*, 2014, Atilola, 2010) because of the frustrations to amend the Act which is embedded in the 1999 constitution of the country.

In July, 2013, federal government also gave a directive to the Presidential Committee on Land Reform to work out ways of repealing the Land Use Act of 1978 and explore options to 'create more transparent and systematic land titling and registration, and establish a National Land Depository to record all land in Nigeria' (Ghebru and Akumo, 2016). The effort again failed to produce the desired results due to the politics and procedures in amending the Constitution. All commissions, committees and bodies set up by previous governments in Nigeria have recommended that the Land Use Act should be removed except that of the National Conference in 2014 that suggested some amendments in the Act especially on the issue of compensation. The suggestion was to allow owners of land to determine the price and value of their land and for government to negotiate with land owners on what compensation to pay them.

Recent moved to repeal the Act in 2017 suffered a set-back in the legislative arm of the government due to politics between the law makers who viewed such Act as resource control sneaking through the back door. Some states Governors are also not in support of the amendment or the removal of the bill because they view such as removal of their power to hold the land in their states.

People's Perceptions on the Nigerian Land Policy

The following are some excerpts from interviews conducted and reported in some Nigerian newspapers:

Excerpt 1: "If you delete the Land Use Act and remove the powers of the federal government over land, it would be easy for the South-South states in Nigeria that have been at the forefront for the control of their oil resources to achieve it" (Excerpt from Guardians Newspaper interview report, July 31, 2017).

Excerpt 2: "If you remove the Land Use Act, the state governments will just legislate on the land in their territories and whatever natural resources lie below the ground will be theirs instead of the federal government. Abolishing the Act therefore is a huge issue not just for the northerners, but also to less endowed states". (The Guardians Newspaper interview report, July 31, 2017).

Excerpt 3: "If anybody has paid for a land, such land should automatically belong to him/her. Going back to government again to seek for permission for either re-selling or mortgaging the land is not a good thing as it exists in the Nigeria Land Use Act. This should be removed in any land policy in Nigeria" (Private Property, 2017).

Excerpt 4: "Some of the governors often exploit under the Nigeria Land Use Act for private economic and political reasons to the detriment of other parties. Let the Act be struck out of the constitution to stand as an ordinary legislature which can easily be amended, and let every state be allowed to independently determine its land tenure system" (The Vanguard Newspaper interview report, October 19, 2017).

The overall perception of all the respondents as observed from the above excerpts show people want the revocation of the Nigerian Land Use Act used in the management of land in the country.

Cases of Land Policy in Some Selected African Countries and Lessons for Nigeria

'Land has been an object of policy intervention from colonial times to the present, and every spot of land in Africa has a history of changing land policies and different forms of land politics' (Adams and Palmer, 2007, Lund, 2011). The French adopted 'the policy of assimilation (later changed to association) and declared that all unoccupied land belonged to the state' (AUC-ECA-AfDB Consortium, 2011). This enabled the colonial authority to grant large tracts of land for plantation development in Côte d'Ivoire. According to the same report, in Mauritania, all unoccupied land was nationalized. Togo adopted a policy of "vacant land without owner" to transfer unoccupied customary lands into the state domain. The policy of indirect rule in Gambia, Ghana, Nigeria and Sierra Leone through local customary structures helped to strengthen the customary structures in land administration. The system however created confusion as the colonial authority established local chiefs and ruled through them.

Findings have also shown that in Guinea Bissau, the Portuguese 'dispossessed the natives of their land rights and categorized land in three ways: urban lands, lands delimited for collective allocation according to local customs, and vacant lands' (AUC-ECA-AfDB Consortium, 2011). In this system, colonial authority was solely responsible for land categorization and through the concept of vacant land expanded the colonial settlement. After independence in 1974 the Guinea Bissau Government nationalized all lands just as we have in Benin land.

In Burkina Faso, access to land and use in rural areas were regulated by the principle of legal dualism: the statutory land legislation inherited from the colonial period and maintained after independence; and customary law and practices. In 1984, government issued a decree addressing land tenure. By the decree, although all land is property of the state, government intended to create a system of all land registration and titling to secure individual as well as collective rights to certain land. The law includes the dictates for land occupation; allocate use rights to an individual wishing to engage in cash crop farming. In 1991, another new land tenure law was created to address issue of privatization allowing government to cede national domain lands to individual for private land title.

Chad did not undergo any major land reform after independence but adopted the colonial legislation which upheld state monopoly over land. In Sierra Leone (SL), the state can acquire freehold rights in the western area but in the provinces it can only acquire a leasehold interest in land (The Government of Sierra Leone, 2015). The customary arrangements in SL is influenced to a large extent by statute where all lands are vested in paramount chiefs and chiefdom councils who hold land in trust for the native community concerned. Grants of land discriminate between natives and strangers. The Creoles from the western area cannot buy land in the provinces since they are deemed to be strangers leading to source of potential conflict.

Land under the Togo 1974 law are classified into three categories: 'individual private lands; land owned by the state as part of its public domain; and national domain lands which consist all unused lands meant for agricultural development for the benefit of the Togolese people' (AUC-ECA-AfDB Consortium, 2011).

Under the 1950 law in Liberia, land is found to be predominantly the property of the state except relatively limited areas held in freehold located mostly in urban areas, some plantations and other commercial farms owned by descendants of Africans returning from America who concluded sale contracts with local chiefs (AUC-ECA-AfDB Consortium, 2011). In 1974, government instituted the Registered Land Law in effort to formalized land registration system by requesting landholders to register their parcels. Process of obtaining approval involves lengthy bureaucratic procedures culminating with the signature of the president himself. Liberia's land tenure system continues to provide for freehold tenure which is secured by title deed. Parallel system of traditional law based on verbal agreement is also prevalent, creating widespread confusion over who owns what. Landowners as a result, often sell to multiple buyers, opening up room for conflict. In 2009, a law was enacted in Liberia to acknowledge customary ownership and community rights to rental and other shares of revenue, as well as community rights to manage less expansive and valuable classes of forests (Namubiru-Mwaura *et al.,* 2012).

Mauritanian Government introduced land reforms that established individual private property through registration. All lands that were not in the public domain or private property were declared to be covered by Islamic law. The implication of this law was that many customary authorities, especially Black Africans in the Senegal Valley, lost their rights over land to people that did not traditionally live in the region, resulting to tension between the users and "owners" of the land.

In Rwanda, prior to the National land reforms of 2004, most of the lands in Rwanda were acquired for a limited tenure through different practices such as inheritance, leasing, borrowing, gifting, informal occupation, and government land allocation. Rwanda therefore undertook various land reforms in previous years to address issues connected to land tenure security in a policy setting that neither really decentralized land governance to local communities nor attempted to introduce it in a manner that promises social and gender equity (African Natural Resources Center, 2011) before the enactment of land policy legislation and institutions to guarantee equitable land rights called the "Rwanda Land Tenure

Regularization Program" (RLTRP) reform initiated in 2008. This is observed to increase efficiency, transparency, citizen participation and development of viable land governance institutions. The reform provides full equal rights to both wife and husband and to all children, through the systematic land registration process (LandLink, 2015).

In Namibia, before Independence, land in communal areas was managed through a combination of Traditional Authorities and colonial officials. But land governance in communal areas continues to be conceded by an unresolved contradiction between customary laws and statutory law requirements (Wolfgang, 2018). Traditional leaders exercise their powers over subjects not residing in areas where the traditional authority is located. Seeking to sustainably allocate, develop and manage natural resources in communal areas therefore led the Government of Namibia to pass the Communal Land Reform Act (CLRA) in 2002. The law establishes State ownership of all communal lands, which are administered by Traditional Authorities who can allocate and revoke land rights to individuals or families according to customary laws. The CLRA establishes a procedure for land claimants to appeal against decisions taken by traditional leaders and / or land boards. Once a land plot is granted under the Communal Land Reform Act, certificates to guarantee the use of the land in perpetuity, and the right to inherit land are issued. The holder of a land right certificate can transfer that right to others, or leave it to the surviving spouse or dependents as an inheritance, or relinquish it to the Traditional Authority.

Ethiopian land tenure has gone through several significant changes but owing to a lack of land tenure security in Ethiopia, rural smallholders under-invested in their agricultural land and experienced conflict over land use and ownership (Deininger *et al.,* 2003, 2008, Zevenbergen *et al.,* 2007). To address these issues, in the late 1990s, the government introduced a land certification program that grants land use rights, while the government maintained ownership of all land. The Government of Ethiopia continued to forbid the sale or exchange of land and maintained national ownership of all lands.

Ghana government has been implementing a land administration reform since 1999. The Land Administration Project (LAP) in Ghana is supported by donors with the aim of strengthening land administration institutions and increase land holders' security of tenure on both state and customary land (Spichiger and Stacey, 2014). The 1999 land policy was in 2002 amended due to some problems following the LAP of 1999 such as high tenure insecurity, increasing land dispute. The amended 2002 land policy was adopted to strengthen land administration institutions and to increase the security of land tenure through land registration, on both state and customary land.

The land tenure situation in the Gambia is complex because of changes in land policies and administrative practices occurring at several different levels. The main laws that regulate the management of lands are: The Land (Provinces) Acts of 1945 and State Lands Act of 1991. There are also Land Use Regulations 1995; Lands Commission Act 2007; State Lands Regulations 1995; and the Development Control Regulations, 1995 (The Republic of Gambia, 1995). The Lands (Provinces) Act vested all land with the district authorities to administer land in accordance with customary law for the benefit of the indigenous communities. The Act introduced leasehold which could be granted by district authorities only with the endorsement of the Provincial Commissioner and the approval of the Ministry of Lands (MoL), now known as the Ministry of Lands and Regional Government (MLRG). The State Lands Act 1991 replaced the Lands Acts makes all land in the Gambia public land. Direct ownership of public land by the State as well as its custodianship of customary land (Freudenberger, 2000). This State Lands Act introduced the deemed leasehold as a recognized land title and empowered the MoL to designate any area in the regions as state land. It stipulates that "foreigners can only have access to residential land for up to 21 years, in areas not larger than 2,500 m^2 located more than 1.5 km from the high water mark as designated by the Minister of Land and Regional Government and that in underdeveloped non-residential, lands cannot legally be leased or assigned to foreigners and, if they are leased, the lease can be terminated without compensation. In addition, foreign entities that acquire customary land must obtain approval from the Governor of the region" (The Republic of Gambia, 1995).

South Africa (SA) implemented a land reform program in1994 after apartheid. The land reform according to SA Department of Land Affairs (DLA) consisted of three dimensions: redistribution (transferring white-owned commercial farm land to African users); restitution (settling claims for land lost under apartheid measures by restoration of holdings or compensation); and land tenure reform. Land tenure reform aims to secure rights of those who are already occupying land with insecure occupation rights (DLA, 1997). SA, land redistribution programme is focused on a range of market-based tools, such as land purchases by beneficiaries, endowed with a cash grant by the state; share-equity schemes (company operations in which tradable shares are owned by farm workers, former owners and other investors); and credit facilities to disburse loans for land purchases" (Lyne and Darroch, 2003).The state or reform beneficiaries with financial support from the state purchase land from right holders at a negotiated price ("willing seller, willing buyer"). South Africa's Communal Property Associations Act 1996 also enables the establishment of associations to own land, and many such associations have been set up, especially to acquire lands under the land restitution and land redistribution programmes.

One common lesson from these countries is that both the French and British colonial land policy was made to promote private ownership of land in order to enhance economic development (AUC-ECA-AfDB Consortium, 2011). Private lands in the form of freeholds occur in Mauritania, Togo, Côte d'Ivoire through the process of immatriculation (Afemikhe Consulting, 2016). Although the land systems adopted during the colonial periods were unable to completely changed local tenure systems, recent development in both Francophone Anglophone countries show movement towards a different set of interests (Toulmin *et al.,* 2002). This led to the complexity of land tenure systems and governance in many countries till today. In Ghana and the Gambia according to report by AUC-ECA-AfDB Consortium, (2011), 'change of use of compulsorily acquired lands without due reference to the purpose of the acquisition has led to discontent among land owners'. The bureaucracy associated with state management of land and associated delays have led to questions being raised as to whether the state should hold title to land and directly manage such lands or it should limit itself to land use regulatory powers. While in Nigeria, Certificates of Occupancy must be signed by state governors, in Liberia allocation of land requires the approval of the president (Dickerman *et al.,* 1989, AUC-ECA-AfDB Consortium, 2011).

Some African countries such as Côte d'Ivoire, Benin and Niger have made efforts to recognize and register customary land rights (Wiley, 2011). Findings from other countries land reforms have also shown that there are limits to the existing land policy tools. Report has shown that 'only about 3% of the land in Nigeria is covered by title deeds' (Olayiwola, 2006) which is probably responsible for the slow pace of agricultural development. Rural farmers are finding it very difficult to secure credit to increase their agricultural production.

There were records of many Africa land policies formulated and amended within the first five years of enactment as a results of impracticability of such policy or politics. For instance, Communal Land Reform Act, 2004 of South Africa was struck down as unconstitutional in 2010 (Wiley, 2011). Women's groups initially brought complaints before the courts on grounds that women's interests were insufficiently provided for under the land policy. Other groups were concerned that the law left too much scope for chiefs to proclaim themselves as owners rather than trustees of land (Thiyane, 2017).

Experiences from most other African countries have shown that land reforms are done to protect governments interest in land, and for effective land governance and management. Most of these reforms have also taken ownership of land from the private to government without protecting their rights with strong resistance from people and members of the communities. The redesigning of this land management system however has changed in most countries such as: Namibian Communal Land Administration System (NCLAS) (Kapitango and Meijs, 2010), the Land Administration Reform in Ghana (Independent Evaluation Group, 2013), Rwanda's Land Tenure Regularization (LTR) (Sagashya and English, 2010), the Rural Land Certification in Ethiopia (Deininger *et al.,* 2008), the Land Tenure Reform in Mozambique (Norfolk and Tanner, 2007), and land reform in South Africa (Benjaminsen *et al.,* 2009) with the recognition of customary land rights and authorities and emphasis on titling.

It is very important that policy on land should be regulated with the involvement of customary, statutory and religious frameworks. Attempt by any government to subvert and interfere on land without full involvement of these stakeholders may always lead to fierce resistance by the customary authorities (Aryeetey *et al.,* 2007).

CONCLUSION AND RECOMMENDATIONS

Land is a primary means of subsistence, investment, accumulation of wealth, transfer of wealth between generations and a major cause of many disputes in Nigeria. It plays a prominent role in the economic development of agricultural production. Evidences from this study revealed that different countries have their own history of land reforms and governance but all are significantly influenced by political factor, and land-related issues usually generate intense emotional reactions. The Land Use Act in Nigeria has restricted the privileges of possession and use of land. Most public lands are acquired by the governments and their agencies not for immediate use but for future thereby preventing these lands for agricultural usage and probably responsible for low agricultural production and encroachment. It is dangerous to deny the people access to land at present only for the purpose of reserving it for future usage. Governors of states have used the Land Use Act to acquire land for selfish interest. In this sense the acquisition of land for public interest is a device to acquire land cheaply in order to reward party loyalist. Thus, there is politics in government land acquisition policy.

Good land policy and governance exist in both theory and practice, if the people are able to participate in meaningful ways in decision making processes about their rights to their land holdings. The process of reviewing and formulating land policies in Nigeria should be inclusive (participatory) and iterative with the participation of all the stakeholders including the civil society groups and alliances in order to match land rights-holders' sense of belonging to the land reform goals. There is a need to amend the Nigeria Land Use Act that will make land easily accessible to individuals. A new system of regulating land markets is needed that harnesses the strengths of capitalism in putting resources to efficient use in generating growth with the regulatory responsibilities of the state to protect the public interest. The ceiling placed on the size of land to be acquired by individuals should be based on the population of the country and the size or extent of land space.

REFERENCES

Abugu, U. (2012). *Land Use and Reform in Nigeria: Law and Practice* (1st ed.). Immaculate Prints.

Act, L. U. (1978). Federal Republic of Nigeria Official Gazette. No.14. *Federal Ministry of Information, Printing Division, Lagos, Nigeria*, *65*, 2–6.

Adams, M., & Palmer, R. (2007). *Independent Review of Land Issues: Eastern and Southern Africa* (vol. 3). Available online at online at https://www.oxfam.org.uk/resources/learning/landrights/downloads/independent_review_land_issues_eastern_and_southern_africa_2006_07.pdf

Adeleye, N., Osabuohien, E. S., Adeogun, S., Fashola, S., Tasie, O., & Adeyemi, G. (2020). Access to Land and Food Security: Analysis of 'Priority Crops' Production in Ogun State, Nigeria. In E. Osabuohien (Ed.), *The Palgrave Handbook of Agricultural and Rural Development in Africa*. Palgrave Macmillan. doi:10.1007/978-3-030-41513-6_14

Amnesty International. (2006). *Nigeria: Making the Destitute Homeless – Forced Evictions in Makoko, Lagos State*. AI Index: AFR 44/001/2006. Available online at http://fra.controlarms.org/library/Index/ENGAFR440012006?open&of=ENG-NGA

ANRC. (2011). *Land tenure regularization in Rwanda: good practices in land reform*. Available online at https://www.afdb.org/fileadmin/uploads/afdb/Documents/Publications/anrc/AfDB_RwandaLandReform_FA.pdf

Aryeetey, E., Ayee, J. R. A., Ninsin, K. A., & Tsikata, D. (2007). *The Politics of Land Tenure Reform in Ghana: From the Crown Land Bills to the Land Administration Project (Technical Report); Institute of Statistical Social & Economic Research (ISSER)*. University of Ghana.

Atilola, O. (2010). *Land Administration Reform in Nigeria*. Paper presented at FIG congress, Sydney, Australia.

AUC-ECA-AfDB Consortium. (2011). *Land Policy in Africa: West Africa Regional Assessment. Published by Economic Commission for Africa (ECA) Publications and Conference Management Section*. PCMS.

Benjaminsen, T. A., Holden, S., Lund, C., & Sjaastad, E. (2009). Formalisation of land rights: Some empirical evidence from Mali, Niger and South Africa. *Land Use Policy*, *26*(1), 28–35. doi:10.1016/j.landusepol.2008.07.003

Butler, S. (2013). Directions in development: Nigerian land markets and the land use law of 1978. International Bank for Reconstruction and Development/the World Bank.

Chikaire, J. U., Anyoha, N. O., Ani, A. O., & Atoma, C. N. (2014). Land tenure reform: A vehicle for achieving agricultural transformation agenda in Nigeria. *Merit Research Journal of Agricultural Science and Soil Sciences*, *2*(9), 114–122.

CIA. (2018). *Nigeria Area. CIA World Fact book*. Available at https://www.cia.gov/library/publications/the-world-factbook/geos/ni.html

Consulting, A. (2016). *The Impact of the Land Use Act on the development of Agriculture in Nigeria*. Available online at http://ssacltd.com/blog/311-2/

Cotula, L., Toulmin, C., & Hesse, C. (2004). *Land tenure and administration in Africa: Lessons of experience and emerging issues.* International Institute for Environment and Development, London. Available online at http://www.hubrural.org/IMG/pdf/iied_lt_cotula.pdf

de Janvry, A., Gordillo, G., Platteau, J. P., & Sadoulet, E. (2001). *Access to Land, Rural Poverty and Public Action.* Oxford University Press. doi:10.1093/acprof:oso/9780199242177.001.0001

Deininger, K., Ali, D. A., Holden, S., & Zevenbergen, J. (2008). Rural land certification in Ethiopia: Process, initial impact, and implications for other African countries. *World Development*, *36*(10), 1786–1812. doi:10.1016/j.worlddev.2007.09.012

Deininger, K., Jin, S., Anenew, B., Gebre-Selassie, S., & Nega, B. (2003). *Tenure security and land-related investment- evidence from Ethiopia.* Policy Research Working Paper, series 2991. World Bank.

Dickerman, C. W., Barnes, G., Bruce, J. W., Green, J. K., Myers, G., Polishuk, R., Stienbarger, D., & Sund, A. (1989). *Security of tenure and land registration in Africa: literature review and synthesis. Land tenure center paper 137.* University of Wisconsin-Madison.

DLA. (1997). *DLA (Department of Land Affairs). White Paper on South African Land Policy DLA, Pretoria.* Available online at http://ww2.ruraldevelopment.gov.za/DLA-Internet//content/document_library/documents/White_paper/WhitePaperLandReform.pdf (accessed 08.20.2010).

Durand-Lasserve, A. (2003). *Land Tenure, Property System Reforms, and Emerging Urban Land Markets in Sub-Saharan Africa.* Lincoln Institute of Land Policy.

EU Task Force. (2004). EU Land Policy Guidelines. EU Task Force on Land Tenure. Brussels: Author.

FAO. (2010). *FAO Gender and Land Rights Database.* Available online at http://www.fao.org/gender-landrights-database/country-profiles/countries-list/national-legal-framework/land-legislation/en/?country_iso3=NGA

FGN. (1990). *Laws of the Federation of Nigeria 1990. Land Use Act. Chapter 202.* Available online at http://www.nigeria-law.org/Land%20Use%20Act.htm

Francis, P. (1987). Land tenure systems and agricultural innovation: The case of alley farming in Nigeria. *Land Use Policy*, *4*(3), 305–319. doi:10.1016/0264-8377(87)90030-5

French Development Corporation. (2009). *Land Governance and Security of Tenure in Developing Countries. White paper report on "Land Tenure and Development" by French Development Cooperation, June 2009.* Available at http://www.foncier-developpement.fr/wp-content/uploads/land-governance-and-security-of-tenure-in-developing-countries.pdf

Freudenberger, M. S. (2000). *Tenure and natural resources in the Gambia: summary of research findings and policy options. working group on resource tenure and land use planning.* Law Reform Commission of the Gambia, and Nancy Ann Sheehan. Working paper, No. 40, Land Tenure Center, University of Wisconsin–Madison.

Ghebru, H., & Akumo, A. (2016). *Land Administration Service Delivery and Its Challenges in Nigeria. A case study of eight states.* Nigeria Strategy Support Program, IFPRI Working Paper 39.

Ghebru, H., Edeh, H., Ali, D., Deininger, K., Okumo, A., & Woldeyohannes, S. (2014). *Tenure Security and Demand for Land Tenure Regularization in Nigeria Empirical Evidence from Ondo and Kano States*. International Food Policy Research Institute.

Guardians Newspaper interview report. (2017). *Land Use Act: Built environment professionals condemn senate's rejection of bill*. Available online at https://www.vanguardngr.com/2017/07/land-use-act-built-environment-professionals-condemn-senates-rejection-bill/

Independent Evaluation Group. (2013). Project Performance Assessment Report: Ghana Land Administration Project. Washington, DC: Author.

Kapitango, D., & Meijs, M. (2010). Land registration using aerial photography in Namibia: cost and lessons. *Innovations in Land Rights Recognition, Administration, and Governance*. Available online at www.worldbank.org/rural

Kironde, J. M. L. (2009). *Improving land Sector Governance in Africa: The Case of Tanzania*. Paper prepared for the "Workshop on "Land Governance in support of the MDGs: Responding to New Challenges," Washington, DC.

LandLinks. (2015). *Rwanda LAND Report: Access to the Land Tenure Administration Systems and Outcomes*. Available online at https://www.land-links.org/document/rwanda-land-report-access-to-the-land-tenure-administration-systems-and-outcomes/

Lund, C. (2011a). *Land Rights and Citizenship in Africa*. Discussion paper 65, Nordiska Afrikainstitutet, Uppsala printed by on demand, Lightning Source UK.

Lund, C. (2011b). Fragmented sovereignty: Land reform and dispossession in Laos. *The Journal of Peasant Studies*, *38*(4), 885–905. doi:10.1080/03066150.2011.607709

Lyne, M. C., & Darroch, M. A. G. (2003). *Land Redistribution in South Africa: Past Performance and Future Policy. In BASIS (Broadening Access and Strengthening Input Market Systems) Collaborative Research Support Program*. University of Wisconsin Madison.

Mabogunje, A. L. (2010). Land reform in Nigeria: progress, problems & prospects. *Proceedings of the annual conference on land policy and administration*, 25.

Maduekwe, N. C. (2014). The land tenure system under the customary law. Proceedings of the Nigerian Institute of Advanced Legal Studies training programme for Judges of the customary courts and area courts, 19. doi:10.2139srn.2813056

Massay, G. E. (2020). Local Politics of Land Acquisitions for Foreign and Domestic Investments in Tanzania. In E. Osabuohien (Ed.), *The Palgrave Handbook of Agricultural and Rural Development in Africa*. Palgrave Macmillan. doi:10.1007/978-3-030-41513-6_20

Michie, J., & Lobao, L. (2012). Ownership, control and economic outcomes. *Cambridge Journal of Regions, Economy and Society*, *5*(3), 307–324. doi:10.1093/cjres/rss015

Moyo, S., & Yeros, P. (2005). Reclaiming the Land. The Resurgence of Rural Movements in Africa. Zed Books.

Myers, G. W. (1991). *Land and power: the impact of the Land Use Act in Southwest Nigeria*. Land Tenure Center (LTC) Research Working Paper 108, University of Wisconsin-Madison.

Namubiru-Mwaura, E. L., Knox, A., & Hughes, A. K. (2012). *Liberia Land Policy & Institutional Support (LPIS) Project Customary Land Tenure in Liberia: Findings and Implications Drawn from 11 Case Studies*. United States Agency for International Development.

Narh, P., Lambini, C. K., Sabbi, M., Pham, V. D., & Nguyen, T. T. (2016). Land Sector Reforms in Ghana, Kenya and Vietnam: A Comparative Analysis of Their Effectiveness. *Land (Basel)*, *5*(2), 8. doi:10.3390/land5020008

Norfolk, S., & Tanner, C. (2007). *Improving tenure security for the rural poor. Mozambique Country case study.* FAO legal empowerment of the poor working paper. Available: http://www.fao.org/3/ak0786e.pdf

Norton, R. D. (2014). Policy Frameworks for International Agricultural and Rural Development. Encyclopedia of Agriculture and Food Systems, 489-503. doi:10.1016/B978-0-444-52512-3.00123-6

Nwocha, M. E. (2016). Impact of the Nigerian Land Use Act on Economic Development in the Country. *Acta Universitatis Danubius. Administratio*, *8*(2), 117–128.

Nzeh, E., Famobuwa, O. S., & Iroechenwu, C. (2017). Land Reform System and Its Implications on Agricultural Production in Nigeria. *Universal Journal of Agricultural Research*, *5*(6), 338–343. doi:10.13189/ujar.2017.050604

Obayelu, A. E., Arowolo, A. O., & Osinowo, O. H. (2017). Land Tenure, Governance and Accountability in Nigeria: The Implications on Food Production to Feed the Present and the Future. [JADE]. *Journal for the Advancement of Developing Economies*, *6*(1), 1–17.

Okonkwo, E. C. (2013). A Closer Look at The Management, Revocation and Compensation Principles Under the Nigerian Land Use Act. Afe Babalola University. *Journal of Sustainable Development Law and Policy*, *1*(1), 21–36.

Olayiwola, L., & Adeleye, O. (2006). *Land Reform Experience form Nigeria*. Paper presented at the FIG Regional Conference Promoting Land Administration and Good Governance, Accra, Ghana.

Oyebola, F., Osabuohien, E. S., & Obasaju, B. O. (2019). Employment and income effects of Nigeria's Agricultural Transformation Agenda: Evidence from cattle value chain. *African Journal of Economic and Management Studies*, *11*(2), 317–329. doi:10.1108/AJEMS-12-2018-0402

Palmer, D., Fricska, S., & Wehrmann, B. (2009). *Towards improved land governance*. Land Tenure Working Paper 11. Rome, Italy: Food and Agriculture Organization of the United Nations (FAO) and UN-Habitat. Retrieved online from https://unhabitat.org/books/towards-improved-landgovernance-land-and-tenure-working/

Platteau, J. (1996). The evolutionary theory of land rights as applied to sub-Saharan Africa: A critical assessment. *Development and Change*, *1996*(27), 29–86. doi:10.1111/j.1467-7660.1996.tb00578.x

Property, P. (2017). *What is Land Use Act: 12 Things Nigerians Should Know*. Available online at https://www.privateproperty.com.ng/news/what-is-land-use-act-12-things-nigerians-should-know/

Republic of Nigeria. (1978). *Land Use Act.* http://www.nigeria-law.org/Land%20Use%20Act.htm

Republic of Nigeria. (1999). *Constitution of the Federal Republic of Nigeria.* Available online at http://www.nigeria-law.org/ConstitutionOfTheFederalRepublicOfNigeria.htm

Sagashya, D., & English, C. (2010). Designing and establishing a land administration system for Rwanda: a technical and economic analysis. In *Innovations in Land Rights Recognition, Administration, and Governance.* Washington, DC: World Bank. Available: https://www.fig.net/resources/proceedings/2009/fig_wb_2009/papers/sys/sys_2_english_sagashya.pdf

Spichiger, R., & Stacey, P. (2014). *Ghana's Land Reform and Gender Equality.* Danish Institute for International Studies (DIIS) Working Paper 2014:01. Available online at https://www.econstor.eu/bitstream/10419/122291/1/782856365.pdf

Subedi, G. P. (2016). *Land administration and its impact on economic development* (Unpublished Ph.D. thesis). University of Reading.

The Government of Sierra Leone. (2015). *Draft National Land Policy of Sierra Leone.* Ministry of Lands, Planning and the Environment, Version 6.

The Republic of Gambia. (1995). State Lands Regulations, 1995. Supplement "A" to 7lze Gambia, Gazette No 1.5 of 3rd May, 995. Available online at http://extwprlegs1.fao.org/docs/pdf/gam5421.pdf

THISDAY. (2017). Politics of Amending the Land Use Act. *THISDAY Newspaper.* Available online at https://www.thisdaylive.com/index.php/2017/08/01/politics-of-amending-the-land-use-act/

Thiyane, D. (2017). *Communal land belongs to the people, not to the chiefs.* Land and Accountability Research Centre. Available online at https://www.customcontested.co.za/communal-land-belongs-people-not-chiefs/

Toulmin, C., Delville, P. L., & Traoré, S. (2002). The dynamics of resource tenure in West Africa. London: International Institute for Environment and Development, GRET, Currey and Heinemann.

Uchendu, V. C. (1979). State, Land and Society in Nigeria: A Critical Assessment of the Land Use Decree, 1978. *Journal of African Studies, 6*(1), 62–74.

Udo, R. K. (1990). *Land Use Policy and Land Ownership in Nigeria.* Ebie Akwa Ventures.

Ukaejiofo, A. N. (2010). *Identifying Appropriate Tools for Effective Land Governance in Nigeria.* FIG Congress 2010 Facing the Challenges – Building the Capacity, Sydney, Australia.

United States Agency for International Development (USAID). (2010). *Nigeria - Property Rights and Resource Governance. USAID Country Profile.* USAID.

USAID. (2010). *USAID country profile property rights and resource governance: Nigeria.* Washington, DC: US Agency for Development Agency. Available online at https://usaidlandtenure.net/wp-content/.../USAID_Land_Tenure_Nigeria_Profile.pdf

USAID. (2014). *Country profile/LandLinks.* Available online at https://www.land-links.org/country-profiles/

Vanguard Newspaper Interview Report. (2017). *Expunge Land Use Act from constitution – town planners*. Available online at https://www.vanguardngr.com/2017/10/expunge-land-use-act-constitution-

Wells-Dang, A., Tu, P. Q., & Burke, A. (2016). Conversion of Land Use in Vietnam through a Political Economy Lens. *Journal of Social Sciences and Humanities*, *2*(2), 131–146.

Wily, L. A. (2011). *Customary Land Tenure in the Modern World Rights to Resources in Crisis: Reviewing the Fate of Customary Tenure in Africa. Brief No 1 of 5. Rights and Resources Initiative*. RRI.

Wolfgang, W. (2018). *Land tenure and governance on communal land in Namibia*. Paper presented at for the Second National Land Conference, Windhoek. Available online at http://dna.nust.na/landconference/submissions_2018/Land_tenure_and_governance.pdf

World Bank. (1996). *Land Reform*. World Band Paper - Rural Development Series.

World Bank. (2003). *Land Policies for Growth and Poverty Reduction*. World Bank.

World Bank. (2016). *Agricultural Land in Nigeria in the Last Decade*. The World Bank.

World Bank. (2017). *Registering Property*. Retrieved May 26, 2020, from World Bank website: https://www.doingbusiness.org/data/exploretopics/registering-property

Wren-Lewis, L. (2013). *Corruption in Land Administration: Roles for Donors to Minimise the Problem*. U4 Brief March 2013:1.

Zevenbergen, J., Holden, S., Ali, D. A., & Deininger, K. (2007). *Rural land certification in Ethiopia: process, initial impact, and implications for other African Countries, Policy*. Research Working Paper, No. WPS 4218. World Bank.

Chapter 15
Business Plan and Industrial Development:
The Case of Family-Owned Food Processing SMEs in Tanzania

Galinoma Gahele Lubawa
https://orcid.org/0000-0001-9198-4495
Institute of Rural Development Planning (IRDP), Tanzania

ABSTRACT

Writing of business plans ensures performance of a business and contributes to enabling countries to achieve sustainable development goals (SDGs). The latter are intended, in part, to promote industrialization, and improved human living and working standards. This chapter identifies and analyses the importance of business plan for family-owned food processing small and medium enterprises (Fo-SMEs). It advocates for the establishment of an "integrated planning" strategy to link Fo-SMEs and government support system for business development. Business-planning forecasts industrial production based on consumers' demands. Integrated planning ensures sustainability of Fo-SMEs, farmers' economic growth, and consequent achievement of SDGs. Tanzania Fo-SMEs serve as a useful lesson for developing economies. Future studies should consider Fo-SMEs' succession planning framework.

INTRODUCTION

To achieve sustainable economic growth and eradicate poverty, the Governments of Tanzania broaden the economic growth base through improved manufacturing and crop processing. Food processing is one of the fast-growing manufacturing sub-sectors in Tanzania and is important in boosting farmers' incomes. Currently, the sector contributes 38.9 per cent of the value-added production and 36.9 per cent of total employment (URT, Economic Survey, 2018) (See Table 1).

DOI: 10.4018/978-1-7998-4817-2.ch015

Table 1. Structure of Tanzania's manufacturing sector, 2018

ISIC (Rev 3)	Description	Value added		Employment	
		Tanzania shillings (million)	% of total	Number	% of total
151–4	Food processing	3,574,901	38.9%	113,052	36.9%
155	Beverages	1,911,174	20.8%	9,279	3.0%
160	Tobacco and cigarettes	767,867	8.4%	6,769	2.2%
171–2, 181	Textile weaving/tailoring apparel	434,041	4.7%	63,930	20.9%
191	Skins and skin products	28,855	0.3%	2,286	0.7%
201–202	Timber and timber products	162,536	1.8%	12,478	4.1%
210-221–222	Paper products, printing	167,430	1.8%	7,409	2.4%
241–2	Chemicals and pharmaceuticals	360,411	3.9	9,852	3.2%
251, 252	Rubber and plastic products	349,590	3.8	5,753	1.9%
261–9	Non-metallic products	622,101	6.7	12,434	4.1%
271–369	Others	814,399	8.8	62,938	20.6%
	Total manufacturing	**9,193,305**		**306,180**	

Source: URT, Economic Survey, 2018 (Percentages computed).

The manufacturing sector focuses on the processing of agricultural goods as determined by the volume of agricultural production (URT, 2010, 2008). Food-processing has a multiplier effect on the country's economy, particularly for rural farmers. The majority of Tanzanians, especially women, are rural smallholder farmers and are dependent on food industries as outlets for their crops (Osabuohien *et al.*, 2019). Among the efforts which continue to be made is the introduction of the Sustainable Industrial Development Policy (SIDP,1996) which empowers the private sector to play its effective role. The role of SIDP is to design and make available a plan for industrializing Tanzania to become semi-industrialized by 2025, expecting that national economy would reach a 40% mark of the Gross Domestic Product (GDP). Globally, most SMEs are family businesses (Daspit *et al.*, 2015) and contribute about 70–90 per cent of the annual GDP of individual countries (Family Firm Institute, 2017).

On this perspective, the author asserts that the business plan's values cannot be underestimated by firms in developing countries that aim to transform their economies to middle-income economy from low-economy through industrialization consistent with SDG's-9. In developing countries, most manufacturing firms (including food processing firms) are privately-owned family (Beecroft *et al.* 2020; URT, 2016). Although research recognizes that business planning is important for the survival of these private firms, however, there is limited literature on the values of the business plan for the current generation of Family-owned food processing SMEs in developing economies. The variation in family firms across generations may have different effects on activity planning. Sonfield and Lussier (2004) observed that there is resistance to succession planning in the first generation family firms. A study by Cater &Schwab (2008) indicates a negative impact of strategic planning across generations. The issue of planning is, therefore, dynamic and requires the support of empirical literature. In essence, this informs the main point of enquiry in this publication, namely – "*what are the values of a business plan in Fo-SMEs?*

The above research question is of relevance for Tanzania since the East African Community (EAC) has already initiated a regional industrialization strategy which aims to leverage industries for its members. Agro-processing firms account for more than 80% of all manufacturing firms in East Africa (The East African Countries region [EAC], United Nation Industries Development Organization [UNIDO] & FAO, 2011). In resonance with such developments, Tanzania needs to modernize its manufacturing sector which is characterized by simple creation of consumer products, low productivity, and low innovation, and creativity (Msami and Wangwe,2016; Nandonde *et al.*, 2015) for effective competition in the regional markets. The country should act before the regional framework is in place by modernizing the Fo-SMEs to make firms more profitable and competitive by improving total productivity, raising quality, upgrading marketing strategy and encouraging new forms of manufacturing systems. These could be achieved through business planning.

This writing provides background information on the food processing sector, the role of planning at the level of the family. It focuses on the theory of planning behaviour and relevant research methodologies. The findings and discussion of the results of the study, and the conclusion and recommendation altogether contribute not only to the relevant body of knowledge but also leverage the growth of Fo-SMEs into sizable industries for the improved industrial development of Tanzania and the country's competitiveness in the East African markets.

SOME BACKGROUND ISSUES

Family firms often engage in some kind of planning activities to achieve intended goals. This planning can either be formally documented or informally to guide business daily. Family business planning practices have been associated with performance, survival, and financing seeking ability from commercial banks and often influence business expansion (Liao & Garter, 2008; Fraser, 2005). Becherer and Helms (2009) and Struebing (1997) link business planning to pertinent business success and the overall performance of a firm. Empirical evidence reveals the importance of planning to the survival, development, and growth of a business. Through regular monitoring and evaluation, a firm's management can easily re-engineer business for effective market response and competitiveness.

The author argues that business planning determines how Family-owned Food Processing SMEs operate in the market economy. Business planning seeks to use relevant information from government policies and elsewhere in the hope to promote industries and regulate prices of products. Achievement of the goals of Fo-SMEs enables a country to realize her economic growth goals. It is estimated that Tanzania's SME accounts for 97 per cent of all accruals from industrial establishments and contribute 27 per cent of the overall GDP (URT, 2016). Fo-SMEs contribute to the country's economy through enhanced employment and payment of due taxes all of which generate multiple effects on economic growth and GDP growth. Food processing and beverage production account for more than half of the country's manufacturing outputs (URT, 2016). Business planning, therefore, relates to establishments that eventually have a growing impact on the country's economic development. A family firm usually operates under two separate but related systems: the family system (driven by emotions) and the business system (driven by economics). To integrate the two systems for the smooth running of a family firm, the author considers business planning as a critical and inevitable requirement.

A business plan may support improvisation, creativity and innovation through enhanced entrepreneurial decision-making. Burke *et al.,* (2010) evidenced that firms with written business plans and which use external support grow faster than those without such plans. While Delmar and Shane (2003) established that business plans benefit firms by providing for improved management, enhanced by staff training and introduction of new routines, Becherer and Helms (2009) found a relationship between the use of a business plan and financial achievement.

Implementation of a business project is not always a smooth path, as in many cases adjustments are needed in iterative planning without affecting the vision and defined goals. The use of a business plan minimizes trial and error in goal setting, management of resources and response to demands from stakeholders. The business planning helps business initiators to undertake development activities in response to defined goals and promote the firm's sales growth, profitability and risks reduction (Masurel & Smit, 2000; Rue & Ibrahim,1998). However, some scholars hold contrasting views that, due to limited scope and activities, SMEs tend to focus more on informal operational planning while leaving formal systems for large companies (Carson and Cromie,1990).

Business planning involves costs. For instance, the time spent to prepare a plan could be used for other activities that have a direct impact on business. If a consultant is engaged to prepare the plan charges involved could be used to run other activities with more immediate impact on the business. According to the author, the cost of business planning is "*opportunity costs.*" The costs are based on the time spent to prepare or review the existing plan. Chwolka and Raith (2012) assert that the time spent on preparing a business plan is in part loss to the business.

Different initiatives have been taken by the government in Tanzania to support SMEs including designing a special banking system for SMEs and loans schemes. Accordingly, financial policies now accommodate the financial requirements of SMEs. Commercial banks in the country now have SMEs' financing packages and facilitate access to needed loans. Such banks include the National Microfinance Bank (NMB Plc), and the CRDB Bank Plc. All these initiatives are the result of Government enactment of the SMEs development policy (2003) which aims to support improvement, and competitiveness of SMEs in the country.

Despite these efforts, the life-span of an SME in Tanzania is still short and characterized by minimal growth due to such challenges as operating without a business plan. According to the National Baseline survey report for Micro, Small and Medium Enterprises (Finscope Survey, 2012), nine out of ten small businesses did not have basic planning documents, which are typical for business management. Establishing a business without a comprehensive business plan limits SME from accessing financial support and this limits the growth and sustainability of business (Kesale, 2017). Financial capacity is one of the key foundations of an SME. It is not surprising, therefore, to see an SME failing partly due to the lack of financial support.

SMEs are challenged by the lack of essential resources including the lack of business plans needed to support financial injection and where the plans exist they are prepared by hired experts. The use of a hired expert provides practical experience (*through learning by doing*) to business owners and employees, though it poses the challenge of high costs involved (Kesale, 2017). The author argues that a comprehensive business plan enables firms to strategically approach emerging opportunities, including searching for financial resources, investment opportunities, and benefits from profits realized. A Fo-SME can achieve its objectives by exploiting identified opportunities and strategies by developing a business plan, which Hormozi *et al.*, (2002) describe as a company operating the machine on paper.

The SMEs sector in Tanzania does not commonly use business plans and this is one among the reasons why the businesses do not qualify for bank loans (Kesale, 2017). There is also a lack of literature on how SMEs should prepare and operate according to business plans. The author thought it prudent to conduct a study focusing on the values of a business plan in the effort to provide the public with the needed knowledge for emerging entrepreneurs to add value to their businesses through changed mindsets in operating according to business plans. Despite such a considered position the saying still stands that "*If you don't know where you are going, any path will get you there*". This illustrates the importance of planning before embarking on any journey. Literature shows that business planning is critical for the survival and growth of any business including SMEs.

Business planning provides the direction with the firm wishes to go, the strategy it will use to achieve the defined goals and focuses on performance targets (Merchant & Van Der Stede, 2007) and forces management to think about and consider the future business projects. SMEs are here to stay as they play a critical role in promoting national economic development and transformation. The author, therefore, agrees that good planning is key to any firm's success (Barton and Hounsell, 1994). The business plan benefits a family by engaging family members to resolve minor family conflicts (Goodluck, 2015), and qualify for funding from financers and possibly attract foreign business partners for joint venture arrangements.

This publication aims to fill the knowledge gap by sharing discerned values relating to business planning for food processing Fo-SMEs. Such SMEs use agricultural products, namely, cereals, fruits, vegetables, oilseeds in processing value-added foods soya-based products and other consumer inviting products such as confectionery. Some of the agricultural products are fermented or mixed with ingredients to improve their palatability or changing them into customer inviting snacks. Since SMEs are increasingly being regarded as important contributors to community or national economic growth, product innovation, employment promotion, and competition in the industrial sector, added literature can facilitate the sustainability and growth of SMEs as part of the overall national economic growth endeavour.

This paper builds on the Theory of Planned Behaviour (TPB), which addresses Fo-SMEs in food processing. This is possible on the rationale that business planning behaviour can promote food processing by focusing on decision making and supporting the need to diversify and foster industrialization for social and economic development with a focus on employment promotion (*Mass employment-creating industries*), forex generation, (*Industries for export goods)* and government revenue collection (*Industries for domestic mass consumption goods*). With a befitting business plan, Tanzania's food processing sub-sector can provide useful lessons for other developing economies. The author focuses on market-orientation where the supply and demand mindsets often lead to the market, where government role remains to be to provide suitable coordination on what the country should produce and where, while concurrently promoting private sector investments, fair trade practices, and improved role of the private sector in promoting direct investments.

Family and Business Planning

Since a business plan is essential for the survival of a firm and supports entrepreneurship, it would be important to consider how a business planning document works in a family setting where two systems overlap: the *family system* (driven by emotions) and the *business system* (driven by principles of economics*)*. This overlap can force a family firm into complexities that require better planning and effective governance compared to non-family firms. Such an arrangement helps to balance both family expectations and formal business demands (see Figure 1).

To ensure the sustainability of an SME, it is inevitable to have and operate under a clear business plan. Figure 1 demonstrates that the befitting plan enables the accommodation of the views of all the family members as well as environmental economic demands and suggests a better direction for the company even at a cost. The concerned family will understand the requirements of the business including what it

Figure 1. Family business plan model
Source: Author, 2020

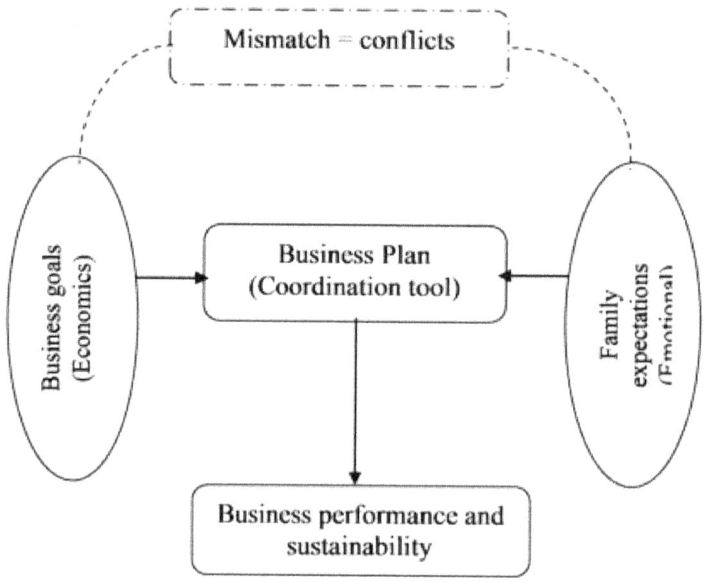

takes for a business to grow, perform, and survive. In the absence of an operational plan, conflicts are likely to arise that might hinder the realization of the business mission and vision. Conflicts are normally caused by a mismatch between the expectations of family members (*family equity*) and business goals (*company equity*). These disputes can lead to the family members' mind-set of … *"Is it either business first or family first?* The author is of the position that the family should consider both perspectives.

A business plan plays the coordinating role of facilitating communication between the two systems, business and family. Practically, the starting point should be the family side where the business partners should meet to determine their values and future vision and involvement in the business. The family values and vision statements should serve as the determinants of what business the family should engage in. The majority of people in developing countries have the fear to invest in the industry simply because they perceive the investment requires a combination of risks. (Mufuruki *et al*, 2017). A business plan provides due guidance of business analysis, identification of risks, suggests mitigation measures and consequent assurance that all fears are eliminated. The most important aspect of business planning is for the concerned family agreeing about what they want to do and the modalities of doing so.

Theory of Planned Behaviour and Family Firm

This theory is based on reasoned action (Fischbein & Ajzen, 1975), and was first used to predict the behaviour of individuals' attitudes, subjective norms, and intentions. Generally, people with intentions can transform their aspirations into actions leading to significant performance and behaviour. (Ajzen & Fishbein, 1977). According to this theory, attitudes refer to a person's individual feelings. Subjective norms refer to how other members in society view a particular behaviour. Behavioural intentions are motivational factors influencing a given mode of conduct where the stronger the behaviour and intention, the more likely the behaviour will be demonstrated. Behavioural control involves a specific mode of conduct. Thus, the combination of the above variables helps in promoting an understanding that human behaviour cannot be explained by using a single factor.

The theory can explain how a family runs a business with or without a business plan. The actions of family members are reflected as they run the business. Family business owners' attitudes and norms serve as the determinants of how a business operates with a business plan. This theory guides family members' decision on whether to follow a business plan or to do things by random decisions and actions. Since the SMEs involved in food processing can implement business plans by hiring a consultant, it is obvious the businesses operate by planning behaviour. Ajzen (1991) argues that individual ability to implement tasks tends to increase the likelihood of attitude change into fruitful behaviours and intentions. If guidelines were to be provided to direct where and when to perform an intended task, the likelihood of successful performance becomes obvious (Orbell *et al.*,1997). The TPB summarized the model formulated by (Ajzen, 1991) and presented in Figure 2.

Figure 2. Source: Ajzen (1991): Theory of planned behaviour

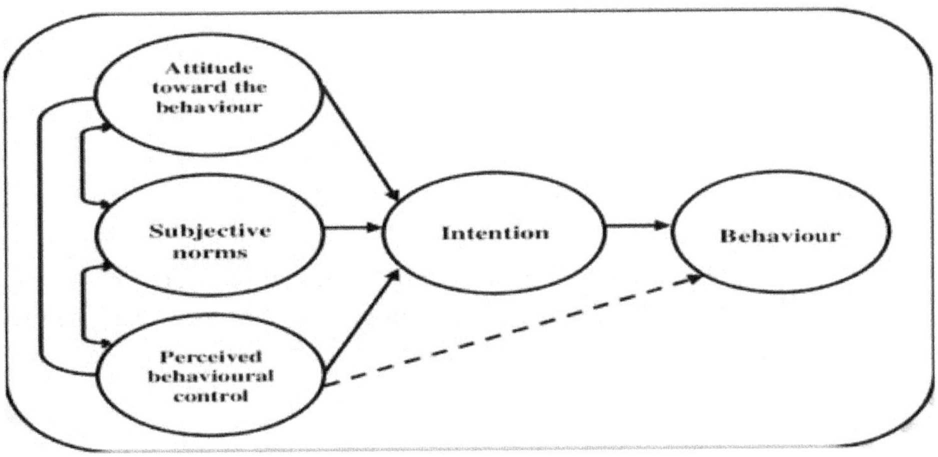

Researchers observe that the TPB applies to family firms where most decision-making appear to be at an individual level, whence the TPB is more concerned with corporate behaviours. The theory has been adopted to maintain consistency with prior literature on family firms (e.g. Koropp *et al.,* 2014). The literature also supports the uniqueness of family firms as organizations in which family members have final decision-making (Sharma *et al.,* 2014).

METHODOLOGY

The author's ten years of experience in the capacity of Business Planner and Adviser (BPA) for 12 SMEs in Iringa, Dar-es-salaam, Dodoma, Morogoro and Singida Regions in Tanzania enabled the production of this work. The firms contracted the BPA to prepare the needed business plans and pertinent implementation modalities, including how to monitor and evaluate businesses. This information was collected between 2012 and 2019 when the BPA engaged in guiding firms to prepare business plans and operate accordingly. This engagement provided the author with more opportunities to learn more about business planning, business monitoring and interaction with concerned family members in business firms. The consultant assisted in writing the business plan leaving the owners-managers responsible to implement the agreed plans (Bracker & Pearson, 1985).

Development of a Business Plan

The preparation of a business plan has several stages involving a participatory open discussion with all the concerned and coordinated and facilitated by the consultant. The BPA collected basic information on past and present business practices from the management and staff. The information collected enhanced understanding of the importance of planning in business and identified the planning capacity of the management and employees. The planning activities included how they are drawn, implemented and evaluated. Priority actions and each employee's responsibilities were drawn. An overall report was prepared incorporating different views that emerged from the participants. This assisted in the preparation of a draft business plan.

The second diagnostic step was the scholarly search for relevant information to facilitate the writing of a business plan. The assignment included a literature review of relevant policies and laws (Acts) including The Tanzania Food, Drug and Cosmetic Act Number 1, of 2003, which directs actors in the agro-based food value chains to increase the production of high-value agro-processed goods for local and international markets. The other reviewed documents were the SMEs policy (2003), Income Tax Act, (2004) and Councils' by-laws. The SMEs were to register their firms and sell their products by the law and to comply with the conditions of the licence granted. The other information gathered included social and economic profiles of production in the food processing sub-sector, business analysis, markets and industry. Other elements were monitoring and evaluation of existing assets and their pertaining life spans, working capacity and technology, annual production cycle, operating costs and possible financing sources. The draft report produced was shared with the business owners for review.

The third stage was to identify how to implement and evaluate the proposed plan. The BPA used verbal protocols to request the business owners, managers and key staff to answer questions about planning as they performed certain business tasks in running the business. The verbal protocols gave the respondents room to "think out loud and recall" how they performed particular tasks. They reported the ways business cases were analysed and solved. The technique was selected because it allowed the participants to recall while engaged in a task or behaviour. Gass and Mackey (2000) defined verbal protocol as the data one gets "by asking individuals to vocalize what is going on through their minds as they solve a problem or perform a task."

For example, the families were asked: what objectives does your business want to achieve in the coming five years? The participants came up with a list, got it organized and wrote a statement. From such data, a discussion ensued where the participants brainstormed and came up with the selected objectives based of the business. Those statements of objectives served as an inspiration for the family for what they want to achieve in their family and their business as a whole.

Thereafter, the BPA finished the work by writing the business plan which involved the entrepreneurs who had more inputs for all the aspects of the business such as ownership, human and financial investment, management structure, and financing. This participatory approach provided the BPA with a more reliable and richer understanding of the value of business plans to the sub-sector. Before business planning work, the BPA also had a series of consultative meetings with management to share their experiences with previous business plans (where available), the values perceived by the firm, and the future activities or plans they intend to incorporate in the proposed new business plan. Before the consultative meetings and fieldwork for participatory data collection, a list was prepared of the main topics (a thematic index) or issues to be researched for the business plan. The consultative meetings enabled the BPA to collect valuable information, which has also influenced the writing of this chapter.

The expected business plan was then translated into Kiswahili order to empower the Owners/employees to easily implement the provisions of the plan. The Owners/ employees got an average of ten days to read and re-read the document before giving it back to the BPA for incorporating the suggested comments and to produce the final draft in both English and Kiswahili and re-submit to the business owners ready for implementation, monitoring, and evaluation (M&E). For effective implementation of the business plan, a periodic review and follow were incorporated. Thus, the BPA planned to periodically visit the food-processing firms to advise accordingly. The employees had the duty of sharing with the BPA the challenges or difficulties faced during the implementation of planned activities. The challenges and difficulties were documented for further review with relevant managements.

Generally, it took an average of 240 to 360 working hours to come up with an actionable business plan. The hours included the time for field research, document review and analysis, consultations, and review for refinement. However, some consultants can accomplish the same task in a shorter period.

FINDINGS AND DISCUSSION

General Characteristics

An important finding of this study included the practices and values relating to the use of a business plan in running a Fo-SMEs. A business plan provides important elements that determine current and future business development. The firm's structure reveals that Fo-SMEs can be harmonious and operated smoothly by a single-family with very few non-family members participating. The key posts (e.g. sales officer and accountant) are held by appointed family members. Contrary to the existing literature by Mufuruki *et al* (2017) that Tanzanian nationals were afraid of engaging in industrial activities, this study found that the ownership of firms is almost wholly in the hands of Tanzanian nationals.

Families involved in SMEs show strong commitment and readiness to run a business successfully through family emotions, and loyalty (*blood is thicker than water*) with the minimum conflicts. Usually, the head of the family (father or mother) are defectors the head of the business system and is so respected based on his or her status in the family to avoid possible conflicts. Such structure ensures continuity, harmony and team spirit in all matters of the family firm management.

The operation of a business plan in family firms is not often linear. Sometimes, there is a mismatch of goals between the family and business systems to the extent that arises a slowing down of implementation of business activities due to minor conflicts on what should be done by who, when and why. The statements such as *"dad planned this way, and not your way, so, you have to do the same way as dad did"*. These are common sources of conflicts between family and non-family employees involved in a business. Such statements that family employees should refrain from interfering with family members' arguments about business but rather wait for a family common position and support it. With the advancements in business technologies and competition, inherited skills are likely to be obsolete. The changes in food processing technologies demand modernization for production techniques and investment in human resources to promote the growth of SMEs and industries (Msami and Wangwe,2016). If family-based businesses were to adhere to expert advice in business planning, the government efforts for national industrialization would bear results sooner than planned or envisioned.

Typically, there is a problem in linking industrial operations and Fo-SMEs planning activities. For instance, the production schedule may not easily go as planned due to family delays in purchasing raw materials, a shortfall caused by the tendency of families to personalize financial plans. Thus, implementation of a business plan can fail to realize set targets if concerned family members do not play their part in good time. To resolve such delays, every concerned family should meet regularly excluding non-family employees to discuss pertaining issues as the dominant planners and operators of family businesses. Non-employees should only be involved in official company meetings. During an interview one of the employees had this to say….

We do not have to say in matters of purchasing sunflower seed; the founder decides the amount to buy and when to buy based on his pocket. As employees simply see a lorry coming in with a bulk of seed stock for oil production and we only have to engage in production based on given directives.

Firm's official meetings are classed as professional by Kotlar and De Massis (2013) usually chaired by an appointed family member to provide operational directive with little if any open discussion of pertaining issues. The BPA recommended how best to shape the official meetings for more open dialogue that builds the firm's culture of shared identity, in return for good performance. Sharma (2004) observes that a family firm achieves good performance, through a shared identity that aligns with the goals which the different members of staff strive to achieve. Having mismatch in perspectives and goals can cause conflicts and endanger the family firm survival (Goodluck, 2015).

Consultative meetings between the family-team and the BPA successfully managed to shape the official meetings and to change the state of mind of family members for actualized shared identity without affecting family ties. Shared identity supports the goals of the Fo-SME. In some Fo-SMEs family members may be given high responsibilities despite the lack of business management competencies. For example, in a Fo-SME, a graduate son, or daughter was given a senior position in management. Such appointees often fail to deliver the goals of the firm and this leads to resentment by non-family employees who may opt to leave the job, and so jeopardizing firm's performance and lowering the family's credibility in the industry. This emphasizes the importance of a clear succession plan which necessitates that concerned family members should undergo training in business management. Experience from outside the business enclave offers family members business acumen and skills and so helps in building self-esteem and confidence in business management (Leach, 2011).

This publication argues that a business plan for the food processing Fo-SME is inevitable due to overlaps that may arise between a family and business systems. The two systems can better work in joint ventures that realize business objectives through a clear business plan and clear demarcations of responsibilities and authority. Business planning can serve as a strategic tool to unite family and non-family employees, to work and communicate as a team. The interrelation between the two systems is very important for the smooth implementation of a business plan. This is because family values and behaviours can develop and shape the firm's culture. The firm's culture is to share a set of beliefs and norms for the motivation of employees and the confidence, trust and reliability of stakeholders.

Business Planning Elements for family-Owned SMEs in Food Processing

Despite the variations in constructing business plan sections, the length and details of a business plan generally depend on the complexity and comprehensiveness of the business, purpose and processes and nature of the business (Sørensen, 2012; Hormozi *et al.,* 2002). In practise, a business plan does not have to be perfect. The truth is, the owner cannot be able to anticipate every situation. Thus, a business plan is always one in progress. Herter (1995) asserts that every business plan should have a purpose and a well-defined format. The literature recommends such contents of a business plan as Executive summary, Introductory elements, Company overview, Industry/Situation Analysis, Market Strategy, Products and Services Description, Organizational design, Location, Management, Critical Risks, Capital Needs, and financial statements and projections (Sørensen, 2012). This chapter suggests the minimum sections for Fo-SMEs' business plan in food processing. The sections are presented in the order in which they usually appear in a typical business plan. However, one should not feel obliged to follow this format exactly if other ways make more sense because of the specifics of the concerned business.

The preparation of a business plan ensures that it is clear, simple, comprehensive and well written (Sørensen, 2012). There are typically eleven sections of a business plan for a food processing firm namely, Introductory section, Business section, Business environment analysis, Marketing Plan, Production plan, Capacity Development Plan, Asset Management Plan, Investment Plan (OIP), Financial Section, Risk Management, Reporting and Monitoring, and Appendices (Figure 3): -

Figure 3. The Fo-SMEs contextual business plan
(Source: Author)

Introductory Sections

The introduction section of a business plan provides the reader with preliminary information such as *cover page, table of contents, and executive summary.*

Cover Page

The cover page informs the reader about the business name and logo (usually *at the top of the page to focuses a reader's attention*). The cover page bears the business name, logo, address, plan title and year, business motto or tagline, branding colour and other attractive features such as sample products, depending on availability of space. Previous experience has shown that most writers of business plans consider this page a minor thing but it should create a powerful impression to set the stage for readers (e.g. financiers) of the plan.

Table of Contents

The table of contents provides the list of sections and sub-sections of the plan. It includes section page numbers to help the reader to easily find the area of particular interest in the text. The cover page and table of contents of a business plan give the potential lender or investor the needed information to guide decisions to give loans.

Executive Summary

The executive summary is the most significant part of the entire business plan. It sets out, in brief, the key aspects of the plan. The potential investors read the executive summary before looking at the rest of the plan to determine whether the business would be of interest to them and may consequently want to learn more about it. The summary indicates the background, mission, vision, objectives, targets, main activities, perceived risks and possible mitigation measures and financial information. The executive summary is usually written last to encourage the reader to "read on".

Business Environment

The business environment outlines the business title, ownership, mission, vision, core values, objectives and strategy; business location, environment analysis, target customers, related industry, principal products/services and management structure. The environment gives the reader an overview of the business and how it is expected to operate.

Business Organization

The business organization embraces its rationale and legal status, its geographical location and including the physical address, plot number, ward, and District, its current organizational design and management structure, staff profiles and experiences, service area covered, services provided, customers served, the main stakeholders, customer care services and the means of communication. The organization also provides for clear duties and responsibilities of every employee such as to minimize unnecessary conflicts. The design enhances good communication and command chain between employees and management watchful for minimized interference from family members in the overall operation of the business.

Industry

This section is written based on researched information guided by the industry assessment model developed by Michael Porter and detailed in his 1980 book on Competitive Strategy between Industries and Competitors. It provides a picture of what is currently ensuing in the food processing industry in the local and international contexts. This is intended to enhance strategies that ensure the success of the firm. In essence, Porter's model describes five competitive forces and the bases for survival when operating in a competitive environment. Porter's competitive forces for business are critical for enhancing the bargaining power of buyers and suppliers, availability of substitute goods, and mechanics of withstanding competitors in compliance set rules and regulations.

According to Porter's industrial analysis is reduced into a short series of paragraphs that provide a clear nature of the industry in terms of size, age, history, technology, opportunities, threats, competitors, pertaining government regulations. The analysis makes the firm known to its readers, financiers, and other potential stakeholders and identifies potential risks. The SMEs must focus on innovation and value creation, efficient and effective productivity…. *no matter what forces are threatening the firm and the same must be recognized, planned for, and dealt with for business sustainability and success* (IFAC, 2006).

Business Products and Services

Business products and services refer to the core undertakings of a firm, namely the specific products produced, their specifications, costing and pricing, quality assurance and control, and what makes the products and pertinent services attractive to customers.

Business Mission, Vision, and Strategy

A mission statement informs what an undertaking aims to accomplish while a vision is the eventual milestone an organization aspires to be in the distant future. The two statements steer everyone in the same direction pursuing defined goals. Kantrabutra (2008) assert that sustained and competitive advantage can be achieved from a well-defined mission and vision, while a faulty or poorly defined vision or mission statement could lead to a firm to failure. Meanwhile, a business strategy operationalizes the mission into time lined specific objectives and activities and defines what a firm aims to actualize in a business plan. A firm's strategy has specific areas of engagement, such as production plan and capacity, customer care, and marketing strategy. In general, the vision, mission, and business strategy remind business owners and operators about what the firm aims and aspires for and the pertaining actions.

Key Drivers

The drivers of a business include the resources, processes and operating conditions. The firm's owners owe their business success to asset – driven economies of scale and product diversification. Business drivers should be shared with all employees as well as stakeholders. In a *family-owned-* food-processing *firm*, the following serves as the key drivers for success:

- **Production efficiency focusing on** customers and how best to produce goods with an optimal combination of inputs for maximum output at minimum cost sellable at affordable prices. This involves efficiently managing inputs, assuring inventory control and decreasing waste.
- **Industrial innovation** implies commitment to the development of new products or new processes serving as the novelty of ideas that give a firm its uniqueness.
- **Organizational innovation** refers to new ways of organizing a business including reshaping the workplace, the introduction of new practices and initiating external relations.

Most business Fo-SMEs' owners and employees indicated that they are unfamiliar with innovation, creativity and drivers for success but are ready to learn for business sustained survival.

Business Environment

The SWOT analysis presents the Strengths and Weaknesses, the Opportunities and Threats available in the operational environment of Fo-SMEs for internal capabilities, physical resources, financial resources, human resources, and intangible resources of the planned firm. By doing a SWOT analysis, a firm successfully identifies its position in terms of objectives, available resources, operating environment and competitors. Internal and external factors determine the effectiveness of business operations. A supportive business environment embraces the strengths and the opportunities while threats and weaknesses are addressed in all ways possible especially as impact the operational environment, internal capabilities, physical, financial, and human resources. Meanwhile, the PESTEL analysis determines the political, socio-cultural, economic, technical, environmental, and legal issues that impact a firm and must be addressed when preparing a business plan.

Production Plan

The production plan of a firm involves efforts to convert raw materials into finished goods/products, which are then sold to the local and external markets. The efforts include plant procurement, installation, or hiring, product processing, quality control and accounting. The production plan should record all activities in the text, figures, and tables (excel) for ease of understanding of all processes and annual production cycles. For example, planning for sunflower oil processing involves the preparation of the soil, planting, harvesting or purchase of raw materials and conversion into the final product. A production plan enables an industry to determine its needed bulk of raw materials and purchase the materials in adequate amounts till the next crop season. Strategically industrial firms should efficiently organize for available resources, management and controls in the execution of production for increased effectiveness of all operations.

Marketing Plan

Every Fo-SME should maintain an extensive marketing campaign to ensure maximum visibility for the products to targeted markets. Every business plan should ensure that a firm stays aligned with marketing objectives and targets. The plan should identify the clear objectives of the firm, its target markets, strategies for enhanced visibility and employee's preparedness to attract, educate, and retain customers (Hormozi et al., 2002). Marketing should consider the existing potential for the Product, selling Price levels, sales Promotion plan and Place, (the 4Ps of marketing), market potential, clear objectives and targets, sales strategy, market growth pattern, and customer relations, product packaging and branding, quality, advertising and distribution channels, all for profit margins to break-even (Sørensen, 2012).

Capacity Development

Experience has shown that most family businesses in developing countries have failed to invest in human resource. The capacity development aspect of a business plan provides for the strengthening of human resource in relevant knowledge and skills for the expedient realization of the objectives of a business within the internal and external environment. It involves two different levels, namely; the ability of individual staff to learn continuously, to acquire knowledge, skills, and new attitudes, and to apply the same to improve organizational performance. A staff training and development program and due financing ensure that set strategic objectives are met by competent staff. The other is organizational, that is the building of institutional structures, operational procedures, clear decision-making system and work processes owned by the whole team of workforce.

Assets Management Plan

Many business plans do not provide for an Asset Management Plan (AMP) mainly because most financiers do not consider AMP as a requirement for loan approval. AMP provides for investment in equipment and machinery, which is in all cases subject to wear and tear. AMPs incorporate preventive maintenance and risk management considerations to ensure that the day to day wear and tear of assets are dealt with promptly and so ensure that the assets reach expected lifetime working effectively and efficiently. The AMP, therefore, is an internal tool for infrastructure and assets assessment and evaluation for regular rehabilitation, maintenance, or replacement.

Financial Controls

Financial projections and controls in business are interlinked and take into account all the factors relating to monetary and resource use for the business. Financial controls also provide a firm with due projections over the planning period and links with the marketing, production, asset management, and investment plans. All financial statements should be prepared following the International Accounting Standards (IAS), including the Financial Position, Comprehensive Income, Cash Flow and other statements showing how the business earns money (profitability), meets short-term obligations (liquidity), uses available assets (efficiency) and manages long-term debts (stability). The projected financial statements should be based on previous records of accomplishment for at least three years.

Risk Management

Risk management is an integral part of good management practice and an essential element of sound business governance. Identifying and managing risks enables a more robust basis for decision-making and facilitates continuous improvement in business performance. Business risks (threats and vulnerabilities) impede the achievement of business objectives and performance targets. Food-processing is likely to meet financial risks such as the supplier non- compliance with contract, low sales, high operating costs, increasing competition, foreign exchange and interest rate risks, liquidity risks, and credit risks. These risks need to be managed and mitigated in the total risk management framework of the firm and incorporated in the business plan. Though these practices are not common for all SMEs, there is the inevitable need to introduce them to all SMEs.

Reporting and Monitoring

Every business plan should incorporate monitoring, evaluation and regular reporting on how the plan progresses and performs. The following are typical elements of the reports:

1. Major review and minor reviews of the production plan (conducted every second and fourth year).
2. Annual summary of achievements of the production and marketing plan goals.
3. Annual satisfaction surveys of customers.
4. Summary of deliberations in meetings involving local stakeholders - farmers, suppliers, banks) invited periodically to collaboratively discuss key issues pertaining.

The management will consequently review its plan against the achievement of objectives and put in place actions for improvement.

Appendix to a Business Plan

The appendix to a business plan (See Appendix 1) serves as the final part of a business plan, as a kind of mini-library, incorporating all the attachments of relating information to supplement and serve as important references in the business plan. Even so, not everything can be shown in the appendix, but only the relevant and supportive information such as credit history, business owners, tax returns, research studies, management and staff curriculum vitae, legal documents, shareholder certificates, copies of patents, permits, licenses, property and equipment leases and rental agreements.

THE VALUES OF A BUSINESS PLAN

Coordinating Tool

Since Fo-SME is a dual operating system where one system is driven by family emotions and the other by economic principles, the overlap of the two systems might create conflicts that might threaten the business performance. A coordination framework will be necessary for the two systems harmonization of the two systems with a common business mission. Family expectations and business demands can be shaped into the business strategy, tactics, and actions. Coordination helps owners and funders to evaluate existing potentials and the managers to set better short and long-term strategic objectives.

Strengthening Communication

A business plan ensures that all that is discussed about the business, whether in formal or informal meetings at the family level, are shared with all staff in matching with business plan objectives. A good business plan provides for a communication system that brings family employees, non-family employees, and the management team together for shared decision making, sharing of ideas, making clarification on each other's roles and dealing with any underlying conflicts, and providing team-building opportunities. This also promotes openness, trust, morale, personal responsibility, and generates useful ideas at all levels in the firm, and keep valuable non-family employees contented.

Strategic Direction

Fo-SME must ensure that there is both family harmony with firm performance. A business plan ensures that the two systems – family and business work towards the same strategic direction. Mintzberg (1993) observes, 'Planning should translate the intended strategies into realized ones, by taking the first step that can lead to effective implementation'.

Financing Tool

A business financial management system is the hardest part to prepare in a business plan. The most preferred financing option for a family business is personal funding (e.g. personal savings, or investment by family and friends), while for firm external financing in the form of bank loans is the most preferred option. The practices from SMEs in food processing show that bank loans are commonly available as the main financing options outside a family funding for a business.

Performance Management

Managing a family-owned business requires fulfilling dual roles. This requires clarity, flexibility, and consistency in achieving the intended business objectives. It also involves a combination of good teamwork management. A good business plan requires each person involved to have relevant academic or professional qualifications and experiences that are relevant to current or proposed future roles. The plan identifies staff training and development needs and ensures that everyone works towards the same goals by setting individual work objectives and priorities in compliance with the business plan timeframe. In this way, a business plan is also a performance management tool and can serve to assess not only business performance but of staff as well.

Selection of the Appropriate Business Model Canvas (BMC)

Every business plan begins with a feasibility study focusing on the commercial, financial, and economic viability of a business environment and serves as a tool for the realization of defined objectives and strategic choices. Osterwalder and Pigneur (2010) defined BMC as the logic supporting the firm, and its mode of operation in creating and delivering new products while capturing new customers and new stakeholders. The selected BMC for food processing Fo-SMEs has nine related blocks, namely, Customers, Resources, Value Proposition, Customer Channels, Key Partnerships, Cost structure, Customer Relationship, Key Activities, and Revenue Stream.

Succession Planning

Since family firms usually undergo periodic changes and restructuring, continuity and smooth succession of ownership and management across generations stand out as critical issues. Succession planning guarantees the survival of a firm, but it has been one of the managerial issues in running family businesses. It affects the survival and performance of a firm. According to Michael et al., (1996) heirs to a business should be experienced and educated and should start at lower levels of employment and only after several years serving in a variety of positions should he or she be assigned to a higher-level position. In this way, there will be sustained loyalty, shared values, common traditions, commitment and trust (Michael et al., 1996).

CONCLUSION

This production has outlined the values of business plans with particular reference to Fo-SMEs. Business plans are inevitable due to the possible emergence of issues, demands and divergent interests between a family and a family business. The values of a business plan vary from country to country and as influenced by levels of economic development and culture. What may be considered valuable in family firms in Asian, European, and American countries might be differently perceived in African countries. For instance: in some countries, banks may grant loans without requiring the loaner to have a business plan (Van Auken & Horton,1994). In Tanzania, loan giving banks demand a fully detailed business proposal. The author encourages family firms in Tanzania to fully use business plans to achieve greater levels of engagement to increase the chances of business survival.

RECOMMENDATIONS

The chapter recommends that the Government should support Fo-SMEs sector. Needless to reiterate but Fo-SMEs do contribute significantly to the economic growth of a country. The Government might consider an inclusive operating model requiring every business to have five-year production plans integrated with agricultural practices for guaranteed sustainability of businesses and improved livelihoods of farmers. The Government should serve as coordinator of the integrated industrial planning by collecting and disseminating relevant statistical information from the processing sub-sector and the agriculture sector. Integrated projects do enhance local agricultural production of industrial raw materials that serve as inputs for processors/industrialists. Integrated projects model under private arrangements may be emulated in other Fo-SMEs with the Government as coordinator, policymaker and regulator. This inclusive business model approach supports industrial businesses, enable developing countries to achieve the SDGs'-9 components and to safely achieve the industrial economy.

ACKNOWLEDGMENT

This chapter is an outcome of the consultant's involvement in the African Finance and Economics Association (AFEA)'s Mentorship Programme. The author, therefore, appreciates the inputs from his

AFEA mentor (Evans Osabuohien, Professor of Economics & Chair, Centre for Economic Policy and Development Research (CEPDeR), Covenant University, Ota, Nigeria).

REFERENCES

Abbrey, J., Bagah, D. A., & Wulifan, J. K. (2015). The Relevance of Business Planning Document for Small and Medium Scale Enterprises in Tamale Metropolis, Northern Ghana. *Journal of Business Administration and Education.*, *7*(1), 34–80.

Abolaji, J. (2010). The interface between Corporate Vision, Mission and Production and Operations Management. *Global Journal of Management and Business Research*, *10*(2), 18–22.

Ajzen, I. (1985). From intentions to actions: a theory of planned behaviuor. In J. Kuhl & J. Beckmann (Eds.). Springer.

Ajzen, I. (1991). The theory of planned behavior. *Organizational Behavior and Human Decision Processes*, *50*(2), 179–211.

Ajzen, I., & Fishbein, M. (1977). Attitude-behavior relations: A theoretical analysis and review of empirical research. *Psychological Bulletin*, *84*(5), 888–918.

Aram, J. D., & Cowen, S. S. (1990). Strategic Planning for Increased Profit in the Small Business. *Long Range Planning*, *23*, 63–70.

Baliga, A, J., Rodrigues, D. L. L. R. (2015). Business Plan- The Secret to Success. *International Journal of Business and Management*, *3*(4), 210–214.

Bangs, H. D. (1985). *Business Planning Guide*. Upstart Publishing Company, Inc.

Barton, F. C., & Hounsell, D. (1994). Accountants Find Success in Business Succession Planning. *Practical Accountant*, *27*, 18–22.

Becherer & Helms.. (2009). The Value of Business Plans for New Ventures: Company and Entrepreneur Outcomes. *Journal of Small Business Strategy, 20*(2).

Beecroft, I., Osabuohien, E., Efobi, U., Olurinola, I., & Osabohien, R. (2020). Manufacturing Export and ICT Infrastructure in West Africa: Investigating the Roles of Economic and Political Institutions. *Institutions and Economies*, *12*(1), 1–36.

Bracker, J. S., & Pearson, J. N. (1985). The Impact of Consultants on Small Firm Strategic Planning. *Journal of Small Business Management*, *23*(3), 23–30.

Burke, A., Fraser, S., & Greene, J. F. (2010, May). The Multiple Effects of Business Planning on New Venture Performance. *Journal of Management Studies*, *47*, 3. doi:10.1111/j.1467-6486.2009.00857

Carlock, R., & Ward, J. (2001). *Strategic Planning for Family Business*. Palgrave.

Carson & Cromie. (1990). Marketing Planning in Small Enterprises: A Model and More Empirical Evidence. *The Journal of Consumer Marketing*, *7*, 5-18.

Cater, J., & Schwab, A. (2008). Turnaround strategies in established small family firms. *Family Business Review*, *21*(1), 31–50.

Chwolka, A., & Raith, M. G. (2012). The value of business planning before start-up - A decision-theoretical perspective. *Journal of Business Venturing*, *27*(3), 385–399. doi:10.1016/j.jbusvent.2011.01.002

Daspit, J. J., Holt, D. T., Chrisman, J. J., & Long, R. G. (2015). Examining family firm succession from a social exchange perspective: A multiphase, multi-stakeholder review. *Family Business Review*, *29*(1), 44–64.

Delmar, F., & Shane, S. (2003). Does Business Planning Facilitate the Development of New Ventures? *Strategic Management Journal*, *24*, 1165–1185.

EAC/UNIDO and FAO. (2011). *Development of Agro-Industries and Agro-Enterprises in the EAC Region*. United Nation Industries Development Organisation.

Family Firm Institute. (2017). *Global data points*. Available at www.ffi.org/page/globaldatapoints

Finch, B. (2010). How to write a business plan (3rd ed.). Academic Press.

Finscope Survey. (2012). *National Baseline Survey Report for Micro, Small, and Medium Enterprises in Tanzania*. Ministry of Industry and Trade, Dar es Salaam; Financial Sector Deepening Trust.

Fraser, S. (2005). *Finance for Small and Medium-Sized Enterprises: A Report on the 2004 UK Survey of SME Finances*. ESRC UK Data Archive: SN 5326.

Goodluck, C. (2015, Jan.). *Effects of nepotism and family conflicts on the performance of family-owned firms in Tanzania: contrasting views. Business Management Review*.

Handler, W. (1991). Key interpersonal relationships of next-generation family members in family firms. *Journal of Small Business Management*, *28*(July), 21–32.

Herter, G. (1995). Business planning boosts your chances. *Accounting Technology*.

Hormozi, A. M., Sutton, G. S., McMinn, R. D., & Lucio, W. (2002). Business Plans for New or Small Businesses: *Paving the Path to Success. Management Decision*, *40*(8), 755–763.

IFAC. (2006). Business Planning Guide: Practical Application for SMEs. The International Federation of Accountants (IFAC).

ILO. (2017). *World employment social outlook. Sustainable enterprises and jobs: formal enterprises and decent work*. International Labour Organisation.

Kantabutra, S. (2008). What do We Know About Vision? *Journal of Applied Business Research*, *24*(2), 127–138.

Kesale, M. A. (2017). Barriers Facing Startup Small and Medium Enterprises (SMEs) in Accessing External Capital in Tanzania. *International Journal of Academic Research in Business and Social Sciences*, *7*(3).

Kessy, S., & Temu, S. S. (2009). Impact on Training on of Micro and Small Enterprises Served by Microfinance Institutions in Tanzania: *Research. Journal of Business and Management*.

Koropp, C., Kellermanns, F.W., Grichnik, D., & Stanley, L. (2014). Financial Decision Making in Family Firms: An Adaptation of the Theory of Planned Behavior. *Family Business Review*, 1 –21. DOI: doi:10.1177/0894486514522483

Kotlar, J., & De Massis, A. (2013). Goal setting in family firms: Goal diversity, social interactions, and collective commitment to family-centred goals. *Entrepreneurship Theory and Practice*, *37*(6), 1263–1288.

Kuratko, D. F., & Hodgetts, R. M. (2001). *Entrepreneurship: A contemporary approach* (5th ed.). Southwestern/Thomson Learning.

Latham, G. P., & Yukl, G. A. (1975). A Review of Research on the Application of Goal Setting in Organizations. *Academy of Management Journal*, *18*, 824–845.

Leach, P. (2011). *Family Businesses: The Essentials*. Profile Books Ltd.

Liao, J., & Gartner, W. B. (2008). The Influence of Pre-Venture Planning on New Venture Creation. *Journal of Small Business Strategy*, *18*(2), 1-21.

Masurel, E., & Smit, H. P. (2000). Planning behaviour of small firms in Central Vietnam. *Journal of Small Business Management*, *38*(2).

Merchant, K. A., & Van der Stede, W. A. (2007). Management Control Systems: Performance Measurement, Evaluation Incentives. Edinburgh Gate: Pearson Education Limited.

Michael, H., & Morris Roy,, W., & Williams. (1996). Factors influencing family business succession. *International Journal of Entrepreneurial Behaviour & Research*, *2*(3), 68–81.

Ministry of Industry and Trade of the United Republic of Tanzania. (2012). *Tanzania Industrial Competitiveness Report*. Author.

Mintzberg, H. (1993). *The Rise and Fall of Strategic Planning*. The Free Press.

Msami, J., & Wangwe, S. (2016). Industrial Development in Tanzania. In Manufacturing Transformation: Comparative Studies of Industrial Development in Africa and Emerging Asia (pp. 155-173). Oxford Scholarship Online.

Mufuruki, A., Mawji, R., Marwa, M., & Kasiga, G. (2017). *Tanzania's Industrialization Journey, 2016 – 2056: From an Agrarian to a Modern Industrialized State in Forty Years, Moran (E, E.)*. Publishers Limited.

Nandonde, F. A., Lubava, G., & Liana, P. J. (2015). Uptake of Market 'Induced Innovation' by Upstream Actors in Tanzania. In C. Machado & D. J. Paulo (Eds.), *Innovation Management: In Research and Industry* (pp. 39–58). Walter de Gruyter. doi:10.1515/9783110358759.39

Orbell, S., Hodgkins, S., & Sheeran, P. (1997). Implementation intentions and the theory of planned behavior. *Personality and Social Psychology Bulletin*, *23*(9), 945–954. PMID:29506445

Osabuohien, E., Efobi, U. R., Herrmann, R., & Gitau, C. M. (2019). Female Labor Outcomes and Large-scale Agricultural Land Investments: Macro-Micro Evidence from Tanzania. *Land Use Policy*, *82*, 716–728.

Osterwalder, A., & Pigneur, Y. (2010). *Business Model Generation*. John Wily & Sons. Inc.

Rue, L. W., & Ibrahim, N. I. (1998). The Relationship Between Planning Sophistication and Performance in Small Business. *Journal of Small Business Management*, *36*, 24–32.

Sharma, P. (2004). An overview of the field of family business studies: Current status and directions for the future. *Family Business Review*, *17*(1), 1–36.

Sonfield, M. C., & Lussier, R. N. (2004). First-, second-, and third-generation family firms: A comparison. *Family Business Review*, *17*(3), 189–202.

Struebing, L. (1997). Recipe for Success: Prepare A Business Plan. *Quality Progress*, *30*(8), 20.

URT. (2008). *Annual Survey of Industrial Production and Performance*. United Republic of Tanzania.

URT. (2010). *Annual Survey of Industrial Production and Performance*. United Republic of Tanzania.

URT. (2016). The 2013 Census of Industrial Production: Analytical Report. National Bureau of Statistics (NBS) & Ministry of Industry, Trade and Investment (MITI).

URT. (2018). *The Economic Survey Report*. Ministry of Finance and Planning DODOMA – TANZANIA.

Van Auken, H., & Horton, H. (1994). Financing Patterns of Minority-Owned Small Business. *Journal of Small Business Strategy*, *5*, 2.

APPENDIX

Table 2. Fo-SME Potential Risks, Impact, and Mitigation

S/N	Type of Risk	Description	Potential Impact	Risk Mitigation
1	**Asset Risks (Existing, new investment)**	Arise from poor infrastructure, forces increase in the cost of raw materials.	• Falling production rate • Low-quality products • Loss of customers	• Plant Rehabilitation, regular Repair and Maintenance, • Assets Management Plan (AMP)
2	**Organizational Risks**	Business contracts/agreements made may be risky (e.g. Sales contracts) Possible breach of contract leads to legal action (legal risk).	Legal liability, fines, and defamed image of the firm.	• Aggressive sales, • Insurance cover.
3	**Operational Risks**	Threats and risks can arise from ordinary business activities., e.g. possible loss of lawsuits, fraud risk.	Frauds	• Strong Internal Control System (ICS) • Staff held accountable for the achievement of assigned internal control objectives. • Improved records management.
4	**Competitive Risks**	Competitive forces hold back the achievement of a business mission and lead to a possible decline in revenue due to competition.	Decreases in revenue.	Improved promotion and sales channels.
5	**Culture Risks**	collective attitudes and behaviours of its people involved that can adversely impact business outcomes.	wrong outcomes for customers and firm	Ensured Culture of Risk Management
6	**Liquidity Risks**	Firm failure to meet obligations with due immediacy.	• Incapability to meet financial obligations • Loss of key suppliers • Loss of market share	Liquidity Risk Appetite fully compliant with regulatory requirements.
7	**Currency Risks**	Posed by exposure to unanticipated changes in the currency exchange rate for exports and imports of goods and services, may involve exchange rate risk into foreign currencies such as US dollars or European euros.	• loss of revenue • Increases in operational costs	• Use of derivatives instruments • Hedge accounting
8	**Financial Risks**	• Involve contracted jobs where cash flows are either known for certain or are conditional. • At some point, the business will be unable to meet its financial obligations.	• Decreases in the value and credibility of the firm • Loss of key stakeholders	Improved Risk Management for Markets, Credits, Liquidity and Operational Risks.

Chapter 16
Technological Innovations in Agriculture in Sub-Saharan Africa

Amadou Tandjigora
Cheikh Anta Diop University, Senegal

ABSTRACT

The purpose of this chapter is to review the literature on technological innovations in general and more specifically on the use of information and communication technologies in agriculture. Emphasis was placed on two main tools, namely the telephone and the internet. The opportunities created by these two tools have been highlighted on the basis of previous studies supported by scientific arguments. Some stylized facts have also made it possible to highlight the level of these ICTs in 20 countries of sub-Saharan Africa. Some countries like Kenya, Nigeria, South Africa, and Rwanda, and, to a lesser extent, Senegal are more advanced in this process of using ICT because they are relatively more economically stable. Finally, the constraints linked to the adoption of these ICTs as well as certain public policy recommendations were formulated.

INTRODUCTION

Agriculture remains the backbone of most economies in Africa, where it alone accounts for 60% of total employment (IFPRI, 2019). It is estimated that 45 percent of the territory is classified as arid, sub-arid or dry sub-humid zones: rainfall is between 300 mm and 800 mm per year. These regions are particularly affected by recent climate change accentuating constraints on agricultural production, making them very vulnerable to fluctuations in production, sources of serious food crises (Clavel, Barro, Belay, Lahmar, & Maraux, 2008). Exposure to risks, shocks and weak incentives for welfare are the main issues facing farm households in Africa (Osabohien, Onanuga, Baderounmu, Matthew & Osabuohien, 2020). According to the same authors, the same is true of market access difficulties (including the poor condition of roads, the failure of marketing infrastructure, lack of information on market opportunities, lack of control over negotiation techniques of the producers), the low technicality of the farmers but also the insufficiency of credits.

DOI: 10.4018/978-1-7998-4817-2.ch016

In addition, according to the World Bank (2020), the continued increase in globalization and the integration of food markets has intensified competition and efficiency in the agricultural sector and created unique opportunities to include more smallholders in supply chains. Yet on a related note, agriculture faces a series of modern and serious challenges, particularly in developing countries exposed to price shocks, climate change and persistent infrastructure deficiencies in rural areas. . Severe and unforeseen weather conditions reduce already limited yields and promote migration from rural areas and rural employment. It is in the context of the globalization of agriculture that the need for information becomes most pressing. Smallholders, who still provide a significant portion of the world's food, need information to advance their work just as much as industrial producers. It therefore becomes necessary to wonder about the question of new methods applicable to agriculture so that it is efficient, more profitable, less painful and more attractive than Information and Communication Technologies (ICT)

ICT can be seen as a tool to increase efficiency and save time. There are a dimension (sub-set) of technology (alongside electricity generation, transport, etc.), which can be considered as an essential indicator of the level of development achieved by an economy and given the trend Current globalization, ICT could be a tool to achieve this goal (Ejemeyovwi & Osabuohien, 2018). This definition generally applies to all sectors of activity including the agricultural sector.

Thus, ICTs, particularly the telephone and the internet, as we wish to address in this chapter, are now tools that farmers in several countries have integrated into their strategies for improving agricultural production, increasing yields and marketing this production. According to the existing literature on ICT in particular the telephone and the Internet, many opportunities are noted for their use such as the facilitation of money transfer to farmers, the marketing of agricultural products, information on weather conditions and market failures etc. Stylized facts on the rate of telephone and internet adoption, however, show low levels in Sub-Saharan Africa as shown in Figure 1 and 2, while they constitute the main tools for receiving meteorological information and coordinating between farmers themselves, but also between farmers and buyers of production and many other roles that will be developed in the body of the chapter.

The main objective of this chapter is to review the literature on information and communication technologies applied to the agricultural sector in Sub-Saharan Africa. This will specifically involve questioning the theoretical review of the literature on technological innovations in general and applied to agriculture in a particular way, a field in which the theme of our chapter fits, but also to highlight the role of two tools, namely the telephone and the Internet, in the facilitation of agricultural work and the flow of production, although access is not sufficient for all countries.

The main research question of this article is what are the opportunities that the information and communication technologies (telephone, Internet) generate for the benefit of the agricultural sector in Sub-Saharan Africa? To answer this question, we will use existing literature to identify the arguments that could be put forward as scientific evidence.

The work is structured in three main parts. The first deals with the theoretical review of the literature on innovations in general. The second concerns the review of the literature on technological innovations in agriculture. The last part deals with the opportunities of Information and Communication Technologies for the benefit of the agricultural sector. It also analyzes with stylized facts the evolution of the rate of subscription to the telephone and the rate of use of the Internet in the Sub-Saharan African countries targeted by the study. The conclusion finally highlights guidelines and recommendations for public policies.

THEORETICAL LITERATURE REVIEW

General Information on Innovation

Innovation, defined as the execution of new productive combinations (Lakomski-laguerre, 2006), or even as a problem-solving process according to the evolutionary economist Dosi (1988), started with the English industrial revolution. However, we cannot approach the subject of innovation without mentioning the work of Joseph Schumpeter. To describe the dynamics of change in this way, Schumpeter uses two concepts: circuit and evolution, developed on the basis of empirically observed facts. According to Marty (as cited by Tremblay, 2003, p. 4), evolution calls for the implementation of innovations, new combinations which drive the economy out of the circular flow.

During the Thirty Glorious Years, Schumpeter's positions were not very successful due to the rise of Keynesian theories which were more current. How can we hope to arouse interest when we proclaim that the economic system is only imbalance, instability, while all Western economies have experienced uninterrupted growth since 1945 (Fournier, 2001)?

Since the 1970s, the return of economic crises has reminded us that the capitalist system, like any economic system, can experience upheavals. The theme of evolution, expensive to Schumpeter, has thus become fully relevant again. If some economists like Arena & Lazaric (2003) have had to challenge the relevance of the evolutionary approach to innovation, but all agree on the importance of Joseph Schumpeter's contribution to the analysis of innovation (Fournier, 2001). Thus, we speak today of technological innovations as if it were a novelty whereas there is perhaps again in this term of innovation only the acceleration and the diffusion of the process (Labini, 2007). According to this author, technological innovation is the essence of modern civilization, the essence of economic development.

Innovation is unpredictable according to Marty (as cited by Tremblay, 2003, p. 13). However, we wonder if this is still the case. For Marx, it constitutes the main mode of seeking profit, even a kind of necessity (Labini, 2007). When driven by the entrepreneur, it modifies existing production structures, creates novelty by upsetting market equilibria and profoundly changes the economy and society as a whole (Lakomski-laguerre, 2006). Innovations also increase labor productivity (Labini, 2007) and it is the increase in labor productivity that in turn tends to determine two particular effects: an increase in average income and a reduction in hours of work.

Innovation and Agriculture, Theoretical Insights

Regarding innovation in the agricultural sector, conceptual works are relatively recent, but are part of a longer history of social science work on technical progress and changes in the agricultural sector (Temple, Chiffoleau, & Touzard, 2018). At the beginning of modern productive development, in the second half of the eighteenth century, most of the population in England still lived on agriculture. The traditional or manufacturing industry was not as developed. Its development has enabled agriculture to experience high productivity in order to support the subsistence of a considerable number of people outside of agriculture. This systematic increase in productivity was itself determined by the application of technological innovations, radical or minor, to agriculture. These were generally innovations related to chemical fertilizers, agricultural machinery and electricity (Labini, 2007). According to some authors, however, the term "innovation" was not yet used in agriculture and one spoke rather of technical progress, which was then gradually evacuated by rural economists and sociologists Temple et al., (2018).

It was not until the twentieth century that innovation will assert itself as a positive concept, qualifying a process generating technical, organizational changes in product or use. It therefore constitutes a field of research, at the interface of different scientific communities (economy, sociology, geography, management, etc.) and in multiple empirical fields, including agriculture and food (Temple et al., 2018). According to these authors, before this period of the 20th century, Physiocrats like Quesnay, had already advanced that the investment of the rich farmers, enlightened by the new methods, would allow an improvement of the efficiency of agriculture, and therefore the creation of national wealth. This wealth creation will be done by concentrating land in agriculture to achieve economies of scale (Kerzazi, 2015). This process in itself also generates social exclusions from the activity, leading to a drastic reduction in the number of farmers in all industrial countries. Technical progress is then considered as the major factor of growth in the continuation of classical economists like Ricardo (1817). The latter identifies two forms of improvement in agriculture, namely those which increase the productive capacities of the earth (new rotations, fertilizers, etc.) and those which, by improving the machines, make it possible to obtain the same product with less work (plow, mechanization of harvests then plowing, treatment etc.). Moreover, according to Pouch (2015), agricultural production has undergone profound changes in recent years, distinguished by more capital mobilized, technicality emanating from scientific, agronomic, biological, economic and financial progress. Such mutations necessarily affect the very identity of the farmer whose image no longer matches that of the sedentary peasant, whose economic activity was almost totally punctuated by the cycle of the seasons.

Besides the benefits expected from innovation for all sectors of activity, including agriculture, some authors have a critical approach to innovation. According to Marx, technical progress leads to an appropriation of living labor by capital, violent for workers and peasants, but which appears necessary for the progress of humanity. The same is true of Kaustky (1900), who developed this analysis in agriculture, arguing that the development of the mechanical, chemical and biological sciences led to its industrialization, favored large farms and the poverty of the peasantry. The thesis was challenged in Russia by Chayanov in the 1920s, but it was not until the 1960s that his ideas were disseminated in the scientific community, showing on the contrary the capacity of peasant or family agriculture to adopt or generate the technical change (Temple et al., 2018).

LITERATURE REVIEW ON TECHNOLOGICAL INNOVATIONS IN AGRICULTURE

The Determinants of the Adoption of Technological Innovations

Beyond the unfavorable climatic conditions, the low yields and agricultural incomes which can strongly influence the decision to generate technological innovations, certain socioeconomic characteristics of farming households in Sub-Saharan Africa could also influence the implication in the technological innovation processes. Among these socioeconomic characteristics, we can cite the perception of farmers (Adesina & Zinnah, 1993), human capital (Kebede, Gunjal, & Coffin, 1990; Chirwa, 2005), household size (Croppenstedt et al., 2003), gender (Chirwa, 2005), degree of risk aversion (Kebede et al., 1990), age (Alene & Manyong, 2006), family heritage (Lambrecht, Vanlauwe, Merckx, & Maertens, 2014), participation in activities non-agricultural (Chirwa 2005), the distance from home to farm or home to market (Hailu, Abrha, & Weldegiorgis, 2014), the social capital acquired via social networks (Bandiera & Rasul, 2006) and contact with agricultural extension agents (Lambrecht et al., 2014), finally, the institutions and organizations that regulate and systematize regulatory frameworks, incentive and sanction systems, and the hybridization of knowledge bases between communities of actors, are at the center of many contemporary works (Touzard, Temple, Faure, & Triomphe, 2015).

Regarding age for example, more recent studies (Gedikoglu, McCann, & Artz (2007); Pandit et al., (2011); Ward, Vestal, Doye, & Lalman (2008) have shown however that this socioeconomic characteristic acts negatively on decision to adopt technological innovations.

Experience would also have a negative impact on the decision to adopt technological innovations according to Caswell, Fuglie, Ingram, Jans, & Kascak (2001), but most studies contradict this assertion, among the authors who have distinguished themselves and whose studies are more recent (Baffoe-Asare, Danqua, Annor-Frempong, 2013 ; Khanna, 2001 ; Kim, Gillespie, & Paudel, 2005 ; Nyaupane & Gillespie, 2009 ; Tosakana et al., 2010).

The element on which many authors like Baffoe-Asare et al., (2013) agree, that is a brake on the adoption of innovations by farmers is the level of debt. Farmers' level of debt would limit significantly the adoption of good agricultural practices which do not necessarily require material or financial investments.

The institutional determinants of the adoption of technological innovations are also referenced in the existence or not of insurance systems or imperfect insurance (Udry, 2010), credit constraints (Croppenstedt et al., 2003; Udry, 2010) and insecurity related to property rights (Udry, 2010).

Risk Aversion in the Adoption of Technological Innovations in Agriculture

In the context of the adoption of innovations in agriculture, the level of risk aversion has been highlighted as a brake on adoption (Feder & Umali, 1993; Kebede et al., 1990). Farm households are generally risk-averse because they need to secure food and household needs. Their risk aversion strongly influences their decision to adopt new technologies. Their desire to minimize production risks and secure their current production negatively affects their propensity to adopt new technologies even if they are accessible (in terms of cost, availability and skills required to implement them), and can improve their productivity and the yields of their farms (Kato, Ringler, Yesuf, & Bryan, 2009). However, risk aversion alone cannot explain farmers' behavior in adopting innovations (Hellerstein, Nathaniel, & Higgins, 2013). In fact, operators make their choice based on their preferences but also on their risk perception (Teno, Lehrer, & Kone, 2018). Regarding this perception of risk, Adesina & Zinnah (1993) show that the decisions to experimentally adopt improved rice varieties by Sierra Leonean farmers depend mainly on their perceptions of these new varieties. More specifically, factors such as cooking, yield ease of husking and grinding play a decisive role in the decision to adopt these varieties of rice.

Farm households that accept risk will be more willing to use the new technology, unlike households that do not accept risk (Foster & Rosenzweig, 2010). To protect themselves, the latter will prefer to wait to see what the new technology is producing for neighboring farmers before making the decision to adopt it. As a result, agricultural households that are rich or have more work space (arable land) are less resistant to the risks of innovation than poor agricultural households (Teno et al., 2018).

Indeed, if innovation fails, the ability of household workers to survive could pose a huge problem, which is not the case for wealthy households. As technological innovation is therefore more adopted by wealthy households than poor ones, it therefore presents in itself the risk of worsening existing social inequalities if the adoption conditions are not freed from the constraints of risk by public policies. The poverty that characterizes most agricultural households in Sub-Saharan Africa could therefore make them risk-averse and therefore less inclined to adopt new technologies (Teno et al., 2018). For De Janvry, Sadoulet, Kyle, & Dar (2015), in seeking an explanation for this problem of technological adoption in agriculture, a certain number of constants stand out; and where the problem arises, agriculture is dominated by smallholders who grow food crops (tropical starch) in potentially profitable but very risky rainy conditions. This challenge of producers' access to agricultural innovations has been at the origin of many reforms within research and extension institutions since the 1970s (Zoundi & Hitimana, 2002).

In this context, decision-making is particularly complex, with high exposure to risk and great heterogeneity in the situation of farmers (De Janvry et al., 2015). However, beyond the risks, other factors may not motivate the use of technological innovations by farm households. Thus, according to Dembele (2001), in the long term, the instability of the agricultural sector (climate, markets) reduces investment and the capacity for technological innovations in agriculture compared to other sectors of the economy. Labor productivity is found to be lower in agriculture than that obtained in other sectors (industrial, services), which may explain the fact that countries whose production system has remained structurally agricultural remain in poverty. This context of low productivity and structural poverty is an element of food insecurity in sub-Saharan Africa.

Innovation can also be rejected if it challenges the rules of access to resources such as land. To be efficient, innovation in organizational structuring must avoid disorganizing the peasant environment or modifying there too deeply the social cohesion systems that allow rural communities to face environmental uncertainties in a context or public institutions performing this function are not yet functional (Alary, 2006).

Constraints in the Agricultural Sector and the need for Technological Innovations

Micro and macroeconomic constraints are believed to be behind the slow development of agriculture in general in Sub-Saharan Africa. For microeconomic constraints, these are low physical and human capital (Duflo et al., 2011; Gollin et al., 2014), difficulties in accessing credit (Croppenstedt et al., 2003), constraints on the valuation of products on the market, including storage constraints (Ricker-gilbert et al., 2015) and the low use of technology or innovative practices (Alene et al., 2006; Lambrecht et al., 2014; Pamuk et al., 2014, as cited by Teno et al., 2018, p. 142) .Macroeconomic constraints can be summed up in different ways. Referring to the experience of European countries, Balie et al., (2008) find that agricultural policies as practiced in Africa do not favor the development of the agricultural sector, which immediately suffers from an unfair commercial practice compared to the outside (as cited by Teno et al. 2018, p. 142).

Beyond these micro and macroeconomic constraints, others linked to the employability of young people are acute. Currently, agriculture alone accounts for around 60 percent of total employment on the continent, and much more when jobs along the food value chain are taken into account. In Ethiopia, Malawi, Mozambique, Tanzania, Uganda and Zambia, for example, the food system is expected to create more jobs between 2010 and 2025 than the rest of the economy, but young people have little interest, or not at all, looking for jobs in the agricultural sector (International food policy research institute [IFPRI], 2019). For the Centre technique de coopération agricole et rurale [CTA] (2019c), the main reasons are related to the poor image that agriculture shows, its precariousness and its lack of competitiveness and support. The agriculture on which they depend remains heavily dependent on rainfall, which has been irregular and unpredictable for some time. However, the fall in agricultural incomes calls into question the hope based on agriculture as a source of employment and as a factor of growth, since a sector which is not capable of generating remunerative activities will not attract young people who are entering the labor market in large numbers (Dupaigre, 2017). According to the author's projections, nine countries would see their farmers' incomes chronically decrease as a result of the collapse in land productivity. These are Senegal, Gambia, Angola, Burundi, Malawi, Rwanda, Nigeria, Comoros and Sao Tome and Principles. As a result, one might expect increased migratory pressures as a result of increased poverty and the frequency of subsistence crises. In addition, according to the review "Grain de sel" (2012), an annual cohort of 200,000 to 300,000 young people from countries of around 15 million people like Senegal, arrives each year on the labor market, which raises questions about remaining in the agricultural sector.

Tandjigora (2019) has also shown that other sectors of activity are more important than that of agriculture. His results showed that in reality, where agriculture brings 1 CFA to his practitioner, the service at the same time gives him 12 CFA, industry, 3.87 CFA, trade, 1.85 CFA against 4, 83 CFA for other services, which represents a significant difference. Rural industries and services would be a real alternative to agriculture for this purpose, constantly facing environmental realities.

Another important factor that stands out is age. The average age in the agricultural sector currently exceeds 50 years and raises the question of generational renewal to ensure the succession in a sector so essential for the economy and the food and nutritional security of populations (CTA, 2019a).

However, growth driven by agriculture generates a greater welfare effect than growth driven by non-agricultural activities, especially for the poorest 20 percent of the population (Schneider & Gugerty, 2011).

Indeed, the large-scale adoption of technological innovations in agriculture and the food chain (irrigation infrastructure, mechanization of transport and processing of products allows households and rural businesses to improve their agricultural production and incomes and food security, to increase livelihoods and participate in the economic growth of their countries (Conseil ouest et centre africain pour la recherche et le développement agricoles [CORAF], 2018). According to this institution, despite efforts to disseminate and promote the adoption of these technologies and innovations, this remains weak, which could explain low agricultural productivity and precarious livelihoods. For other institutions including IFPRI (2019), the increasing use of digital technologies, tools and services would be widely visible, including in the agricultural sector. According to this institution, digital would play a key role for African countries in achieving their goals in poverty reduction, food security and nutrition. From a macroeconomic point of view, technological inequalities between countries would largely explain the differences in GDP per capita and wages between workers in different countries of the world (Teno et al., 2018, Foster & Rosenzweig, 2010). In light of this work, digital technologies hold the promise of transforming the context of employment in the agricultural sector, of creating jobs that require a new set of skills likely to be attractive especially for young people (IFPRI, 2019).

OPPORTUNITIES IN INFORMATION AND COMMUNICATION TECHNOLOGIES

Generalities

If in the past, technological innovations were generally incorporated into machines of different types, they are today incorporated, to a still limited but increasing extent, in mechanisms and tools of electronic type, which one can hardly call machines (Labini, 2007). The idea, however, that digital solutions can be used in agriculture is certainly not new.

Like all industries, agriculture has opened up to information and communication technologies (ICTs). Digital is an increasingly important determinant in agricultural and rural development strategies (Centre de cooperation internationale en recherche agronomique pour le développement [CIRAD], 2019). According to this institution, the use of mobile phones and the Internet is the typical example of technologies that have become essential, when they were only very little adopted by the agricultural world at the turn of the millennium. The adoption of ICTs and related services therefore penetrates an agricultural world connected to modernity and the digital revolution, and this even leads to an agricultural revolution in the modes of production and practices implemented to provide increasingly demanding consumers of food in quantity and quality (CIRAD, 2019). Similarly, according to World Bank (2019), the impressive (but not yet complete) penetration of the Internet and mobile telephone networks, even in remote rural areas of low-income countries, offers new possibilities for the dissemination of technical information and educational materials for farmers and agricultural service providers.

It also figures among the research of other authors such as Saidu, Clarkson, Adamu, Mohammed, & Jibo (2017), that improving market activities, exchanging relevant information, gaining profits, networking the agricultural sector worldwide, carrying out research and developing economic growth strategies for self-sufficiency is one of the possible benefits of ICT in the agricultural sector.

These ICTs also provide access to information. Thus, Oladele (2015) shows in his study carried out among farmers in South Africa that 66.9 percent of farmers had very positive responses that ICT would increase the availability of information, 60.9 percent had very positive responses that ICTs would increase knowledge of farming activities, 60.4 percent were very favorable of ICTs improving the quality of information and record keeping respectively, 58 percent were very favorable of ICTs raising awareness of agricultural events, news and information flow, 55.6 percent had very positive responses that ICT improves information accuracy, 55 percent were very favorable that ICT improved capacity building, 54.4 percent of farmers had very positive responses that ICTs encourage data sharing and dissemination and respectively improve access to agricultural inputs (54.4 percent), strengthening the partnership with research and extension (53.8percent), improving access to agricultural markets (52.7 percent), improving the timeliness of information and improving the relevance of the research respectively (50.3 percent).

IFPRI (2019) also reports that in Kenya, the results show that farmers who participated in an ICT market information systems project, used (or upgraded) seeds and fertilizers more per acre, as well as labor and land productivity. In the same country, other evidence shows that ICTs greatly facilitate the provision of agricultural extension services to farmers, by facilitating the adoption of new agronomic practices, which translates into improved yields and increased income of farm households. These IFPRI claims can be supported by a previous study by Kumar & Sankarakumar (2012). The latter showed that 49 percent of farmers who had not changed the application of pesticides and fertilizers before using ICT in agriculture, had some change in the application of pesticides and fertilizer after using ICT in agriculture; 48.3 percent of farmers who were not in a position to reduce poverty status before benefiting from the application of ICT in agriculture, were in a position to reduce poverty after having used the application of ICT in Agriculture ; 52 percent of farmers who did not experience their improvement in agricultural wealth before using the application of ICT in agriculture, have an improvement in agricultural wealth after using the application of ICT in agriculture; 42.3 percent who had not improved the marketing of agricultural products before using ICT in agriculture, experienced some improvement in the marketing of agricultural products after using ICT in agriculture.

An inclusive and digital-assisted agricultural transformation could help bring significant improvements to the livelihoods of the 250 million smallholder farmers and pastoralists in Africa (CTA, 2019b). These digital tools can improve efficiency, transparency, aggregation and market integration.

However, despite the rapid expansion of digital, not all rural areas and all farmers are familiar with or connected to these innovations (Cosimo, 2016). According to (World Bank, 2016), the digital dividends are also not shared equally, neither geographically nor socially.

Some Opportunities and Stylized Facts on the use of the Telephone and the Evolution of the Internet

Choice of Countries

Sub-Saharan Africa has four geographic sub-regions. Five countries were randomly selected from each sub-region. Some, however, such as Mali, Senegal, Ethiopia, Rwanda, South Africa, Botswana, Gabon were chosen automatically because of the efforts that their respective governments made for the agricultural sector, but also because of the relatively high telephone subscription rate and the high Internet usage rate.

Stylized Facts and Opportunities about Using the Telephone

Figure 1 shows the evolution of the telephone subscription rate between 2000 and 2013 for twenty countries in Sub-Saharan Africa selected from the four main regions that make it up. The trend has generally changed for all countries. This finding is in line with the World Bank's assertion (2019) that over the past decade, telephone subscriptions have become ubiquitous in most countries of the world. Some countries, however, such as Djibouti, Eritrea, Ethiopia, Central Africa, the Democratic Republic of the Congo have rates that have evolved slowly; the subscription rate until 2013 is less than 50 percent, which is in line with Cosimo's assertion (2016) that all farmers are not yet familiar or connected to these innovations. However, others experienced a very rapid evolution and exceeded the 100 percent mark of the subscription rate in 2013. These are mainly Ghana, Mali, South Africa, Botswana, Namibia and Gabon. A third category of country also exists and includes those who have not reached the 100 percent subscriber mark but have largely exceeded the average. These are Cote d'Ivoire, Nigeria, Senegal, Kenya, Lesotho and Swaziland.

Regarding this digital tool, numerous studies have shown the opportunities it can offer. According to Murthy (cited by Chhachhar et al., 2014, p. 283), some farmers use the telephone to obtain the price of the product on the market while others communicate directly with customers to sell their products at a better price. In addition, farmers use SMS services to keep themselves informed of weather conditions and the use of pesticides on their farms. This SMS service also has other positive effects for farmers, in particular on the yields of their farms. Thus, Casaburi et al., (2014) conducted a study in Kenya and found that small-scale sugar cane producers who had received agricultural advice by SMS just when they needed to do tasks, such as watering their crops, have seen their yields increase by 11.5 percent.

In developing countries, farmers have been shown to use mobile phones to obtain information on different markets and weather information, while others communicate with agricultural experts to obtain information on the use of pesticides in their crops holdings (Chhachhar, 2014). In Kenya, for example, cell phones can speed up the way farmers in rural Kenya obtain trade and manipulate information. They rework the way farmers interact with markets and cities. The use of mobile phones can also reduce information asymmetries, allowing users to access marketing opportunities they would otherwise have missed (Muriithi, Bett & Ogaleh, 2009). In the same country, Karakaraa & Osabuohien (2018) have shown that with MPESA, farmers can send and receive money using their MTN mobile phones. In Ghana, too, mobile money services have enabled many rural households that were previously unbanked to save, send and receive money through their mobile phones. The MAKWACHA smart card system in Malawi also enables rural farmers to receive payments and purchase agricultural inputs electronically. This has led the once unbanked rural population to have some form of financial service with the use of their cell phones.

Steinen et al., have shown that the use of mobile phones has a significant effect on the sale price of pineapple and the income derived from agricultural production by the household (as cited by Anselme & Adégbidi, 2012, p. 244). Thus, with mobile phones, producers have more access to information and thus increase their negotiating capacity and therefore the prices they receive. This very significant effect on the price obtained and income, confirms the results of Okello and Okello & Swinton who found that the effect of market access for producers can be significant for crops commercials and precious fruits (cited by Anselme & Adégbidi, 2012, p. 244).

According to Chete & Fasoyiro (2014), the probability of using mobile phones is 0.276 times higher among farmers who practice farming as their main activity compared to those who are not. This is probably due to the fact that the former are more inclined to find buyers for their products in order to increase the income of their daily life and would therefore seek information from the market using several platforms, including mobile phones.

However, not all studies of ICT, including the telephone, have provided positive impact results. For Chavula (2014), only the main telephone lines have a positive and very significant impact on agricultural production, while mobile subscriptions and the use of the Internet have an insignificant impact

Figure 1. Evolution of the Telephone subscription rate in the countries of Sub-Saharan Africa
Source: (Author, Africa Agriculture Status Report 2015)

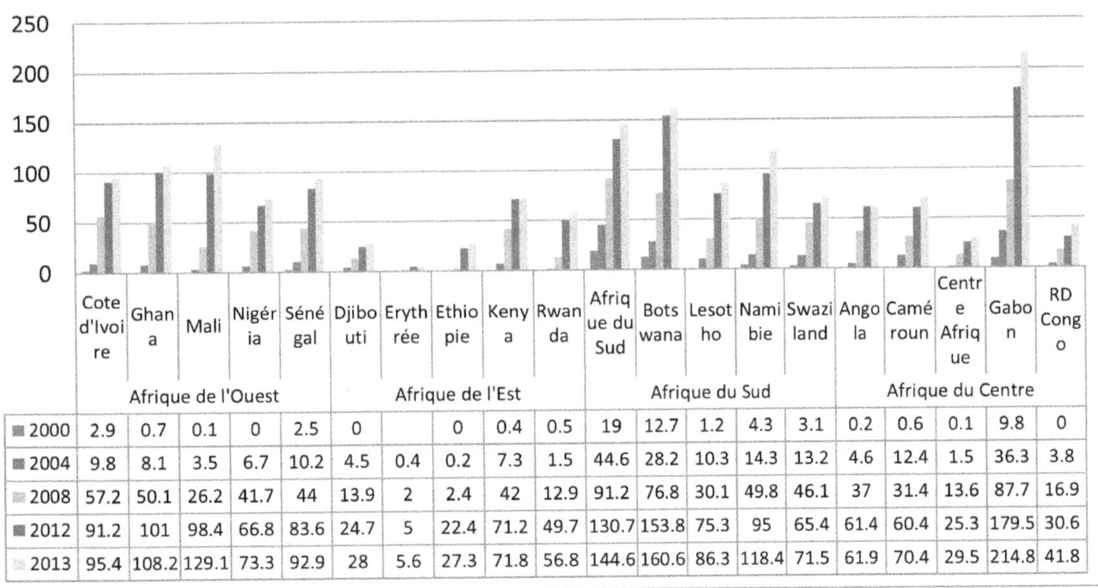

	Afrique de l'Ouest					Afrique de l'Est					Afrique du Sud					Afrique du Centre				
	Cote d'Ivoire	Ghana	Mali	Nigéria	Sénégal	Djibouti	Erythrée	Ethiopie	Kenya	Rwanda	Afrique du Sud	Botswana	Lesotho	Namibie	Swaziland	Angola	Caméroun	Centre Afrique	Gabon	RD Congo
2000	2.9	0.7	0.1	0	2.5	0		0	0.4	0.5	19	12.7	1.2	4.3	3.1	0.2	0.6	0.1	9.8	0
2004	9.8	8.1	3.5	6.7	10.2	4.5	0.4	0.2	7.3	1.5	44.6	28.2	10.3	14.3	13.2	4.6	12.4	1.5	36.3	3.8
2008	57.2	50.1	26.2	41.7	44	13.9	2	2.4	42	12.9	91.2	76.8	30.1	49.8	46.1	37	31.4	13.6	87.7	16.9
2012	91.2	101	98.4	66.8	83.6	24.7	5	22.4	71.2	49.7	130.7	153.8	75.3	95	65.4	61.4	60.4	25.3	179.5	30.6
2013	95.4	108.2	129.1	73.3	92.9	28	5.6	27.3	71.8	56.8	144.6	160.6	86.3	118.4	71.5	61.9	70.4	29.5	214.8	41.8

on agricultural production, which shows the under-use of both technologies in the agricultural sector. Despite the proliferation of mobile phones, this result could show that these technologies, although used effectively in certain agricultural initiatives, could not have had a significant impact on the agricultural production of the sector in the countries of the continent.

The use of the mobile phone also helps to solve the market failures that farmers face. Moreover, Kirui, Okello, Nyikal & Njiraini (2013), showed that the use of money transfer services by mobile phone considerably increased the level of annual use of inputs by households by $ 42, agricultural marketing household income of 37% and annual household income of $ 224.

Role of the Internet and Stylized Facts on Its Evolution

The Internet of Things, a term used to describe the connection of devices to the Internet, makes it possible to generate and transfer huge amounts of data. With an annual growth of 30 percent in the number of connections since 2015, the Internet of Things is developing rapidly in Africa. Estimates in developing countries suggest that each additional 10 percent of Internet penetration can increase GDP growth per capita by 1.35 percent (IFPRI, 2019).

According to Zhou, Song, Xie & Zhang (2013), practice has shown that the Internet of Things is of utmost importance in raising the level of agricultural development, improving the overall efficiency of agriculture, promoting level of modern agricultural transformation.

Figure 2 thus illustrates the evolution from 2000 to 2013 of the Internet access rate of the countries of Sub-Saharan Africa. The countries with the least internet access with a rate less than or equal to 10 percent are by far the most numerous. For West Africa, this concerns Mali with a use rate of 2.3 percent in 2013, Djibouti, Eritrea, Ethiopia and Rwanda for East Africa with respective rates of 9.5 percent, 0.9 percent, 1.9 percent and 8.7 percent. For the southern area of Africa, only Lesotho has a rate below 10 percent, with only 5 percent in 2013. All the countries of Central Africa also have Internet use rates below 10 percent, except Angola which has a rate higher than 10 percent. According to the International Monetary Fund [IMF] (2018), the level of Internet penetration in sub-Saharan Africa is the lowest in the world. It is less than half the world average. This could be linked to the high cost of the Internet. The price of a fixed broadband connection is higher in sub-Saharan Africa than in other regions (IMF, 2018); only mobile broadband prices are similar, in dollars, to those seen in other countries.

The most powered countries remain Nigeria with 38 percent in 2013, Kenya with 39 percent and South Africa with 48.9 percent. The latter represents the highest rate of Internet use in Sub-Saharan Africa. We note, however, that these countries which are the most connected to the Internet are fairly stable economically. South Africa ranks second after Mauritius. According to the African ranking of the most competitive economies of the World Economic Forum, Kenya occupies the eighth place and Nigeria, the sixteenth. However, according to the 2019 report on the digitalization of agriculture, CTA claims that Kenya is the most connected country to the Internet, although no statistics have been provided. Countries like Senegal, Swaziland and Angola also have fairly significant internet access with rates of 20.9 percent, 24.7 percent and 19.1 percent respectively.

However, difficulties are noted at this level also. The first is that women are much less represented in the use of digital technologies in general (25 percent) and the Internet in particular than men (Msengezi & Williams, 2019). They constitute around 45 percent of the agricultural workforce (CTA, 2019b). The second is its high cost. Sub-Saharan Africa is the region where the Internet is most expensive in the world according to the report (2013) of the International Telecommunication Union on international Internet connectivity in

Figure 2. Evolution of the Internet rate in Sub-Saharan African countries
Source: (Africa Agriculture Status Report 2015)

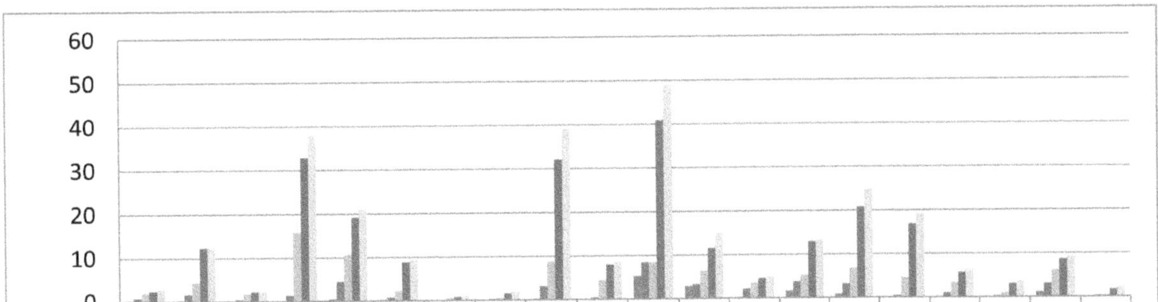

	Afrique de l'Ouest					Afrique de l'Est					Afrique du Sud					Afrique du Centre				
	Cote d'Ivoire	Ghana	Mali	Nigéria	Sénégal	Djibouti	Erythrée	Ethiopie	Kenya	Rwanda	Afrique du Sud	Botswana	Lesotho	Namibie	Swaziland	Angola	Caméroun	Centre Afrique	Gabon	RD Congo
2000	0.2	0.2	0.1	0.1	0.4	0.2	0.1	0	0.3	0.1	5.3	2.9	0.2	1.6	0.9	0.1	0.3	0.1	1.2	0
2004	0.8	1.7	0.4	1.3	4.4	0.8		0.2	3	0.4	8.4	3.3	2.2	3.8	3.2	0.5	1	0.2	3	0.2
2008	1.9	4.3	1.6	15.9	10.6	2.3	0.5	0.5	8.7	4.5	8.4	6.3	3.6	5.3	6.9	4.6	3.4	1	6.2	0.4
2012	2.4	12.3	2.2	32.8	19.2	8.9	0.8	1.5	32.1	8	41	11.5	4.6	12.9	20.8	16.9	5.7	3	8.6	1.7
2013	2.6	12.3	2.3	38	20.9	9.5	0.9	1.9	39	8.7	48.9	15	5	13.2	24.7	19.1	6.4	3.5	9.2	2.2

sub-Saharan Africa. According to this institution, of the twenty countries where connection is more expensive, fourteen are countries of Sub-Saharan Africa, which would not fail to affect the agricultural sector.

A Solution for States

For countries like Rwanda, for example, the government has exploited digital solutions to consolidate agricultural activities, thus facilitating overall decision-making regarding price fixing, storage and supply of inputs for basic products (CTA, 2019c). And that could intensify with the creation of his new Smartphone Company which has already registered its first products.

Digital solutions also help governments make more informed decisions and support agricultural planning, albeit more slowly than food industry (CTA, 2019c). However, for many countries the potential of digital solutions to support macro-level decision-making would be largely untapped.

Figure 3 shows the overall percentage of agricultural spending by states in relation to their total spending. Regardless of spending on digital, countries like Senegal, Ethiopia, Rwanda and the Democratic Republic of Congo are the countries that spent the most on the agricultural sector in 2014 with respective rates of 7.8 percent, 8.2 percent, 9.1percent and 7.2 percent. However, countries like Mali and Ethiopia had higher spending on the agricultural sector in 2008 and 2012, with rates reaching 15.5 percent at times. Some countries such as Djibouti, South Africa, and Angola are the least dynamic countries in agricultural spending with rates between 0.8 and 1.5 percent in 2014.

Figure 3. Evolution of government spending for the agricultural sector in Sub-Saharan African countries
Source: (Africa Agriculture Status Report 2015)

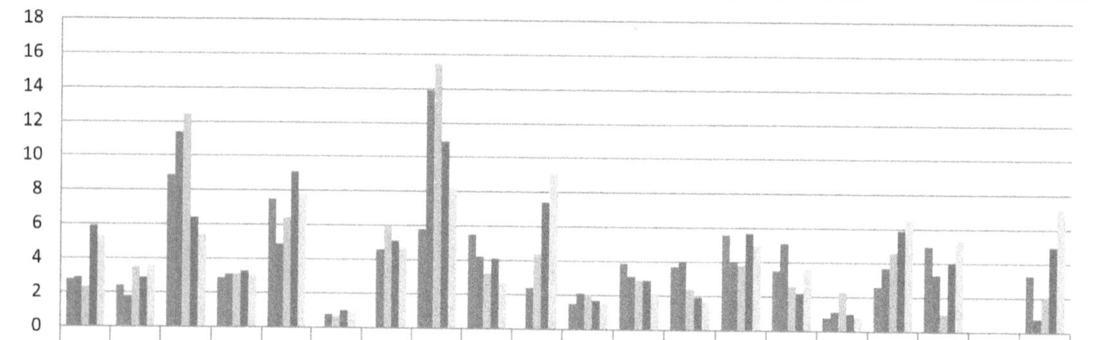

	Afrique de l'Ouest					Afrique de l'Est					Afrique du Sud					Afrique du Centre				
	Cote d'Ivoire	Ghana	Mali	Nigéria	Sénégal	Djibouti	Erythrée	Ethiopie	Kenya	Rwanda	Afrique du Sud	Botswana	Lesotho	Namibie	Swaziland	Angola	Caméroun	Centre Afrique	Gabon	RD Congo
2000	2.8	2.4	8.9	2.9	7.5			5.8	5.5		1.5	3.9	3.7	5.6	3.5	0.8	2.6	5		3.3
2004	2.9	1.8	11.4	3.1	4.9	0.8	4.6	13.9	4.2	2.4	2.1	3.1	4	4	5.1	1.1	3.7	3.3		0.8
2008	2.3	3.5	12.5	3.1	6.4	0.7	6	15.5	3.2	4.4	2	2.9	2.4	3.8	2.6	2.3	4.6	1		2
2012	5.9	2.9	6.4	3.3	9.1	1	5.1	10.9	4.1	7.4	1.7	2.9	1.9	5.7	2.2	1	5.9	4		5
2014	5.3	3.6	5.4	3.1	7.8	0.9	4.7	8.2	2.7	9.1	1.5	2.1	1.7	5	3.6	0.8	6.6	5.3		7.2

Constraints in the Adoption and Success of ICT in the Agricultural Sector

Although Information and Communication Technologies play an important role for farmers, there are many constraints related to it. Many studies conducted in Africa highlight these different constraints. Thus, according to Syed, Urooj, & Meela (2016), one of the constraints is the lack of funding resulting in the non-applicability of information leading to an insignificant impact of ICT on production. For other authors like Kumar & Sankarakumar (2012), poor rainfall and poor irrigation facilities make dispassionate to access ICT application on agriculture, what is another problem associated with availing ICT application in Agriculture and they are ranked in second and third position and their mean score values shows 6.67 and 6.64 respectively.

It is the same for the lack of education of farmers, (which does not respond to access to ICT applications on agriculture), information on market prices, supply and demand, negatively affect the price paid to farmers. Lack of awareness of the application of ICT in agriculture, the inadequate availability of ICT services to rural farmers and the lack of mechanisms to extend the application of ICT to rural areas in turn affects access to the application ICT in agriculture Kumar and Sankarakumar (2012).

For Saidu et al (2017), staff, insufficient infrastructure, harmonization of knowledge and language, electricity consumption and farmers' perception are some of the challenges and problems that hinder the success of the implementation of ICT in agricultural growth.

The study by Chete et al. (2014) also shows a number of constraints in the adoption of information and communication technologies. So, according to their study of a sample of women farmers in Nigeria, 29 percent of respondents had little knowledge of the use of ICT (mobile phone) tools for agricultural transactions, 21 percent had no phones, and 10 percent had a low level of education. At the same time, 9 percent had an inadequate electricity supply, 7 percent had little knowledge of ICT applications, 5 percent had an age-related constraint, and another 5 percent of women farmers were distant from ICT establishment.

A final targeted study classifies the constraints by levels, in this case the severe constraints and the light constraints. Among the serious constraints are the unstable market price, insufficient funding as well as an insufficient supply of innovation as well as the high cost of innovation. Among the light constraints however, there are lighter constraints such as the shortage of land for agriculture and disease attacks (Ayoade & Akintonde, 2012).

CONCLUSION AND RECOMMENDATION

Agriculture represents the most accessible sector in terms of employment in Sub-Saharan Africa, employing 60 percent of the active population (IFPRI, 2019) or just fewer than 70 percent according to other sources such as Organisation Internationale du Travail [OIT] (2018). However, it no longer attracts new incoming to the labor market in a context where the available agricultural active population will structurally increase in the coming decades. This situation is therefore potentially generating a significant increase in migratory flows to cities. Agriculture must therefore make its priority a transformation oriented towards a better ability to adopt new technologies in order to attract these new incoming to the labor market and keep those who are there. The consequences would be a "new" modernization of agriculture, to encourage agricultural entrepreneurship (CTA, 2019b) to include 65 to 75 percent of young African migrants who seek more remunerative jobs on the regional and international market and reduce the food and nutritional insecurity for inclusive growth.

To this end, public policies could focus on two main areas. The first is education in general and education oriented towards the use of digital technologies and services in a particular way. This human capital is necessary, even compulsory, for agricultural actors wishing to integrate into this new deal in agriculture. The latter facilitates agricultural work. The second axis concerns the promotion of research and development. The relative stagnation of agricultural productivity and yields in recent years, particularly in Sub-Saharan Africa, testifies to the great need for new innovative solutions for the agricultural sector, on which more households depend for their survival and their basic needs. Research and development constitutes a lever for transformation of the agricultural sector, which questions the forecasts given by the World Bank (2019) on the decrease in investment in research in Africa and the role that donors play in this decrease.

REFERENCES

Adesina, A. A., & Zinnah, M. M. (1993). Technology characteristics, farmers' perceptions and adoption decisions: A Tobit model application in Sierra Leone. *Agricultural Economics*, *4*(4), 297–311. doi:10.1111/j.1574-0862.1993.tb00276.x

Alary, V. (2006). L'adoption de l'innovation dans les zones agropastorales vulnérables du Maghreb. *De Boeck Supérieur. Afrique Contemporaine*, *219*(3), 81–101. doi:10.3917/afco.219.0081

Alene, A. D., & Manyong, V. M. (2006). Farmer-to-farmer technology diffusion and yield variation among adopters: The case of improved cowpea in northern Nigeria. *Agricultural Economics*, *35*(2), 203–211. doi:10.1111/j.1574-0862.2006.00153.x

Arena, R., & Lazaric, N. (2003). La théorie évolutionniste du changement économique de Nelson et Winter: Une analyse économique ré prospective. *Revue économique*, *54*(2), 329–354. doi:10.3917/reco.542.0329

Ayoade, A. R., & Akintonde, J. O. (2012). Constraints to Adoption of Agricultural Innovations among Women Farmers in Isokan Local Government Area, Osun State. *International Journal of Humanities and Social Science*, *2*(8), 57–61.

Baffoe-Asare, R., Danquah, J. A., & Annor-Frempong, F. (2013). Socioeconomic Factors Influencing Adoption of Codapec and Cocoa High-tech Technologies among Small Holder Farmers in Central Region of Ghana. *American Journal of Experimental Agriculture*, *2*(2), 277–292. doi:10.9734/AJEA/2013/1969

Bandiera, O., & Rasul, I. (2006). Social networks and technology adoption in Northern Mozambique. *Economic Journal (London)*, *116*(514), 869–902. doi:10.1111/j.1468-0297.2006.01115.x

Casaburi, L., & Wills, J. (2014). *Innovations for Poverty Action (IPA): Agricultural Micro insurance for Sugar Cane Farmers in Kenya*. Retrieved February 30, 2020, from: https://www.poverty-action.org/study/agricultural-microinsurance-cane-farmers-kenya

Caswell, M., Fuglie, K., Ingram, C., Jans, S., & Kascak, C. (2001). Adoption of Agricultural Production Practices: Lessons Learned from the U.S. Department of Agriculture Area Studies Project. *Agricultural Economics*, *792*, 1–111.

Centre de coopération internationale en recherche agronomique pour le développement. (2019). *AgriNumA: Le 1er rendez-vous de l'agriculture numérique en Afrique de l'Ouest. 2019*. Récupéré le 15 Février 2020 de: https://www.cirad.fr/actualites/toutes-les-actualites/communiques-de-presse/2019/agriculture-numerique-en-afrique-de-l-ouest

Centre technique de coopération agricole et rurale. (2019b, Juin). Jeunes et emploi: L'agriculture plutôt que l'émigration. *Spore, 193*, 1-48.

Centre technique de coopération agricole et rurale. (2019c). *The digitalisation of African agriculture report 2018–2019*. Bruxelles: CTA.

Centre technique de coopération agricole et rurale (éd.). (2019a). *Ils l'ont fait: Etre jeune et entreprendre dans le secteur agricole: Succes stories*. Bruxelles: CTA.

Chavula, H. P. (2014). The role of ICTs in Agricultural production in Africa. *Journal of Development and Agricultural Economics*, *6*(7), 279–289. doi:10.5897/JDAE2013.0517

Chete, O. B., & Fasoyiro, S. B. (2014). Impact of ICT-based Initiative (Mobile Phone) On Market Access by Women Farmers in Nigeria. *World Rural Observations*, *6*(3), 65–71.

Clavel, D., Barro, A., Belay, T., Lahmar, R., & Maraux, F. (2008). Changements techniques et dynamiques d'innovation agricole en Afrique Sahélienne: Le cas du Zai mécanisé au Burkina Faso et de l'introduction d'une cactée en Ethiopie. *La revue en Sciences de l'environnement*, *8*(3), 1-11.

Conseil Ouest et Centre Africain pour la Recherche et le Développement Agricoles. (2018). *Impulser l'innovation 2018-2027, Plan stratégique*. Récupéré le 27 Juin 2019 de: http://www.coraf.org/wp-content/uploads/2019/03/PlanStrategique.pdf

Cosimo, L., & Abis, S. (2016). Innovation et technologie: quels enjeux pour l'agriculture et le monde rural en Méditerranée? *Tendances économiques*, 58-60.

Croppenstedt, A., Demeke, M., & Meschi, M. M. (2003). Technology adoption in the presence of constraints: The case of fertilizer demand in Ethiopia. *Review of Development Economics*, *7*(1), 58–70. doi:10.1111/1467-9361.00175

De Janvry, A., Sadoulet, E., Kyle, E., & Dar, M. (2015). L'Adoption des technologies agricoles: Quelles leçons tirer des expérimentations de terrain? *Revue d'Economie du Developpement*, *4*(23), 129–153. doi:10.3917/edd.294.0129

Deblock, C. (2012). Introduction: Innovation et développement chez Schumpeter. *Revue Interventions économiques Papers in Political Economy,* (46), 1-15.

Dembele, N. N. (2001). *Sécurité alimentaire en Afrique Sub-saharienne: Quelle Stratégie de Réalisation?* PASIDMA, (Document de Travail no. 1). Récupéré le 05 Juillet 2019 de https://pdfs.semanticscholar.org/3a75/662ca2a9fa7807df408104e9eafb4a19ab09.pdf

Ejemeyovwi, J. O., & Osabuohien, E. S. (2018). Investigating the relevance of mobile technology adoption on inclusive growth in West Africa. *The Journal of Academic Social Science*, 1–15.

Feder, G., & Umali, D. L. (1993). The Adoption of Agricultural Innovations: A review. *Technological Forecasting and Social Change*, *43*(3-4), 255–298. doi:10.1016/0040-1625(93)90053-A

Foster, A. D., & Rosenzweig, M. R. (2010). Microeconomics of technology adoption. Economic Growth Center Discussion, Yale University, Paper No. 984, 1-43. doi:10.1146/annurev.economics.102308.124433

Fournier, E. (2001). Schumpeter (1883-1950): Innovation et capitalisme. *Sciences Humaines*, *8*(119), 1–31.

Gedikoglu, H., McCann, L., & Artz, G. (2011). Off-Farm Employment Effects on Adoption of Nutrient Management Practices. *Agricultural and Resource Economics Review*, *2*(2), 293–306. doi:10.1017/S1068280500008078

Grain de Sel. (2012). *Quelles politiques pour les populations rurales pauvres du Sahel?* Author.

Hailu, B. K., Abrha, B. K., & Weldegiorgis, K. A. (2014). Adoption and impact of agricultural technologies on farm income: Evidence from Southern Tigray, Northern Ethiopia. *International Journal of Food and Agricultural Economics*, *2*(4), 91–106.

Hellerstein, D., & Nathaniel, H. (2013). The predictive power of risk preference measures for farming decisions. *European Review of Agriculture Economics*, *40*(5), 1–27. doi:10.1093/erae/jbs043

International Food Policy Research Institute. (2019). *Byte by Byte: Policy Innovation for Transforming Africa's Food System with Digital Technologies. A Malabo Montpellier Panel Report* (3rd ed.). IFPRI.

International Monetary Fund. (2018). *L'avenir de l'emploi en Afrique subsaharienne. Dans Regional Economic Outlook: Sub-Saharan Africa*. Récupéré de: https://www.imf.org/en/Publications/REO/SSA/Issues/2018/09/20/sreo1018

Karakaraa, A. A., & Osabuohien, E. O. (2018). Households' ICT access and bank patronage in West Africa: Empirical insights from Burkina Faso and Ghana. *Technology in Society*, 116–125.

Kato, E., Ringler, C., Yesuf, M., & Bryan, E. (2009). *Soil and water conservation technologies: a buffer against production risk in the face of climate change? Insights from the Nile basin in Ethiopia*. IFPRI Discussion paper 00871. International Food Policy Research Institute.

Kautsky, K. (1900). *La question agraire: étude sur les tendances de l'agriculture moderne*. Éditions V. Giard et E. Brière.

Kebede, Y., Gunjal, K., & Coffin, G. (1990). Adoption of new technologies in Ethiopian agriculture: The case of Tegulet-Bulga District, Shoa province. *Agricultural Economics*, *1*, 27–43.

Kerzazi, L. (2015). L'innovation au cœur des écoles de pensée économique: Une tentative d'analyse appliquée au secteur agroalimentaire québécois. *La Revue Gestion et Organisation*, *7*(2), 93–105. doi:10.1016/j.rgo.2015.07.001

Khanna, M. (2001). Sequential adoption of site-specific technologies and its implications for nitrogen productivity: A double selectivity model. *American Journal of Agricultural Economics*, *1*(1), 35–51. doi:10.1111/0002-9092.00135

Kim, S., Gillespie, J. M., & Paudel, K. P. (2005). The effect of socioeconomic factors on the adoption of best management practices in beef cattle production. *Journal of Soil and Water Conservation*, *3*, 111–120.

Kirui, O. K., Okello, J. J., Nyikal, R. A., & Njiraini, G. W. (2013). Impact of Mobile Phone-Based Money Transfer Services in Agriculture: Evidence from Kenya. *Zeitschrift für Ausländische Landwirtschaft*, *52*(2), 141–162.

Labini, P. S. (2007). Développements scientifiques, innovations technologiques, croissance et productivité. *Revue d'Economie Industrielle*, *118*(118), 79–90. doi:10.4000/rei.1773

Lakomski-laguerre, O. (2006). Introduction à Schumpeter. Alternatives économiques. *Economics and Politics*, *29*, 82–98.

Lambrecht, I., Vanlauwe, B., Merckx, R., & Maertens, M. (2014). Understanding the process of agricultural technology adoption: Mineral fertilizer in eastern DR Congo. *World Development*, *59*, 132–146. doi:10.1016/j.worlddev.2014.01.024

Msengezi, C., & Williams, Y. (2019). Les femmes et la digitalisation de l'agriculture. *Un bulletin d'alerte pour l'agriculture ACP*, 90. Récupéré le 18 Juin 2019 de https://cgspace.cgiar.org/bitstream/handle/10568/99719/ICTUpdate90F.pdf

Muriithi, A. G., Bett, E., & Ogaleh, S. A. (2009). *Information Technology for Agriculture and Rural Development in Africa: Experiences from Kenya*. Paper presented at the Conference on International Research on Food Security, Natural Resource Management and Rural Development, University of Hamburg.

N'Goulakia, L. P. (2015). Afrique subsaharienne: Une identité plurielle, un destin commun. *Géoéconomie*, *73*(1), 59–72. doi:10.3917/geoec.073.0059

Nyaupane, N. P., & Gillespie, J. (2009). *The influences of land tenancy and rotation selection on crawfish farmers' adoption of best management practices*. Paper presented at the annual meeting of Southern Agricultural Economics Association, Atlanta, GA.

Oladele, O. I. (2015). Effect of information communication technology (ICT) on agricultural information access among extension officers in North West province South Africa. *South African Journal of Agricultural Extension*, *43*(2), 30–41. doi:10.17159/2413-3221/2015/v43n2a344

Osabohien, R., Onanuga, O., Aderounmu, B., Matthew, O., & Osabuohien, E. (2020). Social Protection and Employment in Africa's agricultural Sector. *Business: Theory and Practice*, *21*(2), 494–502. doi:10.3846/btp.2020.11945

Pandit, M., Mishra, A. K., Paudel, K. P., Larkin, S. L., Rejesus, R. M., Lambert, D. M., English, B. C., Larson, J. A., Velandia, M. M., Roberts, R. K., & Kotsiri, S. (2011). *Reasons for Adopting Precision Farming: A Case Study of US Cotton Farmers*. Annual Meeting of Southern Agricultural Economics Association, Corpus Christi, TX.

Pouch, T. (2015). L'agriculture et l'enjeu de l'innovation: Dimensions générales et éclairage méditerranéen. *Watch Letter*, *32*, 1–5.

Ricardo, D. (1817). Des principes de l'économie politique et de l'impôt. Les Classiques des sciences sociales, France.

Sadoulet, E., Kyle, E., & Dar, M. (2015). L'adoption des technologies agricoles: Quelles leçons tirer des expérimentations de terrain? *Revue d'Economie du Developpement*, *23*(4), 129–153. doi:10.3917/edd.294.0129

Saidu, A., Clarkson, A. M., Adamu, S. H., Mohammed, M., & Jibo, I. (2017). Application of ICT in Agriculture: Opportunities and Challenges in Developing Countries. *International Journal of Computer Science and Mathematical Theory*, *3*(1), 8–18.

Schneider, K., & Gugerty, M. K. (2011). Agricultural Productivity and Poverty Reduction: Linkages and Pathways. *The Evans School Review*, *121*(1), 1–19. doi:10.7152/esr.v1i1.12249

Tandjigora, A. (2019). Industries et Services ruraux: Supports de la Transformation Rurale dans le contexte d'une Agriculture en dégradation continue: Evidence du Sénégal. *Journal of Economics and Sustainable Development*, *2*, 36–43.

Temple, L., Chiffoleau, Y., & Touzard, J. M. (2018). Une histoire de l'innovation et de ses usages dans l'agriculture. In Innovation et développement dans les systèmes agricoles et alimentaire (pp. 19-37). Paris: Cairn Info.

Teno, G., Lehrer, K., & Kone, A. (2018). Les facteurs de l'adoption des nouvelles technologies en agriculture en Afrique Subsaharienne: Une revue de la littérature. *African Journal of Agricultural and Resource Economics*, (13), 140–151.

Tosakana, N. S. P., Van Tassell, L. W., Wulfhorst, J. D., Boll, J., Mahler, R., Brooks, E. S., & Kane, S. (2010). Determinants of the adoption of conservation practices by farmers in the Northwest Wheat and Range Region. *Journal of Soil and Water Conservation*, *6*(6), 404–412. doi:10.2489/jswc.65.6.404

Touzard, J. M., Temple, L., Faure, G., & Triomphe, B. (2015). Innovation systems and knowledge communities in the agriculture and agrifood sector: A literature review. *Journal of Innovation Economics and Management*, *17*(2), 117–142. doi:10.3917/jie.017.0117

Tremblay, D. (2003). Innovation, management stratégique et économie: Comment la théorie économique rend-elle compte de l'innovation dans l'entreprise? Présenté à la Sixième Conférence de l'AIMS, Montréal, Canada.

Udry, C. (2010). The economics of agriculture in Africa: Notes toward a research program. *African Journal of Agricultural and Resource Economics*, *1*, 284–299.

Union Internationale des Télécommunications. (2013). *Etude sur la connectivité internationale d'Internet en Afrique subsaharienne*. UIT.

Ward, C. E., Vestal, M. K., Doye, D. G., & Lalman, D. L. (2008). Factors affecting adoption of cow-calf production practices in Oklahoma. *Journal of Agricultural and Applied Economics*, *3*(3), 851–863. doi:10.1017/S1074070800002376

World Bank. (2019). *Harvesting Prosperity: Technology and Productivity in agriculture*. World Bank.

World Bank. (2020). *ICT for agriculture*. Open Learning Campus. Retrieved from https://olc.worldbank.org/content/ict-agriculture

Yung, J. M., & Bosc, P. M. (1999). Schumpeter au Sahel. In L'innovation en agriculture: Questions de méthodes et terrains d'observation (pp.143-168). Paris: IRD. doi:10.4000/books.irdeditions.15741

Zhou, L., Song, L., Xie, C., & Zhang, J. (2013). Applications of Internet of Things in the Facility Agriculture. *International Federation for Information Processing,* 297-303.

Zhou, L., Song, L., Xie, C., & Zhang, J. (2013). Applications of Internet of Things in the Facility Agriculture. *International Federation for Information Processing,* 297-303.

Zoundi, S.J., & Hitimana, L. (2002). Défis de l'accès des exploitations familiales aux innovations agricoles en Afrique de l'Ouest: implications institutionnelles et politiques. *Club du Sahel et de l'Afrique de l'Ouest,* 1-15.

KEY TERMS AND DEFINITIONS

CTA: Technical Center for Agricultural and Rural Cooperation.

IFPRI: International Food Policy and Research Institute.

Internet: Computer network (also available on smartphone) whose access allows having information in real time.

Risk-Averse: Refusal to take risks, to engage in innovation.

Schumpeter: Austrian economist (1883-1950) very famous for his theories on innovation.

SMS: Short Message Service. It allows farmers to have weather information in order to anticipate their production process and have better yields.

Telephone: Information and communication technology tool, allowing people in general and farmers in particular to join at any time and from a distance. It makes it easier for farmers to receive meteorological information and also allows an easy flow of production.

Temple: French economist and researcher from the Center for International Cooperation in Agronomic Research for Development (CIRAD). He is the author of several publications on innovation in agriculture, particularly in Africa.

APPENDIX

Table 1. Evolution of the Telephone subscription rate in the countries of Sub-Saharan Africa

		Année													
		2000	2001	2002	2003	2004	2005	2006	2007	2008	2009	2010	2011	2012	2013
Afrique de l'Ouest	Cote d'Ivoire	2,9	4,4	6,2	7,6	9,8	13,5	23	41,6	57,2	70,9	82,2	89,4	91,2	95,4
	Ghana	0,7	1,3	2	3,9	8,1	13,4	23,7	33,8	50,1	63,8	71,9	85,3	101	108,2
	Mali	0,1	0,2	0,4	2,2	3,5	6,4	12,3	19,9	26,2	32,9	53,2	75,1	98,4	129,1
	Nigéria	0	0,2	1,2	2,4	6,7	13,3	22,6	27,4	41,7	48	54,7	58	66,8	73,3
	Sénégal	2,5	3	5,3	7,3	10,2	15,4	25,8	30,5	44	54,8	64,4	70,2	83,6	92,9
Afrique de l'Est	Djibouti	0	0,4	2	3	4,5	5,7	5,7	8,7	13,9	15,7	19,9	22,8	24,7	28
	Erythrée					0,4	0,8	1,2	1,6	2	2,5	3,2	4,1	5	5,6
	Ethiopie	0	0	0,1	0,1	0,2	0,5	1,1	1,5	2,4	4,8	7,9	15,8	22,4	27,3
	Kenya	0,4	1,9	3,6	4,7	7,3	12,9	20	30,1	42	48,6	61	66,8	71,2	71,8
	Rwanda	0,5	0,7	0,9	1,4	1,5	2,4	3,3	6,4	12,9	23,1	32,7	39,9	49,7	56,8
Afrique du Sud	Afrique du Sud	19	24	30,1	36,6	44,6	71,7	82,6	86,9	91,2	92,8	99,2	124,1	130,7	144,6
	Botswana	12,7	18,6	18,4	24,3	28,2	30,1	43,4	60,1	76,8	96	120	146	153,8	160,6
	Lesotho	1,2	3	7,3	6,6	10,3	13	18,4	24,7	30,1	33,2	49,2	60,7	75,3	86,3
	Namibie	4,3	5,5	7,7	11,3	14,3	22,1	29,7	38,5	49,8	76,1	89,5	99	95	118,4
	Swaziland	3,1	5,1	6,3	7,8	13,2	18,1	22,4	33,5	46,1	56,6	60,8	63,2	65,4	71,5
Afrique du Centre	Angola	0,2	0,5	0,9	2,3	4,6	9,7	17,8	28	37	42,8	48,1	59,8	61,4	61,9
	Caméroun	0,6	2,6	4,2	6,3	12,4	12,4	16,8	23,8	31,4	39,8	41,9	49,6	60,4	70,4
	Centre Afrique	0,1	0,3	0,3	1	1,5	2,5	2,7	8,3	13,6	20,2	22,5	22,4	25,3	29,5
	Gabon	9,8	11,9	21,7	22,8	36,3	53,4	63,6	80,8	87,7	95,4	103,5	148,7	179,5	214,8
	RD Congo	0	0,3	1,1	2,4	3,8	5,1	7,9	11,5	16,9	15,6	19	24,5	30,6	41,8

Source: (Africa Agriculture Status Report 2015)

Table 2. Evolution of the Internet rate in Sub-Saharan African countries

		2000	2001	2002	2003	2004	2005	2006	2007	2008	2009	2010	2011	2012	2013
Afrique de l'Ouest	Cote d'Ivoire	0,2	0,4	0,5	0,8	0,8	1	1,5	1,8	1,9	2	2,1	2,2	2,4	2,6
	Ghana	0,2	0,2	0,8	1,2	1,7	1,8	2,7	3,9	4,3	5,4	7,8	14,1	12,3	12,3
	Mali	0,1	0,2	0,2	0,3	0,4	0,5	0,7	0,8	1,6	1,8	1,9	2	2,2	2,3
	Nigéria	0,1	0,1	0,3	0,6	1,3	3,5	5,5	6,8	15,9	20	24	28,4	32,8	38
	Sénégal	0,4	1	1	2,1	4,4	4,8	5,6	7,7	10,6	14,5	16	17,5	19,2	20,9
Afrique de l'Est	Djibouti	0,2	0,3	0,5	0,6	0,8	1	1,3	1,6	2,3	4	6,5	7	8,9	9,5
	Erythrée	0,1	0,2	0,2					0,4	0,5	0,5	0,6	0,7	0,8	0,9
	Ethiopie	0	0	0,1	0,1	0,2	0,2	0,3	0,4	0,5	0,5	0,8	1,1	1,5	1,9
	Kenya	0,3	0,6	1,2	2,2	3	3,1	7,5	8	8,7	10	14	28	32,1	39
	Rwanda	0,1	0,2	0,3	0,4	0,4	0,6		2,1	4,5	7,7	8	7	8	8,7
Afrique du Sud	Afrique du Sud	5,3	6,3	6,7	7	8,4	7,5	7,6	8,1	8,4	10	24	34	41	48,9
	Botswana	2,9	3,4	3,4	3,3	3,3	3,3	4,3	5,3	6,3	6,2	6	8	11,5	15
	Lesotho	0,2	0,3	1,1	1,5	2,2	2,6	3	3,4	3,6	3,7	3,9	4,2	4,6	5
	Namibie	1,6	2,4	2,6	3,4	3,8	4	4,4	4,8	5,3	6,5	11,6	12	12,9	13,2
	Swaziland	0,9	1,3	1,8	2,4	3,2	3,7	3,7	4,1	6,9	8,9	11	18,1	20,8	24,7
Afrique du Centre	Angola	0,1	0,1	0,3	0,4	0,5	1,1	1,9	3,2	4,6	6	10	14,8	16,9	19,1
	Cameroun	0,3	0,3	0,4	0,6	1	1,4	2	2,9	3,4	3,8	4,3	5	5,7	6,4
	Centre Afrique	0,1	0,1	0,1	0,2	0,2	0,3	0,3	0,4	1	1,8	2	2,2	3	3,5
	Gabon	1,2	1,3	1,9	2,7	3	4,9	5,5	5,8	6,2	6,7	7,2	8	8,6	9,2
	RD Congo	0	0	0,1	0,1	0,2	0,2	0,3	0,4	0,4	0,6	0,7	1,2	1,7	2,2

Source: Africa Agriculture Status Report 2015

Table 3. Evolution of government spending for the agricultural sector in Sub-Saharan African countries

		2000	2001	2002	2003	2004	2005	2006	2007	2008	2009	2010	2011	2012	2013	2014
Afrique de l'Ouest	Cote d'Ivoire	2,8	2,9	2,9	2,9	2,9	2,2	2,7	2,4	2,3	2,7	3	3,3	5,9	5	5,3
	Ghana	2,4	1,2	1,4	1,4	1,8	2,6	2,2	2,5	3,5	2,5	2,7	2,9	2,9	3,4	3,6
	Mali	8,9	12,8	8,9	9,6	11,4	15,5	10,6	10,9	12,5	10	11,8	6,6	6,4	6,3	5,4
	Nigéria	2,9	3,2	3,5	1,9	3,1	3,4	4,1	3,8	3,1	3,6	3,3	2,9	3,3	3,1	3,1
	Sénégal	7,5	4,7	7	7,2	4,9	7,9	7,2	8,9	6,4	9,6	7,6	7,4	9,1	6	7,8
Afrique de l'Est	Djibouti			0,6	0,7	0,8	0,8	0,8	0,7	0,7	0,6	0,7	1	1	0,9	0,9
	Erythrée		5,1	5,1	4,4	4,6	4,3	5,9	6,1	6	6,6	5,6	5,1	5,1	4,9	4,7
	Ethiopie	5,8	8,1	10,2	12,1	13,9	16,5	18,2	16,3	15,5	18,4	11,1	10	10,9	9,1	8,2
	Kenya	5,5	4,8	5	4,6	4,2	3,9	2,8	3,4	3,2	3,9	4,1	4,3	4,1	3,4	2,7
	Rwanda			1,8	2,1	2,4	2,8	3,3	3,4	4,4	3,1	3	6,9	7,4	7,6	9,1
Afrique du Sud	Afrique du Sud	1,5	1,8	2	2,1	2,1	2,3	2,1	2,4	2	1,8	1,7	1,7	1,7	1,5	1,5
	Botswana	3,9	4,1	4,1	3,9	3,1	4,5	3,7	3,4	2,9	2,4	3,4	2,7	2,9	2,1	2,1
	Lesotho	3,7	4,9	3,8	4,2	4	3,8	3,2	2,7	2,4	2,1	1,9	1,8	1,9	1,7	1,7
	Namibie	5,6	5,3	5,2	5	4	6,1	4,6	4,2	3,8	3	7,1	6,4	5,7	4,4	5
	Swaziland	3,5	3,5	3,8	4,1	5,1	3,6	3	3	2,6	2,2	3	2	2,2	3,9	3,6
Afrique du Centre	Angola	0,8	1,3	0,5	0,9	1,1	1,7	1,7	2,8	2,3	2	1,6	1,3	1	1,1	0,8
	Caméroun	2,6	3,1	3	3,3	3,7	3,8	4	4,3	4,6	4,8	5,2	5,5	5,9	6,2	6,6
	Centre Afrique	5	3,1	2,8	3,5	3,3	1,7	1,3	1,2	1	1,7	2,6	2,7	4	4,1	5,3
	Gabon															
	RD Congo	3,3	1	0,8	1,9	0,8	0,7	1,1	1,8	2	3,8	2,4	2,5	5	2,7	7,2

Source: Africa Agriculture Status Report 2015

Chapter 17
Rural-Urban Food Movement:
Role of Road Transportation in Food Chain Analysis

Ayobami Abayomi Popoola
https://orcid.org/0000-0002-9742-0604
University of KwaZulu-Natal, South Africa

Yamah Dele Adeyemi
University of Ibadan, Nigeria

Femi Emmanuel Oni
https://orcid.org/0000-0001-9994-413X
University of KwaZulu-Natal, South Africa

Odunayo Omojola
University of Ibadan, Nigeria

Bamiji Michael Adeleye
Federal University of Technology, Minna, Nigeria

Samuel Medayese
https://orcid.org/0000-0001-6683-0101
University of KwaZulu-Natal, South Africa

Ojoma Gloria Popoola
Kogi State University, Nigeria

ABSTRACT

The production of the food is majorly composite to the rural setting, and the consumption of this food is not only restricted to the rural area. This rural food production and urban area demand/consumption emphasises the need for rural-urban market linkages. This study employed mixed methods to investigate the role of road transport in the flow of food products from rural areas to the urban markets. Ten urban markets were sampled and 250 respondents from urban markets in Ibadan. The study revealed that household collaboration in the production and marketing of food produce exists in Ibadan. It was established that distance and transportation cost plays a vital role in supply volume, pricing, and delivery price. The variance in delivery cost is dependent on factors such as bargaining power, the season of the year, demand, destination, and road condition. In conclusion, improved roads condition and workable traffic policies that eliminate roadblocks are recommended.

DOI: 10.4018/978-1-7998-4817-2.ch017

INTRODUCTION

The fact that nations, settlements cannot survive in isolation brings about interaction and relationship between them. The connection and interaction between settlements is a function of transportation. Transportation is a measure of relationship between places; it helps bring about interaction between human settlements. The nature of relationship between rural settlement and urban centers is dependent on the transport sector. Rural-urban interaction is most times a demand-supply relationship. Rural areas supply the food that the urban centres need for sustainability, while they need these urban centers for their threshold. The rural population most times does not have the population strength (range) to survive in business of food crop production thus it needs the urban centers to demand for food and thus supply (Osabuohien, 2020a; 2020b). What makes interaction easy and feasible is transportation.

Food chain analysis is a concept that helps in understanding the rural and urban market systems developmental impact within a geographical location. Critical to the food system is market linkage, food production and distribution across rural and urban setting in which road transport is imperative.

Transportation as a part of any human activity determines the goods and services available for consumption (Nkegbe et al., 2012). Spatial distribution of facilities, services and goods in space cannot be efficiently maximized if the transport sector is paralyzed. The transport sector is an important component of the economy impacting on development and the welfare of populations. When transport systems are efficient, they provide economic and social opportunities and benefits that result in positive multipliers effects such as better accessibility to markets, employment and additional investments. When transport systems are deficient in terms of capacity or reliability, they can have an economic cost such as reduced or missed opportunities. Studies (Ajiboye and Afolayan, 2009; Tchanche, 2019) noted that road transport is the most common means of transportation and complex network. Its network covers a wide range, physically convenient, highly flexible and usually the most operationally suitable and readily available means of movement of goods and passenger traffic over short, medium and long distances.

Studies (Popoola et al., 2015; Avery et al., 2017) state that transport as a lung to other sector of the economy performs the role of linking supply and demand. Transport contributes to the overall development of a country since it serves as essential means of collecting, moving, transferring and distributing people as well as goods in from place to place. Thus, development is a function of demand for transport. In Northern Nigeria, Yunusa et al. (2002) reported that road improvement in part of rural Kaduna, led to significant increase in agricultural production, farm and non-farm employment and revitalization of economic activities in the area. Buttressing this, Ogunleye et al. (2018) reported that road transport infrastructure investments over the years in Nigeria had brought about an upward movement of agricultural sector in the country. This is because good road networks often ease transport costs and as said by Oni (2000), it tells a great deal about a society and its values. Thus, it can be said that transportation is the life-wire of any environment (Medayese, 2009; Herrero, 2011). Herrero (2011) iterate that transport is an important factor in the context of sustainable development due to the pressure it places on the environment, its, economic and social impacts, and its linkages with other sectors. It is the channel through which information is been diffused from one place to another, knowledge is been shared, and commercial activity takes place. Commercial activity in the instance of this study is focused on the food movement from rural areas to urban market within the food system and analysis.

Agricultural production is very important to the economy of developing nations and Nigeria in particular. Porter (2013) is of the notion that in productive agricultural regions, transport services are essential for the evacuation of produce. In Nigeria, Tunde, and Adeniyi, (2012) stated that, transport is regarded as an important factor involved in agricultural development. This can be postulated that agriculture will depend on transport. Agricultural activities in developing countries are constrained by several factors one of which is poor rural infrastructure and inadequate and poor transport sector. Such is that a poor transport system would necessarily influence costs.

With the challenges of transportation increasing daily and thus varying from one location to another, it is obvious that lack of good transportation networks, poor condition of transport routes, poor planning and traffic congestion are the problems of transportation. These problems have direct effect on the flow of agricultural produce from rural areas to urban centres. The problems militate against the profitable movement of farm products to either rural markets or the urban markets and high selling cost in urban centres. Obinna and Ukoha (2017) narrated the negative effect of poor road condition on cassava farming. Among rural cassava farmers of Abia, Nigeria, it was reported that good road condition and availability of a faster mode (as against the common rickety rural transport system) was key to achieving profitable cassava production and sustainable farming. This is heightened by the fact that neither the farmer nor the rural traders are equipped with enough storage and processing facilities which will enable them access core areas.

The study brasses its argument that three aspects are crucial in effect food delivery system: physical infrastructure, including road networks and affordable transport; relations between producers, traders and consumers; and information on how markets operate, including price fluctuations and consumer preferences. Poor physical infrastructure can have far-reaching consequences on producers' prices, as inadequate roads usually entail prohibitive transport costs.

Badejo (2011) stated that "the transport in Nigeria is better explained as very pathetic and unfortunate, despite huge investment which the sector has enjoyed over the years especially since in independence in 1960". He argued that when measured by all known international standards, the transport situation in Nigeria can be described as severally challenged by many or a combination of different problems which ranges from: corruption, institutional framework problem, poor and lopsided information and data base, unfavourable government policies. The growth and development of other sector of the economy (agricultural production) inclusive is often dependent on an improved transport sector (Popoola et al., 2015). This true as transport helps to close up the demand-supply gap between rural farmlands and urban markets. Against this backdrop, it is considered inevitable to examine the effect of transportation on the flow of farm produce from rural areas to urban centres (markets).

The nature of the agricultural relationship between the rural and urban centres has been between the rural farmlands and urban markets. Urban centres depend heavily and almost entirely on farmers in the rural areas for their requirement of agricultural products (food). The efficiency of the flow of agricultural produce depends on the transport facilities available for use. But this does not mean the productivity level of agriculture is entirely dependent on transportation. Against this backdrop, it is considered inevitable to examine in this chapter the effect of transportation on the flow of farm produce from rural areas to urban centres (markets).*The question that guides this study is what is the role of road transport system on rural-urban food chain analysis.*

STUDY METHODS AND MATERIALS

The case study area-Ibadan is the capital city of Oyo state. The city grew organically as it did not experience any form of conscious physical planning. Ibadan is made-up of eleven (11) local government

Figure 1. Local governments areas of Ibadan

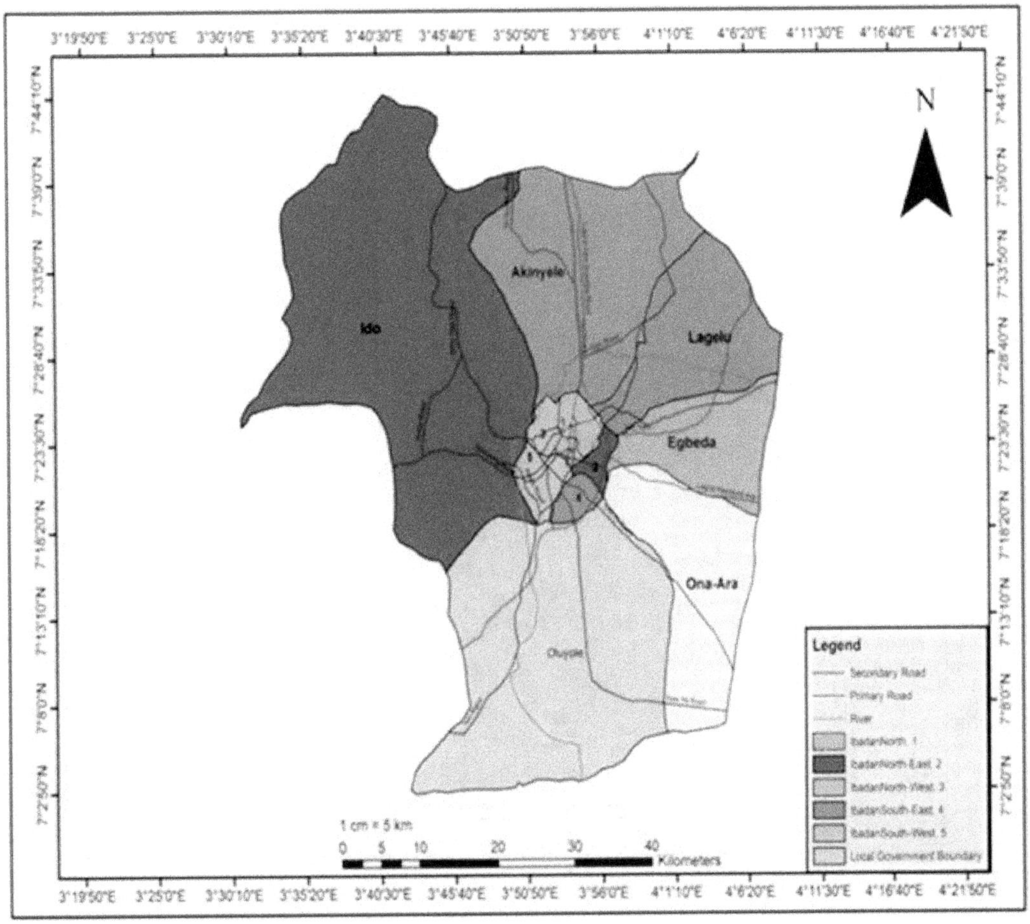

area (LGA), 5 urban metropolitan (Ibadan North West, Ibadan North, Ibadan North East; Ibadan South East; and Ibadan South West) and 6 rural region LGAs (Akinyele; Lagelu; Egbeda; Ona-Ara; Oluyole and Ido) (Figure 1).

Spatially, Ibadan is located near the forest-grassland boundary of south-western Nigeria, 128 km inland northeast of Lagos and 530 km southwest of Abuja, the Federal capital and is a prominent transit point between the coastal region of the south and the areas to the north in the extreme western portion of the country. Despite the metropolitan configuration and urban spatial change of Ibadan (Fabiyi, 2006), agricultural related activities and trading along both formal and informal routes remain two of the major employers of labour in the city (Wahab and Popoola, 2018a&b Wahab et al., 2019). This results in a whooping spatial distribution of markets in the State (Figure 2).

The study made use of survey research design to examine the effect of road transportation on the flow of farm produce from rural areas to urban markets in Ibadan, and the two main types of data that will be used in the study are obtained from both secondary (existing literature) and primary sources in the study. The primary data type to be used for the study is structured questionnaire. Also, to compliment the quantitative data source from questionnaire, the study engaged in an on-spot interview with rural-urban food transport drivers, food crop sellers in urban markets and some rural farmers within the study area.

Figure 2. Identified markets within Ibadan

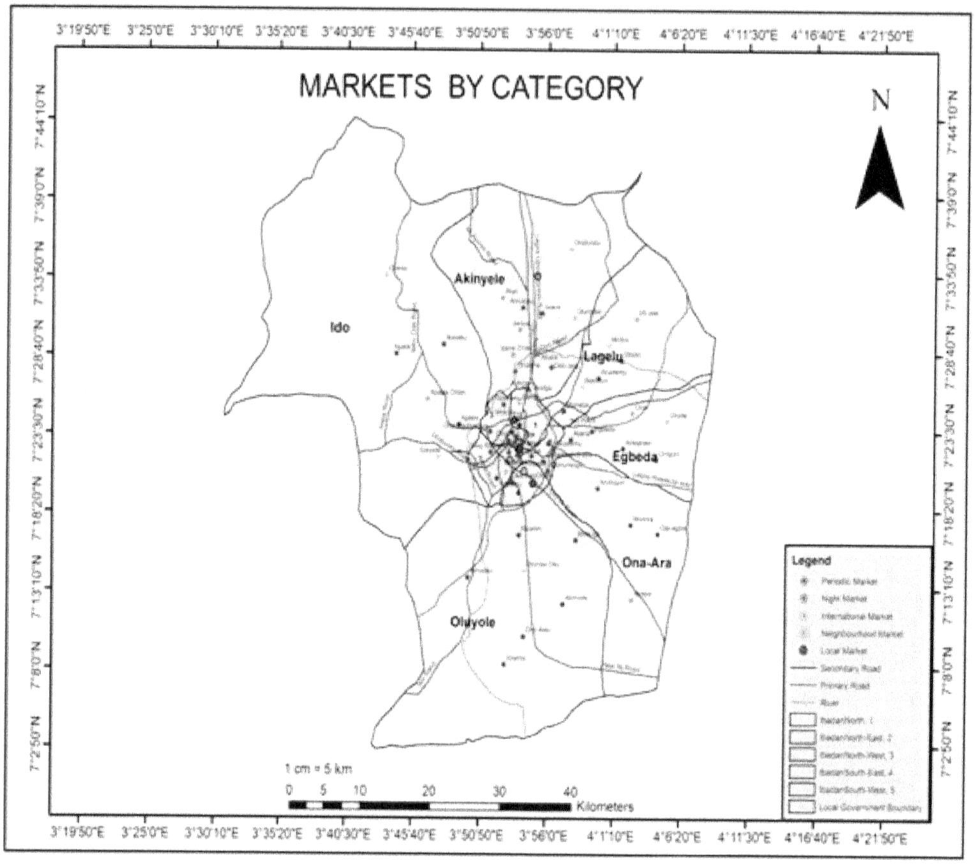

Thematic and narrative analysis was done from the secondary data gathered and the interview responses done in a narrative form such that it was well situated within the thematic discussions. For this study, the main focus of analysis is urban marketers' experiences as relating to the flow of products from rural point of purchase to urban markets. The sample frame for the study comprises of all the urban markets in the five (5) urban local government area of Ibadan (Table 1).

Table 1. Markets in Ibadan metropolis according to LGA

Local Government	Name of Markets in the LGA
Ibadan North	Bodija, Gate, Gbaremu, Sango, Mokola, Sabo, Agbowo, Inalende
Ibadan North East	Oje, Bashorun, Araromi, Agugu, Irefin
Ibadan North West	Dugbe, Agbeni, Alafara-olubadan, Ayeye, Beere, Agbaje, Ifeleye, Ogunpa, Oritamerin
Ibadan South East	Orita-merin, Molete livestock market, Ile-Tuntun, Owode, Oja-oba, Orita-aperin bode
Ibadan South- West	Aleshinloye, Challenge, Orita Challenge.

Source: Oyo State Agricultural Development Programme Office (2017)

For the study, a multi-stage sampling technique was adopted in selecting the study area and the sample size. The urban markets were identified using the data from Oyo State Agricultural Development Programme Office and other markets not mentioned identified in the list where identified purposively. Two (2) markets each was selected from each LGA through balloting making up a total of 10 urban markets. In addition to the balloting, the researcher took into consideration for case study the market's ease of access, popularity, and type (periodic or daily market). Respondents were also chosen purposively (considering the study is focused on food crop- vegetable, fruits pepper and tomatoes traders). For the study, all the markets in the five urban local government areas were identified. Ibadan North has 8 markets, Ibadan north East has 5 markets, Ibadan North West has 9 markets, Ibadan South East has 6 markets, and Ibadan South-West has 3 markets (Figure 3).

Figure 3. Identified markets within the five urban local governments

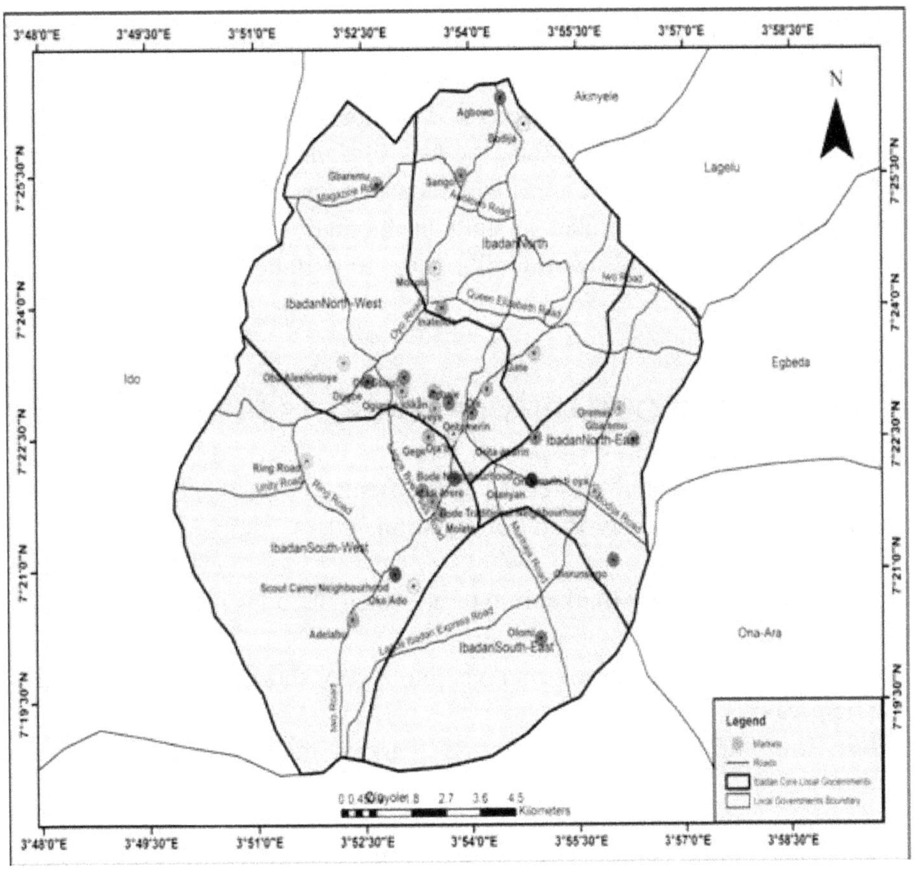

In Ibadan North Local government area Bodija and Sabo market was selected, Bashorun and Oje markets in Ibadan North-East LGA, Beere and Dugbe market in Ibadan North-West LGA, in Ibadan South-East Molete and Orita-aperin market were selected, and Ibadan South-West Challenge and Aleshinloye market were selected (Table 2).

Table 2. List of markets selected for the study according to LGA

Local Government	Name of Markets in the LGA
Ibadan North	Bodija, Sabo.
Ibadan North East	Oje, Bashorun.
Ibadan North West	Dugbe, Beere.
Ibadan South East	Orita-merin, ojaoba.
Ibadan South- West	Molete scout camp, Challenge.

Source: Authors' Field Survey

For proper representation, 25 questionnaires were administered in each of the 10 selected urban markets amounting to a total of 250 respondents. The 25 questionnaire per market was arrived at owing to the difficulty in establishing the total market population (that is food crop traders) in Ibadan markets. Preliminary field observation and informal discussion with the market union leaders reveals that many of the markets do not have stalls, food crop sellers are of transit characteristics, road sellers are many than stall owners and that traditionally it is wrong and cannot be established the total number of market traders of a particular crop. Coupled with this, the lack of database for the number of traders selling crops identified in the local government areas and because most of the markets have no well planned out layout that will give the actual number of stalls in the market. Also, two transporters of the farm products randomly (based on availability and willingness to partake of the study) picked in all the selected markets were interviewed.

CLASSIFICATION AND GEOGRAPHY OF MARKETS IN IBADAN

The complexity of the word "market" makes it very difficult to classify; the market can be classified based on any of the following factors or their combination;

- **Place:** The place factor classify market into three which includes local, national and international markets
- **Time:** This unlike the formal classify markets into a very short period, short period, long period and very long period.
- **Competition:** This, unlike the other two divides markets into a perfect competition and imperfect competition.

For a better understanding of market structure within Ibadan region, the study utilizes the factor of place to categorize markets in the region; thus, each market visited was discussed under local, national and international market. Local Markets also called traditional or indigenous markets are the most common type of market in the study area. This is as a result of the cultural setting of Ibadan. Most of the markets sprung up at the city centre, a warrior's courtyard or front yard, or due to the availability of modern facilities (Schools, transport routes). However, most markets in Ibadan falls within the circle of local markets. This doesn't mean all are predominantly traditional or unplanned. Some of these markets are organized and planned, although become easily deteriorated and look unplanned over the years due to lack of maintenance and sub-standard building material used.

Unplanned local markets example of which is *Oja' Ba /OritaMerin* (see Figure 4) markets are found in the city centre, the markets are dated back to the 80s and they started by people selling farm produce. The market later extended with time and covered a large area in its domain. Oja'ba is patronized both by day and by night; the advent of arterials makes the pattern of the market to be on-street trading with development being of natural, gradual and sense of identity. This gradual development led to Orita-merin market. Another unplanned market *Agbaje/Ayeye markets* are seen as a further extension of the Oja'ba/ Oritamerin market. There is no clear boundary between the two markets, although they are being referred to by users {buyers and sellers} as two separate markets. The stalls are located along the roads. Agbaje is a daily market while Ayeye operates both day and night patronage.

The geography of another unplanned local market called *Inalende market* shows that it is more of a food items markets, it accommodates sellers who are not willing to move to the Mokola market. The market is a linear one as stalls are also positioned along the roads. Its serves as a neighbourhood market for the surrounding residents; *Agbowo market* is a domain of this market was planned for offices and shops; the growth of the University of Ibadan, however, increased the movement of various good sellers to the present day Agbowo market and also *Sango market* emerged as a result of the Old Oyo-Ibadan express road; the market booms because of the presence of its closeness to the Polytechnic of Ibadan. The market features foodstuffs, building materials, cloth and shoes, provisions and cosmetics and plank sellers. These present an argument that the location characteristics present the functioning of a market.

Figure 4. Example of unplanned local market (Oja'ba)
Source: Authors' Field Survey

Planned local markets in Ibadan are born from proper and effective planning decisions. That is, the government decided these market locations. In this study, the example of such a market is the *Mokola market*. The Mokola market came as a result of an attempt to resettle street traders around the Mokola-Roundabout area. The parcel of land was cleared without any stalls put in place by the government. Traders are thus responsible for their stalls. The market, although very small, has all sections ranging from food items to the jewellery section. Another planned market is the Oranyan market: The Oranyan market, unlike the Mokola market, although planned, came into being as a result of the resettlement scheme carried out to enhance renovation of Mapo hall. The Jankara market as being fondly called is much more composed than any other planned local markets. It comprises of livestock, gold, cloth, furniture and light industry sections; although very dirty.

The national market is a form of markets that provides services and goods not only for the area but attract buyers and sellers daily from other parts of the country. It doesn't necessarily mean that these markets must be planned but, they could be once an international market. Examples of national markets identified include Dugbe/ Agbeni Market, Bodija Market and Alesinloye Market. Like national markets that attract nationwide buyers and sellers, *International markets* are markets where both local, national and international goods and services are provided for the consumption of buyers. Activities in this market encompass basic, and non-basic activities and even exportation of locally produced commodities are made possible. Some of the markets visited that qualify as international markets include Bodija and Aleshinloye market.

RURAL-URBAN FLOW OF FARM PRODUCE: THE CONCEPTUAL THINKING

The study was based on the spatial interaction model traced to French geographers' notions of geographic de circulation, including both the movement of physical objects and the communication of intangible ideas. Its fullest development as the most fundamental of all geographic concepts came in the middle 1950s as the seminal contribution of Ed Ullman. Hitherto, geography had been conceptualized as a way of describing the areal differentiation of sites. With the spatial interaction concept, Ullman shifted attention to the situation as a second and equally important locational attribute. Areal differentiation emerged as the outcome of transportation and trade, which permitted specialization in economic activities and concentrations of various social groups. Thus, spatial interaction remains fundamental to understanding the development of distinctive regional geographies.

One methodology of importance to transport geography relates to how to estimate flows between locations, since these flows, known as spatial interactions, enable to evaluate the demand (existing or potential) for transport services. A spatial interaction is a realized movement of people, freight or information between an origin and a destination. It is a transport demand/supply relationship expressed over geographical space. Spatial interactions cover a wide variety of movements such as journeys to work, migrations, tourism, the usage of public facilities, the transmission of information or capital, the market areas of retailing activities, international trade and freight distribution. Economic activities are generating (supply) and attracting (demand) flows. The simple fact that a movement occurs between an origin and a destination underlines that the costs incurred by a spatial interaction are lower than the benefits derived from such an interaction. As such, a commuter is willing to drive one hour because this interaction is linked to an income, while international trade concepts, such as comparative advantages, underline the benefits of specialization and the ensuing generation of trade flows between distant locations.

Spatial interaction is a dynamic flow process from one location to another. It is a general concept that refers to the movement of human beings such as intra-urban commuters or intercontinental migrants but may also refer to traffic in goods such as raw materials or to flows of intangibles such as information. While the origins of the term may be traced French geographers of the early twentieth century, Edward Ullman's (1954) "Geography as Spatial Interaction" is normally cited as the seminal statement of the concept. In Ullman's conception, there were "*three bases for spatial interaction*" or more fundamentally, three reasons for why things move *complementarity, transferability, and intervening opportunity*.

Complementarity explains that there must be a supply and a demand between the interacting locations. Rural farmland (area) is complementary to an urban area (market) because the first is supplying the food while the second is supplying consumers and buyers. The same can be said concerning the complementarity between farmland and urban market buyers. Complementarity refers to the presence of a demand or deficit at one location and a supply or surplus at another without which there is no economic rationale for any movement. Agriculture which comprises of food products according to Hine and Ellis (2001) is best served by consistent high urban, and international, demand, and this is best brought about by an efficient, high volume, transport and marketing system where the transporting and marketing unit costs are low. The rural areas engage in primary activities which form the foundation for any economic development.

Generally, rural areas serve as the base for the production of food and fibre, the major sources of capital formation for a country, and a principal market for domestic manufactures (Olayiwola and Adeleye, 2005). Close to two thirds of the natural wealth in low-income countries is embodied in crop and pasture land (Omiti et al., 2009). Urban areas in Ibadan also depend on the rural areas for such natural wealth such as food for survival. There exists a symbiotic relationship between the rural and urban areas. The rural areas provide the urban centres with farm produce to feed on while the urban areas help in the diffusion of idea and value-added goods to the rural areas. Oluwasola et al. (2008) sermonized that such symbiotic relationship though beneficial to both sides, is expected to specially provide the necessary impetus for improving the economic prospects of the rural areas. Oluwasola et al. (2008) argued that rural-urban linkages represent a powerful strategy for enhancing incomes, increasing productivity, alleviating poverty and promoting employment in the rural areas. While urban centres focuses on the production of value-added commodities, rural areas are advantaged in providing certain goods and services, mainly agricultural products and labour for urban centres (Tacoli, 2003; Satherthwaite, et al., 2010; Mulyana, 2014; Turok and McGranahan, 2019). This process brings into fore the relevance of the transferability principle of the spatial interaction model.

Transferability speaks that freight (food transported), persons (buyer or seller) or information (seasonality of produce and rural farmers contact) being transferred must be supported by transport infrastructures, implying that the origin and the destination must be linked. Costs to overcome distance must not be higher than the benefits of related interaction, even if there is complementarity and no alternative opportunity. Transport infrastructures (modes and terminals) must be present to support an interaction between B and A. Also, these infrastructures must have a capacity and availability which are compatible with the requirements of such an interaction. The goal of spatial interaction is to explain spatial flows. They provide ways to measure flows and predict the consequences of changes in the conditions generating them. Transferability refers to the cost of overcoming distance measured in real economic terms of either time or travel cost.

Settlement functionality is dependent on a good, effective and functioning transport system. Adedeji et al. (2014) stated that sustainable rural development is a function of a number of factors in which transportation is of importance. They went ahead and stated that efficient and effective rural transportation serves as one of the channels for the collection and exchange of goods and services, movement of people, dissemination of information and the promotion of rural economy. Along this line of the relevance of transportation to development, it can be argued that effective transportation eases accessibility to inherent potentials of rural areas which could be harnessed for the development of its economy. In other words, rural transportation provision forms an intrinsic part of rural development strategies, serving as a mechanism and catalyst for rural transformation through the reinforcement of rural development and contributes to poverty reduction by enhancing both equity and efficiency outcomes.

Pushing forward the relevance of good transport infrastructure, Lucas (2010) in his explanation of the concept of transferability, he mentioned that the second factor necessary for an interaction to take pace is transferability. In some cases, it is simply not feasible to transport certain goods (or people) a great distance because the transportation costs are too high in comparison to the price of the product. In all other cases where the transportation costs are not out of line with nee, we say that the product is transferable or that transferability exists. Adedeji et al. (2014) assert that rural transport and infrastructure development in Nigeria have being topical issues and have been identified by many as crucial components for the economic development of the country. According to Oluwasola et al. (2008), a major policy omission in Nigeria is the absence of policies deliberately targeted at fostering rural-urban linkage to improve the income earning potentials of the rural areas through the increased output to satisfy the urban market. Usman et al. (2013) ascertained that rural transport is important for the evacuation and marketing of farm products and the delivery of farm inputs and extension services. It also aids innovation diffusion, expand production and raises incomes (Olukotun, 2007; Osabohien, et al., 2018). In Nigeria, Osabohien, et al. (2018) reported that poor condition of road infrastructure along with rural geographical isolation have contributed to household poverty. It was proposed that improving feeder roads will enhance rural farmers' productivity and profits.

In Bangladesh, studies (Ahmed and Hussain, 1990; Khandker, et al., 2009) reported that rural communities with better access to markets, education enrollment and basic services have lower poverty levels. Such communities had higher agricultural productivity, higher household incomes, better health and higher participation of women in economic production. Ahmed and Nahiduzzaman (2016) went further to report that rural accessibility enhanced through road projects will promote the achievement of SDG goal by limiting rural exclusion. Similarly, in village level surveys carried out in Burkina Faso, Uganda and Zambia, good roads were seen to raise the economic opportunities for people in rural Africa (Barwell, 1996). Improvement in transport stimulates economic development in rural areas through the expansion of opportunities for income and employment. In Peru, Cambodia, and China, some authors (Qin and Zhang, 2016; Flachsbarth, et al., 2017; Idei and Kato, 2018) mentioned that rural roads impacted positively on agriculture, promoted farming income, raise people's welfare level and enhanced non-farm income diversification which resulted in declining poverty index in rural China.

In Nigeria, the issue of rural transportation development has continued to be of national importance. For instance, most of the rural roads are in poor condition, and this has imposed significant cost on the national economy especially to the agricultural activities due to increased vehicle operating costs and travel times (Akintola, 2007). Adedeji et al (2014) argued that the rural areas are indispensable in the supply of food, raw materials to urban centres and the country's economic growth as a whole. The condition of rural transportation has frustrated rural development efforts in the country and this has resulted into series of challenges such as the cutting off of many rural areas in the country from neighbouring larger settlements from which they could access higher order socio-economic services, low productivity, low income and a fall in the standard of living of rural residents and high rate of poverty (Aderamo and Magaji, 2010). Considering the above, it becomes expedient to examine rural transportation problems, so that the extent of the problems can be known, and possible solution proffered to achieving sustainable rural development.

Rural transportation problem in Nigeria relates generally to the provision of access to natural resources like minerals, agriculture, forestry and the provision of access for the rural population so that they can access services at affordable rate. Findings by Ovubude (2000) in Adedeji et al. (2014) have shown that the movement of passengers and freight in rural areas of Nigeria are comparatively smaller than those of intra-urban movement. People in rural areas travel less than their urban counterparts and this is not independent of the absence of reliable and easily affordable means of motorized public transport in those areas. The distance over which motorized transport is required within the rural areas is relatively shorter because of the small and compact nature of the rural settlements generally. Rural transportation problem is accentuated by the dispersed spatial derivation of traffic, this is conditioned by the nature of rural environment and economy, bulkiness and perishable nature of rural product, imbalance in inflow and outflow, and marked variability in demand for transport.

Intervening opportunity principle avers that there must not be another location that may offer a better alternative as a point of origin or as a point of destination. For instance, in order to have an interaction of a customer to a store, there must not be a closer store that offers a similar array of goods. If location C offers the same characteristics (namely complementarity) as location A and is also closer to location B, an interaction between B and A will not occur and will be replaced by an interaction between B and C. This principle presents the roles played by urban farming, modern super stores sale as an outlet to source for food by urban dwellers.

In South Africa, it is estimated that food damages to its road systems from overloaded trucks amounts to annual losses of R600 million (Louw et al. 2004). Many small traders buy peri-urban agricultural produce because they do not have the capital required to transport products over long distances. In a study of traders from Benin, Malawi, and Madagascar, few had weighing equipment, transportation, or storage facilities. Transport costs were the largest share of marketing costs followed by personal travel costs of the trader (Fafchamps et al., 2005).

According to SARRNET, traders in Tanzania preferred to buy cassava from areas closer to Dar Es Salaam at 30 USD per metric ton as opposed to farmers from the Rufiji district at 10 USD per metric ton because the poor road linkages greatly increase the transport costs (SARRNET 2004; Romanik, 2008). In Ethiopia, rural road enhanced households' welfare and resilience to environmental shocks (Nakamura et al., 2019) and vice-versa in road infrastructure limited rural areas.

FINDINGS AND DISCUSSIONS

This section examines the effects of road transportation on the flow of farm produce from rural areas to urban markets. It also identified the problems facing traders in the transportation of farm produce. The average distance travelled, and cost of transportation was also investigated. This section thematically through narrative experience of both the researcher and respondents presents analysis of various data collected from the field. Descriptive analysis where complimented by interviews conducted.

Locational and Demographic Characteristics of Respondents

A total of 250 copies of questionnaires were administered in 10 urban markets of the five (5) local government areas of Ibadan, namely: Ibadan North, Ibadan North-East, Ibadan North-West, Ibadan South-West, and Ibadan South-East. This was made possible because the questionnaires were administered by the researcher themselves and with the assistance of a supervised field assistants. It is no longer gainsaying that rural areas are dependent on the urban centres for product demand. To meet the demand placed by urban markets, traders often shift focus to the adjoining places of farm production to supply them the produce. The question as to the origin of purchase of farm produce shows that the adjoining rural areas are the supplier of the urban markets. The responses present 11.2% purchase their produce from Onidundu in Akinyele local government area, Iware (34.4%), Total (13.4%), Owena (3.2%), Akinyele (6.4%), Olanla (6.4%), while the remaining 24.8% buys from other sources such as Ikire. Although based on classification, the locations of purchase are within the rural LGA, informal discussion with the urban traders perceive that the market of sale can be said to be urban as all the 250 respondents was of the view. The urban perception can be said to be based on the nature of demand and outlook of the market environment.

Table 3. Location and business history where farm produce is bought

Trading location among respondents			Respondents Trading Experience			Average Monthly Income Distribution		
Farm market location	**No.**	**%**	**Number of years in trading**	**No.**	**%**	**Income of respondents**	**No.**	**%**
Onidundun	28	11.2	Less than 5years	113	45.2	Less than #5000	94	37.6
Iware	85	34.4	6-10 years	99	39.5	#5000-#15000	48	19.2
Total	34	13.4	11-20 years	16	6.4	#16000-#25000	100	40.0
Owena	8	3.2	Above 20 years	22	8.8	#26000-#35000	4	1.6
Akinyele	16	6.4	**Total**	**250**	**100.0**	Above #45000	4	1.6
Olanla	16	6.4				**Total**	250	100.0
Others	62	24.8						
Total	**250**	**100.0**						

Source: *Authors' Field Survey*

The socio-demographic configuration of the sampled respondents reveals that many (76.8%) of the respondents are married, many (65.6%) of who are women.Women are often known for their trading capabilities across ages. The economic rationality and quest to meet daily human needs is no restricted to any age grouping and this reflects in the 6.4% aged below 30years, 82.4% between age 31 and 50years and the remaining 11.2% are above 50 years of age. The analysis buttresses that young people less than 50 years (youths) engage in trading of farm produce. Table 3 presents that despite the youthful age composition of the respondents, majority (84.7%) of the respondent have been in the business for less than 10 years while the remaining 15.3% had been in family between 11-20years (6.4%) and over 20 years (8.8%). Although despite the many years in business, evidence shows a high percentage (57.6%) of the respondents either attended adult literacy (44.0%) or primary school (13.6) education while only 1.6%

had post-secondary education experience. This finding presents a preposition that food crop trading can be said to be traditional and mainly practised by less educated people in Ibadan. This finding was also reported by Wahab and Popoola (2018) that illiteracy among urban farmers in Ibadan has limited their adaptation to climate change. This study as presented in the analysis revealed that illiteracy among food crop traders is also high. A hypothetical statement that the research argues accounted for the majority (as only 1.6% earn above #45,000 in a month) of the respondents been classified are low income earners despite their over a decade farming experience (See Table 3).

Origin-Destination Food Chain Analysis

From the field observation, the researcher classified the food crops into tomatoes, fruits, vegetables and grains based on the traders interviewed. It was observed that while some sell only on crop (fruits or grain) some sell a combination of two or more farm produce (for example tomatoes and vegetable sellers). Responding, a tomatoes seller stated that the factors such as demand, profit and season determine what can be patronized. In her words she said "Ah… I sometimes sell ugwu and "efo-green" (a type of vegetable) but my main item of sale is tomatoes, I just add the vegetables to it in my stall or inside tray outside…" Another trader said that she sells vegetable so as to encourage his husband and children. They family has a vegetable farm along the floodplain of University of Ibadan and Samonda. She reported that she sometimes serves as a supplier to the vegetable sellers in the market, but she mainly buys her tomatoes from Onidundu village and another village in Egbeda. In her words she has this to say:

"… Supplier le mi (I am a supplier) … I just sell small vegetable here, I mainly supply to other market people… my husband and son are vegetable farmers, so they bring in the morning while I help them sell and collect money (with small additions on cost as personal gain to her she reported) …" **Tomatoes Trader**

This statement represents a form of household collaboration and representation in food production, marketing and consumptions. Economic rationality and quest to meet daily human needs by urban traders are subjected to some factors. Asked about certain factors that influence demand, traders designate demand, price or distance. From the above, distance was identified as a major determinant to market volume. A driver stated that the farther the distance the higher the cost of transportation.

Downplaying the role of farmers, a trader offloading her grains said the farmer is always willing to sell no matter what as he or she cannot consume all the produce, but it the place is far the cost of transportation is high and this indirectly influences the cost of delivery. One of the respondents who is a rural commercial driver said, "… *Ona Oko O wule Da A Mo yen* (meaning the roads linking to the rural villages of purchase are generally bad) *SuGbon To Nab A Tun Jin, Owo OKO Yo Won Gan (*But if the place is now far, the cost of transport is always high) and this might affect the trader capital budget…". Asked how to quantify distance, he stated that they are familiar with the route owing to history of interaction with a seller. When the trader was asked the effect of distance on delivery cost, she said bluntly "…*NikanTi A Ba Na Ni A O Ta OOO* (meaning it is what is delivered and cost of delivery that is been sold that is determines cost of sale) …"

Why the origin of purchase is usually within the rural areas, source of purchase can be from immediate household farms (28 traders), close fellow farmers within rural areas (199 traders), wholesalers (9 respondents) or from other sources such as from fellow retail market sellers and traders associations

(14 respondents). The researchers denote that the choice of which rural area to patronize is usually dependent on ease of accessibility, modal transportation availability and cost. The argument is that movement of goods and services from places of origin to destination is dependent on efficient and good road infrastructure. From the sampled respondents as presented in Table 4, 87% reported that bad road condition of rural connector and access roads are a major transport problem, while the remaining 13% identified that the state of the vehicle that ply this routes are nothing to write home about. Infact, it was argued by the traders (48%) that continuous axel overload is a major limitation to effective mobility of farm produce from rural to urban market, another 51% states that bad road is the problem associated with the flow of produce from rural areas to urban markets, while the remaining 1% complained about numerous police check-points.Drawing from the respondents' statements it was identified that the major problems associated with the flow of farm produce from rural areas to urban markets majority are bad road and axle overload.

Table 4. Problems associated with the flow of farm produce from rural areas to markets

Variable	Bad road	Over loading	Checking point	Bad vehicle
Transport problems experienced	217 (87%)	-	-	33 (13%)
Rural areas-urban market food flow problem	127 (51%)	121 (48%)	2 (1%)	-
What is the nature of problem encountered in flowing farm produce	241 (96%)	9 (4%)	-	-

Source: *Authors' Field Survey*

Although the most common form of transportation is the use of chartered public buses. It was reported that the choice of mode is often dependent on the proximity from the origin to destination. Most the traders engage in collective transportation in order to ease the cost of transportation. Responding on choice of transportation and cost effect, a trader stated thus:

"... Sometimes when we finish buying from the farm the last bus at the bus stop will have gone to Ibadan which now make transportation difficult as sometimes, we might need to wait till the next day or even days when negotiations are not favourable to us... as the drivers also inflate cost.... so, what some (4-5 traders) of us now do is that we have a permanent transporter who has a pick-up (4X4 open-back Van) that we all use... we come together on a fixed market day and when he should come pick us.... We all charter together and this has greatly reduced our cost of transportation, reduced waiting time, reduce number of spoiled produces, increase our profits and also indirectly reduce cost of delivery..." **Food crop Trader**

Transportation Characteristics

Responding to how it has reduced the number of spoilt produces, a driver said most tomatoes seller owing to scarcity, seasonality, limited availability and poor effectiveness of public transportation along rural roads have to depend on the same taxi with grains sellers. He said in many instances, the weight of the grains ends up meshing the tomatoes and also the vegetables there by increasing their produce loss.

This statement was confirmed in Table 5 as inference shows that only 18% of the participants agreed that means of transportation are readily available. Also when available, it is considered very effective by 16%, effective by 68%, and ineffective by the remaining 16%. The effectiveness in this regard was measured based on the nature of the vehicle and the state of the road in which it travels on. All of which is defined by the chartered vehicle used by traders, driver's choice of route and how much it tend to dictate and influence the cost of delivery.

Ability of traders to pay for available transport means is an important factor in flow of produce, but the availability of the transport mode is another imperative factor. Interview with a driver when asked of the reason why there are limited and seasonality in rural public transport, he said the nature of road dictates the availability of transport means as drivers prefer to ply roads that a motorable and will not damage their cars. In his words he stated thus:

*"... Many things determines this, the season (if raining season drivers including me don't like going to some villages), number of police, village or military check-points (as this increases amount paid for bribery for lack of vehicle documentations), road condition (paved or unpaved) and road security (instances where there are cases of robbery on the road)... "***Driver**

A farmer also reported that the effect of bad roads not only lead to spoiling of farm produce in transit but also indirectly affect cost of produce cost and also the farmers output (how much is produced and profits). He recorded that at several instances he might have harvested waiting on a trader to come purchase only to be informed that the road is bad or that the driver can't come done to the village owing to bad road network. This he said affects production, household income, livelihood survival and often result into debts. He said thus:

*"...Wahala Ona yipo gan, Ojaowa ko ni se Olubara, ke sis se be, Ona ni o Daa (The problem of this road is plenty, sometimes, there are goods to sell but no buyer, and It's not that no buyer but th road is bad to connect them.... Igbamiran to ba tip e nile, a kantaa mole nii Owoti o To kan, kin gbogbe ma lo baje (Sometimes, we have to sell the produce at ridiculous price when we don't see our main buyers to buy and we have already harvested) ... "***Rural Farmer**

Table 5. Availability of transport mode

<table>
<tr><th>Availability of transport</th><th>Frequency</th><th>Percent</th><th>Effectiveness transport</th><th>Frequency</th><th>Percent</th></tr>
<tr><td>Readily available</td><td>46</td><td>18</td><td>Very effective</td><td>40</td><td>16.0</td></tr>
<tr><td>Scarcely available</td><td>204</td><td>82</td><td>Effective</td><td>170</td><td>68.0</td></tr>
<tr><td>Total</td><td>250</td><td>100.0</td><td>Not effective</td><td>40</td><td>16.0</td></tr>
<tr><td colspan="3"></td><td>Total</td><td>250</td><td>100.0</td></tr>
<tr><td colspan="6">Summary of what transport cost account for in delivery price of</td></tr>
<tr><td colspan="2">Variable</td><td colspan="2">Frequency</td><td colspan="2">Percent</td></tr>
<tr><td colspan="2">Less than 10%</td><td colspan="2">208</td><td colspan="2">83.2</td></tr>
<tr><td colspan="2">11 – 50%</td><td colspan="2">42</td><td colspan="2">16.8</td></tr>
<tr><td colspan="2">Total</td><td colspan="2">250</td><td colspan="2">100</td></tr>
</table>

Delivery price can be defined as the selling price of produce at the market. From the sampled respondents, many (94%) opined that transport cost affect selling price of produce. This is because transportation accounts for 10% changes in delivery cost according to 83.2% of the traders and 11 – 50% of the final selling cost by the remaining. The variance in the effect of transport on delivery price is because traders consider distance between farm and residence or market which sometimes takes more than 2 hours as reported by 90.4% of the sampled traders.

The average time travel from residence to farm is dependent on the location of the farm, whether it is located in the same local government area as the residence or in a different local government area. It also shows that travel time of most of the farm produce sellers is above two hours. It was observed that majority of the traders buy their produce outside Ibadan. Of the sample, 215 respondents purchase their produce outside Ibadan (conceptualized and seen as the metropolitan urban or city area) while the remaining 34 buy within Ibadan. For those that buy outside Ibadan, locations where they buy includes Onidundun, Iware, Total, Akinyele, Ikereku, Olanla and Owena. All of which are located within the rural area or outside the state capital. Many of the traders attributed ready supply and cheap cost as to the reason for purchasing outside Ibadan. Speaking, a rural farmer that was accidentally met at the market said the rural areas have the capacity to produce some produce (mainly grain, vegetable, cassava, yam and pepper) for Ibadan consumers and the neighbouring towns. In his words he stated thus:

"... Melo Ni W Ni Ibadan Ti A O Le Pese Ounje Ti A O Je, Ile Lo Perese Ti A o TI Da (What is the population of Ibadan that the rural farmers cannot farm and produce what they will consume, there are many unfarmed rural land)... Ti Awon Oloja Ban Wa Daadaa, A O pese re eeee (If the traders were coming continually and steady demand, the rural farmers will produce foods)..." **Rural Farmer**

This statement according to the farmer connotes and presents an undertone of a shortage in demand from urban areas to rural areas of Ibadan. Although traders are rational about the cost of transport, various factors explain this cost of transporting agricultural products from origin to destination, among these, poor roads, destination, bargaining power, demand and the season of years.. According to the responses gathered in Table 6, bargaining power, season of the year, demand, destination and bad road in that order are the factors that determines the cost of transportation.

Table 6. Factors that determines cost of transportation

	Bad road		Bargaining power		Destination		Season of the year		Demand	
Response	**No.**	**%**	**No.**	**%**	**No.**	**%**	**No.**	**%**	**No.**	**%**
Agree	205	82.4	248	99.2	244	97.6	248	99.2	244	97.6
Disagree	44	17.6	2	.8	6	2.4	2	.8	6	2.4
Total	250	100	250	100	250	100	250	100	250	100

Source: *Authors' Field Survey*

To ascertain the relationship between distance travel and cost of transportation of farm produce, correlation analysis run shows that there exists a weak relationship between distance travel and cost of transportation (Table 7). This shows that there exist other untested variables that account for cost of transportation.

Table 7. Correlations between distance travelled and cost of transportation

			distance in km	how much does it cost you to transport your farm produce to the market
	distance in km	Correlation Coefficient	1.000	-.098
		Sig. (2-tailed)	.	.126
		N	246	246
	how much does it cost you to transport your farm produce to the market	Correlation Coefficient	-.098	1.000
		Sig. (2-tailed)	.126	.
		N	246	250

Source: *Authors' Field Survey*

Buttressing this, a driver said sometimes the main factor that account for cost of transportation can be road-blockage and season. He said transport cost is usually high during raining season and that if there are many check-points the drivers always account for the loss from the trader through a hike in transport cost. He also reported that should the car or bus get spoilt on the road, some drivers are in negotiation with the traders to repair it and this sometimes add to the cost of transportation. He said the sometimes, agreement by drivers during the associational meeting might dictate cost of transportation as in some cases if a new association due or fee is introduced, drivers agree in their meetings to increase transport cost by ascertain percentage in order to accommodate the cost.

All this also indirectly influences the delivery cost and also choice of urban market supply. A trader said, in order to recuperate back her capital and more profit, traders do a quick market survey through phone calls to know the cost of sales and delivery cost at various markets in Ibadan before going there to supply. She said through this, traders create a form of scarcity to create a price hike in a market such that the market with the highest delivery cost is supplied the produce. These assertions are widely true as Figure 5 shows that 64.8% of the respondents reveals that the price dictates the choice of market to supply.

CONCLUSION AND RECOMMENDATION

In conclusion, traders identify improved road condition, drainage facility and workable traffic policy that eliminate road blocks as the factors that can help enhance the smooth flow of farm produce from rural areas to urban markets. The socio-economic development of any society depends largely on the nature and structure of the transportation network of the society since it provides the arteries through which the economic life stream of the society flows. Transportation is an indispensable element of development and socio-economic growth. As engines of economic integration, transport infrastructure and services facility constitute a precondition for facilities trade and persons. Transport development is national and regional trade in a radically changed global environment. Transport infrastructure remains pillar of development with a view to accelerating growth and reducing poverty. Strategic planning and proper management processes needs to be in place in other to appropriate a good rural-urban market system as well as leaving a sustainable progress and development.

Road transportation has been described as a form land transport which involves the movement of people and goods by motor cars, trucks, buses, three wheelers motor cycles and bicycle. The government should provide good road networks to facilitated free movement of farm produces to urban market and transportation is catalysis' to development of any sociality. The government at various level, agencies and ministry of transport should take look at road network in their community to boost the flow of farm produces to urban market. The government should provide public transport to meet high traffic demand which the market and farm are facing in transporting their farm produce to market. The government should create a policy which will rise to fight the shortcoming facing transportation system in the country apart from transportation problem government should create storage facility to preserved that are in surplus.

Figure 5. Factors that influence the choice of the market supply?
Source: *Authors' Field Survey*

REFERENCES

Adedeji, O., Olafiaji, E., Omole, F., Olanibi, J., & Yusuf, L. (2014). An assessment of the impact of road transport on rural development: A case study of Obokun local government area of Osun State, Nigeria. *British Journal of Environmental Sciences, 2*(1), 34–48.

Aderamo, A., & Magaji, S. (2010). Rural transportation and the distribution of public facilities in Nigeria: A case of Edu local government area of Kwara State. *Journal of Human Ecology (Delhi, India), 29*(3), 171–179. doi:10.1080/09709274.2010.11906260

Ahmed, R., & Hussain, M. (1990). *Development impact of rural infrastructure in Bangladesh. research report, No. 83*. International Food Policy Research Institute.

Ahmed, S., & Nahiduzzaman, K. (2016). Impacts of rural accessibility on women empowerment: The case of south west Bangladesh. *Transport and Communications Bulletin for Asia and the Pacific, 86*, 41–57.

Ajiboye, A., & Afolayan, O. (2009). The Impact of Transportation on Agricultural Production in a Developing Country: A Case of Kolanut Production In Nigeria. *International Journal of Agricultural Economics and Rural Development, 2*(2), 49–57.

Akintola, S. (2007). Coping with infrastructural deprivation through collective action among rural people in Nigeria. *Nordic Journal of African Studies, 16*(1), 30–46.

Avery, L., Regmi, M., Joshi, G., & Mohanty, C. 2017. Rural-Urban Connectivity in Achieving Sustainable Regional Development. In *Intergovernmental Tenth Regional Environmentally Sustainable Transport (EST) Forum* (pp. 14-16). Academic Press.

Badejo, B. (2011). *The Transportation Realities, Challenges and Opportunities of Lagos State: The Leadership Imperatives and Synergies*. Paper delivered at the Fiftieth Anniversary Lecture Organized by Great Independence Hall, University of Ibadan.

Barwell, I. (1996). *Transport and the Village: Findings from African Village Level Travel and Transport Surveys and Related Studies*. World Bank Discussion Paper, no. 344. The World Bank.

Fabiyi, O. (2006). Urban Land Use Change Analysis of a Traditional City from Remote Sensing Data: The Case of Ibadan Metropolitan Area, Nigeria. *Humanity & Social Sciences Journal, 1*(1), 42–64.

Fafchamps, M., Gabre-Madhin, E., & Minten, B. (2005). Increasing returns and market efficiency in agricultural trade. *Journal of Development Economics, 78*(2), 406–442. doi:10.1016/j.jdeveco.2004.10.001

Flachsbarth, I., Lay, J., & Garrido, A. (2017). *Rural income dynamics: Understanding poverty and inequality changes in rural Peru* (No. 728-2017-3112). Paper presented at the XV EAAE Congress, "Towards Sustainable Agri-food Systems: Balancing between Markets and Society", Parma, Italy.

Herrero, L. (2011). Transport and mobility: The keys to sustainability. *Lychnos: Notebooks of the Fundacion General CSIC, 04*, 1–6.

Hine, J., & Ellis, S. (2001). *Agricultural marketing and access to transport services: a rural transport knowledge base, rural travel and transport program*. Available at: http://www.transport-links.org/transport_links/index.Asp

Idachaba, F. (1980). *The Green Revolution: A Food Production Plan for Nigeria*. Final Report submitted to the Federal Ministry of Agriculture.

Idei, R., & Kato, H. (2018). How Does Rural Road Improvement Influence Livelihoods of the Poor in a Developing Country? A Case Study in Cambodia. *Asian Transport Studies*, *5*(2), 378–392.

Khandker, S., Bakht, Z., & Koolwal, G. (2009). The poverty impact of rural roads: Evidence from Bangladesh. *Economic Development and Cultural Change*, *57*(4), 685–722. doi:10.1086/598765

Louw, A., Madevu, H., Jordaan, D., & Vermeulen, H. (2004). *Regoverning markets: Securing small producer participation in restructured national and regional agri-food systems. RSA Country Report*. Department of Agricultural Economics, Extension and Rural Development, University of Pretoria.

Medayese, F. (2009). *Transportation systems in Nigeria: problems and prospects*. Available at: http://www.jimoh4bunuland.blogspot.com/

Mulyana, W. (2014). *Rural-Urban Linkages: Indonesia Case Study*. Working Paper Series No. 126. Working Group: Development with Territorial Cohesion. Territorial Cohesion for Development Program. Rimisp, Santiago, Chile.

Nakamura, S., Bundervoet, T., & Nuru, M. (2019). *Rural roads, poverty, and resilience: evidence from Ethiopia*. The World Bank. doi:10.1596/1813-9450-8800

Nkegbe, P., Kuunibe, N., & Abdul-Mumin, Y. (2012). Choice of transport mode by non-resident university students in Ghana. *International Journal of Business and Social Science*, *3*(2), 136–142.

Obinna, L., & Ukoha, J. (2017). Comparative effect of rural road transportations on cassava production among rural farmers in Abia State, Nigeria. *European Journal of Social Sciences Studies*, *2*(3), 117–131.

Ogunleye, O., Ajibola, A., Enilolobo, O., & Shogunle, O. (2018). Influence of road transport infrastructure on agricultural sector development in Nigeria. *Logistics & Sustainable Transport*, *9*(1), 39–50. doi:10.2478/jlst-2018-0004

Olajide, S., & Olayemi, J. (1972). *A Quantitative Analysis of Food Requirement; Supply and Demand in Nigeria. 1968-1985*. Federal Department of Agriculture.

Olayiwola, L., & Adeleye, O. (2005). Rural infrastructural development in Nigeria between 1960-1990-problems and challenges. *Journal of Social Science*, *11*(2), 91–96.

Olukotun, G. (2007). The role of local government in rural transport finance. *Journal of Social Sciences*, *15*(2), 147–152. doi:10.1080/09718923.2007.11892576

Oluwasola, O., Idowu, E., & Osuntogun, D. (2008). Increasing agricultural household incomes through rural-urban linkages in Nigeria. *African Journal of Agricultural Research*, *3*(8), 566–573.

Omiti, J., Otieno, D., Nyanamba, T., & McCullough, E. (2009). Factors influencing the intensity of market participation by smallholder farmers: A case study of rural and peri-urban areas of Kenya. *African Journal of Agricultural and Resource Economics*, *3*(1), 57–82.

Oni, S. (2000). Education and Training for Road Traffic Safety in Nigeria. In *Proceedings of the International Conference CODATU IX* (pp. 913 – 918). Academic Press.

Osabohien, R., Osabuohien, E., & Urhie, E. (2018). Food security, institutional framework and technology: Examining the nexus in Nigeria using ARDL approach. *Current Nutrition and Food Science, 14*(2), 154–163. doi:10.2174/1573401313666170525133853 PMID:29853816

Osabuohien, E. (2020a). *The Palgrave Handbook of Agricultural and Rural Development in Africa*. Palgrave Macmillan. doi:10.1007/978-3-030-41513-6

Osabuohien, E. (2020b). Guest Editorial: Labour Issues in Africa's Agricultural and Rural Transformation. *African Journal of Economic and Management Studies, 11*(2), 185–191. doi:10.1108/AJEMS-06-2020-406

Popoola, A., Ayangbile, O., & Adeleye, B. (2015). Assessment of Solid Waste Management Systems in Ibadan North, Oyo State Using Geo-Spatial Techniques. *Ethiopian Journal of Environmental Studies and Management, 9*(6), 666–679.

Popoola, A., & Magidimisha, H. (2019). Will Rural Areas Disappear? Participatory Governance and Infrastructure Provision in Oyo State, Nigeria. *Proceedings for the 6th International Conference of Development and Investment-Strategied for Africa. DII-2019.*

Porter, G. (2013). *Transport Services and Their Impact on Poverty and Growth In Rural Sub- Saharan Africa*. AFCAP/ Durham University.

Qin, Y., & Zhang, X. (2016). The road to specialization in agricultural production: Evidence from rural China. *World Development, 77*, 1–16. doi:10.1016/j.worlddev.2015.08.007

Romanik, C. (2008). *An urban-rural focus on food markets in Africa*. The Urban Institute. Available at https://www.urban.org/sites/default/files/publication/31436/411604-An-Urban-Rural-Focus-on-Food-Markets-in-Africa.PDF

SAARNET. (2004). *See Southern Africa Root Crops Research Network*. Available at: https://core.ac.uk/download/pdf/6689793.pdf

Satterthwaite, D., McGranahan, G., & Tacoli, C. (2010). Urbanization and its implications for food and farming. *Philosophical Transactions of the Royal Society of London. Series B, Biological Sciences, 365*(1554), 2809–2820. doi:10.1098/rstb.2010.0136 PMID:20713386

Tacoli, C. (2003). The links between urban and rural development. *Environment and Urbanization, 15*(1), 1–12. doi:10.1630/095624703101286376

Tchanche, B. (2019). A view of road transport in Africa. *African Journal of Environmental Science and Technology, 13*(8), 296–302. doi:10.5897/AJEST2018.2575

Tunde, A., & Adeniyi, E. (2012). Impact of Road Transport on Agricultural Development: A Nigerian Example. *Ethiopian Journal of Environmental Studies and Management, 5*(3), 232–238. doi:10.4314/ejesm.v5i3.3

Turok, I., & McGranahan, G. (2019). Urbanisation and Economic Growth: The Arguments and Evidence for Africa and Asia. *Urbanisation, 4*(2), 109–125. doi:10.1177/2455747119890450

Ullman, E. (1954). Geography as spatial interaction. *Annals of the Association of American Geographers, 44*, 283–294.

Usman, B., Adefila, J., & Musa, I. (2013). Impact of rural road transport on agricultural production in Kwara state, Nigeria. *Nigerian Journal of Agriculture. Food and Environment*, *9*(2), 20–25.

Wahab, A., & Popoola, A. (2019). Urban Farmers' Perceptions of and Adaptation Strategies to Climate Variability in Ibadan, Nigeria. In The Geography of Climate Change Adaptation in Urban Africa (pp. 123-154). Palgrave Macmillan.

Wahab, B., & Popoola, A. (2018). Climate-Induced Problems and Adaptation Strategies of Urban Farmers in Ibadan. *Ethiopian Journal of Environmental Studies and Management*, *11*(1), 31–42.

Wahab, B., Popoola, A., & Magidimisha, H. (2018b). Access to Urban Agricultural Land in Ibadan, Nigeria. *Planning Malaysian: Journal of the Malaysian Institute of Planners*, *16*(4), 161–175. doi:10.21837/pmjournal.v16.i8.547

Yunusa, M., Shaibu, I., Ambi, Y., Yusuf, A., & Abdulkarim, B. (2002). Road rehabilitation: The impact on transport and accessibility. In P. Fernando & G. Porter (Eds.), *Balancing the Load: Gender, Women and transport*. Zed Books.

Chapter 18
The Role of Agriculture in Tanzania:
Unpacking Industrialization Prospects and Constraints

Nyanjige Mbembela Mayala
Mwenge Catholic University (MWECAU), Tanzania

ABSTRACT

Agriculture's importance to industrialization efforts in Tanzania goes far beyond its direct impact on the manufacturing sector, but on farmers' incomes, economic stability, and reduction of poverty. The challenges are on both sides; agricultural development initiatives are needed on one hand while manufacturing obstacles are supposed to be dealt with on the other hand. Using literature review approach, the study found that there should be a balance between infrastructure development and agricultural support so that the two may support well the industrialization process. Massive efforts have been myths to the smooth changes which call for serious attention to the planners to review strategies, policies and programme. On the other hand, the potentials of the agricultural sector are observed to support the industrialization process in Tanzania. The potentials include food security, private investments support, employment, and exports enhancement and supply strain stabilization through various crops and produce.

INTRODUCTION

Agriculture in Africa represents a major economic activity and contributes, on average, 15% of gross domestic products (GDP), although this varies widely across the continent, from 2.5% in South Africa to 56% in Sierra Leone (World Bank, 2018a). The agricultural sector employs about 65% of the workforce (Osabuohien, 2020a; World Bank, 2017; FAOSTAT, 2015) and constitutes the primary income generating activity for many especially those in the rural areas. African agriculture is, therefore, believed to have the potential to contribute to eradicating poverty and hunger, by boosting agricultural investment and trade, creating jobs, and improving livelihoods (NEPAD, 2013; Osabuohien, 2020b). Tanzania's agricultural

DOI: 10.4018/978-1-7998-4817-2.ch018

sector is among the most diverse in East Africa. The country's primary export crops include coffee, cotton, tobacco, cashew nut and tea. It also produces significant quantities of fruits and vegetables, pyrethrum – a plant used to make fertilizer – and sisal, which is derived from a species of agave plant and is used to create strong plant fibers for rope, twine and fabric (Katundu, 2020; Osabuohien et al, 2020).

In Tanzania, most of the population (more than 70%) is engaged in agriculture, residing in the rural areas and practicing small scale farming. Thus, Tanzania's agricultural sector makes sense in a number of ways ranging from employment creation, input supplies in the manufacturing sector and food security to the industrial work force and the nation at large a few to mention; not forgetting the constraints facing the agricultural sector to adequately support industrialization on the other side (Massay, 2020; Kumburu and Pande, 2020). Agriculture's importance to economic development goes far beyond its direct impact on farmers' incomes, as it is the driver for the economy and the best hope for the food security in Tanzania, Africa and world at large. Agricultural development has benefited millions through higher income, more plentiful and cheaper food and generates patterns of development that are employment-intensive and benefit both rural and urban areas. More important it has contributed to the economy even outside agriculture where growth and job creation are faster and has raised wages. Tanzania's economy has responded to the structural transformation with steadily increasing shares of total GDP from the services sector. Agricultural activities accounted for 30.1 per cent of the GDP in 2017, from 29.2 per cent in 2016 (URT, 2018). There are some indications of increase in trend for the subsequent years too.

According to the World Bank (2019), the current trends in agriculture in Tanzania offer a tremendous opportunity to catalyze private investment, both local and foreign, and raise the incomes of the poor. Since agriculture already accounts for a quarter of total GDP and two-thirds of jobs, enhanced agricultural growth must be part of the strategy to create more and better jobs and alleviate poverty. Recent signs of transformation in Tanzania's agricultural sector offer encouraging opportunities for acceleration of growth, job creation and poverty reduction, if urgent steps are taken to improve the sector's policy and regulatory environment and investments, according to a new World Bank report (2019).

Realizing the potential of agriculture for Inclusive growth and poverty Reduction, underscore the importance of having supportive public policies and spending which crowds in more private investments needed to catalyze a nascent agriculture transformation (Wolter, 2018). Signs of transformation within the study period (2008-2018) include a growing number of medium-scale farmers which has opened up opportunities for smallholder farmers through positive spillovers. These farms have created jobs for farmers through their demand for extra agricultural inputs and financial, traction rental, and especially, transport services.

With the in trend as explained above, the experience of weak farming practices of farmers are the common in most of developing countries as it is in Tanzania. Farmers normally operate low-technology, businesses on small and fragmented plots of land without access to proper infrastructures, improper inputs and other productivity enhancing methods (Duursma et al., 2012). These weaknesses can be triangulated and used as strength to rectify the system that has been doing thing for traditional for years. For instance, land inheritance to a member of families for cultivation range from 0.2ha to 2ha, besides, 70% of the land is hand tools worked, reliant on rain-fed farming, mostly without the use of proper inputs. The evidence shows that, only 11 percent (about 44 million hectares) of the total arable land under cultivation are owned by smallholder farmers in Tanzania (Wolter, 2018). The planted area has been stable for some years, indicating that land expansion has ceased to be a major source of agricultural growth. Agriculture growth has been stagnated, slowing wider economic growth and exacerbating poverty with it.

This chapter provides an assessment of the agricultural potentials in Tanzania by looking at the wider role to industrialization link process in the country. The major and basic question that will be answered is in this study is whether Agricultural sector is responding to the development challenges in support of the quest for Tanzania to become a middle income country by the year 2025 through the manufacturing transformation process. Using the literature review, we present the role that agriculture plays in the country and making a connection to the industrialization process in Tanzania.

The Theory of Agricultural Development

The main aim of agricultural development is the improvement of material and social welfare of the people. Therefore, it is often seen as integrated approach to improving the environment and well-being of the people of the community (Nwachukwu, 2006). The well-being improvement can be observed in all aspects of development including industrialization. The first step in the process of agricultural development is to abandon the view of agriculture in pre-modern or traditional societies as essential static. However, the problem of agricultural development is not that of transforming a static agricultural sector into a modern dynamic sector, but of accelerating the rate of growth of agricultural output and productivity consistent with the growth of other sectors of a modernizing economy. Therefore, any attempt to embrace a meaningful perspective on the process of agricultural development must abandon the view of agriculture in pre-modern or traditional society as essential stagnant. Hence, a theory of agricultural development should provide insights into the dynamics of agricultural growth and support either into the changing sources of growth, in economies ranging from those in which output is growing at a rate of 1.0% or less to those in which agricultural output is growing at an annual rate of 4.0% or more (Cardno, 2017).

STATUS OF AGRICULTURAL SECTOR IN TANZANIA

Agricultural position is known as a backbone of Tanzania for many decades acknowledged from the fact that it employs many people than any other sector (62.8% 7 in 2013) (NBS, 2014a). About seventy percent of Tanzanian live in rural area and own land or farm and engage at least in one form of agricultural activities. However, the average per capita holdings is 0.12 ha, and majority of farmers are small scale, operating between 0.2 and 2.0 ha, producing for subsistence (NBS, 2017). The reason for producing for subsistence is that agriculture is taken as a last resolution after failing to get opportunity in non-agricultural sector elsewhere. Nevertheless, commercial agriculture requires massive investment on; infrastructure for irrigation, farming skills, research and technology, of which small scale farmer cannot afford. Unfortunately, increase in the cost of living created tension among farmers and non-farmers, with a scenario that, most government employee are engaged in agriculture activities to supplement their low income (Kessy et al, 2017).

Most small scale farmers who operate in the small area for subsistence have very slim profit and low chance for their income to generate opportunities (Mayala et al, 2018). Insufficient effort towards rural development and poverty reduction are exacerbated by the low profitable investment opportunities, or by inability to save. Vast research shows poor households with little wealth have to work on non-agriculture to support their livelihood. Albeit, wealthier households invest in more profitable activities such as keeping cattle and fishing boats, whilst poor household compliment agriculture with casual labour, bricks or charcoal making and or owning trading shops (Sarris et al, 2016). However, population growth has created a demand and pressure for the immediate need for increase in food supply which trigger demand for improving productivity for all farming activities (URT, 2018).

The agriculture is major sector that feed a nation and support other sector to grow easily if social protection, agriculture innovation and investment are prioritized. Furthermore, if crucial supports are like inputs are available to the farmers, market for farmer's produce are in place with minimum cost associated with transportation and reasonable tax re in place. Last but very critical is if the policy support small farmers to grow and encourage more people to invest in the field (Kessy, 2018). To minimize these challenges, and make agriculture supportive to the other sectors of the economy especially with the industrialization process, different authors in the agricultural sector agrees that some issues need to be attended as follows:

Social Protection to Farmer

Conceptually, there is a two-way relationship between social protection and agriculture. On the one hand, poor rural households in Tanzania that mostly rely on agriculture for their livelihoods are often affected by limited access to resources, low agricultural productivity, poorly functioning markets and repeated exposure to covariate and peculiar risks. Social protection can help to alleviate credit, savings and liquidity constraints by providing cash and in-kind support. In addition, the regularity and predictability of social protection instruments help households to better manage risks and to engage in more profitable livelihood and agricultural activities (FAO, 2019). On the other hand, agricultural policies and programmes can help smallholder households manage risk by stimulating farm output, income and overall household welfare. Since social protection and smallholder agricultural interventions often cover the same geographic areas and target the same households, there are opportunities for synergies and complementarities that would strengthen the livelihoods of poor rural households.

Additionally, social protection is important for a minimum level of well-being and social security for people living in rural poor. Well-structured social protection minimizes risk of investment in agriculture and benefit agricultural growth more directly. Assurance of a safety net to farmers in terms of support for the unexpected shocks encourages investment and innovations as well as providing favorable environment for agricultural business (Osabohien et al, 2020a). In fact, social protection is an investment for future growth as it helps families to break poverty cycles through health and education investment for their children (Osabohien et al, 2020b). Actually, careful choice of policy and proper strategies to be implemented in a certain time ensures social protection is complementary to growth (DFID 2015). For instance, implementation of the voucher subsidy input in Tanzania for the period of 2009-2013 allowed poor farmers to acquire inputs that were not able to be afforded before. But on the other side it distorted input market and prices, consequently, there was an increase in dependency for the farmer to the free inputs and reduces a deliberate effort to the agriculture investment. DFID (2015) argued that interventions that target agriculture as a safety net may be less successful than strategies to harness agriculture for growth. This calls for appropriate approaches and policies for agricultural growth.

Investment in Agriculture

In recent years Tanzania has become a darling of Western donors and investors, building on an image of stable democratic reform and economic structural transformation. It is one of the top three aid recipients within Africa and accounts for 5% of all aid given to Africa (OECD, 2015). High levels of multilateral and bilateral donor partner involvement in its agricultural sector account for up to 5.6% of the country's gross national income (World Bank, 2016). However, there is much debate about whether this involvement (and funding) flooding into the country is having a deep and lasting impact on poverty alleviation and social transformation through agricultural development. With a population estimated at 58 million, 28% of all Tanzanians survive below the poverty line and rely predominantly on subsistence farming (World Bank, 2018). The majority of the country's population resides in rural areas; consequently, agriculture is a vital source of economic activity, contributing up to 31% of the country's gross domestic product (GDP) and employing more than 70% of the country's workforce *(ibid)*. Women constitute 55% of the agricultural labour force.

Currently, Tanzania has been announced by the World Bank as a middle-income country with an annual growth rate of 7% per year – the fastest growth recorded in East Africa – with an average income level at $1,150 per capita (GoT, 2019). Despite this high growth rate it did not meet its poverty reduction targets under the Millennium Development Goals (MDGs) moving to the Sustainable Development Goals (SDGs). Initial reports on the poverty alleviation effect of Tanzania's impressive growth rate appear confined to Dar es Salaam, and there seems to be little evidence of gains penetrating the rural areas (World Bank, 2018). The UN Children's Emergency Fund estimates that one in four urban families and one in six rural families live in poverty (UNICEF, 2018).

The status being as explained above, it is further notices that there is insufficient infrastructure and low government support which put the expansion of agriculture into areas where the land cannot support, the areas with good-quality soils being taken for non-agriculture activities leaving bad management of intensive farming caused by poor policies and incentives and the inappropriate use of technologies (Mufuruki et al., 2018). The current strategies for the government of Tanzania is to make sure that good infrastructure are available. However, there should be a balance in public spending to be invested in the roads construction, railway construction, education, irrigation infrastructure and agricultural research to easy farmer's produce supply to the market, better knowledge in agriculture as well as access to the input supply. For example the Indian's green revolution, government spending on agriculture was done by ensuring every rupee invested generated returns of almost nine times the amount increased in agricultural output in the 1960s (DFID 2005). Unfortunately, public investment for agricultural support is very low and is poorly focused (Wolter, 2018). This is from the fact that agriculture is taken as last resort for anyone who failed to get income in non-agricultural sectors, since agriculture is taken as a risk business.

Agricultural Irrigation

The possible and fast way to generate income to local farmers is to reduce obvious risks. Tanzania has possible irrigated land of 90,400 square km, but only 1,843 square km (2013) was the irrigated land, which is about 0.63%. Wolter (2018) reported that out of 29.4 million hectares (i.e. 31 percent of the total land area) with irrigation potential, only 227 490 hectares (less than 1 percent) are under irrigation. This is also reported by NBS (2014b) that the irrigation potential in Tanzania is 29.4 million hectares out of which 2.3 million hectares are high potential, 4.8 million hectares are medium potential and 22.3 million hectares are low potential. Use of development incubator concept or idea-Lab will make quick change. A good example is KickStart Irrigation Pump (Dutt et al., 2007). However, government focuses on Agricultural Sector Development Programme (ASDP) on irrigation since 2013, but there is no significant difference to date (Kessy, 2019). Even though the importance of irrigation to reduce Tanzania's dependency on rainfall is undisputed, yet it would have been better to have a two-fold programme with one part focusing on production-related investments such as irrigation and the other fostering commercial agriculture and the private sector (Wolter, 2018). The concept should be originated from farmers by identifying appropriate product or services that answer local needs inquiries especially to support the industrial sector in terms of raw materials (Dutt et al., 2017).

INDUSTRIALIZATION STATUS IN TANZANIA

Tanzania desires to have industries that will export industrial goods (URT, 2016). This is a good thing because as the country builds ground for export earnings as much as it is needed in terms of foreign currencies with the many and far-reaching advantages of it. In order to be able to export industrial goods, domestic value addition and a move away from the current predominantly export of unprocessed raw materials is important. Among the key implication here is availability of and access to export markets for the 'made in Tanzania' industrial goods (Dutt et al, 2017). Currently the main industrial goods from Tanzania include agro-processed products. In order to access the export market in a meaningful way, there is a need to meet and adhere to the demanded quality and standards across the East African block and across the globe. For food and beverage products for example, issues of sanitary and phytosanitary conditions as well as traceability are very important (Duursma et al., 2017). Important too, in exporting is the ability to meet and adhere to the needed quantity and supply frequencies. Performance of African countries Tanzania included in the African Growth and Opportunity Act (AGOA) market access opportunity should be able to give Tanzania lessons (Duursma et al., 2012).

At the core of succeeding in Tanzania's industrialization move lies understanding of what industrialization means and entails by all key stakeholders. This is because a problem known is a problem half solved. Pass et al, (2000) describe the term industrialization to imply the extensive development of organized economic activity for the purpose of manufacture. It is characterized by inter alia transformation of a primarily agrarian economy into a more specialized, capital as opposed to labour intensive economy. It took the form of Industrial Revolution in Western Europe and North America in the 18th and 19th centuries. Elsewhere in the economic and business literature, industrialization is described as the process in which a country transforms itself from a basically agricultural society into one based on manufacturing of goods and services (Martorano et al., 2017; Pass et al., 2000). Whereas manual labour is more often than not replaced by mechanized and automated high tech-mass production, craftsmen are replaced by assembly lines. Industrialization is associated with the growth and development of large urban centers and suburbs. Tanzania may need to adopt its own definition of industrialization but it should not miss out the key components of a true industrialized economy (BOT, 2017).

The desire is to have 40% of employment in Tanzania coming from the industrial sector by the year 2020 although the current percent is not known. For Tanzania to attain the mass employment-creating industrialization, then it has to opt for labour intensive industrialization if it means jobs coming direct from industries (Martorano et al., 2017). Labour intensive production techniques employ more labour than capital and therefore create more jobs. However, there are several downsides of labour intensive production and by extension labour intensive industrialization. These include limited ability to enjoy economies of scale through large scale production, less speed in production, less efficiency and at times less quality and standardization of products (Dutt et al., 2017). For this type of industrialization, employment can only be mainly created along industrial value chains nodes through backward and forward integration.

It calls for strong inter-sectoral linkages and holistic approach to industrialization. All sectors related to the industrial sector need to be adequately developed. To this end, agricultural development is key.

There are many potential advantages embedded within industrial economy. These include but are not limited to potentials for direct and indirect jobs and therefore incomes creation and improved standards of living (Martorano et al., 2017). Industrialization also poses potentials for foreign exchange earnings through exports and foreign exchange saving through imports substitution. It can also generate government revenues from related taxes and none tax charges (UNIDO, 2012). Furthermore, it stands to develop other sectors of the economy through inter-sectoral linkages via both backward and forward linkages that can trigger development of many other sectors through providing them with markets as well as supplying these sectors with factor inputs both intermediate and finished. The agricultural sector in Tanzania here stands a better chance than any other supportive sector to industrialization as it currently employs many as stated before. As a country, it should not dwell on the potentials only but should make concrete moves to actualize the potentials.

The intention of having manufacturing industries will produce goods for mass consumption. They include industrial goods from agro-processing such as food and related items; textile; footwear and many others. Among other things, these industries will make use of locally available raw materials (Martorano et al., 2017). The agricultural sector therefore has the role of providing the needed quantity and quality of raw materials for agro-processing industries. Apart from the mentioned potentials above, the agricultural sector plays other vital cross-cutting roles in all types of industries. These include but are not limited to the following:

1. The sub-sector is expected to provide various raw materials for agro-processing industries. The raw materials include various kinds of grains (maize, rice, and wheat); seeds (sunflower, groundnuts, sesame, cotton, and coconut), grass (including lemon grass, grass for pellets etc. Others include cashewnuts, cotton and coffee (Balchin et al., 2016).
2. The livestock sub-sector of the agricultural sector plays an important role of providing raw materials to the industries that process these raw materials (Mayala et al., 2017). The raw materials include but are not limited to milk, hides and skin for leather industries that manufacture among others bags, footwear, belts, wallets, horns for key holders and decorations (ornaments like ear rings); bones and blood for animal feed.
3. In the context of inter-sectoral linkages (forward and backward linkages) and input – output relations, the agricultural sector is part of important market for industrial goods both intermediate and final. Agriculture provides markets for such industrial outputs as machinery and equipment as well as fertilizers, pesticides, insecticides, packaging materials etc. Therefore, agricultural sector is the potential and actual market for the industrial sector which in turn is a key factor for industrial development.

Tanzania's industrialization move in general and the role of agriculture in that process in particular stands to encounter a number of challenges. Among the general challenges to industrialization include inadequate resources both financial and none-financial. Other general challenges are those related to investment/business climate (Mufuruki et al., 2017). Various studies and reports have produced a wide range of issues that constitute challenging and constraining business climate in general sectors and sub-sectors in particular. When the business climate issues are short of the needed level they are seen as challenging and constraining (MITI, 2018). They constitute unfriendly, none-conducive, unattractive and none-optimal business climate. They imply a deficit in the desired business environment. Such deficits need to be bridged through various interventions as they constitute issues of concern to business stakeholders including but not limited to the following:

Cost and Quality of Raw and Intermediate Materials

Agriculture remains one of the driving forces of industrialization in Tanzania (Mufuruki et al., 2017). However, the small size of and poor technology used by agricultural production limits its ability to supply adequate raw materials to support industrialization. For instance, Bakhresa Food Products wanted to invest in the UHT coconut cream industry but failed because of a lack of raw materials, and instead imported from Indonesia (Butt et al., 2017). Although Tanzania is the main grower of coconut in Africa, existing supply levels are insufficient to meet the raw material requirements for the factory, given the high demand for raw unprocessed coconut. The use of domestically produced raw material inputs for downstream processing is limited in other areas also. For instance, according to the Bank of Tanzania (2017), only 40% of sunflower oil demand is met domestically (330,000 tons); the remaining 60% is imported. In August 2018, cement manufacturers reported a deficit in coal availability, and government of Tanzania responded by banning exports of coal to meet local demand – but the problem persists (MITI, 2018).

Cost and Quality of Labour

Tanzania has been a macro-economic success story for nearly two decades. The rate of economic growth increased from 3.5 percent in the 1990s to 7 percent in the 2000s. Despite the global financial crisis, growth rates have been remarkably stable over the last decade, and they are expected to continue or even increase in the foreseeable future. At the same time, the country has experienced high population growth from around 45 million in 2012 to around 53 in 2018 at nearly 3 percent growth rate annually. If this growth rate continues, there will be 60 million Tanzanians in 2022 and 100 million in 2042 (World Bank, 2018).

While donors and the government have used significant resources to improve the social sectors, similar necessary support has not been given to agriculture and other productive sectors. Lack of secure land tenure to ensure that the traditional users in the rural districts do not lose their land is one of the most essential issues, constraining investments that could enhance productivity. Processing of food and other agricultural produce and other forms of manufacturing is also very limited in the rural areas creating very few additional employment opportunities.

For the same reason, Tanzania is experiencing significant out-migration of young people from low productivity agriculture to urban informal service sectors, where productivity is just as low. Unemployment is high and growing rapidly, especially in the urban areas and among youth. The official unemployment rate is 12% and is highest in the cities, reaching 32% in Dar es Salaam (ILO, 2018). In addition, one-third of those employed are so-called "working poor": technically employed, but whose income is less than the basic needs poverty line of USD 0.96 per day. They often work either in farming or in the urban informal service sector in low-productivity, part-time jobs. An estimated 700,000 new young job-seekers enter the labour market each year, but only a fraction of them have a realistic possibility of obtaining a stable job that can give them the possibility to provide for a family. The flow from countryside to city of rural-urban migration will continue in years ahead, and Dar es Salaam is already one of the fastest growing cities in Africa *(ibid)*.

However, Tanzania is still well positioned in some areas, with a large unskilled urban workforce readily available and a competitive wage rate of about $60–75 per month, but not in the availability of skilled and semi-skilled labour (BoT, 2017). More could be done to improve the quality and relevance of training provided through the Vocational Educational and Training Authority (VETA) and makes it easier to hire skilled expatriates in Tanzania. The action will complement the need of skilled manpower needed in the industrialization process but also reduce the cost of labour as more and more are trained and exposed to the labour market.

Supporting Infrastructure

The main problems identified to have been frustrating the agricultural sector in Tanzania include but not limited to efficiency of productivity for irrigation schemes encompassed by inadequate water supply caused by deteriorated irrigation and drainage facilities, poor farm roads and an absence of irrigation infrastructure in the undeveloped areas (GoT, 2017). Along with training and increased adoption of new farming technologies, taking rehabilitation measures may lead to positive impact in the local community. Agricultural production will be increased, the value of land will go up and the incidence of water-borne diseases, such as malaria and bilharzias, may fall significantly. Most farmers will be able to enrol their children in school; some may be able to send their children to boarding schools. Most farmers may be able to up-grade their housing by using clay bricks and corrugated iron sheets, rather than trees, soil and grass.

Power represents a significant portion of the costs of production (e.g. 35% for spinning in textile production), such that a fraction of reduction in the cost of power will have an enormous impact on firm-level competitiveness. According to TDU (2017), firms pay $0.12/kwh in Tanzania, which is four times higher than in Ethiopia ($0.04/kwh) and 25% more than in Kenya (which has introduced a subsidy for textile and apparel manufacturers to make it more competitive, bringing the costs down from $0.20/kwh to $0.09/kwh). Nonetheless, recent initiatives to implement energy projects have addressed challenges related to availability, although reliability is still a concern. These initiatives include addressing losses and inefficiencies in power generation, distribution and transmission, and additional capacity to the national grid from Kinyerezi II (167.82 MW) as of April 2018. Clearly, Dar port is a critical asset in reducing costs to improve competitiveness. However, efficiency of customs and other government departments needs further improvement to realize this advantage.

Business and Regulatory Environment

Tanzania enjoys favourable (domestic and export) market opportunities given existing preferential market access and a growing middle class, but the realization of these opportunities is largely hampered by business environment challenges (Balchin, 2017a). These challenges include limited access to affordable finance, shortages in the availability of appropriate skills and difficulties associated with paying taxes. Tanzania's performance has also been deteriorating on a number of relevant Doing Business indicators (Balchin, 2017a). Firms also find it burdensome to comply with multiple charges and taxes by various agencies.

Operationalization of the recently approved Blueprint for Regulatory Reforms to Improve Tanzania's Business Environment will be critical to addressing these challenges. The Blueprint proposes measures to improve the business-enabling environment and put in place a framework that facilitates regular reviews of the business climate in Tanzania (URT, 2018). The document notes that, 'Government acknowledges that Tanzania still faces a number of policy and regulatory challenges which slow down the growth of the private sector and the industrialization' (MITI, 2018). In addition, the Blueprint makes recommendations in a number of specific areas. These include, for instance, the need for tax relief to promote domestic industries (including raw materials for producing animal feed) and backward linkages to agriculture to support industrialization. Other proposed measures include establishment of one-stop-service centres for investment and trade facilitation in order to guide investors, and incentives to the energy sub-sector to support industrialization.

AGRICULTURAL POTENTIALS IN TANZANIA

The importance of the agricultural sector towards the manufacturing lead economy cannot be overemphasized. The industrialization history narrates that, the development in Europe during the industrial revolution benefitted significantly from the agricultural sector (SET, 2018). The revolution was headed by the agricultural revolution towards the manufacturing economy. Thus, the agricultural sector is among the numerous paired sectors for industrialization around the world. According to URT (2017), the government of Tanzania acknowledge that industrial development will be extremely vulnerable if complementary sectors such as agriculture are overlooked. Reflections of lessons from strong economies are presented to include that, agriculture played transformative role in converting the economy from a stagnant agrarian society to a modern industrial one (Osabuohien et al, 2019). Thus, the agricultural sector has key roles to play in the industrialization move too for Tanzania

Tanzania towards its vision of becoming a middle-income economy by 2025, the National Five-Year Development Plan 2016/17–2020/21 (FYDP II), published in 2016, identifies industrialization as the main policy objective and key driver of economic transformation. Indeed, the 5th Phase Government is persistently pursuing industrialization as an overriding priority in the implementation of FYDP II. Such emphasis follows consensus in the literature that industrialization plays a critical role in economic development (Martorano et al., 2017). Despite the importance and priority attached to industrialization, though, progress on the ground has been slow, especially hampered by the overwhelmingly large amount of finance needed to push progress in many of the FYDP II flagship projects. Recently, the Government of Tanzania (GoT) prepared an action plan for implementing FYDP II. On-going monitoring of implementation and progress towards industrialization is necessary to ensure the industrialization agenda remains on track (URT, 2018).

Agriculture is undoubtedly the largest and most important sector of the Tanzanian economy, with the country benefitting from a diverse production base that includes livestock, staple food crops and a variety of cash crops. The sector's contribution to GDP (SET, 2018) has more than tripled in the last 10 years, supported by rising cash crop production, an emerging agro-processing segment and strong domestic demand for processed food. At the same time, farmers and other sector stakeholders face considerable challenges in modernizing the industry to increase yields, exports and value-added processing. Slowing export revenues; land acquisition hurdles; and smallholder farmers struggling to access economically viable technology, adequate storage facilities, markets and credit have affected private investment. Although the country's food self-sufficiency ratio ranged from 88% to 125% between 2000 and 2017, according to government data, the nation continues to rely on imports to meet demand for sugar, edible oil and cereal crops (MIT, 2018)

What is seeing for example is that medium-sized farms grew from 23 percent of all farm land holdings in the country in 2008 to 35 percent in 2017; and these are in the 5–20 hectare (ha) range, compared to the typical smallholding of 1–2 ha, whose numbers are decreasing (Holger and Kray, 2018). Farmers employ, invest in technology and knowledge, and they attract commercial services that can provide a basis for agri-food-based tax revenue. The effect of this is that small-scale farms on average improved their farming outcomes the nearer they were to medium-scale farms, providing an opportunity for more inclusive growth. The presence of medium-scale farms in the country generally builds and deepens markets for agricultural inputs and outputs by enhancing local demand, which attracts suppliers (Holger and Kray, 2018). As a result, small-scale farms are more likely to use improved seed and fertilizer, cultivate a larger proportion of their landholdings, and access agricultural extension services and credit in areas where there are more medium- and large-scale farms. The agriculture sector provides livelihoods directly to around 55 percent of the population (and three quarters of the poor) and indirectly to a further 15 percent within related value chain functions such as traders, transporters and processors (Dutt, 2017). Specifically the potentials of agriculture in Tanzania as part of supporting industrialization are in the following areas:

Employment and Exports

The sector remains an economic mainstay and the largest source of employment, with the Ministry of Finance and Planning (MoFP) reporting in the FYDP 2016/17-2020/21 that 67% of the workforce is engaged in agriculture. Data from the NBS shows that 11.3m people participated in agricultural activities during the 2017/18 season. Roughly 60% of operators were involved in crop production, 38% in crop and livestock activities, and 2% were solely engaged in livestock production. The indicated statistics produce raw materials availability which in turn may be used in industrial sector to make manufactured goods. Moreover, agricultural exports comprise around 30% of total exports and 65% of inputs to the industrial sector, according to the FYDP. However, value-added manufacturing activities which are very limited at present, and the agricultural export base is dominated by raw products and vulnerable to climate change, the potential that can be utilized at the moment is to use the raw materials internally instead of exporting raw as they are which seeks less price in the international markets.

Food Security

Another important area for the country with regards to agriculture is food security, which has shown major improvements towards 2020. The government aims to reach a food self-sufficiency ratio of 140% by that year, and reduce stunting and vitamin-A deficiencies in children younger than five years old to 28% and less than 25%, respectively. Staple crop production will play an important role in meeting these objectives. With the COVID-19 however, crop production have not been affected much as Tanzania was not under lock down. The Tanzania's primary staple crops are maize, rice, millet and wheat although several of these have seen production contract in recent years due to droughts. Nonetheless, these crops have recorded an overall positive growth trend since 2015 (NBS, 2018).

Maize production, which dominates the staple crop segment, grew from 3.32m tons in 2015 to 5.1m tons in 2018, reaching a seven-year peak of 6.73m tons in 2017 before falling by 12.3% in 2018 to 5.9m tons. At the same time, wheat production rose from 94,000 tons in 2018 to a high of 167,000 tons in 2019. Production then fell by 56.9% in 2015 to 72,000 tons, its lowest level since 2010. Millet production, likewise, soared from 204,000 tons in 2017 to reach 1.25m tons in 2018, but fell by 19.2% to 1m tons in 2016 and progressively seems to grow towards 2018. Other crops have recorded a more positive performance. Rice paddy production jumped from 885,000 tons in 2009 to a high of 2.65m in 2010, and then moderated to 1.46m in 2016 and 1.17m in 2018. Production has risen again in recent years, however, to 1.3m tons in 2017, 1.68m in 2016 and 1.94m in 2017 – a 15.2% increase over 2018 levels. Cassava production was up 17.9% in 2017 to hit 1.96m tons, while bean and banana production rose by 6.5% and 12.3%, respectively, in the same year. All these crops potentially indicate stable food security in the country of which supports the work force in the production of raw materials but also the ones that are working in the industrial sector.

Supply Strains Stabilization

In April 2017 the FAO reported that two consecutive below-average harvests have left low-income households in Arusha, Kilimanjaro, Pwani and Tanga "stressed" under the Integrated Food Security Phase Classification system. It noted that as of late March 2017, roughly 309,000 refugees and asylum seekers were living in the border regions of Kigoma and Kagera, due to violence and instability in Burundi and the Democratic Republic of the Congo, further straining the food supply.

The organization reported that maize prices have increased sharply in Tanzania in recent months, doubling between September 2016 and March 2017 in Iringa and Arusha, and rising by 60% in Dar es Salaam over the same period. Maize prices rose by an average of 55% year-on-year in March 2017, with the FAO reporting that these are "near record" levels, exacerbated by poor *vuli* crop production and uncertain prospects for the main *msimu* harvest[1].

The FAO reports that the country produced an estimated 10m tons of aggregate cereals in 2018 which is 9% more than the average of the previous five years while cereal import requirements for the 2016/17 marketing year were estimated at 1m tons, including 190,000 tons of rice. This represents a 6% increase over 2017/18 and a 10% rise over the average of the previous five years. At the end of 2017 the UN Office for the Coordination of Humanitarian Affairs reported that there were 424,000 people in Tanzania at risk of food and livelihood insecurity approximately 7% of the total population. With an increased and well managed agricultural production and more searches for markets of produce, the country will stabilize the economy and lessen the strains.

Private Investment Support

Increased private sector investment in all aspects of the agricultural value chain will play an important role in reducing food imports, improving food security, and supporting mid and long term development plan targets. The government is particularly seeking out new foreign financing for the flagship project Southern Agricultural Growth Corridor of Tanzania (SAGCOT) to quickly develop that region's agricultural potential. Following years of delays after the project was announced at the World Economic Forum on Africa 2010 in Dar es Salaam, the World Bank announced in March 2016 that it had approved a $70m facility for the programme. The entire project seeks to mobilize $2.1bn of private sector investment under a public-private partnership model. SAGCOT is expected to dramatically improve smallholder farmers' links with domestic and international markets, a critical consideration given that 80% of farms in the country are no larger than 2.2 ha (see analysis). The US International Trade Administration (ITA) reported in April 2016 that the government had, by that date, already allocated 63,000 ha of land for development under SAGCOT to be used for the cultivation and processing of sugarcane and rice. These wide-reaching efforts should see production levels of key cash crops return to growth in the coming years, helping boost value-added processing in the cotton, sisal, cashew, livestock, oilseed crop, coffee and tea segments. The whole lot of the production focus by the programme will enhance raw materials for the industrialization support for the country as follows:

Cotton

A potentially critical support mechanism for industrialization, Tanzania's cotton industry is one of its agricultural mainstays. According to the MoFP, between 350,000 and 500,000 smallholder farms grow cotton crops, and the income from this touches 40% of Tanzania's population. The Shinyanga region accounts for 60% of total production, followed by Mwanza at 25%, Mara at 8%, Tabora at 4% and Kagera at 2%. Together these regions comprise the Western Cotton Growing Area, which has seen export growth average 9.8% since 2000. The remaining 1% is grown in the Eastern Cotton Growing Area. Tanzania's primary cotton markets include China and Indonesia each receiving 24% of all cotton exports Vietnam (12%), Thailand (11%) and India (9%).Although cotton production has shown a net positive growth trend since 2006, levels never quite bounced back to the high of 378,000 bales recorded in 2005. Some 267,004 bales were harvested in 2009, rising to 357,130 in 2013, but sinking to 246,767 and 203,312 bales in 2014 and 2015, respectively. Cotton export revenues fell by 30.5% in 2015 to $38m alongside the lower production level.

Tanzania's cotton industry may actually benefit from being underdeveloped and overlooked, with the MoFP reporting that rising labour costs in leading global cotton markets have opened new opportunities for the country to compete on a price basis (see Industry & Retail chapter). In April 2017 the government announced that several levies would be abolished on cash crops as part of the 2017/18 budget in order to support growth opportunities in cotton, coffee, tobacco and tea (see analysis). Challenges remain, however, as input delivery is often delayed and cotton lint is of low quality, with yields often reduced by diseases. Price uncertainty also remains a chronic challenge for producers given global price fluctuations. Adoption of improved cottonseed and other crop husbandry techniques in the Lake Zone could lift between 302,500 and 600,000 people out of poverty, according to the FYDP, boosting the zone's economy by up to 12%.

Sisal

Sisal has been cultivated in Tanzania since German colonial times, with the country standing as the world's largest sisal producer until 1961. Production has recorded a volatile but overall positive growth trajectory since 2002, rising from 23,000 tons that year to reach 33,039 in 2007, dipping to 24,091 in 2010, and recovering to record 34,875 in 2013 and 39,204 in 2015, a 14-year high.

According to regional media, Tanzania is set to benefit from resurgent international demand for natural twine and plant fibres after the global sisal market took a hit with the advent of new synthetic fabrics and fibres, and the country aims to overtake Brazil to become the top global exporter once again. Indeed, NBS data indicates that sisal became the country's third-largest agricultural export earner in 2015 after cashew nuts and tobacco, with receipts soaring by 865% to hit $162.2m against $16.8m in 2014 and $10.9m in 2011. Beyond rope and twine, agave plants can also be processed into sweet syrup, and one of the industrialization interventions in the current FYDP includes the establishment of an agave syrup factory in Tanga. The facility is planned to be financed by the Public Service Pensions Fund and it is expected to be operational by December 2019 (NBS, 2019).

Cashews

Cashew nut production has recorded a positive performance in the last 15 years. The NBS (2018) reported that mainland production rose from 78,000 tons in 2002 to 121,070 in 2010 and 160,000 in 2011. Although production did not exceed 130,000 tons between 2012 and 2014, it surged to 197,933 tons in 2015 which is a 60% increase over 2014 levels. This enabled the crop to surpass tobacco as the nation's top agricultural export earner. Cashews were one of three cash crops to report export revenue growth in 2015, reaching $234m compared to $96.9m in 2011. Just 10% of cashew production is currently processed in the country, according to the ITA. Investment in this area could lead to the rehabilitation of old plants or the launch of new medium-scale processing plants.

Sugar

The last 10 years have seen sugar demand increase to reach an aggregate 580,000 tons in 2016/17. Household demand has been steadily growing, with annual sugar consumption at 445,000 tons. Industry demand for sugar has also increased, hitting 135,000 tons. Production of household sugar registered 326,909 tons in 2016/17, up from 262,879 tons in 2013/14. Meanwhile, industrial sugar is produced entirely abroad, leaving the country's aggregate annual sugar demand gap at about 255,000 tons, which is met through imports. Total sugarcane production rose from 1.81m tons in 2003 to 3.15m tons in 2011. The figures have moderated in the years since, falling to 2.98m tons in 2013 before climbing to 3.03m in 2015/16. It would be possible to double in-country sugar production over the medium term, according to the plan, but the government and private sector will first need to address challenges like excessive sugar imports; low sugarcane yields; the rising cost of primary inputs; the lack of infrastructure development, incentives to attract large-scale investments and access to credit facilities; and inadequate research, training and biosecurity services.

Edible Oils

Import requirements for edible oils are also high. The development plan reports that Tanzania spends more than $150,000 on edible oil imports annually, despite extremely rapid growth in the domestic output of oilseed crops. Indeed, NBS figures show that sunflower production has expanded more than three-fold since 2011, from 786,902 tons that year to 2.76m tons in 2014, and increasing a further 4.5% to 2.88m tons in 2017. Groundnut production rose 182% between 2011 and 2015 to 1.84m tons, and sesame oil production jumped by 229% over the same period to register 1.17m tons. Palm oil production increased by 144% to 41,475 tons in 2015, and soya production rose by 141% to 6030 tons in 2017.

The FYDP reports that with increased output and efficient practices, Tanzanian oilseed crops could hold significant potential to anchor a competitive domestic industry. However, out of 300,000 tons of edible oil demand in 2015, only 40% was sourced domestically. The plan intends to reduce oil import dependency through increased local processing, with a scheme to boost domestic output from 100,000 tons annually in 2015 to 250,000 tons in 2020/21 and 600,000 tons by 2025/26. This will be achieved by focusing on research and the availability of quality seeds, and developing the oilseed value chain to encourage investment in processing so that processing of edible oils is enhanced.

Coffee and Tea

Coffee and tea remain important cash crops for farmers in Tanzania. Production of cured coffee beans rose substantially over 2014, from 51,763 tons to 82,058 tons in 2015. Exports rose as well, from 44,100 tons to 58,000 tons. Corresponding export revenue was up 20.2% to $146m in 2015. Tea production, meanwhile, resulted in 45,750 tons of black tea and 46,230 tons of blended tea in 2015. Exports stayed stable between 2014 and 2015, with each year recording approximately 29,000 tons. However, the value of tea exports dipped 5.9% in 2015, bringing in revenue of $43m compared to $45.7m the year before.

Livestock

Looking beyond crops, livestock production including meat, dairy products, and skins and hides continues to hold great potential for future expansion (Mayala et al, 2017). The NBS reports that total meat production has risen significantly since 2009, from 452,230 tons that year to 532,711 tons in 2012 and 597,757 tons in 2017. This resulted in an average annual growth rate of 19%. Milk production has also risen significantly, from 1.6bn litres in 2009 to 2.06bn litres in 2017, while the number of skins and hides grew from 5.6m in 2009 to 6.45m in 2017, the most recent year for which statistics are available. The development plan also targets reviving the country's leather industry to support mid-term industrialization, creating new opportunities for private investment in meat and dairy production.

Produce

A variety of other produce is grown in Tanzania. The country's most popular fruit crops include mangoes, oranges, pineapples, passion fruits, bananas, avocados, jackfruits, papayas, peaches, pears, guavas, tomatoes and grapes. Vegetable production is dominated by okra and chilis. Vegetable and flower export revenues surged in 2018, rising by 153% over the $62.9m recorded the previous year to reach $159.1m. This growth trend has been building for several years, with the segment's exports totaling $37.8m in 2017. A 2018 report on Tanzanian horticulture by the Netherlands Enterprise Agency credits steady European demand and shrinking flower hectares around the world for the pick-up in Tanzania's flower exports, and growing middle classes in Tanzania's export countries for the increased demand for vegetables. The ITA reports that the country grows around 2.75m tons of produce annually, although just 4% of it is processed locally (ITA, 2018). This low percentage leaves significant potential for the provision of heavy equipment for commercial farming, as well as fruit and vegetable processing which all supports the industrialization processes.

RECOMMENDATIONS AND CONCLUSION

Since Tanzania has a quest for changing the focus of her economy from agricultural stance to manufacturing, at the same time the rate of increase in population is higher, food productivity and raw materials productivity in terms of agricultural produce is required; there is a need to refresh the plan/strategies/

programme and give a special focus on creating effective participation through encouraging full investment, especially in agri-business. Likewise, policies, strategies and programme developed, amended and implemented have to be realistic in portraying and exploring enormous opportunities that are in agriculture to ensure that growth of the economy is benefiting poor farmers as well as special attention is desired on the government spending on agriculture investment, which should focus on providing short and long term solution; including encouraging agriculture investment and well communicated agricultural research between researcher-extension officer-farmers and should encourage feedback from farmers to researchers. There are indications that with appropriate investments in the context of public-private partnership, it is possible to achieve lower costs of production, given that infrastructures and public services are well available to the small-scale farmers and opportunities are available to them to participate in the industrialization process. It is expected that ongoing road, railway and air transport infrastructure development will improve and reduce costs of transport, distribution and reduce unnecessary expenses, especially on post-harvest loss that make local produce uncompetitive versus imported products.

Agriculture plays an important role in the Tanzanian economy and has the potential to advance the country's goal of being middle income country in 2025, and sustaining growth while reducing poverty on one hand and fostering the objective of industrialization to the other hand. It has big share of employment (62.8%), but majority are smallholder farmer mostly producing food for their families and surplus for sale. Since industrialization at the moment is the focus for the country, and that in rural and agriculture is a major economic activity for most population (about 70%), therefore, to make efforts on agricultural development is necessary to improving performance of the agricultural productivity. So it is imperative that increasing in agricultural growth is not only to increase the incomes of farmers but also to support acceleration of development of non-agricultural activities in rural and urban areas, narrowing down inequality and improving lives of rural poor (poverty reduction). Steps must be taken now if the nation is to continue to pursue high level of achievement so that at the far end, less importation of raw materials is done, food production is enhanced to ensure availability of supply of the food and bridge the gap of shortage of food today and in the future. This is a decent obligation of the nation that intends not only to change income of the poor and their life style standard but also ensure re-engineering of the economy towards manufacturing. However, the role of agriculture during growth and structural transformation and the impact in economic development through industrialization has been and still a controversial issue since a lot need to be done from the angle of agricultural development.

REFERENCES

Balchin, N. (2017a). *Tanzania's second five-year development plan 2016/17–2020/21: summary and key action points. SET Policy Brief, August.* ODI.

Balchin, N. (2017b). *Financing Tanzania's national five-year development plan 2016/17 2020/21*. SET Report on Workshop, Dar es Salaam, 27 October. London: ODI

Balchin, N. (2018). *Private sector consultative workshop on effective implementation of Tanzania's second five-year development plan. SET Event Report, October.* ODI.

BOT – Bank of Tanzania. (2017). *Annual economic review 2017.* BOT.

Butty, A. M., Frischknecht, M., Gredler, B., Neuenschwander, S., Moll, J., Bieber, A., Baes, C. F., & Seefried, F. R. (2017). Genetic and genomic analysis of hyperthelia in Brown Swiss cattle. *Journal of Dairy Science, 100*(1), 402–411. doi:10.3168/jds.2016-11420 PMID:27865493

Cardno. (2017). *Agricultural development as a key role in food security and economic development in most of the world's population in rural area.* Academic Press.

Federici, S., Tubiello, F. N., Salvatore, M., Jacobs, H., & Schmidhuber, J. (2015). New estimates of CO2 forest emissions and removals: 1990–2015. *Forest Ecology and Management, 352*, 89–98. doi:10.1016/j.foreco.2015.04.022

Katundu, M. (2020). Fostering Rural Development and Social Inclusion in East Africa: Interrogating the Role of Cooperatives. In E. Osabuohien (Ed.), *The Palgrave Handbook of Agricultural and Rural Development in Africa.* Palgrave Macmillan. doi:10.1007/978-3-030-41513-6_17

Kumburu, N. P., & Pande, V. (2020). Rural Transformation Through Savings and Credit Cooperative Societies in Moshi District, Tanzania. In E. Osabuohien (Ed.), *The Palgrave Handbook of Agricultural and Rural Development in Africa.* Palgrave Macmillan. doi:10.1007/978-3-030-41513-6_15

Martorano, B., Sanfilippo, M., & Haraguchi, N. (2017). *What factors drive successful industrialization? Evidence and implications for developing countries.* Inclusive and Sustainable Industrial Development Working Paper. Vienna: UNIDO.

Massay, G. E. (2020). Local Politics of Land Acquisitions for Foreign and Domestic Investments in Tanzania. In E. Osabuohien (Ed.), *The Palgrave Handbook of Agricultural and Rural Development in Africa.* Palgrave Macmillan. doi:10.1007/978-3-030-41513-6_20

Mayala, N. M., Katundu, M. A., & Msuya, E. E. (2019). Socio-cultural Factors influencing livestock investment decisions among Smallholder Farmers in Mbulu and Bariadi Districts, Tanzania. *Global Business Review, 20*(5), 1214–1230. doi:10.1177/0972150917742556

Mayala, N. M., Msuya, E. E., & Katundu, M. A. (2018). Role of Extension Services on Livestock Investment Decisions by Smallholder Farmers in Mbulu and Bariadi Districts, Tanzania. *Indian Research Journal of Extension Education, 18*(3), 57–70.

MITI – Ministry of Industry, Trade and Investment. (2017a). Strategy for fast-tracking industrialization in Tanzania: 2016-2020. Dar es Salaam: MITI.

MITI – Ministry of Industry, Trade and Investment. (2017b). A joint inter-ministerial programme for supporting implementation of the industrialization agenda. Dar es Salaam: MITI.

MITI – Ministry of Industry, Trade and Investment. (2018). Blueprint for regulatory reforms to improve the business environment. Dar es Salaam: MITI.

Mufuruki, A., Mawji, R., Kasiga, G., & Marwa, M. (2018). *Tanzania's industrialization journey, 2016–2056: from an agrarian to a modern industrialized state in forty years.* Moran Publishers.

NBS – National Bureau of Statistics. (2016). *Report on the 2013 census of industrial production.* NBS.

Nwachukwu, I. (2008). *Planning and evaluation of agricultural and rural development project.* Lambhouse publishers.

OECD. (2016, July). Development Aid at a Glance: Statistics by Region. *Africa, 2015*, 26. https://www.oecd.org/dac/stats/documentupload/2%20Africa%20%20Development%20Aid%20at%20a%20Glance%202015.pdf,accessed

Osabohien, R., Matthew, O., Ohalete, P., & Osabuohien, E. (2020a). Population-Poverty-Inequality Nexus and Social Protection in Africa. *Social Indicators Research, 151*(2), 575–598. Advance online publication. doi:10.100711205-020-02381-0

Osabohien, R., Onanuga, O., Aderounmu, B., Matthew, O., & Osabuohien, E. (2020b). Social Protection and Employment in Africa's agricultural Sector. *Business: Theory and Practice, 21*(2), 494–502. doi:10.3846/btp.2020.11945

Osabuohien, E. (2020a). Guest Editorial: Labour Issues in Africa's Agricultural and Rural Transformation. *African Journal of Economic and Management Studies, 11*(2), 185–191. doi:10.1108/AJEMS-06-2020-406

Osabuohien, E. (2020b). *The Palgrave Handbook of Agricultural and Rural Development in Africa*. Palgrave Macmillan. doi:10.1007/978-3-030-41513-6

Osabuohien, E., Efobi, U., Gitau, C. M., Osabohien, R. A., & Adediran, O. O. (2020). Youth Unemployment and Large-scale Agricultural Land Investments in Africa: Examining the Relevance of Indigenous Institutions and Capacity in Tanzania. In The Palgrave Handbook of Agricultural and Rural Development in Africa (pp. 425-455). Cham, Switzerland: Palgrave Macmillan. DOI: doi:10.1007/978-3-030-41513-6_19

Osabuohien, E., Efobi, U. R., Herrmann, R., & Gitau, C. M. (2019). Female Labour Outcomes and Large-scale Agricultural Land Investments: Macro-Micro Evidence from Tanzania. *Land Use Policy, 82*, 716–728. doi:10.1016/j.landusepol.2019.01.005

SET – Supporting Economic Transformation. (2018). *Manufacturing in Africa: factors for successes.* Paper prepared for the Second African Transformation Forum, June, Accra. London: ODI

UNIDO – United Nations Industrial Development Organization. (2012). *Tanzania industrial competitiveness report 2012*. Dodoma: UNIDO and GoT.

URT - United Republic of Tanzania. (2016). *Cotton-to-clothing Strategy 2016-2020*. ITC.

World Bank. (2016). *Tanzania*. https://data.worldbank.org/country/tanzania?display=graph

World Bank. (2017). *World Bank Annual Report 2017 (English).* Washington, DC: World Bank Group. https://documents.worldbank.org/curated/en/143021506909711004/World-Bank-Annual-Report-2017

World Bank. (2018). *The World Bank Annual Report 2018 (English).* Washington, DC: World Bank Group. https://documents.worldbank.org/curated/en/630671538158537244/The-World-Bank-Annual-Report-2018

ENDNOTE

1 *Vuli* means rainy season for crops planting while *Msimu* means harvesting period.

Section 4

Sustainable Resource Development, Energy, and Environment

Chapter 19
Design of a Food Waste Management Program in Reducing Urban Food Waste

Olubunmi Racheal Ajayi
Griffith University, Australia

Scott R. Baum
https://orcid.org/0000-0003-1711-2087
Griffith University, Australia

Cordia Chu
Griffith University, Australia

ABSTRACT

Sustainable food systems can contribute to addressing food security, poverty alleviation, and economic growth. With 870 million people around the world being undernourished, and food shortages exacerbated by climate change, the United Nations, in 2013, made food security a priority. This study aimed to develop a food waste reduction program model to assist with designing and delivering effective responses in relevant institutions. This study conducted desktop review of literature, detailing proven practices in food waste management systems and synthesised key success factors. Three cases, from San Francisco, Taiwan, and South Korea, were chosen for further analysis because they have a proven track record of success. The study also proposes a program for designing, implementing, and evaluating future food waste management programs. The findings have identified significant policy opportunities for food waste management strategies and have provided an opportunity to develop food waste guidelines as many work towards the 2030 Sustainable Development Goal of halving global food waste.

DOI: 10.4018/978-1-7998-4817-2.ch019

INTRODUCTION

Sustainable development is at the core of our human existence and has evolved as a significant policy concern for governments and business organizations (Mebratu, 1998). The Brundtland report (1987) which brought this concept to the forefront defines sustainable development a "development that meets the needs of the present without compromising the ability of future generations to meet their own needs" (Brundtland, 1987). In 2015, a universal agreement was signed by 193 UN Members States to end poverty. The 17 goals consisting of 169 targets were adopted to address rapidly changing landscapes and developmental initiatives affecting the environment, economies and the social spheres of existence (United Nations, 2015). It is vital to take into cognizance the universal nature of these goals and the freedom embedded in member states to monitor outcomes and progress nationally, using guidelines provided by the United Nations. With projections of global human population increasing to 9.3 billion by 2050 and forty-seven percent of the growth in sub-Saharan Africa (Hanson, 2013), it is pertinent for Africa to combat food insecurity. The Millennium development goals (MDGs) reflect the commitment to sustaining future generations.

Zero waste, one of the most innovative concept of the century (Zaman, 2003 &Zaman, 2004) is a key area for achieving Sustainable development. Several developed countries have implemented zero waste agendas to conserve depleting resources. Many developing economies can benefit from the zero waste concept. This chapter contributes to institutional development in Africa by elaborating on how African countries can use the zero waste concept to their advantage. Overconsumption trends and the materialistic culture of consumers has resulted in unprecedented increases in waste, which cannot be sustained by current purchase, use and dispose of in landfills practice. Zero waste encapsulates holistic (Song et al., 2014) visionary and closed-loop (Park & Lah, 2015) concepts of managing waste as a resource. One of the critical areas where the concept of Zero Waste is crucial is in the area of food waste. Food waste is defined as *'food, which was originally produced for human consumption but then was discarded or was not consumed by humans'* (Thyberg & Tonjes, 2016).

There can be little doubt that food waste continues to be a global problem and one that is increasing over time. Over 2 billion people in the world experience moderate to severe levels of food insecurity. There are increasing levels of hunger in sub regions of Africa (FAO, 2019). As concern grows about the wide-ranging impacts of food waste on human society, the economy and the environment, local, national and international institutions are introducing programs and policies aimed at addressing the problem (Thyberg & Tonjes, 2016). These efforts are laudable and must continue to be implemented in line with the best evidence. Although difficult to measure and quantify, the available empirical evidence suggests that food waste makes up a significant proportion of global food production. It is estimated that globally, food waste accounts for approximately one-third (by weight) of all food produced annually (Hebrok & Boks, 2017; Hamilton et al., 2005). Moreover, it is suggested that while the problem of food waste is more significant in highly developed economies than in less-developed ones, it is becoming an issue across countries as economic development, urbanization and affluence increases (Baig et al, 2018; Koch et al, 2018; Gustavsson et al, 2015).

The impacts of ever-increasing food waste for the planet and society are primarily acknowledged and have been well described in the literature (Park & Lah, 2015; Secondi et al., 2015; Lundqvist, 2008; Asomani-Boateng & Haight, 1999).

Across all levels of analysis from individual consumers to national and international food systems, the impacts of increasing food waste are seen in terms of ever-increasing environmental concerns, fears around the use and sustainability of economic resources and the effects on future food availability and food scarcity (Gustavsson et al, 2011). When food is wasted, so too are all of the resources that went to growing, producing, processing and transporting the food resulting in unnecessary negative environmental and economic impacts. A study estimates that global production of lost and wasted food accounts for 24 per cent of total freshwater resources, 23 per cent of all cropland and 23 per cent of global fertilizer use (Kummu et al, 2012). Other environmental impacts include the release of pollutants into the atmosphere and water bodies through dumping and incineration. In landfills, for example, food waste converts into methane, which has a global warming potential 25 times greater than the equivalent carbon dioxide production (Forster et al, 2007).

Along with environmental impacts, the wasted economic resources associated with the production, distribution and disposal of wasted food is also an area of concern. The FAO reports that food waste has direct economic costs equal to USD1 trillion per year, environmental costs of USD 700 billion and social costs of USD 900 billion. The final impact of food waste and one that has received significant attention is the issue of food security and in particular, the decline in food security across the globe. Access to healthy and nutritious food is vital for human health and development and is also a human right issue (FAO, 2018; FAO, 2013)

The United Nations has identified food security as one of its 17 sustainable development goals, and several authors, including (Reynolds et al, 2014; Lundqvist et al, 2008) have made a vital link between increasing food waste and declining food security. These concerns and the urgent needs for the world to work together to achieve sustainable development goals, including inclusive economic growth, are at the heart of this chapter.

In particular, the chapter will address the issue of food waste by presenting a framework for understanding and building appropriate program responses based on a desktop comparison of three cases drawing from a review of available literature, reports, policy documents and websites. By applying the framework to compare the three cases, we aim to identify the key factors required for food waste reduction programs. The outcomes of this review are then applied to design a step-wise operational model to guide the development and implementation of programs aiming at food waste reduction.

A BRIEF BACKGROUND: DEFINITION, CAUSES AND INTERVENTION

What is Food Waste, and What are its Causes?

Factors characterizing waste vary according to the type of material included, the means of production used and the management approaches adopted (FAO, 2013). Early definitions regarded food waste as the destruction or deterioration of food or the use of crops, livestock and livestock products in ways which return relatively little human food value (kling, 1943). More contemporary definitions consider food waste as a sub-set of food loss. Food loss is defined as a '*decrease in edible food mass throughout the part of the supply chain that specifically leads to edible food for human consumption*'. As a subset of this, food waste is defined as '*food, which was originally produced for human consumption but then was discarded or was not consumed by humans*' (Thyberg & Tonjes, 2016).

Causes of Food Waste

The causes of food waste are variable and have been widely discussed in the literature (Neff et al, 2019; Oelofse & Nahman, 2013; Venkat, 2012; Gustavsson et al, 2011; Morisaku, 2000. The upstream processes such as unharvested crops due to disease, pest infestation and weather fluctuations coupled with stringent quality standards of food production accounts for 54% of food loss and waste. In comparison, 46% is a result of processing operations, distribution and consumption patterns (Mebratu, 1998). While there are likely, many sources of food waste, researchers (Buzby et al, 2014) argue that consumers drive a significant proportion of food waste and that understanding the drivers of food waste is an important step in developing and implementing successful institutional programs. In a wide-ranging systematic review argue that 'food turns to waste within a web of interrelated practices, tools, concerns, skills, knowledge and anxieties' (Hamilton et al, 2005). Broad macro-level factors can include increasing globalization resulting in more complex food supply chains, packaging, labelling, urbanization meaning change in populations and taste and modernization resulting in changes to values and lifestyles (Gooch et al, 2019; Williams et al, 2012; Gustavsson et al, 2011). Once these are distilled down to the level of individuals and households, factors including consumer values, culture, lifestyle and material and structural aspects all are presented as potentially important drivers. (Mena et al,2020).

Values and lifestyles influence the way consumers view and use food, and relate to issues around perceived food abundance and cost of food, willingness to use leftovers and meal planning. Modern living is often associated with convenience and the throw-away society, resulting in significant food waste. Cultural aspects such as wanting to be seen as a good provider or a welcoming host to visitors may lead to increased food purchase and preparation and the potential for waste. Moreover, the ability to safely store food, the availability of refrigeration and the type of food packaging used by producers and retailers will also impact on waste (Rockefeller, 2013).

Food Waste Situation in Africa and Around the World

At a more national and country level, the scale of the food waste problem is also significant. In the United States of America, preventable food waste exceeds 55 metric tons annually, representing around 29% of annual food production (Thyberg & Tonjes, 2016). In the United Kingdom, it is estimated that around half (7 million metric tons) of all food fit for human consumption is wasted. In Australia, households discard AUD $5.2 billion worth of food, which can be broken down to (AUD $616 per household) annually (Reynolds et al., 2014). The story is not different in developing economies because North Africa, Kenya, South Africa and South-East Asia waste 35-40%. China, Beijing (66.19%), Shanghai (71.44); India (35-40%) (Mebratu, 1998). In some African countries such as Nigeria, many households are food insecure (Osabohien et al, 2020) and some cities such as Lagos waste (68.1%), Accra (85.1%), and Kampala (75%) (Asomani-Boateng & Haight, 1999).

Even though there is an ongoing coordinated strategy to manage food waste in developed economies, it is more challenging to implement an effective waste management strategy in developing countries (Rockefeller, 2013). According to the World Bank, developing countries spend 80% of the Municipal Solid Waste Management budget on collection and landfill management. In comparison, developed countries spend less than 10% on collections and allow more funds for creating awareness, treatment facilities and waste segregation (Prasad et al., 2011). Some other challenges in developing countries are low funding for segregation and recycling activities, insufficient and ineffective administrative processes and most importantly, lack of policies and regulations (Rockefeller, 2013). These are all institutional inefficiencies slowing down economic growth especially in Africa. It is pertinent for policymakers to initiate actions acknowledging the positive link between strong institutions and economic progress (Vianna & Mollick, 2018).

Intervening in Food Waste

The inter-related web of drivers associated with food waste means that like other complex 'wicked-problems' food waste requires coordinated action across various sectors, institutions and groups while utilizing combinations of technology-based solutions, public intervention and incentives. While higher-level national or state governmental practices have a role to play, investment in large-scale technology and broad overarching policy (such as the United States Department of Agriculture's food waste reduction goal of 50%) (USDA,2015) programs and national level goals, attention at more local levels is also beneficial. Local municipalities sit in-between individual consumers and national and or state-level governments. Programs used to intervene in reducing food waste, need to influence the behaviour of individual consumers and suppliers, and as a consequence, local municipalities are often best placed to act (Heller, 2019; Peter et al., 2010). The goals of existing food waste programs are diversion of food waste from landfill, strengthening institutions through infrastructural development and capacity building, and behavioural change of consumers and producers to reduce waste production. The following sections will describe the method and highlight salient points from cases of food waste management in other developed countries that could be suited to the institutional context in developing economies in Africa.

Method

The goal of this paper is to present a food waste reduction model that is informed both by the existing literature and three selected cases. The development of this model will enable policymakers and program designers to consider aspects of food waste mitigation and prevention more systematically and is deemed to be a constructed ideal used to approximate reality by selecting and accentuating certain elements. The approach used to develop the model is outlined in figure 1 and detailed further below.

Figure 1. Methodology

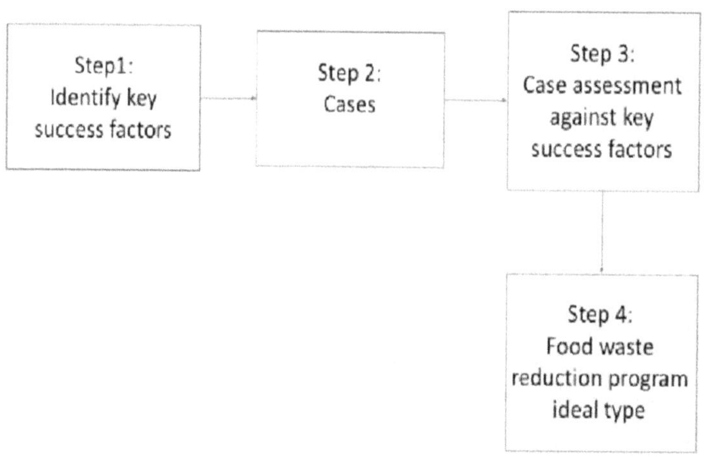

Identifying key Success Factors

A search of appropriate literature was undertaken to identify several key factors which may be important in the development of successful food waste programs. We identified relevant peer-reviewed journals articles and grey literature appearing in Science Direct, Scopus and Google Scholar plus manual reference searches, limiting our search to material published in English between the years 1977 to 2019.

The keyword search strings included 'food waste'. 'food waste strategies', 'food waste systems' 'food waste policies', 'cases on food wastes' and 'best practice and food waste'. Articles were then screened by title and then abstract, and then full papers were reviewed. Information extracted to help develop a summary of key factors that were consistently identified across successful and effective food waste prevention/mitigation programs.

Selected Cases and Their Features

The cases were selected based on the period of operation, replicability of program features, the validity of data and widely known as best practice. The cases were evaluated using a comparative analysis. Some key success factors were identified as critical for their operation. These key success factors were used to help identify and critically assess cases that were selected (or chosen) as exemplary programs based on the review. One program, San Francisco, is based at the municipal level and is guided by national and state-level goals and objectives. At the same time, the remaining two, Taiwan and Korea, are illustrations of national-level programs which are physically enacted at local municipal levels.

Assessment

Supplementary information, where necessary, was gathered on each case, which included grey literature from government sources and additional scientific manuscripts where possible. The use of such literature helped to establish a rich understanding of the cases, and then these cases were assessed concerning the key success factors identified in stage one.

Food Waste Reduction Model

The results of the assessment of the cases against the key success factors then became the background material feeding into the development of the food waste reduction model (stage four). The model was developed concerning the process of Intervention Mapping (IM). Intervention Mapping is a protocol for planning theory-based and evidence-based behaviour change programs, and while it is most often used in health promotion, the potential for its use in other fields has begun to be recognized.[3] As a planning and intervention development tool, it recognizes that behaviors are the function of individuals and the physical, social and organizational environments in which individuals operate in, and that intervention content needs to be developed with these multi-faceted spheres in mind. It also recognizes that interventions at one level may have consequences (intended or unintended) at other levels. Intervention Mapping also acknowledges the requirement to involve stakeholders at all stages of development, rollout and evaluation of a program (Kok et al, 2011). Finally, Intervention Mapping demands programs to be built around relevant theories and evidence (Kok et al, 2017).

RESULTS

Review

The outcome of the systematic search was that a range of key success factors was synthesized from the evidence (see Figure 2). Generally, factors accounting for successful programs are divided into **content factors** and **process factors**. Content factors include the resources adopted to influence or change behaviour or to improve skills or knowledge and the infrastructure required to conduct the program successfully. Process factors relate to the logistics of developing a program and focus on issues including planning, engagement and evaluation. Planning process factors include problem identification, program timing, program goals, including the establishment of baselines, and program integration. Engagement process consists of the engagement of stakeholders and the collaboration across sectors or groups. The evaluation process includes processes around piloting programs and testing programs against goals and baselines.

Figure 2. Key factors in successful food waste management programs

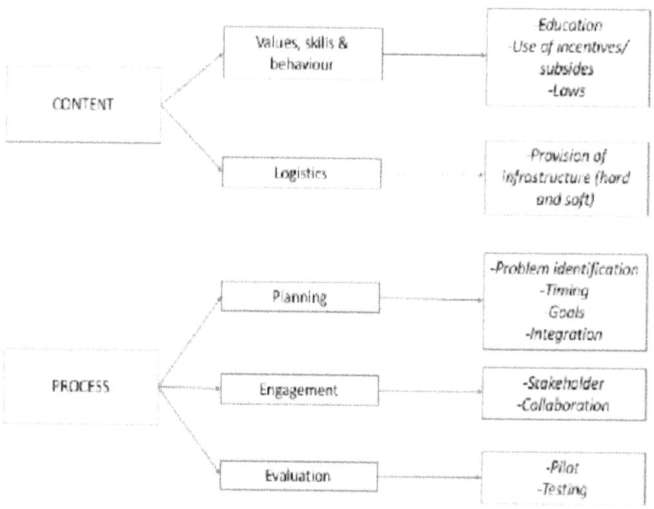

SELECTED CASES AND THEIR PROGRAMS

San Francisco

The San Francisco case represents an example of a food waste reduction and diversion program based at the municipal level. Driven in part by higher-level state and national policies, including California's Integrated Waste Management Act, the food waste program is embedded in the city's broader zero-waste policy. The program is holistic by design and is backed by carefully developed processes, and program content has been subject to extensive stakeholder engagement during development and subsequent evaluation.

The success of San Francisco's food waste recovery program is attributed to strong institutions and exemplary policy leadership. During the development of the program, innovative policy initiatives such as mandatory recycling, composting and modern outreach programs covering residences, commercial, schools and events have all changed in the way food waste has been produced and handled (EPA, 2016; Cote, 2009). After achieving the state-mandated level of 50 per cent waste diversion in 2000 the city's broader zero-waste policy aimed at diverting 75 per cent of municipal waste from landfill by 2010 (higher than the required legislated state level) and moving to zero-waste by 2020 (Cote, 2009). Legislatively, the diversion goal was supported by mandatory municipal ordinance which was launched 2009 and requires all residents in San Francisco separate recyclable, compostable and landfill materials and participate in recycling and composting programs, with enforcement mechanisms and penalties set out for violations of the code (Cote, 2009).

Residents are encouraged to meet the legislative requirements through the provision of appropriate infrastructure and extensive education and outreach campaigns. The city implemented an innovative "Fantastic Three" residential curbside collection program that includes colour-coded rubbish bins for the collection of commingled recyclables; compostable materials, including all food scraps and any remaining trash. The use of the correct bin is achieved via an online 'customizable sign' portal that allows users to develop appropriate recycling signage to meet their specific needs. These signs allow for visual cues regarding the appropriate content to be placed in each bin and are provided in a multi-lingual format. Also, there is composting and organic transfer infrastructure provided for both households and the commercial sector, allowing the sorting and transfer of organic waste material (Dmitriew, 2018). Education is provided through mechanisms including a face-to-face outreach program run by the Department of Environment and an online recycling database. The outreach program involves Department of Environment officers visiting neighbourhoods and identifying households and businesses requiring information regarding the appropriate waste disposal actions. The online database 'recycle where' provides information to residents about the recycling and waste disposal options, while other online resources offer information regarding composting.

Enforcement of the program is carried out through the Department of Environment. Monitoring is undertaken to start during waste collection, with truck driver tagging contaminated bins. Affected customers are consulted and followed up with a 30-day warning letter and another enforcement letter for non-compliance until the customer is reaudited and regains their status.10 Enforcement via a fine is considered to be the last resort with education and face-to-face outreach being the preferred management options. Incentives and subsidies were also introduced for both businesses and households as an inducement to change waste management behaviour. Business organizations are eligible to receive a rate discount based on the amount of waste diversion, providing strong financial incentives to reduce waste, recycle and compost (Dmitriew, 2018).

The compostable material collected includes all food scraps pre and post-consumer with meat, together with food-soiled paper, animal bedding, waxed cardboard and wood crates. The organics are transported to a municipal composting facility where they are mixed, ground and composted using state of the art facilities. The final composted material is sold to agriculture and landscaping users, including organic farmers in the San Francisco Bay area, highway erosion control projects and retail outlets for sale to consumers.

South Korea

The South Korean case is an example of a national food waste strategy set within a broader national level framework and implemented at local municipal levels. The impetus for the development and rollout of the South Korean program was environmental concerns regarding increasing levels of waste products associated with the country's rapid urbanization and the shortage of suitable landfill sites. Developed over several years, the program today focuses on waste reduction, reuse and recycling utilizing incentives, penalties, education campaigns and infrastructural approaches.

Beginning in 1995 with the release of the Food Waste Reduction Masterplan and subsequent plans in 1998 and 2004, South Korea's food waste program has evolved into a highly integrated program. The evolution of the program has included a landfill ban on food waste in 2005, encouragement of composting and recycling as a landfill diversion strategy and the introduction of a cross-sector voluntary food waste reduction program in 2010. The sectors included restaurants, hotels and education institutions. Restaurants were encouraged to use fewer small side-dish plates and adopt eco-friendly menus. At the same time, cafeterias in public institutions such as schools promoted the "no-leftover day" program once a week. One of the most significant advances within the program has been the introduction of Volume-Based Waste Fees (VBWF) as a means of encouraging households to change food waste behavior (EPA, 2019). Up till 1994, the South Korean government had utilized a fixed waste tariff as a means of reducing all types of waste, including food waste. Evaluation of this program identified that rather than reducing waste, it contributed to a gradual increase in the amount of waste produced. This evaluation resulted in the implementation of the current VBWF system in its early form during 1995 by the Korean Ministry of Environment (Park & Lah, 2015; Seo et al., 2004). The South Korean government banned landfilling of food without pre-treatment requiring residents to cautiously separate food scraps collected in the VBWF bags (Park & Lah, 2015).

The main goal of the VBWF system is to pass-on waste treatment costs to each polluter according to the amount of waste produce (Bourtsalas et al., 2019). Local municipalities implement three "pay-as-you- throw" solutions namely paid bio-degradable plastic bags, attached paid sticker or coupons to food - waste bins and technological-based system that weighs individual household waste and record monthly waste totals using Radio Frequency Identification (RFID) Cards. These solutions allow monthly waste disposal charges to be sent to households.

The introduction of the Volume Based Waste Fee system has been supported by a range of ancillary programs and policies. Illegal food waste disposal is discouraged by imposing fine of KRW 1 million (around USD900) levied at individuals caught disposing of waste without the appropriate VBWF bags or unlawfully incinerating waste. Other enforcement tools include mandatory education on appropriate disposal practices and vetoes on waste collection for households found to violate the program practices. Civil servants monitor unlawful activities, and CCTV cameras are installed at problem locations, while local municipalities also operate special reporting centers.

The success and acceptance of the VBWF system have, in large part, been due to the implementation of education programs and continuous evaluation. While the initial rollout resulted in public complaints, the Korean Ministry of Environment developed public promotion campaigns across electronic and print media, including the distribution of promotional materials containing important educational messages. Moreover, workshops, seminars, and symposiums are organized continuously allowing the national ministry and municipal level agencies to evaluate and modify the program where needed.

While installing infrastructural facilities for collection, the government also made provision for the use of the collected food waste in the form of animal feed and fertilizer, which is supporting the growing urban farm movement. Feed safety is guided by several control measures, including certification, registration, strict feed standards coupled with treatment technologies. This introduction and implementation of regulations and laws have not experienced disease outbreaks associated with food waste-derived feeds (Vianna & Mollick, 2018).

Taiwan

The Taiwan case represents an example of a nationally coordinated system aimed at landfill diversion through recycling and reuse. The development of the contemporary program, which includes a range of education, incentives and enforcement tools has been developed through several iterations. In 2001, the Taiwanese Environmental Protection Administration (EPA) set up kitchen waste collection programs throughout the nation. The policy encouraged waste recycling and reuse by providing subsidies to counties and townships to develop food waste recycling systems throughout the country. The subsidy system was provided in a staged rollout, and by 2006, all municipalities had established recycling systems (Chen, 2016). This initiative expanded in 2002 to include separation and collection of food waste from hotels, restaurants and residential areas. Furthermore, in 2003, food waste recycling became part of the official function of the EPA with allotted budgets resulting in incentives being offered for the private establishment of food waste reuse and recycling programs.

Under the current program, households and other food waste producers are required to separate food waste before collection by municipal waste collectors. Failure to comply attracts a fine, in addition to waste collectors refusing to collect the offending items. Of all municipal solid waste collected, food waste accounts for approximately one-tenth with the bulk being used to produce pig feed (71 per cent) and the remainder to compost. In total tonnage, food waste for pig feed has increased from 140,090 tonnes in 2003 (Buzby et al,2014) to 695, 000 tonnes in 2018. Food waste for composting has increased from 23, 092 tonnes in 2003 (Chen, 2016) to 231, 676 tonnes in 2018 (EPA, 2008). In economic terms (Thi et al, 2015) annual benefit of 2.7 billion NT dollars was recorded from the reduced incineration fee and sales revenue of pig food scraps. The power generation potential for the food waste recovered was 68.0 GWh y−1, and the potential excluding composting and swine feeding were 14.0 and 54.5 GWh y−1 in 2006, respectively.

Furthermore, the potential for compost production was 122 MWh y−1 when compared with the energy consumption of chemical fertilizer (ammonium sulfate and calcium superphosphate) production in Taiwan in 2006. These results suggested that recycled food wastes not only reduces the amount of garbage but has immense potentials for power generation and energy conservation (Lai, 2009). Other benefits of Taiwan's food waste recycling program include nationwide awareness of the food waste problem and a National Sustainable Development Award for its contribution towards making Taiwan a Zero waste society (Thi et al, 2015).

Assessment of the Cases Against Key Success Factors

The key success factors presented in figure two were used to assess the three individual case studies as a precursor to the development of a model to assist food waste reduction interventions. The key success factors of food waste reduction listed below are broadly categorized into two main categories; content and process. Content includes key components such as education and awareness, incentives and subsidies and the provision of infrastructure. The method comprises aspects of planning, engagement and evaluation.

All three case studies included the development and implementation of appropriate content focused on changing values, skills and behavior. Although implemented at different times in the planning and implementation stages, each case successfully used educational campaigns or face-to-face outreach to influence the adoption of the new programs and to initiate appropriate change. The San Francisco program emphasizes continuous education through different platforms, including the monthly waste bills of customers and social media (Cote, 2009). While the Taiwanese program also utilized different signages to target the different sectors. Education must be strategic and targeted to different audiences to allow wide-ranging take-up of key messages across different societal groups and communities. Communities with multi-lingual populations must endeavour to translate the education materials and create an awareness strategy that would resonate with the target audience, as demonstrated in the San Francisco Case. Practical demonstrations of how to store the food waste to be collected and compost them where these facilities are available are also helpful and prevent contamination right from the source of production. Targeted and strategic education and continuous awareness are suggested pathways for implementing successful food waste reduction programs.

Content aimed at behaviour change is also introduced in the form of positive and negative incentives or subsidies. Subsidies and incentives can be in terms of inducements to encourage recycling of food waste for individuals and households, up to incentives for industry to invest in large scale food recycling plant (i.e. commercial level composting). An illustration of incentives is the free collection service offered by the South Korean government in 2006, which facilitated the use of food wastes as soil conditioners and animal feed (Seo et al, 2004). In Taiwan, the policy provided subsidies to townships and counties for the development of food waste recycling systems throughout the country.

Associated with the use of incentives and subsidies is the use of legal frameworks to enforce the required outcomes. All of the case studies had well established legal frameworks setting out the boundaries of their programs, including legislation around penalties, responsibilities and scope of programs. San Francisco passed a Mandatory Municipal Recycling and Composting Ordinance in 2009. This local municipal ordinance requires all residents to separate their compostable, recyclables and landfill trash. The strategy kicked off with a clearly defined diversion goal of 75% diversion by 2010 and zero waste by 2020 (Dmitriew, 2018) Monitoring and enforcement are followed through starting with the truck driver who tags every contaminated bin. On enforcing compliance, the non-complying customer is consulted and followed up with a 30-day warning letter and another enforcement letter for non-compliance until the customer is reaudited and regains their status (Cote, 2009).

On the other hand, the South Korean government initiated a phased solution for food waste management by launching a Food waste reduction masterplan in 1995 followed by a recycling programme established in 1998 and revamped in 2004 to include the collection of food waste in residential areas and restaurants. The program evolved into a landfill ban on food waste in 2005 by the South Korean government. In 2010, the Ministry of Environment, in **collaboration** with other ministries, carried out a food **waste reduction** project by signing agreements with different sectors for voluntary cooperation. The sectors included restaurants, hotels, schools etc. Restaurants were encouraged to use fewer small side-dish plates and adopt eco-friendly menus. Cafeterias in public institutions promoted the "no-leftover day" program once a week. In Taiwan's case, the government encouraged the policy of mandatory waste sorting in stages according to Article 12 of the Waste Disposal Act since 2005. It regulates that the discharge of waste from households should be sorted into three categories: "Resources", "Kitchen waste" and "Trash", which shall be respectively sent to resource recycling vehicles, refuse trucks and recycling bins for the kitchen waste (EPA, 2019).

A common theme through the case studies was the provision of necessary infrastructure to enable the successful rollout of programs. The infrastructure can be hard-infrastructure such as massive food waste composting, or treatment facilities, waste collection infrastructure down to the provision of suitable waste containers at the household level, or it can be a term of the provision of soft-infrastructure such as the provision of bureaucratic systems to manage education and enforcement. This is a missing factor in most of Africa's waste disposal systems.

In San Francisco, compostable food materials are collected using semi-automatic side loading, single compartment compactor loadings. In contrast, the recyclables are collected using semi-automatic vertically split dual compartment side-loading compactor vehicles. Collected organics are delivered to the city's transfer station where the material is top-loaded from the refuse pit too large possum belly trailers (Biocycle, 2002). In South Korea, the food waste program operated a Volume-based food waste fee system in 2010, where households pay based on the amount of food waste they generate. Municipalities have *three "pay-as-you-throw" solutions (paid standard plastic bags, attaching paid stickers to food-waste bins- not emptied without labels and a high-tech solution, operating food-waste bins with magnetic card-readers that households must use when disposing of their waste.* Technology has played a significant role in the success of the program. The country's capital Seoul installed 6,000 automated bins fixed with Radio Frequency Identification (RFID) and scales to weigh and charge residents as they deposit the food waste using an II.D.card. City officials claim the recycling machines have led to a reduction of 47,000 tonnes in six years. Residents are encouraged to minimize the weight of their food waste by removing moisture, and this reduces their charges because Food waste contains about 80% moisture and also saved the city $8.4 million in collection charges during the period. While installing infrastructural facilities for collection, the government also made provision for the use of the collected food waste in the form of animal feed and fertilizer, which is supporting the growing urban farm movement. Feed safety is guided by diverse control measures, including certification, registration, strict feed standards coupled with treatment technologies. This introduction and implementation of regulations and laws have not experienced disease outbreaks associated with food waste-derived feeds (Vianna & Mollick, 2018).

While the content of food waste programs is important, several process factors are also required. All of the case studies were developed following extensive planning and after identifying a problem in terms of food waste reduction or waste diversion. In all three cases, clear goals in term of food waste reduction were identified and were used to evaluate and provide ongoing reporting. In the case of San Francisco for example, the city was driven to meet state-mandated targets in terms of waste reduction and these goals became the impetus for developing and managing the food waste problem as part of the overall waste strategy. The success of the case studies was driven by the inclusion of stakeholders during the development and implementation of the programs and through collaboration between different sectors and levels of government. This was especially the case in the South Korean and Taiwanese examples were the national level waste reduction policies and programs had to be filtered down to and instigated at the local level. Finally, all of the case studies included some form of pilot work or staged rollout, and all have completed evaluation periods. South Korea, for example, developed the food waste program over several iterations of policy and program design and have undertaken constant evaluation involving input from stakeholders at various levels.

Intervention Mapping in the Context of Food Waste Program Success Factors

Developing appropriate food waste reduction programs has become increasingly important in developing counties, such as Africa and the success of such programs has the ability to significantly impact on the path of inclusive and sustainable growth (Hanson, 2013). Despite the fact that there are many examples in the literature dealing with issues of food waste and the best approaches to achieve reductions in food waste, it is often the case that approaches are ad-hoc in design. One way to overcome these short-comings is through the adoption of systematic processes of program design. One such approach, which was developed in the field of public health (Bartholomew et al., 1998). but has been expanded to other fields (Kok et al, 2015) is Intervention mapping. Intervention mapping has defined as a planning framework for the development of theory and evidence-based behaviour change programs. It is 'a framework for effective decision making at each step in the intervention development process (Bartholomew et al., 1998). When combined with the key content and process-oriented success factors identified from the three case studies, the intervention mapping protocol can be modified to provide a useful matrix outlining key opportunities, issues and structures (Figure 3).

The benefit of utilising an intervention mapping approach is that it describes an iterative path involving six steps (figure 3) running from problem identification to problem solving to evaluation and provides opportunities for feedback loops to be integrated into the program development process. The completion of various tasks at each step creates a product that feeds-in to subsequent steps. The completion of all of the steps provides a useful blueprint for designing, implementing and evaluating an intervention based on a foundation of theoretical, empirical and practical information.

Step 1: Logic of Model

Developing the logic of the model involves conducting a needs assessment or an analysis of the problem and includes the identification of the extent of the problem and the issues that need to be addressed or changed (Bartholomew et al., 1998). In the context of the success factors identified, this necessarily involves engagement with stakeholders who can help identify suitable data sources dealing with food waste in the local context, identifying potential key informants and understanding food waste in the broader social and economic context. Here program developers and planners would establish the extent of food waste at different organisational and institutional context (farmers, distributors, retails, households) as well as geographic levels (country, regional, municipal, local community/ neighbourhood). They would ask what behaviours need to be targeted and what the target populations are. On completion of step one, program designers and planners, in conjunction with stakeholders, would have developed a list of food waste behaviours and the context in which these behaviours occur.

Step 2: Program Outcomes

The second step in intervention mapping involves identifying the goals for a given food waste reduction program and understanding the who, what and why of program outcomes. Here again stakeholder engagement is important in identifying agreed goals. Developing agreed goals that are built around the broader context of step 1 allows for ownership of programs to be cemented. Depending on context, goals may include farmers reducing waste by a certain number of tonnes or changing to more sustainable crops. At the household level, goals may include reducing the amount of food purchased that is subsequently wasted or changes to other buying habits. In step two the outcome should be a matrix of goals associated with particular contexts that allow for specific targeted program design to be initiated.

Step 3: Program Design

Program design is a crucial stage of intervention mapping and involves understanding the values, skills and behaviours of target groups and brings into play important aspects of planning. It involves linking the matrix of goals developed in step 2 and considering theoretical methods that will result in meeting these goals. Here designers and planners begin to think about links between values, skills and behaviours and particular objectives. As an example, practitioners may consider theories of planned behaviour and consider how they help understand behaviour that will move towards desired goals. The main aim will be to populate the goal matrix from step 2 with broad conceptual ideas that can feed into practical applications.

Step 4: Program Production

Step 4 is closely aligned with program design and involves taking output from the previous step and integrating methods and practical applications into an organized program. Practitioners will now begin to engage with a broad range of context success factors across values, skills and behaviours and logistics. Here, successful case studies can be engaged and modified where necessary to meet particular contexts. Understanding the broader contexts from earlier steps allows practitioners to better grasp the potential for success of any one intervention and undertake pilot programs to test potential interventions. Program production may involve the development of context specific educational packages and approaches, approaches that reward or punish particular behaviour or the development of logistical requirements. The end of the program production stage provides a package of approaches tailored to specific contexts and aimed at reaching specific agreed goals (Kok et al, 2011).

Step 5: Program Implementation

The penultimate step in program design is program implementation and draws on an understanding of context success factors (values, skills and behaviour, logistics) and the associated program design and process success factors (planning). A key in implementation will be to plan for the adoption, implementation and sustainability of the program designed in stage 4. Successful design at this step is important as programs often fail to meet goals and objectives due to poor implementation planning. As with previous steps, step five draws heavily on previous intervention mapping outputs. Practitioners will need to understand linkages between programs and goals and need to consider a number of context specific issues. Will implementation occur all at once or will a staged approach be undertaken? How will different programs be interlinked and how will this impact of the timing and process of implementation. Who will be implementing the programs and in what context? At the implementation stage previous steps may need to be revisited for fine tuning to allow the alignment of goals, programs and implementation.

Step 6: Program Evaluation

The final step of program design in the intervention mapping protocol focuses on evaluation and allows for feedback loops to be considered as a way of improvement of program design. The goal here is for practitioners to generate appropriate evaluation plans drawing on stakeholder input and considering best practice evaluation approaches. In many senses, the evaluation of the programs will be ongoing with practitioners considering outputs from program design onwards and considering how the design and implementation of program will help meet specified goals and targets. Appropriate evaluation will provide information on successes as well as failures and allow these to be understood in the appropriate contexts. For successful outcomes, evaluation will be fed back to stakeholders for use in redesign and future planning.

Figure 3. Intervention Mapping Protocol Matrix

	Case study success criteria				
	Content		*Process*		
Intervention Mapping protocol	Values, skills and behaviour	Logistics	Planning	Engagement	Evaluation
Step 1: Logic of model				X	
Step 2: Program outcomes				X	
Step 3: Program design	X		X		
Step 4: Program production	X	X			
Step 5: Program implementation	X	X	X		
Step 6: Evaluation plan				X	X

CONCLUDING REMARKS

Food waste is a significant and growing concern across the globe with significant implications for sustainable development. Proponents of food waste reduction programs point to the significant benefits that can flow from investing in the development of a sound evidence-based waste reduction program. This paper is developed within the growing concern around food waste and presents an analysis of the key success factors required for the implementation of a successful food waste reduction program and provides an ideal type model for program development.

The review of the example cases suggests that there are several key factors required for a successful food waste programs and that these can be divided into factors related to the content of the program and factors associated with the process surrounding the development of the program. Our findings suggest that pathways for a good food waste program should include: pilots, phased rollouts, education and continuous awareness, convenience, consistency, monitoring and enforcement, measurement of waste collection, key success indicators, integration with existing stakeholders, logical plans and demand for collected food waste. Combining the case study evidence and an intervention mapping protocol the paper outlines an approach to program development that allows for the successful development and monitoring of food waste programs in Africa that are context specific and flexible to need.

ACKNOWLEDGMENT

This work was supported by Griffith University, Australia.

REFERENCES

Asomani-Boateng, R., & Haight, M. (1999). Reusing organic solid waste in urban farming in African cities: A challenge for urban planners. *Third World Planning Review*, *21*(4), 411–428. doi:10.3828/twpr.21.4.5537184137847u14

Baig, M. B., Gorski, I., & Neff, R. A. (2018). Understanding and addressing waste of food in the Kingdom of Saudi Arabia. *Saudi Journal of Biological Sciences*. Advance online publication. doi:10.1016/j.sjbs.2018.08.030 PMID:31762638

Bartholomew, L. K., Parcel, G. S., & Kok, G. (1998). Intervention mapping: A process for developing theory and evidence-based health education programs. *Health Education & Behavior*, *25*(5), 545–563. doi:10.1177/109019819802500502 PMID:9768376

Biocycle. (2002). *Food Residuals put city on track to over 50% diversion*. A publication of the city of San Francisco.

Bourtsalas, A. T., Seo, Y., Alam, M. T., & Seo, Y. C. (2019). The status of waste management and waste to energy for district heating in South Korea. *Waste Management (New York, N.Y.)*, *85*, 304–316. doi:10.1016/j.wasman.2019.01.001 PMID:30803585

Brundtland, G. H. (1987). *World Commission on environment and development: our common future*. Oxford, UK: Oxford University Press.

Buzby, J. C., Farah-Wells, H., & Hyman, J. J. U.-E. E. I. B. (2014). *The estimated amount, value, and calories of postharvest food losses at the retail and consumer levels in the United States*. Academic Press.

Chen, Y. T. (2016). A cost analysis of food waste composing in Taiwan. *Sustainability*, *8*(11), 1210. doi:10.3390u8111210

Coté, J. (2009). SS.F.OO.K.sToughest Recycling Law in UU.S. *San Francisco Chronicle*.

Dmitriew, A. (2018). *Maximizing Organics Recovery: The San Francisco Experience*. Paper presented at Waste Expo, Las Vegas, NV.

EPA. (2008). *Environmental management in Korea: Insights and observations from the 2007 Australia-Korea Young Leaders Exchange Program*. Author.

EPA. (2016). *Zero Waste Case Study: San Francisco*. https://www.epa.gov/transforming-waste- tool/zero-waste-case-study-san-francisco

FAO. (2013). *Food Wastage Footprint. Impacts on Natural Resources: Summary Report*. FAO.

FAO, IFAD, UNICEF, WFP, & WHO. (2018). The State of Food Security and Nutrition in the World. Building climate resilience for food security and nutrition. Rome: Author.

FAO. (2019). *The State of Food Security and Nutrition in the World. Safeguarding against economic slowdowns and downturns*. https://www.unicef.org/media/55921/file/ SOFI-2019-full-report.pdf

Forster, P., Ramaswamy, V., Artaxo, P., Berntsen, T., Betts, R., Fahey, D. W., & Myhre, G. (2007). Changes in atmospheric constituents and in radiative forcing. In *Climate Change 2007*. The Physical Science Basis.

Gjerris, M., & Gaiani, S. J. E. i. p.-N. J. o. A. E. (2013). *Household food waste in Nordic countries: Estimations and ethical implications*. Academic Press.

Gooch, M., Bucknell, D., LaPlain, D., Dent, B., Whitehead, P., Felfel, A., Nikkel, L., & Maguire, M. (2019). *The Avoidable Crisis of Food Waste: Technical Report*. Value Chain Management International and Second Harvest.

Gustavsson, J., Cederberg, C., Sonesson, U., Van Otterdijk, R., & Meybeck, A. (2011). *Global food losses and food waste*. FAO Rome.

Hamilton, C., Denniss, R., & Baker, D. (2005). *Wasteful consumption Australia*. Discussion paper number 77. The Australia Institute, Manuka, Australia. https://www.tai.org.au/documents/dpfulltext/ DP77.pdfIPCC.Working

Hanson, C. (2013). *Food security, inclusive growth, sustainability, and the post-2015 development agenda*. Background Research Paper, High Level Panel on the Post-2015, Development Agenda, World Resources Institute.

Hebrok, M., & Boks, C. (2017). *Household food waste: Drivers and potential intervention points for design–An extensive review*. Academic Press.

Heller, M. (2019). Waste Not, Want Not: Reducing Food Loss and Waste in North America through Life Cycle-Based Approaches. United Nations Environment Programme, North America Office.

Kling, W. (1943). Food waste in distribution and use. *Journal of Farm Economics*, *25*(4), 848–859. doi:10.2307/1231591

Koch, J., Wimmer, F., & Schaldach, R. (2018). Analyzing the relationship between urbanization, food supply and demand, and irrigation requirements in Jordan. *The Science of the Total Environment*, *636*, 1500–1509. doi:10.1016/j.scitotenv.2018.04.058 PMID:29913610

Kok, G., Lo, S. H., Peters, G.-J. Y., & Ruiter, R. A. (2011). Changing energy-related behavior: An Intervention Mapping approach. *Energy Policy*, *39*(9), 5280–5286. doi:10.1016/j.enpol.2011.05.036

Kok, G., Peters, L., & Ruiter, R. (2017). Planning theory-and evidence-based behavior change interventions: Conceptual review of the intervention mapping tool. *Psychology Research and Review*, *30*(1), 19. doi:10.118641155-017-0072-x PMID:32026109

Kummu, M., De Moel, H., Porkka, M., Siebert, S., Varis, O., & Ward, P. J. J. S. o. t. e. (2012). *Lost food, wasted resources: Global food supply chain losses and their impacts on freshwater, cropland, and fertilizer use*. Academic Press.

Lai, Lai, & YuChung. (2009). Potentials of food wastes for power generation and energy conservation in Taiwan. *Renewable Energy, 34*, 1913-1915.

Lundqvist, J., de Fraiture, C., & Molden, D. (2008). *Saving water: from field to fork: curbing losses and wastage in the food chain*. Stockholm International Water Institute Stockholm.

Mebratu, D. (1998). Sustainability and sustainable development: Historical and conceptual review. *Environmental Impact Assessment Review, 18*(6), 493–520. doi:10.1016/S0195-9255(98)00019-5

Mena, C., Adenso-Diaz, B., & Yurt, O. (2011). The causes of Food waste in the supplier-retailer interface: Evidences from the UNK and Spain. *Resources, Conservation and Recycling, 55*(6), 648–658. doi:10.1016/j.resconrec.2010.09.006

Morisaki, I. (2011). *Pattern of Food Losses in Households: A Case Study in Oita-Prefecture, Japan*. Oita, Japan: Ritsumeikan Asia Pacific University. Retrieved April 3 2015 from: http://r-cube.ritsumei.ac.jp/bitstream/10367/2585/1/MORISAKI%20Ikuko.pdf

Neff, R.A., Spiker, M., Rice, C., Schklair, A., Greenberg, S., Broad Leib, E., 2019. Misunderstood food date labels and reported food discards: a survey of UU.S.consumer attitudes and behaviors. *Waste Manage, 86*, 123-132. .023 doi:10.1016/j.wasman.2019.01

Oelofse, S. H., & Nahman, A. (2013). Estimating the magnitude of food waste generated in South Africa. *Waste Management & Research, 31*(1), 80–86. doi:10.1177/0734242X12457117 PMID:22878934

Osabohien, R., Osuagwu, E., Osabuohien, E., Ekhator-Mobayode, U. E., Matthew, O., & Gershon, O. (2020). Household access to agricultural credit and agricultural production in Nigeria: A propensity score matching model. *Suid-Afrikaanse Tydskrif vir Ekonomiese en Bestuurswetenskappe, 22*(1), a2688. doi:10.4102ajems.v23i1.2688

Park, S., & Lah, T. T. J. (2015). Analyzing the success of the volume-based waste fee system South Korea. *Waste Management (New York, N.Y.), 43*, 533–538. doi:10.1016/j.wasman.2015.06.011 PMID:26141278

Peter, L., Peter, W., & Oakdene, H. (2010). *Waste Arising in the Supply of Food and Drink to Households in the UU.K.* Academic Press.

Prasad, M., Vera, W., Moustapha, K. G., Toolseeram, R., Visvanathan, C., Hardy, M. W., Shailendra, M., Louise, G., Andrea, M. B., John, P. A., Zhuohua, T., & Swati, A. (2011). Waste - investing in energy and resource efficiency, towards a green economy. In E. Derek & F. Sheng (Eds.), *United Nations Environment Programme*. UNEP.

Reynolds, C. J., Mavrakis, V., Davison, S., Stine, B. H., Vlaholias, E., & Sharp, A. (2014). Estimating informal household food waste in developed countries: The case of Australia. *Waste Management & Research, 32*(12), 1254–1258. doi:10.1177/0734242X14549797 PMID:25248761

Rockefeller Foundation. (2013). *Waste and Spoilage in the Food Chain*. Decision Intelligence Document.

Secondi, L., Principato, L., & Laureti, T. (2015). Household food waste behaviour in EE.U. 27 countries: A multilevel analysis. *Food Policy, 56*, 25–40. doi:10.1016/j.foodpol.2015.07.007

Seo, S., Aramaki, T., Hwang, Y., & Hanaki, K. (2004). Environmental impact of solid waste treatment methods in Korea. *Journal of Environmental Engineering*, *130*(1), 81–89. doi:10.1061/(ASCE)0733-9372(2004)130:1(81)

Song, Q., Li, J., & Zeng, X. (2014). Minimizing the increasing solid waste through zero waste strategy. *Journal of Cleaner Production*. Advance online publication. doi:10.1016/j.jclepro.2014.08.027

Thi, N. B. D., Kumar, G., & Lin, C. (2015). An overview of food waste management in developing countries: Current status and future perspective. *Journal of Environmental Management, 157*, 220-229.

Thyberg, K. L., & Tonjes, D. J. J. R. (2016). Drivers of food waste and their implications for sustainable policy development. *Conservation & Recycling, 106*, 110-123.

United Nations. (2015). *Sustainable Development Goals*. Retrieved from https://sustainabledevelopment.un.org/?menu=1300

United States Department of Agriculture (USDA). (2015). *Food Waste Reduction Goals*. Retrieved February 2 2016 From:to 47 http://www.usda.gov/wps/portal/usda/usdahome?contentid=2015/09/0257.xml

Venkat, K. (2012). The Climate Change and Economic Impacts of Food Waste in the United States. *Int. J. Food System Dynamics, 2*(4), 431-446.

Vianna, A. C., & Mollick, A. V. (2018). Institutions: Key variable for economic development in Latin America. *Journal of Economics and Business*, *96*, 42–58. doi:10.1016/j.jeconbus.2017.12.002

Williams, H., Wikström, F., Otterbring, T., Löfgren, M., & Gustafsson, A. (2012). Reasons for household food waste with special attention to packaging. *Journal of Cleaner Production*, *24*, 141–148. doi:10.1016/j.jclepro.2011.11.044

Zaman, A. U. (2014). Measuring waste management performance using the ‘zero waste index’. *Journal of Cleaner Production*, *66*, 407–419. doi:10.1016/j.jclepro.2013.10.032

Zaman, A. U. (2015). A Comprehensive review of the development of zero waste management: Lessons learned and guidelines. *Journal of Cleaner Production*, *91*, 12–25. doi:10.1016/j.jclepro.2014.12.013

Chapter 20

NGO Participatory Approaches for Promoting Environmental Consciousness Among Subsistence Farmers in Ghana

Alexis Beyuo
https://orcid.org/0000-0001-6266-0491
Kumasi Centre for Collaborative Research in Tropical Medicine (KCCR), Ghana

ABSTRACT

Agriculture contributes a fifth of the greenhouse gas emissions on earth. To help reduce this large ecological footprint, there is the need for collaborative efforts aimed at increasing farmers' environmental consciousness. This chapter used the ladder of participation as a framework to assess how knowledge co-creation between local farmers in Ghana's Upper West Region and NGO agro-technocrats is associated with farmers' environmental consciousness. Using an exploratory sequential mixed method design, in-depth interviews and focus group discussions were conducted with NGO officers and beneficiary farmers. Probability sampling was then used to select 1,050 beneficiary farmers for interviews and analysed using descriptive statistics and logistic regressions. Results show that the use of robust categories of participation were associated with farmers' increased likelihood of adopting most of the environmentally conscious practices co-created. Conversely, less robust participatory approaches resulted in either a reduced likelihood of adoption or non-adoption among beneficiary farmers.

INTRODUCTION

The International Panel on Climate Change (IPCC) (2018) estimates that humanity is faced with the arduous task of achieving net zero global carbon dioxide emission by mid-century if the deleterious effects of climate change are to be averted. Efforts at achieving this net zero emission target will require improved environmental consciousness, a term that emphasises that humans are merely part of the complex web of life and therefore cannot lay any better claim to the earth than their co-inhabitants (Nazir &

DOI: 10.4018/978-1-7998-4817-2.ch020

Pedretti, 2016). Accordingly, to ensure a sustainable co-existence with their fellow earthlings, humans should endeavour not to push the earth's carrying capacity beyond its limits. Increased environmental consciousness results in better ecosystem services (IPCC, 2019; 2018).

Estimates point to the agricultural sector as one of the biggest greenhouse gas emitters (Ba, 2016; Garnett, 2011; McMichael, Powles, Butler, & Uauy, 2007). Besides, many subsistence farmers in Developing Countries aspire to farm on large scale just as their counterparts in Developed Countries. This heightens the risk of a larger ecological footprint from the agricultural sector if the sector is to continue its business-as-usual production trajectory. Though subsistence farmers have not contributed substantially to the current climate change conundrum, it will be in their interest to help adapt to its consequences since postulations show that economically poor parts of the world, which are dominated by subsistence farmers, will likely bear the brunt of climate change (Afriyie, Ganle, & Santos, 2017; IPCC, 2014; Opare, 2016; Egbetokun et al, 2018; 2020). Indigenous subsistence farmers in the Upper West Region (UWR) do not only live on marginal lands, but also depend on the environment in spite of its increasing vagaries for their livelihood (Adam, Freeman, & Dassah, 2017; Kusakari et al., 2014). They therefore need to heighten their environmental consciousness so as to fully participate in climate change adaptation.

There is a preponderance of literature on climate change adaptation efforts. They include Kuchimachi, Nazareth, Bendapudi, Awasthi and D'Souza's (2019) study of adaptation strategies in Maharashtra, Mataya Vincent and Dougill's (2019) examination of adaptation efforts in Malawi, and Degefu, Assen, Satyal and Budds' (2019) assessment of the implications of villagization on pastoralists' adaptation drive in Middle Awash Valley of Ethiopia. Little is however known about how adaptation efforts can be influenced by the types of participatory approaches employed.

Studies extoling the importance of indigenous knowledge in the promotion of environmental consciousness also abound (e.g. Adom & Kquofi, 2016; Berkes & Usher, 2000; Bernard et al., 2019; Guthiga & Newsham, 2011; Nyong, Adesina, & Elasha, 2007; Opare, 2016; Veihe, 2000). These studies argue that indigenous farmers see themselves as an integral part of the ecosystem, which is needed for their very survival. As such, indigenous farmers often farm in ways that use the land as a natural carbon sink. Little is however known about how grassroots participation can be leveraged to increase environmental consciousness among indigenous subsistence farmers. Nyong et al. (2007) have for instance assessed how indigenous knowledge in the Sahel region of Africa has been relied on for decades by locals to adapt to climate change. These findings are in tandem with those of Berkes and Usher (2000) in their assessment of indigenous knowledge from across cultures in the world. In a similar fashion, Guthiga and Newsham (2011) have conducted a comparative study of scientific rainfall forecast and indigenous rain-making in Kenya and discovered that both approaches converged on similar predictions of rainfall patterns. In the context of Ghana, the indigenous knowledge of the Asante tribe and the Dupong community have also been examined (Adom & Kquofi, 2016; Opare, 2016).

In spite of the relevance of participatory approaches to co-create environmental conscious farming practices, there is little collaborative work between agro-technocrats and indigenous farmers. Agro-technocrats rather seem to downplay the importance of indigenous farming practices. Their inability to learn from indigenous farmers has often resulted in difficulties in tailoring technocratic support to meet indigenous farmers' needs (Chambers, 1998; Gyawal & Thompson, 2016; Pretty, Chambers, & Harris, 2003); a problem described by Nightingale et al. (2019) as the technical trap. Given these challenges, there is the need for a more nuanced application of environmental consciousness in indigenous subsistence farming. This improved behaviour change would require knowledge cross-fertilisation between technocrats and indigenous farmers since such knowledge cross-fertilisation would bring forth environmentally friendly farming practices that neither parties could realise if each worked in silos. Drawing on insights from an Oxfam GB-supported intervention known as the *Enhancing Livelihoods through Climate Change Adaptation Project (ELCAP),* this study seeks to address two related questions. First, what are the environmentally conscious practices promoted by change agents? Second, is there any association between participation and indigenous farmers' likelihood of adopting environmentally conscious practices? Using Sherry Arnstein's (1969, 2011) metaphorical ladder of participation as a theoretical basis, the study finds that environmental consciousness among indigenous subsistence farmers is more likely to be enhanced when change agents employ genuine participation in their work with indigenous farmers. The paper proceeds by discussing its theoretical framework, methodology and descriptive statistics. It then presents the results and discussions which entail the environmentally conscious farming practices promoted by ELCAP, socio-demographic characteristics of likely adopters and the nexus between participation and environmental consciousness before summarising and concluding.

LITERATURE REVIEW

Participation

Extant literature on participation seems to be fraught with controversy. This controversy manifests in two divergent views about its relevance: scepticism versus enthusiasm. While sceptics of participation (such as Arcand & Fafchamps, 2012; Botchway, 2001; Cleaver, 1999; Cooke & Kothari, 2001; Kvartiuk & Curtiss, 2019) argue that participation is often used as a smokescreen by change agents to mask their ineptitude, participation enthusiasts (e.g. Botes & Van-Rensburg, 2000; Chambers, 1985; Chambers & Ghildyal, 1985) on the other hand believe that it is a sine qua non for genuine grassroots development. Arguments adduced by these two sides are further discussed next.

Arguments of Participation Sceptics

One of the seminal critiques of participation comes from Cooke and Kothari (2001) who argue that local participation often perpetuates 'existing dominant power structures' of development agencies (ibid, p. 171). An example of such a hegemony has been studied by Kvartiuk and Curtiss (2019). They assessed how the hierarchical governance structure of rural Ukraine seems to have perverted participation by nudging fledging community-based organisations to tailor their interventions towards their own financial stability rather than meeting local felt needs. In such situations, participation is seen as a prop used by development agencies to source funding aimed at keeping them in business at the expense of making lasting developmental impacts.

Cooke and Kothari (2001) further argue that participation often assumes that local beneficiaries are a monolithic block. This assumption requires consensus building which in turn can dispense with important divergent views that are in the minority. Thus, beyond imposing dominant power structures on the grassroots, participation has been implicated in the problem of elite capture: a situation in which wealthy locals superimpose their desires on the will of the grassroots (Mansuri & Rao, 2012; Platteau, 2004; Platteau & Gaspart, 2003). For example, in their study of the calibre of people who participate in and benefit from community-based development organisations in Burkina Faso and Senegal, Arcand and Fafchamps (2012) found that rather than the grassroots, individuals on the higher pecking order of the social ladder were beneficiaries of these development organisations. Kinyashi's (2006) study of the Village Travel and Transport Project (VTTP) in Tanzania using grassroots participation is also worth mentioning. The VTTP aimed at infrastructural development in rural Tanzania. By so doing, perishable foodstuff produced in villages could find ready markets in towns. Central to the idea of the VTTP was the involvement of villages since they were to be the direct beneficiaries. Well intentioned as this project was, Kinyashi (2006) argues that it was captured by the elite: leaders intentionally deprived members of important project information and that made it impossible for members to assert their right and demand accountability. A similar problem of elite capture was earlier bemoaned by Dulani (1977) in his analysis of the Malawi Social Action Fund (MASAF).

Another drawback of participation has been elucidated by Botchway (2001). The author's study of some participatory approaches used in a rural water project in northern Ghana called the Northern Region Rural Integrated Programme (NORRIP) showed that rather than supporting the self-sufficiency efforts of beneficiaries, the project created a dependency syndrome that made the locals rely on NORRIP for the routine maintenance and repair of the water supply system even after the intervention had ended thereby defeating the sustained use of the intervention beyond the project's lifespan.

Arguments of Participation Enthusiasts

While acknowledging that participation can be perverted to serve the self-interest of some development agencies, Botes and Van-Rensburg (2000) recommend that development practitioners come to terms with the bottlenecks associated with their implementation as this serves as a precondition for fine-tuning them for better implementation. Describing the bottlenecks associated with participation as 'plagues', Botes and Van-Rensburg (2000) proffer twelve approaches to addressing these challenges. These approaches essentially border on the need for reorienting development professionals to plan with, not for their target beneficiaries.

In this vein, Chambers (1998) argues that local level participation ought to be an integral part of development interventions because local beneficiaries more than anyone else are better positioned to articulate their own felt needs. Moreover, he surmises that the hierarchical approach to development interventions often blinds such change agents from the wisdom of rural people themselves. Such change agents gloss over the complexities of local environments and therefore single-handedly impose on local people, interventions that have been tailored by the change agents without due consideration for local felt needs. Beyond breeding apathy, such an approach does not engender cross-fertilisation of ideas between change agents and target beneficiaries.

THE IMPERATIVE OF PARTICIPATION IN ENVIRONMENTAL PROTECTION

It is generally accepted that development must be grounded in demand-driven local level initiatives and commitment if it is to be both sustainable and reach the poor (Moumouni, Vodouhe, & Streiffeler, 2009; Parkinson, 2009). This has become important against the backdrop of environmental degradation resulting from crude farming methods. Increasing agricultural production from economic development in UWR while at the same time sustaining the natural resource base, is an enormous challenge. This is especially so as UWR is one of the most ecologically deprived in Ghana. As the economically poor are expected to be most negatively affected by the ravages of climate change, there is the need for adaptation to climate change as this will help reduce the frequent occurrence of floods and droughts in the UWR. In spite of the importance of participation in the promotion of environmentally conscious farming in the UWR, there is a dearth of literature on the topic and this is the gap the paper seeks to contribute to filling.

THE LADDER OF PARTICIPATION AS A THEORETICAL FRAMEWORK

This study views participation as an instrument for societal improvement. The study therefore defines participation as a 'process in which local communities discover the possibilities of exercising choice and becoming capable of managing what they understand as development' (Botchway, 2001, p. 136). One of the seminal theories on the instrumental value of participation is attributed to Arnstein (1969). Due to its enduring relevance, the theory has been reprinted in the recent past by Cornwall (2011) and LeGates and Stout (2015){LeGates, 2015 #866@@author-year;Arnstein, 2011 #810@@author-year}. The theory has further received attention in the literature on various grassroots-related interventions (examples Choguill, 1996; Collins & Ison, 2009; Connor, 1988; Hart, 1992; Kinyashi, 2006; Ruesga & Knight, 2013; Stelmach, 2016; Tritter & McCallum, 2006). In light of its enduring relevance, this study uses the ladder of participation as a framework for analysing the various categories of participation used by change agents to promote environmental consciousness among indigenous farmers. The three categories of Arnstein's ladder of participation is discussed next.

Arnstein identifies three categories of participation: non-participation, degrees of tokenism and degrees of citizen power/true participation. These categories vary based on the degree of power imbued in indigenous people to make decisions regarding a development intervention (Figure 1). Non-participation is the lowest category of participation often employed by change agents as a means of legitimising whatever intervention they introduce to indigenous people. Change agents often resort to this when they have already fashioned an intervention at the higher echelon of the organisation and need a buy-in from local target beneficiaries. In such cases, change agents only require rubber-stamping from the indigenous people for an intervention to take off. Beneficiaries however have no power to articulate their felt needs for incorporation into the intervention since it is tailor-made at the change agents' level and implemented at the grassroots.

The second category, degrees of tokenism is better than non-participation given that beneficiaries are allowed some level of agency to articulate their feelings and aspirations at the planning stage of the project. Though they are allowed to voice their feelings, the decision to incorporate their voice in the intervention is at the discretion of the change agents. The ideal form of participation in Arnstein's estimation is degrees of citizen power where the change agents and the grassroots are expected to have discussions aimed not only at understanding the collective needs of the indigenes, but to appreciate and build on local knowledge without superimposing the change agents' technocratic knowledge on the indigenes. Appreciating and meeting these local needs become the standard by which the success of the intervention is measured. Beneficiaries are important members of the monitoring and evaluation team that determines the success or otherwise of the intervention (Figure 1).

Figure 1. Ladder of grassroots participation
Source: Arnstein (1969, 2011)

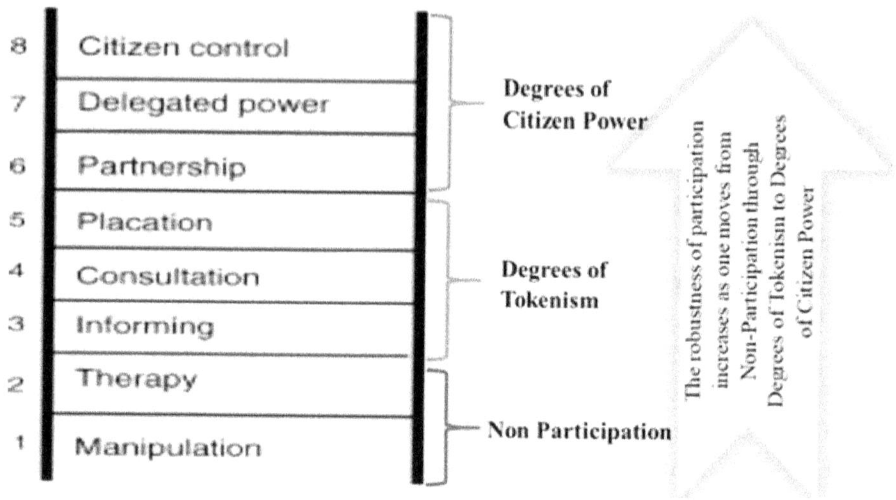

MATERIALS AND METHODS

Study Area, Sampling, Data Collection and Analysis

The UWR is located in north-western Ghana (Figure 2). The region is largely semi-arid with an annual erratic rainfall pattern occurring from June to September (Kusakari et al., 2014). As a result, trees often shed their leaves to retain moisture during these long dry spells. In spite of the drought, the 'Dagaare' indigenes who are predominantly subsistence farmers rely on the vagaries of the weather for farming. The problem of climate change has further accentuated the region's perennial drought (Kusakari et al., 2014). The *Enhancing Livelihoods through Climate Change Adaptation Project (ELCAP),* a brainchild of the International NGO Oxfam GB, was purposefully selected for this study given its focus on helping local farmers adapt to the challenges associated with climate change. ELCAP was a five-year project implemented in two districts; Nadowli and Nandom (Figure 2). The project envisaged that adopting participatory approaches was the medium through which knowledge cross-fertilisation between ELCAP technocrats and indigenous farmers—especially women—could be realised.

An exploratory sequential mixed method design (Creswell, 2009, 2012), which consists of two data collection phases, was used to ascertain how participatory approaches could engender knowledge co-creation between ELCAP and their beneficiaries and how this process was associated with farmers' environmentally conscious farming practices. This approach allowed for the qualitative (first) data collection and analysis phase to feed into the quantitative (second) phase. Thus, not only did the qualitative phase form a basis for the development of a structured questionnaire for the second phase, the two phases were also triangulated (Agula et al., 2019; Hussein, 2009) for more nuanced findings. To this end, the first phase of the study entailed two in-depth interviews with two officers in charge of ELCAP and four focus group discussions with beneficiaries. The two in-depth interviews were held with the Project Manager and the Field Officer of ELCAP in English. Since they were directly involved in rolling out the intervention, they gave insights into the rationale and operationalisation of the intervention, locations of

Figure 2. Map of UWR showing the two study districts in the contexts of Ghana and Africa
Source: Adapted from Ghana Statistical Service (2013)

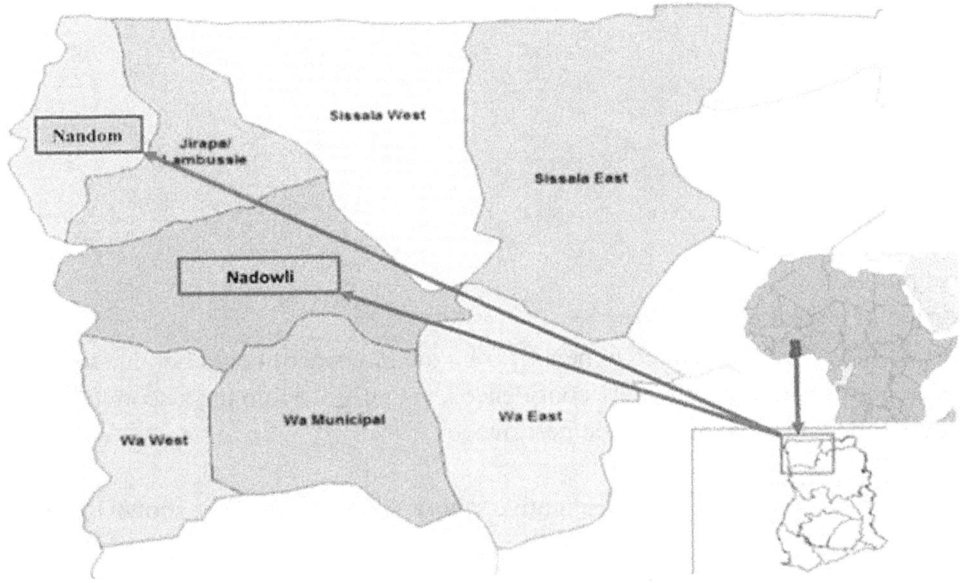

the various beneficiary farmer groupings and the environmentally conscious farming practices ELCAP promoted in the two beneficiary districts. The focus groups were held with cross sections of beneficiaries in 'Dagaare', beneficiaries' local dialect. It ascertained different and common views about how ELCAP was rolled out in beneficiary communities. It also helped unearth some of the indigenous ecologically friendly farming practices farmers engaged in prior to the advent of ELCAP and assessed how the two actors were able to cross-fertilise environmentally conscious ideas using participatory approaches.

Qualitative analysis was done using the Atlas.ti software. First, I read through all transcripts several times to get a general idea of the responses given. Next, I coded the transcripts guided by the two main themes of the study; participation and environmental consciousness. To ensure reliability of the qualitative findings, the intra-coder reliability test, a coding approach mediated by time, which is employed by an individual coder in order to measure the consistency of codes generated from the same set of transcripts (Aikins, 2005) was used. Thus, after the first round of coding, I put the transcripts aside for one month to ensure that the second phase of coding was not biased by my memory of the first round. I then re-started the coding afresh, once again guided by the two sensitising concepts of the study; participation and environmental consciousness. Comparison of the two coding processes were consistent. The entire coding process was iterative given that it was repeated multiple times to get at relevant quotations from respondents. The in-depth interview responses were then cross-referenced with responses from the focus group discussions to identify common and divergent responses. These anonymised quotations from respondents further buttressed findings from the quantitative phase of the study.

The second phase of the exploratory sequential mixed method design consisted of cross-sectional data collected using structured questionnaires administered directly to individual beneficiaries. ELCAP earmarked a total of 1,300 beneficiaries in the Nadowli and Nandom districts. Given that the total target population was less than 10,000, there was the need for a two-stage approach to arrive at the adjusted sample size as recommended by Saunders, Lewis, and Thornhill (2009). This entailed deriving a tentative number using equation 1, followed by the adjusted sample size using equation 2. These two stages consisted of ten steps. Thus, the first six steps (1 to 6) were for computing the tentative sample size and steps 7 to 10 consisted of computing the adjusted sample size.

$$n = p\% \times q\% \times \frac{z^2}{e\%^2} \tag{1}$$

where,

n = tentative number
$p\%$ =proportion of project beneficiaries
$q\%$ =proportion of farmers earmarked to benefit from the project but could not due to limited funds
z = the z value corresponding to the 99% confidence level i.e. ±2.57 on the z score table
$e\%$= the required margin of error (0.01) in percentage.

The formula in equation 1 resulted in a tentative sample size of 5,409.41 as shown in step 6 of Table 1.

Table 1. First stage of sample size determination at 1% significance level

Beneficiaries	Frequency
Step 1. Total number of target beneficiaries farmers	1,300
Step 2. Number of farmers who actually benefitted (p)	1,183
Step 3. Number of farmers earmarked to benefit but could not due to limited funds (q)	117
Step 4. Proportion of beneficiaries ($p\%$)	91%
Step 5. Proportion of farmers earmarked to benefit but could not due to limited funds ($q\%$)	9%
Step 6. Substituting the formula in equation 1 resulted in the tentative number	5,409.41

Given that the total population of beneficiaries was less than 10,000, the formula for adjusted minimum sample size (equation 2) was used.

$$n' = \frac{n}{1+\left(\frac{n}{N}\right)} \tag{2}$$

where

n' = the adjusted minimum sample size
n = the tentative number (5,409.41 as calculated in Table 1) and
N = the total population of target beneficiary farmers

The formula in equation 1 resulted in an adjusted minimum sample size of 1046.46 which is ≈1,050 as shown in step 10 of Table 2.

Table 2. Adjusted minimum sample size at 1% significance level

Beneficiaries	Frequency
Step 7. Total population of target beneficiary farmers	1,300
Step 8. Tentative number	5,409.41
Step 9. Substituting the formula above I arrived at an adjusted sample of	**1,048.12**
Step 10. The adjusted minimum sample was thus approximately equal to	**≈1,050**

Having arrived at the adjusted minimum sample size of 1,050, the two study districts of Nandom and Nadowli served as two strata from which the samples were drawn. Given that they bore similar socio-demographic and ecological characteristics, the adjusted sample size of 1,050 was evenly divided between the two stratified districts resulting in a sample of 525 beneficiaries from each of the two strata. Next, simple random sampling technique without replacement (Cancino & Saborowski, 2005) was used to select 525 beneficiaries from each of the two study districts. This process ensured external validity which facilitated generalizability of results to a larger population (Patton, 2002). Data for the second phase of the research design were analysed using marginal effects derived from the logit model as explicated below.

Empirical Model and Estimation Approach

Following Long and Freese (2001) the study's model was derived from marginal effects of a logistic regression. Therefore, the binary outcome y in equation 3 was used to analyse the probability of a farmer accepting environmentally conscious farming practices after the participatory approaches were introduced by ELCAP.

$$y = \begin{cases} 1, & if\ agree \\ 0, & if\ otherwise \end{cases} \tag{3}$$

where y is a binary dependent variable which takes on two values (i.e. 0 and 1), 1 denoting a beneficiary agreeing that they adopted environmentally conscious farming practices co-created with ELCAP and 0, otherwise.

Taking a cue from the OLS model (which has y as a continuous variable),

$$y = x'^{2} + \Delta \tag{4}$$

The binary outcome model estimating the probability that an individual adopts environmentally conscious farming practices (i.e. y=1) is denoted as

$$p = pr\left[y = 1|x\right] = F\left(x'^{2}\right) \tag{5}$$

As the linear probability model shows,

$$F\left(x'^{2}\right) = x'^{2} \tag{6}$$

Therefore,

$$p = pr\left[y = 1|x\right] = x'^{2} \tag{7}$$

However, the limitation inherent in Equation 7 is that its predicted probabilities are not limited to 0 and 1. To limit the predicted probabilities to 0 and 1, the logit model is used. This is denoted as

$$F\left(x'^{2}\right) = \frac{exp\left(x'^{2}\right)}{1 + exp\left(x'^{2}\right)} \tag{8}$$

where $F\left(x'\beta\right)$ is the cumulative distributive function (CDF) of the logistic distribution. However, one can only interpret the sign of the coefficient resulting from Equation 8 but cannot interpret its magnitude. To interpret both the sign and magnitude, the average marginal effect is derived thus

$$dp/dx_j = \frac{\sum F'\left(x'^{2}\right)}{n}{}^{2}{}_{j}$$ Equation 9

Where the index j denotes the jth independent variable and n, the number of observations. Using Equation 9 (the marginal effect), one can then interpret both sign and magnitude of the results derived

DEPENDENT AND INDEPENDENT VARIABLES

The dependent variables for the study were based on the environmentally conscious practices co-created by ELCAP and its beneficiaries. Eight dichotomous (Yes/No) questions were posed to respondents to gauge their likelihood of adopting each of these eight environmentally conscious practices.

They are shown in Table 3, together with their respective measurements and a priori expectations of the study. Independent variables on the other hand consisted of socio-demographic characteristics and the three categories of grassroots participation as espoused by Arnstein (see Table 4).

Descriptive Statistics

Most respondents (74.90%) were within the economically active age group of 21 to 59 years. Almost all beneficiaries (80.00%) were females (Table 5). This high female representation is in tandem with the

Table 3. Environmental consciousness proxies used as dependent variables

Proxies	Measurement	A priori expectations
1. Planting of trees on farms and neighbourhood	1=Yes, 0=No	+
2. Use of stone bunds[1]	1=Yes, 0=No	+
3. Use of zai micro-dozing[2] on farms	1=Yes, 0=No	+
4. Use of half-moon farming[3] method	1=Yes, 0=No	+
5. Use of energy-saving stoves	1=Yes, 0=No	+
6. Use of compost on farms	1=Yes, 0=No	+
7. Protection of riparian regions/zones[4]	1=Yes, 0=No	+
8. Use of agrochemicals	1=Yes, 0=No	-

Table 4. Description of independent variables

Variables	Measurement	A priori expectations
Respondents' socio-demographic characteristics		
1. Age categories	1=working age group (21-59), 0=Aged (60+)	+
2. Gender	Female=1, Male=0	+
3. Educational status	1=Some level of formal education, 0=No formal education	+
4. Household breadwinner	1=Yes, 0=No	+
Categories of grassroots participation		
1. Nonparticipation	1=Agree, 0=Otherwise	-
2. Degrees of tokenism	1=Agree, 0=Otherwise	-/+
3. Degrees of citizen power	1=Agree, 0=Otherwise	+

raison d'être of the project which was to serve underprivileged women in rural areas. The importance of such an approach is confirmed in the literature which suggests that when women's wellbeing is enhanced, it has far-reaching ripple effects on the socio-economic wellbeing of the entire family (Dollar & Gatti, 1999; World Bank, 2000).

A large proportion of respondents (71.71%) had no formal education (Table 5). The few members with formal education (28.29%) were often secretaries to their beneficiary group. Such members completed at least Junior High School education. A few of the chairpersons and other executives also had some level of education. Females had a disproportionately high representation of people with no formal education compared to males.

About half of respondents (51.14%) were breadwinners of their respective households. This is an important proxy for measuring farmers' commitment levels to the intervention since it is assumed that those with dependants would be more predisposed to giving off their best in the project in order to improve on their ability to meet the economic needs of their dependants.

Table 5. Socio-Demographic characteristics of respondents

Variables	Categories of farmers	
	Frequency	Percentage
Age categories		
21-59 (Active working age group)	786	74.90%
60+ (Aged)	264	25.10%
Total	1,050	100.00%
Gender categories		
Male	210	20.00%
Female	840	80.00%
Total	1,050	100.00%
Formal educational status		
Not educated	297	28.29%
Educated	753	71.71%
Total	1,050	100.00%
Marital status		
Married	750	71.43%
Not married	300	28.57%
Total	1,050	100%
Household breadwinner		
Yes	537	51.14%
No	513	48.86%
Total	**1,050**	**100.00%**

Marital Status

Monogamy was the commonest form of marriage among respondents (56.60%). Widows were the second most populous (24.70%) and if Adinkrah's (2004) observation that widows are in the lower levels of the economic ladder in many parts of rural Ghana is anything to go by, the relatively high percentage of widows gives credence to the fact that the project aimed at supporting the poor. Respondents' marital statuses are shown in Figure 3.

RESULTS AND DISCUSSION

Environmentally Conscious Practices Promoted by ELCAP

Environmentally conscious farming practices promoted by ELCAP were categorized into two: indigenous practices encouraged by ELCAP and add-ons from ELCAP. Indigenous practices encouraged by ELCAP were composting, tree planting and creation of stone bunds. Add-ons from the project were the reduction in agrochemical use, zai micro-dozing, half-moon farming, energy-saving cook-stoves and

Figure 3. Respondents' marital statuses
Source: Fieldwork, 2017

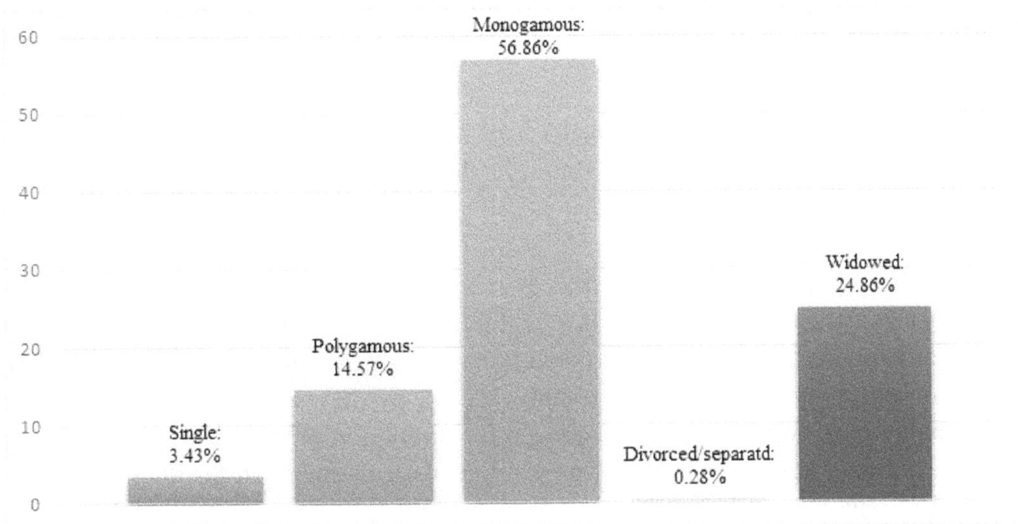

protection of riparian regions. This section discusses these two categories of practices in turns, starting with the indigenous practices, and then practices introduced by ELCAP.

Indigenous Practices

Traditionally, farmers rejuvenated their soils using compost. Farmers were however less inclined to use compost because its preparation is labour-intensive. ELCAP encouraged farmers to revert to the use of compost by helping them reduce the drudgery involved in its preparation. For instance, rather than dig huge holes as was the practice prior to the intervention, ELCAP helped farmers to dig smaller holes into which they put biodegradable materials for composting. This is against the backdrop that composting is environmentally friendly and a cost-effective method of injecting nutrients into soils (Blum, 1992). Extant literature points to increased yield resulting from applying compost and other natural regenerative materials on farms (e.g. Lechenet, Dessaint, Py, Makowski, & Munier-Jolain, 2017).

Given the importance of trees in the ecosystem, another indigenous farming practice encouraged by ELCAP was agroforestry. Apart from their importance in carbon capture and sequestration, trees also provide both timber and non-timber forest products (Binam et al., 2015). Besides, trees are traditionally conduits through which indigenous farmers determine the various seasons of the year. In the words of an elderly male beneficiary farmer in Nadowli during a focus group discussion, 'whenever shea trees start to flower, we know that we are entering the rainy season and so we start our farming.' This finding is consistent with that of Bernard et al. (2019) in their study of indigenous knowledge used by agro-pastoralists in Uganda who discern the onset of the rainy season from the blooming of wild plants and the ubiquitous presence of insects that feed on the flowers. Farmers planted fruit-bearing trees like mangoes (*Mangifera indica*) and interspersed their crops with naturally grown shea (*Vitellaria paradoxica*) and dawadawa (*Parkia biglobosa*) trees prior to ELCAP. The project encouraged this indegenous farming practice by supplying farmers with cashew (*Anacardium occidentale*) and mango (*Mangifera indica*) seedlings.

Another indigenous practice the study found was the protection of soils and waterbodies using local natural resources. Locals combined readily available vetiver grass (*Chrysopogon zizanioides*) with the stone bunding technique to re-inforce the boundaries of their dams to avoid water loss. As a female focus group discussant explained,

To conserve our waters, we use the vetiver, which we have planted along the bank of the dam and enforced the bank with stones so that the water does not break the boundaries of the dam. ~(FGD with ELCAP Beneficiaries, Nadowli, 3rd March, 2017)

To protect the ecosystem, the locals further passed and enforced by-laws against environmental degradation. Though ELCAP itself was not involved in making these by-laws, it encouraged the initiative. The project only created avenues for knowledge sharing regarding the importance of protecting the fragile ecosystem. Farmers were made to understand why they should avoid indiscriminate bush burning and tree felling. Avenues were also created for promotion of tree planting, encouragement of compost use rather than agrochemicals and prevention of slash-and-burn farming. According to the ELCAP Project Manager,

We let them know that the proliferation of diseases, both animal and human, is as a result of climate change which has come about due to indiscriminate cutting of trees and burning and other human factors… and people have come to realise that it is true. The rains are not coming as they used to… so they now believe in what we say. ~(Interview with ELCAP's Project Manager, 4th March, 2017)

To enforce local laws against environmental degradation, local taskforces were commissioned in beneficiary communities. The following comment from a male discussant in a focus group buttresses their collective decision to protect their ecology;

If a tree dies, you must get permission from the local taskforce before using it for fuelwood. They will confirm that the tree has actually died. Then they will let you plant a seedling to replace it before you are allowed to use the dead tree. ~(A male beneficiary during a FGD, Nandom, 10th March, 2017)

Add-Ons From ELCAP

Building on the aforementioned environmentally conscious practices, ELCAP introduced reduction in agrochemical misuse, the use of energy-saving cook-stoves and protection of riparian regions/zones. Other environmentally conscious practices introduced were zai micro-dozing and half-moon farming.

Though respondents revealed that they traditionally did not use agrochemicals, many resorted to it in response to the increasing reduction in their agricultural yields, which is attributable to climate change (Kusakari et al., 2014). Besides, many peasant farmers aspire to use agrochemicals to produce in large scale as in the case of commercial farmers in Developed Countries. The practice of scaling back on agrochemical use was however encouraged by ELCAP because some farmers were predisposed to misusing them. In the words of ELCAP's Field Officer,

We have tried to discourage agrochemical usage because most of the farmers do not use them properly and besides, most of them buy in small quantities due to their poverty situation. The agrochemicals are often misapplied and this can have a lot of effect on the environment, their yield and even the health of the farmer and the consuming public. ~(In-depth interview with ELCAP Field Officer, 5th March, 2017)

Dichloro-Diphenyl-Trichloroetane (DDT) was commonly used to ward off pests on farms prior to ELCAP. Pesticides misuse has long been bemoaned by Carson (1962), a U.S. environmental activist in her ground-breaking publication criticizing the effects of pesticides on biodiversity. This problem persists today as humanity seems to be hooked on pesticides. Though pesticides control insects and pests in agriculture, their misuse can lead to reduced biodiversity and even colony collapse as in the case of bees which are important agents for plant pollination. Smaller insects such as ants and worms, which are important for breaking down biodegradable materials and soil aeration are killed when pesticides are misused in farming. Apart from the environmental consequences of releasing nitous oxide into the atmosphere, the literature also identifies agrochemical misuse as a major socio-economic bane to compromised human health and reduced agricultural yields (Bourguet & Guillemaud, 2016; Chéze, David, & Martinet, 2020; Fianko, Donkor, Lowor, & Yeboah, 2011; Wilson & Tisdell, 2001).

Two other ELCAP add-ons were zai micro-dozing and half-moon farming. These farming practices originated from the semi-arid regions of Burkina Faso (Reij, Tappan, & Smale, 2009). Zai farming involves the precise application of compost in small holes into which crops are planted. This maximises compost utilisation. It also retains water thereby preventing runoffs in the harsh semi-arid climatic region of the UWR where water scarcity is a major bane to farming. Half-moon farming on the other hand involves the creation of semi-circular boundaries on a degraded land into which farmers put compost after loosening the soil. These boundaries are often created to retain water in dry ecological regions like UWR. Before the introduction of zai and half-moon farming, many indigenous farmers simply sprinkled animal droppings on their farms. Others used the laborious traditional composting methods described earlier. These traditional methods hardly improved agricultural yields. Discussing how she and her colleagues felt about the zai micro-dozing and half-moon farming methods, a female beneficiary said

...even the land over there [referring to a hardpan land deprived of vegetation] can be improved if you used the zai and half-moon farming methods the project taught us. ~(A female focus group discussant, Nadowli 13th March, 2017)

ELCAP further facilitated farmers' adoption of energy-saving cook-stoves in an effort to reduce the frequency of tree felling (see right hand side of Figure 4). These improved but cost-effective stoves were constructed from clay, a readily available resource in beneficiary communities. The stove was an improvement on the traditional firewood-consuming method of using three boulders arranged to form a make-shift tripod interspersed with heaps of burning firewood. This make-shift stove was often used for cooking. As the firewood was often exposed, much of the energy was lost thereby requiring more heaps of firewood in order to cook food (see left hand side of Figure 4).

Trees that would have been felled and used as firewood were saved and this contributed to greening the environment and improving on the micro-climate. The following comments by a female beneficiary of this initiative buttresses the relevance of the improved cook-stove:

Figure 4. From traditional firewood-guzzling cooking to improved energy-saving cook-stoves
Source: Fieldwork, 2017

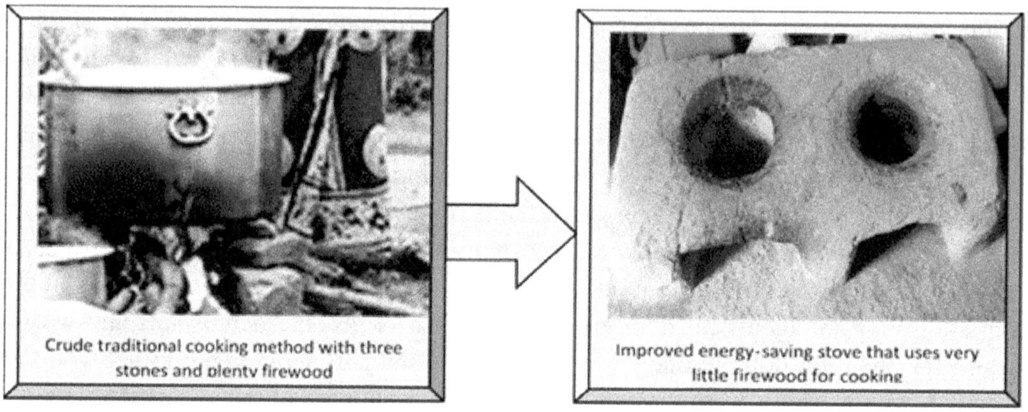

The energy-saving stove has been very helpful. It has reduced our use of firewood. The stove uses just about three to four pieces of firewood. Even the three to four are often burnt half way and the food is cooked. Such firewood is quenched and put away for later use. This is unlike the first where we could use as many as fifteen pieces of firewood for cooking a meal. ~(FGD with female beneficiaries in Nandom, 10th March, 2017)

The final add-on was the protection of riparian regions. Though farmers used vetiver grass and boulders to protect the boundaries of waterbodies prior to ELCAP, they often engaged in the negative environmental practice of farming too close to the banks of riparian regions. This was due to water scarcity in the region. To augment the indigenous environmentally conscious practices of stone bunding and use of vetiver grass, ELCAP sensitised farmers on the need to protect riparian regions. They were for instance sensitised to avoid farming too close to waterbodies as that caused siltation of the waterbodies. These environmentally conscious practices were part of efforts at creating a circular ecology that is self-regenerating.

Environmental Consciousness Based on Respondents' Socio-Demographic Characteristics

Beneficiaries within the working age group (i.e. 18-59 years) were 7.90% more likely to protect riparian regions from environmental degradation than the aged (i.e. 60+ years) (Table 6). In comparison with the aged, beneficiaries within the working age group were also 5.10% more likely to use stone bunds. Compared to beneficiary farmers who had no formal education, those with some form of education were 17.70% more likely to adopt stone bunding. These results are in tandem with the a priori assumption of the study.

Compared to farmers with no formal education, beneficiaries with some level of formal education however recorded a precipitous reduction in their likelihood of adopting zai farming (32.20%). They were also 23.80% less likely to adopt half-moon farming, 9.90% less likely to adopt improved cook-stoves and 14.20% less likely to protect riparian regions (Table 6). Similarly, females, who formed about 80% of beneficiaries of the intervention registered no significant improvement in most of the environmentally conscious interventions relative to men. The only significant change seen for females was a 15.55% reduction in their likelihood of adopting zai farming method in comparison to men. This result is rather counter-intuitive given that females were the intervention's target. Further interrogation revealed that most women felt the zai farming method was too laborious. In the words of a female beneficiary,

[The improved farming methods were] so fascinating. They helped us a lot but the difficulty in gathering cow dung for making compost, scarcity of water and the back-breaking nature of preparing the half-moon and zai methods have made it difficult for us to practice them. ~(A female beneficiary during a FGD, Nandom, 10th March, 2017)

The literature on zai farming (e.g. Danso-Abbeam, Dagunga, & Ehiakpor, 2019) however presents mixed results regarding farmers' probability and intensity of adopting zai micro-dozing.

Relative to educated males, educated females also presented mixed results. They were 13.70% less likely to plant trees, and 10.10% less likely to practice composting on their farms. In line with the study's a priori expectation, they however record significant improvements in their likelihood of adopting the new farming methods introduced by ELCAP. Thus, their likelihood of adopting zai micro-dozing and half-moon farming increased by 30% and 16.70% respectively when compared to their male counterparts. Educated females were also 12.90% more likely to adopt the energy conserving stoves introduced by the project than their male counterparts. Furthermore, beneficiaries who were breadwinners in their various households were 4.70% more likely to adopt zai micro-dozing but were 9.20% less likely to protect riparian regions. They were also 3.30% less likely to adopt the improved stove introduced to protect the fragile environment.

The Participation-Environmental Consciousness Nexus

When assessed in light of the three categories of grassroots participation, results become more consistent with the study's a priori assumption that indigenous farmers' likelihood of adopting the various environmentally conscious practices is contingent on indigenous farmers' degree of participation in the collaborative exercises. For instance, of the three environmentally conscious farming practices embarked on by indigenous farmers prior to the advent of ELCAP, only composting shows a 7.40% significant but negative effect when measured in light of Arnstein's lowest category of participation; non-participation (Table 6). This suggests that farmers were 7.40% less likely to use compost when they were involved through the medium of non-participation. The NGO's use of non-participation in the collaborative exercises was likely to result in no significant improvements in tree planting and use of stone bunding among beneficiaries suggesting that farmers were not likely to change their farming practices even with the advent of ELCAP because the NGO used the lowest category of participation. Even farming practices built on by the NGO were not likely to fare well when introduced to farmers using non-participation. There were for instance a 17.90% probability of reduction in protection of riparian regions, a 9% reduction in probability of adopting zai micro-dozing, a 7.90% probability of reduction in half-moon farming and a 9.40% probability of reduction in the use of energy-conserving cook-stoves. These results show that the use of non-participation either did not amount to the adoption of any of the environmentally conscious practices or worsened these prospects, which is in tandem with Arnstein's theory that non-participation is a charade used by change agents to legitimise decisions already made at the higher echelons of the NGO's command structure with little recourse to the needs of indigenous farmers. This suggests that the use of non-participation makes indigenous farmers view the intervention not as theirs, but the change agent's. Farmers therefore may not show the needed commitment towards it thereby leading to a waste of scarce resources.

Compared to non-participation, ELCAP's use of degrees of tokenism shows better patterns of farmers' likelihood of adopting environmentally conscious practices. For instance, of the three indigenous environmentally conscious activities recorded, only tree planting recorded a 10% significant likelihood of adoption by farmers if farmers participated in the collaborative exercise through the prism of degrees of tokenism. The remaining two indigenous practices encouraged by ELCAP (i.e. composting and stone bunding) recorded highly significant reductions in farmers' likelihood of using them when farmers participated through the medium of Arnstein's category of participation called degrees of tokenism. Most add-ons from ELCAP registered highly significant likelihood of adoption by farmers when the collaborative exercises were rolled out through degrees of tokenism: half-moon farming was 17% more likely to be adopted, zai micro-dozing was 8.90% more likely to be adopted and the use of energy-conserving cook-stoves was 6.40% more likely to be adopted.

These results associated with the category of participation called degrees of tokenism are in tandem with Arnstein's theorization that tokenism allows change agents to have more power than the locals in the decision making process. As such, though locals, or their representatives, have a say in decisions they have no power to ensure the implementation of their felt needs. Though local felt needs can be dispensed with by change agents, their authority they wield to voice out their needs makes degrees of tokenism a better participatory approach than non-participation. The risk associated with the various degrees of tokenism is however when local representatives only serve to rubberstamp decisions made by change agents without due consideration given to local voices. This, according to Arnstein, can be avoided when locals are free to choose their own local representatives without any attempt by the NGO to nudge them into choosing people that would serve the change agent's interest.

Degrees of citizen power, regarded by Arnstein as the gold standard in grassroots participation show significant and direct associations with improvements in farmers' likelihood of adopting environmentally conscious practices (Table 6). Irrespective of whether these farming practices were indigenous to beneficiaries or were add-ons from the ELCAP project, all eight interventions registered highly significant and expected directions of results. Participation through the prism of degrees of citizen power also shows higher magnitudes of improvements than participation under degrees of tokenism, the highest being in farmers' likelihood of protecting riparian regions (i.e. 32.50%). These results suggest that participatory approaches tailored to meet local felt needs increase the likelihood of adoption. The findings are consistent with those of Mataya, Vincent, and Dougill Mataya et al. (2019) who studied the content of capacity building interventions aimed at equipping selected groups in Malawi on climate change adaptation. They find that adaptation efforts tailored towards meeting participants' needs greatly improved participants' ability to adapt to climate change.

SUMMARY AND CONCLUSION

Using Arnstein's (1969, 2011) metaphorical ladder of participation as a theoretical framework, this paper has assessed how the various categories of participation are associated with indigenous farmers' likelihood of adopting environmentally conscious practices in an effort to adapt to climate change. Drawing on insights from ELCAP, a project initiated in the UWR by Oxfam GB, results show that farmers'

Table 6. Association between Arnstein's three categories of participation and farmers' likelihood of adopting environmental consciousness practices

	Indigenous environmentally conscious activities			**ELCAP add-ons**				
VARIABLES	**Tree plant**	**compost**	**bund**	**zai**	**agrochem.**	**moon**	**Stove**	**riparian**
Age categories(ref: Aged)								
Working age	0.028	0.012	0.051*	-0.002	-0.001	0.003	-0.006	0.079***
	(0.029)	(0.022)	(0.031)	(0.028)	(0.023)	(0.027)	(0.016)	(0.026)
Gender (ref: Male)								
Female	0.001	-0.013	-0.004	-0.155**	-0.002	0.048	-0.013	-0.017
	(0.063)	(0.040)	(0.055)	(0.060)	(0.034)	(0.056)	(0.049)	(0.067)
Educational status (ref: no formal education.)								
Some formal education	0.106	-0.064	0.177**	-0.322***	0.039	-0.238***	-0.099*	-0.142*
	(0.077)	(0.045)	(0.073)	(0.083)	(0.036)	(0.078)	(0.051)	(0.075)
Gender#Educated (ref: educated males)								
Educated females	-0.137*	-0.101**	-0.129	0.300***	-0.022	0.167**	0.129**	0.091
	(0.082)	(0.050)	(0.078)	(0.088)	(0.042)	(0.083)	(0.054)	(0.079)
Household breadwinner	-0.030	-0.017	-0.013	0.047*	0.002	0.015	-0.033*	-0.092***
	(0.029)	(0.020)	(0.029)	(0.027)	(0.023)	(0.026)	(0.019)	(0.023)
Categories of grassroots participation								
Non-participation	-0.024	-0.074***	0.006	-0.090***	0.010	-0.079***	-0.094***	-0.179***
	(0.033)	(0.028)	(0.035)	(0.030)	(0.038)	(0.029)	(0.016)	(0.025)
Degrees of tokenism	0.054*	-0.109***	-0.201***	0.089***	-0.176***	0.170***	0.064***	0.018
	(0.032)	(0.020)	(0.031)	(0.029)	(0.038)	(0.026)	(0.020)	(0.024)
Degrees of citizen power	0.232***	0.094***	0.102***	0.283***	-0.156***	0.285***	0.097***	0.325***
	(0.032)	(0.040)	(0.031)	(0.022)	(0.043)	(0.020)	(0.020)	(0.024)
Observations	1,050	1,050	1,050	1,050	1,050	1,050	1,050	1,050

Standard errors in parentheses. *** p<0.01, ** p<0.05, * p<0.1

likelihood of adoption was influenced by the robustness of their participation in ELCAP. Thus, increased farmer participation corresponded with increased environmental consciousness among farmers. Agro-technocrat's use of degrees of citizen power, the most robust category of participation—which entailed actively seeking and incorporating indigenous farmers' opinions in the planning and implementation of ELCAP—resulted in an increased likelihood of knowledge cross-fertilisation between farmers and agro-technocrats. By engaging indigenous farmers through the prism of degrees of citizen power, agro-technocrats were for instance able to build on indigenous compost making by sensitising farmers on how to use compost for zai micro-dozing and half-moon farming. ELCAP's agro-technocrats further supported farmers in agro-forestry and helped farmers to better protect riparian regions. Beyond agricultural practices, farmers also adopted and used improved cook-stoves. This preserved local forest cover and improved carbon capture and sequestration. Farmers' likelihood of adopting environmental conscious practices declined as the robustness of local participation reduced to degrees of tokenism. Adoption likelihood was further reversed when non-participation was employed. This is quite intuitive given that non-participation is a charade to gain legitimacy from donors and other stakeholders (Arnstein, 1969, 2011). These results suggest that subsistence farmers' adaptation to climate change can be accelerated if subsistence farmers are seen as necessary partners rather than passive development aid recipients.

The study thus demonstrates that rather than dwell on transferring knowledge from agro-technocrats to indigenous farmers, both indigenous and technocratic farming approaches can go hand in hand so as to co-create knowledge that can contribute to adapting to the climate change conundrum. Besides, as estimates show, economically disadvantaged groups like subsistence farmers are often hardest-hit by the consequences of climate change. Implementation of the participatory approaches espoused in this study in such disadvantaged groups can therefore contribute to a more just transition into a carbon neutral world by 2050 as envisaged by the IPCC. Agro-technocrats, be they under governments or NGOs, can use the participatory approaches as signposts for ensuring community involvement in efforts to reduce the negative impact of climate change, especially on the vulnerable.

ACKNOWLEDGMENT

This study was funded by the German Academic Exchange Service (DAAD) and the Pan African Doctoral Academy (PADA)

REFERENCES

Adam, J. N., Freeman, C. K., & Dassah, E. Z. (2017). Access to dry season water and small ruminants market integration in the Nadowli District of Upper West Region of Ghana. *Journal of Agricultural Extension and Rural Development*, *9*(11), 262–269. doi:10.5897/JAERD2017.0913

Adom, D., & Kquofi, S. (2016). The high impacts of Asante indigenous knowledge in biodiversity conservation issues in Ghana: The case of the Abono and Essumeja Townships in Ashanti Region. *British Journal of Environmental Sciences*, *4*(3), 63–78.

Afriyie, K., Ganle, J. K., & Santos, E. (2017). 'The floods came and we lost everything': Weather extremes and households' asset vulnerability and adaptation in rural Ghana. *Climate and Development*, *10*(3), 259–274. doi:10.1080/17565529.2017.1291403

Agula, C., Mabe, F. N., Akudugu, M. A., Sittoh, S., Ayambila, S. N., & Bawah, A. (2019). Enhancing healthy ecosystems in Northern Ghana through eco-friendly farm-based practices: Insights from irrigation scheme types. *BMC Ecology*, *19*(1), 38. doi:10.118612898-019-0254-8 PMID:31511000

Aikins, A. D. G. (2005). Healer shopping in Africa: New evidence from rural-urban qualitative study of Ghanaian diabetes experiences. *BMJ (Clinical Research Ed.)*, *331*(7519), 737. doi:10.1136/bmj.331.7519.737 PMID:16195290

Arcand, J. L., & Fafchamps, M. (2012). Matching in community-based organisations. *Journal of Development Economics*, *98*(2), 203–219. doi:10.1016/j.jdeveco.2011.07.002

Arnstein, S. (1969). A ladder of citizen participation. *Journal of the American Institute of Planners*, *35*(4), 216–224. doi:10.1080/01944366908977225

Arnstein, S. (2011). Ladder of participation. In A. Cornwall (Ed.), *The participation reader*. Zed Books.

Ba, M. N. (2016). Analysis of Agricultural Commodities Value Chains and Greenhouse Gas Emission in Rice and Maize in West Africa: Impact on Food Security. *Agricultural Sciences*, *7*(07), 457–468. doi:10.4236/as.2016.77047

Berkes, F., & Usher, P. J. (2000). Sacred knowledge, traditional ecological knowledge and resource management. *Arctic*, *53*(2), 198.

Bernard, B., David, M., Anthony, E., Michael, M. S., James, W., Andrew, A., & Claire, N. (2019). The role of indigenous knowledge (IK) in adaptation to drought by agropastoral smallholder farmers in Uganda. [IJKT]. *Indian Journal of Traditional Knowledge*, *19*(1), 44–52.

Binam, J. N., Place, F., Kalinganire, A., Hamade, S., Boureima, M., Tougiani, A., Dakouo, J., Mounkoro, B., Diaminatou, S., Badji, M., Diop, M., Babou, A. B., & Haglund, E. (2015). Effects of farmer managed natural regeneration on livelihoods in semi-arid West Africa. *Environmental Economics and Policy Studies*, *17*(4), 543–575. doi:10.100710018-015-0107-4

Blum, B. (1992). Composting and the roots of sustainable agriculture. *Agricultural History*, *66*(2), 171–188.

Botchway, K. (2001). Paradox of empowerment: Reflections on a case study from Northern Ghana. *World Development*, *29*(1), 135–153. doi:10.1016/S0305-750X(00)00084-X

Botes, L., & Van-Rensburg, D. (2000). Community participation in development: Nine plagues and twelve commandments. *Community Development Journal: An International Forum*, *35*(1), 41–58. doi:10.1093/cdj/35.1.41

Bourguet, D., & Guillemaud, T. (2016). The hidden and external costs of pesticide use. *Sustainable Agriculture Research*, *19*, 35–120.

Cancino, J., & Saborowski, J. (2005). Comparison of randomized branch sampling with and without replacement at the first stage. *Silva Fennica*, *39*(2), 201–216. doi:10.14214f.384

Carson, R. (1962). *Silent spring*. Houghton Mifflin Harcourt.

Chambers, R. (1985). *Rural development: Putting the last first*. Longman.

Chambers, R. (1998). Whose reality counts? Participatory poverty assessments in Africa. In K. King & S. A. McGrath (Eds.), *Running, Reporting & Researching Africa*. Centre of African Studies, University of Edinburgh.

Chambers, R., & Ghildyal, B. P. (1985). Agricultural research for resource-poor farmers: The farmer-first-and-last model. *Agricultural Administration*, *20*(1), 1–30. doi:10.1016/0309-586X(85)90063-9

Chéze, B., David, M., & Martinet, V. (2020). Understanding farmers' reluctance to reduce pesticide use: A choice experiment. *Ecological Economics*, *167*(106349), 1–13. doi:10.1016/j.ecolecon.2019.06.004

Choguill, M. B. G. (1996). A ladder of community participation for underdeveloped countries. *Habitat International*, *20*(3), 431–444. doi:10.1016/0197-3975(96)00020-3

Cleaver, F. (1999). Paradoxes of participation: Questioning participatory approaches to development. *Journal of International Development*, *11*(4), 597–612. doi:10.1002/(SICI)1099-1328(199906)11:4<597::AID-JID610>3.0.CO;2-Q

Collins, K., & Ison, R. (2009). Jumping off Arnstein's ladder: Social learning as a new policy paradigm for climate change adaptation. *Environmental Policy and Governance*, *19*(6), 358–373. doi:10.1002/eet.523

Connor, D. M. (1988). A new ladder of citizen participation. *National Civic Review*, *77*(3), 249–257. doi:10.1002/ncr.4100770309

Cooke, B., & Kothari, U. (Eds.). (2001). *Participation: The new tyranny?* Zed Books.

Cornwall, A. (2011). *The participation reader*. Zed Books.

Creswell, J. W. (2009). Research Design, Qualitative, Quantitative and Mixed Methods Approaches (Vol. 3). SAGE Publications Inc.

Creswell, J. W. (2012). *Educational research: Planning, conducting and evaluating quantitative and qualitative research* (Vol. 4). Pearson Education Inc.

Danso-Abbeam, G., Dagunga, G., & Ehiakpor, D. S. (2019). Adoption of zai technology for soil fertility management: Evidence from Upper East Region, Ghana. *Journal of Economic Structures*, *8*(1), 32. doi:10.118640008-019-0163-1

Degefu, M. A., Assen, M., Satyal, P., & Budds, J. (2019). Villagization and access to water resources in the Middle Awash Valley of Ethiopia: Implications for climate change adaptation. *Climate and Development*, 1–12. doi:10.1080/17565529.2019.1701973

Dollar, D., & Gatti, R. (1999). Gender Inequality, Income and Growth: Are Good Times Good for Women? *The World Bank Development Research Group, Working paper series, No. 1*, 1-42.

Egbetokun, S., Osabuohien, E., & Akinbobola, T. (2018). Feasible Environmental Kuznets and Institutional Quality in North and Southern African Sub-regions. *International Journal of Energy Economics and Policy*, *8*(1), 104–115.

Egbetokun, S., Osabuohien, E., Onanuga, O., Akinbobola, T., Gershon, O., & Okafor, V. (2020). Environmental Pollution, Economic Growth and Institutional Quality: Exploring the Nexus in Nigeria. *Management of Environmental Quality*, *31*(1), 18–31. doi:10.1108/MEQ-02-2019-0050

Fianko, J. R., Donkor, A., Lowor, S. T., & Yeboah, P. O. (2011). Agrochemicals and the Ghanaian environment, a review. *Journal of Environmental Protection*, *2*(03), 221–230. doi:10.4236/jep.2011.23026

Garnett, T. (2011). Where are the best opportunities for reducing greenhouse gas emissions in the food system (including the food chain)? *Food Policy*, *36*, S23–S32. doi:10.1016/j.foodpol.2010.10.010

Gregory, S. V., Swanson, F. J., McKeen, W. A., & Cummins, K. W. (1991). An ecosystem perspective of riparian zones. *Bioscience*, *4*(8), 540–551. doi:10.2307/1311607

Guthiga, P., & Newsham, A. (2011). Meteorologists meeting rainmakers: Indigenous knowlede and climate policy processes in Kenya. *IDS Bulletin*, *42*(3), 104–109. doi:10.1111/j.1759-5436.2011.00228.x

Gyawal, D., & Thompson, M. (2016). Restoring development dharma with toad's eye science? *IDS Bulletin*, *47*(2A), 180–190. doi:10.19088/1968-2016.173192

Hart, R. (1992). Ladder of participation, children's participation: From Tokenism to citizenship. *Innocenti Essays, 4.*

Hussein, A. (2009). The use of triangulation in social sciences research: Can qualitative and quantitative methods be combined? *Journal of Comparative Social Work*, *4*(1), 106–117. doi:10.31265/jcsw.v4i1.48

Intergovernmental Panel on Climate Change. (2019). *IPCC special report on climate change, desertification, land degradation, sustainable land management, food security and greenhouse gas fluxes in terrestrial ecosystems: summary for policymakers*. Retrieved from https://www.ipcc.ch

IPCC. (2014). [Synthesis Report. Contribution of Working Groups I, II and III to the Fifth Assessment Report of the Intergovernmental Panel on Climate Change. IPCC.]. *Climatic Change*, •••, 2014.

IPCC. (2018). Global worming of 1.5 C, an IPCC special report on the impacts of global worming of 1.5 C above pre-industrial levels and related global greenhouse gas emissions. Retrieved from https://wg1.ipcc.ch/SR/documents.SR1.5_LAM3_Room_Assignments.pdf

Kinyashi, G. F. (2006). Towards genuine participation for the poor: Critical analysis of Village Travel and Transport Project (VTTP) in Morogoro, Tanzania. SPRING Scientific Research Paper.

Kuchimanchi, B., Nazareth, D., Bendapudi, R., Awasthi, S., & D'Souza, M. (2019). Assessing differential vulnerability of communities in the agrarian context in two districts of Maharashtra, India. *Climate and Development*, *11*(10), 918–929. doi:10.1080/17565529.2019.1593815

Kusakari, Y., Asubonteng, K. O., Jasaw, G. S., Dayour, F., Dzivenu, T., Lolig, V., ... Obeng, F. K. (2014). Farmer-perceived effects of climate change on livelihoods in Wa West District, Upper West Region of Ghana. *Journal of Disaster Research*, *9*(4), 516–528. doi:10.20965/jdr.2014.p0516

Kvartiuk, V., & Curtiss, J. (2019). Participatory rural development without participation: Insights from Ukraine. *Journal of Rural Studies*, *69*, 76–86. doi:10.1016/j.jrurstud.2019.04.002

Lechenet, M., Dessaint, F., Py, G., Makowski, D., & Munier-Jolain, N. (2017). *Reducing pesticide use while preserving crop productivity and profitability on arable farms* (Vol. 3). Nature Plants.

LeGates, R. T., & Stout, F. (Eds.). (2015). *A ladder of citizen participation*. Routledge.

Long, J. S., & Freese, J. (2001). *Regression models for categorical dependent variables using Stata*. Stata press.

Mansuri, G., & Rao, V. (2012). *Localizing development: Does participation work?* World Bank Publications. doi:10.1596/978-0-8213-8256-1

Mataya, D. C., Vincent, K., & Dougill, A. J. (2019). How can we effectively build capacity to adapt to climate change? Insights from Malawi. *Climate and Development*, •••, 1–10. doi:10.1080/17565529.2019.1694480

McMichael, A. J., Powles, J. W., Butler, C. D., & Uauy, R. (2007). Food, livestock production, energy, climate change, and health. *Lancet*, *370*(9594), 1253–1263. doi:10.1016/S0140-6736(07)61256-2 PMID:17868818

Moumouni, I. M., Vodouhe, S. D., & Streiffeler, F. (2009). What makes small-scale farmers participate in financing agricultural research extension? Analysis of three case studies from Benin. *Journal of Agricultural Education and Extension*, *15*(3), 301–316. doi:10.1080/13892240903069595

Nazir, J., & Pedretti, E. (2016). Educators' perceptions of bringing students to environmental consciousness through engaging outdoor experiences. *Environmental Education Research*, *22*(2), 288–304. doi:10.1080/13504622.2014.996208

Nightingale, A. J., Eriksen, S., Taylor, M., Forsyth, T., Pelling, M., Newsham, A., & Bezner-Kerr, R. (2019). Beyond technical fixes: Climate solutions and the great deragement. *Climate and Development*, 1–10. doi:10.1080/17565529.2019.1624495

Nyong, A., Adesina, F., & Elasha, B. O. (2007). The value of indigenous knowledge in climate change mitigation and adaptation strategies in the African Sahel. *Mitigation and Adaptation Strategies for Global Change*, *12*(5), 787–797. doi:10.100711027-007-9099-0

Opare, S. (2016). Adaptation to climate change impacts: Coping strategies of an indigenous community in Ghana to declining water supply. *Climate and Development*, *10*(1), 73–83. doi:10.1080/17565529.2016.1184610

Parkinson, S. (2009). When farmers don't want ownership: Reflections on demand-driven extension in sub-Saharan Africa. *Journal of Agricultural Education and Extension*, *15*(4), 417–429. doi:10.1080/13892240903309678

Patton, M. Q. (2002). *Qualitative research & evaluation methods* (Vol. 3). Sage Publications, Inc.

Platteau, J. (2004). Monitoring elite capture in community-driven development. *Blackwell Publishing*, *35*(2), 223–246.

Platteau, J., & Gaspart, F. (2003). The risk of resource misappropriation in community-driven development. *World Development*, *31*(10), 1687–1703. doi:10.1016/S0305-750X(03)00138-4

Pretty, J. N., Chambers, R., & Harris, J. (2003). Towards a learning paradigm: New professionalism and institutions for agriculture. In Rethinking sustainability: power, knowledge, and institutions (pp. 189-227). Academic Press.

Reij, C., Tappan, G., & Smale, M. (2009). Agroenvironmental Transformation in the Sahel: Another kind of "Green Revolution". In D. J. Speilman & R. Pandya-Lorch (Eds.), *Proven Successes in Agricultural Development; A Technical Compenium to Millions Fed*. International Food Policy Research Institute.

Ruesga, G. A., & Knight, B. (2013). The view from the heights of Arnstein's ladder: Resident engagement by community foundations. *National Civic Review*, *102*(3), 13–16. doi:10.1002/ncr.21137

Saunders, M., Lewis, P., & Thornhill, A. (2009). *Research methods for business students* (Vol. 5). Pearson Education Limited.

Stelmach, B. (2016). Parents' participation on school councils analysed through Arnstein's ladder of participation. *School Leadership & Management*, *36*(3), 271–291. doi:10.1080/13632434.2016.1247048

Tritter, J. Q., & McCallum, A. (2006). The snakes and ladders of user involvement: Moving beyond Arnstein. *Health Policy (Amsterdam)*, *76*(2), 156–168. doi:10.1016/j.healthpol.2005.05.008 PMID:16006004

Veihe, A. (2000). Sustainable farming practices: Ghanaian farmers' perception of erosion and their use of conservation measures. *Environmental Management*, *25*(4), 393–402. doi:10.1007002679910031 PMID:10667945

Wilson, C., & Tisdell, C. (2001). Why farmers continue to use pesticides despite environmental, health and sustainability cost. *Ecological Economics*, *39*(3), 449–462. doi:10.1016/S0921-8009(01)00238-5

World Bank. (2000). *Engendering Development Through Gender Equality in Rights, Resources and Voice*. Retrieved from Washington.

ENDNOTES

1 Creating barricades across the slope to prevent soil erosion and water run-offs.

2 Precise application of compost in small holes into which crops are planted. This maximises the use of manure. It also retains water thereby preventing runoffs in the harsh semi-arid climatic region of the UWR where water scarcity is a major bane to farming.

3 The creation of semi-circular boundaries on a degraded land into which the farmer puts compost after loosening the soil. These boundaries are often created to retain water in dry ecological regions like UWR.

4 Gregory, Swanson, McKeen, and Cummins (1991) describe it as '…the interface between terrestrial and aquatic ecosystems.' An example is the bank of a river.

Chapter 21
Thematic Review of Trends in Inclusive Urban Development Studies (2000– 2020)

Samuel Medayese
https://orcid.org/0000-0001-6683-0101
University of KwaZulu-Natal, South Africa

Hangwelani Hope Magidimisha-Chipungu
University of KwaZulu-Natal, South Africa

Ayobami Abayomi Popoola
https://orcid.org/0000-0002-9742-0604
University of KwaZulu-Natal, South Africa

Lovemore Chipungu
University of KwaZulu-Natal, South Africa

Bamiji Michael Adeleye
Federal University of Technology, Minna, Nigeria

ABSTRACT

This study followed a chronological review of literature over the past 20 years. This was able to show relationship between inclusivity and physical development. A variety of discussions were looked into including dimension of inclusivity, definition of inclusivity, scales for measurement of inclusivity, methodology for appraising inclusivity, protagonists of inclusivity, and antagonists of inclusivity. The intricacy of the correlations between inclusive physical development and life expectations of residents are improved upon so as to show the similarities of these parameters. The analysis of the relevant literature indicated the process of enhancing the urban space and ensuring that all interest and strata of groups in the human composition are adequately cared for by employing the best parameters from the conceptualization of the city development, all the indicators of inclusiveness are well thought out.

DOI: 10.4018/978-1-7998-4817-2.ch021

INTRODUCTION

Unequal distribution of resources within the urban space brings into play the resource endowed location and disadvantageous locations. The resultant effect of the lack of some resources in some areas has led to both the uneven distribution of the dividends of the resources within space and introduction of the concept of exclusion (Medayese *et al.*, 2016). Societies and individuals are said to be excluded when they do not enjoy certain infrastructures and services which other societies or individual tend to benefit from (Herrmann et al, 2018; Osabuohien, 2020). Driving for spatial equality and equal access to service and infrastructure within the urban area led to the promotion and advocacy for an inclusive city. Arriving at a more inclusive space prompted the paradigm development of inclusive urban planning and development. Wey (2015:1898) mentioned that a bunch of measures such as outcome-oriented policies aim at improving the quality of lives for the excluded, including inclusionary zoning and public housing have been introduced to enhance the inclusiveness in both outcomes and processes of urban planning. Kooy *et al.* (2018:110) opine that an inclusive development approach emphasizes fairness and social justice and participation in development. Gupta *et al.* (2015:546) defined inclusive development as 'development that includes marginalized people, sectors and countries in social, political and economic processes for increased human wellbeing, social and environmental sustainability, and empowerment.

The objective of inclusive development is not just improving the wellbeing of the worse off along non-income dimensions such as education and health, but to also strengthen the case for migrants and vulnerable groups in the city. For example, the informal urban evicted group, according to Popoola *et al.* (2020) is a city-shaping with less relevance for the urban poor. Especially in the face of emerging estates and urban gated communities. Blakely and Snyder (1997) aver that the appearance of gates, walled, private and facility well-serviced community despite the outlawing of all forms of discrimination in housing, education, public transportation, and public accommodations has been termed *"a new form of discrimination"*. To this end, Schindler (2015) observed that throughout history, people had used varied methods to exclude undesirable individuals from places where they were not wanted. Whereas the real question asked is how much of the sermonized equality have reflected spatial equality in infrastructure planning, service delivery and the allocation of resources within all classes.

Arfvidsson *et al.* (2017) pointed out that various forms of informality are widespread in urban areas of low-income and many middle- income and transitional countries. To this end, improving the lives of slum dwellers by arguing for tenure security as a prerequisite for development and inclusion was suggested by the study (ibid. p. 8).Promoting the income and employment base as introduced in the study of Yuan *et al.* (2020) can be a motivation for inclusive development. In the study, inclusive and sustainable industrial development (ISID) is a call for action to promote industrialization by minimizing the environmental footprint and enhancing social inclusion (Yuan *et al.*, 2020). The ISID, as proposed by the United Nations Industrial Development Organization (UNIDO) (2009), was targeted at promoting inclusiveness through increased industrialization, innovation, and provision of infrastructures. This, according to UNIDO (2019), is a framework that triggers citizens inclusion in environment, economy, and society. As earlier stated, while income growth is one determinant of improvements in education and health, it is not the only one, and there is considerable variation in these achievements at any level of income. Direct intervention along these dimensions to improve the lowest achievements is what is required if inclusive development is going to be acceptable (van de Walle, 2000; Balisacan and Pernia, 2002; Fan and Chan-Kang, 2005; Khandker, Bakht and Koolwal, 2006; Asian Development Bank, 2006;Bryceson, Bradbury and Bradbury, 2008).

Looking at the bias of the inclusive physical development, itemphasizes poor members of the society, migrants, gender mainstreaming, consideration for children and infrastructure that also give priority attention to vulnerable individuals in the city. For example, Pineda (2020) iterates that as much as cities are essential to livelihood and survival, unlocking human potential and innovation can be better improved through inclusive urban policies. The argument was that urban infrastructure and mobility concerns are brought to the forefront as the privatization of public space, and the creation of closed networks reorganize value creation and benefit distribution to those whose connections matter (ibid. p. 30). This reservation provokes the city inclusiveness for people with disabilities. In fact, Thapa and Pathranarakul (2019) identified that a limiting factor to the achieving inclusion for all is lack and limited recognition of diversity (especially across class and gender) within the urban space.

Using women experiences and vulnerability to disaster in Nepal, it was reinforced that there is vulnerability oblivion among women when women's lived realities and the Nepal government's commitment and position to promote gender equality, to empower women and the level of inclusiveness in current disaster risk governance and post-disaster recovery is taken into consideration (ibid. p. 217).The study reported gender risk exposure and social exclusion among women. However, the contention here is the bias for the consumption of environmental space for the provision of infrastructure like housing, transport, commerce and other city functions, for the disadvantaged groups in the city, which is at variance with the urban liveability concept which focus is more broadly approached. But, in the overall analysis, it negates the sustainable development definition which seeks more environmentally focused development and resource conservation.

Varying degrees of examples abound on studies on inclusive physical planning literature across the world. Kaubar and Raumyar (2009) conceptualized inclusive development with application to rural infrastructure and development assistance. This research was carried out in the Philippines a part of the Asian continent. Another research by Gougon *et al.* (2014) in Australia titled a comparative assessment review of measurement instruments to inform and evaluate the effectiveness of disability-inclusive development. Further, Kaubaur (2010) also researched inclusive growth and inclusive development in the Philippines. While a further search by Heeks *et al.* (2014) presented a new model of inclusive innovations for development in Manchester, United Kingdom.

Santiago (2014) also researched inclusive physical development in Ottawa, Canada. Promoting communal and individual innovation, Erjavec and Ruchinskaya (2019) align the idea of co-creation and community participation to arrive for at an inclusive public space. Co-creative techniques give communities and individuals more direct involvement in defining their needs and priorities, collaboratively finding solutions, influencing decisions, and achieving better outcomes (ibid. p.211). The view was that the flexibility of the process achieved by the integration of knowledge of different users and understanding that, what is being created can be changed by the community.

This body of knowledge across a diversity of groups and communities point at the existing variations to the conceptualization of inclusive development. The import of the citations as mentioned above, is that literature abounds on the issues surrounding inclusive development across the world. However, an insight into the spread of this literature across the racial group is also important to drive home the points on its wider exploration and level of acceptability amongst various groups and race across the world, bearing in mind the development peculiarities between developed and developing regions of the world. The aim, therefore, of this review work is to explore available literature resources around inclusive development and establishing the trend in the research discourse of the subject matter. This is with a view to achieving the objectives of establishing the knowledge gap in terms of research spread in the discourse, the different locations of the identified source materials on inclusive development available both in open and closed access sources.

METHODOLOGY

The study methodology was based on the extensive review of the literature. A literature review is to enable the reviewer to understand up to date research that has been carried out on inclusive development studies. This method informed the identification of the gap on inclusive development in the process of understanding the important linkages relating resident's wellbeing and inclusivity. The study review was based on a twenty-year timeline over a period 2000-2020. The post-millennia meta-analysis led to presentations of reality and recommendations for the future studies. The literature search using Google and Google Scholar search software through the use of keywords such as inclusivity, inequality, gender bias, disable mobility, informality and informal housing, and inclusive development resulted in the identification of sizeable number-controlled research material on the topic. The focus of this study centered on the impact of inclusive development on resident's wellbeing in the urban space, the keywords employed include: Social Inclusion, Exclusion, Spatial Configuration, Vulnerable groups, Disability, infrastructure, development, wellbeing, built environments and green spaces.

The materials used for the analysis was from purposively selected from accredited and indexed materials from Science direct journals. The procedure for the study followed a laydown process of identification of the relevant literature, collection of the relevant literature, its classification and analysis to achieve the stated aim.

The collected articles were thenitemized through the references so to separate relevant literature from all the collected literature. Three criteria were employed to classify the literature, which includes: year of publications, the reputation of the journal and top-cited journals.

1. **Year of Publication:** The literature employed for the study were those published between 2000 and 2020. This gives a prospect of determining the paradigm shift in the literature over time, as discovery improves through advanced technological breakthrough physical infrastructure provision.
2. **The reputation of Journal:** Journals were classified based on their wide coverage and open to a vast number of readers. The index employed provided opportunity to classify journals into Q1; Q2; Q3 and Q4. More of the Q1 and Q2 journals were collected because they provided good, quality, and reputable articles. This was achieved because more reputable publishers of journals were used (for example, Elsevier, Taylor and Francis, Springer, Emerald).
3. **Top 10 Cited Paper:** The use of the top ten cited papers for the classification was also employed to analyze the good, quality, and reputable articles.

The analysis of the relevant literature that is earmarked for the study was the last aspect of the methodology employed. The analysis conducted, wascategorized into the following: safety, resilience, Social justice, inequality, social inclusion, social exclusion. This formed the basis for the structure of this study as presented. The effect of these is then linked with the impact on infrastructure planning and development.

RESULTS OF THE FINDINGS

Year of Publication

This study employed the journals that were published between 2000 and 2020 for the analysis, and the total journals employed were 250. The number of papers used for the study is presented in Figure 1. This shows a variation in the number published in different years using three years interval. The analysis shows that between 2018 and 2020, the highest turnout of publication was witnessed at this era, while the least number of publications regarding the subject of inclusive development was recorded between 2011 and 2013. The implication of this as shown in Figure 1 is that from 2000 to 2020, there is a gradual increase in the awareness on the subject of inclusive development across the world even though at certain points there seems to be a drop in between.

Furthermore, it can be inferred from this analysis that the literature increase about inclusivity continues to increase as the awareness level towards the subject from scholars continues to increase over time. It is therefore important in view of the importance and challenges associated with the subject matter to continue to build literature defense wall around the subject in other to ensure that a balance is created on the inequality scale across space and ensure equality amongst the different classes in the city for the purpose of guaranteeing justice in the city over time.

Figure 1. Number of journals articles published by year of publication
Source: *Author's Analysis, 2020*

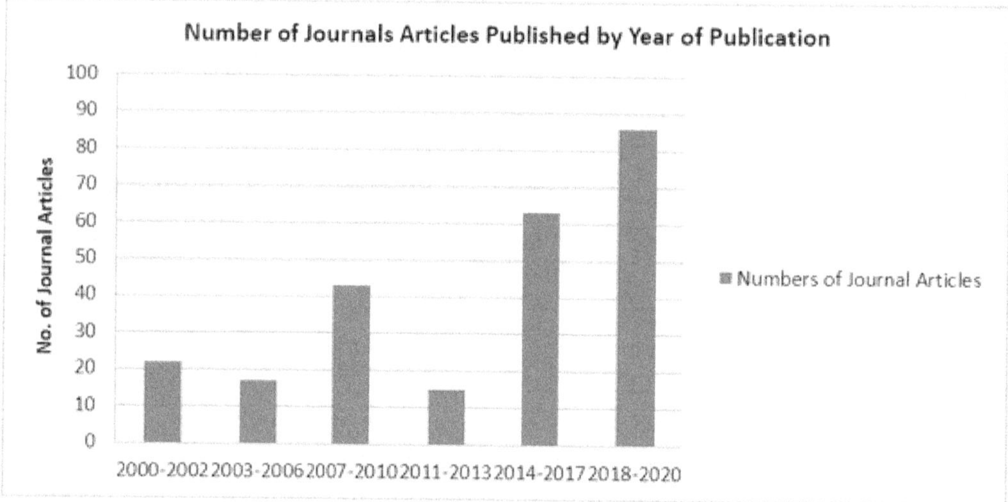

Indexing House of Journal Articles reviewed

The indexing house of each journal involved in the publication of articles regarding inclusive development was also appraised in this review, as shown in Figure 2. According to the classifications laid out in the methodology from Q1 to Q5 which represent the various indexing platforms, the analysis shows that the highest number of publications examined for this review were from the Q1 which were the Social science citation index/Science citation index and Q4 which are the Scopus citation index. This implies that a considerable number of the journals and articles published under the inclusive development theme are considered under reputable indexed journal outlets, and this gives a lot of credit to the findings of the various research publication as being from sources that are of a good level of integrity. Other indexing platforms considered includes the Q3 which is Department of higher education and training (DHET) Q4 which are the emerging source citation index and Q5 which is the International Bibliography of Science citation index (IBSS). All of which have a fair share of publication on the theme of inclusivity which puts the subject on a radius of very important global and scholarly issues worthy of continuous evaluation by the academia until a fair balance is achieved in the balancing of the inequality scale in the city space.

Figure 2. Number of journal articles published by indexing house
Source: *Authors' Analysis, 2020*

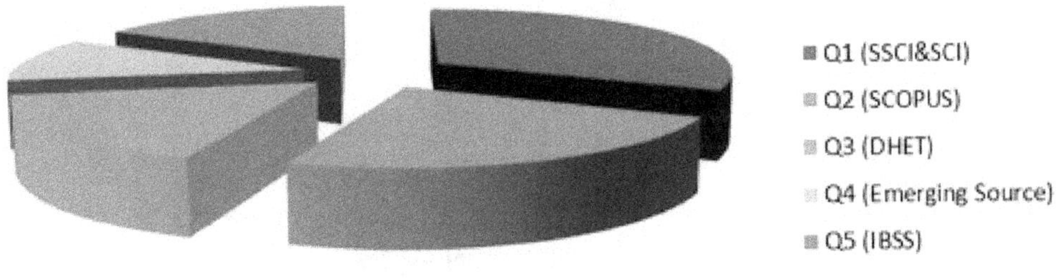

Locational Spread on Studies in Inclusive Physical Development Literature

Another issue appraised in this review in the trend of literature on inclusive physical development is the concerns around the locations of the various studies on the subject matter. This is of great concern in research as is observed in the Figure 3 that the highest number of research publication is associated with Europe as the location of research or case study of the research for most of the empirical research works. It is also observed that quite many of the identified publications also have roots in Australia. Locations in Asia amongst the study locations were also observed to be high in the publication scale, as is shown in Figure 3. However, Africa and the Southern part of America were observed to have the least volume of publication on the subject of inclusivity between 2000 and 2020, this is, however, not because there are no inequalities within these areas, but these are not brought into the front burner as a result of poor scholarly publications from these locations. The implication of the above analysis there is that there is a considerable literature gap in scholarly publications which deals with the situations of Africa and South American Countries as is observed in the analysis and reviews carried out.

Reputation of Journal

The analysis of the reputation of journals indicated that 31 different journals were employed for the study and the analysis presented in Table 1. The journals were selected based on their 5 years impact factors as of 2019. The journal citation was used to rank the journals. The citation plays a significant role in the impact factor estimation. The best journal used was the Journal of Clean Production that has the highest number of contributions to the study (6.395IF and 72,855 citations). In comparison, the least contributor was Journal Architectural Theory Review with no impact factor but 17 citations. Also, there are several other high-quality journal outlets such as The LANCET with over 1.1million citations and impact factor of 3.633, as shown in Table 1.

Figure 3. Number of journal articles published by case study
Source: *Authors' Analysis, 2020*

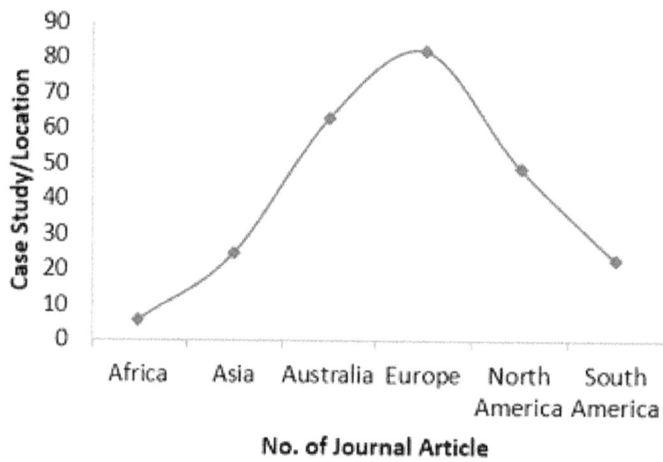

Top 10 Cited Journals

Of the total 250 journals articles deployed for this analysis, the top 10 articles that are cited include the following as shown in Table 2. The highest cited article is Will the real smart city please stand up. In the Journal City analysis of urban trends, culture, theory, policy, action with 2,462 citations between 2000 and 2020, while, the least was Old Age and Poverty in Developing Countries: New Policy Challenges in the World Development cited 55 times between 2000 and 2020.

CONCLUSION AND RECOMMENDATION

This study is based purely on a literature review focused on the analysis of trends in literature publications about inclusive physical development. This research focuses its interest on published articles on inclusivity as a concept for managing physical development and ensuring a balance on the inequality scale in the city space. Though this research is centred mainly on the inclusive development paradigm in development planning, it unlocks opportunity for several studies on Inclusive development and development approach in planning. Other aspects that research can focus on include trends in inclusive transportation, gender balance and inclusivity in the city space, migrants, and sense of belonging in the city space and several other related relationships between inclusivity and the city environment.

Table 1. Journals that are used for this state-of-the-art study

Name of Journal	5 yrs Impact Factor, 2019	Journal citation
Cities	3.853	2,114
Sustainable Cities and Society	4.624	5,871
Journal of Regional Studies		19
Energy Conversion and Management	7.181	29,699
Journal of Cleaner Production	6.395	72,855
City, Culture and Society		230
Environment and Urbanization	3.015	2,288
Habitat International	3.846	2,366
Innovation: The European Journal of Social Science research	1.055	
World Development	3.904	
Journal of Environmental Management	4.865	18,092
Applied Energy	8.426	53,875
Technological Forecasting and Social Change	3.815	6,453
Journal of Early Intervention	2.165	759
Landscape and Urban Planning	5.144	3,823
Current Opinion in Environmental Sustainability	4.258	1,787
Journal of Area Development and Policy		248
Sustainability	2.801	
Social Inclusion	0.785	313
Critical Social Policy	2.185	1,297
Urban Studies	3.272	11,903
Environment and Planning: Economy and Space	3.146	9,985
China Information	1.481	300
Journal of Urban Affairs	1.115	108
The Lancet	59.102	60,620
JournalArchitectural Theory Review		17
Waste Management	5.431	11,336
Journal of City analysis of urban trends, culture, theory, policy, action		1,845
Journal of Special Education	1.537	1,291
Frontiers in Environmental Sciences	3.633	1,100,000
International Environmental Agreements: Politics, Law and Economics	2.404	

Source: Authors' Analysis, 2020

This study has taken chronological documentation of scholarly publications about inclusivity within the city space. This review of relevant literature in the field of inclusive development has itemized trends and the dimensions of publications relating to inclusivity within the city space between 2000 and 2020 a twenty-year period to arrive at the various conclusions on the locations of the publications, the indexing houses and the integrity of the journal outlets that have published the articles on the subject of city

Table 2. Top ten cited papers in this state-of-the-art study

Top 10 cited papers	Number cited
Gerometta, J., Haussermann, H., & Longo, G. (2005). Social Innovation and Civil Society in Urban Governance: Strategies for an Inclusive City. *Urban Studies*, *42*(11), 2007–2021. https://doi.org/10.1080/00420980500279851	386
Douglass, M. (2000). Mega-urban Regions and World City Formation: Globalization, theEconomicCrisis and Urban Policy Issues in Pacific Asia. *Urban Studies*, *37*(12), 2315–2335. https://doi.org/10.1080/00420980020002823	332
Robert G. Hollands (2008) Will the real smart city please stand up? Intelligent, progressive or entrepreneurial? JournalCity analysis of urban trends, culture, theory, policy, actionPages 303-320 https://doi.org/10.1080/13604810802479126	2462
Gupta, J., Vegelin, C. Sustainable development goals and inclusive development. Int Environ Agreements 16, 433–448 (2016). https://doi.org/10.1007/s10784-016-9323-z	178
PeterLloyd-Sherlock (2000). Old Age and Poverty in Developing Countries: New Policy Challenges. World Development Volume 28, Issue 12, Pages 2157-2168 https://doi.org/10.1016/S0305-750X(00)00077-2	55
Sybrand P T Jallingii (2000) Ecology on the edge:Landscape and ecology between town and country. Landscape and Urban Planning Volume 48, Issues 3–4, Pages 103-119 https://doi.org/10.1016/S0169-2046(00)00035-9	137
Agnes Binagwaho et al., (2014) Rwanda 20 years on: investing in life, The Lancet Volume 384, Issue 9940, 26 July–1 August 2014, Pages 371-375 https://doi.org/10.1016/S0140-6736(14)60574-2	171
Brockerhoff, M.P. (2000). BULLETIN A publication of the Population Reference Bureau Population.	316
Ramin Keivani (2010) A review of the main challenges to urban sustainability, International Journal of Urban Sustainable Development, 1:1-2, 5-16, DOI: 10.1080/19463131003704213	115
Healey, P. (2002). On Creating the "City" as a Collective Resource. Urban Studies, 39(10), 1777–1792. https://doi.org/10.1080/0042098022000002957	312

Source: Authors' Analysis, 2020

development and the inclusivity question which is a major challenge for balancing inequality in the city space and giving every inhabitant of the city a sense of belonging a place to thrive. As from the findings from the selected literature, city development planners must begin a rethink towards a good spread of the inclusivity literature to cover areas around Africa and Southern part of America which have been observed from the literature review as seen in this research to have a great deal of limitations on the subject of inclusive physical development.

ACKNOWLEDGMENT

I acknowledge the contributions of the SARChI For Inclusive Cities Ably led by Professor H.H Magidimisha and all members of the Team who contributed to the review and gathering of Literature materials for this research work.

REFERENCES

Arfvidsson, H., Simon, D., Oloko, M., & Moodley, N. (2017). Engaging with and measuring informality in the proposed Urban Sustainable Development Goal. *African Geographical Review*, *36*(1), 100–114. doi:10.1080/19376812.2015.1130636

Blakely, E., & Snyder, M. (1997). Divided We Fall: Gated and Walled Communities in the United States. In Architecture of Fear. New York: Princeton Architectural Press.

Erjavec, I., & Ruchinskaya, T. (2019). A Spotlight of Co-creation and Inclusiveness of Public Open Spaces. In *CyberParks–The Interface Between People, Places and Technology* (pp. 209–223). Springer. doi:10.1007/978-3-030-13417-4_17

Gupta, J., Pouw, N., & Ros-Tonen, M. (2015). Towards an elaborated theory of inclusive development. *European Journal of Development Research*, *27*(4), 541–559. doi:10.1057/ejdr.2015.30

Herrmann, R., Jumbe, C., Bruentrup, M., & Osabuohien, E. (2018). Competition between Biofuel Feedstock and Food Production: Empirical Evidence from Sugarcane Outgrower Settings in Malawi. *Biomass and Bioenergy*, *114*(July), 100–111. doi:10.1016/j.biombioe.2017.09.002

Kooy, M., Walter, C., & Prabaharyaka, I. (2018). Inclusive development of urban water services in Jakarta: The role of groundwater. *Habitat International*, *73*, 109–118. doi:10.1016/j.habitatint.2016.10.006

Medayese, S., Adeleye, B., & Popoola, A. (2016). Exclusion. In Contemporary Concepts in Physical Planning, (vol. 2, pp. 347-366). Ibadan, Nigeria: Department of Urban and Regional Planning, University of Ibadan.

Osabuohien, E. (2020). *The Palgrave Handbook of Agricultural and Rural Development in Africa*. Palgrave Macmillan., doi:10.1007/978-3-030-41513-6

Pineda, V. (2020). *Building the Inclusive City: Governance, Access, and the Urban Transformation of Dubai*. Palgrave Macmillian. doi:10.1007/978-3-030-32988-4

Popoola, A., Olatunde, M., Magidimisha, H., Abiodun, A., Adeleye, B., & Chipungu, L. (2020). Urban Forced Evictions: Experiences in the Metropolitan City of Lagos, Nigeria. *The Indonesian Journal of Geography*, *52*(1), 112–127.

Schindler, S. (2015). Architectural Exclusion: Discrimination and Segregation through Physical Design of the Built Environment. *The Yale Law Journal*, *124*(6), 1836–2201.

Thapa, V., & Pathranarakul, P. (2019). Gender inclusiveness in disaster risk governance for sustainable recovery of 2015 Gorkha Earthquake, Nepal. *International Journal of Disaster Risk Reduction*, *34*, 209–219. doi:10.1016/j.ijdrr.2018.11.019

United Nations Industrial Development Organization. (2009). *Green Industry – UNIDO*. Available at: https://www.unido.org/sites/default/files/2010-11/Green_Industry_Initiative_0.pdf

United Nations Industrial Development Organization. (2019). *ISID Platform*. Available at: https://isid.unido.org/

Wey, W. (2015). Developing the Socio-Economic Urban Sustainable Planning Strategies Based on The Smart and Inclusive Growth Principles. *Journal of Business and Economics*, *6*(11), 1898–1907. doi:10.15341/jbe(2155-7950)/11.06.2015/008

Yuan, Q., Cheng, C., Wang, J., Zhu, T., & Wang, K. (2020). Inclusive and sustainable industrial development in China: An efficiency-based analysis for status and improving potentials. *Applied Energy*, *268*, 114876. doi:10.1016/j.apenergy.2020.114876

Chapter 22
Transition of Ecosystem Services Based on Urban Agroecology

José G. Vargas-Hernández
https://orcid.org/0000-0003-0938-4197
University Center for Economic and Managerial Sciences, University of Guadalajara, Mexico

ABSTRACT

This chapter has the aim to analyze the implications of the transition of ecosystem services based on urban agro ecology. It advances on the debate over the negative effects of the traditional and industrial oriented agricultural production on the ecosystem services, food systems, climate change, etc., and analyses the principles, methods and some practices that supports the transition to urban agro ecology. The method employed is the analytical of the theoretical and empirical literature review. It concludes that a transition from traditional and industrial oriented agriculture towards more urban agro ecology is inevitable to improve the ecological and environmental services, the economic efficiency, the social equity and justice, and the environmental sustainability of cities.

INTRODUCTION

The following essay aims to assess the importance of urban agroecology as a promoter of ecosystem services in cities. In response to a debate over the negative impacts of industrial input-intensive agriculture is leading to consider a feasible transition to other alternative forms capable to provide ecosystem services and produce food. Agroecology emerges in response to the problems associated with the industrial model of agricultural production. The simplified form of agroecosystem is altered with the input substitution that occurs in industrial agro systems. The industrial agriculture framed in the free market economic model has a destructive impact on sustainable natural resources, biodiversity, food security, environmental services and climate change, leading to ecosystem disruption and human hunger. Conventional agriculture is not sustainable for the rarefaction of inputs, global competition, loss of biodiversity and benefits from ecosystem services, and climate change.

DOI: 10.4018/978-1-7998-4817-2.ch022

The current consumption model based on industrial agro culture is disconnected from food production leads towards poor consumption patterns and choices of diets beyond the requirements of urban land planning and development.

There is a gap in the agroecological transitions between the agroecological practices and the ecosystem services delivery. The relationship between agroecology and nature is relevant in the current crisis is framed by the land used for agriculture and the land dedicated to conservation of biodiversity and ecosystem services.

The agroecological struggles leading to demands for right to food, land redistribution, concerns for pollution of soil, land and water, provision of ecosystem services, corporate dismantling and access to fair markets of organic products, etc., are some of the emerging issues in urban environments. To break this pervasive relationship, it is required the incorporation of an integral conservation programs framed by minimizing land use dedicated to agriculture and more to conservation of agroforest ecological biodiversity and other ecosystem services (Herrmann et al, 2018).

Agroecology and food production systems face some economic, social and environmental challenges when economies are organized around a competitive export orientation of crops that have impacts on the ecosystem services integrity, food quality, public health, and disruption of traditional rural livelihoods. The autonomy and solidarity between peoples of rural and urban agroecology displaces the control of global markets.

Research on agroecology is based on the assumption that there is a positive relationship between biodiversity and the rate of ecosystem services. Agroecological research tends to enhance agroecosystem functions of biodiversity systems based on ecological principles such as facilitation, niche partitioning, competition, etc. Sustainable urban agroecology take into consideration the efficient competition of resources between the strategies developed by actors in the urban environment to enhance benefits and securing access to land use.

In this sense, we ask ourselves why is urban agroecology important as a promoter of ecosystem services in cities? To later present analytical perspectives on agroecology, urban agroecological systems and ecosystem services, and in subsequent sections analyze the following: contributions, transitions, transformative strategies for the agroecological transition to urban agro-ecological systems. Starting from a thorough documentary review to analyze the theoretical contributions currently established on these issues.

AGROECOLOGY, URBAN AGROECOLOGY SYSTEMS AND ECOSYSTEMS SERVICES

Many studies have shown the unwanted effects of the current corporate agro-food system, emphasizing the fact of being a reproducer of hunger, disease, depletion of water, soil and energy, extinction of biodiversity, among others (Altieri and Toledo, 2011; Cuéllar-Padilla and Calle-Collado, 2011; De Molina, 2012; De Schutter, 2010). Leaving in evidence the weaknesses of this System, partly caused, because it reproduces the productivity logics of economic growth and capital accumulation, and which operates within the current economic system. A system that established a model for food production, which is developed based on mechanization, the use of monoculture and chemical fertilization (Gliessman, 2007; Ferguson and Morales, 2010; Altieri and Toledo, 2011); ignoring the organic or biological factors that determine food systems themselves (Altieri and Toledo, 2011.

In this field of criticism, agroecology takes on importance. In this sense, as in a polysemy concept, such as science, practice and movement (Ferguson and Morales, 2010; Gliessman and Rosemeyer, 2009; Levidow, Pimbert and Valoqueren, 2014; Wezel and Soldat, 2009). From a more localized perspective, it relies on diversifications and synergies of biological interactions to improve food productivity, soil fertility and resilience through participatory frameworks while achieving high crop production, economic efficiency, sustainable environment. and social inclusion (Pretty, 2006¸Rosset et al. 2011; Méndez, Bacon and Cohen, 2013).

Various experiences have shown that agroecology based on social organization is very powerful. The case of Cuba, for example, where agroecology was key to help the survival of Cubans during the crisis caused by the collapse of the socialist bloc between 1989 and 1990, and the subsequent escalation of the trade embargo of the United States of America (USA). Between 1997 and 2010, a third of the peasant families in Cuba participated in the "Movimiento Campesino a Campesino" promoted by ANAP (Rosset et al. 2011). Consecutively, this movement has been growing by including 200,000 peasant families: approximately half of the Cuban peasantry, in addition to many urban ones (Rosset et al. 2011; Funes and Vázquez 2016). This case shows us the importance of agroecology to overcome situations of vulnerability of food systems.

Agroecology as a practical approach encompasses agricultural systems thinking aimed at supporting local economies, strengthening ecological biodiversity, ecosystem resilience, social justice, and food sovereignty (Fernandez et al. 2012; Ferguson and Morales, 2010; Cuéllar-Padilla and Calle-Collado, 2011; Gliessman, 2007). Agroecology for this is based on various disciplines, for example, to be able to assess the diversity of farms that interact with some agroecological functions, such as the impact on biodiversity, carbon sequestration, climate change, gas emissions, ecosystem resilience, food security, etc. (Duru and Thérond, 2015; Felipe-Lucia et al. 2015; Méndez, Bacon and Cohen, 2013).

In this sense, this idea of agroecology spread to the cities, taking up other perspectives. Urban agroecology as a theoretical and practical approach studies and applies agricultural systems from ecological concepts and principles in a socio-economic perspective to design, manage and implement sustainable agro-ecosystems to increase the sustainability of agro food systems (Altieri, 2002; Altieri et al. 1999; Crawford, 2010). The concept of agro-ecosystem was introduced by the ecologist Odum in 1969 to represent the interaction of ecological, technological and socio-economic factors, expanding the scope of agroecology (Wezel, et al., 2009; Gliessman, 2007).

Urban agroecology can be defined simply, as growing plants and raising animals in and around cities (De Zeeuw, Van Veenhuizen and Dubbeling, 2011). However, by deepening in the social transformations it can promote, it expands. One area is the cultural significance of the urban agroecology experience in its special dimension that values the place as a public right to have access to the dynamics of power (Marques, 2010; Fernandez et al, 2012). So urban and peri-urban agroecology systems are the cultivation, processing, and distribution of agroecological products to feed local residents. These urban agroecosystems have a more social approach than a technical one, it is explicitly rooted in radical political thought and action, becoming part of the fabric of a sustainable urban society (Rojo et al, 2014; Mendez, Bacon and Cohen, 2013; Lovell, 2010).

Urban agroecology can often be confused with urban agriculture, gardening, farming, and subsistence agriculture. However, part of the rise of urban agroecology was the exhaustion of urban gardening, which was perceived as a sign of underdeveloped and poor people who cultivated on a small scale with little experience and diversity (Crawford, 2010; Fernandez et al, 2012). On the other hand, urban agroecology exceeds the dimensions of what is horticulture, becoming an important source of fresh and healthy products for urban populations, not only of vegetables free of agrochemicals but also proteins of animal origin (Companioni et al., 1997). And it is not subsistence because it has a clear political message, which starts from the counter-narrative of globalized agro-food systems.

By expanding the look beyond these agroecosystems in the city, we find nearby consumers, in this way it takes another signified, that is, it becomes a food system (Cuéllar-Padilla and Calle-Collado, 2011). A space that includes production, input, processing, and marketing activities (Gliessman and Rosemeyer, 2009). Urban agroecology requires technology to function under specific conditions of limited spaces and high land values, use of natural and urban resources and waste, direct contacts between producer and consumer (Ferguson and Morales, 2010; Francis and Porter, 2011).

For this reason, it makes use of low-cost and knowledge-intensive technologies and innovations adapted by producers to advance food productivity, social equity and environmental sustainability and to encourage the maintenance and resilience of the ecosystem (Gliessman, 2007; Konijnendijk & Gauthier 2006).

But it can also be a favorable space for the provision of ecosystem services closely related in space and time due to the geographical proximity of resource flows (Lovell et al. 2010; Mouchet et al. 2014). Urban agroecological systems have sustainable impacts for beneficiaries in the provision of environmental and ecosystem services (Lovell, 2010). Agroecology provides food, fuel, fiber, and a wide range of ecosystem services. Ecosystem services are a natural process that results from interdependencies and interactions between nature, the economy and society that have an effect of human dependency. Ecosystem services are the direct and indirect contributions of nature to human well-being (The Economics of Ecosystems and Biodiversity (TEEB) 2010).

In this sense, we could argue that agroecology by promoting beneficial interactions in agroecosystems (Gliessman, 2007) promotes ecosystem services with the following foundations (Altieri, 2002) specifically and genetically diversifies the agroecosystem in time and space, in this way increases biological interactions and synergies between components of biodiversity by promoting key ecological processes and services; improve soil conditions through the management of organic matter and increasing the biotic activity of the soil; increases biomass recycling and thus optimizes the availability and balanced flow of nutrients; favors microclimates and minimizes losses due to flows of solar radiation, air and water; among other strategies. In this way, agroecological techniques can improve yields and increase productivity while improving the supply of critical natural resources and environmental services (Pretty 2006).

The concept of integrated valuation of ecosystem and ecosystem services can be an operational tool to direct the sustainable transition of agroecosystems (Duru and Thérond, 2015). An integrated assessment of ecosystem services should make explicit the feasibility of the expectations that must be met (Cote and Nightingale 2012, Davies et al. 2015). Valuations of ecosystem services in the agro-ecological and agro-environmental context are theoretically limited (Holt et al. 2016; Tscharntke et al. 2005, Prager et al. 2012, Merckx and Pereira 2015).

The relevance of urban agroecology is recognized in any city in the world because it contributes to feeding residents with sustainable approaches. However, the plots are located within the cities of the interior or in the peri-urban spaces that take place inside or outside the parcel of the residences and private, public or semi-public lands; and it is possible that urban and peri-urban soils and vacant lots located near industrial areas and roads may be contaminated, as well as poorly processed organic waste, may contain environmentally risky substances (Nehls et al, 2015; Säumel et al., 2012; Schwarz et al., 2016).

WHAT DOES URBAN AGRICULTURE PROVIDE AS ECOSYSTEM SERVICES TO CITIES?

Urban agroecology is dedicated to food production and has multifunctional economic, social and environmental benefits and other non-economic and non-quantifiable benefits (Hampwaye, 2013). Urban agroecological food production is becoming more familiar in its location and spatial organization in urban spaces and the distribution of activities, feasibility and durability (Lovell et al. 2010; Wiskerke, 2016). In the same way that they relate more easily to the basic principles of agroecology as an alternative food system. Which are based on the diversified and complementary use and recycling of nutrients and energy from ecosystems with the aim of creating a sustainable environment of resilient biodiversity Altieri, 2002; Altieri et al. 1999; Gliessman, 2007).

Returning to the idea of the importance of ecosystem services, we will take the contributions of FAO (2015), which classifies them as follows:

1. Supply services referring to the material benefits that people obtain from ecosystems, for example, the supply of food, water, fibers, wood and fuels;
2. Regulatory services linked to benefits obtained from the regulation of ecosystem processes, for example, soil fertility, crop pollination, among others;
3. Support services that are necessary for the production of all other ecosystem services, for example, offering spaces in which plants and animals live, allowing species diversity and maintaining genetic diversity; and
4. Cultural services that offer us the immaterial benefits that people obtain from ecosystems, for example, the source of inspiration for aesthetic manifestations, cultural identity and spiritual well-being. In the following lines we will emphasize the contributions of urban agriculture to the various modes of ecosystem services.

Contributions of Urban Agriculture to Supply Services

Sustainable urban agroecological agriculture is healthy food production to ensure nutrients and accessible to all, while natural resources are managed to maintain ecosystem functions and ecological services designed to support current and future human needs. In general, the production of fresh urban agroecology is for self-consumption and when there are surpluses, these are either commercialized in a market-oriented economic agent or processed and packaged for later self-consumption or sale (Konijnendijk & Gauthier 2006; Taghavi and Murat 2011).

Urban agroecology meets only part of the global demand for food and does not support the food self-sufficiency of city dwellers. Urban agroecology is part of a widely globalized food system that is experiencing a dramatic increase in trade in food and agricultural products (Busch and Bain, 2004; Wiskerke, 2016). Urban agroecology requires a third of the total urban area to meet global food demand, and only a small proportion is consumed by low-income people with food insecurity and more vulnerable people who do not have access to land and lack the skills to produce it (Lovell, 2010).

Agroecology as a way of life and language of nature is based on ecological principles (Altieri and Toledo, 2011). Agroecological principles are adopted by social food movements linked to struggles for food sovereignty, which is described as the human right to healthy and culturally appropriate food produced through ecologically sustainable methods, and to define agroecological systems (Bohn, 2005;

Cuéllar-Padilla and Calle-Collado, 2011). Agroecology is a mix between principles of agricultural science and ecology that focuses on the diversification of agricultural systems for the benefit of the functions and services of the agroecosystem to improve the environment and mitigate the negative social externalities of the intensified industrial agricultural model (Duru and Thérond, 2015; Fernandez et al, 2012; Francis, 2011).

Urban Agriculture and Contributions to Regulatory Services

Urban agroecology has concerns about maintaining food security and climate change in urban areas, reducing temperatures and food-related greenhouse gas (GHG) emissions. The agroecological approach is well-suited to withstand economic and environmental stresses and the pressures of climate change by avoiding or reducing synthetic chemical inputs in crops such as fossil fuels, fertilizers, and pesticides that poison consumers, workers, and communities. Consumers of agroecological products gain access to healthy and nutritious local food at a fair cost, while supporting urban agroecological agriculture (Taghavi and Murat 2011; Venkatadri et al. 1997; Becker and Steele 1995; Burbidge 1971).

Urban and suburban agroecological farms are an asset to city residents by providing micronutrients and livelihoods during lean seasons, supporting ecosystem health and wild plant habitat, genetic diversity and pollination, supplying and regulating air and water (Galafassi et al. 2017; Francis, 2011; Gliessman, 2007). Urban agroecological agriculture preserves the biodiversity of the urban ecosystem and the quality of local seeds. Urban agroecology is an inextricable component of the conservation of biodiversity and environmental services in the urbanization processes evident in industrialization that drives complicated socioeconomic, political, environmental and ecological dynamics (Holt et al. 2016; Lovell, 2010).

The development of sustainable urban agroecology can recycle nutrients and waste in accordance with the use of local natural resources and agroecological principles for the production of compost and seeds and the protection of organic plants. Urban agroecology is part of the urban environmental and ecological system that solves problems such as the reuse of urban waste as productive resources and the collection of fresh organic waste that can cause health and environmental problems (Lovell et al, 2010; Marques, 2010).

Sustainable agroecology depends on ecological services such as the topsoil and crop pollination (Zhang et al. 2007). Agro-ecologically managed plots have less erosion, retain vegetation, have lower economic losses, and increase the resilience of agricultural ecosystems by improving adaptive capacity and reducing vulnerability to climate change, natural disasters, and crises and stresses economic and environmental.

Urban agroecology can be used to restore degraded lands and turn them into a productive area of green innovation or public space to promote inclusive and sustainable socio-economic activities. Agroecological crops and food production infrastructure in urban green areas and community spaces can serve different and multiple purposes, needs and interests of all stakeholders involved (Lovell, 2010). Community-led urban agroecology food systems play an important role in rebuilding vacant spaces in cities and retraining employment opportunities (Piraux et al, 2010).

Urban agroecological crops are a response to carbon sequestration on farms by climate change and contribute to anthropogenic emissions of greenhouse gases, the supply and conservation of biodiversity and habitat, biogeochemical maintenance, the water cycle and complex trophic interactions, improved community livelihoods, sovereignty and food security (Tscharntke, 2005). Urban agroecology focused on food sovereignty is a concept connected to political methodologies based on a radical framework that can be used in any context between the practical and the political in urban agriculture.

Urban Agriculture and its Contributions to Support Services

Urban agroecology includes food and non-food products from different types of crops, herbs, plants and animals or a combination of these, often high valued but perishable. Urban agroecology revitalizes starchy roots traditional crops expanding production, playing a relevant role in the food system reducing dependencies on foreign food sources, making it widely available through distribution, logistics and consumer networks and improving the socio economic conditions of large urban areas. To reduce agroecological food systems carbon footprint, the producer-consumer links of quality standards and integration of ecological issues, must be strengthening though direct sales, community supported agroecology and value chain (Lev and Stevenson2011; Stevenson et al.2011).

Agroecology has multifunctional functions and dimensions to provide a nutritious, healthy and fresh diet that facilitates equitable and environmental sustainability, increasing ecological resilience (Hampwaye, 2013; Wiskerke, 2016). Agroecology in urban areas improves nutrition, food security, sovereignty and offers economic, social, health and environmental benefits (Gomiero, Pimentel and Paoletti, 2011). Therapeutic activities related to urban agroecology and gardening in communities accessible by urban green innovation areas foster cooperative and inclusive human interactions, knowledge sharing, strengthen mental health, reduce poverty, etc.

The advantages in urban agroecology are related to produce that can be sold fresh due to the fact that cultivations are near consumers. Urban agroecology changes how far healthy and nutritious food travels to a better informed consumer, increasing the access to local grown food and taking the right place for the food system and reintroducing the culture of how food grows seasonally in the region.

Low-resource agroecology systems are based on the use of local resources and the modest use of external inputs that produce most of the grains, roots, tubers and crops. Organic and agroecological farming systems that tend to depend more on local than external inputs and foreign certification seals tend to be less dependent on foreign and volatile markets. However, keeping small organic and agroecological farmers' dependent on input substitution does not motivate them to redesign agricultural ecosystems and tends to perpetuate dependency. In planning and maintaining complex agroecosystems, permaculture offers risks and challenges.

Urban Agriculture and its Contribution To Cultural Services

Agroecology starts from local knowledge, from the dialogue of knowledge (Rosset and Martinez-Torres, 2012), therefore a range of different ways of practicing agriculture appears and in cities it has its manifestations based on the foundations of permaculture, agroforestry and urban forestry.

The multiple functionality of earth movements for water and harvest control are used and traditional agricultural systems and can be used in urban agroecological systems to improve productivity in urban land contexts (Evenari et al. 1982; Bruins et al. 1986; Boyd and Gross 2000; Mussery et al. 2013, Holt-Gimenez 2006, Prein 2002; Smukler et al. 2010). Traditional agriculture and agroecological systems use earthmoving for water and harvest control despite the frequency (Lancaster and Marshall 2008; Frey 2011) and the risks posed by vulnerable and dispersive soils (Sherard et al. 1976).

Permaculture is being positive and nonspecific associated (Leakey 2012; Deb et al. 2008; Lovell et al. 2010) with agrobiodiversity, agroecosystem design, agroforestry and other polycultures (Francis and Porter 2011; Torre Ugarte and Hellwinckel 2010). Permaculture is defined as an integrated and evolving system of perennial and self-perpetuating plant and animal species useful to man, forming an agricultural ecosystem, (Mollison and Holmgren 1978, p. 1). Permaculture is identified more as an alternative agriculture more than explicitly questioned agroecological framework (Gomiero et al. 2011; Pretty 2006; Bavec et al. 2009; Pretty 2005). The agroecological content of the permaculture is the diverse and multifunctional site design at multiple scales to increase the productivity based on heritage agroecosystems, water management and global germplasm to achieve sustainability.

Permaculture grows overlapping with agroecology focusing on ecology and agricultural production in association with environmental movements towards the agroecological transition. Permaculture is an agroecological movement with a potential contribution to the agroecological transition by mobilizing social support for sustainability. The permaculture movement has limited contributions by cultural factors that affect the impact on the agro-ecological transition despite mobilizing social support in various geographic locations. Furthermore, permaculture movements have been accused of inflating land and work in perennial and polyculture systems (Shepard, 2013; Mollison, 1988, 1979).

The other source of inspiration is urban agroforestry - an innovative gap between urban planning and agroecology in contexts of urban sustainability, which increases resilience, biodiversity and carbon sequestration capacity. Agroecological practices in agroforestry improve the provision of ecosystem services. Agroforestry combines recognized agricultural and woody farming as an agroecological practice to address sustainability and community resilience (Nair 1993; Kumar 2006; Nair 2007). Urban agroforestry ecology is an urban resilience strategy to protect urban food and energy supply (Altieri et al. 1999; Lovell 2010; Dubbeling et al. 2009; De Zeeuw et al. 2011) that provides a set of economic services, social and ecological (Konijnendijk and Gauthier 2006).

Similarly, urban agro-food forestry as an interdisciplinary and multifunctional strategy to improve the development of urban sustainability, ecosystem services, ecological resilience, food security, climate change, poverty, public health, etc., by increasing eating more nutrient dense foods. The shade tree in agroecological forestry protects crop plants against fluctuations in soil and temperature in a microclimate that controls evaporation, exposure to sunlight, wind speed and rain.

Finally, it is determined by the configuration of the agroecosystem, thus promoting multiple functions, such as environmental productivity, land, and the labor force of diversified agricultural systems. Agroecosystems benefit from soil rich in organic matter, which improves fertility and increases agroecological production, providing food to society and income for producers (Adhikari and Hartemink 2015). Agroecology provides nutrition and food security benefits for people and to keep the environment and ecosystems healthy. Urban agroecology improves food security by taking into account the supply and distribution of food costs for rural production.

IMPORTANCE OF AGROECOLOGICAL TRANSITION

The dominant model of agriculture is based on corporate control of growing chemical-intensive agro-industrial complexes of growing monocultures for export, diminishing the quality of healthy food, exacerbating global climate change, disrupting traditional rural livelihoods and eroding arable land. The transition to more sustainable agroecological systems aims to achieve resilience that conventional farming systems have not achieved because vertical interdependence easily links breakdown and failure (Servigne and Stevens 2015).

The trend towards agroecological agriculture and the transition of agroecological practices is global. A transition to more environmentally friendly farming systems should be able to substitute agricultural chemicals for more organic inputs Gliessman and Rosemeyer (2009). Describe the transition from conventional agriculture to agroecological practices on a continuum defining four steps. Agroecology that relies on locally produced inputs increases the incomes of small farmers. Ecological small farming systems are more productive and resistant to natural disasters. The local self-sufficiency agenda is the transition initiative that underestimates the benefits of international cooperation in agroecological food.

Agroecological transition is a multi-sectorial project, complex of operating through the involvement of multiple temporal and spatial scales and diverse constituencies (Geels and Kemp 2007; Marques 2010; Piraux et al. 2010). Agroecological literature addresses the transition to diversified and multifunctional production systems (De Schutter 2010, Kremen et al. 2012; Wilson 2008). The agroecological transition is a complex process that requires the evaluation of resources and opportunities supported by disciplines and movements outside the boundaries.

The transition from industrial agriculture to agroecological production requires experiential and scientific knowledge from the collaboration between research institutions, traditional producers, consumers, agroecological movements, and other stakeholders. Stakeholders relate their socio economic values to an agroecological transition by increasing their equity and reducing their power asymmetries in their assessment and decision processes (Felipe-Lucia et al. 2015). Among the various stakeholders of urban agroecology should be stimulated the dialogue and cooperation relationships through the implementation of a multi-actor working team to organize joint analysis in urban development and to coordinate policymaking and sustainable urban planning.

The evaluation of the agro-ecological transition has to measure its impacts and the viability in the different elements of the agro-ecological and conventional agricultural systems in the socio-ecosystem services (Mouchet et al. 2014; Crouzat et al. 2015). The agro-environment scheme is an example of payment for ecosystem services in environmental governance, although limited by the influence and polarization processes of powerful pressure groups and generalized strategic behaviors. Agroecological systems require implementing large-scale institutional changes to integrate evaluations of ecosystem services to support local communities in directing transitions for the sustainability of agroecological systems.

Agricultural research opens up the potential to address the agroecological transition and diversified production systems of staple and complementary crops (Shepard 2013). Ongoing suburbanization, peri-urban transition areas, and urban expansion processes challenge the dichotomy of urban-rural development and related phenomena of land uses of agroecology mixed together in a fragmented mosaic.

Agroecology is a participatory action research to practice science with actors involved in agroecological transitions (Cuéllar Padilla and Calle-Collado 2011; Levidow et al. 2014, Méndez et al. 2013). Actors involved in urban agroecology, such as urban planners, local governments, researchers, producers, etc., face some challenges in urban economic, sociodemographic, and environmental changes resulting from the post-productive rural transition to food production urban agroecological (Wilson, 2009; Almstead et al., 2014; Roche and Argent, 2015). Food consumption patterns, linked to the nutritional transition, are decreasing the availability of water, which is used for irrigation in agriculture (Collette et al. 2011).

Individual residents and land users can contribute to the agro-ecological transition by using simple, practical techniques and depoliticize the agro-ecological transition (de Molina 2012; Lovell et al. 2010; Rosset and Martínez-Torres 2012), simplifying the complexity sociological of challenges and processes.

The negotiation of the agro-ecological transition between the different interests of the stakeholders is a normative political process that involves the emotional dimension (Wezel et al. 2009). To deliver the principles of agroecology in a process of transition to a new paradigm, political actions are required.

STRATEGIES FOR THE TRANSITION TO URBAN AGRICULTURE SYSTEMS

Moving to the incorporation of food systems in cities, involves recognizing the existence of those that already exist. Popular agroecological movements and networks advance the transition from traditional agriculture to agroecology through social and political support (Nelson et al. 2009; Ferguson and Morales 2010; Rosset et al. 2011; Altieri and Toledo 2011).

Urban agroecological production requires the formulation and implementation of strategies aimed at minimizing risks and improving opportunities for biodiversity and ecosystem services to improve climate change, leisure, education, tourism, culture, etc. Agroecological production and processing must be adjusted to mitigate climate change. and other ecosystem stresses.

To improve this situation, it is recommended to provide more extension, education, training and support to agro-economic services. Urban economies benefit from urban agroecology if local governments develop institutions with a policy framework to provide agroecological services, promote sustainable urban development and urban food security with the aim of enabling urban agroecological participants to unlock financial and technical services support. This characterizes the Cuban agroecological movement (Companioni et al. 1997).

The analysis of the theory and practice of agroecology can contribute to the discussion to follow for the institutionalization of agroecological development based on an agricultural system with investments and services supported by network interactions between the state, society and inclusive participatory organizations. A multilevel methodology to analyze the impact of agroecological practices on the flows and processes of environmental services to assess the viability of the agroecological transition.

Common ground achieved through consultation between the various views of stakeholders becomes a basis for a normative vision of the expected agroecosystem. The systemic vision of the agro-ecological system facilitates the trajectories of change in the transition space of ecosystem services. An agroecosystem model is a representation of a complex system of stakeholder perceptions that integrate ecosystem services and their valuable biophysical, economic, and socio-cultural domains (Martín-López et al. 2014) to develop a systematic approach to the framework of agroecological analysis.

Regional spatial urban agroecology follows a combination of economic scale and diversity patterns of urban developments with implications for urban spatial planning and governance. Integrating peri-urban agroecology spatial planning can implement the use of participatory forms of land use and cultural heritage to improve ecosystem services and sustainable urban development (Simon Rojo et al., 2014; Swensen and Jerpåsen, 2008). Urban and peri-urban agroecology becomes part of urban planning and management systems that adopt production methods linked to ecosystem services, sustainable natural resources, ecological waste and sanitation, recreational and leisure services, nature reserves, etc.

The principles of agroecosystem configuration implicit in land use functions seem reasonably supported, but some of them, such as the analysis of spatial relationships, are notoriously absent (Cavazza 1996; Veldkamp et al. 2001; Hatfield 2007; Osty 2008; cited in Benoit et al. 2012).

An agroecological model based on small-scale production that uses ecological methods may not compete with an industrial agriculture model, but it provides improvements for the environment and the living conditions of the producers employed. Urban agroecology often tends to involve urban residents who have access to urban land, natural resources, and water and have available time combined with other household-related activities and tasks and difficult to combine with full-time jobs that require travel. The expansion of agroecology expands the knowledge of the principles, methods and systems used by producers to design and implement policies and strategies aimed at transforming the socioeconomic context and the food system.

Social change and innovation in urban and peri-urban agroecology do not come from the government, but from families of small urban farmers willing to transform living conditions towards a healthier lifestyle. Urban agroecology tends to expand involving innovation and adaptation as the capacities of food systems expand creating more nutritional and healthy resources and more employment opportunities. Technological innovation in agroecology requires the contribution of social and production techniques, organization and dissemination.

The coherent management of urban agroecological policies establishes the standards of a sustainable environment for cultivation techniques and the treatment of natural resources. Agroecological management in urban and peri urban areas must be supported by production, environmental protection, quality and marketing policies integrated into local governance and cultural heritage.

Policy approaches on urban agroecology are related to economic, social and ecological scenarios. Agroecological management of urban and peri-urban areas is a complex process of development and governance strategies and policies to support investments and safeguard ecosystem self-sufficiency. Projects with agroecological funds tend to focus on the links between agroecological biodiversity, functioning, improvement of intercultural and agroecological systems, management of agroecosystems, and agroecological science and management.

Implementing sectoral policies in urban agroecology requires urban institutions to operate in the urban sphere, such as an urban agricultural department or office and an interdepartmental committee to care for urban food production, supply and consumption. Peri-urban agro tourism is being developed and promoted by farmers who offer ecological tourism services in the form of larger agro-recreational parks and family agro tourism that includes accommodation, food, fresh produce, horseback riding, etc.

The agroecological system should include policies to combine knowledge, ensure access to land and self-organize in solidarity towards food sovereignty and justice. Urban agroecological farms rely more on grants, donations, volunteer and social services, and other non-farm income to support their activities. The Social and Solidarity Economy (SSE) refers to cooperatives, companies, organizations, mutual benefit societies, associations, foundations and social companies that produce environmental goods, services and knowledge while pursuing economic, social and environmental objectives and promoting solidarity.

The management of socio-ecological ecosystems has some compensations inherent in the provision of ecosystem services (Armitage et al. 2008, Galafassi et al. 2017) under different agroecological scenarios, although what is lacking is the implementation of transition actions. Urban agroecological systems require a more interdisciplinary and integrated analysis of sustainable urban planning, urban land rights, urban food planning, ecological systems and services, etc. (Bohn and Viljoen 2005). Agroecosystem planning develops design approaches to harness the contributions of incorporating permaculture principles into participatory farmer-oriented research and development to support design solutions and site analysis by stimulating creative problem solving.

CONCLUSION

There is an urgent need for agroecology of change in sustainable global food systems. The new global sustainable food system aims to protect agricultural ecosystems that provide food and ecosystem services based on equity, participation, democracy and justice. Urban farmers can actually take some steps to convert from conventional or industrial agroecosystems to an agroecological farm, such as reducing the use and consumption of inputs that are harmful to the environment, replacing alternative practices, and redesigning based on new agroecological processes.

The economic policy promoting urban agroecological production should create regulatory and financial mechanisms and provide incentives to farmers and urban communities to favor market conditions for food production and ecosystem services. Agroecological production requires the action of local governments and supporting policies, communities, markets and citizens to spread the practices and benefits of crop and livestock production systems and are managed as ecosystem services.

Advanced research for urban agroecology has emerged and highlighted spatial trends and the organization of agro-food systems in urban and peri-urban areas of developing countries. Research in urban agroecology must include democratic and participatory dialogues between scientists, urban planners, farmers, communities, agribusinesses, and other relevant stakeholders. The research potential of urban agroecology goes beyond its food production dimension and the growing concerns about social and environmental changes.

The cultivation of productive urban agroecology in urban green spaces, open spaces and domestic production systems is an intervention strategy that will be carried out to achieve economic, social and environmental benefits, to alleviate poverty and urban hunger and improve urban environmental services.

An ecosystem service valuation framework can help direct agroecological transitions. Assessing the impact of urban agroecology activities on ecosystem services and food justice may vary on its own merits due to the diversity of objectives, scope, scale, type of access, and participants.

Urban agroecology is spreading across empty and marginal urban lands in some cities around the world, embraced by local governments and civil society as a source of healthy food, ecosystem services and job creation.

REFERENCES

Adhikari, K., & Hartemink, A. E. (2015). Linking soils to ecosystem services— A global review. *Geoderma, 262*, 101–111. doi:10.1016/j.geoderma.2015.08.009

Almstead, A., Brouder, P., Karlsson, S., & Lundmark, L. (2014). Beyond post-productivism: From rural policy discourse to rural diversity. *European Countryside, 4*(4), 297–306. doi:10.2478/euco-2014-0016

Altieri, M. A. (2002). Agroecología: principios y estrategias para diseñar sistemas agrarios sustentables. Sarandon, SJ Agroecología: el camino hacia una agricultura sustentable. Buenos Aires–La Plata.

Altieri, M. A., Companioni, N., Cañizares, K., Murphy, C., Rosset, P., Bourque, M., & Nicholls, C. I. (1999). The greening of the "barrios": Urban agriculture for food security in Cuba. *Agriculture and Human Values*, *16*(2), 131–140. doi:10.1023/A:1007545304561

Altieri, M. A., & Toledo, V. M. (2011). The agroecological revolution in Latin America: Rescuing nature, ensuring food sovereignty and empowering peasants. *The Journal of Peasant Studies*, *38*(3), 587–612. doi:10.1080/03066150.2011.582947

Armitage, D., Marschke, M., & Plummer, R. (2008). Adaptive comanagement and the paradox of learning. *Global Environmental Change*, *18*(1), 86–98. doi:10.1016/j.gloenvcha.2007.07.002

Bavec, M., Mlakar, S. G., Rozman, C., Pazek, K., & Bavec, F. (2009). Sustainable agriculture based on integrated and organic guidelines: Understanding terms—the case of Slovenian development and strategy. *Outlook on Agriculture*, *38*(1), 89–95. doi:10.5367/000000009787762824

Becker, F. D., & Steele, F. (1995). *Workplace by design: mapping the high-performance workscape*. Jossey-Bass.

Benoit, M., Rizzo, D., Marraccini, E., Moonen, A. C., Galli, M., Lardon, S., Rapey, H., Thenail, C., & Bonari, E. (2012). Landscape agronomy: A new field for addressing agricultural landscape dynamics. *Landscape Ecology*, *27*(10), 1385–1394. doi:10.100710980-012-9802-8

Bohn, K., & Viljoen, A. (2005). More city with less space: Vision for lifestyle. In A. Viljoen (Ed.), *Continuous Productive Urban Landscapes: Designing Urban Agriculture for Sustainable Cities* (pp. 251–264). Architectural Press.

Boyd, C. E., & Gross, A. (2000). Water use and conservation for inland aquaculture ponds. *Fisheries Management and Ecology*, *7*(1-2), 55–63. doi:10.1046/j.1365-2400.2000.00181.x

Bruins, H. J., Evenari, M., & Nessler, U. (1986). Rainwater-harvesting agriculture for food production in arid zones: The challenge of the African famine. *Applied Geography (Sevenoaks, England)*, *6*(1), 13–32. doi:10.1016/0143-6228(86)90026-3

Burbidge, J. L. (1971). Production flow analysis. *Production Engineering*, *50*(4-5), 139–152. doi:10.1049/tpe.1971.0022

Cavazza, L. (1996). Agronomia aziendale e agronomia del territorio. *Riv Agron*, *30*, 310–319.

Collette. (2011). Thunnus obesus The IUCN Red List of Threatened Species. doi:10.2305/IUCN.UK.2011-2

Companioni, N., Rodríguez Nodals, A., Carrión, M., Alonso, R. M., Ojeda, Y., & Peña, E. (1997). La Agricultura Urbana en Cuba. Su participación en la seguridad alimentaria. Conferencias. III Encuentro Nacional de Agricultura Orgánica. Villa Clara, Cuba: Central University of Las Villas.

Cote, M., & Nightingale, A. J. (2012). Resilience thinking meets social theory: Situating social change in socio-ecological systems (SES) research. *Progress in Human Geography*, *36*(4), 475–489. doi:10.1177/0309132511425708

Crawford, M. (2010). *Creating a forest garden: working with nature to grow edible crops*. Green Books.

Crouzat, E., Mouchet, M., Turkelboom, F., Byczek, C., Meersmans, J., Berger, F., & Lavorel, S. (2015). Assessing bundles of ecosystem services from regional to landscape scale: Insights from the French Alps. *Journal of Applied Ecology*, *52*(5), 1145–1155. doi:10.1111/1365-2664.12502

Cuéllar-Padilla, M., & Calle-Collado, Á. (2011). Can we find solutions with people? Participatory action research with small organic producers in Andalusia. *Journal of Rural Studies*, *27*(4), 372–383. doi:10.1016/j.jrurstud.2011.08.004

Davies, K. K., Fisher, K. T., Dickson, M. E., Thrush, S. F., & Le Heron, R. (2015). Improving ecosystem service frameworks to address wicked problems. *Ecology and Society*, *20*(2), art37. Advance online publication. doi:10.5751/ES-07581-200237

De Molina, M. G. (2012). *Agro ecology and politics. How to get sustainability?* About the necessity for a political agroecologist. *Agroecology and Sustainable Food Systems*, *37*, 45–59. doi:10.1080/10440046.2012.705810

De Schutter, O. (2010). *Report submitted by the special rapporteur on the right to food*. United Nations Human Rights Council.

De Zeeuw, H., Van Veenhuizen, R., & Dubbeling, M. (2011). The role of urban agriculture in building resilient cities in developing countries. *J Agric Sci*, *149*(S1), 153–163. doi:10.1017/S0021859610001279

Deb, S., Barbhuiya, A. R., Arunachalam, A., & Arunachalam, K. (2008). Ecological analysis of traditional agroforest and tropical forest in the foothills of Indian eastern Himalaya: Vegetation, soil and microbial biomass. *Tropical Ecology*, *49*, 73–78.

Dubbeling, M., Campbell, M. C., Hoekstra, F., & van Veenhuizen, R. (2009). Building resilient cities. *Urban Agriculture Magazine*, *22*, 3–11.

Duru, M., Thérond, O., & Fares, M. (2015). Designing agroecological transitions: A review. *Agronomy for Sustainable Development*, *35*(4), 1237–1257. doi:10.100713593-015-0318-x

Evenari, M., Shanan, L., & Tadmor, N. (1982). *The Negev: the challenge of a desert*. Harvard University Press.

FAO. (2015). *Construyendo una visión común para la agricultura y alimentación sostenibles*. Organización de las Naciones Unidas para la Alimentación y la Agricultura.

Felipe-Lucia, M. R., Martín-López, B., Lavorel, S., Berraquero Díaz, L., Escalera-Reyes, J., & Comín, F. A. (2015). Ecosystem services flows: Why stakeholders' power relationships matter. *PLoS One*, *10*(7), e0132232. doi:10.1371/journal.pone.0132232 PMID:26201000

Ferguson, B. G., & Morales, H. (2010). Latin American agroecologists build a powerful scientific and social movement. *Journal of Sustainable Agriculture*, *34*(4), 339–341. doi:10.1080/10440041003680049

Fernandez, M., Goodall, K., Olson, M., & Mendez, E. (2012). Agroecology and alternative agrifood movements in the United States: Towards a sustainable agrifood system. *Agroecology and Sustainable Food Systems*, *37*, 115–126. doi:10.1080/10440046.2012.735633

Francis, C. A., & Porter, P. (2011). Ecology in sustainable agriculture practices and systems. *Critical Reviews in Plant Sciences*, *30*(1-2), 64–73. doi:10.1080/07352689.2011.554353

Frey, D. (2011). *Bioshelter market garden: a permaculture farm*. New Society, Gabriola Island.

Funes, F., & Vázquez, L. (Eds.). (2016). *Avances de la agroecología en Cuba*. Editora Estación Experimental de Pastos y Forrajes Indio Hatuey.

Galafassi, D., Daw, T., Munyi, L., Brown, K., Barnaud, C., & Fazey, I. (2017). Learning about social-ecological trade-offs. *Ecology and Society*, *22*(1), 2. doi:10.5751/ES-08920-220102

Geels, F. W., & Kemp, R. (2007). Dynamics in socio-technical systems: Typology of change processes and contrasting case studies. *Technology in Society*, *29*(4), 441–455. doi:10.1016/j.techsoc.2007.08.009

Gliessman, S. R. (2007). *Agroecology: The ecology of sustainable food systems* (2nd ed.). CRC Press.

Gliessman, S. R., & Rosemeyer, M. (Eds.). (2009). *The conversion to sustainable agriculture: principles, processes, and practices*. CRC Press. doi:10.1201/9781420003598

Gomiero, T., Pimentel, D., & Paoletti, M. G. (2011). Is there a need for a more sustainable agriculture? *Critical Reviews in Plant Sciences*, *30*(1-2), 6–23. doi:10.1080/07352689.2011.553515

Hampwaye, G. (2013). Benefits of urban agriculture: Reality of illusion? *Geoforum*, *49*, R7–R8. doi:10.1016/j.geoforum.2013.03.008

Hatfield, J. (2007). Beyond the edge of the field. *Arch. Soil Sci. Soc. Am.* https://www.soils.org/about-society/presidents-message/archive/13

Herrmann, R., Jumbe, C., Bruentrup, M., & Osabuohien, E. (2018). Competition between Biofuel Feedstock and Food Production: Empirical Evidence from Sugarcane Outgrower Settings in Malawi. *Biomass and Bioenergy*, *114*(July), 100–111. doi:10.1016/j.biombioe.2017.09.002

Holt, A. R., Alix, A., Thompson, A., & Maltby, L. (2016). Food production, ecosystem services and biodiversity: We can't have it all everywhere. *The Science of the Total Environment*, *573*, 1422–1429. doi:10.1016/j.scitotenv.2016.07.139 PMID:27539820

Holt-Gimenez, E. (2006). *Campesino a campesino: voices from Latin America's farmer to farmer movement for sustainable agriculture*. Food First.

Konijnendijk, C., & Gauthier, M. (2006). Urban forestry for multifunctional land use. In *Cities farming for the future: urban agriculture for green and productive cities*. International Development Research Centre, Ottawa. https://www.idrc.ca/en/ev-103884-201-1-DO_TOPIC.html

Kremen, C., & Miles, A. (2012). Ecosystem services in biologically diversified versus conventional farming systems: Benefits, externalities, and trade-offs. *Ecology and Society*, *17*(4), 40. doi:10.5751/ES-05035-170440

Kumar, B. M. (2006). Agroforestry: The new old paradigm for Asian food security. *Journal of Tropical Agriculture*, *44*, 1–14.

Lancaster, B., & Marshall, J. (2008). *Water-harvesting earthworks*. Rainsource.

Leakey, R. R. B. (2012). *Multifunctional agriculture and opportunities for agroforestry: implications of IAASTD. Agroforestry: the future of global land use*. Springer.

Lev, L., & Stevenson, G. W. (2011). Acting collectively to develop midscale food value chains. *Journal of Agriculture, Food Systems, and Community Development, 1*(4), 119–128. doi:10.5304/jafscd.2011.014.014

Levidow, L., Pimbert, M., & Vanloqueren, G. (2014). Agroecological research: conforming—or transforming the dominant agro-food regime? *Agroecology and Sustainable Food Systems, 38*(10), 1127–1155. doi:10.1080/21683565.2014.951459

Lovell, S. (2010). Multifunctional urban agro ecology for sustainable land use planning in the United States. *Sustainability*, *2*(8), 2499–2522. doi:10.3390u2082499

Lovell, S. T., De Santis, S., Nathan, C. A., Olson, M. B., Méndez, V. E., Hisashi, C., Kominami, H. C., Erickson, D. L., & .... (2010). Integrating agroecology and landscape multi-functionality in Vermont: An evolving framework to evaluate the design of agroeco-systems. *Agricultural Systems*, *103*(5), 327–341. doi:10.1016/j.agsy.2010.03.003

Marques, F. (2010) Constructing sociotechnical transitions toward sustainable agriculture. *Proc. Symp. Innov. Sustain. Dev. Agric.*

Martín-López, B., Gómez-Baggethun, E., García-Llorente, M., & Montes, C. (2014). Trade-offs across value-domains in ecosystem services assessment. *Ecological Indicators*, *37*, 220–228. doi:10.1016/j.ecolind.2013.03.003

Méndez, V. E., Bacon, C. M., & Cohen, R. (2013). Agroecology as a transdisciplinary, participa-tory, and action-oriented approach. *Agroecology and Sustainable Food Systems*, *37*(1), 3–18.

Merckx, T., & Pereira, H. M. (2015). Reshaping agrienvironmental subsidies: From marginal farming to large-scale rewilding. *Basic and Applied Ecology*, *16*(2), 95–103. doi:10.1016/j.baae.2014.12.003

Mollison, B. (1988). *Permaculture: a designer's manual*. Tagari.

Mollison, B., & Holmgren, D. (1978). *Permaculture one: a perennial agricultural system for human settlements*. Tagari, Tyalgum.

Mouchet, M. A., Lamarque, P., Martín-López, B., Crouzat, E., Gos, P., Byczek, C., & Lavorel, S. (2014). An interdisciplinary methodological guide for quantifying associations between ecosystem services. *Global Environmental Change*, *28*, 298–308. doi:10.1016/j.gloenvcha.2014.07.012

Mussery, A., Leu, S., Lensky, I., & Budovsky, A. (2013). The effect of planting techniques on arid ecosystems in the northern Negev. *Arid Land Research and Management*, *27*(1), 90–100. doi:10.1080/15324982.2012.719574

Nair, P. K. R. (1993). *An introduction to agroforestry*. Kluwer Academic Publishers. doi:10.1007/978-94-011-1608-4

Nair, P. K. R. (2007). The coming age of agroforestry. *Journal of the Science of Food and Agriculture*, *87*(9), 1613–1619. doi:10.1002/jsfa.2897

Nehls, T., Jiang, Y., Dennehy, C., Zhan, X., & Beesley, L. (2015). From waste to value: urban agriculture enables cycling of resources in cities. In Urban Agriculture Europe, (pp. 170–173). Berlin: Jovis.

Nelson, E., Scott, S., Cukier, J., & Galán, Á. L. (2009). Institutionalizing agroecology: Successes and challenges in Cuba. *Agriculture and Human Values*, *26*(3), 233–243. doi:10.100710460-008-9156-7

Osty, P.-L., Le Ber, F., & Lieber, J. (2008). Raisonnement à partir de cas et agronomie des territoires. *Rev Anthr Connaissances*, *2*(2), 169–193. doi:10.3917/rac.004.0169

Piraux, M., Silveira, L., Diniz, P., Duque, G., Coudel, E., Devautour, H., Soulard, C., & Hubert, B. (2010). Agroecological transition as a socio-territorial innovation: the case of the territory of Borborema in Brazilian semi-arid. *Proc. Symp. Innov. Sustain. Dev. Agric. Food Montp.*

Prager, Reed, & Scott. (2012). Encouraging collaboration for the provision of ecosystem services at a landscape scale—rethinking agri-environmental payments. *Land Use Policy, 29*(1), 244–249. .landusepol.2011.06.012 doi:10.1016/j

Prein, P. (2002). Integration of aquaculture into crop–animal systems in Asia. *Agricultural Systems*, *71*(1-2), 127–146. doi:10.1016/S0308-521X(01)00040-3

Pretty, J. (2005). Sustainability in agriculture: Recent progress and emergent challenges. Issues. *Environmental Science & Technology*, *21*, 1–15.

Pretty, J. (2006). *Agroecological approaches to agricultural development*. World Bank.

Roche, M., & Argent, N. (2012). The fall and rise of agricultural productivism? An Antipodean viewpoint. *Progress in Human Geography*, *39*(5), 621–635. doi:10.1177/0309132515582058

Rojo, S. M., Moratalla, A. Z., Alonso, N. M., & Jimenez, V. H. (2014). Pathways towards the integration of peri-urban agrarian ecosystems into the spatial planning system. *Ecological Processes*, *3*(13), 16.

Rosset, P. M., & Martínez-Torres, M. E. (2012). Rural social movements and agroecology: Context, theory, and process. *Ecology and Society*, *17*(3), 17. doi:10.5751/ES-05000-170317

Rosset, P. M., Sosa, B. M., Jaime, A. M. R., & Lozano, D. R. Á. (2011). The campesino-to-campesino agroecology movement of ANAP in Cuba: Social process methodology in the construction of sustainable peasant agriculture and food sovereignty. *The Journal of Peasant Studies*, *38*(1), 161–191. doi:10.1080/03066150.2010.538584 PMID:21284238

Säumel, I., Kotsyuk, I., Hölscher, M., Lenkereit, C., Weber, F., & Kowarik, I. (2012). How healthy is urban horticulture in high traffic areas? Trace metal concentrations in vegetable crops from plantings within inner city neighbourhoods in Berlin, Germany. *Environmental Pollution*, *165*, 124–132. doi:10.1016/j.envpol.2012.02.019 PMID:22445920

Schwarz, K., Cutts, B. B., London, J. K., & Cadenasso, M. L. (2016). Growing gardens in shrinking cities: A Solution to the Soil Lead Problem? *Sustainability*, *8*(2), 1–11. doi:10.3390u8020141

Servigne, P., & Stevens, R. (2015). *Comment tout peut s'effondrer. Petit manuel de collapsologie à l'usage des générations présentes*. Seuil.

Shepard, M. (2013). *Restoration agriculture: real world permaculture for farmers*. Acres U.S.A.

Sherard, J. L., Decker, R. S., & Dunnigan, L. P. (1976). Identification and nature of dispersive soils. *Journal of the Geotechnical Engineering Division, 102*, 287–301.

Smukler, S., Sánchez-Moreno, S., Fonte, S., Ferris, H., Klonsky, K., O'Geen, A., Scow, K., Steenwerth, K., & Jackson, L. (2010). Biodiversity and multiple ecosystem functions in an organic farmscape. *Agriculture, Ecosystems & Environment, 139*(1-2), 80–97. doi:10.1016/j.agee.2010.07.004

Stevenson, G. W., Clancy, K., King, R., Lev, L., Ostrom, M., & Smith, S. (2011). Midscale food value chains: An introduction. *Journal of Agriculture, Food Systems, and Community Development, 1*(4), 1–8. doi:10.5304/jafscd.2011.014.007

Swensen, G., & Jerpåsen, G. P. (2008). Cultural heritage in suburban landscape planning. A case study in Southern Norway. *Landscape and Urban Planning, 87*(4), 289–300. doi:10.1016/j.landurbplan.2008.07.001

Taghavi, A., & Murat, A. (2011). A heuristic procedure for the integrated facility layout design and flow assignment problem. *Computers & Industrial Engineering, 61*(1), 55–63. doi:10.1016/j.cie.2011.02.011

The Economics of Ecosystems and Biodiversity (TEEB). (2010). *Mainstreaming the economics of nature: a synthesis of the approach, conclusions and recommendations of TEEB*. TEEB.

Torre Ugarte, D. G., & Hellwinckel, C. C. (2010). The problem is the solution: the role of biofuels in the transition to a regenerative agriculture. In P. Mascia, J. Scheffran, & J. Widholm (Eds.), *Plant biotechnology for sustainable production of energy and co-products* (pp. 365–384). Springer. doi:10.1007/978-3-642-13440-1_14

Tscharntke, T., Klein, A. M., Kruess, A., Steffan-Dewenter, I., & Thies, C. (2005). Landscape perspectives on agricultural intensification and biodiversity-ecosystem service management. *Ecology Letters, 8*(8), 857–874. doi:10.1111/j.1461-0248.2005.00782.x

Veldkamp, A., Kok, K., De Koning, G. H. J., Schoorl, J. M., Sonneveld, M. P. W., & Verburg, P. H. (2001). Multi-scale system approaches in agronomic research at the landscape level. *Soil & Tillage Research, 58*(3-4), 129–140. doi:10.1016/S0167-1987(00)00163-X

Venkatadri, U., Rardin, R. L., & Montreuil, B. (1997). A design methodology for fractal layout organization. *IIE Transactions, 29*(10), 911–924. doi:10.1080/07408179708966411

Wezel, A., & Soldat, V. (2009). A quantitative and qualitative historical analysis of the scientific discipline agroecology. *International Journal of Agricultural Sustainability, 7*(1), 3–18. doi:10.3763/ijas.2009.0400

Wilson, G. A. (2008). From "weak" to "strong" multifunctionality: Conceptualising farm-level multifunctional transitional pathways. *Journal of Rural Studies, 24*(3), 367–383. doi:10.1016/j.jrurstud.2007.12.010

Wilson, G. A. (2009). Post-Productivist and multifunctional agriculture. International Encyclopedia of Human Geography, 379–386. doi:10.1016/B978-008044910-4.00895-6

Wiskerke, J. S. C. (2016). Urban food systems. In Cities and Agriculture. Developing resilient urban food systems (pp. 1–26). New York: Routledge.

Zhang, W., Ricketts, T. H., Kremen, C., Carney, K., & Swinton, S. M. (2007). Ecosystem services and dis-services to agriculture. *Ecological Economics, 64*(2), 253–260. doi:10.1016/j.ecolecon.2007.02.024

KEY TERMS AND DEFINITIONS

Agroecology: Is the discipline that is responsible for administering the ecological principles of the production of food, fuels, fibers, and pharmaceuticals. This encompasses a wide range of approaches and they consider it a science and a way of seeing life, whether organic, conventional, intensive, or extensive.

Ecosystem Services: They are resources or processes of natural ecosystems (goods and services) that benefit human beings. It includes products such as clean drinking water and processes such as waste decomposition.

Environmental Development: An economic and social development that respects the environment. The objective of sustainable development is to define viable projects and reconcile the economic, social, and environmental aspects of human activities; It is about making progress in these areas without having to destroy the environment.

Food System: Refers to food produced, processed, distributed, and consumed locally.

Transition: Step or change from one state, way of being, etc., to another. Intermediate state between an older one and another that is reached in a change.

Urban Agroecology: Is called agroecological practices that are developed in or near cities. ... Urban agroecology usually develops on the roofs of buildings, on the walls of houses and on the balconies and terraces of buildings.

Chapter 23
Participatory Exclusion in Community-Based Forest Management:
The Case of Semi-Arid Ghana

Enoch Akwasi Kosoe
https://orcid.org/0000-0002-1484-5755
SDD University of Business and Integrated Development Studies, Ghana

Alexis Beyuo
https://orcid.org/0000-0001-6266-0491
Kumasi Centre for Collaborative Research in Tropical Medicine (KCCR), Ghana

Reginald Addy-Morton
SDD University of Business and Integrated Development Studies, Ghana

ABSTRACT

The inherent benefits of community participation are sometimes used by local power holders as a façade to perpetuate non-participation in the management and use of forest resources. Guided by the concept of participatory exclusion, the study assessed the perceptions of inhabitants around the Wa Community Forest Reserve (WCFR), concerning the categories of people that benefit from the forest and the factors influencing community participation in the management of the forest reserve. Data was collected from 200 households in three communities and analysed using mainly descriptive statistics and binary logistic regression. The study found that community participation in the forest reserve management is below average. Gender, age, and livelihood options of households were significant determinants of one's participation in forest reserve management. Lack of community cooperation and logistical challenges were impediments to the effective management of the forest reserve. Local authorities should therefore encourage women to co-manage the forest reserve with men and local authorities for its sustenance.

DOI: 10.4018/978-1-7998-4817-2.ch023

INTRODUCTION

Forests play an important role in livelihoods, especially of rural households given their indispensable role in the provision of ecosystem services, as timber and non-timber products the world over (Blomley, 2013; Blomley, Pflienger, Isango, Zahabu, & Burgess, 2008). The competing interests in the ownership and use of forest resources have, however, led to resource use and management-based problems such as forest resource mismanagement, litigations and conflicts in many parts of the world (Appiah, 2001; Schreckenberg & Luttrell, 2009). As a consequence, the world's forest resources are experiencing a tremendous decline, resulting from human-induced activities. Farm spaces in the tropics have been converted into agricultural lands, thereby unleashing lots of carbon dioxide (CO_2) sequestered by forests (Sharma, Chauhan, & Tripathi, 2016). Given that humanity's subsistence is contingent on judicious use of the ecosystem, it is incumbent for humanity to stem the tide of the current spate of deforestation by bringing on board the interests of all stakeholders.

In the Ghanaian context, the nation's natural forest cover has experienced substantial degradation over the past century (Nsiah, 2010). One major implication of this alarming situation is the effect on households and forest- fringe communities, whose livelihoods are hinged on forest resources (Appiah, 2001). Barrow, Clarke, Grundy, Jones, and Tessema (2002), argue that exclusion and expropriation have alienated many rural people from forest resources close to them for a long time, resulting in local encroachment and forest degradation. Though northern Ghana is bedevilled with the challenge of creeping desertification as a result of climate change (Akudugu, Dittoh, & Mahama, 2012; Issahaku & Maharjan, 2014; Kusakari et al., 2014; Nyantakyi-Frimpong & Bezner-Kerr, 2015), the Wa Municipality, located in the North-Western part of Ghana, has 2.48 km^2 forest plantation with, a total perimeter of 6.24 km, with the state as a major stakeholder in its management.

Extant literature, however, shows that strict forest management approaches used by formal institutions hardly involve local communities, leading to an alienation of fringe communities from co-managing forests with formal institutions (Awung & Marchant, 2016; Bhattarai, 2011). A case in point is Awung and Marchant (2016), regarding the management of Mount Cameroon National Park. Top-down management, such as the establishment of strict conservation zones without the involvement of surrounding local communities resulted in saboteurs, arising from within fringe communities against the strict rules. To placate the locals, authorities of the National Park employed a subtle form of pseudo-participation by merely employing some community members as labourers or passive members of the community forest protection committee. Such members simply rubber-stamped decisions already taken by the authorities in charge of the Mount Cameroon National Park. Similarly, participatory exclusion has been assessed in the area of natural disaster management. Nadiruzzaman and Wrathall (2015) assessed how the power structure of communities affected by Cyclone Sidr in Bangladesh, determined the extent to which victims were marginalised or supported. They found that individuals at the lower pecking order of the social structure bore the brunt of the disaster resulting from the cyclone. Apart from these and a few other similar studies, the researchers have not sighted much literature on how participatory exclusion plays out in communities.

As a result of the challenges associated with the identification of subtle forms of pseudo-participation, there is the need to involve the various categories of people in rural communities in the protection of these fragile ecosystem services provided by forests. Guided by the concept of participatory exclusion, this study examined the extent of local-level participation in the management and use of the Wa Community Forest Reserve (WCFR). It assessed the perceptions of the various categories of residents around the

WCFR, concerning whether one's position on the social ladder is associated with one's level of access to forest resources. Specifically, the study had two objectives:

1. To examine the categories of inhabitants benefitting from the forest reserve.
2. To assess the factors influencing the exclusion of some segments of forest fringe communities.

Forms of Community Involvement in Forest Management

Community involvement in forest management can take two main forms: bottom-up or top-down (Fraser, Dougill, Mabee, Reed, & McAlpine, 2005). Bottom-up approaches allow for incorporation of community members' views and aspirations in the management of forests. Classic examples of such bottom-up approaches have been studied: Lepetu and Garekae (2015), Keller (2009), Shrestha (2013), and Bhattarai (2011); Lepetu and Garekae (2015) for instance, find in Botswana that many local communities participate in forest management through forest conservation projects such as tree planting. Bhattarai (2011), of the Mid-Hill District of Nepal, indicates that to have transparency, forest projects often include people from disadvantaged communities in their decision-making processes. Keller (2009), adds that in Sri Lanka, one of the ways local communities participate in sustainable forest management, is through the construction of fire belts, uprooting mana grass, planting fire-resistant species and employing committees to patrol the forest. By participating in community forest management, local people can submit themselves to rules for forest protection and management and share in its benefits (Shrestha, 2013). Besides, local communities subsidize the conservation of forests on behalf of the society by bearing the burden of its opportunity cost. Therefore, to make sure that households actively partake in the protection of community forests, policymakers need to devise alternative income-generating activities to ease economic constraints among forest-adjacent communities (Ogada, 2012). The benefits derived from involving communities in forest management are contingent on genuine participation of the communities.

Keller (2009), reports of a conservation group in Sri Lanka, called Human and Environment Development Organization (HEDO), which used genuinely participatory approaches to enlist the support of surrounding communities in the management of a forest reserve. Using this bottom-up approach, HEDO did not undergo the drudgery of employing extra hands for patrolling the forest reserve. Besides, local farmers regularly climbed tall trees in the forest to tap the palms for sap, and as they go about this, they can observe potential intruders and avert dangers, including fires. In the light of the importance of community participation in forest management, Ogada (2012), recommends that forest management needs to allow entry into forests for extraction of specified forest products because complete restriction may discourage households from joining the community forest association and participating in the devolved forest management arrangement.

The extant literature suggests that the involvement of local people in forest management can yield positive results. This, however, becomes effective when the livelihood of the people is tied to the forest management and community members can view their participation as an economic activity (Barrow, Clarke, Grundy, Jones, & Tessema, 2002). This argument is further buttressed by Lepetu and Garekae (2015), of a forest reserve in Botswana. Their study shows a positive relationship between household income and participation. Thus, given that people's incomes are dependent on the forest resources, through avenues such as ecotourism, they are motivated to participate in the management of forests. Thus, a right to benefit from forest resources must be linked to responsibilities for forest management.

Incentives and realistic pricing structures must augment the security of tenure so that private people can responsibly manage the benefits from forest resources on their lands (Barrow et al., 2002).

Top-down approaches, on the other hand, are associated with situations where community members are side-lined from the management of forest resources or are made to feel that the participatory approach used is merely a charade. In such situations, community apathy creeps in, thereby defeating the purpose of the concept of genuine community participation. A case in point is reported by Awung and Marchant (2016), regarding the management of Mount Cameroon National Park. Top-down management such as the establishment of strict conservation zones without the involvement of surrounding local communities resulted in saboteurs arising from within fringe communities against the strict rules. To placate the locals, authorities of the National Park merely employed some community members as labourers or passive members of the community forest protection committee, to rubber-stamp decisions already taken by the authorities in charge of the Mount Cameroon National Park. This, however, did not engender genuine community participation and ownership of the National Park. In such situations, where management of forest resources is left with community members, it stands the risk of being exposed to what Kopytoff (1971) and Mendosa (1976), described as the 'eldership complex', in many African traditional settings. Accordingly, this occurs when local elders who wield respect in traditional settings, superimpose their will on the rest of the community.

Notwithstanding the observed and potential benefits of community participation in the management of forests, studies have shown the challenges that are encountered by local communities in managing community forestry. In the Southern and Eastern parts of Africa, for instance, despite efforts to improve community participation, little transfer of power has been seen because the government remains the land-owner and the dominant stakeholder. This has resulted in disinclination on the part of the government to implement decentralized policies beyond the usual rhetoric (Mogaka, Simons, Turpie, Emerton, & Karanja, 2001). Barrow et al. (2002), states that forest authorities justify their reluctance to cede control of community forests to local people in the belief that rural folks are unable to effectively and sustainably manage their natural resources. According to Des Grades, Fakultät, and Guthiga (2007), from the local and national perspective, the opportunity costs of conserving the forest outweigh the benefits.

Another challenging factor in the management of community forests is women's inactiveness in decision-making processes. Chhetri (2005), has, for instance, argued against the low participation of women in decision-making in certain parts of rural India. The author further contends that the marginalization of people of the lower caste in decision-making is due to low levels of education. In Cameroon, Awung and Marchant (2016), found that some local communities did not support an introduced conservation project because they were not involved in decisions regarding the use of their lands. They, therefore, resisted because they felt that their lands had been seized for the conservation project without any proper consultation, thereby giving credence to the fact that insecure tenure reduces project support for local engagement.

Also, Nsiah (2010) in Ghana, reveals that regulations that prohibit the harvesting of trees and transportation of timber from private lands, as well as uncertainty in tree tenure, emanating from ambiguous policy frameworks negatively influenced the establishment of smallholder forest reserve on farmers' agricultural land. These forest management practices are examples of pseudo-participation; given that they exclude the stakeholders found at the lower pecking order of society. This is also reminiscent of the concept of participatory exclusion, which is briefly discussed next, to put the study into a clearer perspective.

Participatory Exclusion as a Framework for Analysing WCFR

Agarwal (2011, p. 1623) defines the concept as 'exclusions within seemingly participatory institutions.' Though participatory exclusion at first glance comes across as an oxymoron, at its core, the concept connotes the use of local involvement by power holders as a camouflage to deprive their constituents of their access to and use of common-pool resources (Nadiruzzaman & Wrathall, 2015). Participatory exclusion as a concept is synonymous with placation in Arnstein (1969), typology of participation in development initiatives. In the context of community forestry management, participatory exclusion serves as an avenue for power holders to deny the marginalised their right to access and use of ecosystem services derived from forests. As such, the concept of participatory exclusion aptly serves as a framework for this study.

STUDY AREA, MATERIALS AND METHODS

Study Area

The Wa Municipality, one of eleven districts in the Upper West Region (UWR) of Ghana, is the regional capital of the UWR and is bounded to the north by the Nadowli District, Wa East district to the east and Wa West District to the West. The Municipality is located between latitudes 1°40'N to 2°45'N and longitudes 9°32'W to 10°20'W and covers about 6.4% of the UWR with an area of about 234.74km2 (Ghana Statistical Service, 2014). The most recent District Analytical Report of the GSS (2010), estimates the population of the Wa Municipality to be 107,214, with females constituting a little over half (i.e. 50.6%) of this population. About 31% of households in the Municipality depend on agriculture as their mainstay (Ghana Statistical Service, 2013). Figure 1 gives the locations of the three communities sampled for this study.

MATERIALS AND METHODS

Cross-sectional data were collected from 200 randomly selected households in three selected communities living along with the Wa Forest Reserve, using a semi-structured questionnaire. The three communities, Kunta, Tampalipaani and Danko, were purposively selected due to their proximity to the forest reserve. The sample size was arrived at using the table developed by Krejcie and Morgan (1970). The study employed stratified quota sampling to proportionally allocate the total sample size of 200 households to the three communities, since the number of households per community was not equal. To select the actual households for the study, a sampling frame was constructed for each community, comprising households within each community. Households within each sampling frame were allocated different numbers, after which the random sampling tool in Microsoft Excel was used to select the required share of the sample size for each community. Heads of the households corresponding to those selected were located and interviewed.

The questionnaire devised for the study was devoted to the collection of data regarding the background information of the respondents, community participation in forest management, the forms of participation, factors influencing participation, and the challenges associated with the management of the forest. Open-ended questions, aimed at respondents' feelings about how they participated in and benefited from

Figure 1. A map of the Wa Municipality, showing the study communities and forest reserve in the context of Africa, Ghana and the Upper West Region

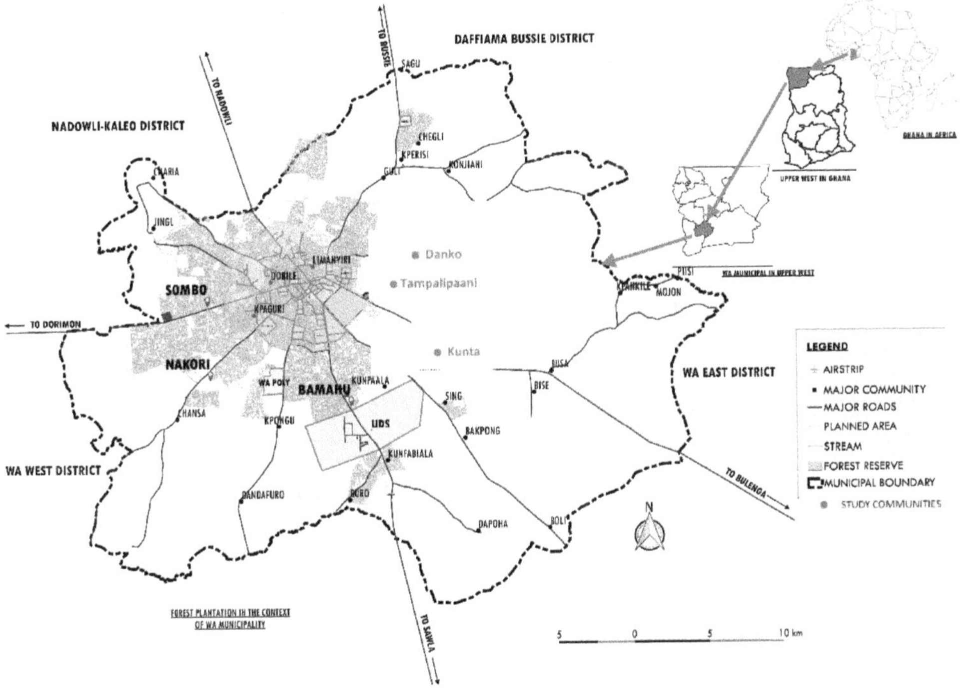

management of the forest, were embedded in the questionnaire. This approach gave in-depth explanations of the findings through probing.

Following Long and Freese (2001), logistic regressions were used for analysis. One's ability to participate or not was considered as a mutually exclusive event that yielded a binary outcome variable. Thus, participation, the dependent variable, assumed two values, where respondents who participated in the management of the WCFR took the value of 1 and 0 otherwise. The cumulative logistic distribution function is specified as:

$$P_i = \frac{1}{1+e^{-Z_i}} = \frac{e^{z_i}}{1+e^{z_i}} \tag{1}$$

Where: P_i= the probability of an individual participating in the management of Wa Community forest reserve. Hence, the researchers specify $1-P_i$ to represent the probability of non-participation.

$$z_i = \beta_0 + \beta_i X_i \tag{2}$$

Where: X_i= The vector of explanatory variables

$\beta 0$ = The vector of the constant term

βi = The vector of the regression coefficient

As Z ranges from -∞ to ∞, P_i ranges from 0 to 1.

The relative effect of each independent variable on the likelihood that an individual participates in the management of the WCFR is given by the marginal effect as:

$$\frac{\partial(P_i)}{\partial(X_i)} = \beta_i\left[\bar{P}\left(1-\bar{P}\right)\right] \tag{3}$$

Where Ṕ is the mean of the dependent variable (participation). The empirical estimation of the model for participation or non-participation is given as:

$$ln\left(\frac{P_i}{1-P_i}\right) = \beta_0 + \beta_1 Gen + \beta_2 Age + \beta_3 Married + \beta_4 HH_{Size} + \beta_5 Access + \beta_6 Livelihood + \beta_7 Remove + \beta_8 Condition \tag{4}$$

The independent variables consist of household demographic characteristics, benefits of the plantation and views on the management of the forest reserve. These were considered as the factors that can influence participation and non-participation in the management of the community forest reserve (see Table 1).

Table 1. Variable labelling, measurement and expected signs

Variable Name	Label	Measurement	Expected Sign
Gen	Gender	0 = male; 1 = female	+
Age	Age of respondents	Years	-/+
Married	Marital status	1 = married; 0 = otherwise	-/+
HH_Size	Household Size	Number of people	-/+
Access	Respondents have access to the forest	1 = Access; 0 = otherwise	+
Livelihood	Respondents derive livelihood from the forest	1 = yes; 0 = otherwise	+
Remove	Whether to remove the forest	1 = yes; 0 = otherwise	-
Conditions	Whether respondents prefer the current condition of the forest	1 = yes; 0 = otherwise	-/+

Further, Kendall's Coefficient of Concordance Test was used in the analysis of respondents' rating of the benefits of the Wa Community Forest Reserve. The procedure for analysis involved respondents ranking the benefits of the forest reserve identified, in order of importance. The purpose was to identify whether there exists any agreement among the respondents on the order of importance of the benefits of the Forest Reserve. Eight (8) of the benefits were identified from the field, and hence, a value of 8 was assigned to the most beneficial and 1 assigned to the least beneficial. The value of Kendall's coefficient (W) ranges from 0 to 1. Hence, a value of 1 represents perfect agreement, and 0 means perfect disagreement, on the order of the benefits of the forest reserve. A statistical significance of W, therefore, means that it is different from 0 and the null hypothesis of no agreement should be rejected. The significance of the estimated value (W) is validated using the Chi-square statistics.

RESULTS AND DISCUSSION

Categories of Inhabitants Benefitting from the Forest Reserve

The analysis shows that while 41% of the sampled respondents were within the age group of 20-29 years and more than half (52%) of them were females (see Table 2). The results of the age structure of respondents show that most of them were youthful and served as forest guards. They were, however, not involved in decision-making regarding the Forest Reserve. More than half (58.5%) of respondents were not involved at all in the management of the forest reserve. About 41.5%, of household heads who reported that they participated, nonetheless maintained that their participation was at the lower level of decision-making; by serving as forest guards. Elders of the sampled communities made decisions for implementation by the youth. This is quite counter-intuitive, given that only 6% of the respondents were elderly (i.e. between the ages of 50-59 years, and 3% were 60 years and above, as shown in Table 2). This finding is reminiscent of the concept of elite capture; a situation in which the few local leaders superimpose their interest on those of the grassroots (Mansuri & Rao, 2012; Platteau, 2004). It is also in tandem with findings from Blomley (2013). The writer identified lessons concerning community forest management in Africa and concludes that most community members lacked full rights such as the right to establish, implement and enforce rules governing access to, as well as the use of forest resources.

The study further revealed that among those involved in managing the forest reserve, there were more males (87%) than females (13%). The dominance of men implies that decision-making regarding gender roles in forest management and related activities, especially farming rests with men. This is yet another manifestation of participatory exclusion, given that though the power to use the resources has been devolved to the community level, males seemed to have superimposed their power over the use of the ecosystem services emanating from the forest reserve, to the neglect of females. Given that the study area is mostly patriarchal, males wielded more power over common pool resources such as forests and the ecosystem services derived from them. This finding conforms to extant literature about the category of people who have control over natural resources in developing countries (e.g. Osabuohien, et al., 2020; Osabuohien, et al., 2019; Osabuohien & Karakara, 2020; Chhetri, 2005). Osabuohien et al., (2019), has for example examined the extent to which large-scale agricultural land investment has impacted rural women in Tanzania and found that female-headed households working on such lands earned lower agricultural wage, compared to their counterparts not working on large-scale agricultural lands. Similarly, Chhetri (2005), a study of marginalisation of females and people in the lower caste of rural India, shows that a low level of education among the less privileged is the root cause of the marginalisation. Given the relevance of female economic emancipation, it is not surprising that in their assessment of the causal effects of women empowerment on household food security in the Savannah Accelerated Development Authority (SADA) zone of Ghana, Asitik and Abu (2020), found that when women participated in crop and livestock decision-making in the household, and when they had access to cultivable lands, their households had lower probabilities of being severely or moderately hungry.

Table 2. Background information of respondents

		Frequency	Percent
Gender	Male	96	48%
	Female	104	52%
	Total	**200**	**100%**
Age	20-29	82	41.00%
	30-39	54	27.00%
	40-49	46	23.00%
	50-59	12	6.00%
	60+	6	3.00%
	Total	**200**	**100.00%**
Education	Primary	17	8.50%
	JHS	33	16.50%
	SHS	57	28.50%
	Tertiary	81	40.50%
	No formal education	12	6.00%
	Total	**200**	**100.00%**

Source: Field Survey (2018)

On the various ways in which respondents participated in the management of the forest, respondents maintained that they participated through enforcement of regulations, protection of biodiversity, protection of the forest from theft (illegal lumbering), protection from fire, and prevention of dumping of waste in the forest. The frequencies and proportion of respondents indicating their direct role in the forest management are presented in Table 3.

Table 3. Respondents' roles in forest reserve management

Direct role in forest management	Frequency
Enforcing regulation	71
Protecting forest reserve for biodiversity	57
Protecting forest reserve from theft	79
Protecting forest reserve from fire	47
Protecting forest reserve from being used for disposal of waste	13

Note: *Multiple responses were considered*
Source: Field Survey (2018).

Respondents' level of satisfaction with their involvement in the community in the decision-making process of the Wa Forest Reserve was mixed. Responses ranged from totally satisfied to no opinion. About 42% of the respondents did not comment when asked to rate the satisfaction of the community participation and management of the Forest Reserve. This could be due to fear of upsetting power holders, by discussing how they felt about their exclusion from the management and use of the forest resources. However, 30.5% of respondents opened up by expressing total dissatisfaction with the rate of community involvement in decision-making. They indicated that they had nothing to show for their involvement. In contrast, 10.5% said they were totally satisfied with how the community is involved in decision-making. Details on the level of satisfaction of respondents in the management of the forest are

Table 4. Levels of satisfaction with involvement in decision making

Satisfaction with involvement in decision making	Frequency	Percent
Totally satisfied	21	10.50%
Somewhat satisfied	14	7.00%
Neither satisfied nor dissatisfied	11	5.50%
Somewhat dissatisfied	9	4.50%
Totally dissatisfied	61	30.50%
No opinion	84	42.00%
Total	**200**	**100.00%**

Source: Field Survey (2018)

presented in Table 4.

Most respondents were dissatisfied with the management of the forest reserve because of the rampant burning of the forest reserve every season, especially in the dry season. Since they had no decision-making authority over the forest reserve, respondents argued that they could not ward off people who burnt sections of the forest reserve. They added that this negatively affects the forest reserve and therefore concluded that managers of the forest reserve had not given it the needed attention. Thirty-nine and a half percent (39.5%) of the sampled respondents were totally dissatisfied with the forest reserve's current condition, with 23% not even knowing the current condition of the forest reserve and hence having no opinion (see Table 5). This further shows that because the locals had no control over the forest, they were apathetic about it. These findings are consistent with those of Awung and Marchant (2016), of the Mount Cameroon National Park,which reveals that due to the management style of local authorities, many inhabitants living close to the park were apathetic about its maintenance. In light of this, Osabuohien, Okorie and Osabuohien (2018), a study of the importance of indigenous institutional arrangements in rice production and processing in Ogun State of Nigeria, recommend the active participation of indigenous rice farmer groups in decision-making, as this improves local wellbeing.

Respondents indicated that the poor management of the forest reserve, stemming from the lack of involvement of communities, is the cause of its poor state. Respondents revealed that many negative environmental practices take place in the Forest Reserve, which defeats the conservation practices. They include tree cutting for charcoal production, dumping of solid and liquid waste and defecating in the forest reserve. Figure 2 presents open defecation and dumping of solid waste in and around the forest reserve.

The details in Figure 2 correspond with the position of the Wa Municipal Assembly (2018), that in Wa, about 47.7% of households practice open defecation (Wa Municipal Assembly, 2018). This situation is also consistent with previous studies (Osumanu & Kosoe, 2013; Osumanu et al., 2016; Kosoe &

Table 5. Levels of satisfaction with current condition of the forest reserve

Satisfied with the condition of the Forest Reserve	Frequency	Percent
Totally satisfied	3	1.50%
Somewhat satisfied	41	20.50%
Neither satisfied nor dissatisfied	10	5.00%
Somewhat dissatisfied	21	10.50%
Totally dissatisfied	79	39.50%
No opinion	46	23.00%
Total	**200**	**100.00%**

Source: Field Survey (2018)

Osumanu, 2018; Osumanu et al., 2019), which indicate the inadequacy of toilet facilities and the general practice of open defecation. Specifically, Osumanu & Kosoe, (2013); Osumanu et al., (2016); Kosoe & Osumanu, (2018), noted that households without any form of toilet facilities in their homes, who mostly claim that they use public toilets to answer nature's call, usually ease themselves in available bushes, uncompleted buildings, and open spaces including the Wa forest reserve.

Figure 2. Dumping and open defecation spots in the Wa forest reserve

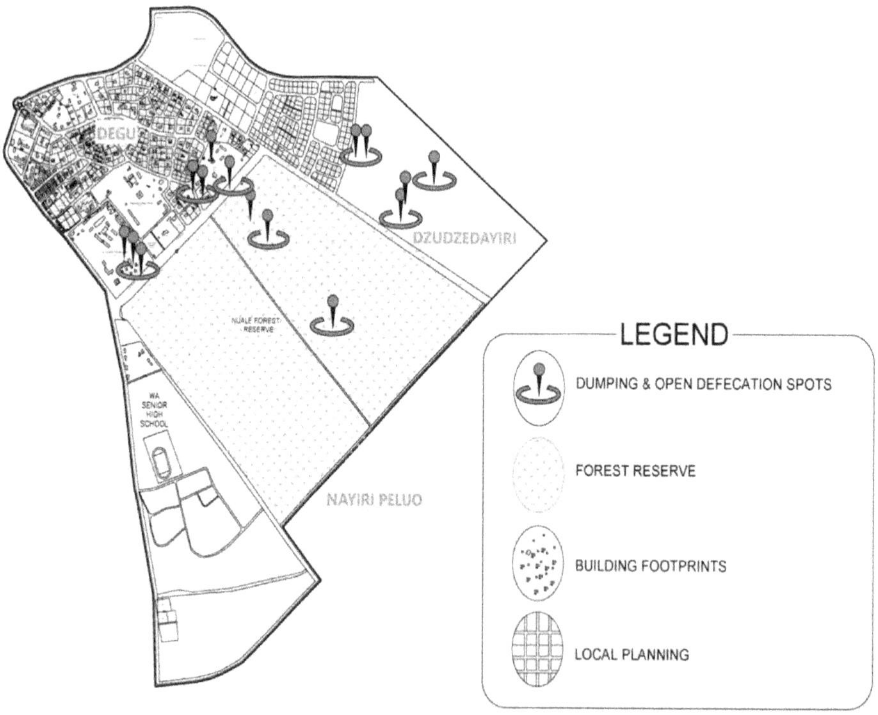

BENEFITS OF THE WA COMMUNITY FOREST RESERVE

Respondents mentioned that if properly managed, the forest reserve could serve as a recreational centre. It could also become a green belt for study purposes, as well as provide fruits, firewood, herbs and also serve as hunting grounds. The forest reserve could also provide trees for logging and farming. Having listed these potential benefits, respondents were then asked to rank these potential socio-economic benefits of the forest in order of importance. This was analysed using the Kendall coefficient of concordance analysis, as presented in Table 6.

Table 6. Ranking of the potential benefits of the forest reserve

Benefits of Forest Reserve	Mean Score	Rank
Recreation	7.71	1
Conservation of biodiversity	6.5	2
Collection of wild fruits	5.6	3
Source of firewood	4.56	4
Harvesting of herbs	4.39	5
Hunting	3.05	6
Logging	2.52	7
Farming	1.68	8
Test Statistics N = 200, Kendall's W = 0.720, Chi-Square = 1007.819, df = 7, Asymp. Sig. = 0.000		

Source: Field Survey (2018)

The results of Kendall's analysis as presented in Table 6, show that recreation, with the highest mean score of 7.71, was confirmed by the sampled respondents as the most important potential benefit of the Wa forest reserve. Conservation of biodiversity was ranked second importance in the order of potential benefits, with a mean score of 6.5. Further, with a mean score of 1.68, farming was ranked as the least benefit that community members derive from the Wa Forest Reserve. The value of Kendall's W (0.720) was found to be significant at 1%. This means that about 72% of the respondents agreed with the order of the ranking. This means that the respondents considered recreation as potentially the most beneficial use of the WCFR and farming as the least beneficial of the forest.

Further, given that Kendall's coefficient of concordance of 0.72, indicates that up to 72% of the managers interviewed agreed to the rankings of the challenges, the study finds that there is a high degree of unanimity among the owners regarding their ranking of challenges. Thus, the rankings of the potential benefits of the forest reserve are not random but have strong statistical underpinning, implying that valid conclusions and generalisations can be made from the rankings provided.

FACTORS INFLUENCING THE EXCLUSION OF SOME RESIDENTS OF FOREST FRINGE COMMUNITIES

The Logistic Regression framework was used to examine the factors that influence participatory exclusion in the management of the community forest reserve. One's ability to participate or not, is the dependent variable and this was regressed on the explanatory variables. Gender of household head, age of household head, household head's marital status, household size, access to the Forest Reserve, livelihood, removal of forest and current condition of the forest comprised the explanatory variables. Livelihood is a dummy variable measured by whether individuals in the selected household derived their livelihoods from the Forest Reserve (1) or not (0). Removal of the forest reserve is also a dummy variable and is measured by the respondent's opinion on whether the forest should be removed for other development activities to take place (1), or maintained as a forest reserve. Again, condition of the forest reserve was a dummy variable measuring respondents' assessment of the current condition of the forest whether satisfactory (1), or unsatisfactory (0).The results are depicted in Table 7.

Table 7. Logistics regression estimates of factors influencing participation in community forest management

Logistic estimates of Variables	Marginal Effect
Respondents' Demographics	
Gender (Ref: Male)	
Female	-0.298***(0.096)
Age	0.011**(0.005)
Married	0.132(0.095)
HH_size	-0.007(0.013)
Access	-0.053(0.091)
Livelihood	0.129*(0.077)
Remove	0.125(0.091)
Condition	0.452***(0.099)

***, ** and * represent significance at 1%, 5% and 10% respectively. Figures in parenthesis are standard errors

As shown in Table 7, four (4) out of the eight variables; gender, age, livelihood and "condition" have a significant influence on the decision to participate in the management of the forest reserve. The significant variables imply that the demographic characteristics of the study population, as well as their opinions on the management and condition of the forest reserve, influence their decision to take part in its management. The coefficient of gender is negative and significant at 1%, implying that females are less likely to participate than their male counterparts. The marginal effect of -0.298 means that females are 29.80% less likely to participate in the management and use of the forest reserve than their male counterparts. Besides this, women felt unsafe entering the Forest reserve. Reacting to this, the women complained that increasing criminal activities in the forest deter them from entering it. A female respondent bore this out from Tampalipaani who revealed:

I cannot just get up and enter the forest without the permission of my husband because I am under his care. He will blame me, if 'weed' smokers [who often use the forest cover as a hideout for smoking 'weed', a banned substance] attack me in there (A female respondent in Tampalipaani, 11th November 2018).

This supports earlier studies that women are not active participants in the management of forests in developing countries (Chhetri, 2005; Shrestha, 2013). Considering the contributions of forest resources to household food security, it is surprising that women, who happen to be at the forefront of the household food supply in the study area, are less involved in managing the forest. This finding is in tandem with the theory of participatory exclusion, given that females, who are expected to depend on the ecosystem services provided by the forest, have limited access to this resource compared with men.

The findings further show that more men than women are used as forest guards and volunteers for management of the forest reserve. Men also have better access to forest resources than women. This finding may not augur well for improved forest management in the study communities. It also runs counter to Agarwal's (2010), a position that women's inclusion in forest management and their effective participation in decision-making have direct links with improved forest governance and resource sustainability.

The age structure of respondents also shows a significant (at 5%), and positive association with participation. This suggests that participation increases with age. The marginal effect of 0.011 (Table 7), indicates that as an individual adds a year to his or her age, the likelihood of participating in the management of the WCFR is 1.1%. This supports earlier findings by Nsiah (2010), regarding the effect of age in forestry management. This finding is also reminiscent of the concept of participatory exclusion (Agarwal, 2011; Nadiruzzaman & Wrathall, 2015), given that access to and use of the forest resources is contingent on the age of individuals. It is also comparable to what Kopytoff (1971) and Mendosa (1976), describe as the 'eldership complex', in many African traditional settings. This is a situation common to many African traditional societies, where there is overwhelming respect for older (often male) members of the society. As such, the elderly often make decisions that affect the entire community.

The livelihood coefficient is positive and significant at 10% (Table 7), and the corresponding marginal effect of 0.129 explains that community members whose livelihood depends on the forest reserve have about 12.90% likelihood of participating in the management of the forest reserve than those whose livelihoods are independent of the forest reserve. The finding is also in tandem with those of Chhetri (2005) and Bhattarai (2011), who have argued that beneficiaries of forests tend to be more willing to participate in its management than those who do not derive any livelihood from it.

Finally, the results in Table 7 show that the condition variable is positive and significant at 1%. The marginal effect of 0.452 for the variable means that those who considered the current condition of the forest reserve as good, have 45.2% probability of participating in its management than those who considered it as bad. This may be because those who considered it as bad are pessimistic about the potential benefits of the forest and are unlikely to take any part in its management. This further shows that for individuals to participate in the management of the forest reserve, they must be allowed to share in its benefits as well.

CONCLUSION

Given the difficulties in rolling-out genuine participation, many development agencies resort to less robust participatory approaches in their work with local people they seek to support (Cooke &Kothari,

2001). In some cases, these participatory approaches do not inure to the benefit of target beneficiaries (Botchway, 2001). In light of these complexities, this study sought to identify less robust participatory approaches that practically exclude the marginalised in the management and use of forest resources in Ghana. The findings suggest that the gender, age and livelihood condition of the people, are the key factors influencing participation in the management of the forest reserve. In line with the theory of participatory exclusion, the results further show that males are more predisposed to participate in the management of the forest than females. This is because men are usually the heads of the household and arrogate to themselves, decisions that favour them. Rather than being core beneficiaries of the Wa Forest Reserve, women were involved in the fringes, including picking dead tree branches for firewood.

Furthermore, community participation was manifested through local forest guards' efforts at protecting the forest from wildfires and illegal logging, as well as ensuring general enforcement of regulations protecting the WCFR. These efforts were, however, hampered by problems of illicit activities, poor coordination between government agencies and communities, inadequate personnel to guard the forest, as well as inadequate training opportunities and logistical constraints. Thus, limited participation of communities in forest resource management inhibited proper management of these resources, thereby perpetuating the problem of participatory exclusion in the management of community natural resources.

The findings are relevant for government institutions involved in the management of forest resources in Ghana and the African continent as a whole. They are also relevant for NGOs that support governments in natural resource management. Their ability to identify pseudo-participatory activities is an important step in their co-management of ecosystem services with local communities.

It is therefore recommended that communities around the forest be empowered by the central government and other civil society organisations, to team up and co-manage the forest reserve and to arrest intruders and seize forest products from people acting illegally. They should be encouraged to volunteer to keep guard of the forest resources and to protect them from depletion. Cordial cooperation between the government management agency and the communities is recommended to form a coherent unit to end illegality in the Forest reserve and to enhance sustainability for optimal community benefit. This is because community participation in forests is a way of improving the livelihood and welfare of forest fringe communities. The principle of participation, therefore, calls for the incorporation of all, especially women in decisions regarding the use and management of the forest resource. This will engender a much broader understanding and commitment to the development and protection of the natural resources among women.

REFERENCES

Agarwal, B. (2011). Participatory exclusions, community forestry and gender: An analysis for South Asia and a conceptual framework. *World Development*, *29*(10), 1623–1648. doi:10.1016/S0305-750X(01)00066-3

Akudugu, M. A., Dittoh, S., & Mahama, E. S. (2012). The implications of climate change on food security and rural livelihoods: Experiences from Northern Ghana. *Journal of Environment and Earth Science*, *2*(3), 21–29.

Appiah, M. (2001). Co-partnership in forest management: The Gwira-Banso joint forest management project in Ghana. *Environment, Development and Sustainability*, *3*(4), 343–360. doi:10.1023/A:1020879510134

Asitik, A. J., & Abu, B. M. (2020). Women empowerment in agriculture and food security in Savannah Accelerated Development Authority zone of Ghana. *African Journal of Economic and Management Studies*, *11*(2), 253–270. doi:10.1108/AJEMS-03-2019-0102

Awung, N., & Marchant, R. (2016). Investigating the role of local communities as co-managers of the Mount Cameroon National Park Conservation Project. *Environments*, *3*(4), 36. doi:10.3390/environments3040036

Barrow, E., Clarke, J., Grundy, I., Jones, K., & Tessema, Y. (2002). *Analysis of stakeholder power and responsibility in community involvement in forestry management in eastern and southern Africa*. IUCN.

Bhattarai, R. C. (2011). Economic impact of community forestry in Nepal: A case of mid hill districts of Nepal. *Economic Journal of Development, 1*(13).

Blomley, T. (2013). *Lessons learnt from community forestry in Africa and their relevance for REDD*. United States Agency for International Development.

Blomley, T., Pflienger, K., Isango, J., Zahabu, A. A., & Burgess, N. (2008). Seeing the wood for the trees: an assessment of the impact of participatory forest management on forest condition in Tanzania *Fauna &Flora International, 42*(3), 380-391.

Botchway, K. (2001). Paradox of empowerment: Reflections on a case study of Northern Ghana. *World Development*, *29*(1), 135–253. doi:10.1016/S0305-750X(00)00084-X

Chhetri, B. B. K. (2005). *Community forestry programme in the hills of Nepal: Determinants of user participation and household dependency*. Norwegian University of Life Sciences.

Cooke, B., & Kothari, U. (n.d.). Paradox of empowerment: reflections on a case study from Northern Ghana. World Development, 29(1), 135-153.

Des Grades, E., Fakultät, H. L., & Guthiga, P. M. (2007). Economic analysis of different management approaches of Kakamega Forest in Kenya: Cost-benefit and local community satisfaction analysis. *Forests and Climate Change Adaptation and Mitigation, 66*.

Fraser, E. D. G., Dougill, A. J., Mabee, W. E., Reed, M., & McAlpine, P. (2005). Bottomup and top down: analysis of participatory processes for sustainability indicator idetification as a pathway to community empowerment and sustainable environmental management. *Environmental Management, 78*(2006), 114-127.

Ghana Statistical Service. (2013). *2010 population and housing census: regional analytical report, Upper West Region*. Retrieved from www.statsghana.gov.gh/

Ghana Statistical Service. (2014). *Distict Analytical Report, Nadowli*. Retrieved from Ghana http://www.statsghana.gov.gh/docfiles/2010_District_Report/Upper%20West/NADOWLI.pdf

Issahaku, Z. A., & Maharjan, K. L. (2014). Crop substitution behavior among food crop farmers in Ghana: An efficient adaptation to climate change or costly stagnation in traditional agricultural production system? *Agricultural and Food Economics*, *2*(1), 1–14.

Keller, D. (2009). Community participation in sustainable forest management *Forests and Climate Change Adaptation and Mitigation, 66.*

Kopytoff, I. (1971). Ancestors as Elders in Africa. *International African Institute, 41*(2), 129–142. doi:10.2307/1159423

Kosoe, A. E., & Osumanu, K. I. (2018). Entertaining risks to health: The state of human faecal matter management in Wa, Ghana. *Ghana Journal of Development Studies, 15*(1), 149–170. doi:10.4314/gjds.v15i1.8

Krejcie, R. V., & Morgan, D. W. (1970). Developing Sample Size for Reseach Activities. *Educational and Psychological Measurement, 30*(3), 607–610. doi:10.1177/001316447003000308

Kusakari, Y., Asubonteng, K. O., Jasaw, G. S., Dayour, F., Dzivenu, T., Lolig, V., ... Obeng, F. K. (2014). Farmer-perceived effects of climate change on livelihoods in Wa West District, Upper West Region of Ghana. *Journal of Disaster Research, 9*(4), 516–528. doi:10.20965/jdr.2014.p0516

Lepetu, J. P., & Garekae, H. (2015). Attitudes of local communities towards forest management practices in Botswana: The case study of Kasane Forest Plantation. *International Journal of Agriculture and Forestry, 5*(2), 138–145.

Long, J. S., & Freese, J. (2001). *Regression models for categorical dependent variables using Stata.* Stata Press.

Mansuri, G., & Rao, V. (2012). *Localizing development: does participation work?* World Bank Publications. doi:10.1596/978-0-8213-8256-1

Mendosa, E. L. (1976). Elders, office-holders and ancestors among Sisala of Northern Ghana. *Africa, 46*(1), 57–65. doi:10.2307/1159093

Mogaka, H., Simons, G., Turpie, J., Emerton, L., & Karanja, F. (2001). *Economic aspects of community involvement in sustainable forest management in eastern and southern Africa.* IUCN.

Nadiruzzaman, M., & Wrathall, D. (2015). Participatory exclusion - Cycle Sidr and its aftermath. *Geoforum, 64*, 196–204. doi:10.1016/j.geoforum.2015.06.026

Nsiah, B. (2010). Contribution of farm forest plantation management to the livelihood strategies of farm households in the high forest zone of Ghana. *FakultätForst-, Geo- und Hydrowissenschaften.*

Nyantakyi-Frimpong, H., & Bezner-Kerr, R. (2015). The relative importance of climate change in the context of multiple stressors in semi-arid Ghana. *Global Environmental Change, 32*, 40–56. doi:10.1016/j.gloenvcha.2015.03.003

Ogada, M. J. (2012). *Forest management decentralisation in Kenya: Effects on household farm forestry decisions in Kakamenga.* Paper presented at the Triennial Conference of the International Association of Agricultural Economists, Brazil.

Osabuohien, E., Efobi, U., Gitau, C. M., Osabohien, R. A., & Adediran, O. O. (2020). Youth Unemployment and Large-scale Agricultural Land Investments in Africa: Examining the Relevance of Indigenous Institutions and Capacity in Tanzania. In The Palgrave Handbook of Agricultural and Rural Development in Africa (pp. 425-455). Cham, Switzerland: Palgrave Macmillan. DOI: doi:10.1007/978-3-030-41513-6_19

Osabuohien, E., & Karakara, A. A. (2020). Conclusion: Agricultural investments and Rural Development in Africa—Salient Issues and Imperatives. In The Palgrave Handbook of Agricultural and Rural Development in Africa (pp. 627-640). Cham, Switzerland: Palgrave Macmillan. DOI: doi:10.1007/978-3-030-41513-6_28

Osabuohien, E., Okorie, U., & Osabohien, R. (2018). Rice Production and Processing in Ogun State, Nigeria: Qualitative Insights from Farmers' Association. In E. Obayelu (Ed.), *Food Systems Sustainability and Environmental Policies in Modern Economics* (pp. 188–216). IGI Global. doi:10.4018/978-1-5225-3631-4.ch009

Osabuohien, E. S., Efobi, U. R., Hermann, R. T., & Gitau, C. M. (2019). Female labour outcomes and lage-scale agricultural land investments: Macro-micro evidence from Tanzania. *Land Use Policy*, *82*, 716–728. doi:10.1016/j.landusepol.2019.01.005

Osumanu, K. I., & Kosoe, A. E. (2013). Where do I answer nature's call? An assessment of accessibility and utilisation of toilet facilities in Wa, Ghana. *Ghana Journal of Geography*, *5*, 17–31.

Osumanu, K. I., Kosoe, A. E., & Ategeeng F. (2019). Determinants of open defecation in the Wa Municipality of Ghana: Empirical findings highlighting sociocultural and economic dynamics among households. *Journal of Environmental and Public Health*. doi:10.1155/2019/3075840

Osumanu, K. I., Kosoe, A. E., & Dapilah, F. (2016). Residential housing in Ghana's low-income urban areas: An analysis of households living conditions in the Wa Municipality. *Journal of Geography and Regional Planning*, *9*(7), 139–153.

Platteau, J. (2004). Monitoring elite capture in community-driven development. *Blackwell Publishing*, *35*(2), 223–246.

Schreckenberg, K., & Luttrell, C. (2009). Participatory forest management: A route to povety reduction? *Commonwealth Forestry Association*, *11*(2), 221–238. doi:10.1505/ifor.11.2.221

Sharma, R., Chauhan, S. K., & Tripathi, A. M. (2016). Carbon sequestration potential in agroforestry systems in India: An analysis for carbon project. *Agroforestry Systems*, *90*(4), 631–644. doi:10.100710457-015-9840-8

Shrestha, R. (2013). *People's participation in community forestry managementl A study of Siddhicharan community forestry user group of Bigutar*. Okhaldhungu.

Chapter 24
Neoliberal Reforms in Sub-Saharan Africa's Electricity Sector:
Implementation, Experiences, and Impacts

Chigozie Nweke-Eze
Institute of Geography, University of Bonn, Germany

ABSTRACT

Based on literature review and documents analyses, this contribution discusses the processes, implementation, experiences and impacts of the neoliberal electricity-sector reform in Sub-Saharan Africa (SSA). The study generally finds poor implementation status and experiences as well as little improvement in the performance of the electricity sector as a result of the reforms, in the reviewed and analyzed SSA countries. The study identifies the reasons for the general poor outcomes of the reforms to be non-existence of truly independent electricity regulatory agencies, weak institutions and non-existence of unhampered competition among players in the electricity markets in most SSA context. The study suggests implementation of more tailored reform alternatives which suit existing political, social, and institutional characteristics and conditions of the SSA countries, namely: hybrid electricity markets and complementary regulatory measures.

INTRODUCTION

Over the last thirty years, almost half of the countries of the world have implemented electricity sector reforms in varying degrees (Erdogdu, 2013a). Sub-Saharan African (SSA) countries were included. Billions of dollars have already been spent worldwide in achieving this goal (Erdogdu, 2013b). The typical reform model involves the processes of: 1) corporatization and commercialization of state-owned utilities; 2) adoption of new electricity sector legislation which approves the liberalization of the utilities and provides for the establishment of independent regulatory bodies; 3) unbundling of utilities; 4)

DOI: 10.4018/978-1-7998-4817-2.ch024

introduction of competition through private sector participation (PSP); and 5) provision of incentives for investment (Newbery, 2002; Pollitt, 2012; Jamasb, Nepal and Timilsina, 2015). This chapter calls this model of reform: the neo-liberalized model of electricity sector reform.

Many researchers, in this area of study, believe that a well-designed and regulated implementation of the liberalized model of electricity sector reform will: 1) improve the technical and financial performance of the sector; 2) improve access to electricity; and 3) make-up for government's inability to mobilize sufficient capital investment for electricity sector development and expansion in the implemented countries (Zhang, Parker and Kirkpatrick, 2008; Sen and Jamasb, 2012; Kessides, 2012; Erdogdu, 2013b). This argument is also in line with the traditional theoretical arguments for market liberalization, which posits that liberalization and privatization of economic sectors lead to higher investments, outputs and efficiency (Singh, 2002; Megginson and Netter, 2001; Jamasb et al., 2015). In SSA, the widespread implementation of the liberalized model of electricity sector reform is mainly driven by the desire to achieve optimal allocation of resources; technical and economic efficiency; improve social welfare; as well as to increase investment in the sector (Jamasb et al.; 2015; Eberhard and Gratwick, 2016; Bacon and Beasant-Jones, 2001). It is estimated that an investment of USD 120-160 billion per annum is required to meet the growing demand for electricity in SSA countries combined (IEA, 2014).

The liberalized model of electricity sector reforms has, however, not yet been fully implemented in many SSA countries (AICD, 2008; Eberhard et al. 2011; Eberhard and Gratwick, 2016). However, since the 1990's, there has been the implementation of PSP in the electricity sector of 33 out of 48 SSA countries (World Bank, 2016). The implementation of PSP in these countries is an essential part of the process of liberalization of the electricity sector in the countries. The PSP adopted by the individual countries were in the form of management or lease contracts; concession contracts; independent power projects; and divestitures (World Bank, 2016). As of 2015, a total of 210 electricity sector projects with PSP reached financial closure with a total investment of more than USD32.7 billion in the studied 33 SSA countries between 1990 and 2015 (World Bank, 2016).

Despite this widespread implementation of PSP in the region, there has been little or no improvement in the performance of the power sector. The privatization reform process has been complex, inefficient and slow in the SSA countries where reforms have begun (Vagliasindi, Maria, and Nellis, 2010; Nepal and Jamasb, 2012; Eberhard et al., 2011; Prasad, 2011 and 2008). State-owned utilities still retain most ownership and management of unbundled electricity utilities, thereby limiting most private sector participation to mainly the generation sector—where the private investors are Independent Power Producers (IPPs) (Gratwick and Eberhard, 2008; Eberhard et al., 2011). Many private management contracts have been awarded, yet there is no visible effect on the performance of the electricity sectors (Gboney, 2009; Eberhard et al., 2011). Only a few out of the many issued private leases and concessions have survived (Nellis, 2008; Eberhard et al., 2011). These trends question the effectiveness of the currently implemented liberalized model of electricity sector reform in improving the performance of the electricity sector in SSA. Meanwhile, several studies on institutions and development in SSA note that most SSA countries have weak institutions—a characteristic that can impede the success of planned economic reforms (Acemoglu and Robinson, 2010; Parker, 2002; Nepal and Jamasb, 2012, Nepal, 2013).

Based on general literature review and documents analyses, this contribution discusses the processes and drivers of implementation of the liberalized model of electricity sector reform as well as its applications, implementation status, experiences and impacts in Sub-Saharan Africa (SSA). SSA consists of 4 regions. They include Central Africa, East Africa, Southern Africa and West Africa (IEA 2016; KPMG, 2016). The region consists of 49 countries, with a total estimated population of 900 million people (IEA,

2016). The region has seen a rapidly rising economic growth over the last past years (World Bank, 2016). This rise in economic growth has also seen an increase in demand of electricity as well as the need for improvement in private sector investment in the electricity sector to meet the growing demand (IEA, 2014). In recent years, however, economic growth has declined across the region with an overall 2015 GDP slowing down to 3.5% from 5.1% in 2014 (World Bank, 2016). Yet, this decline in economic growth does not slow down electricity demand (IEA, 2014). Improvement in electrification rates has been one of the major challenges of the region (IEA, 2016). This challenge is common among the countries in the region, yet, the solution to it varies and are country-specific (IEA, 2016; KPMG, 2016). The region has a total installed capacity of 70GW, yet, about one-quarter of its generation does not reach the population due to poor facility performance (IEA, 2016; KPMG, 2016). Many of the countries experience severe power shortages, costing the economies about two percent of their GDP (IEA, 2016; KPMG, 2016).

STRUCTURE OF THE ELECTRICITY INDUSTRY AND ELECTRICITY MARKET MODELS

Structure of the Electricity Industry

A typical electricity enterprise consists of generation, transmission and distribution utilities (EIA, 2000). The generation utilities begin the process of delivery of electricity to consumers by generating electric power from primary energy sources. The generated electricity is then stepped-up and ran through network switchyards (EIA, 2000). The transmission utilities transport bulk generated electrical energy to the distribution utilities through transmission networks with the use of transformers—which lowers the transmission voltage (EIA, 2000). The distribution entities then carry the electricity to the individual consumers.

Electricity Market Models

Before the first-ever electricity sector reform in Chile in 1982, which saw a widespread implementation of liberalized and competitive electricity markets, electricity enterprises in most countries were state-run natural monopoly markets (Joskow, 2008). Natural monopolistic and competitive markets are explained herein.

Natural Monopoly

A natural monopoly is a market system where all or most of market activities are dominated and run by one firm. It is characterized by having a huge capital investment, being the sole market supplier, and having considerable cost advantage due to economies of scale—meaning that they can satisfy market demand for goods and services at a lower cost (Makwe et al.; 2012).

The cost structure of a natural monopoly is characterized by declining long-run average cost and a constant marginal cost (Makwe et al.; 2012). A natural monopolist can set the price above marginal cost using its market advantage, if unregulated (Makwe et al.; 2012). Natural monopolies, as a result, can lead to market distortion by creating artificially high prices; foster inefficient production and management, and result in delivery of low-quality goods or services (Makwe et al.; 2012).

Competitive Market

Since the Chilean electricity sector restructuring and privatization reform, an increasing number of developed and developing countries have pursued and implemented liberalized electricity sector reforms in the following years (Kessides, 2012). Liberalization of the electricity markets implies introducing competition in the markets through privatization of entities and involvement of private sector market players (Kessides, 2012). Privatization is a process where the government transfers its firm ownership and management to private sector firms or organizations (Shirley, 1992). In a competitive market model, competition among several producers or suppliers drives down the cost of production; leads to improved performance and more efficiency in the firms; curbs government rent-seeking interests; leads to increase in national revenue and reduction in national debts (Singh, 2002; Kessides, 2012). When compared with a monopoly market model, many economic literatures have argued in favour of a privatized competitive market (Singh, 2002; Megginson and Netter, 2001; Jamasb et al., 2015).

PROCESSES OF IMPLEMENTATION OF NEOLIBERAL ELECTRICITY SECTOR REFORMS

A standard liberalized model of the electricity industry reform involves the implementation of following reform processes:

1. Corporatization and commercialization of state-owned utilities into separate legal entities that can make profits;
2. Adoption of new legislation which enforces the restructuring process;
3. Establishment of well informed and independent regulatory agencies to promote fair-play among competitors, efficiency and access to utilities, and to guide efficient investment in the sector;
4. Facilitation of market entry and competition through vertical restructuring—which involves separating the industry into separate segments of generation, transmission and distribution— and horizontal restructuring (usually applied in large countries and economies)—which involves separating natural monopoly government utilities into smaller utilities across regions and districts;
5. Privatization of assets—which seeks to promote financial discipline, cost efficiency and prevent undue and harmful political interference;
6. Introduction of Independent Power Producers (IPPs)—to increase investment in generation capacity and foster competition;
7. Appointment of Independent System Operator (ISO)—to oversee the working efficiency, expansion and safety of operation of the interconnected electric utility systems.

(AICD, 2008; Newberry 2002, Ljung 2007, Kessides 2012, Politt 2012, Jamasb et al., 2015). Table 1 below depicts these processes.

The reform process generally progresses from process 'i' to 'vii' to achieve full-scale reform implementation. The processes are discussed in details below.

Table 1. Summary of Implementation processes of reforms

	Implementation Processes of Reforms
i	Corporatization and Commercialization
ii	Adoption of new electricity legislations
iii	Establishment of Independent Regulatory agencies
iv	Vertical and Horizontal Restructuring
v	Privatization of Assets
vi	Introduction of Independent Power Producers
vii	Appointment of an Independent system operator

Sources: Author's Summary (2017) from AICD, 2008; Newberry 2002, Ljung 2007, Kessides 2012, Politt 2012, Jamasb et al., 2015

CORPORATIZATION AND COMMERCIALIZATION

In this process, all the state utilities (former investors and operators) are transformed to commercial entities which operate with commercial principles where: utilities are independent owners and operators; pay taxes and market interest; and earn market returns on invested equities (Bacon and Beasant-Jones, 2001). Government establishes and executes policies that foster commercialization (Jena, 2015). Competition is introduced in the generation and distribution entities, and consumers can switch between suppliers according to the cost of purchase (Jena, 2015).

Transmission utilities usually remain natural monopolies run by the state. The distribution utilities are often the first and the most important utility to commercialize—because most of the inefficiencies come from there (Jamasb, 2004). However, it is essential to provide regulatory incentives to the transmission, and the distribution entities in order to promote capacity building and efficiency (Joskow, 2008).

ADOPTION OF NEW ELECTRICITY LEGISLATIONS

It is important that electricity sector reforms are supported with the enactment and adaptation of laws and acts which serves as a legal basis for the restructuring processes (Jamasb, 2004). When these legal provisions are explicit, they reduce tendencies for conflicts in utility functions and on issues relating to property rights (Jamasb, 2004). The existence electricity legislations and the degree of compliance to legislative provisions were one of the critical questions used by the World Bank in determining the degree of success of electricity reforms in 115 developing countries (Bacon & Beasan-Jones, 2001). New reform legislations often fail to provide rules or regulations that promote or encourage electricity generation and distribution efficiency—particularly in East and Southern Africa regions (UNIDO, forthcoming).

ESTABLISHMENT OF INDEPENDENT REGULATORY AGENCIES

Independent regulators are established to oversee and regulate the privatized market (Jamasb, 2004). They prevent unwanted practices in the market and make sure that market players operate according to set rules (Jena, 2015). They prevent non-competitive tendencies in the wholesale market and try to balance out the needs of suppliers and consumers in the retail market (Jena, 2015).

VERTICAL AND HORIZONTAL RESTRUCTURING

This process involves the separation of generation, transmission and distribution utilities and giving room for the introduction of competition in the generation and distribution utilities (Jena, 2015). Limits on maximum market power are set (Jena, 2015). Formation of cartels is forbidden by law (Bacon and Beasan-Jones, 2001). Competition in the unbundled entities is enhanced with an increase in the number of business players within the unbundled entities (Jamasb, 2004).

PRIVATIZATION OF ASSETS

After the entities have been unbundled, they are privatized under different ownerships (Jena, 2015). Competitions in the privatized entities promote efficiency in technical operation, financial and managerial performances (Jamasb, 2004).

Introduction of Independent Power Producers

Allowing entry of IPPs increases the propensity of competition in the generation entities (Jamasb, 2004). Number of IPPs in reform is an essential indicator of reform's success (Jena, 2015).

APPOINTMENT OF INDEPENDENT SYSTEM OPERATORS (ISOS)

Appointment of ISOs for dispatching generated electricity and ensuring network stability is also important for increasing competition and promoting efficiency (Newberry, 2002).

DRIVERS OF ELECTRICITY SECTOR REFORM IN SSA

Electricity sector reform in SSA was driven by two major concerns: first, the dissatisfaction with the government-controlled electricity sector which was characterized by poor technical efficiency; lack of maintenance of the technology which led to dilapidating infrastructure; inability to acquire spare-parts; lack of funding and capital for investment in new infrastructure and expansion of existing ones; huge utility debt burdens; lack of payment for electricity by customers; poor management and corruption and consequent low access to electricity (Jamasb et al., 2015; Vagliasindi et al., 2010; Kessides, 2012; Davies, Wright & Price, 2006). Second, the unsuccessful attempts to improve these technical, financial and management conditions and hence to enhance the performance of the sector—especially financial performance as it was increasingly more difficult to mobilize more funds for electricity sector investments and maintenance (Jamasb et al., 2015; Vagliasindi et al., 2010; Kessides, 2012; Davies et al., 2006).

Other drivers of the reforms identified by some researchers (Jamasb et al., 2015; Vagliasindi et al., 2010; Kessides, 2012; AICD, 2008; Eberhard, 2007; Davies et al., 2006) include:

1. The inability of the government to meet the rising demand for electricity;
2. The desire to ease up the financial stress placed on government to run and maintain electricity utilities and to free up more public funds for other public projects,
3. The desire to introduce competition in the sector which will increase the number of players in the market, increase efficiency and lower cost of tariffs,
4. The desire to make tariffs reflect the original market costs by removing the burden of government subsidies
5. And the desire to limit the inefficient government involvement in the sector by relegating management and regulatory duties to independent agencies.

According to Newberry (1995), power shortages are caused by inadequate investment and inefficiencies in operation. A functional competitive market will create an environment and incentive for higher investments—through ploughed back profits or borrowings—and higher efficiency due to competition (Newberry, 1995; Jamasb et al., 2005; Kessides, 2012). Higher investments increase output and lowers cost of production, as the prices adjust to marginal costs (Newberry, 1995; Kessides, 2012). This competition can only occur when there are adequate utility capacities and many IPPs to guarantee that there is competition at all times (Newberry, 1995). The full potentials of a competitive market can also be achieved when there is a well-designed regulatory framework and credible institution which ensures that tariffs are reflective of marginal costs of utility operation (Jamasb et al., 2005).

Some researchers (Jamasb et al., 2015; Vagliasindi et al., 2010; Kessides, 2012; AICD, 2008; Eberhard, 2007; Davies et al., 2006) noted that some macroeconomic external factors also played a role in the drive for electricity sector reforms. They include:

1. Faith in liberalized economy among economists and politicians;
2. Generally low government revenue;
3. Poor allocation of factors of production;
4. Accumulated credit from lending institutions and governments;
5. Widespread criticisms on how economy was run and the resultant economic liberalization and structural adjustment policies encouraged and championed by the World Bank and IMF—the World Bank and the IMF made sure that African and other developing countries who were seeking funding from them had met the requirement of a more liberalized economy through the Structural Adjustment Program (SAP);
6. And the general limitation and difficulty in raising and sourcing international capital and loans.

Table 2 summarizes the drivers of the liberalized model of electricity sector reform.

It is, however, important to note that the electricity sector reforms in SSA were generally not targeted towards increasing sustainable electricity production through renewable energy production or to improve energy efficiency (Akinyemi et al. 2017). Neither were they explicitly targeted towards improving electricity access to the poor (Akinyemi et al. 2019).

Table 2. Drivers of electricity sector reform in SSA

Internal Drivers	External Drivers
Poor technical, financial and management performance	Faith in economic liberalization ideology
Poor finance source for investment in the sector	Low economic resources
Detrimental government influence and corruption	poor allocation of factors of production
high electric utility inefficiencies and losses	Accumulated debt
limited energy access	International influences from international agencies—World Bank and IMF
low service quality	

Sources: Author's Summary from Jamasb et al., 2015; Vagliasindi et al., 2010; Kessides, 2012; AICD, 2008; Eberhard, 2007; Davies et al., 2006.

STATUS AND EXPERIENCES OF ELECTRICITY SECTOR REFORM IN SSA

Over the years, most of the SSA countries have implemented some form of electricity sector reforms. They include: enacting new electricity sector laws and creation of new regulatory agencies; unbundling of utilities; awarding of new private management and concession contracts; investment through IPPs; divestitures (Eberhard and Gratwick, 2016; Eberhard, 2007; AICD, 2008). However, only a few have adopted all of these reforms, and the extent of implementation is still limited (Eberhard and Gratwick, 2016; Eberhard, 2007; AICD, 2008). As of 2006, almost all of the 24 SSA countries covered in the Africa Infrastructure Country Diagnostic (AICD) had reformed their electricity sector laws, 18 have initiated some form of PSP. Also, 16 have implemented privatization and established independent regulatory bodies, and Up to 8 had active independent power producers' involvement (Eberhard and Gratwick, 2016; Eberhard, 2007; AICD, 2008). About 6 of the countries have adopted 3 or 4 of the reform components (Eberhard and Gratwick, 2016). Nigeria is the only country where full-scale implementation has taken place since 2015 (Eberhard and Gratwick, 2016).

Majority of reforms covered in most SSA countries involve vertical restructuring and privatization (Eberhard, et al., 2011). Nigeria is also the only SSA country where horizontal restructuring is taking place (Eberhard and Gratwick, 2016). Full-scale privatization of generation and distribution entities has not taken place in the countries (AICD, 2008; World Bank, 2016). Neither all generation nor distribution entities in the SSA countries are entirely owned by either the private or the public sector (AICD, 2008; World Bank, 2016). Instead, the privatization of the entities had largely taken the form of partial private sector ownership through equities, awarding of concessions and management contracts (AICD, 2008; World Bank, 2016). As such competition among players is still limited.

According to the World Bank PPI database (2016), SSA countries such as: Ghana, Cote d'Ivoire, Kenya, Tanzania, Mauritius, and Nigeria are implementing more than one IPPs. Few of the IPPs have been successful (for example, the case of Kenya) (Eberhard and Gatwick, 2016). There are some potential positive effects of IPPs in improving generation capacity, even though acquiring them have been costly as a result of procurement difficulties and currency devaluation (Gratwick and Eberhard, 2008). Many of the management contracts, concessions and leases have been unsuccessful. About one-third of the projects have been cancelled (Eberhard and Gatwick, 2016). Eberhard & Gratwick (2016), in their review of public-private transactions in the power sector in SSA, writes that even in countries where management contracts, leases and concession were not an option due to unfavorable political climate, some donors still saw the need to continue to fund the projects with the hope that they can survive long enough to allow stronger institutions to sustain them. Eberhard & Gratwick (2016) further writes that even though the concerned governments deemed the ventures as infeasible, they allowed them anyways—for the sake of getting the much-needed funding for their power sectors. Successful long-term concessions have, however, survived in countries such as Uganda, Cape Verde, Gabon, Mali, Cote d'Ivoire and Cameroon (Eberhard and Gatwick, 2016).

While an increasing number of SSA countries are making progressive efforts towards full privatization by selling off more and more government shares in electric utilities, some other countries such as Senegal and Mali have reversed back to the national monopoly of electricity utilities (Eberhard and Gatwick, 2016). However, while examining some countries in the region such as Mauritius, South Africa and Zimbabwe, where utilities perform relatively better even without privatization, an important question of whether the liberalized model of power sector reform is the ultimate and only route to improved electricity sector performance comes up (Eberhard and Gatwick, 2016). Besant-Jones (2006), in his study on the power sector reform across countries, concluded that liberalized power sector reforms suites large economies with capacities to support multiple electricity utilities. This condition does not apply to most SSA countries.

The sub-section below discusses the experiences of selected SSA countries in implementing key electricity sector reform.

CORPORATIZATION

Being the first stage of the reform process, most SSA countries have commercialized their electricity sector (AICD, 2008; Eberhard & Gratwick, 2016). In most of the SSA countries where corporatization has taken place, it is a commonplace that government is the major shareholder (AICD, 2008; Eberhard & Gratwick, 2016). Experience shows that in comparison with state-owned utilities, commercialized utilities have indeed appeared to be more successful in improving the financial performance of SSA's electricity sector, by enhancing recovery of the cost of electricity production (tariff) and reduction in subsidies directed to the sector (Erdogdu, 2013; Kessides, 2012). This development has, however, led to increase in tariffs in the concerned countries (Jamasb et al., 2015). Table 3 below shows percentage tariff increases as of 2005 in selected countries.

Management Contracts

Management contracts are part of the larger process of corporatization in reformed countries (Pollitt, 2012). It is, therefore, a commonplace, particularly in West Africa (AICD, 2008; KPMG, 2016; UNIDO, 2005). Other countries that have contracted out their electricity utilities to private entities include: Uganda, Tanzania, Ghana, Malawi, Togo, and Guinea Bissau (Eberhard & Gratwick, 2016; AICD, 2008; UNIDO, 2005). In any case, these contracts are usually limited to operation management of utilities (Eberhard & Gratwick, 2016; AICD, 2008; UNIDO, 2005). Most of the assets and investment decisions are still held and made by the state (Eberhard & Gratwick, 2016; AICD, 2008). Most of the contracts have been majorly acquired by foreign private entities—particularly the French entities (Eberhard & Gratwick, 2016; AICD, 2008; UNIDO, 2005). However, in recent times African entities—championed by South African entities—are increasing their dominance in acquiring the management contracts (Eberhard &

Gratwick, 2016; AICD, 2008; UNIDO, 2005). Table 4 below shows case examples of the implementation of management contracts in selected SSA countries.

It is, however, important to note that there has been a recorded degree of dissatisfaction in the performance of the management contractors particularly in: Mali, Cameroon, Senegal, and to some extent in Cote d'Ivoire. There have been premature termination of management contracts in Senegal and Mali (Eberhard & Gratwick, 2016; AICD, 2008; UNIDO, 2005).

Table 3. Recent tariff Increases in selected SSA countries

Country	Average tariff Increase	Year of tariff review	Motive for tariff review
Ghana	326%	1998	General tariff review
Zimbabwe	70%	2000	Annual tariff review
Uganda	56%	2001	General tariff review
Malawi	35%	2000	Effect of foreign exchange adjustment
Kenya	25%	1999	General tariff review
Ethiopia	26%	1998	General tariff review
Eritrea	18%	2003	Annual tariff review
Namibia	10%	2001	Annual tariff review
Cameroon	8%	2004	Annual tariff review
Niger	6%	2002	Annual tariff review
South Africa	6%	2001	Annual tariff review

Sources: Author's Summary from UNIDO, 2005; AICD, 2008

Table 4. Implementation of management contracts in selected SSA countries

Country	Year first signed	Details and case examples
Cote d' Ivoire	1990	contract was signed between Energie Electricite de la Côte d'Ivoire (EECI) and the Compagnie Ivorienne d' Électricité (CIE)—comprising of French utilities as major shareholders. The contract was reviewed again in 2005 to last until 2016.
Guinea Bissau	1997	A private company called Société Guinéenne d' Électricité (SOGEL) was contracted to invest, oversee and manage renewable projects for 10 years. A supervisory authority regularly set the tariff.
Ghana	1997	The Ghanaian government through its electricity board, contracted EdF/SAUR to manage its utility customer service
Togo	2000	The *Compaigne d' Énergie Electrique du* Togo (CEET) contracted a renewable utility project for 5 years to be run and managed by Elyo-France and the Quebec Hydro.
Uganda	1999	Mr Paul Mare, who previously worked for Eskom, was contracted by the Ugandan Energy Board to be the new managing director of its electricity utilities.
Malawi	2001	—
Rwanda	2001	Electrogaz was placed under bid for the management contract.
Tanzania	2002	The Tanzanian Government contracted the Swedish/Swiss Asea Brown Bovery (ABB) and the South African Net Group Solutions (NGS) to run its gas turbines and its Tanzania Electric Service Company (TANESCO), respectively.

Sources: Author's Summary from UNIDO, 2005; AICD, 2008; Eberhard & Gratwick, 2016

Unbundling

Unbundling the electricity sector utilities in SSA were aimed at increasing competition among players as IPPs; and at gaining deeper and better insight into the performance of the now fragmentized utility systems (Jamasb et al., 2015, Kessides, 2012). This process was envisioned to have major positive impacts on the technical and financial performance of the utilities (Jamasb et al., 2015, Erdogdu, 2013). Horizontal unbundling has already taken place on a wide scale in many SSA countries (Jamasb et al., 2015). On the other hand, Vertical unbundling has been sparsely implemented (Eberhard & Gratwick, 2016; AICD, 2008; UNIDO, 2005). Table 5 below summarizes the few implementation cases of vertical unbundling.

Table 5. Cases of the implementation of vertical unbundling in selected SSA countries

Country	Date	Details	status
Kenya	1998	National utility was unbundled into generation and Transmission & distribution. The Generation utility was called the Kenyan Electricity Generation company. While the transmission & distribution utility was called the Kenyan Power and lightening company.	Implemented
Uganda	2001	The Uganda Energy Board (UEB) was unbundled, and three separate companies comprising of generation, transmission and distribution were created. There were the Uganda Electricity Generation Company, the Uganda Electricity Transmission Company, and the Uganda Electricity Distribution Company. The government also legislated for the creation of a Rural Electrification Agency as well as an independent regulator.	Implemented
Malawi	2002	The Electricity Supply Commission of Malawi was unbundled into generation and Transmission & distribution.	Implemented
South Africa	—	The South African government splitter out a regional distribution agency which is also responsible for electrification programmes.	Implemented
Zimbabwe	2002	National utility was split into generation and Transmission & distribution.	Implemented
Tanzania	—	In Tanzania, the national utility was also unbundled into generation and Transmission & distribution.	Implemented

Sources: Author's Summary from UNIDO (2005); AICD (2008).

Independent Power Producers (IPPs)

Independent Power Producers have increasingly played a role as private entities in electricity sector investment and operation in a high-demand-low-supply SSA electricity sector (Eberhard & Gratwick, 2016). By the end of 2002, about 40% of independent power projects were already operational, and another 20% were being planned (UNIDO, 2005). Table 6 below shows case examples of the implementation status of IPPs in selected SSA countries. Companies marked with an asterisk (*) are foreign firms.

Overall, there has been an increase in the growth of IPPs in SSA since the 1990s (World Bank, 2016; Eberhard & Gratwick, 2016). Most of the IPPs were large scale which required high capital investment, high technology knowledge (Eberhard & Gratwick, 2016; AICD, 2008; UNIDO, 2005). These kinds of large-scale projects mostly originated from foreign private investors (from the US, Western Europe and China) or the rich rent-seeking local investors (Eberhard & Gratwick, 2016; AICD, 2008; UNIDO, 2005). However, smaller-scale projects like small hydro and cogeneration plants were spearheaded by local investors; of which entry points were usually renewable energy projects (Eberhard & Gratwick, 2016; AICD, 2008; UNIDO, 2005).

Table 6. Implementation status of IPPs in selected SSA countries

Country	Name of IPPs	Total Size	Total Investment	Fuel	Companies	Implementation status
Ghana	Takoradi II; Tema	550 MW	$414 m	Oil, gas	CMS, VRA, KMR, Marubeni	Complete
Kenya	Tsavo; Kipevu II; Nairobi South plant; Olkaria III; Mombasa Barge-Mounted Power Project; Sondu Miriu; Olkaria III; Lanet and Eldoret	419 MW	$532.5 m	Oil, Geothermal, Hydro.	Tsavo Power Company*(synergy between Kenyan firms and foreign firms)	Complete
Cote d'Ivoire	Azito; Vridi	660 MW	$322.5 m	Gas	Cinergy, CIPREL	Complete
Tanzania	IPLT Power Project; Ubungo, Songo Songo	210 MW	$540 m	Oil, Gas	Tanwart* (synergy between Tanzanian firms and Malaysian firm), CDC, AES	Complete
Senegal	GTI-Dakar	50 MW	$62 m	Oil	General Electric*, IFC, Sondel*	Complete
Zambia	Lusemfwa Hydro Power Company, Itezhi-tezhi, Kafue Gorge Lower	1080 MW	$557.7 m	Hydro	OPPPI, Eskom Enterprises	Complete
Uganda	Bujagali, Kakira Sugar Works	262 MW	$561.3 m	Hydro, Bagasse	AES, Kakira Sugar Works	Complete
Sudan	Khartoum	200 MW	$267 m	Hydro	Harpen Wang Chen*	Complete

Sources: Author's Summary from UNIDO, 2005; AICD, 2008; and Eberhard & Gratwick, 2016

Electricity Law Amendment

The Electricity Act contains the legal, regulatory framework in most SSA countries (Eberhard & Gratwick, 2016; Gboney, 2009). These acts which catered for a monopolized government-owned utilities are then amended to provide for the pursued liberalized electric utilities in the respective countries (AICD, 2008; UNIDO, 2005). Most SSA countries where the electricity reforms are going on have amended their acts, except Tanzania (Eberhard & Gratwick, 2016; AICD, 2008; UNIDO, 2005). The amendments usually provide for the establishment of an independent regulatory agency, private sector participation, renewable and cogeneration electrification, among others (Eberhard & Gratwick, 2016; AICD, 2008; UNIDO, 2005). Table 7 below shows changes in the legal and regulatory framework in electricity sector reform in implemented SSA countries.

IMPACTS OF ELECTRICITY SECTOR REFORMS ON ELECTRICITY SECTOR PERFORMANCE IN SSA

This section reviews empirical studies on the impacts of electricity sector reform on electricity sector performance in SSA. They are discussed under the sub-sections of: productivity and economic efficiency; quality of service and system efficiency; electricity pricing; and electricity access.

Table 7. Changes in the legal and regulatory framework in electricity sector reform in implemented SSA countries

Provision in the electricity act	Previous legal and regulatory framework	New legal and regulatory framework
Regulatory agency	regulated by the state ministry in cooperation with the public utility	regulated by an independent regulatory agency
Rural Electrification Agency	administered by state ministry concerned with national electricity	administered by an independent body
Licensing of IPPs for own use	application through concerned state ministry through the public utility	administered mainly through the Electricity Regulatory Board (ERB); with a few exceptions (example, Kenya) where application is still through concerned state ministry—but with advice from the ERB
Licensing of IPPs for sale to public utility	None existence. The national public utility reserves the sole responsibility of generation of electricity	administered through Power Purchase Agreement (PPA) approved by the ERB
Licensing of Independent Power Distributors (IPDs)	None existence. The national public utility reserves the sole responsibility of distribution of electricity	administered by the ERB
Gazette of license application and license granted	Not mandatory. Private power generations are licensed for applicants' private utilization.	License applications are mandatory requirements for the regulatory agency or the applicant. License granted are also mandatory in some countries.
Tariff setting	proposed by the utility and approved by the ministry	proposed by utility and administered by the regulatory body. The regulatory agency in some countries (for example, Kenya) reserves the right to review the tariff without consultation with the utility.
Appeals and dispute resolution	through the state law courts	through the regulatory body, ministry, arbitration tribunals and state law courts.

Sources: Author's Summary from UNIDO, 2005 and AICD, 2008

Impacts on Productivity and Economic Efficiency

The extensive privatization efforts of the electricity sector of SSA countries were driven by the need to improve productivity and economic efficiency in electricity production and delivery (Jamasb et al., 2015). Impacts of the reforms on productivity and efficiency have, however, been sparsely studied in SSA. Most studies have been on other regions or have been restricted on a global scale. There is, however, evidence that countries with privatized electricity sector have better-performed utilities than those without privatization. These evidence manifest in the form of increase in labor productivity and technical scale efficiency as found in the research carried out by Politt 2008; Fischer, Gutierrey and Serra, 2003; Cullman and von Hirschhausen, 2008; and Celen, 2013.

However, the extent of improvement in performance differs across countries and economies (Ramos-Real et al., 2009; Galan and Pollitt, 2014). In a non-parametric study of 27 least developing countries, Yuno and Hawdon (1997) found that competition is an important prerequisite for privatization to lead to higher efficiency and productivity. They write that simple exchange of ownership and management of assets does not lead to improved productivity and efficiency in itself (Yuno and Hawdon, 1997). Competition in privatized utilities in SSA has been proven to be often hampered as a result of undue government interference in the contract awarding process and undue influences on regulatory agencies (Politt, 1995). Yuno and Hawdon (1997) also noted significant differences in productivity and efficiency of small and large-scale providers; with higher productivity found in large-scale investments. This implies that the mostly smaller-scale investments in SSA electricity utilities also mean relatively lower average productivity and efficiency. ESMAP (2011) identifies the existence of an independent regulator as another important prerequisite.

Plane (1999), in his parametric analysis of the impact of the privatization of electricity sector in Cote d'Ivoire, reported a significant increase in utility productivity and performance after privatization have been implemented. He, however, noted that the increase in performance, especially technical efficiency and productivity, have been irregular over the post-privatization years. Estache, Tovar and Trujillo (2008), using a non-parametric analysis on a sample of 12 operators from 12 Southern African countries to measure the impact of reforms on total factor productivity (TFP), records a similar performance and efficiency level across the examined countries but notes an unclear relationship between adoption of the liberalized electricity sector reform and increase in efficiency.

Impacts on Quality of Service and System Efficiency

One of the main aims of the widespread reforms of the electricity sector of SSA countries were to increase the efficiency of existing capacities, reduce energy losses, increase the quality of service of utilities, add new capacities to existing ones; and by so doing improve access to the quality electricity supply (Joskow, 1998; Briceno-Garmendia, Estache and Nemat, 2004). A panel data analyses of impacts on technical and distribution (T&D) loses in SSA countries carried out by ESMAP (2009), proves otherwise. Average T&D loses in SSA stood at about 28% in 2009, with huge variations across countries—with Angola having an average system loss of 14.5% and Swaziland 68% (ESMAP, 2009).

Cubbin and Stern (2004 & 2006) and Zhang et al. (2005 & 2008) in their panel analyses of a set of developing countries (including SSA countries), show that the existence of independent regulatory agency and competition is a condition that must be satisfied for a meaningful increase in per capita electricity generation, capacity and quality of service of utilities. These findings were supported by Nagayama (2010) in his multi-country panel data analyses of developing and developed countries. Nagayama (2010) found that IPPs, unbundling, wholesale market and regulatory bodies, together, lead to a reduction in transmission and distribution losses.

Nepal and Jamasb (2012) confirm that privatization on its own did not lead to an improvement in electricity sector performance. Yunos and Hawdon (1997) also observe that privatization without accompanying competition does not have any effect on the efficiency of electricity supply. Many of these conditions are yet to be fulfilled in most of the countries analyzed in this study. There are often no or irregular efficiency gains as a result of privatized management in most developing economies (Plane, 1999; Estache, Tovar and Trujillo, 2008). In some developing countries cases, public utilities were found to be more efficient in the management of electric utilities than private utilities (Jamasb et al., 2015; Erdogdu 2013b; AICD, 2008).

Progress in reforms has led to increases in system losses in many developing countries due to the simultaneous decrease in national government research and utility development investments (Hall, 1999 and Erdogdu, 2013b). This may also be a contributing factor to the increase in system losses in some of the implementing SSA countries.

Impacts on Electricity Pricing

The liberalized model of electricity sector reform is expected to introduce competition in the industry by attracting many new players into the market (Fan, Liao & Wei, 2007). The competition introduced through the reforms is expected to increase efficiency and decrease the cost of electricity production; thereby bringing electricity prices to an optimal lower level (Yang and Sharma, 2012). However, the impacts of the reforms on electricity tariff in most developing countries are not significant. In other cases, the outcomes are mixed. Politt (1995) and Nagayama (2007) in their analyses of these impacts write that country-level political interference in investment decision making, awarding of contracts and IPPs, and undue influences of independent regulatory agencies; limits and prevent the significant positive impact of electricity sector reforms on the electricity tariff. ESMAP (2011) study of the impact using a panel data of 20 countries with varied system sizes show that vertical unbundling has reduced electricity tariff by an average of just 10%.

Electricity subsidies often make the capturing of the true impacts of reforms on the tariffs unclear (Jamasb et al., 2015). Nagayama (2009), in his panel data analyses of 75 developed, developing and transitioning economies, shows a decline in national electricity subsidies after the commencement of reforms in many developing countries, including in some SSA countries. Situations like this make it difficult to measure the impact of the reforms on electricity prices if the subsidies are not taken into consideration. There have always been relatively high tariffs before the reforms in SSA countries (Jamasb et al., 2015). Electricity prices have remained constant or have slightly increased regardless of the reforms in most SSA countries, but this has also been accompanied by the reduction in electricity tariff subsidies in some cases (Eberhard et al, 2011). However, in SSA countries such as Angola, Malawi, South Africa, Zambia, Nigeria and Zimbabwe, high tariffs exist with high electricity tariff subsidies (Eberhard et al, 2011).

Impacts on Electricity Access

Increasing national population access to electricity was also one of the major reasons for the widespread liberalization of the electricity sector in SSA (Jamasb et al., 2015). Participation of the private sector was expected to increase the number of investors in electricity generation and capacity thereby increasing access to electricity (Zhang et al., 2008). Several findings, however, prove that this is not always the case in SSA (Zhang et al., 2008; Eberhard et al, 2011). There is also scarce information on the impact on access to the poor and coverage for people who live in rural areas. Prasad (2008) in his multi-country analysis of SSA countries find that access is only improved when reforms are specifically targeted towards improving access to the poor. Multi-country analyses by ESMAP (2011) show that the existence of independent regulatory agencies helps to improve general electricity access by 50%. This finding was supported by Erdogdu's (2014) finding that reforms can lead to system supply self-sufficiency only in the presence of necessary prerequisites—independent regulatory agencies and competition.

CONCLUSIONS, POLICY IMPLICATIONS AND RECOMMENDATIONS

The existence of independent regulatory agencies, institutional quality, and competition seem to be major determinant factors in the success of the electricity sector reforms in many developing countries, particularly in SSA countries (Jamasb et al., 2015; Nepal, 2013; Eberhard et al., 2011). Several of the reviewed studies found that they have a significant positive impact on electricity access, electricity installation and generation as well as on the efficiency of supply (example, Jamasb et al., 2015; Nepal, 2013; Eberhard et al., 2011; Vagliasindi et al., 2010). They have also been shown to be important in keeping the balance between increased investment, welfare and equality of access (Jamasb et al., 2015; ESMAP, 2005; Davies et al., 2006). There has to be an existing suitable political and social framework suited according to the needs of individual countries to ensure and guide the implementation of reform if success is to be achieved (Jamasb et al., 2015; Zhang et al., 2008).

Explanation of the reform processes, objectives, and importance as well as transparency in the implementation of the reform will go a long way to counter the problems of theft, reluctant and non-payment of electricity tariffs in many SSA countries (Eberhard and Gratwick, 2016; Jamasb et al., 2015). The price increase burden as a result of reform implementation due to accompanying removal of electricity subsidies should be well planned and mapped out in phases to reduce adverse impacts on electricity consumers (Eberhard and Gratwick, 2016; Jamasb et al., 2015). It is also essential to chart specific reform routes for individual countries according to existing political, social and institutional circumstances in the countries instead of relying on international paradigm or ideologies of electricity sector reform will go a long way to improving reform outcome in SSA countries (Nepal and Jamasb, 2012; Nepal, 2013; Eberhard et al., 2011).

Two ways for improving the effectiveness of reforms are by implementing hybrid electricity markets and by ensuring the effectiveness of regulatory institutions through complementary regulatory measures (Eberhard and Gratwick, 2016; Kessides, 2012). These two recommendations are discussed below.

Hybrid Markets as Alternative

Following the ineffectiveness of the liberalized electricity reform model in most SSA countries, some recent researchers have supported hybrid markets as alternatives (Eberhard, 2007; Eberhard and Gratwick, 2016; Kessides, 2012). Hybrid electricity market implies that the state has control over electricity utilities, but simultaneously creates room for potential PSP for complementarity (Eberhard, 2007; Eberhard and Gratwick, 2016). It often manifests in the form of PPP. The Hybrid electricity market structure is particularly beneficial in the African context because it can curtail corruption on the part of government and selfishness on the part of private investors. In this way, optimal outcomes can be achieved through embedded checks and balances.

This market structure, however, comes with challenges such as uncertainty on whose responsibility it is to ensure adequate and reliable electricity supply or to make plans for procuring new electric utility infrastructure (a typical case for Tanzania and Rwanda) (AICD, 2008). Plans for procurement of new electricity utility infrastructure should be left in hands of state-owned utilities—who usually have relatively more resources and professional staff (Eberhard and Gratwick, 2016; Eberhard, 2007; Kessides, 2012). Procurement plans should also consider least possible cost options through competitive bidding processes (Eberhard and Gratwick, 2016; Kessides, 2012).

There should also be a strong monitoring oversight for detecting potential and viable opportunities for new capacity investment; setting clear and transparent criteria for building new IPPs among existing state-owned utilities as well as for takeoff of operations of completed projects; ensure adequate and reliable electricity supply; all in a manner that suits national interest as opposed to utilities interests (Jamasb et al., 2015; Eberhard and Gratwick, 2016; Kessides, 2012; Eberhard, 2007). These monitory functions can also be integrated into the functions of already existing regulatory agencies in the concerned countries (Eberhard and Gratwick, 2016; Eberhard, 2007; Kessides, 2012).

Complementary Regulatory Frameworks

State regulatory agencies were initially set up to: 1) ensure financial viability and fair tariff; 2) attract new investments and 3) encourage cost and performance efficiency (Newbery, 2002; Pollitt, 2012). These regulatory institutions were later made independent to ensure the actualization of these duties without undue political influences (Newbery, 2002; Pollitt, 2012). Notwithstanding the existence of independent regulatory agencies in some SSA countries, and the extents of implementation in these countries are still unclear (Zhang et al., 2008; Jamasb et al., 2015). These agencies have been criticized for being weak and for lacking in capacity and experiences for making such important decision which has social and political consequences—thereby exacerbating existing regulatory problems (Eberhard, 2007; Eberhard and Gratwick, 2016).

Strategies some developing countries have used in improving the independence of their regulatory oversights include: contracting regulatory functions to foreign agencies usually located in their former colonial countries (Cubbin and Stern, 2004; Eberhard and Gratwick, 2016); outsourcing regulatory functions to technical consultants and expert panels funded by the state ministries (Eberhard and Gratwick, 2016); and establishing panels which serve as arbitrators in issues or conflicts between regulators and utilities (Eberhard and Gratwick, 2016).

The efficiency of regulatory institution in SSA have been shown to improve significantly when there are co-existence of different forms of regulatory agencies—such as the co-existence of established independent regulatory agency in a country with foreign regulatory agencies inform of contracts; or the co-existence of established independent regulatory agency in a country with regulatory technical consultants and expert panels (Zhang et al., 2008; Jamasb et al., 2015; Nepal, 2013; Nepal and Jamasb; 2012).

REFERENCES

Acemoglu, D., & Robinson, J. L. (2010). The Role of Institutions in Growth and Development. *Revista de Economia Institucional*, *1*(2), 1–33.

AICD – Africa Infrastructure Country Diagnostic. (2008). *Power Sector Database*. World Bank.

Akinyemi, O., Efobi, U., Asongu, S., & Osabuohien, E. (2019). Renewable energy, trade performance and the conditional role of finance and institutional capacity in sub-Saharan African Countries. *Energy Policy*, *132*, 490–498. doi:10.1016/j.enpol.2019.06.012

Akinyemi, O., Osabuohien, E., Alege, P., & Ogundipe, A. (2017). Energy Security, Trade and Transition to Green Economy in Africa. *International Journal of Energy Economics and Policy*, *7*(3), 127–136.

Bacon, R. W., & Besant-Jones, J. (2001). Global Electric Power Reform: Privatization and Liberalization of the Electric Power Industry in Developing Countries. *Annual Review of Energy and the Environment*, *26*(1), 33–59. doi:10.1146/annurev.energy.26.1.331

Besant-Jones, J. E. (2006). *Reforming Power Markets in Developing Countries: What Have We Learnt?* Energy and Mining Sector Board Discussion Paper, the World Bank Group No. 19.

Briceno-Garmendia, C., Estache, A., & Nemat, S. (2004). *Infrastructure Services in Developing Countries: Access, Quality, Costs and Policy Reform*. Policy Research Working Paper Series 3468, the World Bank.

Celen, A. (2013). Efficiency and Productivity (TFP) of the Turkish Electricity Distribution Companies: An Application of Two-Stage (DEA & Tobit) Analysis. *Energy Policy*, *63*(10), 300–310. doi:10.1016/j.enpol.2013.09.034

Cubbin, J., & Stern, J. (2004). *Regulatory Effectiveness: The Impact of Good Regulatory Governance on Electricity Industry Capacity and Efficiency in Developing Countries*. Policy Research Working Paper 3536, the World Bank, Washington D.C.

Cubbin, J., & Stern, J. (2006). The Impact of Regulatory Governance and Privatization on Electricity Industry Generation Capacity in Developing Economies. *The World Bank Economic Review*, *20*(1), 115–141. doi:10.1093/wber/lhj004

Cullmann, A., & Hirschhausen, C. V. (2008). From Transition to Competition. *Economics of Transition*, *16*(2), 335–357. doi:10.1111/j.1468-0351.2008.00312.x

Davies, L., Wright, K., & Price, C. W. (2006). *Experience of Privatization, Regulation and Competition: Lessons for Governments*. ESRC Centre for Competition Policy, University of East Anglia, UK. CCP Working Paper 05-5.

Dilip, J. (2015). *What are the key indicators of successful reforms? A comparative analysis of United Kingdom (UK) and Ghana*. University of Dundee, CEPMLP - Centre for Energy, Petroleum and Mineral Law and Policy, Graduate Student. Academia.edu. https://www.academia.edu/10473243/What_are_the_key_indicators_of_successful_reforms_A_comparative_analysis_of_United_Kingdom_UK_and_Ghana

Eberhard, A. (2007). *Matching Regulatory Design to Country Circumstances: The Potential of Hybrid and Transitional Models. Gridlines Note 23, PPIAF*. World Bank.

Eberhard, A., & Gratwick, K. N. (2016). *New Models to Scale up Investment in Power Generation in Sub-Saharan Africa*. World Bank.

Eberhard, R., & Shkaratan, V. (2011). *Africa's Power Infrastructure: Investment, Integration, Efficiency*. The World Bank. doi:10.1596/978-0-8213-8455-8

EIA. (2000). *The Changing Structure of the Electric Power Industry 2000: An Update. Energy Information Administration*. Office of Coal, Nuclear, Electric and Alternate Fuels, U.S. Department of Energy. Washington, DC 20585. DOE/EIA-0562(00). Distribution Category UC-950. October.

Erdogdu, E. (2013a). *Essays on Electricity Market Reforms: A Cross-Country Applied Approach* (PhD Thesis). University of Cambridge, UK.

Erdogdu, E. (2013b). Implications of Liberalization Policies on Government Support to R&D: Lessons for Electricity Markets. *Renewable & Sustainable Energy Reviews*, *17*(1), 110–118. doi:10.1016/j.rser.2012.09.030

Erdogdu, E. (2014). Investment, Security of Supply and Sustainability in the Aftermath of Three Decades of Power Sector Reform. *Renewable & Sustainable Energy Reviews*, *31*(3), 1–8. doi:10.1016/j.rser.2013.11.014

ESMAP. (2005). *Power Sector Reform in Africa: Assessing Impact on Poor People*. The Joint UNDP/World Bank Energy Sector Management Assistance Program (ESMAP). Report 306/05. August.

ESMAP. (2009). *Monitoring Performance of Electric Utilities: Indicators and Benchmarking in Sub-Saharan Africa. The Energy Sector Management Assistance Program*. The World Bank.

ESMAP. (2011). *Revisiting Policy Options on the Market Structure in the Power Sector. The Energy Sector and Mining Assistance Program (ESMAP)*. The World Bank.

Estache, A., Tovar, B., & Trujillo, L. (2008). How Efficient are African Electricity Companies? Evidence from the Southern African Countries. *Energy Policy*, *36*(6), 1969–1979. doi:10.1016/j.enpol.2008.02.011

Fan, Y., Liao, H., & Wei, Y.-M. (2007). Can Market Oriented Economic Reforms Contribute to Energy Efficiency Improvement? Evidence from China. *Energy Policy*, *35*(4), 2287–2295. doi:10.1016/j.enpol.2006.07.011

Fischer, R., Gutierrez, R., & Serra, P. (2003). *The Effects of Privatization on Firms and on Social Welfare: The Chilean Case*. Inter-American Development Bank Research Network Working Paper R-456, May.

Galan, J. E., & Pollitt, M. (2014). *Inefficiency Persistence and Heterogeneity in Colombian Electricity Distribution Utilities*. EPRG Working Paper 1403, Faculty of economics, University of Cambridge.

Gboney, W. K. (2009). *Econometric Assessment of the Impact of Power Sector Reforms in Africa: A Study of the Generation, Transmission and Distribution Sectors* (PhD thesis). City University, London.

Gratwick, K., & Eberhard, A. (2008). Demise of the Standard Model for Power sector Reform and the Emergence of Hybrid Power Markets. *Energy Policy*, *36*(10), 3948–3960. doi:10.1016/j.enpol.2008.07.021

Gratwick, K. N., & Eberhard, A. (2008). An Analysis of Independent Power Projects in Africa: Understanding Development and Investment Outcomes. *Development Policy Review*, *26*(3), 309–338. doi:10.1111/j.1467-7679.2008.00412.x

Hall, D. (1999). *Electricity Restructuring, Privatization and Liberalization: Some International Experiences*. Public Services International Research Unit, University of Greenwich, October.

IEA. (2014). *Africa Energy Outlook: A Focus on Energy Prospects in Sub-Saharan Africa. World Energy Outlook Special Report*. World Energy Outlook series. International Energy Agency. https://www.iea.org/publications/freepublications/publication/WEO2014_AfricaEnergyOutlook.pdf

IEA. (2016). *Boosting the Power Sector in Sub-Saharan Africa: China's Involvement*. International Energy Agency. https://www.iea.org/publications/freepublications/publication/Partner_Country_SeriesChinaBoosting_the_Power_Sector_in_SubSaharan_Africa_Chinas_Involvement.pdf

Jamasb, T. (2004). Between the state and market: Electricity Sector Reform in Developing Countries. *Utilities Policies*, 14-30.

Jamasb, T., Nepal, R., & Timilsina, G. R. (2015). *A Quarter Century Effort Yet to Come of Age: A Survey of Power Sector Reforms in Developing Countries*. Policy Research Working Paper No 7330. World Bank Group, Washington DC.

Joskow, P. L. (1998). Electricity Sectors in Transition. *Energy Journal, 19*(2), 25–28. doi:10.5547/ISSN0195-6574-EJ-Vol19-No2-3

Joskow. P. L. (2008). Lessons Learned From Electricity Market Liberalization. *The Energy Journal, 0*(S1), p. 9-42.

Kessides, I. N. (2012, July). The Impacts of Electricity Sector Reforms in Developing Countries. *The Electricity Journal, 25*(6), 79–88. doi:10.1016/j.tej.2012.07.002

KPMG. (2016). *Sub-Saharan Africa Power Outlook 2016*. KPMG Africa Infrastructure. https://assets.kpmg.com/content/dam/kpmg/pdf/2016/05/kpmg-sub-saharan-africa-power-outlook.pdf

Ljung, P. (2007). *Energy Sector Reform: Strategies for Growth, Equity and Sustainability. Sidastudies no. 20*. Swedish International Development Cooperation Agency.

Makwe, J., Akinwale, Y., & Atoyebi, M. (2012). An Economic Assessment of the Reform of Nigerian Electricity Market. *Energy and Power, 2*(3), 24–32. doi:10.5923/j.ep.20120203.01

Megginson, W. L., & Netter, J. M. (2001). From State to Market: A Survey of Empirical Studies on Privatization. *Journal of Economic Literature, 39*(2), 321–389. doi:10.1257/jel.39.2.321

Nagayama, H. (2007). Effects of Regulatory reforms in the Electricity Supply Industry on Electricity Prices in Developing Countries. *Energy Policy, 35*(6), 3440–3462. doi:10.1016/j.enpol.2006.12.018

Nagayama, H. (2010). Impacts on Investments, and Transmission/Distribution Loss through Power Sector Reforms. *Energy Policy, 38*(7), 3453–3467. doi:10.1016/j.enpol.2010.02.019

Nellis, J. (2008). *Private Management Contracts in Power Sector in Sub-Saharan Africa. Internal note, Africa Infrastructure Country Diagnostic*. World Bank.

Nepal, R. (2013). *From State to Market: Essays on Electricity Sector Reforms* (PhD Thesis). Heriot-Watt University, Edinburgh, UK.

Nepal, R., & Jamasb, T. (2012). Reforming the Power Sector in Transition: Do Institutions Matter? *Energy Economics, 34*(5), 1675–1682. doi:10.1016/j.eneco.2012.02.002

Newbery, D. (1995). Power Markets and Market Power. *Energy Journal, 16*(3), 41–66. doi:10.5547/ISSN0195-6574-EJ-Vol16-No3-2

Newbery, D. (2002). *Issues and options for restructuring electricity supply industries*. DAE Working Paper WP 0210. Cambridge: Department of Applied Economics, University of Cambridge.

Plane, P. (1999). Privatization, Technical Efficiency and Welfare Consequences: The Case of the Côte d'Ivorie Electricity Company (CIE). *World Development, 27*(2), 343–360. doi:10.1016/S0305-750X(98)00139-9

Pollitt, M. (2008). Electricity reform in Argentina: Lessons for Developing Countries. *Energy Economics, 30*(4), 1536–1567. doi:10.1016/j.eneco.2007.12.012

Pollitt, M. G. (1995). *Technical Efficiency in Electrical Power Plants*. Cambridge Working Papers in Economics 9422, Faculty of Economics, University of Cambridge.

Pollitt, M. G. (2012). The Role of Policy in Energy Transitions: Lessons from the Energy Liberalisation Era. *Energy Policy*, *50*, 128–137. doi:10.1016/j.enpol.2012.03.004

Prasad, G. (2008). Energy sector reform, Energy Transitions and the Poor in Africa. *Energy Policy*, *36*(8), 2806–2811. doi:10.1016/j.enpol.2008.02.042

Prasad, G. (2011). Improving Access to Energy in Sub-Saharan Africa. *Energy Policy*, *3*(4), 248–253.

Ramos-Real, F. J., Tovar, B., de Almeida, E. F., & Pinto, H. Q. (2009). The Evolution and Main Determinants of Productivity in the Brazilian Electricity Distribution 1998-2005: An Empirical Analysis. *Energy Economics*, *31*(2), 298–305. doi:10.1016/j.eneco.2008.11.002

Sen, A., & Jamasb, T. (2012). Diversity in Unity: An Empirical Analysis of Electricity Deregulation in Indian States. *Energy Journal*, *33*(1), 83–130. doi:10.5547/ISSN0195-6574-EJ-Vol33-No1-4

Singh, A. (2002). *Competition and Competition Policy in Emerging Markets: International and Developmental Dimensions*. Research papers for the Intergovernmental Group of Twenty-Four on International Monetary Affairs. G-24 Discussion Paper No. 18. September.

UNIDO. (2005). *The reform of the power sector in Africa*. Sustainable energy regulation and policymaking training manual. Module 4.

UNIDO. (forthcoming). *Impact of Different Power Sector Reform Options on Energy Efficiency in Africa. Sustainable Energy Regulation and Policymaking for Africa*. Advance Copy. https://www.unido.org/fileadmin/import/83270_Module16.pdf

Vagliasindi, M., & Nellis, J. (2010). *Evaluating Africa's Experience with Institutional Reform in Infrastructure Sectors*. AICD Working Paper 22, World Bank, Washington, DC.

World Bank. (2016). *Private Participation in Infrastructure (PPI) Database*. Washington, DC: World Bank. https://ppi.worldbank.org/data

Yang, M., & Sharma, D. (2012, February). *The Impacts of Electricity Reforms on Electricity Prices. 3rd IAEE Asian Conference*, Tokyo, Japan.

Yunos, J. M., & Hawdon, D. (1997). The Efficiency of the National Electricity Board in Malaysia: An Inter-country Comparison Using DEA. *Energy Economics*, *19*(2), 255–269. doi:10.1016/S0140-9883(96)01018-3

Zhang, Y. F., Parker, D., & Kirkpatrick, C. (2005). Competition, Regulation and Privatization of Electricity Generation in Developing Countries: Does the Sequencing of the Reforms Matter? *The Quarterly Review of Economics and Finance*, *45*(2-3), 358–379. doi:10.1016/j.qref.2004.12.009

Zhang, Y.-F., Parker, D., & Kirkpatrick, C. (2008). Electricity Sector Reform in Developing Countries: An Econometric Assessment of the Effects of Privatization, Competition and Regulation. *Journal of Regulatory Economics*, *33*(2), 159–178. doi:10.100711149-007-9039-7

Compilation of References

Abbrey, J., Bagah, D. A., & Wulifan, J. K. (2015). The Relevance of Business Planning Document for Small and Medium Scale Enterprises in Tamale Metropolis, Northern Ghana. *Journal of Business Administration and Education.*, *7*(1), 34–80.

Abolaji, J. (2010). The interface between Corporate Vision, Mission and Production and Operations Management. *Global Journal of Management and Business Research, 10*(2), 18–22.

Abraha, M., & Savage, M. (2006). Potential impacts of climate change on the grain yield of maize for the midlands of KwaZulu-Natal, South Africa. *Agriculture, Ecosystems & Environment, 115*(1-4), 150–160. doi:10.1016/j.agee.2005.12.020

Abubakar, I. R. (2017). Access to sanitation facilities among Nigerian households: Determinants and sustainability implications. *Sustainability, 9*(4), 547. doi:10.3390/su9040547

Abubakar, S. (2020). Institutional Quality and Economic Growth: Evidence from Nigeria. *African Journal of Economic Review, 8*(I).

Abugu, U. (2012). *Land Use and Reform in Nigeria: Law and Practice* (1st ed.). Immaculate Prints.

Acemoglu, D., & Johnson, S. (2005). Unbundling Institutions. *Journal of Political Economy, 113*(5), 949–995. doi:10.1086/432166

Acemoglu, D., Johnson, S., & Robinson, J. A. (2001). The colonial origins of comparative development: An empirical investigation. *The American Economic Review, 91*(5), 1369–1401. doi:10.1257/aer.91.5.1369

Acemoglu, D., & Robinson, J. (2012). *Why Nations Fail: The Origins of Power, Prosperity, and Poverty.* Crown Business Publisher.

Acemoglu, D., & Robinson, J. L. (2010). The Role of Institutions in Growth and Development. *Revista de Economia Institucional, 1*(2), 1–33.

Action Plan, E. U. (2019). Stepping up EU Action to Protect and Restore the World's Forests. Communication from the Commission to the European Parliament, the Council, the European Economic and Social Committee and the Committee of the Regions.

Act, L. U. (1978). Federal Republic of Nigeria Official Gazette. No.14. *Federal Ministry of Information, Printing Division, Lagos, Nigeria, 65*, 2–6.

Adam, J. N., Freeman, C. K., & Dassah, E. Z. (2017). Access to dry season water and small ruminants market integration in the Nadowli District of Upper West Region of Ghana. *Journal of Agricultural Extension and Rural Development, 9*(11), 262–269. doi:10.5897/JAERD2017.0913

Adams, M., & Palmer, R. (2007). *Independent Review of Land Issues: Eastern and Southern Africa* (vol. 3). Available online at online at https://www.oxfam.org.uk/resources/learning/landrights/downloads/independent_review_land_issues_eastern_and_southern_africa_2006_07.pdf

Adedeji, O., Olafiaji, E., Omole, F., Olanibi, J., & Yusuf, L. (2014). An assessment of the impact of road transport on rural development: A case study of Obokun local government area of Osun State, Nigeria. *British Journal of Environmental Sciences*, *2*(1), 34–48.

Adeleye, N., Osabuohien, E. S., Adeogun, S., Fashola, S., Tasie, O., & Adeyemi, G. (2020). Access to Land and Food Security: Analysis of 'Priority Crops' Production in Ogun State, Nigeria. In E. Osabuohien (Ed.), *The Palgrave Handbook of Agricultural and Rural Development in Africa*. Palgrave Macmillan. doi:10.1007/978-3-030-41513-6_14

Adeleye, N., Osabuohien, E., & Asongu, S. (2020). Agro-Industrialisation and Financial Intermediation in Nigeria. *African Journal of Economic and Management Studies*, *11*(3), 443–456. Advance online publication. doi:10.1108/AJEMS-02-2019-0078

Adeleye, N., Osabuohien, E., & Bowale, E. (2017). The Role of Institutions in the Finance-Inequality Nexus in Sub-Saharan Africa. *Journal of Contextual Economics*, *137*(1-2), 173–192. doi:10.3790/jce.137.1-2.173

Aderamo, A., & Magaji, S. (2010). Rural transportation and the distribution of public facilities in Nigeria: A case of Edu local government area of Kwara State. *Journal of Human Ecology (Delhi, India)*, *29*(3), 171–179. doi:10.1080/09709274.2010.11906260

Adesina, A. A., & Zinnah, M. M. (1993). Technology characteristics, farmers' perceptions and adoption decisions: A Tobit model application in Sierra Leone. *Agricultural Economics*, *4*(4), 297–311. doi:10.1111/j.1574-0862.1993.tb00276.x

Adewole, M. A., & Osabuohien, E. S. (2007). Analysis of the Cost of Governance and Options for Its Reduction in Nigeria. *The Nigerian Journal of Economic and Social Studies*, *49*(1), 137–159.

Adger, W. N. (2003). Social Capital, Collective Action, and Adaptation to Climate Change. *Economic Geography*, *79*(4), 387–404. doi:10.1111/j.1944-8287.2003.tb00220.x

Adhikari, K., & Hartemink, A. E. (2015). Linking soils to ecosystem services— A global review. *Geoderma*, *262*, 101–111. doi:10.1016/j.geoderma.2015.08.009

Adom, D., & Kquofi, S. (2016). The high impacts of Asante indigenous knowledge in biodiversity conservation issues in Ghana: The case of the Abono and Essumeja Townships in Ashanti Region. *British Journal of Environmental Sciences*, *4*(3), 63–78.

Adu, G., Marbuah, G., & Mensah, J. T. (2013). Financial development and economic growth in Ghana: Does the measure of financial development matter? *Review of Development Finance*, *3*(4), 192–203. doi:10.1016/j.rdf.2013.11.001

Adusei, M. (2013). Financial development and economic growth: Evidence from Ghana. *International Journal of Business and Finance Research*, *7*(5), 61–76.

African Development Bank (AfDB). (2018). *African economic outlook, 2018*. African Development Bank. Retrieved from www.afdb.org

African Development Bank (AfDB). (2020). *Socio-economic database*. Retrieved from: https://dataportal.opendataforafrica.org/nbyenxf/afdb-socio-economic-database-1960-2020

African Development Bank -AfDB Report. (2008). *Hydropower Resource Assessment in Africa*. Report of the Ministerial Conference, Libyan Arab Jamahiriya.

African Union Development Agency – NEPAD. (2020, February). First Continental Report on the Implementation of Agenda 2063. Midrand, South Africa: NEPAD.

African Union, Economic Commission for Africa, African Development Bank, & United Nations Development Programme. (2016). MDGs to Agenda 2063/SDGsTransition Report 2016. Towards an integrated and coherent approach to sustainable development in Africa. Addis Ababa: AU, ECA, AfDP, UNDP.

Afriyie, K., Ganle, J. K., & Santos, E. (2017). 'The floods came and we lost everything': Weather extremes and households' asset vulnerability and adaptation in rural Ghana. *Climate and Development*, *10*(3), 259–274. doi:10.1080/17565529.2017.1291403

Aga & Peria. (2014). *International remittances and financial inclusion in Africa*. World Bank.

Agarwal, B. (2011). Participatory exclusions, community forestry and gender: An analysis for South Asia and a conceptual framework. *World Development*, *29*(10), 1623–1648. doi:10.1016/S0305-750X(01)00066-3

Aggarwal, R., Demirguc-Kunt, A., Soledad, M., & Peria, M. (2011). Do Emittances Promote Financial Development? *Journal of Development Economics*, *96*(2), 255–264. doi:10.1016/j.jdeveco.2010.10.005

Aguilar, G. R., & Sumner, A. (2020). Who are the world's poor? A new profile of global multidimensional poverty. *World Development*, *126*, 104716. doi:10.1016/j.worlddev.2019.104716

Agula, C., Mabe, F. N., Akudugu, M. A., Sittoh, S., Ayambila, S. N., & Bawah, A. (2019). Enhancing healthy ecosystems in Northern Ghana through eco-friendly farm-based practices: Insights from irrigation scheme types. *BMC Ecology*, *19*(1), 38. doi:10.118612898-019-0254-8 PMID:31511000

Ahlborg, H., & Hammar, L. (2014). Drivers and barriers to rural electrification in Tanzania and Mozambique: Grid extension, off-grid and renewable energy technologies. *Renewable Energy*, *61*, 117–124. doi:10.1016/j.renene.2012.09.057

Ahmed, A., & Gong, J. (2017). Assessment of Electricity Generation Mix in Ghana. Degree Project in Technology, First Cycle, 15 Credits, Stockholm, Sweden.

Ahmed, R., & Hussain, M. (1990). *Development impact of rural infrastructure in Bangladesh. research report, No. 83*. International Food Policy Research Institute.

Ahmed, S., & Nahiduzzaman, K. (2016). Impacts of rural accessibility on women empowerment: The case of south west Bangladesh. *Transport and Communications Bulletin for Asia and the Pacific*, *86*, 41–57.

AICD – Africa Infrastructure Country Diagnostic. (2008). *Power Sector Database*. World Bank.

Aigbokhan, B. E. (2004). Wage Determination in Nigerian Manufacturing Sector: A Test of Competing Theories. *The Nigerian Journal of Economic and Social Studies*, *46*(2), 105–124.

Aikins, A. D. G. (2005). Healer shopping in Africa: New evidence from rural-urban qualitative study of Ghanaian diabetes experiences. *BMJ (Clinical Research Ed.)*, *331*(7519), 737. doi:10.1136/bmj.331.7519.737 PMID:16195290

Ajefu, J. B., & Ogebe, J. (2019). Migrant Remittances and Financial Inclusion among Households in Nigeria. *Oxford Development Studies*, *47*(3), 319–335. doi:10.1080/13600818.2019.1575349

Ajiboye, A., & Afolayan, O. (2009). The Impact of Transportation on Agricultural Production in a Developing Country: A Case of Kolanut Production In Nigeria. *International Journal of Agricultural Economics and Rural Development*, *2*(2), 49–57.

Ajmi, A. N., Hammoudeh, S., Nguyen, D. K., & Sato, J. R. (2015). On the relationships between CO2 emissions, energy consumption and income: The importance of time variation. *Energy Economics*, *49*, 629–638. doi:10.1016/j.eneco.2015.02.007

Ajzen, I. (1985). From intentions to actions: a theory of planned behaviuor. In J. Kuhl & J. Beckmann (Eds.). Springer.

Ajzen, I. (1991). The theory of planned behavior. *Organizational Behavior and Human Decision Processes*, *50*(2), 179–211.

Ajzen, I., & Fishbein, M. (1977). Attitude-behavior relations: A theoretical analysis and review of empirical research. *Psychological Bulletin*, *84*(5), 888–918.

Akintola, S. (2007). Coping with infrastructural deprivation through collective action among rural people in Nigeria. *Nordic Journal of African Studies*, *16*(1), 30–46.

Akinyemi, O., Efobi, U., Asongu, S., & Osabuohien, E. (2019b). Renewable energy, trade performance and the conditional role of finance and institutional capacity in sub-Sahara African Countries. *Energy Policy*, *132*, 490–498. doi:10.1016/j.enpol.2019.06.012Akinyemi, O., Osabuohien, E., Alege, P., & Ogundipe, A. (2017). Energy Security, Trade and Transition to Green Economy in Africa. *International Journal of Energy Economics and Policy*, *7*(3), 127–136.

Akinyemi, O., Efobi, U., Osabuohien, E., & Alege, P. (2019a). Regional Integration and Energy Sustainability in Africa: Exploring the Challenges and Prospects for ECOWAS. *African Development Review*, *31*(4), 517–528. doi:10.1111/1467-8268.12406

Akinyemi, O., Osabuohien, E., Alege, P., & Ogundipe, A. (2017). Energy Security, Trade and Transition to Green Economy in Africa. *International Journal of Energy Economics and Policy*, *7*(3), 127–136.

Akudugu, M. A., Dittoh, S., & Mahama, E. S. (2012). The implications of climate change on food security and rural livelihoods: Experiences from Northern Ghana. *Journal of Environment and Earth Science*, *2*(3), 21–29.

Alary, V. (2006). L'adoption de l'innovation dans les zones agropastorales vulnérables du Maghreb. *De Boeck Supérieur. Afrique Contemporaine*, *219*(3), 81–101. doi:10.3917/afco.219.0081

Alene, A. D., & Manyong, V. M. (2006). Farmer-to-farmer technology diffusion and yield variation among adopters: The case of improved cowpea in northern Nigeria. *Agricultural Economics*, *35*(2), 203–211. doi:10.1111/j.1574-0862.2006.00153.x

Alesina, A., & Dollar, D. (2000). Who gives Foreign Aid to Whom and Why? *Journal of Economic Growth*, *5*(1), 33–63. doi:10.1023/A:1009874203400

Ali, A. M., & Isse, H. S. (2003). Determinants of Economic Corruption: A Cross-Country Comparison. *The Cato Journal*, *22*(3), 449–466.

Allison, T. D., Diffendorfer, J. E., Baerwald, E. F., Beston, J. A., Drake, D., Hale, A. M., Hein, C. D., Huso, M. M., Loss, S. R., Lovich, J. E., Strickland, M. D., Williams, K. A., & Winder, V. L. (2009). *Impacts to Wildlife of Wind Energy Siting and Operation in the United States.* Issues in Ecology, Report No 21, Fall 2009.

Almstead, A., Brouder, P., Karlsson, S., & Lundmark, L. (2014). Beyond post-productivism: From rural policy discourse to rural diversity. *European Countryside*, *4*(4), 297–306. doi:10.2478/euco-2014-0016

Altieri, M. A. (2002). Agroecología: principios y estrategias para diseñar sistemas agrarios sustentables. Sarandon, SJ Agroecología: el camino hacia una agricultura sustentable. Buenos Aires–La Plata.

Altieri, M. A., Companioni, N., Cañizares, K., Murphy, C., Rosset, P., Bourque, M., & Nicholls, C. I. (1999). The greening of the "barrios": Urban agriculture for food security in Cuba. *Agriculture and Human Values*, *16*(2), 131–140. doi:10.1023/A:1007545304561

Altieri, M. A., & Toledo, V. M. (2011). The agroecological revolution in Latin America: Rescuing nature, ensuring food sovereignty and empowering peasants. *The Journal of Peasant Studies*, *38*(3), 587–612. doi:10.1080/03066150.2011.582947

Aluko O., I., & Mawere, M. (2017). Breaking the Cycle of Poverty: Rethinking Africa's Socio-political Economy. *The Political Economy of Poverty, Vulnerability and Disaster Risk Management: Building Bridges of Resilience, Entrepreneurship, 63.*

Aluko O.I (2019) Caging the Leviathan. *Dynamics of Public Administration*, *39*(1).

Aluko, O. I., & Aderinola, G. T. (2019). E-Governance and Corruption Impasse in Nigeria: A Developmental Expedition Synopsis. In Security Frameworks in Contemporary Electronic Government (pp. 129-149). IGI Global. doi:10.4018/978-1-5225-5984-9.ch006

Aluko, O.I. (2018). Entangled in the "New World Order": Africa's (In-) Security Quandaries and Prospects. *Rethinking Securities in an Emergent Technoscientific New World Order: Retracing the Contours for Africa's Hi-jacked Futures, 171.*

Aluko, O. I. (2015). Political Economy of Crony Capitalism: The Prospect and the Bane. *Journal of Economics Library*, *2*(3), 192–197.

Aluko, O. I. (2020a). Backdoor Politics: Permitting Informalities for Formal Development in African Democracy *TEME. Journal for Social Sciences*, *44*(1), 209–229.

Aluko, O. I. (2020b). Breaking the Cycle of Corruption in Nigeria. *The Myth and Reality Journal of Co-operative and Business Studies*, *5*(1), 115–125.

Al-Yousif, Y. K. (2002). Financial development and economic growth: Another look at the evidence from developing countries. *Review of Financial Economics*, *11*(2), 131–150. doi:10.1016/S1058-3300(02)00039-3

Amare, Z. Y., Ayoade, J. O., Adelekan, I. O., & Zeleke, M. T. (2018). Barriers to and determinants of the choice of crop management strategies to combat climate change in Dejen District, Nile Basin of Ethiopia. *Agriculture & Food Security*, *7*(1), 37. doi:10.118640066-018-0188-y

Ambrosius, C. (2016). Remittances and financial access: Is there really a link and for whom? Evidence from Mexican household data. *World Economy*, *39*(7), 964–982. doi:10.1111/twec.12287

Ambrosius, C., & Cuecuecha, A. (2016). Remittances and the Use of Formal and Informal Financial Services. *World Development*, *77*, 80–98. doi:10.1016/j.worlddev.2015.08.010

Ambrosius, C., Fritz, B., & Stiegler, U. (2014). Remittances for Financial Access: Lessons from Latin American Microfinance. *Development Policy Review*, *32*(6), 733–753. doi:10.1111/dpr.12087

Amnesty International. (2006). *Nigeria: Making the Destitute Homeless – Forced Evictions in Makoko, Lagos State*. AI Index: AFR 44/001/2006. Available online at http://fra.controlarms.org/library/Index/ENGAFR440012006?open&of=ENG-NGA

Amsden, A. (2001). *The Rise of "The Rest:" Challenges to the West from Late-Industrializing Economies*. Oxford University Press. doi:10.1093/0195139690.001.0001

Anderson, W., & Juma, S. (2011). Factors Constraining the Linkages between the Tourism Industry and Local Suppliers of Meats in Zanzibar. *New Alliances for Tourism, Conservation, and Development in Eastern and Southern Africa*, 49-62.

Anderson, W. (2018). Linkages between tourism and agriculture for inclusive development in Tanzania: A value chain perspective. *Journal of Hospitality and Tourism Insights*, *1*(2), 168–184. doi:10.1108/JHTI-11-2017-0021

Andonova, L. B., Betsill, M. M., & Bulkeley, H. (2009). Transnational climate governance. *Global Environmental Politics*, *9*(2), 52–73. doi:10.1162/glep.2009.9.2.52

Andonova, L. B., Hale, T. L., & Roger, C. B. (2017). National policy and transnational governance of climate change: Substitutes or complements? *International Studies Quarterly*, *61*(2), 253–268. Advance online publication. doi:10.1093/isq/sqx014

André, M., Amidzic, G., & Massara, A. (2017). Assessing Countries' Financial Inclusion Standing – A New Composite Index. *Journal of Banking and Financial Economics*, *2*(8), 105–126. doi:10.7172/23536845.jbfe.2017.2.5

Andrianaivo, M., & Kpodar, K. (2012). Mobile phone use spurs economic growth through financial inclusion. *Revista de Economia Institucional*, *3*(2).

ANRC. (2011). *Land tenure regularization in Rwanda: good practices in land reform.* Available online at https://www.afdb.org/fileadmin/uploads/afdb/Documents/Publications/anrc/AfDB_RwandaLandReform_FA.pdf

Ansari, M. F., Kharb, R. K., Luthra, S., Shimmi, S. L., & Chatterji, S. (2016). Analysis of barriers to implement solar power installations in India using interpretive structural modeling technique. *Renewable & Sustainable Energy Reviews*, *27*, 163–174. doi:10.1016/j.rser.2013.07.002

Ansu, Y. (2013). Industrial policy and economic transformation in Africa: Strategies for development and a research agenda. In J. E. Stiglitz, J. L. Yifu, & E. Patel (Eds.), *The industrial policy revolution II. International Economic Association Series*. Palgrave Macmillan. doi:10.1057/9781137335234_19

Antonakakis, N., Chatziantoniou, I., & Filis, G. (2017). Energy consumption, CO2 emissions, and economic growth: An ethical dilemma. *Renewable and Sustainable Energy Reviews, 68,* 808–824. .rser.2016.09.105 doi:10.1016/j

Anyanwu, J., & Erhijakpor, A. (2014). Does Oil Wealth Affect Democracy in Africa? *African Development Review*, *26*(1), 15–37. doi:10.1111/1467-8268.12061

Anzoategui, D., Demirguc-Kunt, A., & Peria, M. S. M. (2014). Remittances and Financial Inclusion: Evidence from El Salvador. *World Development*, *54*, 338–349. doi:10.1016/j.worlddev.2013.10.006

Apergis, N., & Payne, J. (2009). CO_2 emissions, energy usage, and output in Central America. *Energy Policy*, *37*(8), 3282–3286. doi:10.1016/j.enpol.2009.03.048

Appiah, M. (2001). Co-partnership in forest management: The Gwira-Banso joint forest management project in Ghana. *Environment, Development and Sustainability*, *3*(4), 343–360. doi:10.1023/A:1020879510134

Aram, J. D., & Cowen, S. S. (1990). Strategic Planning for Increased Profit in the Small Business. *Long Range Planning*, *23*, 63–70.

Arcand, J. L., & Fafchamps, M. (2012). Matching in community-based organisations. *Journal of Development Economics*, *98*(2), 203–219. doi:10.1016/j.jdeveco.2011.07.002

AREI Framework. (2015). *A Framework for Transforming Africa Towards a Renewable Energy Powered Future with Access to All.* Author.

Arellano, M., & Bond, S. (1991). Some tests of specification for panel data: Monte Carlo evidence and an application to employment equations. *The Review of Economic Studies*, *58*(2), 277–297. doi:10.2307/2297968

Arellano, M., & Bover, O. (1995). Another look at the instrumental variable estimation of error-components models. *Journal of Econometrics*, *68*(1), 29–51. doi:10.1016/0304-4076(94)01642-D

Arena, R., & Lazaric, N. (2003). La théorie évolutionniste du changement économique de Nelson et Winter: Une analyse économique ré prospective. *Revue économique*, *54*(2), 329–354. doi:10.3917/reco.542.0329

Areo, F., Gershon, O., & Osabuohien, E. (2020). Improved Public Services and Tax Compliance of Small and Medium Scale Enterprises in Nigeria: A Generalised Ordered Logistic Regression. *Asian Economic and Financial Review*, *10*(7), 833–860. doi:10.18488/journal.aefr.2020.107.833.860

Arfvidsson, H., Simon, D., Oloko, M., & Moodley, N. (2017). Engaging with and measuring informality in the proposed Urban Sustainable Development Goal. *African Geographical Review*, *36*(1), 100–114. doi:10.1080/19376812.2015.1130636

Armitage, D., Marschke, M., & Plummer, R. (2008). Adaptive comanagement and the paradox of learning. *Global Environmental Change*, *18*(1), 86–98. doi:10.1016/j.gloenvcha.2007.07.002

Arndt, C., & Tarp, F. (2017). Measuring Poverty and Wellbeing in Developing Countries: Motivation and Overview. In *Measuring Poverty and Wellbeing in Developing Countries*. Oxford University Press.

Arnold, U., & Yildiz, Ö. (2015). Economic risk analysis of decentralized renewable energy infrastructures: A Monte Carlo simulation approach. *Renewable Energy*, *77*, 227–239. doi:10.1016/j.renene.2014.11.059

Arnstein, S. (1969). A ladder of citizen participation. *Journal of the American Institute of Planners*, *35*(4), 216–224. doi:10.1080/01944366908977225

Arnstein, S. (2011). Ladder of participation. In A. Cornwall (Ed.), *The participation reader*. Zed Books.

Arpaia, A., & Turrini, A. (2008). *Government Expenditure and Economic Growth in the EU: Long-Run Tendencies and Short-Term Adjustment. Economic Papers 300*. European Commission.

Arthur, K. E., Musau, S. M., & Wanjohi, F. M. (2020). Diaspora Remittances and Financial Inclusion in Kenya. *European Journal of Business and Management Research*, *5*(2). Advance online publication. doi:10.24018/ejbmr.2020.5.2.289

Arun, T., & Ulku, H. (2011). Determinants of Remittances: The Case of the South Asian Community in Manchester. *The Journal of Development Studies*, *47*(6), 894–912. doi:10.1080/00220388.2010.527951

Aryeetey, E., Ayee, J. R. A., Ninsin, K. A., & Tsikata, D. (2007). *The Politics of Land Tenure Reform in Ghana: From the Crown Land Bills to the Land Administration Project (Technical Report); Institute of Statistical Social & Economic Research (ISSER)*. University of Ghana.

Asiedu, E. (2002). On the Determinants of Foreign Direct Investment to Developing Countries: Is Africa Different? *World Development*, *30*(1), 107–199. doi:10.1016/S0305-750X(01)00100-0

Asiedu, E. (2005). Foreign Direct Investment in Africa: The Role of Natural Resources, Market Size, Government Policy, Institutions and Political Instability. *World Economy*, *29*(1), 63–77. doi:10.1111/j.1467-9701.2006.00758.x

Asiedu, E., Jin, Y., & Kanyama, I. (2015). The Impact of HIV/AIDS on Foreign Direct Investment in Developing Countries. *Journal of African Trade*, *2*(1), 1–17. doi:10.1016/j.joat.2015.01.001

Asitik, A. J., & Abu, B. M. (2020). Women empowerment in agriculture and food security in Savannah Accelerated Development Authority zone of Ghana. *African Journal of Economic and Management Studies*, *11*(2), 253–270. doi:10.1108/AJEMS-03-2019-0102

Asomani-Boateng, R., & Haight, M. (1999). Reusing organic solid waste in urban farming in African cities: A challenge for urban planners. *Third World Planning Review*, *21*(4), 411–428. doi:10.3828/twpr.21.4.5537184137847u14

Asongu, S. A. (2017). *The Comparative Sustainable Development in Sub-Saharan Africa*. African Governance and Development Institute working paper no. WP/17/060

Asongu, S. A. (2013). African Stock Market Performance Dynamics: A Multidimensional Convergence Assessment. *Journal of African Business*, *40*(3), 186–201. doi:10.1080/15228916.2013.844043

Asongu, S. A. (2016). Law and investment in Africa. *Institutions, Etc.*, *8*(2), 91–120.

Asumadu-Sarkodie, S., & Owusu, A. (2016). A Review of Ghana's Energy Sector National Energy Statistics and Policy Framework. *Cogent Engineering*, *3*(1), 1155274. doi:10.1080/23311916.2016.1155274

Atilola, O. (2010). *Land Administration Reform in Nigeria*. Paper presented at FIG congress, Sydney, Australia.

Attwood, D. W., Bruneau, T. C., Galaty, J. G., & Attwood, D. W. (2019). *Power and poverty: development and development projects in the Third World*. Routledge. doi:10.4324/9780429302817

AU Energy Report. (2015). *The African Union Bioenergy Development in Africa Programme*. Author.

AUC-ECA-AfDB Consortium. (2011). *Land Policy in Africa: West Africa Regional Assessment. Published by Economic Commission for Africa (ECA) Publications and Conference Management Section*. PCMS.

Auerbach, A. J., & Gorodnichenko, Y. (2013). Fiscal multipliers in recession and expansion. In A. Alesina & F. Giavazzi (Eds.), *Fiscal Policy after the Financial Crisis* (pp. 63–98). University of Chicago Press. doi:10.7208/chicago/9780226018584.003.0003

Avery, L., Regmi, M., Joshi, G., & Mohanty, C. 2017. Rural-Urban Connectivity in Achieving Sustainable Regional Development. In *Intergovernmental Tenth Regional Environmentally Sustainable Transport (EST) Forum* (pp. 14-16). Academic Press.

Awung, N., & Marchant, R. (2016). Investigating the role of local communities as co-managers of the Mount Cameroon National Park Conservation Project. *Environments*, *3*(4), 36. doi:10.3390/environments3040036

Aye, C. (2019). *Fiscal policy uncertainty and economic activity in South Africa: An asymmetric analysis* (UP Working Paper No.2019/22). Retrieved from https://www.up.ac.za/media/shared/61/WP/wp_2019_22.zp170505.pdf

Aye, C., & Harris, L. (2019). *The effect of real exchange rate uncertainty on income distribution in South Africa* (WIDER Working Paper No. 2019/29). Retrieved from https://www.wider.unu.edu/publication/effect-real-exchange-rate-volatility-income-distribution-south-africa

Aye, G. C. & Edoja, P. E. (2017). Effect of economic growth on CO2 emission in developing countries: Evidence from a dynamic panel threshold model. *Cogent Economics & Finance*, *5*(1). Doi:10.1080/23322039.2017.137923

Ayoade, A. R., & Akintonde, J. O. (2012). Constraints to Adoption of Agricultural Innovations among Women Farmers in Isokan Local Government Area, Osun State. *International Journal of Humanities and Social Science*, *2*(8), 57–61.

Bacon, R. W., & Besant-Jones, J. (2001). Global Electric Power Reform: Privatization and Liberalization of the Electric Power Industry in Developing Countries. *Annual Review of Energy and the Environment*, *26*(1), 33–59. doi:10.1146/annurev.energy.26.1.331

Badejo, B. (2011). *The Transportation Realities, Challenges and Opportunities of Lagos State: The Leadership Imperatives and Synergies*. Paper delivered at the Fiftieth Anniversary Lecture Organized by Great Independence Hall, University of Ibadan.

Baffoe-Asare, R., Danquah, J. A., & Annor-Frempong, F. (2013). Socioeconomic Factors Influencing Adoption of Codapec and Cocoa High-tech Technologies among Small Holder Farmers in Central Region of Ghana. *American Journal of Experimental Agriculture*, *2*(2), 277–292. doi:10.9734/AJEA/2013/1969

Bagehot, W. (1873). *Lombard street: a description of the money market*. John Murray.

Baig, M. B., Gorski, I., & Neff, R. A. (2018). Understanding and addressing waste of food in the Kingdom of Saudi Arabia. *Saudi Journal of Biological Sciences*. Advance online publication. doi:10.1016/j.sjbs.2018.08.030 PMID:31762638

Bakker, M. (2019). A conceptual framework for identifying the binding constraints to tourism-driven inclusive growth. *Tourism Planning & Development*, *16*(5), 575–590. doi:10.1080/21568316.2018.1541817

Balchin, N. (2017b). *Financing Tanzania's national five-year development plan 2016/17 2020/21*. SET Report on Workshop, Dar es Salaam, 27 October. London: ODI

Balchin, N. (2017a). *Tanzania's second five-year development plan 2016/17–2020/21: summary and key action points. SET Policy Brief, August*. ODI.

Balchin, N. (2018). *Private sector consultative workshop on effective implementation of Tanzania's second five-year development plan. SET Event Report, October*. ODI.

Baliamoune-Lutz, M. (2003). An Analysis of the Determinants and Effects of ICT Diffusion in Developing Countries. *Information Technology for Development*, *10*(3), 151–169. doi:10.1002/itdj.1590100303

Baliga, A, J., Rodrigues, D. L. L. R. (2015). Business Plan- The Secret to Success. *International Journal of Business and Management*, *3*(4), 210–214.

Ba, M. N. (2016). Analysis of Agricultural Commodities Value Chains and Greenhouse Gas Emission in Rice and Maize in West Africa: Impact on Food Security. *Agricultural Sciences*, *7*(07), 457–468. doi:10.4236/as.2016.77047

Bandiera, O., & Rasul, I. (2006). Social networks and technology adoption in Northern Mozambique. *Economic Journal (London)*, *116*(514), 869–902. doi:10.1111/j.1468-0297.2006.01115.x

Bangs, H. D. (1985). *Business Planning Guide*. Upstart Publishing Company, Inc.

Barbier, E. B., & Hochard, J. P. (2019). Poverty-Environment Traps. *Environmental and Resource Economics*, *74*(3), 1239–1271. doi:10.100710640-019-00366-3

Barrow, E., Clarke, J., Grundy, I., Jones, K., & Tessema, Y. (2002). *Analysis of stakeholder power and responsibility in community involvement in forestry management in eastern and southern Africa*. IUCN.

Bartholomew, L. K., Parcel, G. S., & Kok, G. (1998). Intervention mapping: A process for developing theory and evidence-based health education programs. *Health Education & Behavior*, *25*(5), 545–563. doi:10.1177/109019819802500502 PMID:9768376

Bartley, T. (2007). Institutional emergence in an era of globalization: The rise of transnational private regulation of labour and environment conditions. *American Journal of Sociology*, *113*(2), 297–351. doi:10.1086/518871

Barton, F. C., & Hounsell, D. (1994). Accountants Find Success in Business Succession Planning. *Practical Accountant*, *27*, 18–22.

Barwell, I. (1996). *Transport and the Village: Findings from African Village Level Travel and Transport Surveys and Related Studies*. World Bank Discussion Paper, no. 344. The World Bank.

Bauhr, M. (2016). *Does Corruption reduce Public Support for Foreign Aid? Aid Effectiveness, Accountability and Foreign Aid Cuts*. Paper Presented at "Public Opinion and Foreign Aid: Policy and Methodology Perspectives" Conference. Retrieved from https://ncgg-new.princeton.edu/sites/ncgg/files/media/bauhr_public_opinion_and_foreign_aid.pdf

Bavec, M., Mlakar, S. G., Rozman, C., Pazek, K., & Bavec, F. (2009). Sustainable agriculture based on integrated and organic guidelines: Understanding terms—the case of Slovenian development and strategy. *Outlook on Agriculture, 38*(1), 89–95. doi:10.5367/000000009787762824

Becherer & Helms.. (2009). The Value of Business Plans for New Ventures: Company and Entrepreneur Outcomes. *Journal of Small Business Strategy, 20*(2).

Becker, F. D., & Steele, F. (1995). *Workplace by design: mapping the high-performance workscape*. Jossey-Bass.

Beck, T., Demirguc-Kunt, A., & Levine, R. (2007). Finance, Inequality and the Poor. *Journal of Economic Growth, 12*(1), 27–49. doi:10.100710887-007-9010-6

Beck, T., Demirguc-Kunt, A., & Peria, M. S. M. (2007). Reaching out: Access to and use of banking services across countries. *Journal of Financial Economics, 85*(1), 234–266. doi:10.1016/j.jfineco.2006.07.002

Beck, T., Hans, D., & Christiane, K. (2014). Is more finance better? Disentangling intermediation and size effects of financial systems. *Journal of Financial Stability, 10*, 50–64. doi:10.1016/j.jfs.2013.03.005

Beecroft, I., Osabuohien, E. S., Efobi, U. R., Olurinola, I., & Osabohien, R. A. (2020). Manufacturing export and ICT infrastructure in West Africa: Investigating the roles of economic and political institutions. *Institutions, Etc., 12*(1), 1–36.

Beecroft, I., Osabuohien, E. S., & Olurinola, I. O. (2018). Institutions, Fiscal Performance and Development Trajectories in ECOWAS: Implications for Sustainability. In U. R. Efobi & S. Asongu (Eds.), *Financing Sustainable Development in Africa* (pp. 121–141). Palgrave-Macmillan. doi:10.1007/978-3-319-78843-2_6

Beecroft, I., Osabuohien, E., Efobi, U., Olurinola, I., & Osabohien, R. (2020). Manufacturing Export and ICT Infrastructure in West Africa: Investigating the Roles of Economic and Political Institutions. *Institutions and Economies, 12*(1), 1–36.

Beecroft, I., Osabuohien, E., Efobi, U., Olurinola, I., & Osabohien, R. (2020). Manufacturing Export and ICT Infrastructure in West Africa: Investigating the Roles of Economic and Political Institutions. *Institutions, Etc., 12*(1), 1–36.

Begum, R. A., Sohag, K., Abdullah, S. M. S., & Jaafar, M. (2015). CO_2 emissions, energy consumption, economic and population growth in Malaysia. *Renewable & Sustainable Energy Reviews, 41*(January), 594–601. doi:10.1016/j.rser.2014.07.205

Benhin, J. K. (2006). *Climate change and South African agriculture: Impacts and adaptation options*. CEEPA discussion paper.

Benjaminsen, T. A., Holden, S., Lund, C., & Sjaastad, E. (2009). Formalisation of land rights: Some empirical evidence from Mali, Niger and South Africa. *Land Use Policy, 26*(1), 28–35. doi:10.1016/j.landusepol.2008.07.003

Benoit, M., Rizzo, D., Marraccini, E., Moonen, A. C., Galli, M., Lardon, S., Rapey, H., Thenail, C., & Bonari, E. (2012). Landscape agronomy: A new field for addressing agricultural landscape dynamics. *Landscape Ecology, 27*(10), 1385–1394. doi:10.100710980-012-9802-8

Berkes, F., & Usher, P. J. (2000). Sacred knowledge, traditional ecological knowledge and resource management. *Arctic, 53*(2), 198.

Bernard, B., David, M., Anthony, E., Michael, M. S., James, W., Andrew, A., & Claire, N. (2019). The role of indigenous knowledge (IK) in adaptation to drought by agropastoral smallholder farmers in Uganda. [IJKT]. *Indian Journal of Traditional Knowledge, 19*(1), 44–52.

Besant-Jones, J. E. (2006). *Reforming Power Markets in Developing Countries: What Have We Learnt?* Energy and Mining Sector Board Discussion Paper, the World Bank Group No. 19.

Betsill, M. M., & Harriet Bulkeley, H. (2004). Transnational networks and global environmental governance: The cities for climate protection program. *International Studies Quarterly, 48*(2), 471–493. doi:10.1111/j.0020-8833.2004.00310.x

Betül, M. (2014). The relationship between financial development and economic growth for Turkey. *Journal of Economic Policy Researches, 1*(2), 85–115.

Beyer, C. (2016). *Violent globalisms: conflict in response to empire*. Routledge. doi:10.4324/9781315548111

Bhandari, B., Lee, K., Lee, G., Cho, Y., & Ahn, S. (2015). Optimization of hybrid renewable energy power systems: A review. *Int. J. Precis. Eng. Manuf. Green Technol., 2*(1), 99–112. doi:10.100740684-015-0013-z

Bhattarai, R. C. (2011). Economic impact of community forestry in Nepal: A case of mid hill districts of Nepal. *Economic Journal of Development, 1*(13).

Biddulph, R., & Scheyvens, R. (2018). Introducing inclusive tourism. *Tourism Geographies, 20*(4), 583–588. doi:10.1080/14616688.2018.1486880

Biekart, K., & Fowler, A. (2018). Ownership dynamics in local multi-stakeholder initiatives. *Third World Quarterly, 39*(9), 1692–1910. doi:10.1080/01436597.2018.1450139

Binam, J. N., Place, F., Kalinganire, A., Hamade, S., Boureima, M., Tougiani, A., Dakouo, J., Mounkoro, B., Diaminatou, S., Badji, M., Diop, M., Babou, A. B., & Haglund, E. (2015). Effects of farmer managed natural regeneration on livelihoods in semi-arid West Africa. *Environmental Economics and Policy Studies, 17*(4), 543–575. doi:10.100710018-015-0107-4

Binswanger, M. (2001). Technological progress and sustainable development: What about the rebound effect? *Ecological Economics, 36*(1), 119–132. doi:10.1016/S0921-8009(00)00214-7

Biocycle. (2002). *Food Residuals put city on track to over 50% diversion.* A publication of the city of San Francisco.

Blaauw, P.F. (2006). The dual labour market theory and the informal sector in South Africa. *Acta Commercii*, 248-257.

Blakely, E., & Snyder, M. (1997). Divided We Fall: Gated and Walled Communities in the United States. In Architecture of Fear. New York: Princeton Architectural Press.

Blanchard, O., & Perotti, R. (2002). An empirical characterization of the dynamic effects of changes in government spending and taxes on output. *The Quarterly Journal of Economics, 117*(4), 1329–1368. doi:10.1162/003355302320935043

Blomley, T., Pflienger, K., Isango, J., Zahabu, A. A., & Burgess, N. (2008). Seeing the wood for the trees: an assessment of the impact of participatory forest management on forest condition in Tanzania *Fauna &Flora International, 42*(3), 380-391.

Blomley, T. (2013). *Lessons learnt from community forestry in Africa and their relevance for REDD.* United States Agency for International Development.

Bluemenstock, J. E. (2016). Fighting Poverty with Data. *Science, 353*(6301), 753–754. doi:10.1126cience.aah5217 PMID:27540154

Blum, B. (1992). Composting and the roots of sustainable agriculture. *Agricultural History, 66*(2), 171–188.

Blundell, R., & Bond, S. (1998). Initial conditions and moment restrictions in dynamic panel data models. *Journal of Econometrics*, *87*(1), 115–143. doi:10.1016/S0304-4076(98)00009-8

Bochańczyk-Kupka, D., & Pęciak, R. (2015). Institutions in the context of sustainable development. *The Macrotheme Review*, *4*(5), 29–41.

Bodart, C., Brink, A. B., Donnay, F., Lupi, A., Mayaux, P., & Achard, F. (2013). Continental Estimates of Forest Cover Changes in the Dry Ecosystems of Africa Between 1990 and 2000. *Journal of Biogeography*, *40*(6), 1036–1047. doi:10.1111/jbi.12084 PMID:23935237

Bohn, K., & Viljoen, A. (2005). More city with less space: Vision for lifestyle. In A. Viljoen (Ed.), *Continuous Productive Urban Landscapes: Designing Urban Agriculture for Sustainable Cities* (pp. 251–264). Architectural Press.

Börzel, T. A., & Risse, T. (2010). Governance without a state: Can it work? *Regulation & Governance*, *4*(2), 113–134. doi:10.1111/j.1748-5991.2010.01076.x

BOT – Bank of Tanzania. (2017). *Annual economic review 2017*. BOT.

Botchway, K. (2001). Paradox of empowerment: Reflections on a case study from Northern Ghana. *World Development*, *29*(1), 135–153. doi:10.1016/S0305-750X(00)00084-X

Botes, L., & Van-Rensburg, D. (2000). Community participation in development: Nine plagues and twelve commandments. *Community Development Journal: An International Forum*, *35*(1), 41–58. doi:10.1093/cdj/35.1.41

Bourguet, D., & Guillemaud, T. (2016). The hidden and external costs of pesticide use. *Sustainable Agriculture Research*, *19*, 35–120.

Bourtsalas, A. T., Seo, Y., Alam, M. T., & Seo, Y. C. (2019). The status of waste management and waste to energy for district heating in South Korea. *Waste Management (New York, N.Y.)*, *85*, 304–316. doi:10.1016/j.wasman.2019.01.001 PMID:30803585

Boyd, C. E., & Gross, A. (2000). Water use and conservation for inland aquaculture ponds. *Fisheries Management and Ecology*, *7*(1-2), 55–63. doi:10.1046/j.1365-2400.2000.00181.x

Brack, D. (2017). *The Impacts of the Demand for Woody Biomass for Power and Heat on Climate and \forests*. Environment, Energy and Resources Department.

Bracker, J. S., & Pearson, J. N. (1985). The Impact of Consultants on Small Firm Strategic Planning. *Journal of Small Business Management*, *23*(3), 23–30.

Brainard, W. & Cooper, R. (1968). Uncertainty and diversification of international trade. *Food Research Institute Studies in Agricultural Economics, Trade, and Development, 8,* 257-85.

Brian, M., & Odhiambo, N. M. (2018). South Africa's financial development and its role in investment. *Journal of Central Banking Theory and Practice*, *7*(1), 101–120. doi:10.2478/jcbtp-2018-0005

Briceno-Garmendia, C., Estache, A., & Nemat, S. (2004). *Infrastructure Services in Developing Countries: Access, Quality, Costs and Policy Reform.* Policy Research Working Paper Series 3468, the World Bank.

Briguglio, L. P. (2016). Exposure to external shocks and economic resilience of countries: Evidence from global indicators. *Journal of Economic Studies (Glasgow, Scotland)*, *43*(6), 1057–1078. doi:10.1108/JES-12-2014-0203

Brown, R. P. C., Carmignani, F., & Fayad, G. (2013). Migrants' Remittances and Financial Development: Macro- and Micro-level Evidence of a Perverse Relationship. *World Economy*, *36*(5), 636–660. doi:10.1111/twec.12016

Bruenig, M. (2014). *Two Theories of Poverty*. https://www.demos.org/policy-shop/Matt%20Bruenig

Bruins, H. J., Evenari, M., & Nessler, U. (1986). Rainwater-harvesting agriculture for food production in arid zones: The challenge of the African famine. *Applied Geography (Sevenoaks, England)*, *6*(1), 13–32. doi:10.1016/0143-6228(86)90026-3

Brundtland Commission. (1987). *Our Common Future*. Oxford University Press.

Brundtland, G. H. (1987). *World Commission on environment and development: our common future*. Oxford, UK: Oxford University Press.

Buffie, E. F. (1984). Financial repression, the new structuralist, and stabilization policy in semi- industrialized economies. *Journal of Development Economics*, *14*(3), 305–322. doi:10.1016/0304-3878(84)90061-0

Burbidge, J. L. (1971). Production flow analysis. *Production Engineering*, *50*(4-5), 139–152. doi:10.1049/tpe.1971.0022

Burchardt, T., Le Grand, J., & Piachaud, C. (2002). Degrees of exclusion: developing a dynamic multidimensional measure. In J. Hills, J. Le Grand, & D. Piachaud (Eds.), *Understanding Social Exclusion*. Oxford University Press.

Burke, D. (2016). Voluntary initiatives in corporate global governance; a case study on the UN Global Compact. Erasmus University. https://thesis.eur.nl/pub/36662/DoreenBurkeThesis-26072016-1.pdf

Burke, A., Fraser, S., & Greene, J. F. (2010, May). The Multiple Effects of Business Planning on New Venture Performance. *Journal of Management Studies*, *47*, 3. doi:10.1111/j.1467-6486.2009.00857

Burton, I. (2006). *Adaptation to climate change: international policy options*. Citeseer.

Busse, M., & Hefeker, C. (2007). Political Risk, Institutions and Foreign Direct Investment. *European Journal of Political Economy*, *23*(2), 397–415. doi:10.1016/j.ejpoleco.2006.02.003

Büthe, T., & Milner, H. V. (2008). The politics of foreign direct investment into developing countries: Increasing FDI through international trade agreements? *American Journal of Political Science*, *52*(4), 741–762. doi:10.1111/j.1540-5907.2008.00340.x

Butler, S. (2013). Directions in development: Nigerian land markets and the land use law of 1978. International Bank for Reconstruction and Development/the World Bank.

Butty, A. M., Frischknecht, M., Gredler, B., Neuenschwander, S., Moll, J., Bieber, A., Baes, C. F., & Seefried, F. R. (2017). Genetic and genomic analysis of hyperthelia in Brown Swiss cattle. *Journal of Dairy Science*, *100*(1), 402–411. doi:10.3168/jds.2016-11420 PMID:27865493

Buzby, J. C., Farah-Wells, H., & Hyman, J. J. U.-E. E. I. B. (2014). *The estimated amount, value, and calories of postharvest food losses at the retail and consumer levels in the United States*. Academic Press.

Cabrera, J. J. V., Herrero, S. P., Gómez, I. P., & Camacho, X. G. O. (2017). Causal attributions of poverty in less developed countries: Comparing among undergraduates from nations with different development levels. *The Journal of Psychology*, *51*(1), 4.

Cairns, J. E. (2012). Maize production in a changing climate: impacts, adaptation, and mitigation strategies. Advances in Agronomy, 114, 1-58. doi:10.1016/B978-0-12-394275-3.00006-7

Calderon, C., & Liu, L. (2003). The direction of causality between financial development and economic growth. *Journal of Development Economics*, *72*(1), 321–334. doi:10.1016/S0304-3878(03)00079-8

Cancino, J., & Saborowski, J. (2005). Comparison of randomized branch sampling with and without replacement at the first stage. *Silva Fennica*, *39*(2), 201–216. doi:10.14214f.384

Cardno. (2017). *Agricultural development as a key role in food security and economic development in most of the world's population in rural area*. Academic Press.

CAREInternational. (2009). *CARE International. Climate vulnerability and Adaptive capacity Analysis*. Handbook.

Carlock, R., & Ward, J. (2001). *Strategic Planning for Family Business*. Palgrave.

Carson & Cromie. (1990). Marketing Planning in Small Enterprises: A Model and More Empirical Evidence. *The Journal of Consumer Marketing*, *7*, 5-18.

Carson, R. (1962). *Silent spring*. Houghton Mifflin Harcourt.

Casaburi, L., & Wills, J. (2014). *Innovations for Poverty Action (IPA): Agricultural Micro insurance for Sugar Cane Farmers in Kenya*. Retrieved February 30, 2020, from: https://www.poverty-action.org/study/agricultural-microinsurance-cane-farmers-kenya

Cashore, B. (2002). Legitimacy and the privatization of environmental governance: How non-state market-driven (NSMD) governance systems gain rule-making authority. *Governance: An International Journal of Policy, Administration and Institutions*, *15*(4), 503–529. doi:10.1111/1468-0491.00199

Castalia-GIZ & Government of Ghana, (2015). *Renewable Energy Policy Review, Identification of Gaps and Solutions in Ghana*. Author.

Caswell, M., Fuglie, K., Ingram, C., Jans, S., & Kascak, C. (2001). Adoption of Agricultural Production Practices: Lessons Learned from the U.S. Department of Agriculture Area Studies Project. *Agricultural Economics*, *792*, 1–111.

Cater, J., & Schwab, A. (2008). Turnaround strategies in established small family firms. *Family Business Review*, *21*(1), 31–50.

Catrinescu, N., Leon-Ledesma, M., Piracha, M., & Quillin, B. (2009). Remittances, Institutions and Economic Growth. *World Development*, *37*(1), 81–92. doi:10.1016/j.worlddev.2008.02.004

Cavalcanti, T., Magalhaes, A. M., & Tavares, J. (2008). Institutions and Economic Development in Brazil. *The Quarterly Review of Economics and Finance*, *48*(2), 412–432. doi:10.1016/j.qref.2006.12.019

Cavazza, L. (1996). Agronomia aziendale e agronomia del territorio. *Riv Agron*, *30*, 310–319.

Ceccon, E., & Miramontes, O. (2008). Revenue Déforestation? Bioenergy and Society in Two Brazilian Models. *Ecological Economics*, *67*(2), 311–317. doi:10.1016/j.ecolecon.2007.12.008

CEIF Report, . (2008). *Proposals for Clean Energy Investment Framework for Africa: Role of African Development Bank Group*. Final Version.

Celen, A. (2013). Efficiency and Productivity (TFP) of the Turkish Electricity Distribution Companies: An Application of Two-Stage (DEA & Tobit) Analysis. *Energy Policy*, *63*(10), 300–310. doi:10.1016/j.enpol.2013.09.034

Central Bank of Nigeria. (2017). *Statistical Bulletin*. Central Bank of Nigeria.

Centre de coopération internationale en recherche agronomique pour le développement. (2019). *AgriNumA: Le 1er rendez-vous de l'agriculture numérique en Afrique de l'Ouest. 2019*. Récupéré le 15 Février 2020 de: https://www.cirad.fr/actualites/toutes-les-actualites/communiques-de-presse/2019/agriculture-numerique-en-afrique-de-l-ouest

Centre technique de coopération agricole et rurale (éd.). (2019a). *Ils l'ont fait: Etre jeune et entreprendre dans le secteur agricole: Succes stories*. Bruxelles: CTA.

Centre technique de coopération agricole et rurale. (2019b, Juin). Jeunes et emploi: L'agriculture plutôt que l'émigration. *Spore, 193*, 1-48.

Centre technique de coopération agricole et rurale. (2019c). *The digitalisation of African agriculture report 2018–2019*. Bruxelles: CTA.

Cerin, P. (2006). Bringing economic opportunity into line with environmental influence: A discussion on the coase theorem and the Porter and van der Linde hypothesis. *Ecological Economics, 56*(2), 209–225. doi:10.1016/j.ecolecon.2005.01.016

Chambers, R. (1985). *Rural development: Putting the last first*. Longman.

Chambers, R. (1998). Whose reality counts? Participatory poverty assessments in Africa. In K. King & S. A. McGrath (Eds.), *Running, Reporting & Researching Africa*. Centre of African Studies, University of Edinburgh.

Chambers, R., & Ghildyal, B. P. (1985). Agricultural research for resource-poor farmers: The farmer-first-and-last model. *Agricultural Administration, 20*(1), 1–30. doi:10.1016/0309-586X(85)90063-9

Chami, R., Fullenkamp, C., & Jahjah, S. (2005). Are Immigrant Remittance Flows a Source of Capital for Development? *IMF Economic Review, 52*, 55–81. doi:10.2307/30035948

Chandrasekhar, C. P. (2015). National Development Banks in a Comparative Perspective. In Rethinking Development Strategies after the Financial Crisis. United Nations Conference on Trade and Development and Fachhochschule für Technik und Wirtschaft Berlin.

Chandra, V., & Khan, M. A. (1993). Foreign investment in the presence of an informal sector. *Economica, 60*(237), 79–103. doi:10.2307/2554732

Chauhan, A., & Saini, R. P. (2015). Renewable energy based off-grid rural electrification in Uttarakhand state of India: Technology options, modelling method, barriers and recommendations. *Renewable & Sustainable Energy Reviews, 51*(December), 662–681. doi:10.1016/j.rser.2015.06.043

Chavula, H. P. (2014). The role of ICTs in Agricultural production in Africa. *Journal of Development and Agricultural Economics, 6*(7), 279–289. doi:10.5897/JDAE2013.0517

Chen, Y. T. (2016). A cost analysis of food waste composing in Taiwan. *Sustainability, 8*(11), 1210. doi:10.3390u8111210

Chete, O. B., & Fasoyiro, S. B. (2014). Impact of ICT-based Initiative (Mobile Phone) On Market Access by Women Farmers in Nigeria. *World Rural Observations, 6*(3), 65–71.

Cheung, H. Y., & Chan, A. W. (2008). Corruption across countries: Impacts from education and cultural dimensions. *The Social Science Journal, 45*(2), 223–239. doi:10.1016/j.soscij.2008.03.002

Chéze, B., David, M., & Martinet, V. (2020). Understanding farmers' reluctance to reduce pesticide use: A choice experiment. *Ecological Economics, 167*(106349), 1–13. doi:10.1016/j.ecolecon.2019.06.004

Chhetri, B. B. K. (2005). *Community forestry programme in the hills of Nepal: Determinants of user participation and household dependency*. Norwegian University of Life Sciences.

Chikaire, J. U., Anyoha, N. O., Ani, A. O., & Atoma, C. N. (2014). Land tenure reform: A vehicle for achieving agricultural transformation agenda in Nigeria. *Merit Research Journal of Agricultural Science and Soil Sciences, 2*(9), 114–122.

Chipumbu, G. M. (1993). The Impact of External Debt on African Economies. *International Journal on World Peace, 10*(1), 43–56.

Chirambo, D. (2016). Addressing the Renewable Energy Financing Gap in Africa to Promote Universal Energy Access: Integrated Renewable Energy Financing in Malawi. *Renewable & Sustainable Energy Reviews*, *62*, 793–803. doi:10.1016/j.rser.2016.05.046

Cho, C., Yang, L., Chu, Y., & Yang, H. (2013). Renewable energy and renewable R&D in EU countries. *Cointegrat. Anal.*, *2*(1), 10–16.

Choguill, M. B. G. (1996). A ladder of community participation for underdeveloped countries. *Habitat International*, *20*(3), 431–444. doi:10.1016/0197-3975(96)00020-3

Chwolka, A., & Raith, M. G. (2012). The value of business planning before start-up - A decision-theoretical perspective. *Journal of Business Venturing*, *27*(3), 385–399. doi:10.1016/j.jbusvent.2011.01.002

CIA. (2018). *Nigeria Area. CIA World Fact book.* Available at https://www.cia.gov/library/publications/the-world-factbook/geos/ni.html

Clark, D., Renato, L., & Charles, S. (2016). Stages of diversification in Africa. *Economics Letters*, *144*, 68–70. doi:10.1016/j.econlet.2016.05.001

Clavel, D., Barro, A., Belay, T., Lahmar, R., & Maraux, F. (2008). Changements techniques et dynamiques d'innovation agricole en Afrique Sahélienne: Le cas du Zai mécanisé au Burkina Faso et de l'introduction d'une cactée en Ethiopie. *La revue en Sciences de l'environnement*, *8*(3), 1-11.

Cleaver, F. (1999). Paradoxes of participation: Questioning participatory approaches to development. *Journal of International Development*, *11*(4), 597–612. doi:10.1002/(SICI)1099-1328(199906)11:4<597::AID-JID610>3.0.CO;2-Q

Collette. (2011). Thunnus obesus The IUCN Red List of Threatened Species. doi:10.2305/IUCN.UK.2011-2

Collier, U. (2004). *Hydropower and the Environment: Towards Better Decision-making.* Paper submitted to the United Nations Symposium on Hydropower and Sustainable Development, Beijing, China.

Collins, K., & Ison, R. (2009). Jumping off Arnstein's ladder: Social learning as a new policy paradigm for climate change adaptation. *Environmental Policy and Governance*, *19*(6), 358–373. doi:10.1002/eet.523

Commission on Global Governance (Ed.). (1995). *Our global neighborhood.* Oxford University Press.

Companioni, N., Rodríguez Nodals, A., Carrión, M., Alonso, R. M., Ojeda, Y., & Peña, E. (1997). La Agricultura Urbana en Cuba. Su participación en la seguridad alimentaria. Conferencias. III Encuentro Nacional de Agricultura Orgánica. Villa Clara, Cuba: Central University of Las Villas.

Connor, D. M. (1988). A new ladder of citizen participation. *National Civic Review*, *77*(3), 249–257. doi:10.1002/ncr.4100770309

Conseil Ouest et Centre Africain pour la Recherche et le Développement Agricoles. (2018). *Impulser l'innovation 2018-2027, Plan stratégique.* Récupéré le 27 Juin 2019 de: http://www.coraf.org/wp-content/uploads/2019/03/PlanStrategique.pdf

Consulting, A. (2016). *The Impact of the Land Use Act on the development of Agriculture in Nigeria.* Available online at http://ssacltd.com/blog/311-2/

Cooke, B., & Kothari, U. (n.d.). Paradox of empowerment: reflections on a case study from Northern Ghana. World Development, 29(1), 135-153.

Cooke, B., & Kothari, U. (Eds.). (2001). *Participation: The new tyranny?* Zed Books.

Cornwall, A. (2011). *The participation reader.* Zed Books.

Cosimo, L., & Abis, S. (2016). Innovation et technologie: quels enjeux pour l'agriculture et le monde rural en Méditerranée? *Tendances économiques*, 58-60.

Coté, J. (2009). SS.F.OO.K.sToughest Recycling Law in UU.S. *San Francisco Chronicle.*

Cote, M., & Nightingale, A. J. (2012). Resilience thinking meets social theory: Situating social change in socio-ecological systems (SES) research. *Progress in Human Geography*, *36*(4), 475–489. doi:10.1177/0309132511425708

Cotula, L., Toulmin, C., & Hesse, C. (2004). *Land tenure and administration in Africa: Lessons of experience and emerging issues.* International Institute for Environment and Development, London. Available online at http://www.hubrural.org/IMG/pdf/iied_lt_cotula.pdf

Coubès, M. L. (2005). Movilidad en la trayectoria laboral: Transición entre sector formal-informal del empleo. In M. L. Coubès, M. E. Zavala, & R. Zenteno (Eds.), *Cambio demográfico y social en México en el siglo XX. Una perspectiva de historias de vida* (pp. 259–282). Cámara de Diputados EGAP, Tecnológico de Monterrey, El Colegio de la Frontera Norte, Miguel Ángel Porrúa. Available from http://bibliotecasibe.ecosur.mx/sibe/book/000038678

Cramer, C. (1999). *The economics of political economy of conflict in sub-Saharan Africa.* CDPR Discussion Paper 1099. Retrieved from www.soas.ac.uk

Crawford, M. (2010). *Creating a forest garden: working with nature to grow edible crops.* Green Books.

Creswell, J. W. (2009). Research Design, Qualitative, Quantitative and Mixed Methods Approaches (Vol. 3). SAGE Publications Inc.

Creswell, J. W. (2012). *Educational research: Planning, conducting and evaluating quantitative and qualitative research* (Vol. 4). Pearson Education Inc.

Croppenstedt, A., Demeke, M., & Meschi, M. M. (2003). Technology adoption in the presence of constraints: The case of fertilizer demand in Ethiopia. *Review of Development Economics*, *7*(1), 58–70. doi:10.1111/1467-9361.00175

Crouzat, E., Mouchet, M., Turkelboom, F., Byczek, C., Meersmans, J., Berger, F., & Lavorel, S. (2015). Assessing bundles of ecosystem services from regional to landscape scale: Insights from the French Alps. *Journal of Applied Ecology*, *52*(5), 1145–1155. doi:10.1111/1365-2664.12502

Cubbin, J., & Stern, J. (2004). *Regulatory Effectiveness: The Impact of Good Regulatory Governance on Electricity Industry Capacity and Efficiency in Developing Countries.* Policy Research Working Paper 3536, the World Bank, Washington D.C.

Cubbin, J., & Stern, J. (2006). The Impact of Regulatory Governance and Privatization on Electricity Industry Generation Capacity in Developing Economies. *The World Bank Economic Review*, *20*(1), 115–141. doi:10.1093/wber/lhj004

Cuéllar-Padilla, M., & Calle-Collado, Á. (2011). Can we find solutions with people? Participatory action research with small organic producers in Andalusia. *Journal of Rural Studies*, *27*(4), 372–383. doi:10.1016/j.jrurstud.2011.08.004

Cullmann, A., & Hirschhausen, C. V. (2008). From Transition to Competition. *Economics of Transition*, *16*(2), 335–357. doi:10.1111/j.1468-0351.2008.00312.x

Culpeper, R., & Bhushan, A. (2010). Why Enhance Domestic Resource Mobilisation in Africa? *Trade Negotiations Insights*, *9*(6), 5–7.

Danso-Abbeam, G., Dagunga, G., & Ehiakpor, D. S. (2019). Adoption of zai technology for soil fertility management: Evidence from Upper East Region, Ghana. *Journal of Economic Structures*, *8*(1), 32. doi:10.118640008-019-0163-1

Daron, D. (2014). *Regional Climate Messages: East Africa. Scientific report from the CARIAA Adaptation at Scale in Semi-Arid Regions (ASSAR) Project, December 2014, Cape Town, South Africa.* Retrieved from http://www. uct. ac.za

Daspit, J. J., Holt, D. T., Chrisman, J. J., & Long, R. G. (2015). Examining family firm succession from a social exchange perspective: A multiphase, multi-stakeholder review. *Family Business Review*, *29*(1), 44–64.

Dass, P., Muller, C., Brovkin, V., & Cramer, W. (2013). Can Bioenergy Cropping Compensate High Carbon Emissions from Large Scale Deforestation of High Latitudes? *Earth System Dynamics*, *4*(2), 409–424. doi:10.5194/esd-4-409-2013

Datt, G., Ravallion, M., & Murgai, R. (2020). Poverty and Growth in India over Six Decades. *American Journal of Agricultural Economics*, *102*(1), 4–27. doi:10.1093/ajae/aaz043

Davies, L., Wright, K., & Price, C. W. (2006). *Experience of Privatization, Regulation and Competition: Lessons for Governments.* ESRC Centre for Competition Policy, University of East Anglia, UK. CCP Working Paper 05-5.

Davies, K. K., Fisher, K. T., Dickson, M. E., Thrush, S. F., & Le Heron, R. (2015). Improving ecosystem service frameworks to address wicked problems. *Ecology and Society*, *20*(2), art37. Advance online publication. doi:10.5751/ES-07581-200237

De Gregorio, J., & Guidotti, P. E. (1995). Financial development and economic growth. *World Development*, *23*(3), 433–448. doi:10.1016/0305-750X(94)00132-I

de Janvry, A., Gordillo, G., Platteau, J. P., & Sadoulet, E. (2001). *Access to Land, Rural Poverty and Public Action.* Oxford University Press. doi:10.1093/acprof:oso/9780199242177.001.0001

De Janvry, A., Sadoulet, E., Kyle, E., & Dar, M. (2015). L'Adoption des technologies agricoles: Quelles leçons tirer des expérimentations de terrain? *Revue d'Economie du Developpement*, *4*(23), 129–153. doi:10.3917/edd.294.0129

De Molina, M. G. (2012). *Agro ecology and politics. How to get sustainability?* About the necessity for a political agro-ecologist. *Agroecology and Sustainable Food Systems*, *37*, 45–59. doi:10.1080/10440046.2012.705810

De Schutter, O. (2010). *Report submitted by the special rapporteur on the right to food.* United Nations Human Rights Council.

De Zeeuw, H., Van Veenhuizen, R., & Dubbeling, M. (2011). The role of urban agriculture in building resilient cities in developing countries. *J Agric Sci*, *149*(S1), 153–163. doi:10.1017/S0021859610001279

Deblock, C. (2012). Introduction: Innovation et développement chez Schumpeter. *Revue Interventions économiques Papers in Political Economy*, (46), 1-15.

Deb, S., Barbhuiya, A. R., Arunachalam, A., & Arunachalam, K. (2008). Ecological analysis of traditional agroforest and tropical forest in the foothills of Indian eastern Himalaya: Vegetation, soil and microbial biomass. *Tropical Ecology*, *49*, 73–78.

Degefu, M. A., Assen, M., Satyal, P., & Budds, J. (2019). Villagization and access to water resources in the Middle Awash Valley of Ethiopia: Implications for climate change adaptation. *Climate and Development*, 1–12. doi:10.1080/17565529.2019.1701973

Deininger, K., Jin, S., Anenew, B., Gebre-Selassie, S., & Nega, B. (2003). *Tenure security and land-related investment-evidence from Ethiopia.* Policy Research Working Paper, series 2991. World Bank.

Deininger, K., Ali, D. A., Holden, S., & Zevenbergen, J. (2008). Rural land certification in Ethiopia: Process, initial impact, and implications for other African countries. *World Development*, *36*(10), 1786–1812. doi:10.1016/j.worlddev.2007.09.012

Delmar, F., & Shane, S. (2003). Does Business Planning Facilitate the Development of New Ventures? *Strategic Management Journal, 24*, 1165–1185.

Dembele, N. N. (2001). *Sécurité alimentaire en Afrique Sub-saharienne: Quelle Stratégie de Réalisation?* PASIDMA, (Document de Travail no. 1). Récupéré le 05 Juillet 2019 de https://pdfs.semanticscholar.org/3a75/662ca2a9fa7807df408104e9eafb4a19ab09.pdf

Demirgüç-Kunt, A., & Levine, R. (2008). *Finance, financial sector policies, and long-run growth* (WB Policy Research Working Paper No. 4469). doi:10.1596/1813-9450-4469

Demirguc-Kunt, A., Lopez Cordova, E., Martınez Perıa, M. S., & Woodruff, C. (2011). Remittances and Banking Sector Breadth and Depth: Evidence from Mexico. *Journal of Development Economics, 95*(2), 229–241. doi:10.1016/j.jdeveco.2010.04.002

Des Grades, E., Fakultät, H. L., & Guthiga, P. M. (2007). Economic analysis of different management approaches of Kakamega Forest in Kenya: Cost-benefit and local community satisfaction analysis. *Forests and Climate Change Adaptation and Mitigation, 66*.

Desai, R. M., & Rudra, N. (2019). Trade, poverty, and social protection in developing countries. *European Journal of Political Economy, 60*, 101744. doi:10.1016/j.ejpoleco.2018.08.008

DFID Report. (2007). *Water Storage and: Supporting Growth, Resilience and Low Carbon Development.* A DFID Evidence-into-Action Paper.

Dhrifi, A., Jaziri, R., & Alnahdi, S. (2020). Does foreign direct investment and environmental degradation matter for poverty? Evidence from developing countries. *Structural Change and Economic Dynamics, 52*, 13–21. doi:10.1016/j.strueco.2019.09.008

Diao, X. D., Zeng, S. X., Tam, C. M., & Tam, V. W. Y. (2009). EKC Analysis for Studying Economic Growth and Environmental Quality: A Case Study in China. *Journal of Cleaner Production, 17*(5), 541–548. doi:10.1016/j.jclepro.2008.09.007

Dickerman, C. W., Barnes, G., Bruce, J. W., Green, J. K., Myers, G., Polishuk, R., Stienbarger, D., & Sund, A. (1989). *Security of tenure and land registration in Africa: literature review and synthesis. Land tenure center paper 137.* University of Wisconsin-Madison.

Didia, O. D. (2015). *Ten reasons why sub-Saharan Africa has failed to develop economically: Can Africans succeed by themselves?* Edwin Mellen Press.

Dilip, J. (2015). *What are the key indicators of successful reforms? A comparative analysis of United Kingdom (UK) and Ghana.* University of Dundee, CEPMLP - Centre for Energy, Petroleum and Mineral Law and Policy, Graduate Student. Academia.edu. https://www.academia.edu/10473243/What_are_the_key_indicators_of_successful_reforms_A_comparative_analysis_of_United_Kingdom_UK_and_Ghana

Djelic, M.-L., & Sahlin-Andersson, K. (Eds.). (2006). *Transnational governance: institutional dynamics of regulation.* Cambridge University Press., doi:10.1017/CBO9780511488665.

DLA. (1997). *DLA (Department of Land Affairs). White Paper on South African Land Policy DLA, Pretoria.* Available online at http://ww2.ruraldevelopment.gov.za/DLA-Internet//content/document_library/documents/White_paper/WhitePaperLandReform.pdf (accessed 08.20.2010).

Dmitriew, A. (2018). *Maximizing Organics Recovery: The San Francisco Experience.* Paper presented at Waste Expo, Las Vegas, NV.

Docquier, F., Rapoport, H., & Salomone, S. (2012). Remittances, Migrants' Education and Immigration Policy: Theory and Evidence from Bilateral Data. *Regional Science and Urban Economics*, *42*(5), 817–828. doi:10.1016/j.regsciurbeco.2011.10.005

Dollar, D., & Gatti, R. (1999). Gender Inequality, Income and Growth: Are Good Times Good for Women? *The World Bank Development Research Group, Working paper series, No. 1*, 1-42.

Draper, P., Freytag, A., Dörffel, C., & Schuhmann, S. (2019). Trade, Inclusive Development, and the Global Order. *Global Summitry*, *4*(1), 30–49. doi:10.1093/global/guz001

Dubbeling, M., Campbell, M. C., Hoekstra, F., & van Veenhuizen, R. (2009). Building resilient cities. *Urban Agriculture Magazine*, *22*, 3–11.

Dulal, H. B., Shah, K. U., Sapkota, C., Uma, G., & Kandel, B. R. (2013). Renewable energy diffusion in Asia: Can it happen without government support? *Energy Policy*, *59*(April), 301–311. doi:10.1016/j.enpol.2013.03.040

Dumitrescu, E.-I., & Hurlin, C. (2012). Testing for Granger non-causality in heterogeneous panels. *Economic Modelling*, *29*(4), 1450–1460. doi:10.1016/j.econmod.2012.02.014

Durand-Lasserve, A. (2003). *Land Tenure, Property System Reforms, and Emerging Urban Land Markets in Sub-Saharan Africa*. Lincoln Institute of Land Policy.

Duru, M., Thérond, O., & Fares, M. (2015). Designing agroecological transitions: A review. *Agronomy for Sustainable Development*, *35*(4), 1237–1257. doi:10.100713593-015-0318-x

Dzebo, A. (2019). Effective governance of transnational adaptation initiatives. *International Environmental Agreement: Politics, Law and Economics*, *19*(4-5), 447–466. doi:10.1007/s10784-019-09445-8

EAC/UNIDO and FAO. (2011). *Development of Agro-Industries and Agro-Enterprises in the EAC Region*. United Nation Industries Development Organisation.

Eberhard, A. (2007). *Matching Regulatory Design to Country Circumstances: The Potential of Hybrid and Transitional Models. Gridlines Note 23, PPIAF*. World Bank.

Eberhard, A., & Gratwick, K. N. (2016). *New Models to Scale up Investment in Power Generation in Sub-Saharan Africa*. World Bank.

Eberhard, R., & Shkaratan, V. (2011). *Africa's Power Infrastructure: Investment, Integration, Efficiency*. The World Bank. doi:10.1596/978-0-8213-8455-8

Ebru, T. (2016). Reexamining finance-growth nexus: A new literature survey. *EcoForum*, *5*, 1–7.

Efobi, U. (2015). Politicians' Attributes and Institutional Quality in Africa: A Focus on Corruption. *Journal of Economic Issues*, *49*(3), 787–813. doi:10.1080/00213624.2015.1072393

Efobi, U. R., Osabuohien, E. S., & Oluwatobi, S. (2015). One Dollar, One Bank Account: Remittance and Bank Breadth in Nigeria. *Journal of International Migration and Integration*, *16*(3), 761–781. doi:10.100712134-014-0358-0

Efobi, U., & Osabuohien, E. (2011). Promotion of Non-Oil Export in Nigeria: Empirical Assessment of Agricultural Credit Guarantee Scheme Fund. *Current Research Journal of Economic Theory*, *3*(1), 20–28.

Efobi, U., & Osabuohien, E. (2016). Manufacturing exports, Infrastructure and Institutions in Africa: Reflections from ECOWAS. In D. Seck (Ed.), *In Accelerated Economic Growth in West Africa* (pp. 157–179). Springer International Publishing. doi:10.1007/978-3-319-16826-5_8

Egbetokun, S., Osabuohien, E., & Akinbobola, T. (2018). Feasible Environmental Kuznets and Institutional Quality in North and Southern African Sub-regions. *International Journal of Energy Economics and Policy*, *8*(1), 104–115.

Egbetokun, S., Osabuohien, E., & Akinboloa, T. (2018). Feasible Environmental Kuznets and Institutional Quality in North and Southern African Sub-regions. *International Journal of Energy Economics and Policy*, *8*(1), 104–115.

Egbetokun, S., Osabuohien, E., Onanuga, O., Akinbobola, T., Gershon, O., & Okafor, V. (2020). Environmental Pollution, Economic Growth and Institutional Quality: Exploring the Nexus in Nigeria. *Management of Environmental Quality*, *31*(1), 18–31. doi:10.1108/MEQ-02-2019-0050

EIA. (2000). *The Changing Structure of the Electric Power Industry 2000: An Update. Energy Information Administration*. Office of Coal, Nuclear, Electric and Alternate Fuels, U.S. Department of Energy. Washington, DC 20585. DOE/EIA-0562(00). Distribution Category UC-950. October.

Eicher, T., García-Peñalosa, C., & Van Ypersele, T. (2009). Education, corruption, and the distribution of income. *Journal of Economic Growth*, *14*(3), 205–231. doi:10.100710887-009-9043-0

Ejemeyovwi, J. O., & Osabuohien, E. S. (2018). Investigating the relevance of mobile technology adoption on inclusive growth in West Africa. *The Journal of Academic Social Science*, 1–15.

Ejemeyovwi, J. O., & Osabuohien, E. S. (2020). Investigating the Relevance of Mobile Technology Adoption on Inclusive Growth in West Africa. *Contemporary Social Science*, *15*(1), 48–61. doi:10.1080/21582041.2018.1503320

Ejemeyovwi, J. O., Osabuohien, E. S., Johnson, O. D., & Bowale, E. I. K. (2019). Internet Usage, Innovation and Human Development Nexus in Africa: The Case of ECOWAS. *Journal of Economic Structures*, *8*(5). Advance online publication. doi:10.118640008-019-0146-2

Ejemeyovwi, J. O., Osabuohien, E. S., & Osabohien, R. (2018). ICT investments, human capital development and institutions in ECOWAS. *International Journal of E-Business Research*, *15*(4), 463.

Ejemeyovwi, J. O., Osabuohien, E. S., & Osabohien, R. (2018). ICT Investments, Human Capital Development and Institutions in ECOWAS. *International Journal of E-Business Research*, *15*(4), 463–474.

Ekpo, A. H. (2013). *Rethinking institutions and economic development: is there a new framework?* Paper presented at the 54th Annual Conference of the Nigerian Economic Society, Abuja.

Ekpo, A. H. (2016). Education and economic diversification for self-reliance in Nigeria. *West African Financial and Economic Review*, *11*(2), 1–22.

Elbahnasawy, N. G., & Revier, C. F. (2012). The determinants of corruption: Cross-country-panel-data analysis. *The Developing Economies*, *50*(4), 311–333. doi:10.1111/j.1746-1049.2012.00177.x

El-katiri, L. (2014). *A roadmap for renewable energy in the Middle East and North Africa*. Academic Press.

Emodi, V. N., Yusuf, S. D., & Boo, K. (2014). The necessity of the development of standards for renewable energy technologies in Nigeria. *Smart Grid and Renewable Energy*, *5*(November), 259–274. doi:10.4236gre.2014.511024

Energiforsk Report. (2018). *Wind Power in Forests II*. Author.

Enevoldsen, P. (2017). *Managing Risks of Wind Farms in Forested Areas: Design Principles for Northern Europe*. Industrial PhD Dissertation at the School of Business and Social Sciences, Aarhus University.

Engel, R. F., & Granger, C. W. J. (1987). Cointegration and error correction representation, estimation and testing. *Econometrica*, *55*(2), 251–276. doi:10.2307/1913236

EPA. (2008). *Environmental management in Korea: Insights and observations from the 2007 Australia-Korea Young Leaders Exchange Program.* Author.

EPA. (2016). *Zero Waste Case Study: San Francisco.* https://www.epa.gov/transforming-waste- tool/zero-waste-case-study-san-francisco

Erdogdu, E. (2013a). *Essays on Electricity Market Reforms: A Cross-Country Applied Approach* (PhD Thesis). University of Cambridge, UK.

Erdogdu, E. (2013b). Implications of Liberalization Policies on Government Support to R&D: Lessons for Electricity Markets. *Renewable & Sustainable Energy Reviews, 17*(1), 110–118. doi:10.1016/j.rser.2012.09.030

Erdogdu, E. (2014). Investment, Security of Supply and Sustainability in the Aftermath of Three Decades of Power Sector Reform. *Renewable & Sustainable Energy Reviews, 31*(3), 1–8. doi:10.1016/j.rser.2013.11.014

Eregha, P. B., & Mesagan, E. P. (2017). *The emergence of inclusive growth: Issues, challenges and policy options for Nigeria.* Munich Personal RePEc Archive (MPRA), Paper No. 95671. Available at: https://www.researchgate.net/deref/https%3A%2F%2Fmpra.ub.uni muenchen.de%2F95671%2F

Erjavec, I., & Ruchinskaya, T. (2019). A Spotlight of Co-creation and Inclusiveness of Public Open Spaces. In *CyberParks–The Interface Between People, Places and Technology* (pp. 209–223). Springer. doi:10.1007/978-3-030-13417-4_17

Esanow, A. (2012). *Economic diversification: Dynamics, determinants and policy implications.* Review Watch Institute.

ESMAP. (2005). *Power Sector Reform in Africa: Assessing Impact on Poor People.* The Joint UNDP/World Bank Energy Sector Management Assistance Program (ESMAP). Report 306/05. August.

ESMAP. (2009). *Monitoring Performance of Electric Utilities: Indicators and Benchmarking in Sub-Saharan Africa. The Energy Sector Management Assistance Program.* The World Bank.

ESMAP. (2011). *Revisiting Policy Options on the Market Structure in the Power Sector. The Energy Sector and Mining Assistance Program (ESMAP).* The World Bank.

Esso, L. J. (2010). Threshold cointegration and causality relationship between energy use and growth in seven African countries. *Energy Economics, 32*(6), 1383–1391. doi:10.1016/j.eneco.2010.08.003

Estache, A., Tovar, B., & Trujillo, L. (2008). How Efficient are African Electricity Companies? Evidence from the Southern African Countries. *Energy Policy, 36*(6), 1969–1979. doi:10.1016/j.enpol.2008.02.011

Etzioni, A. (2008). *Security first: for a muscular, moral foreign policy.* Yale University Press.

EU Task Force. (2004). EU Land Policy Guidelines. EU Task Force on Land Tenure. Brussels: Author.

EUEI. (2017). *Partnership Dialogue Facility (EUEI PDF), Phase II bis report.* EUEI.

Evans, O. (2018). *connecting the poor: the internet, mobile phones and financial inclusion in Africa.* Digital Policy Regulation and Governance.

Evenari, M., Shanan, L., & Tadmor, N. (1982). *The Negev: the challenge of a desert.* Harvard University Press.

Evrensel, A. Y. (2010). Institutional and economic determinants of corruption: A cross-section analysis. *Applied Economics Letters, 17*(6), 551–554. doi:10.1080/13504850802297814

Fabiyi, O. (2006). Urban Land Use Change Analysis of a Traditional City from Remote Sensing Data: The Case of Ibadan Metropolitan Area, Nigeria. *Humanity & Social Sciences Journal, 1*(1), 42–64.

Fafchamps, M., Gabre-Madhin, E., & Minten, B. (2005). Increasing returns and market efficiency in agricultural trade. *Journal of Development Economics*, *78*(2), 406–442. doi:10.1016/j.jdeveco.2004.10.001

Fajnzylber, P., Maloney, W., & Rojas, G. M. (2006). Microenterprise dynamics in developing countries: How similar are they to those in the industrialized world? Evidence from Mexico. *fir. Economic Review (Federal Reserve Bank of Atlanta)*, *20*(3), 389–419. doi:10.1093/wber/lhl005

Falkner, R. (2003). Private environmental governance and international relations: Exploring the links. *Global Environmental Politics*, *3*(2), 72–87. doi:10.1162/152638003322068227

Family Firm Institute. (2017). *Global data points*. Available at www.ffi.org/page/globaldatapoints

Fan, Y., Liao, H., & Wei, Y.-M. (2007). Can Market Oriented Economic Reforms Contribute to Energy Efficiency Improvement? Evidence from China. *Energy Policy*, *35*(4), 2287–2295. doi:10.1016/j.enpol.2006.07.011

Fan, Y., Liu, L. C., Wu, G., & Wei, Y. M. (2006). Analyzing impact factors of CO_2 emissions using the STIRPAT model. *Environmental Impact Assessment Review*, *26*(4), 377–395. doi:10.1016/j.eiar.2005.11.007

FAO, IFAD, UNICEF, WFP, & WHO. (2018). The State of Food Security and Nutrition in the World. Building climate resilience for food security and nutrition. Rome: Author.

FAO. (2007). *Forests and Energy in OECD Countries.* Forests and Energy Working Paper 1.

FAO. (2009). State of the World's Forests. Viale delle Terme di Caracalla.

FAO. (2010). *FAO Gender and Land Rights Database*. Available online at http://www.fao.org/gender-landrights-database/country-profiles/countries-list/national-legal-framework/land-legislation/en/?country_iso3=NGA

FAO. (2013). *Food Wastage Footprint. Impacts on Natural Resources: Summary Report*. FAO.

FAO. (2015). *Construyendo una visión común para la agricultura y alimentación sostenibles*. Organización de las Naciones Unidas para la Alimentación y la Agricultura.

FAO. (2019). *The State of Food Security and Nutrition in the World. Safeguarding against economic slowdowns and downturns*. https://www.unicef.org/media/55921/file/ SOFI-2019-full-report.pdf

Feder, G., & Umali, D. L. (1993). The Adoption of Agricultural Innovations: A review. *Technological Forecasting and Social Change*, *43*(3-4), 255–298. doi:10.1016/0040-1625(93)90053-A

Federici, S., Tubiello, F. N., Salvatore, M., Jacobs, H., & Schmidhuber, J. (2015). New estimates of CO2 forest emissions and removals: 1990–2015. *Forest Ecology and Management*, *352*, 89–98. doi:10.1016/j.foreco.2015.04.022

Felipe-Lucia, M. R., Martín-López, B., Lavorel, S., Berraquero Díaz, L., Escalera-Reyes, J., & Comín, F. A. (2015). Ecosystem services flows: Why stakeholders' power relationships matter. *PLoS One*, *10*(7), e0132232. doi:10.1371/journal.pone.0132232 PMID:26201000

Ferguson, B. G., & Morales, H. (2010). Latin American agroecologists build a powerful scientific and social movement. *Journal of Sustainable Agriculture*, *34*(4), 339–341. doi:10.1080/10440041003680049

Fernandez, M., Goodall, K., Olson, M., & Mendez, E. (2012). Agroecology and alternative agrifood movements in the United States: Towards a sustainable agrifood system. *Agroecology and Sustainable Food Systems*, *37*, 115–126. doi:10.1080/10440046.2012.735633

FGN. (1990). *Laws of the Federation of Nigeria 1990. Land Use Act. Chapter 202*. Available online at http://www.nigeria-law.org/Land%20Use%20Act.htm

Fianko, J. R., Donkor, A., Lowor, S. T., & Yeboah, P. O. (2011). Agrochemicals and the Ghanaian environment, a review. *Journal of Environmental Protection*, *2*(03), 221–230. doi:10.4236/jep.2011.23026

Fields, G. S. (1975). Rural-urban migration, urban unemployment and underemployment, and job-search activity in LDCs. *Journal of Development Economics*, *2*(2), 165–187. doi:10.1016/0304-3878(75)90014-0 PMID:12265914

Fields, G. S. (2019). *Self-employment and poverty in developing countries*. IZA World of Labor. doi:10.15185/izawol.60.v2

Finch, B. (2010). How to write a business plan (3rd ed.). Academic Press.

Findex, G. (2017). Measuring financial inclusion and Fintex revolution. Academic Press.

Finscope Survey. (2012). *National Baseline Survey Report for Micro, Small, and Medium Enterprises in Tanzania*. Ministry of Industry and Trade, Dar es Salaam; Financial Sector Deepening Trust.

Fiorini, M., & Hoekman, B. (2018). *Restrictiveness of Services Trade Policy and the Sustainable Development Goals. ADBI Working Paper 903*. Asian Development Bank Institute. Available https://www.adb.org/publications/restrictiveness-services-trade-policy-sustainable-development-goals

Fischer, R., Gutierrez, R., & Serra, P. (2003). *The Effects of Privatization on Firms and on Social Welfare: The Chilean Case*. Inter-American Development Bank Research Network Working Paper R-456, May.

Flachsbarth, I., Lay, J., & Garrido, A. (2017). *Rural income dynamics: Understanding poverty and inequality changes in rural Peru* (No. 728-2017-3112). Paper presented at the XV EAAE Congress, "Towards Sustainable Agri-food Systems: Balancing between Markets and Society", Parma, Italy.

Folke, C., Carpenter, S. R., Walker, B., Scheffer, M., Chapin, T., & Rockström, J. (2010). Resilience thinking: Integrating resilience, adaptability and transformability. *Ecology and Society*, *15*(4), art20. doi:10.5751/ES-03610-150420

Food and Agricultural Organisation. (2018). *Institutions, economic freedom and structural transformation in 11 SSA countries*. FAO Agricultural Development Economics Working Paper 18-01. Rome: Food and Agricultural Organisation of United Nations.

Forster, P., Ramaswamy, V., Artaxo, P., Berntsen, T., Betts, R., Fahey, D. W., & Myhre, G. (2007). Changes in atmospheric constituents and in radiative forcing. In *Climate Change 2007*. The Physical Science Basis.

Foster, A. D., & Rosenzweig, M. R. (2010). Microeconomics of technology adoption. Economic Growth Center Discussion, Yale University, Paper No. 984, 1-43. doi:10.1146/annurev.economics.102308.124433

Fosu, A. K. (2017). Growth, inequality, and poverty reduction in developing countries: Recent global evidence. *Research in Economics*, *71*(2), 306–336. doi:10.1016/j.rie.2016.05.005

Fourie, J. (2016). *Finweek*. Retrieved from https://www.pressreader.com/south-africa/finweek-english-edition/20160908/281492160750259

Fournier, E. (2001). Schumpeter (1883-1950): Innovation et capitalisme. *Sciences Humaines*, *8*(119), 1–31.

Fowler, A., & Biekart, K. (2017). Multi-stakeholder initiatives for Sustainable Development Goals: The importance of interlocutors. *Public Administration and Development*, *37*(2), 81–89. doi:10.1002/pad.1795

Francis, C. A., & Porter, P. (2011). Ecology in sustainable agriculture practices and systems. *Critical Reviews in Plant Sciences*, *30*(1-2), 64–73. doi:10.1080/07352689.2011.554353

Francis, P. (1987). Land tenure systems and agricultural innovation: The case of alley farming in Nigeria. *Land Use Policy*, *4*(3), 305–319. doi:10.1016/0264-8377(87)90030-5

Frankel, J., & Romer, D. (1999). Does Trade Cause Growth. *The American Economic Review*, *39*(3), 379–399. doi:10.1257/aer.89.3.379

Fraser, E. D. G., Dougill, A. J., Mabee, W. E., Reed, M., & McAlpine, P. (2005). Bottomup and top down: analysis of participatory processes for sustainability indicator idetification as a pathway to community empowerment and sustainable environmental management. *Environmental Management, 78*(2006), 114-127.

Fraser, S. (2005). *Finance for Small and Medium-Sized Enterprises: A Report on the 2004 UK Survey of SME Finances*. ESRC UK Data Archive: SN 5326.

Frechette, G. R. (2006). *Panel data analysis of the time-varying determinants of corruption (No. 2006s-28)*. Cirano.

French Development Corporation. (2009). *Land Governance and Security of Tenure in Developing Countries. White paper report on "Land Tenure and Development" by French Development Cooperation, June 2009*. Available at http://www.foncier-developpement.fr/wp-content/uploads/land-governance-and-security-of-tenure-in-developing-countries.pdf

Freudenberger, M. S. (2000). *Tenure and natural resources in the Gambia: summary of research findings and policy options. working group on resource tenure and land use planning*. Law Reform Commission of the Gambia, and Nancy Ann Sheehan. Working paper, No. 40, Land Tenure Center, University of Wisconsin–Madison.

Freund, C., & Spatafora, N. (2008). Remittances, transaction costs, and informality. *Journal of Development Economics*, *86*(2), 356–366. doi:10.1016/j.jdeveco.2007.09.002

Frey, D. (2011). *Bioshelter market garden: a permaculture farm*. New Society, Gabriola Island.

Freyburg, T., Krizic, I., Lavenex, S., & O'flynn, C. (2017, January). Democratic governance and transgovernmental networks. *SUPW and PEIO Conference*.

Fujihara, Y., Tanaka, K., Watanabe, T., Nagano, T., & Kojiri, T. (2008). Assessing the impacts of climate change on the water resources of the Seyhan River Basin in Turkey: Use of dynamically downscaled data for hydrologic simulations. *Journal of Hydrology (Amsterdam)*, *353*(1-2), 33–48. doi:10.1016/j.jhydrol.2008.01.024

Funes, F., & Vázquez, L. (Eds.). (2016). *Avances de la agroecología en Cuba*. Editora Estación Experimental de Pastos y Forrajes Indio Hatuey.

Füssel, H.-M. (2007). Vulnerability: A generally applicable conceptual framework for climate change research. *Global Environmental Change*, *17*(2), 155–167. doi:10.1016/j.gloenvcha.2006.05.002

Galafassi, D., Daw, T., Munyi, L., Brown, K., Barnaud, C., & Fazey, I. (2017). Learning about social-ecological trade-offs. *Ecology and Society*, *22*(1), 2. doi:10.5751/ES-08920-220102

Galan, J. E., & Pollitt, M. (2014). *Inefficiency Persistence and Heterogeneity in Colombian Electricity Distribution Utilities*. EPRG Working Paper 1403, Faculty of economics, University of Cambridge.

Garnett, T. (2011). Where are the best opportunities for reducing greenhouse gas emissions in the food system (including the food chain)? *Food Policy*, *36*, S23–S32. doi:10.1016/j.foodpol.2010.10.010

Gasparatos, A., Doll, C. N. H., Esteban, M., Ahmed, A., & Olang, T. A. (2017). Renewable Energy and Biodiversity: Implications for Transitioning to a Green Economy. *Renewable & Sustainable Energy Reviews*, *70*, 161–184. doi:10.1016/j.rser.2016.08.030

Gautam, D. P. (2019). *Do remittances promote financial inclusion?* (J. C. Hall & S. Harper, Eds.). Economic and Political Institutions and Development., doi:10.1007/978-3-030-06049-7_6

Gboney, W. K. (2009). *Econometric Assessment of the Impact of Power Sector Reforms in Africa: A Study of the Generation, Transmission and Distribution Sectors* (PhD thesis). City University, London.

Gedikoglu, H., McCann, L., & Artz, G. (2011). Off-Farm Employment Effects on Adoption of Nutrient Management Practices. *Agricultural and Resource Economics Review*, *2*(2), 293–306. doi:10.1017/S1068280500008078

Geels, F. W., & Kemp, R. (2007). Dynamics in socio-technical systems: Typology of change processes and contrasting case studies. *Technology in Society*, *29*(4), 441–455. doi:10.1016/j.techsoc.2007.08.009

George, B. P., & Henthorne, T. L. (2007). Tourism and the general agreement on trade in services: Sustainability and other developmental concerns. *International Journal of Social Economics*, *34*(3), 136–146. doi:10.1108/03068290710726702

Gerschenkron, A. (1962). *Economic backwardness in historical perspective. A Book of Essays*. The Belknap Press of Harvard University Press.

Ghana Statistical Service. (2013). *2010 population and housing census: regional analytical report, Upper West Region.* Retrieved from www.statsghana.gov.gh/

Ghana Statistical Service. (2014). *Distict Analytical Report, Nadowli.* Retrieved from Ghana http://www.statsghana.gov.gh/docfiles/2010_District_Report/Upper%20West/NADOWLI.pdf

Ghartey, E. E. (2015). Causal relationship between financial development and economic growth in South Africa. *Applied Econometrics and International Development*, *15*(1), 1255–142.

Ghebru, H., & Akumo, A. (2016). *Land Administration Service Delivery and Its Challenges in Nigeria. A case study of eight states*. Nigeria Strategy Support Program, IFPRI Working Paper 39.

Ghebru, H., Edeh, H., Ali, D., Deininger, K., Okumo, A., & Woldeyohannes, S. (2014). *Tenure Security and Demand for Land Tenure Regularization in Nigeria Empirical Evidence from Ondo and Kano States*. International Food Policy Research Institute.

Giuliano, P., & Ruiz-Arranz, M. (2009). Remittances, Financial Development, and Growth. *Journal of Development Economics*, *90*(1), 144–152. doi:10.1016/j.jdeveco.2008.10.005

GIZ. (2018). *Best Practises on Renewable Energy in Africa*. GIZ.

Gjerris, M., & Gaiani, S. J. E. i. p.-N. J. o. A. E. (2013). *Household food waste in Nordic countries: Estimations and ethical implications*. Academic Press.

Gliessman, S. R. (2007). *Agroecology: The ecology of sustainable food systems* (2nd ed.). CRC Press.

Gliessman, S. R., & Rosemeyer, M. (Eds.). (2009). *The conversion to sustainable agriculture: principles, processes, and practices*. CRC Press. doi:10.1201/9781420003598

Global Migration Group. (2017). *Migration, remittances and financial inclusion: challenges and opportunities for women's Economic Empowerment*. GMG Report.

Gnangnon, S. K. (2019). Does multilateral trade liberalization help reduce poverty in developing countries? *Oxford Development Studies*, *47*(4), 435–451. doi:10.1080/13600818.2019.1612866

Goel, R. K., & Nelson, M. A. (2005). Economic freedom versus political freedom: Cross-country influences on corruption. *Australian Economic Papers*, *44*(2), 121–133. doi:10.1111/j.1467-8454.2005.00253.x

Gök, A. (2017). The Role of Governance on Outward Foreign Direct Investment in Emerging Market Economies. In Outward Foreign Direct Investment (FDI) in Emerging Market Economies (pp. 77-101). IGI Global.

Goldsmiths, K.R. (2015). *Barriers and solutions to the development of renewable energy technologies in the Caribbean.* Academic Press.

Gomes, M. V. P., & Merchán, C. R. (2017). Transnational governance: Definitions, approaches and research agenda. *Journal of Contemporary Management, 12*(1). Advance online publication. doi:10.1590/1982- 7849rac2017150332

Gomiero, T., Pimentel, D., & Paoletti, M. G. (2011). Is there a need for a more sustainable agriculture? *Critical Reviews in Plant Sciences, 30*(1-2), 6–23. doi:10.1080/07352689.2011.553515

Gooch, M., Bucknell, D., LaPlain, D., Dent, B., Whitehead, P., Felfel, A., Nikkel, L., & Maguire, M. (2019). *The Avoidable Crisis of Food Waste: Technical Report.* Value Chain Management International and Second Harvest.

Goodluck, C. (2015, Jan.). *Effects of nepotism and family conflicts on the performance of family-owned firms in Tanzania: contrasting views. Business Management Review.*

Grain de Sel. (2012). *Quelles politiques pour les populations rurales pauvres du Sahel?* Author.

Gratwick, K. N., & Eberhard, A. (2008). An Analysis of Independent Power Projects in Africa: Understanding Development and Investment Outcomes. *Development Policy Review, 26*(3), 309–338. doi:10.1111/j.1467-7679.2008.00412.x

Gratwick, K., & Eberhard, A. (2008). Demise of the Standard Model for Power sector Reform and the Emergence of Hybrid Power Markets. *Energy Policy, 36*(10), 3948–3960. doi:10.1016/j.enpol.2008.07.021

Greene, G., Moffett, J., Meyer, S., & Middelkoop, M. J. (2002). Industry codes of practice and other voluntary initiatives: their application to the mining and metals sector. London: International Institute for Environment and Development (IIED).

Green, J. F. (2013). *Rethinking private authority: Agents and entrepreneurs in global environmental governance.* Princeton University Press.

Gregory, S. V., Swanson, F. J., McKeen, W. A., & Cummins, K. W. (1991). An ecosystem perspective of riparian zones. *Bioscience, 4*(8), 540–551. doi:10.2307/1311607

Grossman, G. M., & Krueger, A. B. (1991). *Environmental Impacts of a North American Free Trade Agreement.* National Bureau of Economic Research. doi:10.3386/w3914

Guardians Newspaper interview report. (2017). *Land Use Act: Built environment professionals condemn senate's rejection of bill.* Available online at https://www.vanguardngr.com/2017/07/land-use-act-built-environment-professionals-condemn-senates-rejection-bill/

Guerrieri, P., Luciani, M., & Meliciani, V. (2011). *The Determinants of Investment in Information and Communication Technologies. Bruges European Economic* Research Papers. Nos. 16.

Guo, K., & Stepanyan, V. (2011). *Determinants of bank credit in emerging market economies* (IMF Working Paper No. 11/51). Retrieved from https://www.imf.org/en/Publications/WP/Issues/2016/12/31/Determinants-of-Bank-Credit-in-Emerging-Market-Economies-24698

Gupta, J., Pouw, N., & Ros-Tonen, M. (2015). Towards an elaborated theory of inclusive development. *European Journal of Development Research, 27*(4), 541–559. doi:10.1057/ejdr.2015.30

Gupta, S., Pattillo, C., & Wagh, S. (2009). Effect of Remittances on Poverty and Financial Development in Sub-Saharan Africa. *World Development, 37*(1), 104–115. doi:10.1016/j.worlddev.2008.05.007

Guru, B., & Yadav, I. (2019). Financial development and economic growth: Panel evidence from BRICS. *Journal of Economics, Finance and Administrative Science, 24*(47), 113–126. doi:10.1108/JEFAS-12-2017-0125

Gustavsson, J., Cederberg, C., Sonesson, U., Van Otterdijk, R., & Meybeck, A. (2011). *Global food losses and food waste*. FAO Rome.

Guthiga, P., & Newsham, A. (2011). Meteorologists meeting rainmakers: Indigenous knowlede and climate policy processes in Kenya. *IDS Bulletin, 42*(3), 104–109. doi:10.1111/j.1759-5436.2011.00228.x

Gutierrez, I. A., Kumar, K. B., Mahmud, M., Munshi, F., & Nataraj, S. (2019). Transitions between informal and formal employment: Result from a worker survey in Bangladesh. *IZA Journal of Development and Migration, 9*(3), 2–27. doi:10.118640176-019-0141-2

Gyawal, D., & Thompson, M. (2016). Restoring development dharma with toad's eye science? *IDS Bulletin, 47*(2A), 180–190. doi:10.19088/1968-2016.173192

Hachen, D. S. Jr. (1990). Three Models of Job Mobility in Labour Markets. *Work and Occupations, 17*(3), 320–354. doi:10.1177/0730888490017003004

Hailu, B. K., Abrha, B. K., & Weldegiorgis, K. A. (2014). Adoption and impact of agricultural technologies on farm income: Evidence from Southern Tigray, Northern Ethiopia. *International Journal of Food and Agricultural Economics, 2*(4), 91–106.

Halabi, M. A., Al-qattan, A., & Al-otaibi, A. (2015). Application of solar energy in the oil industry: Current status and future prospects. *Renewable & Sustainable Energy Reviews, 43*, 296–314. doi:10.1016/j.rser.2014.11.030

Hales, T., & Held, D. (Eds.). (2011). *Handbook of transnational governance: Institutions and innovations*. Polity Press.

Hall, D. (1999). *Electricity Restructuring, Privatization and Liberalization: Some International Experiences*. Public Services International Research Unit, University of Greenwich, October.

Hamilton, C., Denniss, R., & Baker, D. (2005). *Wasteful consumption Australia*. Discussion paper number 77. The Australia Institute, Manuka, Australia. https://www.tai.org.au/documents/dpfulltext/DP77.pdfIPCC.Working

Hampwaye, G. (2013). Benefits of urban agriculture: Reality of illusion? *Geoforum, 49*, R7–R8. doi:10.1016/j.geoforum.2013.03.008

Handler, W. (1991). Key interpersonal relationships of next-generation family members in family firms. *Journal of Small Business Management, 28*(July), 21–32.

Hanson, C. (2013). *Food security, inclusive growth, sustainability, and the post-2015 development agenda*. Background Research Paper, High Level Panel on the Post-2015, Development Agenda, World Resources Institute.

Harris, J. R., & Todaro, M. P. (1970). Migration, unemployment and development: A two-sector analysis. *The American Economic Review, 60*(1), 126–142.

Hart, R. (1992). Ladder of participation, children's participation: From Tokenism to citizenship. *Innocenti Essays, 4*.

Hassan & Nhemachena. (2008). Determinants of African farmers' strategies for adapting to climate change: Multinomial choice analysis. *African Journal of Agricultural and Resource Economics, 2*, 83.

Hatfield, J. (2007). Beyond the edge of the field. *Arch. Soil Sci. Soc. Am.* https://www.soils.org/about-society/presidents-message/archive/13

Hebrok, M., & Boks, C. (2017). *Household food waste: Drivers and potential intervention points for design–An extensive review.* Academic Press.

He, J., & Richard, P. (2010). Environmental Kuznets Curve for CO_2 in Canada. *Ecological Economics*, *69*(5), 1083–1093. doi:10.1016/j.ecolecon.2009.11.030

Heller, M. (2019). Waste Not, Want Not: Reducing Food Loss and Waste in North America through Life Cycle-Based Approaches. United Nations Environment Programme, North America Office.

Hellerstein, D., & Nathaniel, H. (2013). The predictive power of risk preference measures for farming decisions. *European Review of Agriculture Economics*, *40*(5), 1–27. doi:10.1093/erae/jbs043

Henri-Bernard, S. L. (2010). Taxation for Development in Africa: A Shared Responsibility. *Trade Negotiations Insights*, *9*(6), 3–4.

Henry, B. P. (2006). *Capital account liberalization: Theory, evidence, and speculation* (NBER Working Paper No. 12698). Retrieved from https://www.nber.org/papers/w12698.pdf

Hernandez, R. R., Easter, S. B., & Murphy-Mariscal, M. L. (2013). Environmental Impacts of Utility-Scale Solar Energy. *Renewable & Sustainable Energy Reviews*, *29*. Advance online publication. doi:10.1016/j.rser.2013.08.041

Herrero, L. (2011). Transport and mobility: The keys to sustainability. *Lychnos: Notebooks of the Fundacion General CSIC*, *04*, 1–6.

Herrmann, R., Jumbe, C., Bruentrup, M., & Osabuohien, E. (2018). Competition between Biofuel Feedstock and Food Production: Empirical Evidence from Sugarcane Outgrower Settings in Malawi. *Biomass and Bioenergy*, *114*(July), 100–111. doi:10.1016/j.biombioe.2017.09.002

Herter, G. (1995). Business planning boosts your chances. *Accounting Technology*.

Hicks, J. (1969). *A theory of economic history*. Claredon Press.

Higley, C. J., Convery, F., & Lévêque, F. (2001). Voluntary approaches: an introduction. In C. J. Higley & F. Lévêque (Eds.), Environmental Voluntary Approaches: Research Insights for Policy-Makers (pp. 4-13). Paris: Centre d'économie Industrielle.

Hine, J., & Ellis, S. (2001). *Agricultural marketing and access to transport services: a rural transport knowledge base, rural travel and transport program*. Available at: http://www.transport-links.org/transport_links/index.Asp

Holt, A. R., Alix, A., Thompson, A., & Maltby, L. (2016). Food production, ecosystem services and biodiversity: We can't have it all everywhere. *The Science of the Total Environment*, *573*, 1422–1429. doi:10.1016/j.scitotenv.2016.07.139 PMID:27539820

Holt-Gimenez, E. (2006). *Campesino a campesino: voices from Latin America's farmer to farmer movement for sustainable agriculture*. Food First.

Holtz-Eakin, D., & Selden, T. M. (1995). Stoking the ðres? CO_2 emissions and economic growth. *Journal of Public Economics*, *57*(1), 85–101. doi:10.1016/0047-2727(94)01449-X

Hormozi, A. M., Sutton, G. S., McMinn, R. D., & Lucio, W. (2002). Business Plans for New or Small Businesses: *Paving the Path to Success. Management Decision*, *40*(8), 755–763.

Huang, Y., & Quibria, M. G. (2013). *The global partnership for inclusive growth*. WIDER Working Paper No. 2013/059.

Huang, S., Lo, S., & Lin, Y. (2013). To re-explore the causality between barriers to renewable energy eevelopment: A case study of wind energy. *Energies*, *6*(9), 4465–4488. doi:10.3390/en6094465

Hunte, C. K. (2004). Workers' Remittances, Remittance Decay and Financial Deepening in Developing Countries. *The American Economist*, *48*(2), 82–94. doi:10.1177/056943450404800208

Hussein, A. (2009). The use of triangulation in social sciences research: Can qualitative and quantitative methods be combined? *Journal of Comparative Social Work*, *4*(1), 106–117. doi:10.31265/jcsw.v4i1.48

Huxster, J. K., Uribe-Zarain, X., & Kempton, W. (2015). Undergraduate Understanding of Climate Change: The Influences of College Major and Environmental Group Membership on Survey Knowledge Scores. *The Journal of Environmental Education*, *46*(3), 149–165. doi:10.1080/00958964.2015.1021661

Ibrahim, M., & Alagidede, P. (2018). *Effect of financial development on economic growth in sub-Saharan Africa: Does sectoral growth Matter?* (ERSA working paper No.754). Retrieved from https://www.econrsa.org/system/files/publications/working_papers/working_paper_754.pdf

ICCIC. (2014). *Israeli Climate Change Information Center (ICCIC). 2014. Adaptation to climate change in Israel recommendations and knowledge gaps, Jerusalem, Israel.* ICCIC.

Idachaba, F. (1980). *The Green Revolution: A Food Production Plan for Nigeria*. Final Report submitted to the Federal Ministry of Agriculture.

Idei, R., & Kato, H. (2018). How Does Rural Road Improvement Influence Livelihoods of the Poor in a Developing Country? A Case Study in Cambodia. *Asian Transport Studies*, *5*(2), 378–392.

IEA. (2014). *Africa Energy Outlook: A Focus on Energy Prospects in Sub-Saharan Africa. World Energy Outlook Special Report*. World Energy Outlook series. International Energy Agency. https://www.iea.org/publications/freepublications/publication/WEO2014_AfricaEnergyOutlook.pdf

IEA. (2016). *Boosting the Power Sector in Sub-Saharan Africa: China's Involvement*. International Energy Agency. https://www.iea.org/publications/freepublications/publication/Partner_Country_SeriesChinaBoosting_the_Power_Sector_in_SubSaharan_Africa_Chinas_Involvement.pdf

IFAC. (2006). Business Planning Guide: Practical Application for SMEs. The International Federation of Accountants (IFAC).

Iizumi, T., & Ramankutty, N. (2015). How do weather and climate influence cropping area and intensity? *Global Food Security*, *4*, 46–50. doi:10.1016/j.gfs.2014.11.003

ILO. (2017). *World employment social outlook. Sustainable enterprises and jobs: formal enterprises and decent work*. International Labour Organisation.

Imbaya, B. O., Nthiga, R. W., Sitati, N. W., & Lenaiyasa, P. (2019). Capacity building for inclusive growth in community-based tourism initiatives in Kenya. *Tourism Management Perspectives*, *30*, 11–18. doi:10.1016/j.tmp.2019.01.003

Imbs, J., & Wacziarg, R. (2003). Stages of diversification. *The American Economic Review*, *93*(1), 63–86. doi:10.1257/000282803321455160

Independent Evaluation Group. (2013). Project Performance Assessment Report: Ghana Land Administration Project. Washington, DC: Author.

Industrial Labour Organisation (ILO). (2014). Global Employment Trends 2014: Risk of a jobless recovery? International Labour Office.

Inoue, T., & Hamori, S. (2016). Do Workers' Remittances Promote Access to Finance? Evidence from Asia-Pacific Developing Countries. *Emerging Markets Finance & Trade*, *52*(3), 765–774. doi:10.1080/1540496X.2016.1116287

Intergovernmental Panel on Climate Change. (2019). *IPCC special report on climate change, desertification, land degradation, sustainable land management, food security and greenhouse gas fluxes in terrestrial ecosystems: summary for policymakers*. Retrieved from https://www.ipcc.ch

International Food Policy Research Institute. (2019). *Byte by Byte: Policy Innovation for Transforming Africa's Food System with Digital Technologies. A Malabo Montpellier Panel Report* (3rd ed.). IFPRI.

International Monetary Fund (IMF). (2014). *Long-run growth and macroeconomic stability in low-income countries: The role of structural transformation and diversification. IMF Policy Paper*. International Monetary Fund.

International Monetary Fund. (2018). *L'avenir de l'emploi en Afrique subsaharienne. Dans Regional Economic Outlook: Sub-Saharan Africa*. Récupéré de: https://www.imf.org/en/Publications/REO/SSA/Issues/2018/09/20/sreo1018

International Trade Centre. (2017). Trade and sustainable tourism. International Trade Centre.

Iossifov, P. K., & Khamis, M. Y. (2009). *Credit growth in sub-Saharan Africa - sources, risks, and policy responses* (IMF Working Paper No. 09/180). Retrieved from https://www.imf.org/en/Publications/WP/Issues/2016/12/31/Credit-Growth-in-Sub-Saharan-Africa-Sources-Risks-and-Policy-Responses-23229

IPCC. (2001). Intergovernmental Panel On Climate. *Climatic Change*, 2007.

IPCC. (2007). Intergovernmental Panel on Climate Change, Mitigation of Climate Change.

IPCC. (2007). *Solomon, Susan,climate change the physical science basis*. AGU Fall Meeting Abstracts.

IPCC. (2014). [Synthesis Report. Contribution of Working Groups I, II and III to the Fifth Assessment Report of the Intergovernmental Panel on Climate Change. IPCC.]. *Climatic Change*, •••, 2014.

IPCC. (2018). Global worming of 1.5 C, an IPCC special report on the impacts of global worming of 1.5 C above pre-industrial levels and related global greenhouse gas emissions. Retrieved from https://wg1.ipcc.ch/SR/documents. SR1.5_LAM3_Room_Assignments.pdf

Ireland, P. N. (1994). Money and growth: An alternative approach. *The American Economic Review*, *84*(1), 47–65.

IRENA Africa Impact Report. (2020). *Scaling Up Renewable Energy Deployment in Africa: Detailed Overview of IRENA's Engagement and Impact*. Author.

IRENA Impact Report. (2019). *Scaling Up Renewable Energy Deployment in Africa: Impact of IRENA's Engagement*. Author.

Issahaku, Z. A., & Maharjan, K. L. (2014). Crop substitution behavior among food crop farmers in Ghana: An efficient adaptation to climate change or costly stagnation in traditional agricultural production system? *Agricultural and Food Economics*, *2*(1), 1–14.

Isukul, A. C., Chizea, J. J., & Agbugba, I. K. (2019). Economic diversification in Nigeria: Lessons from other countries of Africa. *DBN Journal of Economics and Sustainable Development*. Retrieved from www.devbankng.com

Iyoboyi, M., & Pedro, L. M. (2013). The Demand for Money in the Nigeria: Evidence from Bounds Testing Approach. *Business and Economic Journal*, *76*, 1–13.

Iyoha, F. O., Gberevbie, D. E., Iruonagbe, C. T., & Egharevba, M. E. (2015). Cost of Governance in Nigeria: In Whose Interest? International Journal of Social, Education, Economics and Management Engineering, 9(1), 252-259.

Izadbakhsh, M., Gandomkar, M., Rezvani, A., & Ahmadi, A. (2015). Short-term resource scheduling of a renewable energy based micro grid. *Renewable Energy*, *75*(March), 598–606. doi:10.1016/j.renene.2014.10.043

Jacob, K., Guske, A. L., Antoni-Komar, I., Funcke, S., Gruchmann, T., Kny, J., Naber, E., Ruppert-Winkel, C., Sauer, P. C., Stumpf, K. H., & Volk, R. (2019). Governance for the sustainable economy. Institutional innovation from the bottom up? GAIA Ecological Perspectives on Science and Society, 28(1), 204–209. doi:10.14512/gaia.28.S1.6

Jagadish, P. B. (2018). Financial development and economic growth: Evidence from a panel of 16 African and non-African low-income countries. *Cogent Economics and Finance*, *6*(1), 1449780–144. doi:10.1080/23322039.2018.1449780

Jamasb, T. (2004). Between the state and market: Electricity Sector Reform in Developing Countries. *Utilities Policies*, 14-30.

Jamasb, T., Nepal, R., & Timilsina, G. R. (2015). *A Quarter Century Effort Yet to Come of Age: A Survey of Power Sector Reforms in Developing Countries*. Policy Research Working Paper No 7330. World Bank Group, Washington DC.

Jianjun, J., & Chen, D. S. (2014). Willingness to pay for renewable electricity: A contingent valuation study in Beijing, China. *Energy Policy*, *68*(May), 340–347.

Jo-Ansie. (2007). *Political Leaders in Africa: Presidents, Patrons and Profiteers?* Occasional Paper Series 2, 1. African Centre for the Constructive Resolution of Disputes (ACCORD).

Johansen, S., & Juselius, K. (1990). Maximum likelihood estimation and inference on cointegration with application to the demand for money. *Oxford Bulletin of Economics and Statistics*, *52*(2), 169–210. doi:10.1111/j.1468-0084.1990.mp52002003.x

Jordà, Ò. (2005). Estimation and inference of impulse responses by local projections. *The American Economic Review*, *95*(1), 161–182. doi:10.1257/0002828053828518

José, A.F., Miguel, D.F., Matheus, B., & António, C.M. (2019). The nexus between financial development and economic growth: Evidence from European countries. *Journal of Economics Studies and Research*.

Josephsen, L. (2017). Approaches to the implementation of the Sustainable Development Goals – some considerations on the theoretical underpinnings of the 2030 Agenda. Economics Discussion Papers, No 2017-60, Kiel Institute for the World Economy. http://www.economics-ejournal.org/economics/discussionpapers/2017-60

Joskow. P. L. (2008). Lessons Learned From Electricity Market Liberalization. *The Energy Journal, 0*(S1), p. 9-42.

Joskow, P. L. (1998). Electricity Sectors in Transition. *Energy Journal*, *19*(2), 25–28. doi:10.5547/ISSN0195-6574-EJ-Vol19-No2-3

Jung, W. S. (1986). Financial development and economic growth: International evidence. *Economic Development and Cultural Change*, *34*(2), 334–346. doi:10.1086/451531

Kais, S., & Ben Mbarek, M. (2017). Dynamic relationship between CO2 emissions, energy consumption and economic growth in three North African countries. *International Journal of Sustainable Energy*, *36*(9), 840–854. doi:10.1080/14786451.2015.1102910

Kalfagianni, A., Partzsch, L., & Widerberg, O. (2020). Transnational institutions and networks. In F. Biermann & K. Rakhyun (Eds.), *Architectures of Earth System Governance: Institutional Complexity and Structural Transformation*. Cambridge University Press., doi:10.1017/9781108784641.004.

Kang, Y., Khan, S., & Ma, X. (2009). Climate change impacts on crop yield, crop water productivity and food security–A review. *Progress in Natural Science*, *19*(12), 1665–1674. doi:10.1016/j.pnsc.2009.08.001

Kanie, N., Zondervan, R., & Stevens, C. (2014). Ideas on Governance 'of' and 'for' Sustainable Development Goals: UNU-IAS/POST2015 Conference Report. Tokyo: United Nations University Institute for the Advanced Study of Sustainability.

Kantabutra, S. (2008). What do We Know About Vision? *Journal of Applied Business Research, 24*(2), 127–138.

Kapitango, D., & Meijs, M. (2010). Land registration using aerial photography in Namibia: cost and lessons. *Innovations in Land Rights Recognition, Administration, and Governance*. Available online at www.worldbank.org/rural

Karakara, A. A. (2017). Technological Change and Sustainable Development: The Case of Plastic Products Producers in Ghana. *ADRRI Journal of Arts and Social Sciences, 5*(3), 17 – 33.

Karakara, A. A., & Osabuohien, E. (2019). Households' ICT Access and Bank Patronage in West Africa: Empirical Insights from Burkina Faso and Ghana. *Technology in Society, 56*, 116–125. doi:10.1016/j.techsoc.2018.09.010

Karakara, A. A., & Osabuohien, E. (2020). ICT Adoption, Competition and Innovation of Informal Firms in West Africa: Comparative Study of Ghana and Nigeria. *Journal of Enterprising Communities, 14*(3), 397–414. doi:10.1108/JEC-03-2020-0022

Karakaraa, A. A., & Osabuohien, E. O. (2018). Households' ICT access and bank patronage in West Africa: Empirical insights from Burkina Faso and Ghana. *Technology in Society*, 116–125.

Karakaya, E., & Sriwannawit, P. (2015). Barriers to the adoption of photovoltaic systems: The state of the art. *Renewable & Sustainable Energy Reviews, 49*, 60–66. doi:10.1016/j.rser.2015.04.058

Karekezi, S., & Kithyoma, W. (2003). Renewable Energy in Africa: Prospects and Limits. The Workshop for African Energy Experts on Operationalising the NEPAD Energy Initiative, 2-4 June 2003, Novetel, Dakar, Senegal.

Karienye, J. M. (2018). Influence of Rainfall Variability on Tomato Production among Small Scale Farmers in Kieni East Sub County. Academic Press.

Kato, E., Ringler, C., Yesuf, M., & Bryan, E. (2009). *Soil and water conservation technologies: a buffer against production risk in the face of climate change? Insights from the Nile basin in Ethiopia*. IFPRI Discussion paper 00871. International Food Policy Research Institute.

Katundu, M. (2020). Fostering Rural Development and Social Inclusion in East Africa: Interrogating the Role of Cooperatives. In E. Osabuohien (Ed.), *The Palgrave Handbook of Agricultural and Rural Development in Africa*. Palgrave Macmillan. doi:10.1007/978-3-030-41513-6_17

Kaufmann, D. (2009). Aid Effectiveness and Governance: The Good, the Bad and the Ugly. *Development Outreach, 11*(1), 26–29. doi:10.1596/1020-797X-11_1_26

Kautsky, K. (1900). *La question agraire: étude sur les tendances de l'agriculture moderne*. Éditions V. Giard et E. Brière.

Kayiranga, A., Kurban, A., Nahayo, L., & Ndayisaba, F. (2018). Assessing Forest Cover Changes in Volcanoes Parks Region of East-central Africa Using Landsat Imagery. *Journal of Environmental Protection and Sustainable Development, 4*(2), 16–25.

Kazimierczuk, A. H. (2019). Wind Energy in Kenya: A Status and Policy Framework Review. *Renewable & Sustainable Energy Reviews, 107*, 434–445. doi:10.1016/j.rser.2018.12.061

Kazuzuru, B. (2014). History, Performance, and Challenges of Tourism Industry in Tanzania. *International Journal of Business and Social Science, 5*(11), 120–131.

Kebede, Y., Gunjal, K., & Coffin, G. (1990). Adoption of new technologies in Ethiopian agriculture: The case of Tegulet-Bulga District, Shoa province. *Agricultural Economics, 1*, 27–43.

Keller, D. (2009). Community participation in sustainable forest management *Forests and Climate Change Adaptation and Mitigation, 66*.

Kempson, E., Atkinson, A., & Pilley, O. (2004). Policy level response to financial exclusion in developed economies: lessons for developing countries. Report of Personal Finance Research Centre, University of Bristol.

Kenny, C. (2017). How Much Aid is Really Lost to Corruption? *Centre for Global Development*. Retrieved from https://www.cgdev.org/blog/how-much-aid-really-lost-corruption

Keping, Y. (2018). Governance and good governance: A new framework for political analysis. Fudan Journal of the Humanities and Social Sciences, 11(1), 1–8. doi:10.1007/s40647-017-0197-4

Kerzazi, L. (2015). L'innovation au cœur des écoles de pensée économique: Une tentative d'analyse appliquée au secteur agroalimentaire québécois. *La Revue Gestion et Organisation*, *7*(2), 93–105. doi:10.1016/j.rgo.2015.07.001

Kesale, M. A. (2017). Barriers Facing Startup Small and Medium Enterprises (SMEs) in Accessing External Capital in Tanzania. *International Journal of Academic Research in Business and Social Sciences, 7*(3).

Kessides, I. N. (2012, July). The Impacts of Electricity Sector Reforms in Developing Countries. *The Electricity Journal*, *25*(6), 79–88. doi:10.1016/j.tej.2012.07.002

Kessy, S., & Temu, S. S. (2009). Impact on Training on of Micro and Small Enterprises Served by Microfinance Institutions in Tanzania: *Research. Journal of Business and Management.*

Khandker, S., Bakht, Z., & Koolwal, G. (2009). The poverty impact of rural roads: Evidence from Bangladesh. *Economic Development and Cultural Change*, *57*(4), 685–722. doi:10.1086/598765

Khanna, M. (2001). Sequential adoption of site-specific technologies and its implications for nitrogen productivity: A double selectivity model. *American Journal of Agricultural Economics*, *1*(1), 35–51. doi:10.1111/0002-9092.00135

Khatiwada, S. (2009). *Stimulus packages to counter global economic crisis: A review* (Discussion Paper 196). Retrieved from https://www.ilo.org/ inst/publication/discussion-papers/WCMS_193154/lang--en/index.htm

Khellaf, A. (2018). Overview of Economic Viability and Social Impact of Renewable Energy Deployment in Africa. *Africa-EU Renewable Energy Research and Innovation Symposium.*

Kim, K. B., Zhai, F., & Huynh, P. (2016). Regional Trade Agreements, Employment, and Inclusiveness. In ASEAN Economic Community (pp. 175-195). Palgrave Macmillan.

Kim, H. (2019). Beyond monetary poverty analysis: The dynamics of multidimensional child poverty in developing countries. *Social Indicators Research*, *141*(3), 1107–1136. doi:10.100711205-018-1878-3

Kim, S., Gillespie, J. M., & Paudel, K. P. (2005). The effect of socioeconomic factors on the adoption of best management practices in beef cattle production. *Journal of Soil and Water Conservation*, *3*, 111–120.

King, R. G., & Levine, R. (1993). Finance, entrepreneurship and growth. *Journal of Monetary Economics*, *32*(3), 30–71. doi:10.1016/0304-3932(93)90028-E

Kinyashi, G. F. (2006). Towards genuine participation for the poor: Critical analysis of Village Travel and Transport Project (VTTP) in Morogoro, Tanzania. SPRING Scientific Research Paper.

Kironde, J. M. L. (2009). *Improving land Sector Governance in Africa: The Case of Tanzania*. Paper prepared for the "Workshop on "Land Governance in support of the MDGs: Responding to New Challenges," Washington, DC.

Kirui, O. K., Okello, J. J., Nyikal, R. A., & Njiraini, G. W. (2013). Impact of Mobile Phone-Based Money Transfer Services in Agriculture: Evidence from Kenya. *Zeitschrift für Ausländische Landwirtschaft*, *52*(2), 141–162.

Klarin, T. (2018). The concept of sustainable development: From its beginning to the contemporary issues. Zagreb International Review of Economics and Business, 21(1), 67–94. doi:10.2478/zireb-2018-0005

Klein, R. J. (2003). Adaptation to climate variability and change: what is optimal and appropriate. *Climate Change in the Mediterranean: Socio-Economic Perspectives of Impacts, Vulnerability and Adaptation, 32.*

Kling, W. (1943). Food waste in distribution and use. *Journal of Farm Economics*, *25*(4), 848–859. doi:10.2307/1231591

Koch, J., Wimmer, F., & Schaldach, R. (2018). Analyzing the relationship between urbanization, food supply and demand, and irrigation requirements in Jordan. *The Science of the Total Environment*, *636*, 1500–1509. doi:10.1016/j.scitotenv.2018.04.058 PMID:29913610

Kok, G., Lo, S. H., Peters, G.-J. Y., & Ruiter, R. A. (2011). Changing energy-related behavior: An Intervention Mapping approach. *Energy Policy*, *39*(9), 5280–5286. doi:10.1016/j.enpol.2011.05.036

Kok, G., Peters, L., & Ruiter, R. (2017). Planning theory-and evidence-based behavior change interventions: Conceptual review of the intervention mapping tool. *Psychology Research and Review*, *30*(1), 19. doi:10.118641155-017-0072-x PMID:32026109

Kolawole, B. O. (2016). Public spending, institutional quality and inclusive growth in Nigeria: An econometric assessment. *Proceedings of the 2015 Nigerian Economic Society Conference*, 235-264.

Konijnendijk, C., & Gauthier, M. (2006). Urban forestry for multifunctional land use. In *Cities farming for the future: urban agriculture for green and productive cities*. International Development Research Centre, Ottawa. https://www.idrc.ca/en/ev-103884-201-1-DO_TOPIC.html

Kooy, M., Walter, C., & Prabaharyaka, I. (2018). Inclusive development of urban water services in Jakarta: The role of groundwater. *Habitat International*, *73*, 109–118. doi:10.1016/j.habitatint.2016.10.006

Kopytoff, I. (1971). Ancestors as Elders in Africa. *International African Institute*, *41*(2), 129–142. doi:10.2307/1159423

Koropp, C., Kellermanns, F.W., Grichnik, D., & Stanley, L. (2014). Financial Decision Making in Family Firms: An Adaptation of the Theory of Planned Behavior. *Family Business Review*, 1 –21. Doi:10.1177/0894486514522483

Kosoe, A. E., & Osumanu, K. I. (2018). Entertaining risks to health: The state of human faecal matter management in Wa, Ghana. *Ghana Journal of Development Studies*, *15*(1), 149–170. doi:10.4314/gjds.v15i1.8

Kotlar, J., & De Massis, A. (2013). Goal setting in family firms: Goal diversity, social interactions, and collective commitment to family-centred goals. *Entrepreneurship Theory and Practice*, *37*(6), 1263–1288.

KPMG. (2016). *Sub-Saharan Africa Power Outlook 2016*. KPMG Africa Infrastructure. https://assets.kpmg.com/content/dam/kpmg/pdf/2016/05/kpmg-sub-saharan-africa-power-outlook.pdf

Kpodar, K., & Andrianaivo, M. (2011). *ICT, Financial Inclusion, and Growth Evidence from African Countries*. IMF Working Paper/11/73.

Krejcie, R. V., & Morgan, D. W. (1970). Developing Sample Size for Reseach Activities. *Educational and Psychological Measurement*, *30*(3), 607–610. doi:10.1177/001316447003000308

Kremen, C., & Miles, A. (2012). Ecosystem services in biologically diversified versus conventional farming systems: Benefits, externalities, and trade-offs. *Ecology and Society*, *17*(4), 40. doi:10.5751/ES-05035-170440

Kuchimanchi, B., Nazareth, D., Bendapudi, R., Awasthi, S., & D'Souza, M. (2019). Assessing differential vulnerability of communities in the agrarian context in two districts of Maharashtra, India. *Climate and Development*, *11*(10), 918–929. doi:10.1080/17565529.2019.1593815

Kumar, B. M. (2006). Agroforestry: The new old paradigm for Asian food security. *Journal of Tropical Agriculture, 44*, 1–14.

Kumburu, N. P., & Pande, V. (2020). Rural Transformation Through Savings and Credit Cooperative Societies in Moshi District, Tanzania. In E. Osabuohien (Ed.), *The Palgrave Handbook of Agricultural and Rural Development in Africa*. Palgrave Macmillan. doi:10.1007/978-3-030-41513-6_15

Kummu, M., De Moel, H., Porkka, M., Siebert, S., Varis, O., & Ward, P. J. J. S. o. t. t. e. (2012). *Lost food, wasted resources: Global food supply chain losses and their impacts on freshwater, cropland, and fertilizer use*. Academic Press.

Kuratko, D. F., & Hodgetts, R. M. (2001). *Entrepreneurship: A contemporary approach* (5th ed.). Southwestern/Thomson Learning.

Kusakari, Y., Asubonteng, K. O., Jasaw, G. S., Dayour, F., Dzivenu, T., Lolig, V., ... Obeng, F. K. (2014). Farmer-perceived effects of climate change on livelihoods in Wa West District, Upper West Region of Ghana. *Journal of Disaster Research, 9*(4), 516–528. doi:10.20965/jdr.2014.p0516

Kvartiuk, V., & Curtiss, J. (2019). Participatory rural development without participation: Insights from Ukraine. *Journal of Rural Studies, 69*, 76–86. doi:10.1016/j.jrurstud.2019.04.002

Labini, P. S. (2007). Développements scientifiques, innovations technologiques, croissance et productivité. *Revue d'Economie Industrielle, 118*(118), 79–90. doi:10.4000/rei.1773

Laha. (2015). Association between financial inclusion and human development in south asia: A cross-country analysis with special reference to India. *Journal of Economic Policy and Research, 10*(2).

Lai, Lai, & YuChung. (2009). Potentials of food wastes for power generation and energy conservation in Taiwan. *Renewable Energy, 34*, 1913-1915.

Lakomski-laguerre, O. (2006). Introduction à Schumpeter. Alternatives économiques. *Economics and Politics, 29*, 82–98.

Lambrecht, I., Vanlauwe, B., Merckx, R., & Maertens, M. (2014). Understanding the process of agricultural technology adoption: Mineral fertilizer in eastern DR Congo. *World Development, 59*, 132–146. doi:10.1016/j.worlddev.2014.01.024

Lancaster, B., & Marshall, J. (2008). *Water-harvesting earthworks*. Rainsource.

LandLinks. (2015). *Rwanda LAND Report: Access to the Land Tenure Administration Systems and Outcomes*. Available online at https://www.land-links.org/document/rwanda-land-report-access-to-the-land-tenure-administration-systems-and-outcomes/

Latham, G. P., & Yukl, G. A. (1975). A Review of Research on the Application of Goal Setting in Organizations. *Academy of Management Journal, 18*, 824–845.

Leach, P. (2011). *Family Businesses: The Essentials*. Profile Books Ltd.

Leakey, R. R. B. (2012). *Multifunctional agriculture and opportunities for agroforestry: implications of IAASTD. Agroforestry: the future of global land use*. Springer.

Lechenet, M., Dessaint, F., Py, G., Makowski, D., & Munier-Jolain, N. (2017). *Reducing pesticide use while preserving crop productivity and profitability on arable farms* (Vol. 3). Nature Plants.

Lederman, D., Loayza, N. V., & Soares, R. R. (2005). Accountability and corruption: Political institutions matter. *Economics and Politics, 17*(1), 1–35. doi:10.1111/j.1468-0343.2005.00145.x

LeGates, R. T., & Stout, F. (Eds.). (2015). *A ladder of citizen participation*. Routledge.

Lenk, S. K., & Barik, R. (2018). Has expansion of mobile phone and internet use spurred financial inclusion in the SAARC countries? *Financial Innovation*, *4*(5), 5. Advance online publication. doi:10.118640854-018-0089-x

Lepetu, J. P., & Garekae, H. (2015). Attitudes of local communities towards forest management practices in Botswana: The case study of Kasane Forest Plantation. *International Journal of Agriculture and Forestry*, *5*(2), 138–145.

Levidow, L., Pimbert, M., & Vanloqueren, G. (2014). Agroecological research: conforming—or transforming the dominant agro-food regime? *Agroecology and Sustainable Food Systems*, *38*(10), 1127–1155. doi:10.1080/21683565.2014.951459

Levine, R. (2005). Finance and Growth: Theory and Evidence. In P. Aghion & S. Durlauf (Eds.), *Handbook of Economic Growth*. Elsevier Science.

Lev, L., & Stevenson, G. W. (2011). Acting collectively to develop midscale food value chains. *Journal of Agriculture, Food Systems, and Community Development*, *1*(4), 119–128. doi:10.5304/jafscd.2011.014.014

Levy, S., & Székely, M. (2016, October 19). Más escolaridad, menos informalidad Un análisis de cohortes para México y América Latina. *El Trimestre Economico*, *332*(332), 499–548. doi:10.20430/ete.v83i332.232

Lewis, O. (1961). *Five families: Mexican case studies in the culture of poverty*. Basic Books.

Liang, Z., Appleton, S., & Song, L. (2016). *Informal Employment in China: Trends, Patterns and Determinants of Entry*. IZA DP No. 10139.

Liao, J., & Gartner, W. B. (2008). The Influence of Pre-Venture Planning on New Venture Creation. *Journal of Small Business Strategy*, *18*(2), 1-21.

Ljung, P. (2007). *Energy Sector Reform: Strategies for Growth, Equity and Sustainability. Sidastudies no. 20*. Swedish International Development Cooperation Agency.

Long, J. S., & Freese, J. (2001). *Regression models for categorical dependent variables using Stata*. Stata press.

Louw, A., Madevu, H., Jordaan, D., & Vermeulen, H. (2004). *Regoverning markets: Securing small producer participation in restructured national and regional agri-food systems. RSA Country Report*. Department of Agricultural Economics, Extension and Rural Development, University of Pretoria.

Lovell, S. (2010). Multifunctional urban agro ecology for sustainable land use planning in the United States. *Sustainability*, *2*(8), 2499–2522. doi:10.3390u2082499

Lovell, S. T., De Santis, S., Nathan, C. A., Olson, M. B., Méndez, V. E., Hisashi, C., Kominami, H. C., Erickson, D. L., & … . (2010). Integrating agroecology and landscape multi-functionality in Vermont: An evolving framework to evaluate the design of agroeco-systems. *Agricultural Systems*, *103*(5), 327–341. doi:10.1016/j.agsy.2010.03.003

Lucas, R. E. B., & Stark, O. (1985). Motivations to Remit: Evidence from Botswana. *Journal of Political Economy*, *93*(5), 901–918. doi:10.1086/261341

Lund, C. (2011a). *Land Rights and Citizenship in Africa*. Discussion paper 65, Nordiska Afrikainstitutet, Uppsala printed by on demand, Lightning Source UK.

Lund, C. (2011b). Fragmented sovereignty: Land reform and dispossession in Laos. *The Journal of Peasant Studies*, *38*(4), 885–905. doi:10.1080/03066150.2011.607709

Lundqvist, J., de Fraiture, C., & Molden, D. (2008). *Saving water: from field to fork: curbing losses and wastage in the food chain*. Stockholm International Water Institute Stockholm.

Luvanga, N. E., & Shitundu, J. L. (2003). *The role of tourism in poverty alleviation in Tanzania* (Vol. 3). Mkuki Na Nyoka Publications.

Lyne, M. C., & Darroch, M. A. G. (2003). *Land Redistribution in South Africa: Past Performance and Future Policy. In BASIS (Broadening Access and Strengthening Input Market Systems) Collaborative Research Support Program.* University of Wisconsin Madison.

Mabogunje, A. L. (2010). Land reform in Nigeria: progress, problems & prospects. *Proceedings of the annual conference on land policy and administration*, 25.

Madichie, C. V., Osagu, F., & Eze, A. E. (2018). Economic diversification: Imperative for trade and industrial policies in Nigeria. *Timisoara Journal of Economics and Business*, *11*(1), 67–86. doi:10.2478/tjeb-2018-0005

Madison, D. (2006). *The Perception and Adaptation to Climate Change in Africa*. Policy Research Working Paper 4308. University of Pretoria: Centre for Environmental Economics and Policy in Africa.

Maduekwe, N. C. (2014). The land tenure system under the customary law. Proceedings of the Nigerian Institute of Advanced Legal Studies training programme for Judges of the customary courts and area courts, 19. doi:10.2139srn.2813056

Mahembe, E., & Odhiambo, N. M. (2018). The dynamics of extreme poverty in developing countries. Studia Universitatis „Vasile Goldis. *Arad–Economics Series*, *28*(2), 18–35.

Maiwada, N. A., El-Ladan, A. H., & Abdullahi, U. S. (2014). The Role of Renewable Energy in Mitigating Deforestation and Climate Change in Nigeria. *Journal of Natural Sciences Research*, *4*(24).

Makina, D., & Masenge, A. (2015). The Time Pattern of Remittances and the Decay Hypothesis: Evidence from Migrants in South Africa. *Migration Letters: An International Journal of Migration Studies*, *12*(1), 79–90. doi:10.33182/ml.v12i1.258

Makwe, J., Akinwale, Y., & Atoyebi, M. (2012). An Economic Assessment of the Reform of Nigerian Electricity Market. *Energy and Power*, *2*(3), 24–32. doi:10.5923/j.ep.20120203.01

Maloney, W. F. (1997). *The Structure of Labor Market in Developing Countries: Time Series Evidence on Competing Views. Mimeo*. World Bank.

Maloney, W. F. (1999). Does informality imply segmentation in urban labor markets? Evidence from sectoral transitions in Mexico. *The World Bank Economic Review*, *13*(2), 275–302. doi:10.1093/wber/13.2.275

Mandiefe, P. S. (2015). *The impact of financial sector development on economic growth: analysis of the financial development gap between Cameroon and South Africa* (MPRA Paper No. 64694). Retrieved from https://mpra.ub.uni-muenchen.de/64694/

Mandira, S. (2015). Measuring financial inclusion. *Economic Bulletin*, *35*(1), 604–611.

Mansuri, G., & Rao, V. (2012). *Localizing development: Does participation work?* World Bank Publications. doi:10.1596/978-0-8213-8256-1

Maphosa, F. (2007). Remittances and development: The impact of migration to South Africa on rural livelihoods in southern Zimbabwe. *Development Southern Africa*, *24*(1), 123–136. doi:10.1080/03768350601165942

Marques, F. (2010) Constructing sociotechnical transitions toward sustainable agriculture. *Proc. Symp. Innov. Sustain. Dev. Agric.*

Martín-López, B., Gómez-Baggethun, E., García-Llorente, M., & Montes, C. (2014). Trade-offs across value-domains in ecosystem services assessment. *Ecological Indicators*, *37*, 220–228. doi:10.1016/j.ecolind.2013.03.003

Martorano, B., Sanfilippo, M., & Haraguchi, N. (2017). *What factors drive successful industrialization? Evidence and implications for developing countries*. Inclusive and Sustainable Industrial Development Working Paper. Vienna: UNIDO.

Masron, T. A., & Subramaniam, Y. (2019). Does poverty cause environmental degradation? Evidence from developing countries. *Journal of Poverty*, *23*(1), 44–64. doi:10.1080/10875549.2018.1500969

Massay, G. E. (2020). Local Politics of Land Acquisitions for Foreign and Domestic Investments in Tanzania. In E. Osabuohien (Ed.), *The Palgrave Handbook of Agricultural and Rural Development in Africa*. Palgrave Macmillan. doi:10.1007/978-3-030-41513-6_20

Masurel, E., & Smit, H. P. (2000). Planning behaviour of small firms in Central Vietnam. *Journal of Small Business Management*, *38*(2).

Mataya, D. C., Vincent, K., & Dougill, A. J. (2019). How can we effectively build capacity to adapt to climate change? Insights from Malawi. *Climate and Development*, •••, 1–10. doi:10.1080/17565529.2019.1694480

Mayala, N. M., Katundu, M. A., & Msuya, E. E. (2019). Socio-cultural Factors influencing livestock investment decisions among Smallholder Farmers in Mbulu and Bariadi Districts, Tanzania. *Global Business Review*, *20*(5), 1214–1230. doi:10.1177/0972150917742556

Mayala, N. M., Msuya, E. E., & Katundu, M. A. (2018). Role of Extension Services on Livestock Investment Decisions by Smallholder Farmers in Mbulu and Bariadi Districts, Tanzania. *Indian Research Journal of Extension Education*, *18*(3), 57–70.

Mazumdar, D. (2020). The Problems of Development Gap between Developed and Developing Nations: Is There Any Sign of Convergence? In Wealth Creation and Poverty Reduction: Breakthroughs in Research and Practice (pp. 515-536). IGI Global.

McKinnon, R. I. (1973). *Money and capital in economic development*. Brookings Institution Press.

McMichael, A. J., Powles, J. W., Butler, C. D., & Uauy, R. (2007). Food, livestock production, energy, climate change, and health. *Lancet*, *370*(9594), 1253–1263. doi:10.1016/S0140-6736(07)61256-2 PMID:17868818

Mebratu, D. (1998). Sustainability and sustainable development: Historical and conceptual review. *Environmental Impact Assessment Review*, *18*(6), 493–520. doi:10.1016/S0195-9255(98)00019-5

Medayese, F. (2009). *Transportation systems in Nigeria: problems and prospects*. Available at: http://www.jimoh4bunuland.blogspot.com/

Medayese, S., Adeleye, B., & Popoola, A. (2016). Exclusion. In Contemporary Concepts in Physical Planning, (vol. 2, pp. 347-366). Ibadan, Nigeria: Department of Urban and Regional Planning, University of Ibadan.

Medina, L., Jonelis, A., & Cangul, M. (2016). *The Informal Economy in Sub-Saharan Africa: Size and Determinants*. IMF working paper 156. (WP/17/156).

Megginson, W. L., & Netter, J. M. (2001). From State to Market: A Survey of Empirical Studies on Privatization. *Journal of Economic Literature*, *39*(2), 321–389. doi:10.1257/jel.39.2.321

Mena, C., Adenso-Diaz, B., & Yurt, O. (2011). The causes of Food waste in the supplier-retailer interface: Evidences from the UNK and Spain. *Resources, Conservation and Recycling*, *55*(6), 648–658. doi:10.1016/j.resconrec.2010.09.006

Menard, C., & Shirley, M. M. (2005). *Handbook of new institutional economics*. Springer. doi:10.1007/b106770

Méndez, V. E., Bacon, C. M., & Cohen, R. (2013). Agroecology as a transdisciplinary, participa-tory, and action-oriented approach. *Agroecology and Sustainable Food Systems*, *37*(1), 3–18.

Mendosa, E. L. (1976). Elders, office-holders and ancestors among Sisala of Northern Ghana. *Africa, 46*(1), 57–65. doi:10.2307/1159093

Mensah, J. (2019). Sustainable development: Meaning, history, principles, pillars, and implications for human action: Literature review. *Cogent Social Sciences, 5*. Advance online publication. doi:10.1080/23311886.2019.1653531

Mercado-Bettin, D., Salazar, J. F., & Villegas, J. C. (2017). Global Synthesis of Forest Cover Effects on Long-term Water Balance Partitioning in Large Basins. *Hydrology and Earth System Sciences Discussions, 550*. Advance online publication. doi:10.5194/hess-2017-550

Merchant, K. A., & Van der Stede, W. A. (2007). Management Control Systems: Performance Measurement, Evaluation Incentives. Edinburgh Gate: Pearson Education Limited.

Merckx, T., & Pereira, H. M. (2015). Reshaping agrienvironmental subsidies: From marginal farming to large-scale rewilding. *Basic and Applied Ecology, 16*(2), 95–103. doi:10.1016/j.baae.2014.12.003

Mertz, O., Mbow, C., Reenberg, A., & Diouf, A. (2009). Farmers' perceptions of climate change and agricultural adaptation strategies in rural Sahel. *Environmental Management, 43*(5), 804–816. doi:10.100700267-008-9197-0 PMID:18810526

Metu, A. G., Igbanugo, I. C., & Okonji, S. O. (2018). Economic diversification, institutional environment and industrialization in Nigeria. *International Journal of Economics, Commerce and Management, 6*(12), 10-25. Retrieved from http://ijecm.co.uk/

Metu, A. G., Maduka, O. D., Eze, A. E., & Ajudua, E. (2019). Impact of fiscal policy on inclusive growth in Nigeria. *African Journal of Sustainable Development, 9*(2).

Michael, H., & Morris Roy,, W., & Williams. (1996). Factors influencing family business succession. *International Journal of Entrepreneurial Behaviour & Research, 2*(3), 68–81.

Michie, J., & Lobao, L. (2012). Ownership, control and economic outcomes. *Cambridge Journal of Regions, Economy and Society, 5*(3), 307–324. doi:10.1093/cjres/rss015

Ministry of Industry and Trade of the United Republic of Tanzania. (2012). *Tanzania Industrial Competitiveness Report*. Author.

Mintzberg, H. (1993). *The Rise and Fall of Strategic Planning*. The Free Press.

Misati, R., & Kamau, A. (2018). *Do Migrant Remittances Matter for Financial Development in Kenya?* The Kenya Bankers Association (KBA) Working Papers, no. 30, WPS/08/18.

MITI – Ministry of Industry, Trade and Investment. (2017a). Strategy for fast-tracking industrialization in Tanzania: 2016-2020. Dar es Salaam: MITI.

MITI – Ministry of Industry, Trade and Investment. (2017b). A joint inter-ministerial programme for supporting implementation of the industrialization agenda. Dar es Salaam: MITI.

MITI – Ministry of Industry, Trade and Investment. (2018). Blueprint for regulatory reforms to improve the business environment. Dar es Salaam: MITI.

Mo Ibrahim Foundation. (2019, October). Agendas 2063 & 2030: Is Africa on track? The African Governance Report.

Mogaka, H., Simons, G., Turpie, J., Emerton, L., & Karanja, F. (2001). *Economic aspects of community involvement in sustainable forest management in eastern and southern Africa*. IUCN.

Moghaddasi, R., Sadeghi, E., Hosseini, S., & Mohammadi, A. (2017). Export diversification and agricultural growth: Evidence from developed countries. *Journal of Economics*, *1*, 1–13. doi:10.1016/j.econ.2017.07.001

Mollison, B., & Holmgren, D. (1978). *Permaculture one: a perennial agricultural system for human settlements*. Tagari, Tyalgum.

Mollison, B. (1988). *Permaculture: a designer's manual*. Tagari.

Moomaw, W. R., & Unruh, G. C. (1997). Are environmental Kuznets curves misleading us? The case of CO_2 emissions. *Environment and Development Economics*, *2*(4), 451–463. doi:10.1017/S1355770X97000247

Moomaw, W., Yamba, F., Kamimoto, M., Maurice, L., Nyboer, J., Urama, K., & Weir, T. (2011). Introduction. In *IPCC Special Report on Renewable Energy Sources and Climate Change Mitigation*. Cambridge University Press.

Moon, H., & Solomon, T. (2018). Forest Decline in Africa: Trends and Impacts of Foreign Direct Investment: A Review. *International Journal of Current Advanced Research*, *7*(11), 16356–16361. doi:10.24327/ijcar.2018

Morisaki, I. (2011). *Pattern of Food Losses in Households: A Case Study in Oita-Prefecture, Japan*. Oita, Japan: Ritsumeikan Asia Pacific University. Retrieved April 3 2015 from: http://r-cube.ritsumei.ac.jp/bitstream/10367/2585/1/MORISAKI%20Ikuko.pdf

Mouchet, M. A., Lamarque, P., Martín-López, B., Crouzat, E., Gos, P., Byczek, C., & Lavorel, S. (2014). An interdisciplinary methodological guide for quantifying associations between ecosystem services. *Global Environmental Change*, *28*, 298–308. doi:10.1016/j.gloenvcha.2014.07.012

Moumouni, I. M., Vodouhe, S. D., & Streiffeler, F. (2009). What makes small-scale farmers participate in financing agricultural research extension? Analysis of three case studies from Benin. *Journal of Agricultural Education and Extension*, *15*(3), 301–316. doi:10.1080/13892240903069595

Moyo, S., & Yeros, P. (2005). Reclaiming the Land. The Resurgence of Rural Movements in Africa. Zed Books.

Msami, J., & Wangwe, S. (2016). Industrial Development in Tanzania. In Manufacturing Transformation: Comparative Studies of Industrial Development in Africa and Emerging Asia (pp. 155-173). Oxford Scholarship Online.

Msengezi, C., & Williams, Y. (2019). Les femmes et la digitalisation de l'agriculture. *Un bulletin d'alerte pour l'agriculture ACP*, 90. Récupéré le 18 Juin 2019 de https://cgspace.cgiar.org/bitstream/handle/10568/99719/ICTUpdate90F.pdf

Mufuruki, A., Mawji, R., Kasiga, G., & Marwa, M. (2018). *Tanzania's industrialization journey, 2016–2056: from an agrarian to a modern industrialized state in forty years*. Moran Publishers.

Mufuruki, A., Mawji, R., Marwa, M., & Kasiga, G. (2017). *Tanzania's Industrialization Journey, 2016 – 2056: From an Agrarian to a Modern Industrialized State in Forty Years, Moran (E, E.)*. Publishers Limited.

Mukasa, A. D., Mutambatsere, E., Arvanitis, Y., & Triki, T. (2012). *Development of Wind Energy in Africa*. African Development Bank Group Working Paper Series No 152- June, 2012.

Mukasa, A. D., Mutambatsere, E., Arvanitis, Y., & Triki, T. (2013). *Development of Wind Energy in Africa*. African Development Bank Group Working Paper Series No 170- March 2013.

Mulyana, W. (2014). *Rural-Urban Linkages: Indonesia Case Study*. Working Paper Series No. 126. Working Group: Development with Territorial Cohesion. Territorial Cohesion for Development Program. Rimisp, Santiago, Chile.

Muriithi, A. G., Bett, E., & Ogaleh, S. A. (2009). *Information Technology for Agriculture and Rural Development in Africa: Experiences from Kenya*. Paper presented at the Conference on International Research on Food Security, Natural Resource Management and Rural Development, University of Hamburg.

Musolesi, A., Mazzanti, M., & Zoboli, R. (2010). A panel data heterogeneous Bayesian estimation of environmental Kuznets curves for CO_2 emissions. *Applied Economics*, *42*(18), 2275–2287. doi:10.1080/00036840701858034

Mussery, A., Leu, S., Lensky, I., & Budovsky, A. (2013). The effect of planting techniques on arid ecosystems in the northern Negev. *Arid Land Research and Management*, *27*(1), 90–100. doi:10.1080/15324982.2012.719574

Myers, G. W. (1991). *Land and power: the impact of the Land Use Act in Southwest Nigeria*. Land Tenure Center (LTC) Research Working Paper 108, University of Wisconsin-Madison.

N'Goulakia, L. P. (2015). Afrique subsaharienne: Une identité plurielle, un destin commun. *Géoéconomie*, *73*(1), 59–72. doi:10.3917/geoec.073.0059

Nabila, A., & Zakir, H. (2014). Financial development, trade openness and economic growth in developing countries: Recent evidence from panel data. *Pakistan Economic and Social Review*, *52*(2), 99–126.

Nadiruzzaman, M., & Wrathall, D. (2015). Participatory exclusion - Cycle Sidr and its aftermath. *Geoforum*, *64*, 196–204. doi:10.1016/j.geoforum.2015.06.026

Nagayama, H. (2007). Effects of Regulatory reforms in the Electricity Supply Industry on Electricity Prices in Developing Countries. *Energy Policy*, *35*(6), 3440–3462. doi:10.1016/j.enpol.2006.12.018

Nagayama, H. (2010). Impacts on Investments, and Transmission/Distribution Loss through Power Sector Reforms. *Energy Policy*, *38*(7), 3453–3467. doi:10.1016/j.enpol.2010.02.019

Nair, P. K. R. (1993). *An introduction to agroforestry*. Kluwer Academic Publishers. doi:10.1007/978-94-011-1608-4

Nair, P. K. R. (2007). The coming age of agroforestry. *Journal of the Science of Food and Agriculture*, *87*(9), 1613–1619. doi:10.1002/jsfa.2897

Nakamura, S., Bundervoet, T., & Nuru, M. (2019). *Rural roads, poverty, and resilience: evidence from Ethiopia*. The World Bank. doi:10.1596/1813-9450-8800

Namubiru-Mwaura, E. L., Knox, A., & Hughes, A. K. (2012). *Liberia Land Policy & Institutional Support (LPIS) Project Customary Land Tenure in Liberia: Findings and Implications Drawn from 11 Case Studies*. United States Agency for International Development.

Nandonde, F. A., Lubava, G., & Liana, P. J. (2015). Uptake of Market 'Induced Innovation' by Upstream Actors in Tanzania. In C. Machado & D. J. Paulo (Eds.), *Innovation Management: In Research and Industry* (pp. 39–58). Walter de Gruyter. doi:10.1515/9783110358759.39

Narh, P., Lambini, C. K., Sabbi, M., Pham, V. D., & Nguyen, T. T. (2016). Land Sector Reforms in Ghana, Kenya and Vietnam: A Comparative Analysis of Their Effectiveness. *Land (Basel)*, *5*(2), 8. doi:10.3390/land5020008

Nasirov, S., Silva, C., & Agostini, C. A. (2015). Investors' perspectives on barriers to the deployment of renewable energy sources in Chile. *Energies*, *8*(5), 3794–3814. doi:10.3390/en8053794

Nazir, J., & Pedretti, E. (2016). Educators' perceptions of bringing students to environmental consciousness through engaging outdoor experiences. *Environmental Education Research*, *22*(2), 288–304. doi:10.1080/13504622.2014.996208

NBS – National Bureau of Statistics. (2016). *Report on the 2013 census of industrial production*. NBS.

Neff, R.A., Spiker, M., Rice, C., Schklair, A., Greenberg, S., Broad Leib, E., 2019. Misunderstood food date labels and reported food discards: a survey of UU.S.consumer attitudes and behaviors. *Waste Manage, 86*, 123-132. .023 doi:10.1016/j.wasman.2019.01

Negasi, S., Hishe, H., Annang, T., Pabi, O., Asante, I. K., & Birhane, E. (2018). Forest Cover Change, Key Drivers and Community Perception of Wujig Mahgo Waren Forest of Northern Ethiopia. *Land (Basel)*, *7*(1), 32. doi:10.3390/land7010032

Nehls, T., Jiang, Y., Dennehy, C., Zhan, X., & Beesley, L. (2015). From waste to value: urban agriculture enables cycling of resources in cities. In Urban Agriculture Europe, (pp. 170–173). Berlin: Jovis.

Nellis, J. (2008). *Private Management Contracts in Power Sector in Sub-Saharan Africa. Internal note, Africa Infrastructure Country Diagnostic*. World Bank.

Nelson, E., Scott, S., Cukier, J., & Galán, Á. L. (2009). Institutionalizing agroecology: Successes and challenges in Cuba. *Agriculture and Human Values*, *26*(3), 233–243. doi:10.100710460-008-9156-7

Nepal, R. (2013). *From State to Market: Essays on Electricity Sector Reforms* (PhD Thesis). Heriot-Watt University, Edinburgh, UK.

Nepal, R., & Jamasb, T. (2012). Reforming the Power Sector in Transition: Do Institutions Matter? *Energy Economics*, *34*(5), 1675–1682. doi:10.1016/j.eneco.2012.02.002

Nesamalar, J. J. D., Venkatesh, P., & Raja, S. C. (2017). The drive of renewable energy in Tamilnadu: Status, barriers and future prospect. *Renewable & Sustainable Energy Reviews*, *73*(June), 115–124. doi:10.1016/j.rser.2017.01.123

Newbery, D. (2002). *Issues and options for restructuring electricity supply industries*. DAE Working Paper WP 0210. Cambridge: Department of Applied Economics, University of Cambridge.

Newbery, D. (1995). Power Markets and Market Power. *Energy Journal*, *16*(3), 41–66. doi:10.5547/ISSN0195-6574-EJ-Vol16-No3-2

Nhamo, L. (2019). Preparedness or repeated short-term relief aid? Building drought resilience through early warning in southern Africa. *Water S.A.*, *45*(1), 75–85.

Nhamo, L., Mathcaya, G., Mabhaudhi, T., Nhlengethwa, S., Nhemachena, C., & Mpandeli, S. (2019). Cereal production trends under climate change: Impacts and adaptation strategies in southern Africa. *Agriculture*, *9*(2), 30. doi:10.3390/agriculture9020030

Niang, Ruppel, Abdrabo, Essel, Lennard, Padgham, & Urquhart. (2014). Africa. In Climate Change: Impacts, Adaptation, and Vulnerability (pp. 1199–1265). Cambridge University Press.

Nigeria Sovereign Investment Authority – NSIA. (2018). *Background on Nigeria Sovereign Investment Authority*. Retrieved from https://www.swfinstitute.org/swfs/excess-crude-account/

Nightingale, A. J., Eriksen, S., Taylor, M., Forsyth, T., Pelling, M., Newsham, A., & Bezner-Kerr, R. (2019). Beyond technical fixes: Climate solutions and the great deragement. *Climate and Development*, 1–10. doi:10.1080/17565529.2019.1624495

Njoroge, M. (2019*). Linking entrepreneurial orientation and corporate sustainability: A study of tourist hotels in Tanzania* [Unpublished doctoral thesis]. University of Dar es Salaam, Dar es Salaam, Tanzania.

Njoroge, M. (in press). Tourism Sustainability: Reconceptualization and Measurements In Tourism, and Sustainable Development in Tanzania. Academic Press.

Nkegbe, P., Kuunibe, N., & Abdul-Mumin, Y. (2012). Choice of transport mode by non-resident university students in Ghana. *International Journal of Business and Social Science*, *3*(2), 136–142.

Nkume, N. (2018). Financing Mechanisms African Governments Should Pursue in Financing Sustainable Development in the Next 20 Years. In Financing Sustainable Development in Africa. Palgrave Macmillan.

Nordman, C. J., Rakotomanana, F., & Roubaud, F. (2016). *Informal versus Formal: A Panel Data Analysis of Earnings Gaps in Madagascar. IZA Discussion Papers, No. 9970. Institute for the Study of Labour.* IZA.

Nordman, C. J., Rakotomanana, F., & Roubaud, F. (2016). Informal versus formal: A panel data analysis of earnings gaps in Madagascar. *World Development, 86*, 1–17. doi:10.1016/j.worlddev.2016.05.006

Norfolk, S., & Tanner, C. (2007). *Improving tenure security for the rural poor. Mozambique Country case study.* FAO legal empowerment of the poor working paper. Available: http://www.fao.org/3/ak0786e.pdf

North, D. C. (1990). *Institutions, Institutional Change and Economic Performance.* University Press. doi:10.1017/CBO9780511808678

North, D. C. (1991). Institutions. *The Journal of Economic Perspectives, 5*(1), 97–112. doi:10.1257/jep.5.1.97

Norton, R. D. (2014). Policy Frameworks for International Agricultural and Rural Development. Encyclopedia of Agriculture and Food Systems, 489-503. doi:10.1016/B978-0-444-52512-3.00123-6

Nsiah, B. (2010). Contribution of farm forest plantation management to the livelihood strategies of farm households in the high forest zone of Ghana. *FakultätForst-, Geo- und Hydrowissenschaften.*

Nwachukwu, I. (2008). *Planning and evaluation of agricultural and rural development project.* Lambhouse publishers.

Nwaobi, G. C. (2001). Modern econometric modelling for developing economies I. Lagos: Quantitative Economic Research Bureau (QUANTERB).

Nwocha, M. E. (2016). Impact of the Nigerian Land Use Act on Economic Development in the Country. *Acta Universitatis Danubius. Administratio, 8*(2), 117–128.

Nyantakyi-Frimpong, H., & Bezner-Kerr, R. (2015). The relative importance of climate change in the context of multiple stressors in semi-arid Ghana. *Global Environmental Change, 32*, 40–56. doi:10.1016/j.gloenvcha.2015.03.003

Nyaupane, N. P., & Gillespie, J. (2009). *The influences of land tenancy and rotation selection on crawfish farmers' adoption of best management practices.* Paper presented at the annual meeting of Southern Agricultural Economics Association, Atlanta, GA.

Nyong, A., Adesina, F., & Elasha, B. O. (2007). The value of indigenous knowledge in climate change mitigation and adaptation strategies in the African Sahel. *Mitigation and Adaptation Strategies for Global Change, 12*(5), 787–797. doi:10.100711027-007-9099-0

Nzeh, E., Famobuwa, O. S., & Iroechenwu, C. (2017). Land Reform System and Its Implications on Agricultural Production in Nigeria. *Universal Journal of Agricultural Research, 5*(6), 338–343. doi:10.13189/ujar.2017.050604

Obayelu, A. E., Arowolo, A. O., & Osinowo, O. H. (2017). Land Tenure, Governance and Accountability in Nigeria: The Implications on Food Production to Feed the Present and the Future. [JADE]. *Journal for the Advancement of Developing Economies, 6*(1), 1–17.

Obinna, L., & Ukoha, J. (2017). Comparative effect of rural road transportations on cassava production among rural farmers in Abia State, Nigeria. *European Journal of Social Sciences Studies, 2*(3), 117–131.

OECD Policy Brief. (2015). *Linking Renewable Energy to Rural Development.* Author.

OECD. (2002). *Foreign Direct Investment for Development: Maximising Benefits, Minimising Costs.* OECD.

OECD. (2016, July). Development Aid at a Glance: Statistics by Region. *Africa, 2015*, 26. https://www.oecd.org/dac/stats/documentupload/2%20Africa%20%20Development%20Aid%20at%20a%20Glance%202015.pdf,accessed

OECD/IEA. (2017). *FAO*. Bioenergy Roadmap Development and Implementation.

OECD/WTO. (2017). *Aid for Trade at a Glance 2017: Promoting Trade, Inclusiveness and Connectivity for Sustainable Development*. WTO/OECD Publishing.

Oelofse, S. H., & Nahman, A. (2013). Estimating the magnitude of food waste generated in South Africa. *Waste Management & Research*, *31*(1), 80–86. doi:10.1177/0734242X12457117 PMID:22878934

Ogada, M. J. (2012). *Forest management decentralisation in Kenya: Effects on household farm forestry decisions in Kakamenga*. Paper presented at the Triennial Conference of the International Association of Agricultural Economists, Brazil.

Ogunleye, O., Ajibola, A., Enilolobo, O., & Shogunle, O. (2018). Influence of road transport infrastructure on agricultural sector development in Nigeria. *Logistics & Sustainable Transport*, *9*(1), 39–50. doi:10.2478/jlst-2018-0004

Ogunrinola, I. O., & Osabuohien, E. S. (2010). Globalization and Employment Generation in Nigeria's Manufacturing Sector (1990-2006). *European Journal of Soil Science*, *12*(4), 581–593.

Ohunakin, O. S., Adaramola, M. S., Oyewola, O. M., & Fagbenle, R. O. (2014). Solar energy applications and development in Nigeria: Drivers and barriers. *Renewable & Sustainable Energy Reviews*, *32*, 294–301. doi:10.1016/j.rser.2014.01.014

Okonkwo, E. C. (2013). A Closer Look at The Management, Revocation and Compensation Principles Under the Nigerian Land Use Act. Afe Babalola University. *Journal of Sustainable Development Law and Policy*, *1*(1), 21–36.

Okorie, U., Osabuohien, E., & Oaikhenan, H. (2020). Electricity Consumption, Public Agricultural Expenditure and Output in Nigeria: A Time Series Dynamic Approach. *International Journal Energy Economics and Policy*, *10*(2), 113–123. doi:10.32479/ijeep.8436

Okoro, S. U., Schickhoff, U., & Schneider, A. (2018). Impacts of Bioenergy Policies on Land- Use Change in Nigeria. *Energies*, *11*(152). Advance online publication. doi:10.3390/en11010152

Oladele, O. I. (2015). Effect of information communication technology (ICT) on agricultural information access among extension officers in North West province South Africa. *South African Journal of Agricultural Extension*, *43*(2), 30–41. doi:10.17159/2413-3221/2015/v43n2a344

Olajide, S., & Olayemi, J. (1972). *A Quantitative Analysis of Food Requirement; Supply and Demand in Nigeria. 1968-1985*. Federal Department of Agriculture.

Olawumi, T. O., & Chan, D. W. M. (2018). A scientometric review of global research on sustainability and sustainable development. *Journal of Cleaner Production*, *183*, 231–250. doi:10.1016/j.jclepro.2018.02.162

Olayiwola, L., & Adeleye, O. (2006). *Land Reform Experience form Nigeria*. Paper presented at the FIG Regional Conference Promoting Land Administration and Good Governance, Accra, Ghana.

Olayiwola, L., & Adeleye, O. (2005). Rural infrastructural development in Nigeria between 1960-1990- problems and challenges. *Journal of Social Science*, *11*(2), 91–96.

Olayiwola, W., Osabuohien, E., & Efobi, U. (2012). Inflation and Financial Development in Nigeria. In O. Olaniyan, A. O. Lawson, & B. Alayande (Eds.), *Financial Sector Issues and Economic Development in Nigeria II* (pp. 49–67). University Press.

Olukotun, G. (2007). The role of local government in rural transport finance. *Journal of Social Sciences*, *15*(2), 147–152. doi:10.1080/09718923.2007.11892576

Oluwasola, O., Idowu, E., & Osuntogun, D. (2008). Increasing agricultural household incomes through rural-urban linkages in Nigeria. *African Journal of Agricultural Research*, *3*(8), 566–573.

Omiti, J., Otieno, D., Nyanamba, T., & McCullough, E. (2009). Factors influencing the intensity of market participation by smallholder farmers: A case study of rural and peri-urban areas of Kenya. *African Journal of Agricultural and Resource Economics*, *3*(1), 57–82.

Omotola, J. S., & Saliu, H. (2009). Foreign aid, debt relief and Africa's development: Problems and prospects. *South African Journal of International Affairs*, *16*(1), 87–102. doi:10.1080/10220460902986180

Onakoya, A., Johnson, B., & Ogundajo, G. (2019). Poverty and trade liberalization: Empirical evidence from 21 African countries. *Economic research-. Ekonomska Istrazivanja*, *32*(1), 635–656. doi:10.1080/1331677X.2018.1561320

Oni, S. (2000). Education and Training for Road Traffic Safety in Nigeria. In *Proceedings of the International Conference CODATU IX* (pp. 913 – 918). Academic Press.

Oparah, E. N. (2018). Diversification of the Nigerian economy: The role of Nigerian institute of Leather and Science Technology (NILEST), Zaria Kaduna Nigeria. In B. Anan & A. S. Antai (Eds.), The Nigerian economy: Recession, recovery and growth plan (pp. 2-8). KEJA Publications.

Opare, S. (2016). Adaptation to climate change impacts: Coping strategies of an indigenous community in Ghana to declining water supply. *Climate and Development*, *10*(1), 73–83. doi:10.1080/17565529.2016.1184610

Orbell, S., Hodgkins, S., & Sheeran, P. (1997). Implementation intentions and the theory of planned behavior. *Personality and Social Psychology Bulletin*, *23*(9), 945–954. PMID:29506445

Organization for Economic Cooperation & Development-OECD. (2011). *Economic Diversification in Africa: A Review of Selected Countries*. OECD Publishing.

Orozco & Fedewa. (2006). *Leveraging Efforts on Remittances and Financial Intermediation*. INTAL-ITD: Inter-American Development Bank.

Ortiz, R., Sayre, K. D., Govaerts, B., Gupta, R., Subbarao, G. V., Ban, T., Hodson, D., Dixon, J. M., Iván Ortiz-Monasterio, J., & Reynolds, M. (2008). Climate change: Can wheat beat the heat? *Agriculture, Ecosystems & Environment*, *126*(1-2), 46–58. doi:10.1016/j.agee.2008.01.019

Osabohien, R., Matthew, O., Ohalete, P., & Osabuohien, E. (2020). Population-Poverty-Inequality Nexus and Social Protection in Africa. *Social Indicators Research*, *151*(2), 575–598. Advance online publication. doi:10.1007/s11205-020-02381-0

Osabohien, R., Onanuga, O., Aderounmu, B., Matthew, O., & Osabuohien, E. (2020). Social Protection and Employment in Africa's agricultural Sector. *Business: Theory and Practice*, *21*(2), 494–502. doi:10.3846/btp.2020.11945

Osabohien, R., Osabuohien, E., & Ohalete, P. (2019). Agricultural Sector Performance, Institutional Framework and Food Security in Nigeria. *Bio-Based and Applied Economics*, *8*(2), 161–178.

Osabohien, R., Osabuohien, E., & Urhie, E. (2018). Food security, institutional framework and technology: Examining the nexus in Nigeria using ARDL approach. *Current Nutrition and Food Science*, *14*(2), 154–163. doi:10.2174/1573401313666170525133853 PMID:29853816

Osabohien, R., Osuagwu, E., Osabuohien, E., Ekhator-Mobayode, U. E., Matthew, O., & Gershon, O. (2020). Household access to agricultural credit and agricultural production in Nigeria: A propensity score matching model. *Suid-Afrikaanse Tydskrif vir Ekonomiese en Bestuurswetenskappe*, *22*(1), a2688. doi:10.4102ajems.v23i1.2688

Osabohien, R., Ufua, D., Moses, C. L., & Osabuohien, E. (2020). Accountability in agricultural governance and food security in Nigeria. *Brazilian Journal of Food Technology, 23*, e2019054. doi:10.1590/1981-6723.08919

Osabuohien, E. S., Efobi, U. R., & Gitau, C. M. W. (2013). External Intrusion, Internal Tragedy: Environmental Pollution and Multinational Corporations in Sub-Saharan Africa. In L. Leonard & M. A.Gonzalez-Perez (Eds.), Principles and Strategies to Balance Ethical, Social and Environmental Concerns with Corporate Requirements (pp. 93-118). Emerald Group Publishing doi:10.1108/S2051-5030(2013)0000012010

Osabuohien, E., & Ike, D. N. (2011). Economic Transformation and Institutional Framework in Nigeria – Lessons from Botswana and South Korea. *Selected Papers at the 2011 Annual Conference of Nigerian Economic Society,* 382-414.

Osabuohien, E., & Karakara, A. A. (2020). Conclusion: Agricultural investments and Rural Development in Africa—Salient Issues and Imperatives. In The Palgrave Handbook of Agricultural and Rural Development in Africa (pp. 627-640). Cham, Switzerland: Palgrave Macmillan. Doi:10.1007/978-3-030-41513-6_28

Osabuohien, E., Efobi, U., Gitau, C. M., Osabohien, R. A., & Adediran, O. O. (2020). Youth Unemployment and Large-scale Agricultural Land Investments in Africa: Examining the Relevance of Indigenous Institutions and Capacity in Tanzania. In The Palgrave Handbook of Agricultural and Rural Development in Africa (pp. 425-455). Cham, Switzerland: Palgrave Macmillan. Doi:10.1007/978-3-030-41513-6_19

Osabuohien, E. (2020a). *The Palgrave Handbook of Agricultural and Rural Development in Africa.* Palgrave Macmillan., doi:10.1007/978-3-030-41513-6.

Osabuohien, E. (2020b). Guest Editorial: Labour Issues in Africa's Agricultural and Rural Transformation. *African Journal of Economic and Management Studies, 11*(2), 185–191. doi:10.1108/AJEMS-06-2020-406

Osabuohien, E. S. (2014). Large-scale Agricultural Land Investments and Local Institutions in Africa: The Nigerian Case. *Land Use Policy, 39*(July), 155–165. doi:10.1016/j.landusepol.2014.02.019

Osabuohien, E. S., Beecroft, I., & Efobi, U. R. (2018). Global trade and trade protection in a globalised world. *Transnational Corporations Review, 10*(1), 43–52. doi:10.1080/19186444.2018.1436650

Osabuohien, E. S., & Efobi, U. R. (2013). Africa's Money in Africa. *The South African Journal of Economics, 81*(2), 292–306. doi:10.1111aje.12012

Osabuohien, E. S., & Efobi, U. R. (2014). Africa's Money in Africa: Human and Physical Capital Dimensions. In S. Sahoo & B. K. Pattanaik (Eds.), *Global Diaspora and Development: Socioeconomic, Cultural and Policy Perspectives* (pp. 87–104). Springer. doi:10.1007/978-81-322-1047-4_5

Osabuohien, E. S., Efobi, U. R., & Gitau, C. M. W. (2014). Beyond the Environmental Kuznets Curve in Africa: Evidence from Panel Cointegration. *Journal of Environmental Policy and Planning, 16*(4), 517–538. doi:10.1080/1523908X.2013.867802

Osabuohien, E. S., Efobi, U. R., & Gitau, C. M. W. (2015). Environmental Challenges in Africa: Further Dimensions to the Trade, MNCs and Energy Debate. *Management of Environmental Quality, 26*(1), 118–137. doi:10.1108/MEQ-04-2014-0058

Osabuohien, E., & Efobi, U. (2011). Trade Outcomes in Africa's Regional Economic Communities and Institutional Quality: Some Policy Prescriptions. *Economic Insights - Trends and Challenges, LXIII*(4), 19–32.

Osabuohien, E., & Efobi, U. (2012). Technology Diffusion and Economic Progress in Africa: Challenges and Opportunities. In N. Ekekwe & N. Islam (Eds.), *Disruptive Technologies, Innovation and Global Redesign: Emerging Implications* (pp. 425–440). Information Science Reference. doi:10.4018/978-1-4666-0134-5.ch024

Osabuohien, E., Efobi, U. R., Herrmann, R., & Gitau, C. M. (2019). Female Labor Outcomes and Large-scale Agricultural Land Investments: Macro-Micro Evidence from Tanzania. *Land Use Policy*, *82*, 716–728.

Osabuohien, E., Efobi, U. R., Herrmann, R., & Gitau, C. M. (2019). Female Labour Outcomes and Large-scale Agricultural Land Investments: Macro-Micro Evidence from Tanzania. *Land Use Policy*, *82*, 716–728. doi:10.1016/j.landusepol.2019.01.005

Osabuohien, E., Obiekwe, E., Urhie, E., & Osabohien, R. (2018, Spring). Inflation Rate, Exchange Rate Volatility and Exchange Rate Pass-Through Interactions: The Nigerian experience. *Journal of Applied Economic Sciences*, *13*(2), 574–585.

Osabuohien, E., Okorie, U., & Osabohien, R. (2018). Rice Production and Processing in Ogun State, Nigeria: Qualitative Insights from Farmers' Association. In E. Obayelu (Ed.), *Food Systems Sustainability and Environmental Policies in Modern Economics* (pp. 188–216). IGI Global. doi:10.4018/978-1-5225-3631-4.ch009

Osterwalder, A., & Pigneur, Y. (2010). *Business Model Generation*. John Wily & Sons. Inc.

Ostrom, E. (1990). *Governing the commons: The evolution of institutions for collective action*. Cambridge University Press. doi:10.1017/CBO9780511807763

Osty, P.-L., Le Ber, F., & Lieber, J. (2008). Raisonnement à partir de cas et agronomie des territoires. *Rev Anthr Connaissances*, *2*(2), 169–193. doi:10.3917/rac.004.0169

Osumanu, K. I., Kosoe, A. E., & Ategeeng F. (2019). Determinants of open defecation in the Wa Municipality of Ghana: Empirical findings highlighting sociocultural and economic dynamics among households. *Journal of Environmental and Public Health*. doi:10.1155/2019/3075840

Osumanu, K. I., & Kosoe, A. E. (2013). Where do I answer nature's call? An assessment of accessibility and utilisation of toilet facilities in Wa, Ghana. *Ghana Journal of Geography*, *5*, 17–31.

Osumanu, K. I., Kosoe, A. E., & Dapilah, F. (2016). Residential housing in Ghana's low-income urban areas: An analysis of households living conditions in the Wa Municipality. *Journal of Geography and Regional Planning*, *9*(7), 139–153.

Owusu, P. A., & Asumadu-Sarkodie, S. (2016). A Review of Renewable Energy Sources, Sustainability Issues and Climate Change Mitigation. *Cogent Engineering*, *3*(1), 1167990. doi:10.1080/23311916.2016.1167990

Oyebola, P. O., Osabuohien, E., & Obasaju, B. (2020). Employment and Income Effects of Nigeria's Agricultural Transformation Agenda: Evidence from Cattle Value Chain. *African Journal of Economic and Management Studies*, *11*(2), 317–329. doi:10.1108/AJEMS-12-2018-0402

Oyelami & Ogundipe. (2020). An empirical investigation of remittances and financial inclusion nexus in Sub-Saharan Africa. *Cogent Business & Management*. doi:10.1080/23311975.2020.1712126

Oyinola, O. A. (2011). Corruption Eradication in Nigeria: An Appraisal. *Library Philosophy and Practice*. Available at http://www.webpages.uidaho.edu/~mbolin/ayobami.htm

Ozturk, I., & Acaravci, A. (2010). CO2 emissions, energy consumption and economic growth in Turkey. *Renewable & Sustainable Energy Reviews*, *14*(9), 3220–3225. doi:10.1016/j.rser.2010.07.005

Painuly, J. P. (2001). Barriers to renewable energy penetration; a framework for analysis. *Renewable Energy*, *24*(1), 73–89. doi:10.1016/S0960-1481(00)00186-5

Palmer, D., Fricska, S., & Wehrmann, B. (2009). *Towards improved land governance*. Land Tenure Working Paper 11. Rome, Italy: Food and Agriculture Organization of the United Nations (FAO) and UN-Habitat. Retrieved online from https://unhabitat.org/books/towards-improved-landgovernance-land-and-tenure-working/

Pandit, M., Mishra, A. K., Paudel, K. P., Larkin, S. L., Rejesus, R. M., Lambert, D. M., English, B. C., Larson, J. A., Velandia, M. M., Roberts, R. K., & Kotsiri, S. (2011). *Reasons for Adopting Precision Farming: A Case Study of US Cotton Farmers*. Annual Meeting of Southern Agricultural Economics Association, Corpus Christi, TX.

Paravantis, J., Stigka, E., Mihalakakou, G. (2014). An analysis of public attitudes towards renewable energy in Western Greece. *Renew. Sustain. Energy Rev., 32*(March), 100-106.

Parkinson, S. (2009). When farmers don't want ownership: Reflections on demand-driven extension in sub-Saharan Africa. *Journal of Agricultural Education and Extension, 15*(4), 417–429. doi:10.1080/13892240903309678

Park, S., & Lah, T. T. J. (2015). Analyzing the success of the volume-based waste fee system South Korea. *Waste Management (New York, N.Y.), 43*, 533–538. doi:10.1016/j.wasman.2015.06.011 PMID:26141278

Partida, V., & Pacheco, M. E. (2016). *Changing Jobs in Mexico: Hopping between Formal and Informal Economic Sectors, Unemployment - Perspectives and Solutions*. Intech Open. Available from: https://www.intechopen.com/books/unemployment-perspectives-and-solutions/changing-jobs-in-mexico-hopping-between-formal-and-informal-economic-sectors

Patrick, H. T. (1966). Financial development and economic growth in underdeveloped countries. *Economic Development and Cultural Change, 14*(2), 174–189. doi:10.1086/450153

Pattberg, P., & Widerberg, O. (2016). Transnational multistakeholder partnerships for sustainable development: Conditions for success. *Ambio, 45*(1), 42–51. doi:10.1007/s13280-015-0684-2 PubMed

Patton, M. Q. (2002). *Qualitative research & evaluation methods* (Vol. 3). Sage Publications, Inc.

Pender, J., Hazell, P., & Garrett, J. L. (2020). *Reducing Poverty and Protecting the Environment. The overlooked potential of less-favoured lands*. Unfinished Agenda IFPRI Publication.

Perman, R., & Stern, D. I. (2003). Evidence from panel unit root and cointegration tests that the Environmental Kuznets Curve does not exist. *The Australian Journal of Agricultural and Resource Economics, 47*(3), 325–347. doi:10.1111/1467-8489.00216

Pesaran, M. H. (2003). *Estimation and inference in large heterogenous panels with cross section dependence*. CESifo Working Paper Series.

Pesaran, M. H. (2004). *General diagnostic tests for cross section dependence in panels*. CESifo working paper series No 1219.

Pesaran, M. H. (2007). A simple panel unit root test in the presence of cross-sectional dependence. *Journal of Applied Econometrics, 22*(2), 265–312. doi:10.1002/jae.951

Pesaran, M. H. (2015). Testing weak cross-sectional dependence in large panels. *Econometric Reviews, 34*(6-10), 1089–1117. doi:10.1080/07474938.2014.956623

Pesaran, M. H., Shin, Y., & Smith, R. P. (1999). Pooled mean group estimation of dynamic heterogeneous panels. *Journal of the American Statistical Association, 94*(446), 621–634. doi:10.1080/01621459.1999.10474156

Peter, L., Peter, W., & Oakdene, H. (2010). *Waste Arising in the Supply of Food and Drink to Households in the UU.K.* Academic Press.

Pineda, V. (2020). *Building the Inclusive City: Governance, Access, and the Urban Transformation of Dubai*. Palgrave Macmillian. doi:10.1007/978-3-030-32988-4

Piraux, M., Silveira, L., Diniz, P., Duque, G., Coudel, E., Devautour, H., Soulard, C., & Hubert, B. (2010). Agroecological transition as a socio-territorial innovation: the case of the territory of Borborema in Brazilian semi-arid. *Proc. Symp. Innov. Sustain. Dev. Agric. Food Montp.*

Plane, P. (1999). Privatization, Technical Efficiency and Welfare Consequences: The Case of the Côte d'Ivorie Electricity Company (CIE). *World Development, 27*(2), 343–360. doi:10.1016/S0305-750X(98)00139-9

Platteau, J. (1996). The evolutionary theory of land rights as applied to sub-Saharan Africa: A critical assessment. *Development and Change, 1996*(27), 29–86. doi:10.1111/j.1467-7660.1996.tb00578.x

Platteau, J. (2004). Monitoring elite capture in community-driven development. *Blackwell Publishing, 35*(2), 223–246.

Platteau, J., & Gaspart, F. (2003). The risk of resource misappropriation in community-driven development. *World Development, 31*(10), 1687–1703. doi:10.1016/S0305-750X(03)00138-4

Pollitt, M. G. (1995). *Technical Efficiency in Electrical Power Plants.* Cambridge Working Papers in Economics 9422, Faculty of Economics, University of Cambridge.

Pollitt, M. (2008). Electricity reform in Argentina: Lessons for Developing Countries. *Energy Economics, 30*(4), 1536–1567. doi:10.1016/j.eneco.2007.12.012

Pollitt, M. G. (2012). The Role of Policy in Energy Transitions: Lessons from the Energy Liberalisation Era. *Energy Policy, 50*, 128–137. doi:10.1016/j.enpol.2012.03.004

Pomare, C. (2018). A multiple framework approach to sustainable development goals (SDGs) and entrepreneurship. Entrepreneurship and the Sustainable Development Goals Contemporary Issues in Entrepreneurship Research, 8, 11–31. doi:10.1108/S2040-724620180000008006

Popoola, A., & Magidimisha, H. (2019). Will Rural Areas Disappear? Participatory Governance and Infrastructure Provision in Oyo State, Nigeria. *Proceedings for the 6th International Conference of Development and Investment-Strategied for Africa. DII-2019.*

Popoola, A., Ayangbile, O., & Adeleye, B. (2015). Assessment of Solid Waste Management Systems in Ibadan North, Oyo State Using Geo-Spatial Techniques. *Ethiopian Journal of Environmental Studies and Management, 9*(6), 666–679.

Popoola, A., Olatunde, M., Magidimisha, H., Abiodun, A., Adeleye, B., & Chipungu, L. (2020). Urban Forced Evictions: Experiences in the Metropolitan City of Lagos, Nigeria. *The Indonesian Journal of Geography, 52*(1), 112–127.

Popp, J., Lakner, Z., Harangi-Rakos, M., & Fari, M. (2014). The Effect of Bioenergy Expansion: Food, Energy and Environment. *Renewable & Sustainable Energy Reviews, 32*, 559–578. doi:10.1016/j.rser.2014.01.056

Porter, G. (2013). *Transport Services and Their Impact on Poverty and Growth In Rural Sub- Saharan Africa.* AFCAP/ Durham University.

Pouch, T. (2015). L'agriculture et l'enjeu de l'innovation: Dimensions générales et éclairage méditerranéen. *Watch Letter, 32*, 1–5.

Prasad, A., Rogoff, K., Wei, S., & Kose, M. A. (2004). *Financial globalization, growth and volatility in developing countries* (Working Paper Series No. 10942). doi:10.3386/w10942

Prasad, G. (2008). Energy sector reform, Energy Transitions and the Poor in Africa. *Energy Policy, 36*(8), 2806–2811. doi:10.1016/j.enpol.2008.02.042

Prasad, G. (2011). Improving Access to Energy in Sub-Saharan Africa. *Energy Policy, 3*(4), 248–253.

Prasad, M., Vera, W., Moustapha, K. G., Toolseeram, R., Visvanathan, C., Hardy, M. W., Shailendra, M., Louise, G., Andrea, M. B., John, P. A., Zhuohua, T., & Swati, A. (2011). Waste - investing in energy and resource efficiency, towards a green economy. In E. Derek & F. Sheng (Eds.), *United Nations Environment Programme*. UNEP.

Prein, P. (2002). Integration of aquaculture into crop–animal systems in Asia. *Agricultural Systems*, *71*(1-2), 127–146. doi:10.1016/S0308-521X(01)00040-3

Pretty, J. N., Chambers, R., & Harris, J. (2003). Towards a learning paradigm: New professionalism and institutions for agriculture. In Rethinking sustainability: power, knowledge, and institutions (pp. 189-227). Academic Press.

Pretty, J. (2005). Sustainability in agriculture: Recent progress and emergent challenges. Issues. *Environmental Science & Technology*, *21*, 1–15.

Pretty, J. (2006). *Agroecological approaches to agricultural development*. World Bank.

Property, P. (2017). *What is Land Use Act: 12 Things Nigerians Should Know*. Available online at https://www.privateproperty.com.ng/news/what-is-land-use-act-12-things-nigerians-should-know/

Qin, Y., & Zhang, X. (2016). The road to specialization in agricultural production: Evidence from rural China. *World Development*, *77*, 1–16. doi:10.1016/j.worlddev.2015.08.007

Quitzow, R., Roehrkasten, S., Jacobs, D, Bayer, B., Jamea, E., Waweru, Y. & Matschoss, P. (2016). *The Future of Africa's Energy Supply*. Institute for Advanced Sustainability Studies (IASS).

Rahman, M. I. (2013). Climate change: A theoretical review. *Interdisciplinary Description of Complex Systems: INDECS*, *11*(1), 1–13. doi:10.7906/indecs.11.1.1

Ramey, V. A., & Zubairy, S. (2018). Government spending multipliers in good times and in bad: Evidence from U.S. historical data. *Journal of Political Economy*, *126*(2), 850–901. doi:10.1086/696277

Ramos-Real, F. J., Tovar, B., de Almeida, E. F., & Pinto, H. Q. (2009). The Evolution and Main Determinants of Productivity in the Brazilian Electricity Distribution 1998-2005: An Empirical Analysis. *Energy Economics*, *31*(2), 298–305. doi:10.1016/j.eneco.2008.11.002

Randriamaro, Z. (2006). *Gender and Trade: Overview Report. Bridge*. University of Sussex.

Rapid Assessment and Gap Analysis – RAGA. (2013). *Sustainable Energy for All in Nigeria*. Author.

Rasche, A., & Gilbert, D. U. (2012). Institutionalizing global governance: The role of the United Nations Global Compact. Business Ethics: The European Review, 21(1), 100–114. doi:10.1111/j.1467-8608.2011.01642.x

Ratha, D., Mohapatra, S., & Silwal, A. (2010). *Migration and remittances factbook 2011*. World Bank Group.

Raza, W., Saula, H., Islam, S. U., Ayub, M., Saleem, M., & Raza, N. (2015). Renewable energy resources: Current status and barriers in their adaptation for Pakistan. *J. Bioprocess. Chem. Eng*, *3*(3), 1–9.

Reddy, V., & Pachepsky, Y. A. (2000). Predicting crop yields under climate change conditions from monthly GCM weather projections. *Environmental Modelling & Software*, *15*(1), 79–86. doi:10.1016/S1364-8152(99)00011-0

Rehman, H. U., & Naveed, A. (2007). Determinants of corruption and its relation to GDP (A panel study). *Journal of Political Studies*, *12*(2), 27–59.

Reich, M., Gordon, D. M., & Edwards, R. C. (1973). *Dual labour markets: A theory of labour market segmentation. Economics Department Faculty Publications, Economics Commons*. University of Nebraska.

Reij, C., Tappan, G., & Smale, M. (2009). Agroenvironmental Transformation in the Sahel: Another kind of "Green Revolution". In D. J. Speilman & R. Pandya-Lorch (Eds.), *Proven Successes in Agricultural Development; A Technical Compenium to Millions Fed*. International Food Policy Research Institute.

Republic of Nigeria. (1978). *Land Use Act*. http://www.nigeria-law.org/Land%20Use%20Act.htm

Republic of Nigeria. (1999). *Constitution of the Federal Republic of Nigeria*. Available online at http://www.nigeria-law.org/ConstitutionOfTheFederalRepublicOfNigeria.htm

Reynolds, C. J., Mavrakis, V., Davison, S., Stine, B. H., Vlaholias, E., & Sharp, A. (2014). Estimating informal household food waste in developed countries: The case of Australia. *Waste Management & Research*, *32*(12), 1254–1258. doi:10.1177/0734242X14549797 PMID:25248761

Ricardo, D. (1817). Des principes de l'économie politique et de l'impôt. Les Classiques des sciences sociales, France.

Risse-Kappen, T. (1995). Bringing transnational relations back. In *Bringing Transnational Relations Back In: Non-State Actors, Domestic Structures and International Institutions* (pp. 3–36). Cambridge University Press., doi:10.1017/CBO9780511598760.

Roa, M. J. (2015). *Financial Inclusion in Latin America and the Caribbean: Access, Usage and Quality. Research Papers 19*. CEMLA.

Roche, M., & Argent, N. (2012). The fall and rise of agricultural productivism? An Antipodean viewpoint. *Progress in Human Geography*, *39*(5), 621–635. doi:10.1177/0309132515582058

Rockefeller Foundation. (2013). *Waste and Spoilage in the Food Chain*. Decision Intelligence Document.

Rockström, J., Steffen, W., Noone, K., Persson, A., Chapin, F. S. III, Lambin, E., Lenton, T. M., Scheffer, M., Folke, C., Schellnhuber, H. J., Nykvist, B., de Wit, C. A., Hughes, T., van der Leeuw, S., Rodhe, H., Sörlin, S., Snyder, P. K., Costanza, R., Svedin, U., ... Foley, J. (2009). Planetary boundaries: Exploring the safe operating space for humanity. *Ecology and Society*, *14*(2), 32. doi:10.5751/ES-03180-140232

Rodgers, A.M., Esman, M.N., & Eliud, D.M. (2014). The relationship between financial development and economic growth in Africa. *Research in Applied Economics, 6*(2).

Rodrik, D. (1998). Why is Trade Reform so difficult in Africa? *Journal of African Economies*, *7*(Supplement 1), 10–36. doi:10.1093/jafeco/7.suppl_1.10

Rojo, S. M., Moratalla, A. Z., Alonso, N. M., & Jimenez, V. H. (2014). Pathways towards the integration of peri-urban agrarian ecosystems into the spatial planning system. *Ecological Processes*, *3*(13), 16.

Romanik, C. (2008). *An urban-rural focus on food markets in Africa*. The Urban Institute. Available at https://www.urban.org/sites/default/files/publication/31436/411604-An-Urban-Rural-Focus-on-Food-Markets-in-Africa.PDF

Romualdas, G., Gitana, D., Martin, S., & Kęstutis, P. (2019). The inter-linkages between financial and economic development in the European Union countries. *Economic Research-EkonomskaIstraživanja*, *32*(1), 3309–3326.

Roodman, D. (2009). How to do xtabond2: An introduction to difference and system GMM in Stata. *The Stata Journal*, *9*(1), 86–136. doi:10.1177/1536867X0900900106

Ross, L. (2005). Finance and growth: Theory and evidence. In Handbook of Economic Growth, (pp. 865-934). Elsevier.

Rosset, P. M., & Martínez-Torres, M. E. (2012). Rural social movements and agroecology: Context, theory, and process. *Ecology and Society*, *17*(3), 17. doi:10.5751/ES-05000-170317

Rosset, P. M., Sosa, B. M., Jaime, A. M. R., & Lozano, D. R. Á. (2011). The campesino-to-campesino agroecology movement of ANAP in Cuba: Social process methodology in the construction of sustainable peasant agriculture and food sovereignty. *The Journal of Peasant Studies*, *38*(1), 161–191. doi:10.1080/03066150.2010.538584 PMID:21284238

Rue, L. W., & Ibrahim, N. I. (1998). The Relationship Between Planning Sophistication and Performance in Small Business. *Journal of Small Business Management*, *36*, 24–32.

Ruesga, G. A., & Knight, B. (2013). The view from the heights of Arnstein's ladder: Resident engagement by community foundations. *National Civic Review*, *102*(3), 13–16. doi:10.1002/ncr.21137

Ryan, P. (2014). *Do Not Block Grant and Expanding Opportunity in America*. http://budget.house.gov/uploadedfiles/expanding_opportunity_in_america.pdfhttp://www.demos.org/blog/7/24/14/response-paul-ryan-expand-eitc-do-not-block-grant-anything Assessed on 12/6/2017

SAARNET. (2004). *See Southern Africa Root Crops Research Network*. Available at: https://core.ac.uk/download/pdf/6689793.pdf

Sagashya, D., & English, C. (2010). Designing and establishing a land administration system for Rwanda: a technical and economic analysis. In *Innovations in Land Rights Recognition, Administration, and Governance*. Washington, DC: World Bank. Available: https://www.fig.net/resources/proceedings/2009/fig_wb_2009/papers/sys/sys_2_english_sagashya.pdf

Saidu, A., Clarkson, A. M., Adamu, S. H., Mohammed, M., & Jibo, I. (2017). Application of ICT in Agriculture: Opportunities and Challenges in Developing Countries. *International Journal of Computer Science and Mathematical Theory*, *3*(1), 8–18.

Sala-i-Martin, X., & Subramanian, A. (2013). Addressing the Natural Resource Curse: An Illustration from Nigeria. *Journal of African Economies*, *22*(4, Supplement 1), 15–48. doi:10.1093/jae/ejs033

Saqib, N., Masnoon, M., & Rafique, N. (2013). Impact of foreign direct investment on economic growth of Pakistan. *Advances in Management & Applied Economics*, *3*(1), 35–45.

Sarma, M. (2008). *Index of Financial Inclusion*. ICRIER Working Paper 215.

Sarma, M., & Pais, J. (2011). Financial Inclusion and Development. *Journal of International Development*, *23*(5), 613–628. doi:10.1002/jid.1698

Satterthwaite, D., McGranahan, G., & Tacoli, C. (2010). Urbanization and its implications for food and farming. *Philosophical Transactions of the Royal Society of London. Series B, Biological Sciences*, *365*(1554), 2809–2820. doi:10.1098/rstb.2010.0136 PMID:20713386

Sauer, P. C., & Hiete, M. (2020). Multi-stakeholder initiatives as social innovation for governance and practice: A review of responsible mining initiatives. *Sustainability*, *12*(1), 236. doi:10.3390/su12010236

Säumel, I., Kotsyuk, I., Hölscher, M., Lenkereit, C., Weber, F., & Kowarik, I. (2012). How healthy is urban horticulture in high traffic areas? Trace metal concentrations in vegetable crops from plantings within inner city neighbourhoods in Berlin, Germany. *Environmental Pollution*, *165*, 124–132. doi:10.1016/j.envpol.2012.02.019 PMID:22445920

Saunders, M., Lewis, P., & Thornhill, A. (2009). *Research methods for business students* (Vol. 5). Pearson Education Limited.

Scheyvens, R., & Biddulph, R. (2018). Inclusive tourism development. *Tourism Geographies*, *20*(4), 589–609. doi:10.1080/14616688.2017.1381985

Schindler, S. (2015). Architectural Exclusion: Discrimination and Segregation through Physical Design of the Built Environment. *The Yale Law Journal*, *124*(6), 1836–2201.

Schneider, K., & Gugerty, M. K. (2011). Agricultural Productivity and Poverty Reduction: Linkages and Pathways. *The Evans School Review*, *121*(1), 1–19. doi:10.7152/esr.v1i1.12249

Schreckenberg, K., & Luttrell, C. (2009). Participatory forest management: A route to povety reduction? *Commonwealth Forestry Association*, *11*(2), 221–238. doi:10.1505/ifor.11.2.221

Schumpeter, J. (1912). Theorie der Wirtschaftlichen, Entwicklung [The theory of economic development]. Leipzig: Dunker and Humblot.

Schumpeter, J. (1911). *The theory of economic development: An inquiry into profits, capital, credit, interest and the business cycle*. Oxford University Press.

Schwarz, K., Cutts, B. B., London, J. K., & Cadenasso, M. L. (2016). Growing gardens in shrinking cities: A Solution to the Soil Lead Problem? *Sustainability*, *8*(2), 1–11. doi:10.3390u8020141

Searchinger, T. D., Beringer, T., Holtsmark, B., Kammen, D. M., Lambiri, E. F., Lucht, W., Raven, P., & van Ypersele, J. (2018). Europe's Renewable Energy Directive Poised to Harm Global Forests. *Nature Communications*, *9*(3741). Advance online publication. doi:10.103841467-018- 06175-4 PMID:30209361

Secondi, L., Principato, L., & Laureti, T. (2015). Household food waste behaviour in EE.U. 27 countries: A multilevel analysis. *Food Policy*, *56*, 25–40. doi:10.1016/j.foodpol.2015.07.007

Segerson, K. (2013). Voluntary approaches to environmental protection and resource management. *Annual Review of Resource Economics*, *5*(1), 161–180. doi:10.1146/annurev-resource-091912-151945

Sekkat, K. (2017). Urban concentration and poverty in developing countries. *Growth and Change*, *48*(3), 435–458. doi:10.1111/grow.12166

Seldadyo, H., & De Haan, J. (2005). The determinants of corruption. *The Economist, 66*, 1-60.

Sen, A. (1981). *Poverty and Famines: An Essay on Entitlement and Deprivation*. Oxford University Press.

Sen, A., & Jamasb, T. (2012). Diversity in Unity: An Empirical Analysis of Electricity Deregulation in Indian States. *Energy Journal*, *33*(1), 83–130. doi:10.5547/ISSN0195-6574-EJ-Vol33-No1-4

Sen, R., & Bhattacharyya, S. C. (2014). Off-grid electricity generation with renewable energy technologies in India: An application of HOMER. *Renewable Energy*, *62*, 388–398. doi:10.1016/j.renene.2013.07.028

Seo, S., Aramaki, T., Hwang, Y., & Hanaki, K. (2004). Environmental impact of solid waste treatment methods in Korea. *Journal of Environmental Engineering*, *130*(1), 81–89. doi:10.1061/(ASCE)0733-9372(2004)130:1(81)

Serena, L., & Andrea, Z. (2011). Increasing Public Expenditures: Wagner's Law in OECD Countries. *German Economic Review*, *12*(2), 149–164. doi:10.1111/j.1468-0475.2010.00517.x

Servigne, P., & Stevens, R. (2015). *Comment tout peut s'effondrer. Petit manuel de collapsologie à l'usage des générations présentes*. Seuil.

SET – Supporting Economic Transformation. (2018). *Manufacturing in Africa: factors for successes.* Paper prepared for the Second African Transformation Forum, June, Accra. London: ODI

Shabbir, G., & Anwar, M. (2007). Determinants of corruption in developing countries. *Pakistan Development Review*, *46*(4II), 751–764. doi:10.30541/v46i4IIpp.751-764

Shalley, C., Hitt, M. A., Zhou, J., Raffaelli, R., & Glynn, M. A. (2015). Institutional innovation. In C. Shalley, M. A. Hitt, & J. Zhou (Eds.), *The Oxford Handbook of Creativity, Innovation, and Entrepreneurship*. Oxford University Press., doi:10.1093/oxfordhb/9780199927678.013.0019.

Sharma, N. P., Rietbergen, S., Heimo, C. R., & Patel, J. (1994). *A Strategy for the Forest Sector in Sub-Saharan Africa.* World Bank Technical Paper Number 251, Africa Technical Department Series.

Sharma, P. (2004). An overview of the field of family business studies: Current status and directions for the future. *Family Business Review, 17*(1), 1–36.

Sharma, R., Chauhan, S. K., & Tripathi, A. M. (2016). Carbon sequestration potential in agroforestry systems in India: An analysis for carbon project. *Agroforestry Systems, 90*(4), 631–644. doi:10.100710457-015-9840-8

Shaw, E. S. (1973). *Financial deepening in economic development*. Oxford University Press.

Shepard, M. (2013). *Restoration agriculture: real world permaculture for farmers*. Acres U.S.A.

Sherard, J. L., Decker, R. S., & Dunnigan, L. P. (1976). Identification and nature of dispersive soils. *Journal of the Geotechnical Engineering Division, 102*, 287–301.

Shrestha, R. (2013). *People's participation in community forestry managementl A study of Siddhicharan community forestry user group of Bigutar*. Okhaldhungu.

Singh, A. (2002). *Competition and Competition Policy in Emerging Markets: International and Developmental Dimensions.* Research papers for the Intergovernmental Group of Twenty-Four on International Monetary Affairs. G-24 Discussion Paper No. 18. September.

Singh, P. K., & Chudasama, H. (2020). Evaluating poverty alleviation strategies in a developing country. *PLoS One, 15*(1), e0227176. doi:10.1371/journal.pone.0227176 PMID:31929549

Slaughter, A.-M. (2004). *A new world order*. Princeton University Press.

Smit, B., Burton, I., Klein, R. J. T., & Street, R. (1999). The science of adaptation: A framework for assessment. *Mitigation and Adaptation Strategies for Global Change, 4*(3-4), 199–213. doi:10.1023/A:1009652531101

Smit, B., & Wandel, J. (2006). Adaptation, adaptive capacity and vulnerability. *Global Environmental Change, 16*(3), 282–292. doi:10.1016/j.gloenvcha.2006.03.008

Smith, A. (1776). *An inquiry into the nature and the causes of the wealth of nations*. University of Chicago Press. doi:10.1093/oseo/instance.00043218

Smukler, S., Sánchez-Moreno, S., Fonte, S., Ferris, H., Klonsky, K., O'Geen, A., Scow, K., Steenwerth, K., & Jackson, L. (2010). Biodiversity and multiple ecosystem functions in an organic farmscape. *Agriculture, Ecosystems & Environment, 139*(1-2), 80–97. doi:10.1016/j.agee.2010.07.004

Soares, F. V. (2015). *Do informal workers queue for formal jobs in Brazil?* Discussion Paper No. 130, Institute for Applied Economic Research, Brazil.

Sonfield, M. C., & Lussier, R. N. (2004). First-, second-, and third-generation family firms: A comparison. *Family Business Review, 17*(3), 189–202.

Song, Q., Li, J., & Zeng, X. (2014). Minimizing the increasing solid waste through zero waste strategy. *Journal of Cleaner Production*. Advance online publication. doi:10.1016/j.jclepro.2014.08.027

South African Energy Sector Report. (2018). *Energy Data Collection, Management and Analysis*. Author.

Spichiger, R., & Stacey, P. (2014). *Ghana's Land Reform and Gender Equality*. Danish Institute for International Studies (DIIS) Working Paper 2014:01. Available online at https://www.econstor.eu/bitstream/10419/122291/1/782856365.pdf

Stark, O. (1991). The Economics of International Labour Migration. *Population Studies*, *44*(1), 181–182. doi:10.1080/0032472031000144516

Stelmach, B. (2016). Parents' participation on school councils analysed through Arnstein's ladder of participation. *School Leadership & Management*, *36*(3), 271–291. doi:10.1080/13632434.2016.1247048

Stern, D. I. (2004). The Rise and Fall of the Environmental Kuznets Curve. *World Development*, *32*(8), 1419–1439. doi:10.1016/j.worlddev.2004.03.004

Stevenson, G. W., Clancy, K., King, R., Lev, L., Ostrom, M., & Smith, S. (2011). Midscale food value chains: An introduction. *Journal of Agriculture, Food Systems, and Community Development*, *1*(4), 1–8. doi:10.5304/jafscd.2011.014.007

Stewart, W., Powers, R.F., McGown, K., Chiono, L. & Chuang, T. (2011). *Potential Positive and Negative Environmental Impacts of Increased Woody Biomass Use for California.* Public Interest Energy Research – PIER Program Final project report.

Stickler, C.M., Coe, M.T., Costa, M.H., Nepstad, D.C., McGrath, D.G., Dias, L.C.P., Rodrigues, H.O. & Soares-Filho, B.S. (2013). Dependence of Hydropower Energy Generation on Forests in the Amazon Basin at Local and Regional Scales. *PNAS Early Edition,* 1-6.

Stokes, L. C. (2013). The politics of renewable energy policies: The case of feed-in tariffs in Ontario, Canada. *Energy Policy*, *56*, 490–500. doi:10.1016/j.enpol.2013.01.009

Stone, D. (2008). Global public policy, transnational policy communities, and their networks. *Policy Studies Journal: the Journal of the Policy Studies Organization*, *36*(1), 19–38. doi:10.1111/j.1541-0072.2007.00251.x

Struebing, L. (1997). Recipe for Success: Prepare A Business Plan. *Quality Progress*, *30*(8), 20.

Stumbitz, B., Lewis, S., Kyei, A. A., & Lyon, F. (2018). Maternity protection in formal and informal economy workplaces: The case of Ghana. *World Development*, *110*, 373–378. doi:10.1016/j.worlddev.2018.06.007

Subedi, G. P. (2016). *Land administration and its impact on economic development* (Unpublished Ph.D. thesis). University of Reading.

Sun, P., & Nie, P. (2015). A comparative study of feed-in tariff and renewable portfolio standard policy in renewable energy industry. *Renewable Energy*, *74*(February), 255–262. doi:10.1016/j.renene.2014.08.027

Sustainable Energy Regulation Policymaking -SERP. (2005). *Overview of Renewable Energy and Energy Efficiency*. Academic Press.

Sutter, C., Bruton, G. D., & Chen, J. (2019). Entrepreneurship as a solution to extreme poverty: A review and future research directions. *Journal of Business Venturing*, *34*(1), 197–214. doi:10.1016/j.jbusvent.2018.06.003

Suuronen, A. (2017). Ecological and Social Impacts of Photovoltaic Solar Power Plants and Optimization of their Locations in Northern Chile. *Jyvaskyla Studies in Biological and Environmental Science, 338.*

Suzuki, M. (2013). *What are the roles of national and international institutions to overcome barriers in diffusing clean energy technologies in Asia? Matching barriers in technology diffusion with the roles of institutions*. Retrieved from: http://cdn.intechopen.com/pdfs/43765/InTech-What_are_the_roles_of_national_and_international_institutions_to_overcome_barriers_in_diffusing_clean_energy_technologies_in_asia_matching_barriers_in_technology_diffusion_with_the_roles_of_institutions.pdf

Swanson, A. (2015). Why trying to help poor countries might actually hurt them. *Washington Post*. Retrieved from https://www.washingtonpost.com/news/wonk/wp/2015/10/13/why-trying-to-help-poor-countries-might-actually-hurt-them/?noredirect=on&utm_term=.cdc7a88cc142

Swensen, G., & Jerpåsen, G. P. (2008). Cultural heritage in suburban landscape planning. A case study in Southern Norway. *Landscape and Urban Planning*, *87*(4), 289–300. doi:10.1016/j.landurbplan.2008.07.001

Tacoli, C. (2003). The links between urban and rural development. *Environment and Urbanization*, *15*(1), 1–12. doi:10.1630/095624703101286376

Tafirenyika, S. (2012). *Financial sector development and economic growth nexus in South Africa* (MPRA Paper No. 86633). Retrieved from https://mpra.ub.uni-muenchen.de/86633/

Taghavi, A., & Murat, A. (2011). A heuristic procedure for the integrated facility layout design and flow assignment problem. *Computers & Industrial Engineering*, *61*(1), 55–63. doi:10.1016/j.cie.2011.02.011

Tan, K., & Phang, S. (2005). *From Efficiency-Driven to Innovation-Driven Economic Growth: Perspectives from Singapore*. Policy, Research Working Paper No. WPS 3569. Washington, DC: World Bank.

Tandjigora, A. (2019). Industries et Services ruraux: Supports de la Transformation Rurale dans le contexte d'une Agriculture en dégradation continue: Evidence du Sénégal. *Journal of Economics and Sustainable Development*, *2*, 36–43.

Tansel, A., & Ozdemir, Z. A. (2014). *Determinant of transitions across formal / informal sectors in Egypt*. Working Paper 899, Economic Research Forum.

Taylor. (2009). *Adaptation key terms*. Retrieved 29 May2019 from https://www.weadapt.org/knowledge-base/adaptation-decision-making/adaptation-versus-coping

Tchanche, B. (2019). A view of road transport in Africa. *African Journal of Environmental Science and Technology*, *13*(8), 296–302. doi:10.5897/AJEST2018.2575

Temple, L., Chiffoleau, Y., & Touzard, J. M. (2018). Une histoire de l'innovation et de ses usages dans l'agriculture. In Innovation et développement dans les systèmes agricoles et alimentaire (pp. 19-37). Paris: Cairn Info.

Teno, G., Lehrer, K., & Kone, A. (2018). Les facteurs de l'adoption des nouvelles technologies en agriculture en Afrique Subsaharienne: Une revue de la littérature. *African Journal of Agricultural and Resource Economics*, (13), 140–151.

Thapa, V., & Pathranarakul, P. (2019). Gender inclusiveness in disaster risk governance for sustainable recovery of 2015 Gorkha Earthquake, Nepal. *International Journal of Disaster Risk Reduction*, *34*, 209–219. doi:10.1016/j.ijdrr.2018.11.019

The African Union Commission (2015, September). Agenda 2063: The Africa We Want. First Ten-year Implementation Plan 2014-2023. Author.

The Economics of Ecosystems and Biodiversity (TEEB). (2010). *Mainstreaming the economics of nature: a synthesis of the approach, conclusions and recommendations of TEEB*. TEEB.

The Economist Intelligent Unit. (2016). *Power Up: Delivering Renewable Energy in Africa*. Author.

The Government of Sierra Leone. (2015). *Draft National Land Policy of Sierra Leone*. Ministry of Lands, Planning and the Environment, Version 6.

The Republic of Gambia. (1995). State Lands Regulations, 1995. Supplement "A" to 7lze Gambia, Gazette No 1.5 of 3rd May, 995. Available online at http://extwprlegs1.fao.org/docs/pdf/gam5421.pdf

The Sustainable Development Goals Center for Africa & Sustainable Development Solutions Network. (2020). *Africa SDG Index and Dashboards Report 2020*. SDGCA & SDSN.

Thi, N. B. D., Kumar, G., & Lin, C. (2015). An overview of food waste management in developing countries: Current status and future perspective. *Journal of Environmental Management, 157*, 220-229.

Thindwa, J. (2015 July 7). Multi-stakeholders initiatives: Platforms of collective governance for development. World Bank Blogs. https://blogs.worldbank.org/governance/multi-stakeholder-initiatives-platforms-collective-governance-development

THISDAY. (2017). Politics of Amending the Land Use Act. *THISDAY Newspaper*. Available online at https://www.thisdaylive.com/index.php/2017/08/01/politics-of-amending-the-land-use-act/

Thiyane, D. (2017). *Communal land belongs to the people, not to the chiefs*. Land and Accountability Research Centre. Available online at https://www.customcontested.co.za/communal-land-belongs-people-not-chiefs/

Thyberg, K. L., & Tonjes, D. J. R. (2016). Drivers of food waste and their implications for sustainable policy development. *Conservation & Recycling, 106*, 110-123.

Tokman, V. (2004). Una voz en el camino. Empleo y equidad en América Latina: 40 años de búsqueda. México: Fondo de Cultura Económica, 389.

Tokman, V. (1979). Dinámica del mercado de trabajo urbano: El sector informal urbano en América Latina. In K. Rubén & J. L. Reyna (Eds.), *Fuerza de trabajo y movimientos laborales en América Latina* (pp. 68–102). El Colegio de México. doi:10.2307/j.ctv233mg4.6

Torabi, G. (2015). Foreign Direct Investment and Human Development: The Law and Economics of International Investment Agreements. *Journal of Human Development and Capabilities: A Multi-Disciplinary Journal for People-Centered Development, 16*(2) doi:10.1080/19452829.2015.1028813

Torre Ugarte, D. G., & Hellwinckel, C. C. (2010). The problem is the solution: the role of biofuels in the transition to a regenerative agriculture. In P. Mascia, J. Scheffran, & J. Widholm (Eds.), *Plant biotechnology for sustainable production of energy and co-products* (pp. 365–384). Springer. doi:10.1007/978-3-642-13440-1_14

Tosakana, N. S. P., Van Tassell, L. W., Wulfhorst, J. D., Boll, J., Mahler, R., Brooks, E. S., & Kane, S. (2010). Determinants of the adoption of conservation practices by farmers in the Northwest Wheat and Range Region. *Journal of Soil and Water Conservation, 6*(6), 404–412. doi:10.2489/jswc.65.6.404

Toulmin, C., Delville, P. L., & Traoré, S. (2002). The dynamics of resource tenure in West Africa. London: International Institute for Environment and Development, GRET, Currey and Heinemann.

Touzard, J. M., Temple, L., Faure, G., & Triomphe, B. (2015). Innovation systems and knowledge communities in the agriculture and agrifood sector: A literature review. *Journal of Innovation Economics and Management, 17*(2), 117–142. doi:10.3917/jie.017.0117

Townsend, P. (1979). *Poverty in the United Kingdom: a survey of household resources and standards of living*. Penguin.

Tran-Nguyen, A. N., & Zampetti, A. B. (2004). *Trade and Gender: Opportunities and Challenges for Developing Countries*. UNCTAD.

Tremblay, D. (2003). Innovation, management stratégique et économie: Comment la théorie économique rend-elle compte de l'innovation dans l'entreprise? Présenté à la Sixième Conférence de l'AIMS, Montréal, Canada.

Tritter, J. Q., & McCallum, A. (2006). The snakes and ladders of user involvement: Moving beyond Arnstein. *Health Policy (Amsterdam)*, *76*(2), 156–168. doi:10.1016/j.healthpol.2005.05.008 PMID:16006004

Tscharntke, T., Klein, A. M., Kruess, A., Steffan-Dewenter, I., & Thies, C. (2005). Landscape perspectives on agricultural intensification and biodiversity-ecosystem service management. *Ecology Letters*, *8*(8), 857–874. doi:10.1111/j.1461-0248.2005.00782.x

Tsoutsos, T., Frantzeskaki, N., & Gekas, V. (2009). Environmental Impacts from the Solar Energy Technologies. *Energy Policy*, *33*(3), 289–296. doi:10.1016/S0301-4215(03)00241-6

Tu, C. A., Nguyet, T. M. P., Tuan, L. Q., Yoshino, N., Sarker, T., & Taghizadeh-Hesary, F. (2019). *Remittance inflows, financial inclusion, and economic development: an empirical analysis of the world sample.* ADBI Working Paper Series, No. 1000.

Tunde, A., & Adeniyi, E. (2012). Impact of Road Transport on Agricultural Development: A Nigerian Example. *Ethiopian Journal of Environmental Studies and Management*, *5*(3), 232–238. doi:10.4314/ejesm.v5i3.3

Turney, D., & Fthenakis, V. (2011). Environmental Impacts from the Installation and Operation of Large-scale Solar Power Plants. *Renewable & Sustainable Energy Reviews*, *15*(6), 3261–3270. doi:10.1016/j.rser.2011.04.023

Turok, I., & McGranahan, G. (2019). Urbanisation and Economic Growth: The Arguments and Evidence for Africa and Asia. *Urbanisation*, *4*(2), 109–125. doi:10.1177/2455747119890450

Ty, P.H. & Nghi, T.H. (2017). Hydropower Plant Development and Forest Recompensing Plantation in Vietnam. *Tropics of Vietnam.*

Uchendu, V. C. (1979). State, Land and Society in Nigeria: A Critical Assessment of the Land Use Decree, 1978. *Journal of African Studies*, *6*(1), 62–74.

Udo, R. K. (1990). *Land Use Policy and Land Ownership in Nigeria*. Ebie Akwa Ventures.

Udry, C. (2010). The economics of agriculture in Africa: Notes toward a research program. *African Journal of Agricultural and Resource Economics*, *1*, 284–299.

Ukaejiofo, A. N. (2010). *Identifying Appropriate Tools for Effective Land Governance in Nigeria*. FIG Congress 2010 Facing the Challenges – Building the Capacity, Sydney, Australia.

Ullman, E. (1954). Geography as spatial interaction. *Annals of the Association of American Geographers*, *44*, 283–294.

UNCTAD. (2016). *Structural Transformation and Industrial Policy*. UNCTAD.

UNCTAD. (2018). World Investment Report – Investment and New Industrial Policies, Geneva: UNCTAD Mangasini, K., (2018), The Role of Cooperative Organizations in Tanzania's Industrialization. In U. Efobi & S. Asongu (Eds.), *Financing Sustainable Development in Africa*. Palgrave Macmillan.

UNECE Report. (2014). *Development of Renewable Energy: The Water-Energy-Food- Ecosystem Nexus Approach to Support the Sustainable Development Goals*. Author.

UNEP and WTO. (2005). *Making Tourism More Sustainable: A Guide to Policy Makers*. International Policy Publishing.

UNEP. (1998). *United Nations Environmental Program (UNDP). Hand Book on Methods for Climate Change Impact Assessment and Adaptation Strategies*. UNEP and IES.

UNFCC. (2007). *United Nations Framework Convention on Climate Change (UNFCC). Climate Change: Impacts, Vulnerabilities, and Adaptation in Developing Countries*. United Nations Framework Convention on Climate Change Secretariat.

UNIDO – United Nations Industrial Development Organization. (2012). *Tanzania industrial competitiveness report 2012*. Dodoma: UNIDO and GoT.

UNIDO. (2005). *The reform of the power sector in Africa*. Sustainable energy regulation and policymaking training manual. Module 4.

UNIDO. (2009). *Scaling Up Renewable Energy in Africa*. 12th Ordinary Session of Heads of State and Governments of the African Union, Addis Ababa, Ethiopia.

UNIDO. (forthcoming). *Impact of Different Power Sector Reform Options on Energy Efficiency in Africa. Sustainable Energy Regulation and Policymaking for Africa*. Advance Copy. https://www.unido.org/fileadmin/import/83270_Module16.pdf

Union Internationale des Télécommunications. (2013). *Etude sur la connectivité internationale d'Internet en Afrique subsaharienne*. UIT.

United Nations Conference on Trade and Development. (2018). *Trade and development report 2018*. UNCTAD. Retrieved from www.unctad.org

United Nations Development Programme. (2011). *Sustainability and equity: A better future for all*. Palgrave Macmillan.

United Nations Economic Commission for Africa (UNECA). (2017). Integrating Agenda 2063 and 2030 Agenda for Sustainable Development into national development plans. http://mif.media/gr-2019-uneca.

United Nations Economic Commission for Africa. (2005). *Sustainable Development on Africa*. Author.

United Nations Economic Commission for Africa. (2012). *Progress towards Sustainable Development in West Africa*. United Nations Economic Commission for Africa.

United Nations Economic Commission for Africa. (2019). *Drivers of inclusive growth in Africa*. Economic Commission for Africa.

United Nations Industrial Development Organization. (2009). *Green Industry – UNIDO*. Available at: https://www.unido.org/sites/default/files/2010-11/Green_Industry_Initiative_0.pdf

United Nations Industrial Development Organization. (2019). *ISID Platform*. Available at: https://isid.unido.org/

United Nations. (2015). *Sustainable Development Goals*. Retrieved from https://sustainabledevelopment.un.org/?menu=1300

United States Agency for International Development (USAID). (2010). *Nigeria - Property Rights and Resource Governance. USAID Country Profile*. USAID.

United States Department of Agriculture (USDA). (2015). *Food Waste Reduction Goals*. Retrieved February 2 2016 From:to 47 http://www.usda.gov/wps/portal/usda/usdahome?contentid=2015/09/0257.xml

URT - United Republic of Tanzania. (2016). *Cotton-to-clothing Strategy 2016-2020*. ITC.

URT. (2008). *Annual Survey of Industrial Production and Performance*. United Republic of Tanzania.

URT. (2016). The 2013 Census of Industrial Production: Analytical Report. National Bureau of Statistics (NBS) & Ministry of Industry, Trade and Investment (MITI).

URT. (2018). *The Economic Survey Report*. Ministry of Finance and Planning DODOMA – TANZANIA.

USAID. (2010). *USAID country profile property rights and resource governance: Nigeria*. Washington, DC: US Agency for Development Agency. Available online at https://usaidlandtenure.net/wp-content/.../USAID_Land_Tenure_Nigeria_Profile.pdf

USAID. (2014). *Country profile/LandLinks*. Available online at https://www.land-links.org/country-profiles/

Usman, B., Adefila, J., & Musa, I. (2013). Impact of rural road transport on agricultural production in Kwara state, Nigeria. *Nigerian Journal of Agriculture. Food and Environment*, *9*(2), 20–25.

Uzonwanne, M. C. (2015). Economic diversification in Nigeria in the face of dwindling oil revenue. *Journal of Economics and Sustainable Development*, *6*(4), 61–67.

Vagliasindi, M., & Nellis, J. (2010). *Evaluating Africa's Experience with Institutional Reform in Infrastructure Sectors*. AICD Working Paper 22, World Bank, Washington, DC.

Vaknin, S. (2007, May). *Foreign direct investments (FDI)-Pros and Cons*. In Based on a lecture given at the Euro College Student Union Business Forum, Kumanovo, Macedonia.

Van Auken, H., & Horton, H. (1994). Financing Patterns of Minority-Owned Small Business. *Journal of Small Business Strategy*, *5*, 2.

Van den Brande, K., Happaerts, S., & Bruyninckx, H. (2008). The role of the subnational level of government in decision-making for sustainable development: a multi-level governance perspective. Katholieke Universiteit Leuven Working Paper No 4.

Van, W. J-A. (2007). Political Leaders in Africa: Presidents, Patrons and Profiteers? Durban: ACCORD.

Vanguard Newspaper Interview Report. (2017). *Expunge Land Use Act from constitution – town planners*. Available online at https://www.vanguardngr.com/2017/10/expunge-land-use-act-constitution-

Van, W. S. (1983). Credit policy, inflation and growth in a financially repressed economy. *Journal of Development Economics*, *13*(1-2), 45–65. doi:10.1016/0304-3878(83)90049-4

Veihe, A. (2000). Sustainable farming practices: Ghanaian farmers' perception of erosion and their use of conservation measures. *Environmental Management*, *25*(4), 393–402. doi:10.1007002679910031 PMID:10667945

Velde, D. W. (2006). *Foreign Direct Investment and Development: An Historical Perspective*. Overseas Development Institute, Working Paper. Retrieved from https://www.odi.org/sites/odi.org.uk/files/odi-assets/publications-opinion-files/850.pdf

Veldkamp, A., Kok, K., De Koning, G. H. J., Schoorl, J. M., Sonneveld, M. P. W., & Verburg, P. H. (2001). Multi-scale system approaches in agronomic research at the landscape level. *Soil & Tillage Research*, *58*(3-4), 129–140. doi:10.1016/S0167-1987(00)00163-X

Venkat, K. (2012). The Climate Change and Economic Impacts of Food Waste in the United States. *Int. J. Food System Dynamics, 2*(4), 431-446.

Venkatadri, U., Rardin, R. L., & Montreuil, B. (1997). A design methodology for fractal layout organization. *IIE Transactions*, *29*(10), 911–924. doi:10.1080/07408179708966411

Vianna, A. C., & Mollick, A. V. (2018). Institutions: Key variable for economic development in Latin America. *Journal of Economics and Business*, *96*, 42–58. doi:10.1016/j.jeconbus.2017.12.002

Vogel, D. (2008). Private global business regulation. *Annual Review of Political Science*, *11*(1), 261–282. doi:10.1146/annurev.polisci.11.053106.141706

Wahab, A., & Popoola, A. (2019). Urban Farmers' Perceptions of and Adaptation Strategies to Climate Variability in Ibadan, Nigeria. In The Geography of Climate Change Adaptation in Urban Africa (pp. 123-154). Palgrave Macmillan.

Wahab, B., & Popoola, A. (2018). Climate-Induced Problems and Adaptation Strategies of Urban Farmers in Ibadan. *Ethiopian Journal of Environmental Studies and Management, 11*(1), 31–42.

Wahab, B., Popoola, A., & Magidimisha, H. (2018b). Access to Urban Agricultural Land in Ibadan, Nigeria. *Planning Malaysian: Journal of the Malaysian Institute of Planners, 16*(4), 161–175. doi:10.21837/pmjournal.v16.i8.547

Waheed, R., Chang, D., Sarwar, S., & Chen, W. (2017). Forest, Agriculture, Renewable Energy and CO_2 Emission. *Journal of Cleaner Production*, 1–8.

Wang, C., Wang, F., Zhang, X., Yang, Y., Su, Y., Ye, Y., & Zhang, H. (2017b). Examining the driving factors of energy related carbon emissions using the extended STIRPAT model based on IPAT identity in Xinjiang. *Renewable & Sustainable Energy Reviews, 67*, 51–61. doi:10.1016/j.rser.2016.09.006

Wang, C., Yang, S., Liu, C., & Li, S. (2018). How Would Economic Development Inñuence Carbon Productivity? A Case from Hubei in China. *International Journal of Environmental Research and Public Health, 15*(8), 1730. doi:10.3390/ijerph15081730

Wang, X., & Guan, J. (2017). Financial Inclusion: Measurement, spatial effects, and influencing factors. *Applied Economics, 49*(18), 1751–1762. doi:10.1080/00036846.2016.1226488

Wang, Z. X., Hao, P., & Yao, P. Y. (2017a). Non-Linear Relationship between Economic Growth and CO2 Emissions in China: An Empirical Study Based on Panel Smooth Transition Regression Models. *International Journal of Environmental Research and Public Health, 14*(12), 1568. doi:10.3390/ijerph14121568

Ward, C. E., Vestal, M. K., Doye, D. G., & Lalman, D. L. (2008). Factors affecting adoption of cow-calf production practices in Oklahoma. *Journal of Agricultural and Applied Economics, 3*(3), 851–863. doi:10.1017/S1074070800002376

WDI. (2019). *Worldwide Development Indicators, World Bank.* Retrieved from https://databank.worldbank.org/reports.aspx?source=2&series=SI.POV.DDAY&country=WLD

Wells-Dang, A., Tu, P. Q., & Burke, A. (2016). Conversion of Land Use in Vietnam through a Political Economy Lens. *Journal of Social Sciences and Humanities, 2*(2), 131–146.

Welshman, J. (2013). From the Cycle of Deprivation to Troubled Families: Ethnicity and the underclass concept. In Migration, Health and Ethnicity in the ModernWorld (pp. 174-194). Palgrave Macmillan.

Wey, W. (2015). Developing the Socio-Economic Urban Sustainable Planning Strategies Based on The Smart and Inclusive Growth Principles. *Journal of Business and Economics, 6*(11), 1898–1907. doi:10.15341/jbe(2155-7950)/11.06.2015/008

Wezel, A., & Soldat, V. (2009). A quantitative and qualitative historical analysis of the scientific discipline agroecology. *International Journal of Agricultural Sustainability, 7*(1), 3–18. doi:10.3763/ijas.2009.0400

WGI. (2019). *Worldwide Governance Indicators, World Bank.* Retrieved from https://databank.worldbank.org/source/worldwide-governance-indicators/Type/TABLE/preview/on

Williams, H., Wikström, F., Otterbring, T., Löfgren, M., & Gustafsson, A. (2012). Reasons for household food waste with special attention to packaging. *Journal of Cleaner Production, 24*, 141–148. doi:10.1016/j.jclepro.2011.11.044

Williamson, J. (2011). *Trade and Poverty: When the Third World Fell Behind.* MIT Press. doi:10.7551/mitpress/9780262015158.001.0001

Williamson, O. E. (1975). *Markets and hierarchies: Analysis and antitrust implications.* Free Press.

Williamson, O. E. (1985). *The economic institutions of capitalism*. Free Press.

Williamson, O. E. (2000). The New Institutional Economics: Taking Stock, Looking Ahead. *Journal of Economic Literature, 38*(3), 595–613. doi:10.1257/jel.38.3.595

Wilson, G. A. (2009). Post-Productivist and multifunctional agriculture. International Encyclopedia of Human Geography, 379–386. doi:10.1016/B978-008044910-4.00895-6

Wilson, C., & Tisdell, C. (2001). Why farmers continue to use pesticides despite environmental, health and sustainability cost. *Ecological Economics, 39*(3), 449–462. doi:10.1016/S0921-8009(01)00238-5

Wilson, G. A. (2008). From "weak" to "strong" multifunctionality: Conceptualising farm-level multifunctional transitional pathways. *Journal of Rural Studies, 24*(3), 367–383. doi:10.1016/j.jrurstud.2007.12.010

Wily, L. A. (2011). *Customary Land Tenure in the Modern World Rights to Resources in Crisis: Reviewing the Fate of Customary Tenure in Africa. Brief No 1 of 5. Rights and Resources Initiative*. RRI.

Wiskerke, J. S. C. (2016). Urban food systems. In Cities and Agriculture. Developing resilient urban food systems (pp. 1–26). New York: Routledge.

Wolfgang, W. (2018). *Land tenure and governance on communal land in Namibia*. Paper presented at for the Second National Land Conference, Windhoek. Available online at http://dna.nust.na/landconference/submissions_2018/Land_tenure_and_governance.pdf

World Bank & Knomad. (2019). *Migration and remittances: recent developments and outlook. Migration and Development Brief 31*. Author.

World Bank Energy Report. (2018). Best Practises on Renewable Energy in Africa. *The Status*.

World Bank Report. (2016). *Managing Environmental and Social Impacts of Hydro-power in Bhutan*. A Final Report Prepared in Collaboration with the Royal Government of Bhutan.

World Bank. (1989). *From crisis to sustainable growth – sub Saharan Arica: a long-term perspective study*. The World Bank.

World Bank. (1996). *Land Reform*. World Band Paper - Rural Development Series.

World Bank. (2000). *Engendering Development Through Gender Equality in Rights, Resources and Voice*. Retrieved from Washington.

World Bank. (2003). *Land Policies for Growth and Poverty Reduction*. World Bank.

World Bank. (2005). *Global Economic Prospects Report 2006: Economic Implications of Remittances and Migration*. World Bank.

World Bank. (2009). *Directions in Scaling Up for Development*. Water Working Notes 49017, No. 21, June 2009.

World Bank. (2014). *Global Economic Prospectus*. Author.

World Bank. (2016). *Agricultural Land in Nigeria in the Last Decade*. The World Bank.

World Bank. (2016). *Doing Business: Measuring Business Regulations*. The World Bank.

World Bank. (2016). *Private Participation in Infrastructure (PPI) Database*. Washington, DC: World Bank. https://ppi.worldbank.org/data

World Bank. (2016). *Tanzania*. https://data.worldbank.org/country/tanzania?display=graph

World Bank. (2017). *Registering Property*. Retrieved May 26, 2020, from World Bank website: https://www.doingbusiness.org/data/exploretopics/registering-property

World Bank. (2017). *World Bank Annual Report 2017 (English)*. Washington, DC: World Bank Group. https://documents.worldbank.org/curated/en/143021506909711004/World-Bank-Annual-Report-2017

World Bank. (2017a). *Worldwide Governance Indicators*. The World Bank.

World Bank. (2017b). *World Development Indicators*. The World Bank.

World Bank. (2018). *Strengthening economic diversification in Nigeria through connectivity*. Retrieved from https://www.worldbank.org/en/country/nigeria/publication/strengthening-economic-diversification-in-nigeria-through-connectivity

World Bank. (2018). *The World Bank Annual Report 2018 (English)*. Washington, DC: World Bank Group. https://documents.worldbank.org/curated/en/630671538158537244/The-World-Bank-Annual-Report-2018

World Bank. (2019). *Harvesting Prosperity: Technology and Productivity in agriculture*. World Bank.

World Bank. (2019). *The World Bank in Nigeria*. Retrieved from https://www.worldbank.org/en/country/nigeria/overview

World Bank. (2020). *ICT for agriculture*. Open Learning Campus. Retrieved from https://olc.worldbank.org/content/ict-agriculture

World Commission on Environment and Development. (1987). *Our common future*. Oxford University Press.

World Economic Forum. (2012). *The Informal Sector in Francophone Africa, Firm Size, Productivity, and Institutions*. International Bank for Reconstruction and Development / The World Bank. Retrieved from. https://documents.worldbank.org/curated/en/737371468202815116/pdf/699350PUB0Publ067869B09780821395370.pdf

World Economic Forum. (2019). *The global competitiveness report 2019*. World Economic Forum. Retried from www.weforum.org/gcr

World Economic Forum. (2019). *Travel and Tourism Competitiveness Report*. World Economic Forum.

Wren-Lewis, L. (2013). *Corruption in Land Administration: Roles for Donors to Minimise the Problem*. U4 Brief March 2013:1.

WTO. (2019). *Trade Policy Review Report for the East African Community* (WT/TPR/S/384/Rev.1). WTO.

WTTC. (2019). *Economic Impact of Travel & Tourism World Report 2018*. WTTC.

WWF Technical Report. (2014). *Renewable Energy Vision 2030 – South Africa*. Author.

Xu, G., & Song, D. (2011). An Empirical Study on the Environmental Kuznets Curve for China's Carbon Emissions: Based on Provincial Panel Data. *China Journal of Population and Resource Environment*, *9*(3), 66–76. doi:10.1080/10042857.2011.10685040

Yang, M., & Sharma, D. (2012, February). *The Impacts of Electricity Reforms on Electricity Prices. 3rd IAEE Asian Conference*, Tokyo, Japan.

Yesuf, M. (2008). *The impact of climate change and adaptation on food production in low-income countries: evidence from the Nile Basin*. Intl Food Policy Res Inst.

Yoshino, N., Morgan, P. J., & Trinh, L. Q. (2017). *Financial Literacy in Japan: Determinants and Impacts.* ADBI Working Paper 796.

Yoshino, T.-H. & Otsuka. (2017). *International Remittances and Poverty Reduction: Evidence from Asian Developing Countries.* ADBI Working Paper 759. Tokyo: Asian Development Bank Institute.

Yuan, Q., Cheng, C., Wang, J., Zhu, T., & Wang, K. (2020). Inclusive and sustainable industrial development in China: An efficiency-based analysis for status and improving potentials. *Applied Energy, 268*, 114876. doi:10.1016/j.apenergy.2020.114876

Yung, J. M., & Bosc, P. M. (1999). Schumpeter au Sahel. In L'innovation en agriculture: Questions de méthodes et terrains d'observation (pp.143-168). Paris: IRD. doi:10.4000/books.irdeditions.15741

Yunos, J. M., & Hawdon, D. (1997). The Efficiency of the National Electricity Board in Malaysia: An Inter-country Comparison Using DEA. *Energy Economics, 19*(2), 255–269. doi:10.1016/S0140-9883(96)01018-3

Yunusa, M., Shaibu, I., Ambi, Y., Yusuf, A., & Abdulkarim, B. (2002). Road rehabilitation: The impact on transport and accessibility. In P. Fernando & G. Porter (Eds.), *Balancing the Load: Gender, Women and transport.* Zed Books.

Zaman, A. U. (2014). Measuring waste management performance using the 'zero waste index'. *Journal of Cleaner Production, 66*, 407–419. doi:10.1016/j.jclepro.2013.10.032

Zaman, A. U. (2015). A Comprehensive review of the development of zero waste management: Lessons learned and guidelines. *Journal of Cleaner Production, 91*, 12–25. doi:10.1016/j.jclepro.2014.12.013

Zapata Campos, M. J., Hall, C. M., & Backlund, S. (2018). Can MNCs promote more inclusive tourism? Apollo tour operator's sustainability work. *Tourism Geographies, 20*(4), 630–652. doi:10.1080/14616688.2018.1457074

Zevenbergen, J., Holden, S., Ali, D. A., & Deininger, K. (2007). *Rural land certification in Ethiopia: process, initial impact, and implications for other African Countries, Policy.* Research Working Paper, No. WPS 4218. World Bank.

Zhang, H., Li, L., Zhou, D., & Zhou, P. (2014). Political connections, government subsidies and firm financial performance: Evidence from renewable energy manufacturing in. *Renewable Energy, 63*, 330–336. doi:10.1016/j.renene.2013.09.029

Zhang, W., Ricketts, T. H., Kremen, C., Carney, K., & Swinton, S. M. (2007). Ecosystem services and dis-services to agriculture. *Ecological Economics, 64*(2), 253–260. doi:10.1016/j.ecolecon.2007.02.024

Zhang, Y. F., Parker, D., & Kirkpatrick, C. (2005). Competition, Regulation and Privatization of Electricity Generation in Developing Countries: Does the Sequencing of the Reforms Matter? *The Quarterly Review of Economics and Finance, 45*(2-3), 358–379. doi:10.1016/j.qref.2004.12.009

Zhang, Y.-F., Parker, D., & Kirkpatrick, C. (2008). Electricity Sector Reform in Developing Countries: An Econometric Assessment of the Effects of Privatization, Competition and Regulation. *Journal of Regulatory Economics, 33*(2), 159–178. doi:10.100711149-007-9039-7

Zhao, Z., Chang, R., & Chen, Y. (2016). What hinders the further development of wind power in China? A socio-technical barrier study. *Energy Policy, 88*(January), 465–476. doi:10.1016/j.enpol.2015.11.004

Zhou, L., Song, L., Xie, C., & Zhang, J. (2013). Applications of Internet of Things in the Facility Agriculture. *International Federation for Information Processing,* 297-303.

Zoundi, S.J., & Hitimana, L. (2002). Défis de l'accès des exploitations familiales aux innovations agricoles en Afrique de l'Ouest: implications institutionnelles et politiques. *Club du Sahel et de l'Afrique de l'Ouest*, 1-15.

About the Contributors

Evans Osabuohien holds B.Sc, M.Sc and Ph.D in Economics. He is endowed with a pleasant personality and capability to work effectively in multi-cultural environments. He has executed funded research projects as an individual, team leader, and team member. He is astute in research, which has resulted in over 120 publications and has participated in conferences/workshops/short courses across the world. He was appointed as the Head of Department (HOD) in 2016, emerging as the Youngest HOD in Covenant University. He received a Double Promotion to the Rank of a Full Professor of Economics in December 2017, which made him the Youngest Professor in the University. In May 2020, he was recognised as 'One of the 6 Youngest Professors Nigeria Ever Had'. He is the Chair at the Centre for Economic Policy and Development Research (CEPDeR) as well as the Chair for Regional Centre of Expertise, Ogun State (RCE Ogun), Covenant University. He is a member of numerous International Learned Societies/Professional Associations. He is a Visiting Professor at Witten/Herdecke University, Germany. He is the Editor of 'Handbook of Research on In-Country Determinants and Implications of Foreign Land Acquisitions' (2015) and 'The Palgrave Handbook of Agricultural and Rural Development in Africa' (2020) as well as the Guest Editor for African Journal of Economic and Management Studies (Emerald) on 'Labour Issues in Africa's Agricultural and Rural Transformation' (2020). He is Guest Editing 'Socioeconomic Shocks, Inequality and Food Systems in the Global South for Contemporary Social Science (Taylor & Francis).

Emmanuel Oduntan holds a Ph.D. degree in Statistics with a speciality in Econometrics from the University of Ibadan, Nigeria. Early in life, he had a successful career that spanned over many years in both the public service and the private sector in Nigeria. At the completion of his doctorate degree, he took up a faculty position at the Department of Mathematics, Lagos State University, Nigeria, and later at the Department of Economics and Development Studies, Covenant University, Nigeria. He is a Senior Research Fellow at the Centre for Economic Policy and Development Research (CEPDeR) and currently an Assistant Professor of Statistics at the American University of Nigeria.

Obindah Gershon holds B.Sc, M.Sc and Ph.D in Energy Studies. He is a Senior Lecturer at the Department of Economics and Development Studies and serves as the Co-Chair, Centre for Economic Policy and Development Research (CEPDeR), Covenant University. Previously, he was Director of the Vice Chancellor's Office in Covenant University and taught at Georgetown University. He is an outstanding researcher and expert in energy and natural resource economics - having studied at the foremost Centre for Energy, Petroleum and Mineral Law and Policy, University of Dundee in the United Kingdom. He is a Visiting Professor to Eduardo Mondlane University, Mozambique, St. Jerome University,

Cameroon and Emerald Energy Institute, University of Port Harcourt, Nigeria. He is a member of the International Association for Energy Economics (IAEE), Nigeria Association for Energy Economics, British Institute for Energy Economics (BIEE), Official Monetary and Financial Institutions Forum (OMFIF). He has many publications in journal, published a book in International Gas Pricing, and is a reviewer for many journals. He is Co-Editing 'Decarbonisation Pathways for African Cities' (2021) - an upcoming volume in the Palgrave Studies in Climate Resilient Societies series. [Email: obindah.gershon@covenantuniversity.edu.ng].

Olaronke Onanuga is currently a Research Fellow at the Centre for Economic Policy and Development Research (CEPDeR), Covenant University. She holds a PhD in Economics from the University of South Africa. Her research interest lies in economic and sustainable development. She was a lecturer at Hallmark University, Covenant University and KolaDaisi University after completing her PhD. She was the secretary to the conference organising committee (COC) of the 2019 International Conference on Africa Development and the secretary of the CEPDeR Committee. She is a grant and award-winning researcher: She won the Jean Monnet Network; Trade & Investment in Services Associates (TIISA) Young Scholar Paper Award (2020). She has published in internationally recognised journal outlets like Management of Environmental Quality, Journal on Food System Dynamics, Business: Theory and Practice, and Journal of Contemporary African Studies.

Oluyomi Ola-David is a development economist who is concerned about global development. She currently holds a faculty position at the Department of Economics and Development of Covenant University, Nigeria. She enjoys generating solutions, influencing policy and providing clarity.

* * *

Reginald Addy-Morton is a 41-year-old Ghanaian lecturer with the Department of Economics and Entrepreneurship Development, University for Development Studies with a Bachelor of Arts Degree in Integrated Development Studies and Master of Philosophy Degree in Development Studies. Research focus includes Small Business Management, Social Entrepreneurship, Credit and Microfinance for Small Businesses, Livelihood Management and Human Resource Management. I have experience in assisting and teaching Principles of Entrepreneurship, Marketing, Human Resource Management, Development Economics, Theories of Business Growth and Principles of Microfinance.

Bamiji Adeleye is a lecturer in the Department of Urban and Regional Planning, Federal University of Technology Minna, Nigeria. He is presently undergoing his research in the Planning Department of Makarere University, Uganda.

Yamah Adeyemi is a graduate student of the Department of urban and regional planning, University of Ibadan.

Abdul-Wakeel Alhassan is a postgraduate researcher at the School of Economics, University of Cape Coast, Ghana. He started researching when he served as a Research Assistant for Educational Network for West And Central Africa (ENWACA), in May – June 2009. He had his first degree in Economics, MSc. Economics of Technology and Development as well as Master of Philosophy in Economics all from the University of Cape Coast, Ghana. Alhassan A. Karakara has published some articles in peer review journals with other several articles co-authored with Prof. Evans Osabuohien which are under peer review in various Journals. He has served as a discussant and presenter in international conferences across the African Continent. He was a panel in the African Innovation Summit II, in Kigali Rwanda in June 2018. His research interests include poverty, the economics of innovation and technology, development economics, and international trade with emphasis on developing economies.

Opeyemi Aluko is a proficient scholar in the field of Political Science. He is a lecturer in the Political Science Department Ajayi Crowther University Oyo, Oyo State Nigeria. His areas of research are Judicial Studies, Security Studies, Comparative politics and Research Methodology. He is currently a doctoral candidate in the Political Science Department Kwara State University Malete Kwara State Nigeria.

Uchenna Nnanna Anyanwu is a lecturer with the Department of Economics Nnamdi Azikiwe University Awka and a facilitator with NOUN. He obtained a BSc in Economics from Nnamdi Azikiwe University Awka; MSc Economics and MSc Banking and Finance from Imo State University and Michael Okpara University Umudike respectively. His PhD is in Public Sector Economics. Uche has written publications for both international and local journals. He is a member of the Nigeria Economic Society (NES).

Ewere Evelyn Anyokwu is a Junior Researcher and a PhD student at the Center for Development Research (ZEF), University of Bonn, Germany. Her research interests are issues related to economics of renewable energy, sustainable resource use and climate change.

Simplice Asongu is a Professor of Economics; and the lead economist of African Governance Development Institute (AGDI).

Scott Baum is a Professor in the Cities Research Institute and the Policy Innovation Hub, Griffith University. Trained in Economics and Sociology his research interests include understanding social, economic and ecological disadvantage and injustice in urban and regional settings. He has published in excess of 100 journal articles and book chapters and has been lead researchers or co-lead researcher on grants worth in excess of AUD $11 million.

Ibukun Beecroft is an Economist with experience in empirical research and evaluating policies towards proffering relevant solutions to policy makers, as well as impacting knowledge through teaching in a World Class Institution. She has successfully collaborated on competitive research grants to aid the operations of international organisations towards economic development. Her research is centered around Institutions, Public Economics, International and Development Economics.

Alexis Beyuo is a Post-Doctoral Research Fellow at the Kumasi Centre for Collaborative Research (KCC), Ghana. He has a PhD in Development Studies from the University of Ghana, MSc. in Sustainable Development from the University of St. Andrews, Scotland and a Bachelor of Arts in Integrated Development Studies from the University for Development Studies. His area of interest is in participatory approaches for sustainable agriculture.

Kolade Kamilu Bolarinwa obtained Bachelor of Agricultural Extension in University of Nigeria Nsukka Nigeria in 1986, He obtained his Master of Science Degree and Ph, D. degree in Department of Agricultural Extension and Rural Development in 1997 and 2007 respectively. His area of specialization is conflict management and livelihood impact assessment. He obtained several scholarships and prizes. Bolarinwa has 18 years' experience in the world bank Agricultural Development Programme - an Agricultural Extension arms of the Ministry of Agriculture in Nigeria. He was saddled with the responsibility of disseminating relevant information from the research station to farmers. He has contributed extensively to emerging issues in agriculture and agricultural innovation and consultancies for international and national organizations. Dr. Bolarinwa has participated in several baseline surveys and impact evaluation and data collection using both quantitative and qualitative techniques, participatory rural conflict appraisal (PRA) using information-gathering tools such as questionnaires, interview schedules, focus group discussion, pair ranking and use of key informants. He has 65 papers published in local and international journals. He is currently a Reader and Head of the Department of the Agricultural Administration, Federal University of Agriculture Abeokuta. He was one of those agricultural extension practitioners that have agricultural extension field experience and become Assistant Director of the extension before he crossed to University where he acquired research and teaching experiences. He is a member of many professional associations and societies.

Lovemore Chipungu is a senior lecturer in the Department of Housing at UKZN. He has his research interest in Planning Policy development, land administration and urban development.

Cordia Chu is the director of the Centre for Environment and Population Health, Griffith University. With a background in medical anthropology and sociology, her key areas of research expertise are global health, eco-friendly healthy settings; reproductive health; integrated health planning; workplace health promotion and safety management; community needs assessment; and policy development. She is committed to ensuring that research is useful and used through translational research and capacity-building, particularly in linking the environment, health strategies and sustainable development. Awarded the Member of the Order of Australia in 2013, she has published over 200 articles and book chapters, delivered two policy/guidelines, four commissioned research communication booklets, five documentary films, twenty-one international consultancy reports, one WHO regional guideline, and has presented over 80 keynote addresses in conferences. She has graduated 45 PhDs and in 2018 she won a national commendation for excellence in research supervision by the Australian Council for Graduate Research.

Hayelom Yrgaw Gereziher is a lecturer of Economics at Adigrat University, College of Business and Economics, Department of Economics, Ethiopia. He has published articles in international peer reviewed journals. He has also recently secured research grant from UNU- WIDER. He presented his research findings in international workshops and conferences.

Adem Gök is currently employed in Department of Economics at Kırklareli University, Turkey as an assistant professor. He received his bachelor degree in economics from Boğaziçi University in 2008 and master degree in economics (English) from Marmara University in 2012. He holds a Ph.D in economics (English) from Marmara University since 2016. His main research areas include economic growth, economics of governance and foreign direct investment. His current research area is economics of education.

Okezie Ihugba is a Senior Lecturer in the Department of Economics Alvan Ikoku Federal College of Education Owerri, Imo State. Okezie was the Coordinator of NCE Project, Department of Economics from 2012-2014; Coordinator of Degree Project, Department of Economics from 2016-2017. He is currently the Head, Department of Economics. He is a member of Nigeria of Economic Society (NES); Royal Economic Society (RES); American Economists Association (AEA); Canadian Economists Association (CEA); Institute of Economists of Nigeria (INEN); Global Association for Teachers of Economics (GATE); International Research and Development Institute (IRDI) and has published over 40 articles in local and international journals.

Christopher U. Kalu is a Senior Lecturer in the Economics Department, Nnamdi Azikiwe University Awka, Nigeria. Chris obtained a PhD in Development Economics from Nnamdi Azikiwe University Awka and is a Fellow of the United Nations African Institute for Economic Development and Planning Dakar, Senegal. His research area includes Health Economics, Financial Economics and Development.

Enoch Akwasi Kosoe holds a Master of Science degree in Environmental Resource Management from the Kwame Nkrumah University of Science and Technology (KNUST), Kumasi, Ghana. He lectures several environmental related courses such as waste management, pollution control and monitoring, environmental economics, consumer culture and the environment, biodiversity conservation, water resources development, land-use and rural Environment. He is a member of the Ghana Geographical Association (GGA) and has several research articles published in peer reviewed journals in the area of potable water supply and solid waste management. Mr. Kosoe research interest and experience is in the following areas: Sanitation – issues on access to household toilet facilities, household sanitary practices, policy issues on sanitation; and Waste Management – access to solid waste management services in urban and rural areas, household solid waste management, policy discourse on waste management; Water Resource Management – access to household water supply, small-town water supply management, water quality issues, policy issues. He also has research interest in Community Based Natural Resource Management – Forestry and Tourism; Community Based Wildfire Management; Sustainable Environmental Management; and Biodiversity Conservation.

Galinoma Lubawa has extensive experience in preparation of Corporate/SMEs Business Plan, Investment Profiles for Local Government Authorities(LGAs), Local Government Revenue Planning, Financial Modelling and Investment/business planning training on all aspects of Corporate Finance, Financial Reporting, International Finance, Taxation and Entrepreneurship. He has consulted several companies including; International Executive Services Corps(IESC) USA, Cereal and Other Produce Board of Tanzania (CPB), Arusha Urban Water Supply and Sanitation Authority(AUWSA), Geita Gold Mining Limited (GGM), Kibaigwa International Market (Ltd), and Dodoma Urban Water Supply and Sanitation Authority (DUWASA) among others. He is also working as a Lecturer at the Department of Development Finance and Management Studies at the Institute of Rural Development Planning (IRDP), in Dodoma Tanzania.

Chekwube V. Madichie has B.Sc. in Economics from Anambra State University, and M.Sc. in Quantitative Economics from Nnamdi Azikiwe University. He is a gifted teacher and an erudite scholar who is highly motivated to embrace new challenges. His research interest borders on Quantitative Economics and Development, with particular interest in Econometric Analysis of both time series and panel data. He's the creator of the YouTube channel @ViData Solutions where he shares videos on how to use Eviews to perform various analyses of both time series and panel data, with more than 20 videos already shared.

Hope Magidimisha is a Professor of Town and Regional Planning, who currently is the Acadmic Leader for Town and Regional Planning at the University of KwaZuulu Natal, She is also the SARChI Chair for Inclusive cities sponsored by South African City Network and UKZN. Her research focus currently traverse subjects such as city inclusivity, gender advocacy and infrastructure development in African Cities.

Nyanjige M. Mayala works for the Moshi Co-operative University (MoCU) as a Lecturer in the Department of Management teaching a number of business management related courses. She have a 20 years experience in research and consultancy undertakings in Tanzania and across Africa. She currently Head the Department of Management and serve as a Chief Editor for the East African Journal of Social and Applied Sciences (EAJ-SAS).

Samuel Medayese is a Ph.D. candidate in the Department of Town and Regional Planning. Also a Lecturer in the Department of Urban and Regional Planning, Federal University of Technology, Minna, Nigeria. His areas of interest are sustainable transport planning, city liveability, and inclusive physical development.

Amaka Metu is a Senior Lecturer in the Department of Economics, Nnamdi Azikiwe University Awka Nigeria. Amaka's research interest includes Development Economics, Entrepreneurship, Institutional Economics and Migration Studies. Amaka is the Managing Editor of the Journal of Economic Studies (JES) and The Nigerian Journal of Energy and Environmental Economics (NJEEE), published by the Department of Economics, NAU Awka.

Msafiri Njoroge is a PhD holder in Business Administration focusing on linking Entrepreneurial Orientation with Corporate Sustainability in Tourism. In his PhD, Msafiri has benefited from the Scholarship Project No. 2208 on Innovation and Sustainability in Tourism under the UDSM-Sida Programme 2015-2020. Msafiri also holds Masters in International Trade (MIT) and Bachelor of Commerce (Accounting) [B.Com]. Professionally, Msafiri is Certified Public Accountant [CPA (T)]. Msafiri is a Lecturer at Faculty of Business Management, the Open University of Tanzania. His research interests include Entrepreneurship; Corporate Sustainability; Sustainable Tourism; International Business; Taxation; and Financial Management.

Naser Yenus Nuru is Assistant Professor of Economics at Adigrat University, Ethiopia. He has published articles in international peer reviewed journals. He has also recently secured research grant from UNU- WIDER. He presented his research findings in international workshops and conferences. He is also going to make a research visit to KU-Leuven, Belgium in April, 2021.

Chigozie Nweke-Eze is a Research associate and PhD candidate at the Institute of Geography, University of Bonn. He researches the governance, financing and infrastructures for renewable energies from development economics and economic geography perspectives.

Abiodun Obayelu is a seasoned scholar with about 10 years of experience of teaching, research, consultancy and community service. He has a PhD (Agricultural Economics) from University of Ibadan, Nigeria. He currently Lectures at the Federal University of Agriculture, Abeokuta, Nigeria. He has participated as team member (Agricultural and Food Economist) in a number of funded research and consultancy works, playing one or more roles in the conceptualization and designed of research, facilitation of field work and data collection, data analysis and report writing, facilitation of stakeholders meeting, liaison with government officials of the federal ministry of agriculture, agencies and Non-Governmental Organization (NGOs) for possible mainstreaming of research project and findings into agricultural development policy of Nigeria. Dr. Obayelu A. E is the editor of the book "Food Systems Sustainability and Environmental Policies in Modern Economies" published by IGI International, USA in 2018. He has over 65 publications in reputable local and international journals and more than 12 chapters in books.

Odunayo Omojola is a trained planner with specialty in transport planning. His MSc. research was focused on bystanders' role and pre-hospital care of injured road crash victims.

Femi Oni is an expert in Development studies. His sphere of influence ranges from Agricultural Economics, food security, environmental sustainability to social identity issues. He is a graduate of the department of development studies where he finished his masters in development studies. He is a vast researcher with private educational consultancy services. He is also a part-time lecturer at the Durban University of Technology, Durban. South Africa, taking environmental sustainability modules.

Olalekan Oyekunle is a Senior Lecturer at the Federal University of Agriculture, Abeokuta Ogun State, Nigeria. He holds a B. Agric. (Agricultural Extension and Rural Sociology), M. Agric and Ph.D in Agricultural Communication, Postgraduate Diplomas in Mass Communication and a Postgraduate Diploma in Education (PGDE). His research focus or interest is on innovative use of Media Resources for the facilitation of Agro-information flow between researchers and smallholder farmers for improved productivity, as well as translation of agricultural research findings into Agricultural Media Materials with main emphasis on video, audio, printed materials and other multimedia tools for the dissemination of information to all stakeholders in agriculture. He is a reputable Academic who actively carries out Teaching, Research and Extension Services. As a member of the University Radio Management Board, Dr. Oyekunle coordinates and produces Farm Broadcasts on Radio to support field level Agricultural Extension Services in Southwest Nigeria. He is proficient in the use of Information and Communication Technology (ICT) tools. Dr. Oyekunle is an active member of Professional Associations including Agricultural Extension Society of Nigeria (AESON), Rural Sociological Society of Nigeria (RuSAN), Farm Management Association of Nigeria (FAMAN) and the National Research and Development Network of Youth in Agriculture Programme (CYIAP). He has over 40 Publications in reputable International and Local Learned Journals and Conference proceedings.

Ayobami Abayomi Popoola is a trained Geographer and now an Urban and Regional Planner with lifelong interest on Human Wellbeing and Livelihood. His interest is how planning and plans shape human livelihood and wellbeing. This He displayed in His PhD research in the Department of Town and Regional Planning, UKZN where He studied Rural Physical Development and how it impacts household livelihood. This study explains rural household wellbeing from the tripod of rural governance, infrastructure and planning. He is presently a researcher with the SARChI Chair for Inclusive Cities at the University of KwaZulu-Natal, South Africa. He is the author of eleven Chapters in highly-rated books published by reputable international publishers and over eighteen peer-reviewed international and local journal articles. Most of these publications are in the area of rural, city, land-use planning, food security, climate change, environmental and sustainable planning and management, human livelihood and wellbeing. Dr Popoola is currently a team in the SARChI Chair for Inclusive Cities project located in the Department of Town and Regional Planning, School of Built Environment and Development Studies, UKZN. The research chair is funded by NRF, South African Cities Network and others.

Amadou Tandjigora is a PhD student in Economics at the Cheikh Anta Diop University of Dakar where he has done all his university studies. After his Master's degree, he became interested in agricultural and rural issues. He has participated in several scientific meetings in Senegal including the Senegalese Institute of Agricultural Research, the Laboratory of Economic and Monetary Research and abroad especially at the University of Social Sciences and Management of Bamako. He is passionate about research, especially agriculture and related works. He published in 2019 "Industries and Rural Services: The Rural transformation Support in the context of continuing Degradation Agriculture: Evidence from Senegal", in French. He is also the author of the chapter entitled "Impact of Non-Agricultural Activities on Farmers' Income: Evidence from the Senegalese Arachid Area" of a research manual entitled: "The Palgrave Handbook of Agricultural and Rural Development in Africa" edited by Professor Evans Osabuohien.

Efobi Uchenna is a faculty of the College of Business and Social Sciences, Covenant University. He is also a Research Fellow at the Centre for Economic Policy and Development Research - Covenant University, and Merian Institute for Advanced Studies in Africa – University of Ghana. He has a PhD from Covenant University, with a research focus on International capital flow and financial regulations in Africa.

José G. Vargas-Hernández, M.B.A., Ph.D., Member of the National System of Researchers of Mexico and a research professor at University Center for Economic and Managerial Sciences, University of Guadalajara. Professor Vargas-Hernández has a Ph. D. in Public Administration and a Ph.D. in Organizational Economics. He has undertaken studies in Organisational Behaviour and has a Master of Business Administration, published four books and more than 200 papers in international journals and reviews (some translated to English, French, German, Portuguese, Farsi, Chinese, etc.) and more than 300 essays in national journals and reviews. He has obtained several international Awards and recognition.

Zerihun Yohannes Amare holds his Ph.D. degree in Environmental Management specialization in Climate change and Development from Pan African University (PAULESI), University of Ibadan, Nigeria. He has a Master's degree in Urban Management specialization in Urban Environmental Planning and Management, International Cooperation and Humanitarian Aid. His Ph.D. thesis was titled "perception, vulnerability and adaptation strategies of rural communities to climate change in Dejen District, Amhara Regional State, Ethiopia. His Master's thesis was titled the "Socio-economic and Environmental Benefits of interventions in Biogas Energy Production and Use". He scored excellent grades for both his Ph.D. and MSc thesis. He received continental awards for outstanding performance at the Pan African University, University of Ibadan, Nigeria (22Feb2018). He has five years of work experience working directly in the community of both urban and rural settings. He is a member of IAIA (International Association for Impact Assessment) since 2014, USA, YALI-Young African leaders' initiative, and Ethiopian Red Cross society.

Index

M

N

O

P

R

S

T

U

V

www.ingramcontent.com/pod-product-compliance
Lightning Source LLC
LaVergne TN
LVHW060349300926
849162LV00006B/1232
* 9 7 8 1 7 9 9 8 4 8 1 7 2 *